THE DK
GEOGRAPHY
OF THE
WORLD

The Friday Mosque at Mopti in Mali

Chinese boy writing characters

Street scene in Tokyo, Japan

Black pepper plant and peppercorns from the Pacific Islands

Traditional house built by the Tswana people from Botswana

High, windswept plains, called the altiplano, in Bolivia

Aymará Indians from the altiplano in Bolivia

A variety of different crops grown on small farms in Italy

Wine and cheeses from Germany

Copper from Namibia

Street market in Lausanne, Switzerland

UNITED
KINGDOM

PHILIPPINES

ARGENTINA

NEW ZEALAND

CANADA

BRUNEI

PARAGUAY

KAZAKHSTAN

BAHAMAS

SUDAN

UNITED STATES
OF AMERICA

JAPAN

CHINA

BHUTAN

RUSSIAN
FEDERATION

ITALY

VENEZUELA

SWEDEN

PANAMA

GHANA

PORTUGAL

IVORY COAST

BELGIUM

BRAZIL

KENYA

MEXICO

SPAIN

NORWAY

IRAQ

INDIA

CHILE

THE DK
GEOGRAPHY
OF THE
WORLD

SAUDI ARABIA

NETHERLANDS

GERMANY

JAMAICA

FRANCE

GREECE

SOUTH AFRICA

INDONESIA

SENEGAL

THAILAND

AUSTRALIA

AZERBAIJAN

TUVALU

A Dorling Kindersley Book

KIRIBATI

MALAYSIA

MONGOLIA

SI

DK

Dorling Kindersley
London, New York, Munich, Melbourne, Delhi

Senior Art Editor
Rachael Foster

Senior Editor
Susan Peach

Art Editors
Marcus James, Tina Robinson,
Gillian Shaw, Jane Tetzlaff

Editors
Marie Greenwood, Nic Kynaston,
Fran Jones, Veronica Pennycook

US Editor Camela Decaire

Deputy Art Director Miranda Kennedy
Deputy Editorial Director Sophie Mitchell

Senior DTP designer Mathew Birch
DTP designer Almudena Díaz
Cartography Jan Clark, Robin Giddings
Picture research Rachel Leach, Jo Haddon
Research Robert Graham
Special photography Andy Crawford
Production Catherine Semark, Louise Barratt

Chief consultant Dr. David Green

Consultants
Dr. Kathy Baker, Professor Mark Blacksell, Dr. Tanya Bowyer-Bower, Dr. Robert Bradnock, Dr. Edward Brown,
Dr. Brian Chalkley, Professor Roman Cybriwsky, Professor Dennis Dwyer, Professor Alan Gilbert,
St. John Gould, Professor Ian Hamilton, Robert Headland, Dr. Michael Heffernan, Professor Eleanore Kofman,
Keith Lye, Professor Robert Mason, Professor W.R. Mead, Professor William Morgan, Susan Murrell,
Jenny Nemko, Dr. Rewi Newnham, Professor Robert Potter, Dr. Jonathan Rigg, Dr. David Simon,
Dr. David Turnock, John Wright and Nicholas Awde, Dr. Ted Yates

Authors Simon Adams, Anita Ganeri, Ann Kay
Additional text by Ann Kramer, Claire Watts

First American Edition, 1996
This Edition, 2003
2 4 6 8 10 9 7 5 3 1
Published in the United States by
DK Publishing, Inc., 95 Madison Avenue, New York, New York 10016

Published in Great Britain by Dorling Kindersley Limited.
Distributed by Houghton Mifflin Company, Boston.

Library of Congress Cataloging-in-Publication Data
DK geography of the world. – – 2nd American ed.
p. cm.
Includes index.
Summary: Maps and text describe countries around the world and the ways of life of the inhabitants.
ISBN 0-7894-594-X
1. Geography – – Juvenile literature. [1. Geography.]
G133.D58 1996 910 – – dc20   96-15129 CIP AC

Color reproduction by Colourscan, Singapore
Printed and bound in Slovakia by Neografia
See our complete catalog at www.dk.com

CONTENTS

132 ASIA

HOW TO USE THIS BOOK

THIS BOOK IS DIVIDED INTO six continental sections – North America, Central and South America, Europe, Asia, Africa, and Australasia and Oceania. At the start of each section there is a map showing the whole continent, and pages describing the peoples that live there. Each country, or group of countries, then has an individual map showing its cities, towns, and main geographical features. This is followed by country pages which go into detail about life in the countries. The reference section can be used to find out more about subjects of general interest, such as world religions or political systems. There is also a glossary, a gazetteer, and an index. These two pages explain the symbols and information found throughout the book.

COUNTRY PAGES

The country pages, like this one for Japan, have been designed to give you as much information as possible about the way of life in a country – its people, their traditions, politics, and the economy. All the countries of the world are featured in the book.

COLOR BORDERS
Each continental section has a different color border to help you locate that section easily. This page on Japan has the color used for all the countries in Asia.

HEADING
Every page in the book has a heading telling you the name of the section followed by the name of the country featured on that page.

FACT BOXES
Each country page has a box with important statistics about that country, such as its area, the size of its population, its capital city, and its currency. The notes below explain some other entries that appear in most fact boxes.

JAPAN
Capital city: Tokyo

Area: 145,869 sq miles (377,800 sq km)

Population: 123,611,167

Official language: Japanese

Major religions: Shinto and Buddhist 92%, other 8%

Government: Multiparty democracy

Currency: Yen

Adult literacy rate: 99%

Life expectancy: 79 years

People per doctor: 610

Televisions: 620 per 1,000 people

Locator map
This shows the position of a country, or countries, in relation to its neighbors. This locator map shows where Japan lies off the coast of mainland Asia.

Major religions
The figures provide a breakdown of the religious beliefs of the people. All the main religions are explained in detail on pages 274–275.

Government
This describes how a country is ruled, or governed. The main types of government are explained on pages 270–271.

Adult literacy rate
This is the percentage of people in a country that can read and write. Literacy rates are based on the ability of people aged 15 or over to read and write a simple sentence. Find out more about literacy on page 277.

People per doctor
This figure shows how many people there are for every one doctor. It gives a rough guide as to whether people have easy access to medical attention. Find out more on page 276.

Life expectancy
The number shows how long the average person in a country can expect to live. Figures are a combination of the average life expectancy for men and women. There is more about life expectancy on page 276.

Abbreviations used in the book:

Imperial

ft	feet
in	inches
sq miles	square miles
mph	miles per hour
°F	degrees Fahrenheit

Metric

m	meters
mm	millimeters
cm	centimeters
km	kilometers
sq km	square kilometers
km/h	kilometers per hour
°C	degrees Centigrade

Other abbreviations

BC	Before Christ
AD	Anno Domini
US	United States
UK	United Kingdom

Find out more
EARTHQUAKES: *13*
GROWING CITIES: *17, 136*
LIFE EXPECTANCY: *276*
PACIFIC RIM ECONOMIES: *137*

FIND OUT MORE BOXES
At the end of each country entry there is a Find out more box. This directs you to other pages in the book where you can discover more about a particular subject. For example, one of the pages on Japan explains how the country suffers from hundreds of earthquakes a year. You can find out more about earthquakes and why they occur by turning to page 13 in the book.

MAP PAGES

Each country appears on one of the regional maps, like this one of Southern Africa, shown below. These maps show many geographical features, such as mountain ranges, deserts, rivers, and lakes, along with capital cities and other major towns. The key on the far right shows you what these features look like on the maps. A compass point fixes the direction of the region in relation to North (N).

This figure is the page number.

This figure gives the grid reference on the map.

Durango *Town* Mexico 39 E5
Durban *Town* South Africa 247 I10
Dushanbe *Town* Tajikistan 161 G8
Düsseldorf *Town* Germany 95 D6
Dvina (Northern, Western) *River* Russian Federation 78 I8, L6, 109 G6, J8, 138 E5
Dzhugdzhur Range *Mountain range* Russian Federation 133 O6, 139 Q8

E

East China Sea China 10 K6, 133 L10, 265 A3
East Frisian Islands Germany 95 E3

USING THE GRID

The grid around the outside of the page helps you find places on the map. For example, to find the city of Durban, look up its name in the gazetteer on pages 284–295. Next to the word Durban are the reference numbers 247 I10. The first number shows that Durban is on page 247. The second number shows it is in square I10 of the grid. Turn to page 247. Trace down from the letter I on the grid, and then across from the number 10. You will find Durban situated in the square where the number and the letter meet.

Find out more about climate on pages 14–15.

Key to features on the maps

International border

Disputed border

State or province border

River

Wadi

Lake

Seasonal lake

Waterfall

Dam

Capital city

Major town

Special feature

Volcanic mountain

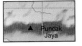
Mountain

SCALE

Each map features a scale which shows how distances on the map relate to miles and kilometers. The scale can be used to see how big a country is, or how far it is from one place to another. Not all maps in the book are drawn to the same scale.

```
0   100  200  300  400  500 km
0      100      200      300 miles
```

LOCATOR MAP

This map shows the position of the country, or countries, within the continental section. It also shows how near the country is to the equator, the Tropics of Cancer and Capricorn, or the Arctic or Antarctic Circle. This gives an indication of how hot or cold a country is.

AFRICA • SOUTHERN AFRICA

THINGS TO LOOK FOR ON THE MAP
Longest river: Zambezi, Mozambique/Zimbabwe/Zambia/Namibia/Angola, 1,678 miles (2,700 km) *Map J5*
Highest point: Mt. Thabana-Ntlenyana, Lesotho, 11,424 ft (3,482 m) *Map H10*
Largest lake: L. Nyasa, Mozambique/Malawi/Tanzania 11,000 sq miles (28,490 sq km) *Map J4*

Francistown, Botswana
Jan 77°F (25°C)
July 58°F (15°C)
Jan 4.2 in (107 mm)
July 0 in (0 mm)

Port Elizabeth, South Africa
Jan 70°F (21°C)
July 56°F (13°C)
Jan 1.2 in (31 mm)
July 1.9 in (48 mm)

CITY GROWTH
Across southern Africa, people are leaving the countryside and moving to the cities in search of work. The outlying areas surrounding such cities as Johannesburg in South Africa are crammed with shanty towns which are now a permanent feature of the landscape. Maputo, the capital of Mozambique (right), doubled in size between 1975 and 1983, and now contains more than 1.5 million people.

WOMEN'S ROLE
In traditional African society, women generally acted as wives and mothers and were responsible for routine household tasks and growing crops. Today, many African men work away from home in the mines and cities for one or two years at a time, leaving women to form a majority in their villages. This means that women are now taking on more responsibility in the communities.

Angola   *Namibia*

COUNTRY FLAGS

The national flag for each country or territory appears around the edge of the map. The designs often reflect the culture or religion of the country.

WEATHER FACTS

The average temperature and amount of rainfall recorded in January and July are shown around the main map. Weather facts are given for several places on the map to show how temperature and rainfall can vary within an area. The weather inland, for example, will generally be hotter than that near the coast.

The sun symbol represents the average temperature.

Francistown, Botswana
Jan 77°F (25°C)
July 58°F (15°C)
Jan 4.2 in (107 mm)
July 0 in (0 mm)

The cloud symbol represents the average rainfall.

Abbreviations used on maps

L.	Lake
I. or Is.	Island(s)
R.	River
Mt. or Mts.	Mountain(s)
St.	Saint
C.	Cape
Res.	Reservoir

THE PHYSICAL WORLD

THE EARTH, OUR HOME in the Universe, is one of the nine planets that circles around the Sun. It is the only planet scientists know of that can support life – thanks to the oxygen in its atmosphere and the water in its oceans. More than two-thirds of the Earth is covered with water in the form of oceans, seas, rivers, and lakes. The remainder is made up of seven vast expanses of land, called continents, each with remarkably varied physical features. Among the most notable features are mountain ranges, rivers, and deserts, which can be found on this world map.

CONTINENTS

The seven continents that make up the world's land mass are, from largest to smallest: Asia, Africa, North America, South America, Antarctica, Europe, and Australia. The polar regions, not completely visible on the flat map, surround the North and South poles and are shown on the globes left and below.

Only 29 percent of the Earth's surface is land. The percentage area of each continent is shown here.

Earth's surface
Water: 71%
Land: 29%

Australia: 5%
Europe: 7%

Asia: 30%
Africa: 20%
North America: 16.5%
South America: 12%
Antarctica: 9.5%

THINGS TO LOOK FOR ON THE MAP

Highest point on Earth: Mt. Everest, China/Nepal, 29,029 ft (8,848 m) *Map H6*

Lowest point on Earth: Mariana Trench, Pacific Ocean, 35,840 ft (10,924 m) below sea level *Map L8*

Longest river: Nile, Egypt/Sudan/Uganda, 4,187 miles (6,738 km) *Map E7*

Largest lake: Caspian Sea, Azerbaijan/Iran/Turkmenistan/Kazakhstan/Russian Federation, 146,101 sq miles (378,400 sq km) *Map F5*

Largest ocean: Pacific Ocean, 63,804,540 sq miles (165,241,000 sq km) *Map Q7*

Map labels: ARCTIC CIRCLE, TROPIC OF CANCER, EQUATOR

Greenland, GREENLAND SEA, ARCTIC CIRCLE, Ellesmere I., Devon I., Baffin Bay, Baffin I., Davis Strait, Melville I., Banks I., Victoria I., Great Bear L., Great Slave L., Hudson Bay, LABRADOR SEA, Newfoundland, Azores

EAST SIBERIAN SEA, CHUKCHI SEA, BEAUFORT SEA, Bering Strait, Yukon, Mackenzie, BERING SEA, Aleutian Is., Gulf of Alaska, ROCKY MOUNTAINS, COAST MTS., COAST RANGES, NORTH AMERICA, GREAT PLAINS, Missouri, Great Lakes, APPALACHIAN MTS., ATLANTIC OCEAN, Bermuda Is., SONORAN DESERT, Rio Grande, Mississippi, SIERRA MADRE, Gulf of Mexico, Bahamas, TROPIC OF CANCER

Midway Is., Hawaiian Is., PACIFIC OCEAN, Marshall Is., Gilbert Is., Tuvalu, Phoenix Is., Marquesas Is., Samoa, Tonga, Vanuatu, New Caledonia, Fiji, Society Is., Cook Is., Tahiti, Tuamotu, Tubuai Is., CENTRAL AMERICA, Greater Antilles, CARIBBEAN SEA, Lesser Antilles, Galápagos Is., LLANOS, ANDES, AMAZONIA, Amazon, SOUTH AMERICA, São Francisco, L. Titicaca, PLATEAU OF MATO GROSSO, TROPIC OF CAPRICORN, EQUATOR, Juan Fernández Is., ATACAMA DESERT, ANDES, PAMPAS, Paraná, PATAGONIA, ATLANTIC OCEAN

New Zealand, Chatham Is., Bounty Is., Antipodes Is., Auckland Is., Falkland Is., Cape Horn

Grid columns: N O P Q R S T U V W X Y A
Grid rows: 1 2 3 4 5 6 7 8 9 10 11 12 13

MOVING CONTINENTS

THE CONTINENTS THAT MAKE UP most of the Earth's land surface
are always on the move, shifted around by forces deep inside the
Earth. This is known as continental drift. Movement, or drift,
takes place because of intense heat generated within the Earth.
The heat is carried upward where it disturbs the cool, rocky
surface, or crust, forcing sections of it, called plates, to move.
Each year the continents, parts of the plates, drift nearly half
an inch (about a centimeter), some getting closer together,
others moving farther apart, some grinding past each other.
As this happens, many of the Earth's natural features
are created or changed.

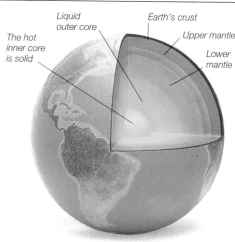

INSIDE THE EARTH
The Earth is not a solid ball, but is made up of
many different layers. The crust which forms
the continents and the ocean floors is a thin
layer of rock that covers the Earth like a shell.
The mantle beneath is 1,864 miles (3,000 km)
thick and made of hot rock, some of which is
molten (liquid). At the center is the core, the
hot metallic center of the Earth. This is liquid
on the outside and solid on the inside.

IN THE BEGINNING
Scientists believe that some
300 million years ago all the
land on Earth was joined together
in one "supercontinent" called Pangaea. It
was surrounded by a giant ocean, Panthalassa. About
200 million years ago, as the plates moved, Pangaea
began to split into two great landmasses, Laurasia in
the north, and Gondwanaland in the south. These were
separated by the Tethys Sea. As the plates continued to
move, the two landmasses split and moved farther apart,
eventually forming the continents on the map below.

200 million years ago

180 million years ago

65 million years ago

RESTLESS EARTH

Because the Earth appears to stand still, it is difficult to imagine that the crust is moving. In fact, its plates move in three main ways – as spreading ridges, subduction zones, and transform faults, all shown on the artwork below. It is possible to see the effect this activity has had on the landscape. The Rocky Mountains in North America were formed when two plates collided, while the Great Rift Valley in Africa is the result of plates pulling apart. Volcanoes and earthquakes are also dramatic reminders that the plates are moving.

At Thingvellir, Iceland, the spreading ridge between the North American and Eurasian plates appears as a long gash in the landscape.

SPREADING RIDGES

A spreading ridge occurs where two plates start to pull apart and molten rocks from the Earth's mantle well up to fill the gap. If this happens along the ocean floor, it creates an underwater mountain chain such as the Mid-Atlantic Ridge. Sometimes the peaks of these mountains break the surface as volcanic islands, as happened with Iceland. When a spreading ridge occurs on land, it creates a steep-sided rift valley.

Chains of volcanoes are often found along subduction zones.

A mid-ocean ridge where two plates are pulling apart

Plates slide past each other along a transform fault.

At a subduction zone, the crust is forced down into the mantle, where it melts.

When plates collide, the crust buckles and folds and may be pushed up to form mountains.

TRANSFORM FAULT

At a transform fault two plates grind past each other in opposite directions or in the same direction but at different speeds. No crust is made or destroyed in the process, but the movement creates deep cracks in the ground. The sliding movement often occurs in short bursts, which are felt on the surface as earthquakes. The San Andreas fault in California is an active earthquake zone.

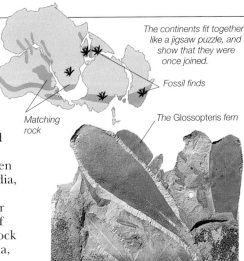

The San Andreas fault is the point where the Pacific and North American plates meet.

SUBDUCTION ZONE

When two plates meet, the edge of one can be pushed down (subducted) under the other and into the mantle below. The rocks from the crust melt in the mantle. Often these molten rocks force their way to the surface as a volcano. The many volcanoes around the edge of the Pacific plate, such as Mt. Mihara, Japan, were formed this way. Sometimes when plates collide, rocks are forced up, forming great mountain ranges.

LOOKING AT THE EVIDENCE

When the German scientist Alfred Wegener first proposed his theory of moving plates in 1923, people dismissed his ideas as nonsense. Since then, evidence had proved him correct. Fossils of the fern *Glossopteris* for example, have been found in rocks as far apart as India, Australia, and Africa. All these places were once joined together as Gondwanaland. Further proof comes from matching types of rock that have been found in Australia, Antarctica, and South America.

The continents fit together like a jigsaw puzzle, and show that they were once joined.

Fossil finds

Matching rock

The Glossopteris fern

CLIMATE AND VEGETATION

CLIMATE IS THE AVERAGE PATTERN of weather and temperature in a particular area over a long period of time. Similar types of climates are found in different places around the world. For example, there are regions of hot, dry desert in Africa and North America, as well as across central Australia. It is a region's climate, together with its physical landscape, that determines the sort of vegetation, or plant life, that is usually found there. Cold areas near the poles and icy mountain peaks support little, or no, vegetation. Hot, wet rain forests near the equator, however, encourage the fast growth of a variety of plants.

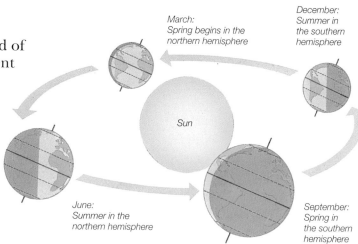

March:
Spring begins in the northern hemisphere

December:
Summer in the southern hemisphere

Sun

June:
Summer in the northern hemisphere

September:
Spring in the southern hemisphere

The Earth's axis is tilted at 23.5 degrees

Earth spins on its axis

North Pole

Places close to the Equator are hot all year round. This is because the Sun's rays strike the equator directly and their heating power is very strong.

ARCTIC CIRCLE

TROPIC OF CANCER

EQUATOR

0 degrees longitude

Places near the North and South poles have the coldest climates because the Sun's rays hit them at an angle. This means any warmth is spread out over a wider area.

TROPIC OF CAPRICORN

ANTARCTIC CIRCLE

0 degrees latitude

South Pole

SEASONS OF THE YEAR

As the Earth travels around the Sun, the tilt on its axis means that each place leans gradually nearer the Sun, and then farther away from it. This causes the seasons. When the northern hemisphere leans toward the Sun it has summer. When it tilts away it has winter. In the southern hemisphere this is reversed. Between the warm days of summer and the cold days of winter come spring and fall. The Earth also spins on its axis, turning once every 24 hours to give us day and night. The side facing the Sun has day, while the other side has night.

LATITUDE AND LONGITUDE

A region's climate is influenced by how far to the north or south of the equator it lies. This is called its latitude. The equator, an imaginary line running around the Earth, lies at 0 degrees latitude. Other lines of latitude include the Tropics of Cancer and Capricorn. Regions around the equator are the hottest in the world, while the closer to the poles you go, the colder it gets. There are also longitude lines that run from north to south, known as meridians.

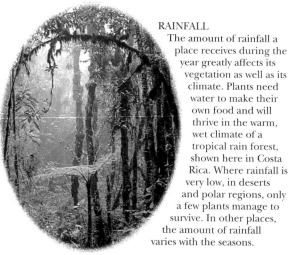

RAINFALL
The amount of rainfall a place receives during the year greatly affects its vegetation as well as its climate. Plants need water to make their own food and will thrive in the warm, wet climate of a tropical rain forest, shown here in Costa Rica. Where rainfall is very low, in deserts and polar regions, only a few plants manage to survive. In other places, the amount of rainfall varies with the seasons.

LAND AND SEA
The climate of a region is affected by altitude – how high a place is above sea level. The higher a place, the colder its climate, even if it lies near the equator or the Tropics, like these Atlas Mountains in Morocco. Another important influence is how close a place is to the sea. The sea warms and cools more slowly than land, so coastal areas often have fewer extremes in temperature.

CHANGES IN WORLD CLIMATE
The world's climate can be changed by both natural as well as human events. When Mt. Pinatubo, a volcano in the Philippines, erupted in 1991, it threw ash and dust high into the atmosphere. Locally, this caused dark skies, heavy rainfall, and high winds. The distance the ash was carried can be seen from this satellite photo. Equally, events such as the massive oil fires in Kuwait, started during the Gulf War, can have a long-term effect on climate.

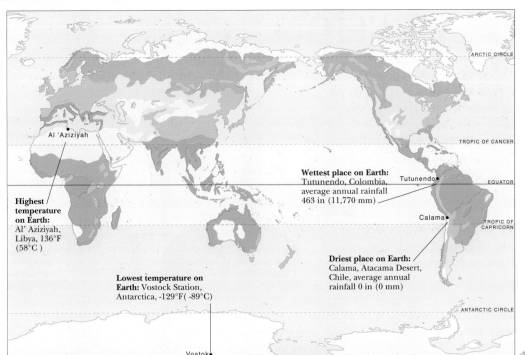

VEGETATION ZONES

Scientists divide the Earth into a number of different vegetation zones, also known as "biomes," shown on the map, left. The plant and animal life found in each zone depends on the region's climate, landscape, and latitude. Over millions of years, plants and animals have adapted to life in this range of climates, often developing special features that have helped them to survive. The map also highlights how similar landscapes, such as taiga or desert, occur at the same latitude across the world.

Wettest place on Earth: Tutunendo, Colombia, average annual rainfall 463 in (11,770 mm)

Highest temperature on Earth: Al' Aziziyah, Libya, 136°F (58°C)

Driest place on Earth: Calama, Atacama Desert, Chile, average annual rainfall 0 in (0 mm)

Lowest temperature on Earth: Vostock Station, Antarctica, -129°F (-89°C)

POLAR AND TUNDRA

The areas around the North and South poles are freezing cold and covered in ice. South of the North Pole lies a region called the tundra, where the lower layers of soil are permanently frozen. Hardy mosses, lichens, and shrubs are the only plants that can survive here.

TAIGA

In Russian, the word taiga means "cold forest." It describes the vast evergreen forests that stretch across northern Canada, Scandinavia, and the Russian Federation. Evergreen trees, such as fir, spruce, and pine, are well-adapted to the long, snowy winters.

MOUNTAIN REGIONS

The higher up a mountain you go, the colder it gets. Trees and plants grow on the lower slopes of many mountains. But above a certain level, called the tree line, it is too cold and windy for plants to survive. High mountain peaks are often covered in snow all year round.

TEMPERATE FOREST

Much of the land in northern Europe and North America was once covered by deciduous forests (trees that lose their leaves in winter). Most of these have now been cut down. Deciduous trees grow well in temperate climates where it is never very hot or very cold.

MEDITERRANEAN

Areas with a Mediterranean climate have hot, dry summers and cool, wet winters. They include land around the Mediterranean Sea and other similar places, such as California in the US. Plants and trees, such as olives, have adapted to survive the lack of water in summer.

DRY GRASSLAND

Vast grasslands cover the centers of some of the continents. They include the South American pampas and the North American prairies. They have hot, dry summers and very cold winters. Large parts of these grasslands are now plowed for wheat or used to raise cattle.

TROPICAL RAIN FOREST

Around the equator, the climate is hot and wet all year round, and providing ideal conditions for lush, green tropical forests to thrive. The world's rain forests may contain 50,000 different types of trees, as well as millions of other species of plants and animals.

HOT DESERT

Deserts are the hottest, driest places on Earth. Despite heat during the day, temperatures may plunge to below freezing at night. In some deserts, years pass without rain. Deserts often contain sandy soil that can only support plants such as cacti.

TROPICAL GRASSLAND

Between the hot deserts and tropical rain forests lie tropical grasslands, such as the African savanna. The climate here is always hot, but the year is divided into a wet and a dry season. Tall grasses, as well as low trees and shrubs, grow in these hot areas.

WORLD POPULATION

PEOPLE HAVE LIVED ON EARTH for at least 2 million years. For most of that time, population size remained steady, because the number of people born roughly equaled the number that died. Disease and famine ensured that the size of the population did not overtake supplies of food and other resources. However, as farming methods became more efficient and medical knowledge improved, population size rapidly began to increase. It now stands in excess of 6 billion people, with more than one million babies born every four days. In many parts of the world, rapid population growth has created serious problems, such as food shortages and overcrowding in cities.

WHERE PEOPLE LIVE

People are not evenly distributed among the world's continents. The fact that a continent is large, such as North America, does not necessarily mean that it has a large population. Some regions cannot support more than a few people, while others, with fertile soils and good communications, can support many. The world map below shows the average number of people who live in a square mile, or kilometer, in each country. This is called population density.

Asia: 62%

Africa: 12.9%

Australasia and Oceania: 0.5%

North America: 6.8%

Europe: 11%

This chart shows the size of each continent or region, together with the percentage of the world's population living on it. Far more people live in Asia than anywhere else on Earth.

Antarctica: 0%

South America: 6.8%

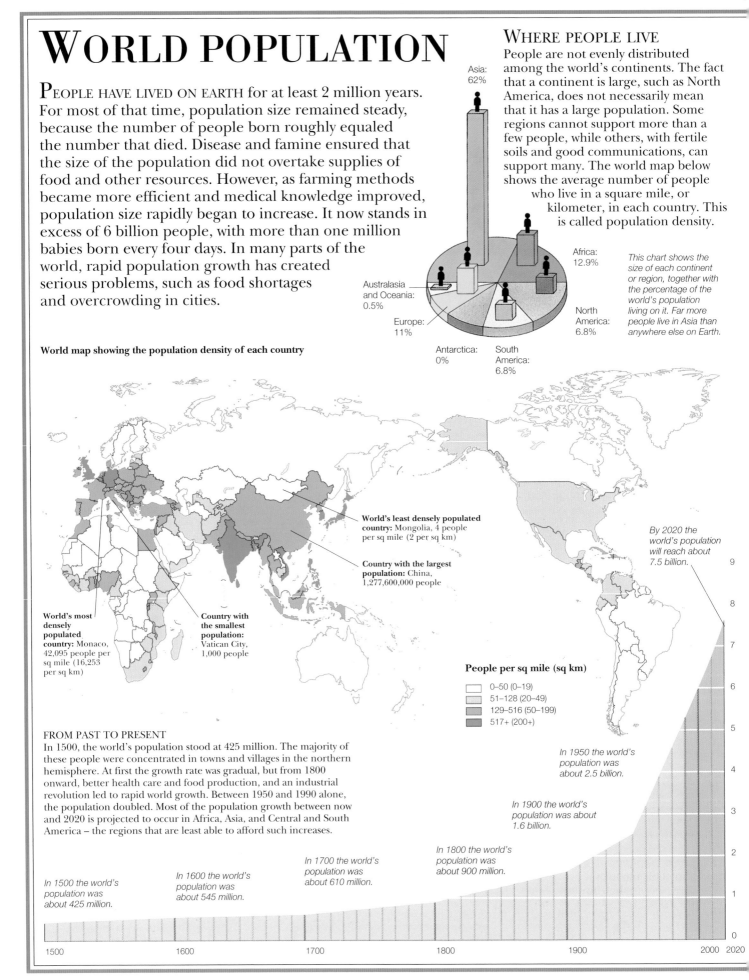

World map showing the population density of each country

World's least densely populated country: Mongolia, 4 people per sq mile (2 per sq km)

Country with the largest population: China, 1,277,600,000 people

World's most densely populated country: Monaco, 42,095 people per sq mile (16,253 per sq km)

Country with the smallest population: Vatican City, 1,000 people

By 2020 the world's population will reach about 7.5 billion.

People per sq mile (sq km)
- 0–50 (0–19)
- 51–128 (20–49)
- 129–516 (50–199)
- 517+ (200+)

FROM PAST TO PRESENT

In 1500, the world's population stood at 425 million. The majority of these people were concentrated in towns and villages in the northern hemisphere. At first the growth rate was gradual, but from 1800 onward, better health care and food production, and an industrial revolution led to rapid world growth. Between 1950 and 1990 alone, the population doubled. Most of the population growth between now and 2020 is projected to occur in Africa, Asia, and Central and South America – the regions that are least able to afford such increases.

In 1950 the world's population was about 2.5 billion.

In 1900 the world's population was about 1.6 billion.

In 1800 the world's population was about 900 million.

In 1700 the world's population was about 610 million.

In 1600 the world's population was about 545 million.

In 1500 the world's population was about 425 million.

1500 1600 1700 1800 1900 2000 2020

Percentage growth of city dwellers

People living in the cities (urban)   People living in the countryside (rural)

Asia: 16% 23% 34% 37%

North America: 64% 74% 75% 76%

South America: 43% 60% 75% 75%

1950   1970   1990   2000   Rural areas

BIRTH AND DEATH

The number of babies a woman has varies from one country to another. In the Sudan, above, the birth rate is high, with an average of 4.9 babies per mother. Better health care, even in the poorer countries of the world, means that fewer babies now die of hunger or disease, and fewer women die in childbirth. In wealthy countries, such as Canada, the birth rate is low because people can choose to have small families. Advances in medical knowledge also mean that people are living longer.

Highest and lowest birth rates within each continent

Rwanda: 8.3
Yemen: 7.3
Guatemala: 4.9
Papua New Guinea: 4.8
Mexico: 3.3
Albania: 2.9

San Marino: 1.5
Canada: 1.8
Uruguay: 2.5
Australia: 1.8
Hong Kong: 1.3
Tunisia: 3

URBAN GROWTH

At the start of the 20th century, only one in ten people lived in a city. The vast majority lived in rural areas and worked on the land. Today, about half the world's population consists of city dwellers. There are various reasons for this growth. For example, in South America people have been pushed out of the countryside by poverty and loss of land and are drawn to the cities in search of work. By 2020, if the growth continues, almost half of all people will live in a city.

WORLD'S BIGGEST CITIES IN 1950	
New York, US	12,300,000
London, UK	8,700,000
Tokyo, Japan	6,700,000
Paris, France	5,400,000
Shanghai, China	5,300,000

WORLD'S BIGGEST CITIES IN 2000	
Tokyo, Japan	26,400,000
Mexico City, Mexico	18,100,000
Mumbai (Bombay), India	18,100,000
São Paulo, Brazil	17,800,000
New York, US	16,600,000

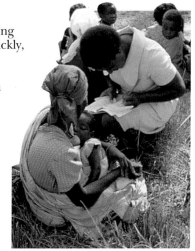

CITY SLUMS

One effect of the move of large numbers of people from the countryside to the cities is overcrowding. There are simply not enough houses and resources to go around. In many large cities, such as Mumbai (Bombay), India, this has led to the growth of sprawling shanty towns on the edges of cities. Conditions in these city slums are often unhygienic. Families survive in crowded homes made of makeshift materials, often with no electricity or running water.

SUPER CITIES

Before the 19th century, cities with more than a million people were rare. In the last 100 years, however, the number of large cities has grown dramatically. Today, several cities, such as Tokyo, already have populations of around 20 million. This means that some cities have more people than some entire countries do, such as New Zealand or Sweden. Large cities often suffer from pollution, caused by car exhausts, factory emissions, and domestic waste.

LOOKING TO THE FUTURE

Although world population growth is showing signs of slowing, numbers are still rising quickly, especially in developing countries. To encourage people to have fewer children, programs have been set up to teach women about family planning and health care so that they have more control over the size and health of their families. Today, almost half the married women in the developing world report that they or their partner use birth control, compared with less than a quarter in 1980.

This doctor is writing out a prescription for contraceptives, now used by 43 percent of the women in Zimbabwe.

THE POLITICAL WORLD

IN ADDITION TO BEING DIVIDED into physical land masses, the world is also split into countries. These countries are separated from one another by language, government, and culture, and this creates the political world. As recently as 1950, there were only 82 countries. Today there are more than twice that many – some vast, others tiny. New countries are created when people want freedom from their past colonial rulers or when separate peoples living within one country seek independence. The breakup of Yugoslavia in the 1990s, for example, created new countries.

KEY
1 NETHERLANDS
2 BELGIUM
3 LUXEMBOURG
4 SWITZERLAND
5 LIECHTENSTEIN
6 MOLDOVA
7 ANDORRA
8 MONACO
9 SAN MARINO
10 VATICAN CITY
11 SLOVENIA
12 CROATIA
13 BOSNIA & HERZEGOVINA
14 YUGOSLAVIA
15 ALBANIA
16 MACEDONIA

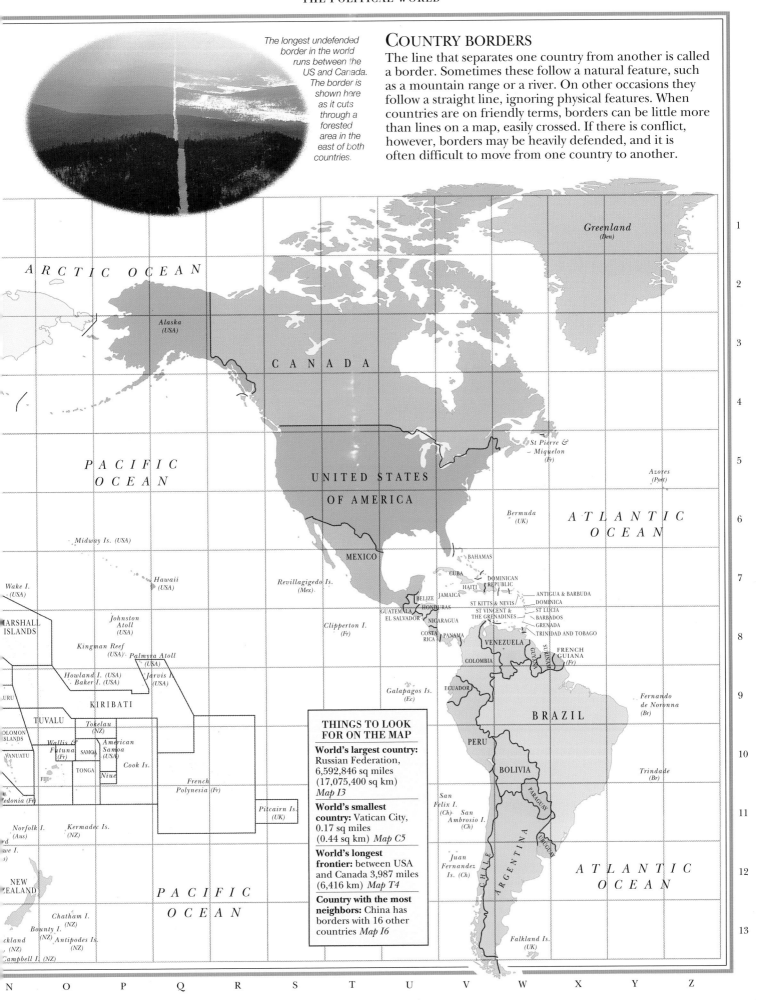

The longest undefended border in the world runs between the US and Canada. The border is shown here as it cuts through a forested area in the east of both countries.

COUNTRY BORDERS

The line that separates one country from another is called a border. Sometimes these follow a natural feature, such as a mountain range or a river. On other occasions they follow a straight line, ignoring physical features. When countries are on friendly terms, borders can be little more than lines on a map, easily crossed. If there is conflict, however, borders may be heavily defended, and it is often difficult to move from one country to another.

Greenland
(Den)

ARCTIC OCEAN

Alaska
(USA)

CANADA

PACIFIC
OCEAN

St Pierre &
Miquelon
(Fr)

Azores
(Port)

UNITED STATES

OF AMERICA

Bermuda
(UK)

ATLANTIC
OCEAN

Midway Is. (USA)

MEXICO

BAHAMAS

Wake I.
(USA)

Hawaii
(USA)

Revillagigedo Is.
(Mex)

CUBA

DOMINICAN
REPUBLIC

HAITI

ANTIGUA & BARBUDA

JAMAICA

DOMINICA

MARSHALL
ISLANDS

Johnston
Atoll
(USA)

Clipperton I.
(Fr)

BELIZE

ST KITTS & NEVIS

ST LUCIA

GUATEMALA

HONDURAS

ST VINCENT &
THE GRENADINES

BARBADOS

Kingman Reef
(USA)

Palmyra Atoll
(USA)

EL SALVADOR

NICARAGUA

GRENADA

COSTA
RICA

PANAMA

TRINIDAD AND TOBAGO

Howland I. (USA)

Baker I. (USA)

Jarvis I.
(USA)

VENEZUELA

FRENCH
GUIANA
(Fr)

URU

KIRIBATI

Galapagos Is.
(Ec)

ECUADOR

COLOMBIA

Fernando
de Noronna
(Br)

TUVALU

Tokelau
(NZ)

BRAZIL

SOLOMON
ISLANDS

Wallis &
Futuna
(Fr)

American
Samoa
(USA)

SAMOA

PERU

VANUATU

TONGA

Niue

Cook Is.

BOLIVIA

Trindade
(Br)

FIJI

French
Polynesia (Fr)

San
Felix I.
(Ch)

San
Ambrosio I.
(Ch)

edonia (Fr)

Pitcairn Is.
(UK)

PARAGUAY

Norfolk I.
(Aus)

Kermadec Is.
(NZ)

URUGUAY

we I.
s)

Juan
Fernandez
Is. (Ch)

CHILE

ATLANTIC
OCEAN

NEW
ZEALAND

PACIFIC
OCEAN

ARGENTINA

Chatham I.
(NZ)

Bounty I.
(NZ)

kland
(NZ)

Antipodes Is.
(NZ)

Falkland Is.
(UK)

Campbell I. (NZ)

THINGS TO LOOK FOR ON THE MAP

World's largest country: Russian Federation, 6,592,846 sq miles (17,075,400 sq km) *Map I3*

World's smallest country: Vatican City, 0.17 sq miles (0.44 sq km) *Map C5*

World's longest frontier: between USA and Canada 3,987 miles (6,416 km) *Map T4*

Country with the most neighbors: China has borders with 16 other countries *Map I6*

N   O   P   Q   R   S   T   U   V   W   X   Y   Z

1   2   3   4   5   6   7   8   9   10   11   12   13

NORTH AMERICA

NORTH AMERICA INCLUDES THE COUNTRIES of Canada, the United States, and Mexico, as well as the world's largest island, Greenland. During the last Ice Age, a great sheet of ice flowed across the continent scouring the landscape, deepening the depressions that now hold the Great Lakes, and dumping fertile soil onto the central plains. The Rocky Mountains form the backbone of the continent, running from Alaska to New Mexico. In the east are the Appalachian Mountains, flanked by coastal lowlands to the east and south. In eastern Canada lies the Canadian Shield, a huge basin of ancient eroded rocks now covered with thin soils. Deserts stretch from the southwestern United States down into northern Mexico.

Section across the US

San Francisco · Rocky Mountains · Great Plains · Great Lakes · Appalachian Mountains · Washington DC

MOUNTAIN RANGES

The main mountain ranges of North America, the snowcapped Rockies and the forested Appalachians, vary greatly in appearance (see above cross-section). The difference can be explained by their age. The Rockies, shown right, are relatively young mountains that have not yet been worn down. The Appalachians, however, are among the world's oldest mountains and have been gradually eroded by the scouring action of wind, water, and the movement of glaciers.

This view shows the Rockies in Canada.

THE GRAND CANYON
The Grand Canyon was formed over millions of years as the waters of the Colorado River and its tributaries carved their way through the solid rock. At some points the canyon is 1 mile (1.6 km) deep, and cuts through rocks that are 2,000 million years old. Different types of fossils found in the canyon walls reveal the dates of its changing history.

THE GREAT PLAINS

Across the center of Canada and the US lie the Great Plains, also called the prairies. This huge area has hot summers and cold, snowy winters. Trees are rare except along rivers and lakeshores, but the region was once covered with grasses grazed by millions of buffalo. Today, little natural prairie survives, and in its place farmers cultivate vast fields of corn and wheat.

THE GREAT LAKES
Estimated to contain one-fifth of the world's freshwater, the five Great Lakes straddle the border between Canada and the US. Only Lake Michigan, shown left, lies entirely within the US. The lakes are linked by waterways and drained by the St. Lawrence River, which empties into the Atlantic Ocean. The Niagara River, which joins lakes Erie and Ontario, passes over the famous Niagara Falls.

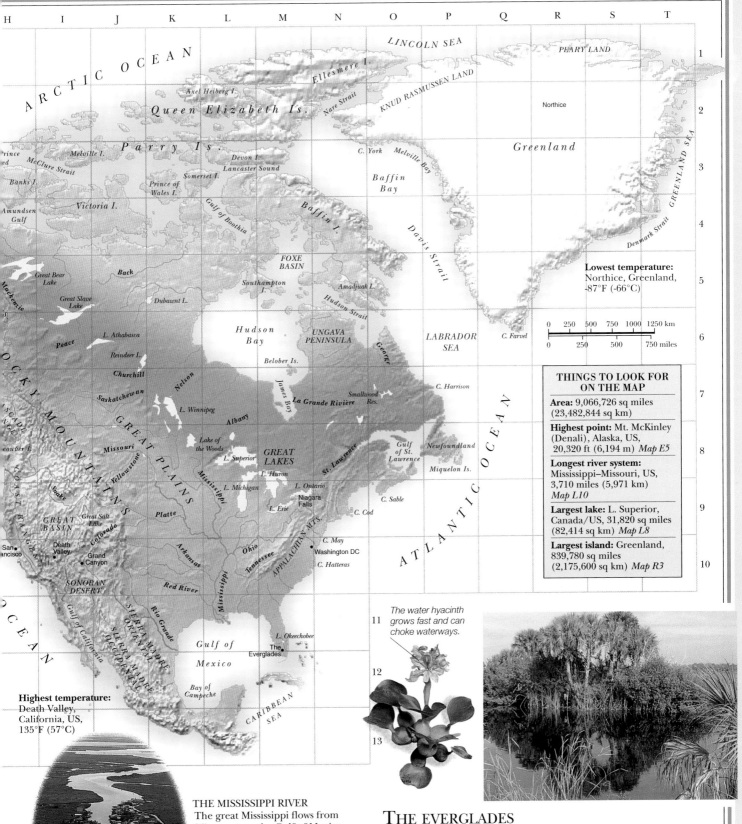

H I J K L M N O P Q R S T
1 2 3 4 5 6 7 8 9 10 11 12 13

ARCTIC OCEAN

LINCOLN SEA

PEARY LAND

Axel Heiberg I.

Queen Elizabeth Is.

Ellesmere I.

KNUD RASMUSSEN LAND

Northice

Parry Is.

Prince
ed
McClure Strait

Melville I.

Devon I.
Lancaster Sound

Somerset I.

Prince of
Wales I.

Nare Strait

C. York
Melville Bay

Greenland

GREENLAND SEA

Banks I.

Gulf of Boothia

Baffin I.

Baffin
Bay

Amundsen
Gulf

Victoria I.

Denmark Strait

FOXE
BASIN

Davis Strait

Great Bear
Lake

Back

Southampton
I.

Amadjuak L.

Lowest temperature:
Northice, Greenland,
-87°F (-66°C)

Mackenzie

Great Slave
Lake

Dubawnt L.

Hudson Strait

Hudson
Bay

UNGAVA
PENINSULA

LABRADOR
SEA

C. Farvel

0   250 500 750 1000 1250 km
0   250   500   750 miles

L. Athabasca

Peace

Reindeer L.

Belober Is.

George

Churchill

Nelson

James Bay

La Grande Rivière

Smallwood
Res.

C. Harrison

ATLANTIC OCEAN

**THINGS TO LOOK FOR
ON THE MAP**

Area: 9,066,726 sq miles
(23,482,844 sq km)

Saskatchewan

L. Winnipeg

Albany

Highest point: Mt. McKinley
(Denali), Alaska, US,
20,320 ft (6,194 m) *Map E5*

ROCKY MOUNTAINS

GREAT PLAINS

Lake of
the Woods

Missouri

Yellowstone

L. Superior

Mississippi

GREAT
LAKES

L. Huron

St. Lawrence

Gulf
of St.
Lawrence

Newfoundland

Miquelon Is.

Longest river system:
Mississippi–Missouri, US,
3,710 miles (5,971 km)
Map L10

CASCADE
RANGE

couver I.

Snake

L. Michigan

L. Ontario

Niagara
Falls

L. Erie

C. Sable

Largest lake: L. Superior,
Canada/US, 31,820 sq miles
(82,414 sq km) *Map L8*

COAST RANGES

GREAT
BASIN

Great Salt
Lake

Platte

Colorado

Ohio

Tennessee

APPALACHIAN MTS.

C. May
Washington DC

C. Hatteras

Largest island: Greenland,
839,780 sq miles
(2,175,600 sq km) *Map R3*

San
ancisco

Death
Valley

Grand
Canyon

Arkansas

C. Cod

SONORAN
DESERT

Red River

Mississippi

Rio Grande

SIERRA MADRE ORIENTAL

SIERRA MADRE OCCIDENTAL

Gulf of California

OCEAN

Gulf of
Mexico

L. Okeechobee
The
Everglades

*The water hyacinth
grows fast and can
choke waterways.*

Bay of
Campeche

CARIBBEAN
SEA

Highest temperature:
Death Valley,
California, US,
135°F (57°C)

THE MISSISSIPPI RIVER
The great Mississippi flows from
Minnesota to the Gulf of Mexico.
At the turn of the last century,
the destruction of forest and the
plowing of prairies around the
river basin caused severe soil
erosion. Soil washed into the river,
raised the water level, and caused
floods. Replanting forests and building
dams has helped control the flow, but
exceptionally heavy rains still cause floods.

THE EVERGLADES
Florida's Everglades are a protected wetland habitat,
home to many rare plants and animals. Originally covering
a much larger area, part of the Everglades has been
drained and used for the cultivation of sugarcane. The
northern part of the surviving wetland is now a sawgrass
prairie, covered by shallow water with islands of higher
land. In the south, freshwater mixes with water from the
sea, creating saltmarshes fringed by mangrove swamps.

PEOPLES OF NORTH AMERICA

ONCE POPULATED BY TRIBES of native peoples who lived off the land, the vast majority of North America's population now consists of immigrants who arrived over the last 400 years. Today, in terms of both population and economic wealth, the continent is dominated by the US, the richest country in the world. To the north, Canada covers a vast area, but much of it is cold and inhospitable, and so it has a much smaller population. Both countries were once British colonies and are still mostly English speaking. In contrast, Mexico is Spanish speaking, reflecting its past as a Spanish colony. Mexico is a relatively poor country, despite its vast oil and gas reserves.

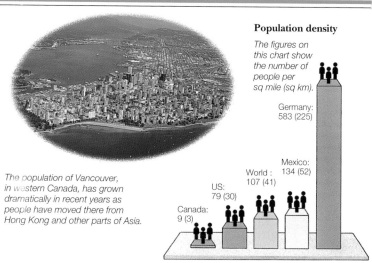

The population of Vancouver, in western Canada, has grown dramatically in recent years as people have moved there from Hong Kong and other parts of Asia.

Population density

The figures on this chart show the number of people per sq mile (sq km).

Germany: 583 (225)

Mexico: 134 (52)

World: 107 (41)

US: 79 (30)

Canada: 9 (3)

POPULATION DISTRIBUTION
In general, North America is one of the most sparsely populated continents. Over two-thirds of the population lives in the US. Mexico has the next largest population, followed by Canada. Historically, the eastern US has been the most densely populated area, but in the past few decades, many people have moved to the warmer southern and western states. In Canada, people have also left the east coast for the Great Lakes and cities such as Toronto, or for west coast cities such as Vancouver.

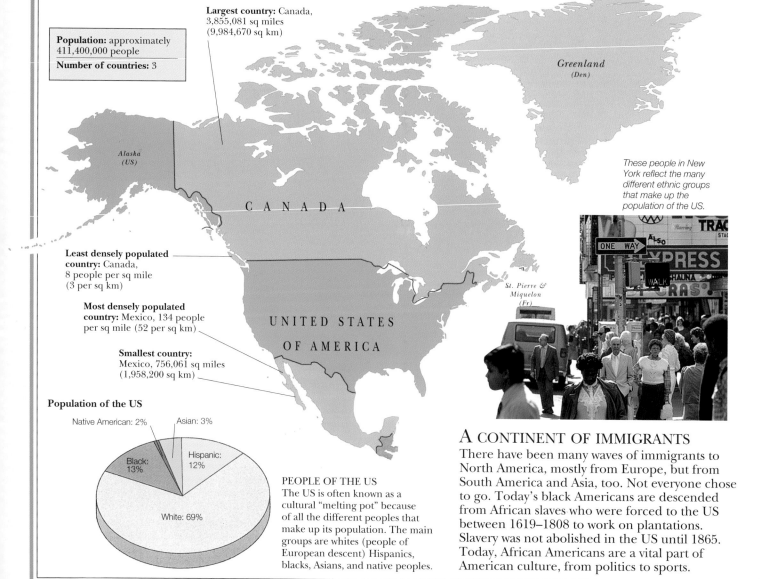

Largest country: Canada, 3,855,081 sq miles (9,984,670 sq km)

Population: approximately 411,400,000 people

Number of countries: 3

Greenland (Den)

Alaska (US)

C A N A D A

These people in New York reflect the many different ethnic groups that make up the population of the US.

Least densely populated country: Canada, 8 people per sq mile (3 per sq km)

Most densely populated country: Mexico, 134 people per sq mile (52 per sq km)

Smallest country: Mexico, 756,061 sq miles (1,958,200 sq km)

St. Pierre & Miquelon (Fr)

UNITED STATES OF AMERICA

Population of the US

Native American: 2%

Asian: 3%

Hispanic: 12%

Black: 13%

White: 69%

PEOPLE OF THE US
The US is often known as a cultural "melting pot" because of all the different peoples that make up its population. The main groups are whites (people of European descent) Hispanics, blacks, Asians, and native peoples.

A CONTINENT OF IMMIGRANTS
There have been many waves of immigrants to North America, mostly from Europe, but from South America and Asia, too. Not everyone chose to go. Today's black Americans are descended from African slaves who were forced to the US between 1619–1808 to work on plantations. Slavery was not abolished in the US until 1865. Today, African Americans are a vital part of American culture, from politics to sports.

CANADIAN CULTURE

Canadians often display their distinctive maple-leaf flag outside their homes. They are very proud of their country with its wide open spaces, lakes, mountains, and extensive national and provincial parks. But there is always the issue of US entertainment and culture flooding across the border and dominating the Canadian identity. To encourage Canada's own cultural development, the government gives grants to the arts, and the broadcasting, publishing, and film industries.

This Canadian "patriotic workshop" is painted in the colors of the country's flag.

This Mayan family is cooking tortillas.

NATIVE PEOPLES

Native Americans are the descendants of people who probably migrated from Asia via a land bridge across the Bering Strait about 50,000 years ago. Today, native peoples form only a small proportion of the population of the US and Canada. In the US, many Native Americans were moved onto special reservations in the 19th century as settlers took over their lands. In Mexico, native peoples, like these Maya, form about 30 percent of the population and are spread throughout the country.

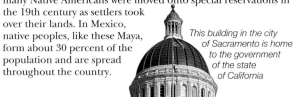

This building in the city of Sacramento is home to the government of the state of California

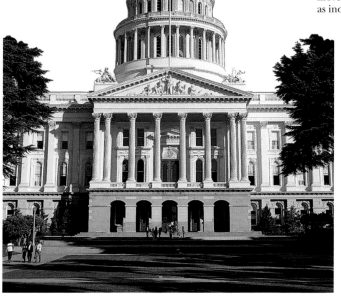

GOOD NEIGHBORS

There has not been a war between the countries of North America for nearly 150 years. Recently, Canada, the US, and Mexico agreed to abolish trade barriers and open their markets to each other's exports. The full effects of this agreement are yet to be discovered, but Mexican workers like these farmers have already lost out, as cheaper US food and goods have flooded into Mexico. By contrast, cheaper food can benefit the poor.

EUROPEAN SETTLERS

Europeans have been settling in the US and Canada since the 16th century, but in the 19th century, immigrants began to flood in. They were often driven from Europe by economic hardship, political unrest, and religious persecution. North America was seen as a land of opportunity, where there was plenty of cheap land and people were promised freedom. The first immigrants settled on the east coast, but began to move northeast in the 1800s as industry began to grow.

State government		Federal government	
📖	Education	💼	Foreign policy
🚌	Highways	$	Currency
🏠	Housing	✚	Health care
🚓	State police	🌲	National parks

In the US, local matters, such as police, hospital, and highway services, are taken care of by individual states. Matters that affect all the states, such as foreign policy, defense, and issuing currency, are dealt with centrally.

FEDERAL GOVERNMENTS

All three countries in North America have federal systems of government. This means that each country is divided into a number of states or provinces. These make their own local laws and also have representatives in the national government. Tension sometimes develops between the interests of the individual states or provinces and the interests of the country as a whole. In Canada, for example, a strong independence movement has grown up in the French-speaking province of Québec.

CANADA

THE SECOND LARGEST COUNTRY in the world, Canada occupies two-fifths of the North American continent, stretches across five time zones, and is divided into 10 provinces and three territories. It was once inhabited only by native peoples including the Inuit. The French were the first Europeans to settle in Canada, but after years of fighting the British gained control in 1763. Gradually they took over the rest of the country, as pioneers and settlers moved west and north. Today, Canada is an important industrial nation and one of the world's richest countries. Most of its manufacturing is based on the natural resources of wood, metals, and mineral fuels.

CANADA	
Capital city: Ottawa	
Area: 3,855,081 sq miles (9,984,670 sq km)	
Population: 31,414,000	
Official languages: English, French	
Major religions: Christian 83%, other 17%	
Government: Multiparty democracy	
Currency: Canadian dollar	
Adult literacy rate: 99%	
Life expectancy: 79 years	
People per doctor: 540	
Televisions: 715 per 1,000 people	

OTTAWA
Ottawa, which is named after the native people who used to live in the area, was chosen as Canada's capital city in 1857 by Queen Victoria of Britain. Today, the city boasts many magnificent copper-roofed government buildings, museums, and art galleries, and a park-lined canal that turns into the world's longest skating rink once the winter freeze sets in.

Canadian vegetation zones

Tundra and polar

Mountain

Taiga

Grassland

Temperate forest

THE CHANGING LANDSCAPE
About one-third of Canada lies within the Arctic Circle and can remain frozen for up to nine months of the year. In these cold northern areas, known as the tundra, any vegetation is limited to lichens, grasses, and small shrubs and trees. Farther south, large areas of land are covered by dense coniferous forests known as taiga. Toward the border with the US lie the mixed, temperate forests and the grasslands of the Prairies.

Edmonton
Calgary
Vancouver
Winnipeg
Montreal
Ottawa
Toronto
Hamilton
Great Lakes

WHERE PEOPLE LIVE
Canada is such a large country, much of it uninhabitable, that on average there are only eight people living in each square mile (three per square kilometer). Around three quarters of the population lives near the US border, in towns and cities around the shores of the Great Lakes and along the St. Lawrence River. The rest live in fishing villages along the coasts or on farms and villages inland.

PEOPLE OF CANADA
Until quite recently, most Canadians were descendants of British or French settlers. Most of the French, like those at the winter carnival shown here, live in Québec province. Germans and Italians are also large ethnic groups but, recently, increased numbers of people have come from eastern Europe, South America, and southeast Asia. Native peoples make up less than 3 percent of the population.

CALGARY STAMPEDE
Every year since 1923, thousands of people have flocked to Calgary for the famous Calgary Stampede. People dress up cowboy style to celebrate the old Wild West and Alberta's origins as a cattle trading center. Attractions include a rodeo, complete with bucking broncos.

THE FIRST CANADIANS

Native peoples, including the Inuit, are sometimes called Canada's "First Nations" because they lived in Canada long before European settlers arrived and took over their lands. Since 1970, the government has tried to draw these peoples into Canadian society, but many prefer their own culture and traditions. Across Canada colorful ceremonies and festivals demonstrate their proud spirit. Recently, First Nations have begun to win battles for their rights to ancestral lands. In 1999, the Nunavut area in the Northwest Territories became a self-governing Inuit territory, the first part of Canada to be governed by native Canadians in modern history.

The Inuit live in such cold conditions that they depend on warm clothing for survival.

Caribou fur is used by the Inuit as it traps warm air between each of the hairs.

Traditional Inuit jacket, called a parka

Insulated boots keep feet warm in freezing winter weather.

JAMES BAY

In 1971, construction began on a vast hydroelectric project to dam the rivers that flow into James Bay and Hudson Bay, generating electricity for use in Canada and the US. However, the project threatens thousands of Cree Indians who live in this region. There has been strong opposition from the Cree as well as from environmental groups, and the future of the project is uncertain.

CANADIAN PACIFIC RAILWAY

The last spike of the transcontinental rail link of the Canadian Pacific Railway was pounded in at Eagle Pass, British Columbia, on November 7, 1885. It was the start of a new era for Canada, opening up the west for trade and settlement, and finally making the vast country seem like one nation. One of the railroad's most amazing engineering feats is a spiral tunnel-road drilled into the Rocky Mountains. Curving steadily around, the tunnel rises for more than 3,000 ft (914 m). In spite of quicker alternatives, tourists often take the spectacular trip across Canada by train. However, the railroad is mostly used for cargo.

MINERAL WEALTH

Most of Canada's wealth comes from its abundance of natural resources, many of them mineral. It is the world's largest producer of uranium, zinc, and nickel, and also has reserves of aluminum, gold, copper, and silver.
Underground work has begun on what are thought to be some of the world's richest diamond deposits in an area near Yellowknife in the Northwest Territories.

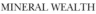

Zinc can be galvanized onto steel to prevent it from rusting.

Nickel can be mixed with other metals to make jet engines.

Main cargo loads

Containers and trailers: 23%

Forest products: 10%

Cars and other products: 22%

Grain: 22%

Coal: 13%

Fertilizers: 10%

AGRICULTURE

Wheat and cattle farming dominate Canada's main farming area, the prairies. Elsewhere, a wide variety of fruits and vegetables are grown. Apples, shown growing here in British Columbia, are the country's most important fruit crop. Between lakes Ontario and Erie lies the Niagara fruit belt. The lakes protect this area from the worst of Canada's weather, making it the ideal place for growing tender fruits such as pears, plums, peaches, and cherries.

COPING WITH THE COLD

Winters are long and cold throughout Canada but when the first snow falls, snow plows and salt trucks are out making sure the roads are safe. Next to some parking places there are even electric outlets where drivers can plug in heaters to keep their car's engine warm. During winter people can play hockey on frozen lakes and ponds. Skiing and snowboarding are also popular winter sports.

Snow plows clear the roads to make them safe.

Find out more

DIAMONDS: *150, 226, 248*
EARLY SETTLERS: *23, 31*
INUIT: *266*
VEGETATION ZONES: *15*

WESTERN CANADA

A WEALTH OF NATURAL RESOURCES first attracted European settlers to the wilds of western Canada. Fur trappers, gold prospectors, and loggers all hoped to make their fortune from the land. Today, natural resources are still the basis of the economy. The fertile soils of the prairie provinces of Alberta, Manitoba, and Saskatchewan make up four-fifths of Canada's farmland. Fishing is a major industry along the Pacific coast, where the main catch is salmon, most of which is canned for export. By contrast, the remote Yukon, Northwest, and Nunavut territories have important reserves of gold, zinc, and lead. These territories are also the only part of Canada where the native peoples form the majority of the population.

The most used softwood trees are spruce, shown left, then pine and fir.

VANCOUVER
Situated between the mountains and the sea, Vancouver is an attractive city and an industrial center, as well as a busy port. Its ice-free harbor provides Canada with year-round access for trade with Asian countries across the Pacific Ocean. Many Chinese families settled here rather than staying in Hong Kong when it reverted to China in 1997.

The most used hardwood trees are poplar, then birch, shown right, and maple.

TIMBER INDUSTRY
Moist winds from the Pacific Ocean deposit rain on the western slopes of the Rocky Mountains, making conditions ideal for trees to grow to enormous sizes. Canada is the world's largest exporter of forest products, and the province of British Columbia produces almost half of Canada's timber. Some logs are still floated to the sawmills, but today logs are often transported by road or helicopter. Most of the timber is softwood, used for building materials as well as for chopsticks for Japan.

At the sawmill the timber is cut into planks or pulped for papermaking.

Logs may be floated downriver from the forests to the sawmills in the form of huge rafts.

Logs are sawn when they are still "green," or full of sap. The method shown here produces boards with a decorative grain.

TOTEM POLES
For generations, native peoples of the northwestern coast carved wooden totem poles to record their family trees. Part of a pole shows which of the main clans a family belongs to, such as the raven or the wolf clan. Totem poles often guarded doorways to village homes.

The animals carved on the totem pole are symbols of the family's ancestors.

COAL, OIL, AND GAS WEALTH
Once grain and beef processing centers for the prairies, Edmonton and Calgary grew rich during the 1970s from the coal, oil, and gas found in the prairies and nearby Rocky Mountains. Now Edmonton boasts a gigantic shopping mall with a hockey rink, a swimming pool, a roller-coaster, and a hotel where people can stay during a shopping trip.

LIVING IN THE WILD
Large parts of the extreme north of Canada are home to more animals than people. Although part of the area is forested most of it is icy wilderness known as tundra. Animals that live here are adapted to the very cold conditions, and waterproof fur helps them to survive the snow and ice. Caribou, or reindeer, live on the tundra but migrate to the forests farther south in winter to escape the cold. Grizzly bears are found in the Rocky Mountains and can be dangerous.

A B C D E F G H I J K L

1 2 3 4 5 6 7 8 9 10 11 12 13 14 15

CANADA

N

THINGS TO LOOK FOR ON THE MAP

Longest river: Mackenzie, 2,650 miles (4,241 km) *Map D9*

Highest point: Mt. Logan, 19,850 ft (6,050 m) *Map A9*

Largest lake: Great Bear Lake, 12,095 sq miles (31,328 sq km) *Map D8*

ARCTIC CIRCLE

TROPIC OF CANCER

0 100 200 300 400 500 km
0 100 200 300 miles

ARCTIC OCEAN

Nares Strait

Ellesmere Island

Queen Elizabeth Islands

Axel Heiberg I.

Parry Islands

Mackenzie King I.

Bathurst I.

Devon Island

Baffin Bay

Melville I.

Cornwallis I.

Resolute

Lancaster Sound

McClure Strait

Viscount Melville Sound

Somerset I.

Arctic Bay

Davis Strait

Banks Island

Prince of Wales I.

Gulf of Boothia

Baffin Island

Pangnirtung

Amundsen Gulf

Victoria Island

McClintock Channel

Prince Charles I.

Cumberland Sound

Mackenzie Bay

Tuktoyaktuk

Old Crow

Inuvik

Fort McPherson

King William I.

Foxe Basin

IQALUIT

Frobisher Bay

Arctic Bay, Nunavut
☀ Jan 21°F (-30°C-)
July 44°F (7°C)
🌧 Jan 0.3 in (8 mm)
July 0.7 in (18 mm)

BEAUFORT SEA

ALASKA (U.S.)

Dawson

Kugluktuk

NORTHWEST TERRITORIES

Great Bear L.

Contwoyto L.

Garry L.

NUNAVUT

Southampton Island

Hudson Strait

YUKON

Norman Wells

Coats I.

Yukon

Kluane L.

Faro

Pelly

MACKENZIE MTS

Lac la Martre

Coppermine

Chesterfield Inlet

Mt. Logan

Haines Junction

WHITEHORSE

C A N A D A

Fort Simpson

YELLOWKNIFE

Dubawnt L.

Rankin Inlet

Arviat

Churchill, Manitoba
☀ Jan -19°F (-28°C)
July 54°F (12°C)
🌧 Jan 0.5 in (13 mm)
July 2.2 in (56 mm)

Teslin L.

Watson Lake

Great Slave L.

Nonacho L.

Fort Resolution

Hay River

Fort Smith

Slave

Hudson Bay

Fort Nelson

Uranium City

Seal

Churchill

ROCKY MOUNTAINS

Peace

L. Athabasca

Wollaston L.

Churchill

Alexander Archipelago

Fort Vermilion

Athabasca

Cree L.

Reindeer L.

MANITOBA

Fort St John

Fort McMurray

Frobisher L.

Lynn Lake

Nelson

Hayes

Prince Rupert

Kitimat

Dawson Creek

Lesser Slave L.

Thompson

Queen Charlotte Is.

Prince George

Grande Prairie

Flin Flon

ONTARIO

Nechako

Athabasca

SASKATCHEWAN

The Pas

Queen Charlotte Sound

BRITISH COLUMBIA

ALBERTA

Saskatchewan

L. Winnipeg

Fraser

EDMONTON

Leduc

Lloydminster

Prince Albert

L. Winnipegosis

Port Mice

Jasper

Wetaskiwin

North Battleford

Saskatoon

Selkirk

Campbell River

Red Deer

Yorkton

Kamloops

Columbia

Drumheller

L. Louise

Melville

Squamish

Vernon

Calgary

REGINA

Vancouver

Penticton

Medicine Hat

Moose Jaw

Brandon

WINNIPEG

VICTORIA

Cranbrook

Lethbridge

Swift Current

Weyburn

Estevan

PACIFIC OCEAN

Vancouver I.

UNITED STATES OF AMERICA

Edmonton, Alberta
☀ Jan 6°F (-14°C)
July 63°F (17°C)
🌧 Jan 0.9 in (23 mm)
July 3.3 in (84 mm)

Sunflower oil is made from the seeds of the tiny central flowers.

THE PRAIRIES
Wheat, the most important crop in Canada, is grown on the fertile grasslands known as the prairies. The province of Saskatchewan is the major producer. Sunflowers and canola are also important crops, grown to make cooking and industrial oils as well as animal feed.

EASTERN CANADA

SOME OF THE RICHEST AND POOREST areas of Canada are found within the eastern part of the country. The provinces of Ontario and Québec that lie around the Great Lakes and the St. Lawrence River form Canada's wealthy industrial region and contain most of the population. Canada's capital, Ottawa, and other major cities, including Toronto and Montreal, are in this region. At the end of Lake Erie, on the border with the United States, is Niagara Falls, one of the main tourist attractions in the region. The Atlantic, or Maritime, provinces along the stormy east coast have few natural resources and are suffering from a decline in the fishing industry, but enjoy a distinctive culture, and a rugged coastline and landscape.

HOCKEY
Canadians take advantage of long winters by playing hockey on frozen lakes and ponds, as well as community ice rinks. Hockey is the world's fastest team game, with the puck moving at speeds of up to 118 miles (190 km) per hour. It can get rough, and the action stops frequently, when players are sent to sit out penalties in the "sin bin."

ST. LAWRENCE SEAWAY
Completed in 1959, the Great Lakes–St. Lawrence Seaway system made it possible for ships to travel 2,342 miles (3,769 km) from the industrial center of North America to the Atlantic Ocean. Ships carrying cargoes of grain, timber, iron ore, and coal descend 600 ft (183 m) from Lake Ontario to sea level through a system of locks. Tolls are charged for ships that use the system. The Seaway is closed due to ice for four months during the winter.

TORONTO
On the north shore of Lake Ontario lies Toronto, Canada's leading industrial city, financial capital, and fastest growing urban area. The city has a reputation for being safe, with the lowest crime rate of any major city in North America. It also boasts the SkyDome, the first stadium with a retractable roof, and the Canadian National (CN) Tower, the tallest free-standing structure in the world.

GOLDEN HORSESHOE
Canada's leading industrial region, known as the Golden Horseshoe, curves around the western end of Lake Ontario, from the car-industry center of Oshawa, through Toronto and Hamilton and on to Niagara. Its location makes it easy to move products by water, by rail, and by road via a major highway called the Queen Elizabeth Way (QEW). Plentiful job opportunities attract people here and they earn some of the highest incomes in Canada.

Car assembly   Steelworks   Shipbuilding
Aircraft assembly   Finance   Fruit canning

QUÉBEC
In 1608, Frenchman Samuel de Champlain set up a fur trading post on the St. Lawrence River at a place the native peoples called Kébec. By 1763, the French settlements had been taken over by the British. Under British control, the province grew into a major commercial center. Today, over 80 percent of Canadians whose native language is French live in the province of Québec. Although laws guarantee the right of French Canadians to their own language, laws, and culture, some Québecois want to separate from the rest of Canada.

Cranberrries are used to make juice, sauces, and syrups.

CRANBERRIES
Along the coast of New Brunswick the land is marshy and ideal for growing cranberries. The plants are grown in bogs and the ripe berries are collected by hand or by special machines that scoop the fruit from the water. Berries are ready to pick in September or October.

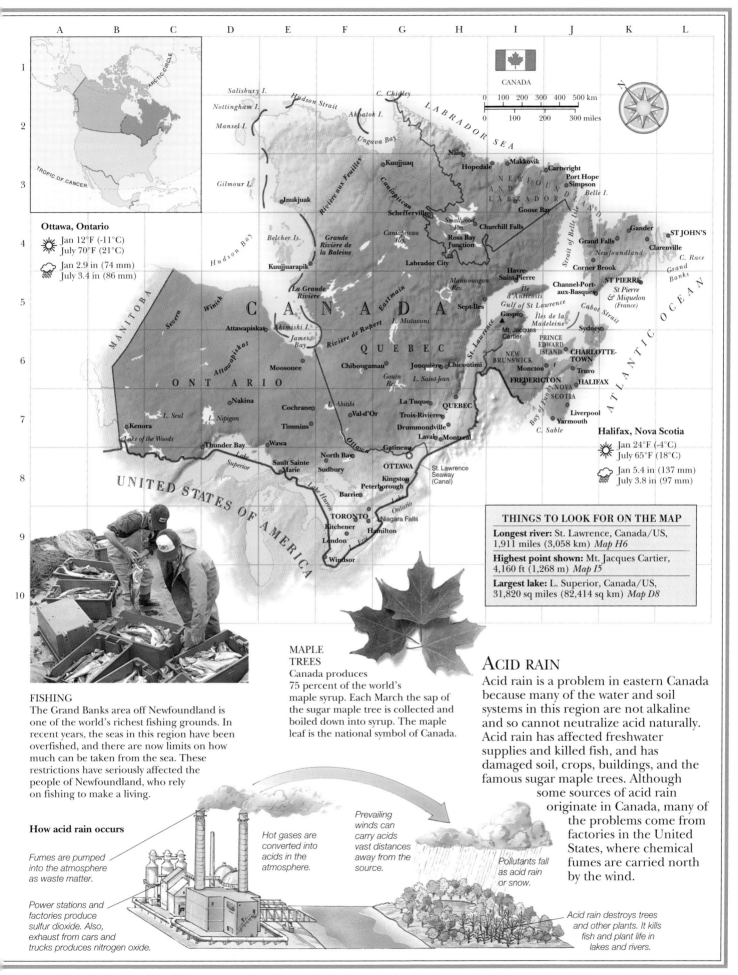

A B C D E F G H I J K L

1 2 3 4 5 6 7 8 9 10

CANADA

0 100 200 300 400 500 km
0 100 200 300 miles

Salisbury I.
Nottingham I.
Mansel I.
Hudson Strait
Akpatok I.
C. Chidley
LABRADOR SEA
Ungava Bay

Gilmour L.
Inukjuak
Rivière aux Feuilles
Kuujjuaq
Nain
Hopedale
Makkovik
Cartwright
Port Hope Simpson
Belle I.
NEWFOUNDLAND AND LABRADOR
Scheffervilie
Caniapiscau
Smallwood Res.
Churchill Falls
Goose Bay
Gander
ST JOHN'S
Grand Falls
Clarenville
C. Race
Newfoundland
Corner Brook
Grand Banks

Belcher Is.
Grande Rivière de la Baleine
Caniapiscau Res.
Labrador City
Ross Bay Junction
Havre Saint-Pierre
Channel-Port-aux-Basques
ST PIERRE
St Pierre & Miquelon (France)

Hudson Bay
Kuujjuarapik
La Grande Rivière
La Grande Rivière
Eastmain
Manicouagan Res.
Sept-Îles
Île d'Anticosti
Gulf of St Lawrence
Gaspé
Îles de la Madeleine
Cabot Strait
Sydney

MANITOBA
Winisk
Severn
Attawapiskat
Akimiski I.
James Bay
Rivière de Rupert
L. Mistassini
Mt. Jacques Cartier
PRINCE EDWARD ISLAND
CHARLOTTE-TOWN
NEW BRUNSWICK
Moncton
Truro
FREDERICTON
NOVA SCOTIA
HALIFAX

CANADA
Attawapiskat
QUEBEC
Chibougamau
Gouin Res.
Jonquière
Chicoutimi
L. Saint-Jean

ONTARIO
Moosonee
Nakina
L. Seul
L. Nipigon
Kenora
Lake of the Woods
Thunder Bay
Cochrane
Timmins
Wawa
L. Abitibi
Val-d'Or
La Tuque
Trois-Rivières
Drummondville
QUEBEC
Laval
Montreal
Liverpool
Yarmouth
C. Sable
Bay of Fundy

UNITED STATES OF AMERICA
Sault Sainte Marie
Lake Superior
North Bay
Sudbury
Lake Huron
Gatineau
OTTAWA
St. Lawrence Seaway (Canal)
Kingston
Peterborough
Barrie
Lake Ontario
TORONTO
Kitchener
Hamilton
Niagara Falls
London
Lake Erie
Windsor
St. Lawrence

Ottawa, Ontario
☀ Jan 12°F (-11°C)
   July 70°F (21°C)
☁ Jan 2.9 in (74 mm)
   July 3.4 in (86 mm)

Halifax, Nova Scotia
☀ Jan 24°F (-4°C)
   July 65°F (18°C)
☁ Jan 5.4 in (137 mm)
   July 3.8 in (97 mm)

THINGS TO LOOK FOR ON THE MAP
Longest river: St. Lawrence, Canada/US, 1,911 miles (3,058 km) *Map H6*
Highest point shown: Mt. Jacques Cartier, 4,160 ft (1,268 m) *Map I5*
Largest lake: L. Superior, Canada/US, 31,820 sq miles (82,414 sq km) *Map D8*

FISHING
The Grand Banks area off Newfoundland is one of the world's richest fishing grounds. In recent years, the seas in this region have been overfished, and there are now limits on how much can be taken from the sea. These restrictions have seriously affected the people of Newfoundland, who rely on fishing to make a living.

MAPLE TREES
Canada produces 75 percent of the world's maple syrup. Each March the sap of the sugar maple tree is collected and boiled down into syrup. The maple leaf is the national symbol of Canada.

ACID RAIN
Acid rain is a problem in eastern Canada because many of the water and soil systems in this region are not alkaline and so cannot neutralize acid naturally. Acid rain has affected freshwater supplies and killed fish, and has damaged soil, crops, buildings, and the famous sugar maple trees. Although some sources of acid rain originate in Canada, many of the problems come from factories in the United States, where chemical fumes are carried north by the wind.

How acid rain occurs

Fumes are pumped into the atmosphere as waste matter.

Hot gases are converted into acids in the atmosphere.

Prevailing winds can carry acids vast distances away from the source.

Pollutants fall as acid rain or snow.

Power stations and factories produce sulfur dioxide. Also, exhaust from cars and trucks produces nitrogen oxide.

Acid rain destroys trees and other plants. It kills fish and plant life in lakes and rivers.

UNITED STATES OF AMERICA

IN LESS THAN 400 YEARS, the United States of America (USA) has grown from wild countryside inhabited by native peoples to the world's most powerful industrial nation. The country is made up of 50 states, including Alaska in the far north and Hawaii in the Pacific Ocean. There are two major mountain ranges, the Appalachians to the east and the Rockies to the west, while much of its center is covered by the gently sloping Great Plains. Vast supplies of coal, oil, and minerals, together with mass immigration in the 19th and early 20th centuries, helped business and industry grow fast. Today, American products and culture are recognized throughout the world.

UNITED STATES OF AMERICA

Capital city: Washington, DC

Area: 3,539,224 sq miles (9,166,600 sq km)

Population: 281,400,000

Official language: English

Major religions: Christian 86%, Jewish 2%, other 12%

Government: Multiparty democracy

Currency: Dollar

Adult literacy rate: 99%

Life expectancy: 77 years

People per doctor: 400

Televisions: 847 per 1,000 people

STARS AND STRIPES
On the US flag, the stars stand for the 50 modern states, while the stripes represent the original 13 colonies on the East Coast. Until independence in 1776, these were governed by Britain. Today, each state has its own laws but is ruled by the national government in Washington, District of Columbia.

PEOPLE OF AMERICA

People in the US belong to a wide range of different groups and races. Most are descended from immigrants – people who moved there from other parts of the world, such as Europe and Asia. Many African-Americans are descendants of slaves forced to the US in the 17th, 18th, and early 19th centuries. Today, the population is increasingly Hispanic (Spanish speaking), Asian, and African-American. By 2050, these groups will make up more than half the population.

This girl has a mother who is part Hawaiian and part Korean.

This child has Japanese parents who moved to the US during the 1970s.

African-Americans now make up 12 percent of the population.

WORLD LEADER
The US is the world's richest country, and its leading products include iron and steel, timber and paper products, electronic equipment, cars, and aircraft, shown above. These industries create many jobs, and women now make up almost half of the country's total workforce.

LIVING IN THE CITY

More than 75 percent of Americans live in cities or the surrounding suburbs. Most people who live in the suburbs own their own homes and travel to work by car. New York is the biggest city, with more than 17 million inhabitants, followed by Los Angeles, and then Chicago. People from different backgrounds mingle in most cities. Often they have their own neighborhoods, with names such as Little Italy or Chinatown. This view shows midtown Manhattan, New York.

As cities became more crowded, and land more expensive, architects began to design taller and taller buildings where people could live and work.

Every day, half a million people use Grand Central Station to get to work.

Many US cities are laid out on a simple grid system where main roads, or avenues, run north to south, and streets run east to west.

Americans live in a variety of homes – detached houses, townhouses, and high-rise apartment buildings.

Skyscrapers, such as the Empire State Building, now dominate the skyline of most cities in the US.

Places of worship, like the Holy Family Church, can be found in every city.

MOVING WEST

The population of America has always been mobile, moving to new states in search of work or a better lifestyle. Major events, such as the Great Depression in the 1930s, also forced people to move in the hope of finding work. The general pattern of movement since settlers first arrived is shown on this map. Over the past 30 years or so, more and more people have moved to the "Sunbelt" states of the south and west. These include California, Arizona, Texas, and Florida.

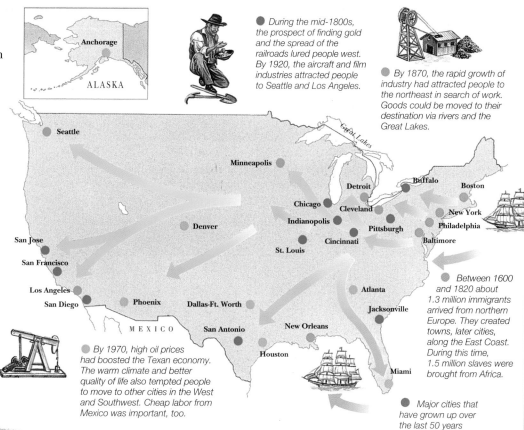

● During the mid-1800s, the prospect of finding gold and the spread of the railroads lured people west. By 1920, the aircraft and film industries attracted people to Seattle and Los Angeles.

● By 1870, the rapid growth of industry had attracted people to the northeast in search of work. Goods could be moved to their destination via rivers and the Great Lakes.

● Between 1600 and 1820 about 1.3 million immigrants arrived from northern Europe. They created towns, later cities, along the East Coast. During this time, 1.5 million slaves were brought from Africa.

● By 1970, high oil prices had boosted the Texan economy. The warm climate and better quality of life also tempted people to move to other cities in the West and Southwest. Cheap labor from Mexico was important, too.

● Major cities that have grown up over the last 50 years

NATIONAL PARKS

Large areas of America's most spectacular countryside are protected in more than 350 national parks. Yellowstone National Park, in Wyoming and Montana, was the first park to open, in 1872. Yellowstone provides a safe environment for animals, including bison, elk, antelope, grizzly bear, moose, and deer.

BASEBALL

Baseball is the country's national sport. The first game played between two organized teams took place in New Jersey in 1846. The National League was formed in 1876, the American League in 1901, and today baseball is the most popular spectator sport in the US. It is traditional for the President to pitch the first ball at the start of each new baseball season.

THE FIRST AMERICANS

Native Americans, the first inhabitants of the US, today make up less than 1 percent of the population. When Europeans arrived in the 1500s, Native American tribes were decimated by disease. They lost many of their homelands and were forced over time to live on reservations, land allotted to them by the government. Despite these hardships, many tribal traditions and languages still survive.

LARGEST TRIBES	
Cherokee	308,000
Navajo	219,000
Chippewa	104,000
Sioux	103,000
Choctaw	82,000
Pueblo	53,000

This Zuni artist, a member of the Pueblo tribe, makes and sells silver and turquoise jewelry.

AMERICAN CULTURE

The influence of US culture can be seen all over the world. Fast foods, such as hamburgers, hot dogs, and soft drinks, as well as characters from films and TV shows, are recognized in cities from Berlin to Beijing. This "selling of America" is a billion-dollar industry and plays a vital part in the US economy.

Strawberry milkshake

Double hamburger

Find out more

NATIVE PEOPLES: 22–23
SETTLING THE CONTINENT: 23, 24–25
US GOVERNMENT: 23, 270

US: WESTERN STATES

FROM THE ICY LANDSCAPE OF ALASKA, through the deserts of Nevada and Arizona, to the semitropical islands of Hawaii, the western states cover a dramatic range of scenery. Down the West Coast, large cities such as Seattle, Portland, and San Francisco ship timber, fish, and fruit all over the world. The West is also home to Hollywood, capital of the multimillion dollar film industry, and Silicon Valley, a stretch of northern California that lies at the heart of the high-tech computer business. Sun Valley, in Idaho, ranks as one of the country's leading ski and summer resorts.

THE NORTHERN FORESTS
Great forests of pine, cedar, and fir trees thrive in the wet climate near the coasts of Oregon and Washington. These states are the country's major suppliers of timber and wood pulp. The trees are cut into logs and transported by road to the coast. Environmental groups are now trying to protect the trees, many of which are more than 200 years old.

EARTHQUAKE COUNTRY

People in California have to live with the constant threat of earthquakes. The area lies on the boundary, or fault line, between two plates of the Earth's crust. When these plates push and slide against each other, it causes earthquakes, which can destroy roads and homes. It is difficult to predict an earthquake, so most people keep a survival kit in case they are trapped or left without supplies. Some of the items included in such a kit are displayed here.

Lightweight bag of emergency items, including first-aid supplies (not shown)

Bar of dried food with vitamins

Mini rolls of toilet tissue

Towelette

Disposable toothbrush with toothpaste

FAULT LINES
The San Andreas fault runs for 750 miles (1,207 km) across California, passing through the cities of San Francisco and Los Angeles. There are also hundreds of other smaller faults that constantly cause minor tremors.

—— Major fault
—— Minor faults

OREGON

Heavy-duty flashlight

San Francisco

NEVADA

CALIFORNIA

San Andreas Fault

P A C I F I C   O C E A N

Los Angeles

MEXICO

Packet of pure drinking water

Light sticks work for 12 hours and do not need batteries.

Emergency blanket designed to reflect body heat

SOUTH OF THE BORDER
The majority of immigrants living in the western states come from nearby Mexico. They are called Hispanics because their ancestors came from Spain and they speak Spanish. Many still follow the religion and festivals of Mexico. Hispanics also arrive from Cuba, Puerto Rico, and El Salvador.

FIELDS OF PLENTY

Fertile soil, plenty of sunshine, and water, diverted from rivers that flow from the Sierra Nevada Mountains, make California the leading agricultural state. The land is used to grow more than 40 percent of the fresh fruit and vegetables eaten in the US, such as peaches, oranges, and strawberries, as well as artichokes and brussels sprouts. Mexicans often cross into the country illegally to find work on the fruit farms. The Napa Valley, north of San Francisco, is an important grape-growing and wine-producing area.

CAR CULTURE
When Henry Ford introduced the first cheap car in 1910, it promised freedom on the open road. Today, there are more cars on the road in the US than in any other country. Networks of six-lane highways weave across cities such as Los Angeles, shown above. Fumes from the cars contribute to city smog problems.

CARS PER 100 PEOPLE		
US		74
France		48
Denmark		37
Brazil		8.5
India		0.7

UNITED STATES
OF AMERICA

Fairbanks, Alaska
☀ Jan -11°F (-24°C)
July 60°F (16°C)
🌧 Jan 0.9 in (23 mm)
July 1.9 in (48 mm)

Boise, Idaho
☀ Jan 30°F (-1°C)
July 74°F (23°C)
🌧 Jan 1.9 in (48 mm)
July 0.2 in (5 mm)

THINGS TO LOOK FOR ON THE MAP

Longest river: Colorado, US/Mexico, 1,400 miles (2,253 km) *Map I12*

Highest point: Mt. McKinley (Denali), 20,320 ft (6,194 m) *Map C2*

Largest lake: Great Salt Lake, 1,361 sq miles (3,525 sq km) *Map J8*

World's largest land gorge: Grand Canyon, 217 miles (349 km) long, 6,234 ft (1,900 m) deep *Map J10*

LIVING IN THE DESERT
The Sonoran Desert was once home only to creatures adapted to the heat. Today, Phoenix, Arizona, is one of the fastest-growing US cities, despite its location in the middle of the desert. Between 1960–1990, its population grew by more than 300 percent. Part of the reason why the Colorado River fails to reach the ocean is because of demands for water from Phoenix.

Cactus plants can survive the desert heat.

The collared lizard of the southwestern deserts hides under a rock at night and comes out in the morning to warm up in the sun.

This extraordinary road runner rarely flies, but can run very fast. It uses its long tail as a brake, or as a rudder to change direction.

Honolulu, Hawaii
☀ Jan 72°F (22°C)
July 77°F (25°C)
🌧 Jan 4.1 in (104 mm)
July 0.9 in (23 mm)

US: CENTRAL STATES

FAMOUS FOR COWBOYS AND CATTLE RANCHES, the central states of the US are also the country's "bread basket" and oil refinery. This vast region includes high mountains, fertile plains, and the Mississippi River system. Texas and Oklahoma have major oil and gas fields, while coal is mined in Wyoming and Montana. The Rocky Mountains contain important national parks, such as Yellowstone and Glacier, and are rich in mineral resources. Hot summers and cold winters, as well as violent hailstorms and tornadoes, make the region's climate one of extremes.

Ears of the type of wheat used for making bread

Grains of wheat

TORNADO ALLEY
Several hundred tornadoes a year strike "Tornado Alley," an area that runs through Kansas, Oklahoma, and Missouri. They occur when hot air from the Gulf of Mexico hits cold, dry air from Canada. The violent storms, known as "twisters," cut through towns and countryside, destroying everything in their path.

A twisting column of rising air forms beneath a thunder cloud.

The air spirals up the column and sucks up dirt and objects in its way.

Tornadoes can travel at 112 mph (180 km/h).

THE GREAT PLAINS
Once home to millions of buffalo, the vast open plains between the Rocky Mountains and the Mississippi River are now planted with cereal grains. Farmers on the Great Plains produce more wheat and corn than anywhere else on Earth. Farming is highly mechanized, with huge machines to harvest the grain. In drier parts, the land can be farmed only if it is irrigated, often using water taken from a natural underground reservoir, called an aquifer.

RURAL AMERICA
Today, most Americans live in cities and towns, but at the start of the 20th century, two out of every five adults lived on farms. There are still many small towns with populations of less than 10,000 people. These towns are often in farming country and are where people go for supplies, to attend school, church, or special events, such as this fair.

COWBOY COUNTRY
Cattle are raised on the Great Plains and foothills of the Rocky Mountains. In summer, cowboys on horseback used to drive the cattle to fresh pastures; in winter, they herded them back to the ranch to be sold at auction for food. Hollywood films turned cowboys into heroes, but life in the saddle was not easy. Pay was poor, and men often spent 15 hours a day on horseback in scorching heat or driving rain. Today, ranches are smaller and cowboys and horses may be ferried from ranch to pasture by truck and trailer.

Hats keep off the sun and the rain, and were once used to carry water.

Leather cuffs

Chaps protect the rider from cattle horns.

Fringe helps to drain away any rainwater.

Spurs

A lasso is used to rope cattle.

Boots have heels to keep feet firmly in the stirrups.

CITIES OF THE DEAD
Cemeteries in New Orleans are built above ground to protect them when the Mississippi floods. The burial grounds are called Cities of the Dead.

A wreath of flowers

MISSISSIPPI RIVER
From Minnesota in the north to its enormous delta in the Gulf of Mexico, the mighty Mississippi River flows through the central states. It is one of the world's busiest waterways, suitable for cargo boats for almost 1,802 miles (2,900 km). This view of the river shows it flowing through Iowa, where it forms a natural border with Illinois and Wisconsin. In the south, severe flooding often occurs after heavy rains.

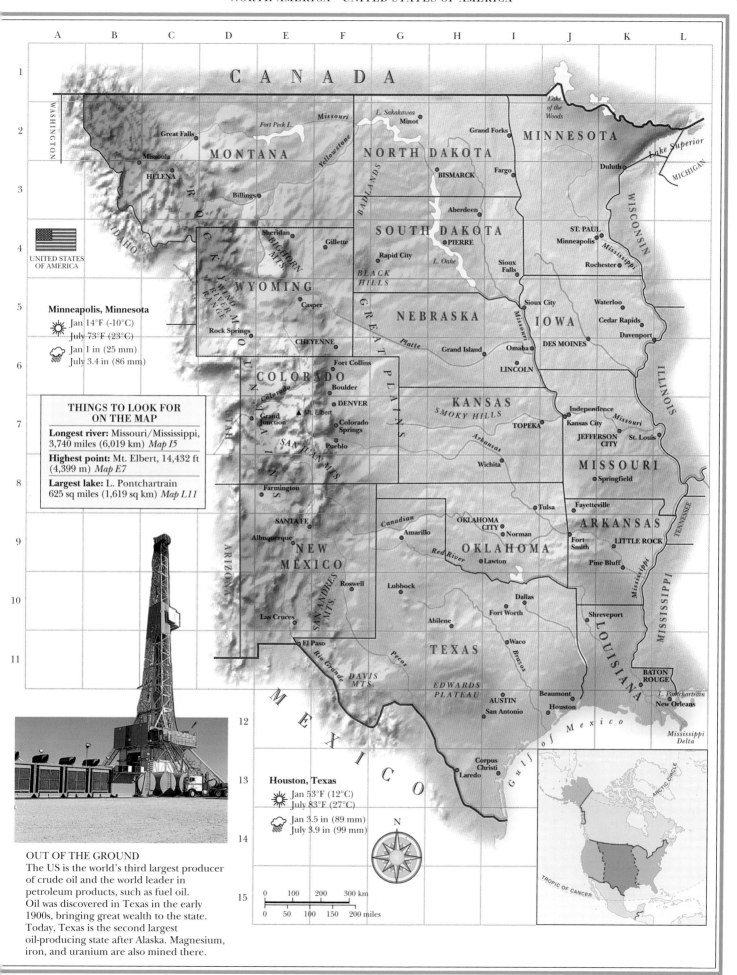

CANADA

WASHINGTON

MONTANA

Great Falls
Missoula
HELENA
Billings

Fort Peck L.
Missouri
Yellowstone

L. Sakakawea
Minot

NORTH DAKOTA
BISMARCK
Fargo

Grand Forks

Lake
of the
Woods

MINNESOTA

Duluth

Lake Superior

MICHIGAN

WISCONSIN

BADLANDS

Aberdeen

SOUTH DAKOTA
PIERRE

ST. PAUL
Minneapolis
Rochester

Mississippi

IDAHO

ROCKY

Sheridan
Gillette

BIGHORN MTS.

Rapid City

L. Oahe

BLACK
HILLS

Sioux
Falls

WYOMING

WIND RIVER RANGE

Casper

Rock Springs

CHEYENNE

GREAT

NEBRASKA

Platte

Sioux City

Missouri

IOWA

Waterloo
Cedar Rapids
Davenport

DES MOINES

Minneapolis, Minnesota
Jan 14°F (-10°C)
July 73°F (23°C)
Jan 1 in (25 mm)
July 3.4 in (86 mm)

Fort Collins
Boulder
DENVER
Colorado Springs
Pueblo

COLORADO

Mt. Elbert

Grand
Junction

Colorado

SAN JUAN MTS.

Grand Island

Omaha

LINCOLN

PLAINS

KANSAS
SMOKY HILLS

TOPEKA

Arkansas

Wichita

Independence
Kansas City
JEFFERSON
CITY

Missouri

St. Louis

MISSOURI

Springfield

ILLINOIS

**THINGS TO LOOK FOR
ON THE MAP**
Longest river: Missouri/Mississippi,
3,740 miles (6,019 km) *Map I5*
Highest point: Mt. Elbert, 14,432 ft
(4,399 m) *Map E7*
Largest lake: L. Pontchartrain
625 sq miles (1,619 sq km) *Map L11*

Farmington

SANTA FE

Albuquerque

ARIZONA

NEW
MEXICO

UTAH

Canadian

Amarillo

Red River

OKLAHOMA
CITY
Norman

Lawton

OKLAHOMA

Tulsa

Fort
Smith

Fayetteville

ARKANSAS

LITTLE ROCK

Pine Bluff

Mississippi

TENNESSEE

Roswell

SAN ANDRES MTS.

Lubbock

Abilene

Dallas
Fort Worth

Waco

Shreveport

LOUISIANA

Las Cruces

El Paso

Rio Grande

DAVIS
MTS.

Pecos

Brazos

EDWARDS
PLATEAU

TEXAS

AUSTIN
San Antonio

Beaumont
Houston

BATON
ROUGE

L. Pontchartrain
New Orleans

Mississippi
Delta

MEXICO

Houston, Texas
Jan 53°F (12°C)
July 83°F (27°C)
Jan 3.5 in (89 mm)
July 3.9 in (99 mm)

Corpus
Christi
Laredo

Gulf of Mexico

N

0   100   200   300 km
0   50   100   150   200 miles

ARCTIC CIRCLE

TROPIC OF CANCER

OUT OF THE GROUND
The US is the world's third largest producer
of crude oil and the world leader in
petroleum products, such as fuel oil.
Oil was discovered in Texas in the early
1900s, bringing great wealth to the state.
Today, Texas is the second largest
oil-producing state after Alaska. Magnesium,
iron, and uranium are also mined there.

UNITED STATES
OF AMERICA

US: EASTERN STATES

EXCELLENT HARBORS, FERTILE LAND, and rich mineral resources have made this region one of the most densely populated in the country. It was along the East Coast that the first settlers from Europe arrived in the 16th century. Today, the area includes some of the country's largest cities, such as New York and Washington, DC, as well as the once-great industrial centers of Chicago, Detroit, and Cleveland on the Great Lakes. Farther south, farmers use the land to cultivate cotton, tobacco, and vegetables grown for their oil. Hurricanes are a threat to people living on the Gulf and Atlantic coasts.

The White House has been the home of every US president since 1800.

RULING THE COUNTRY
The US has a written set of laws, known as a constitution, that sets out how the country should be governed. The center of government is Washington, DC, where the President and his family live in The White House. The President is the head of state and is chosen in elections that are held once every four years.

THE APPALACHIANS
The Appalachian Mountains run through North Carolina, Virginia, and West Virginia. For many years, coal was mined here and used to power steel mills. Today, many mines and factories have closed, eliminating jobs. Despite a plan to open up the area to tourists, Appalachia remains one of the poorest parts of the US.

BIG BUSINESS IN NEW YORK

Originally a fur-trading post at the mouth of the Hudson River, New York is now the US's financial capital. Wall Street, so called because it marked the line of the old city wall, is the home of the New York Stock Exchange. Financial deals worth billions of dollars are made there every day. Nasdaq, short for National Association of Securities Dealers Automated Quotation System, based in New York, was the world's first electronic stock market. Because it is a purely computer-based system, shares can be traded around the globe, 24 hours a day.

This huge machine picks the cotton bolls from the plant.

Flower buds form on the cotton plants.

Flowers turn pink and then fall off.

The sign on this blues club in Memphis, Tennessee, is shaped like a giant guitar.

THE BIRTH OF THE BLUES
This part of the US is the birthplace of some of the world's most popular music. Jazz and blues were based on the spiritual and work songs of the black population. Country music began as poor white people's music in Kentucky and Tennessee, and the soul label Motown grew up in Detroit, or Motor Town.

Neon, used to light up so many buildings across America, was first invented in 1898.

After the flower falls off, a tiny seed ripens and grows into a pod, or boll.

The cotton boll opens into a fluffy fiber ready for harvesting.

Cotton is woven into fabric for shirts, pants, and towels, which are sold at home and abroad.

COTTON – FROM FIELD TO FABRIC

In the mid-1800s, the southern states produced 80 percent of the world's cotton and grew rich on the profits. Cotton was grown on huge plantations, then handpicked by black slaves who had been brought by force from Africa. Slavery was finally abolished in the US in 1865. Cotton is still an important crop, although modern machinery now does the hard work. Soy beans, used mainly for oil, are now the biggest crop in this region.

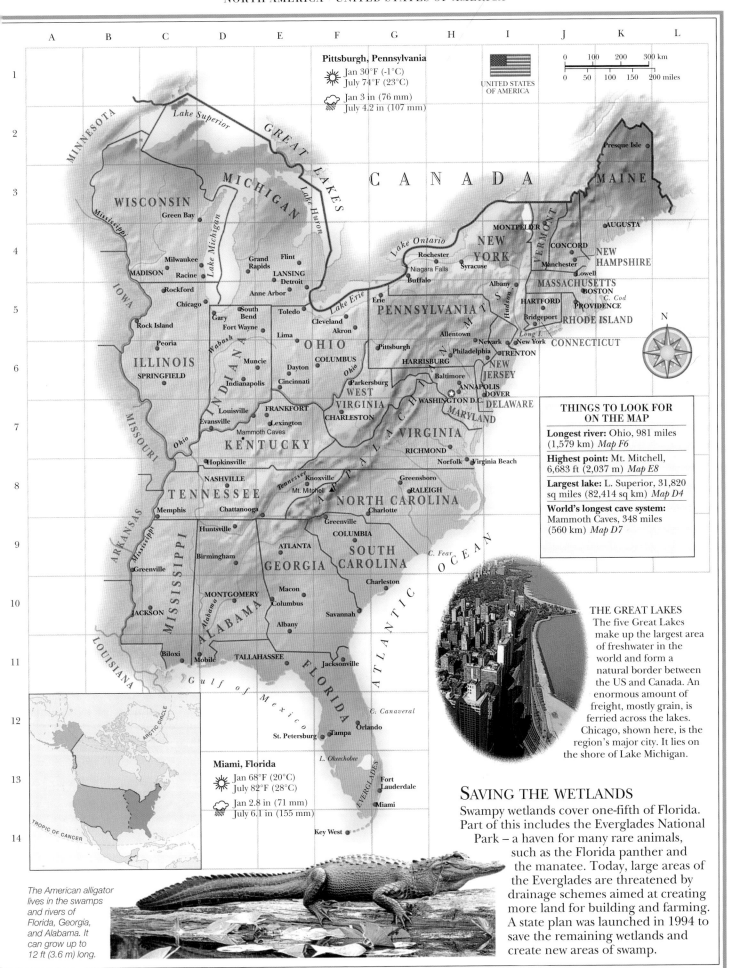

Pittsburgh, Pennsylvania
☀ Jan 30°F (-1°C)
July 74°F (23°C)
🌧 Jan 3 in (76 mm)
July 4.2 in (107 mm)

UNITED STATES
OF AMERICA

0   100   200   300 km
0   50   100   150   200 miles

**THINGS TO LOOK FOR
ON THE MAP**

Longest river: Ohio, 981 miles
(1,579 km) *Map F6*

Highest point: Mt. Mitchell,
6,683 ft (2,037 m) *Map E8*

Largest lake: L. Superior, 31,820
sq miles (82,414 sq km) *Map D4*

World's longest cave system:
Mammoth Caves, 348 miles
(560 km) *Map D7*

THE GREAT LAKES
The five Great Lakes
make up the largest area
of freshwater in the
world and form a
natural border between
the US and Canada. An
enormous amount of
freight, mostly grain, is
ferried across the lakes.
Chicago, shown here, is the
region's major city. It lies on
the shore of Lake Michigan.

SAVING THE WETLANDS
Swampy wetlands cover one-fifth of Florida.
Part of this includes the Everglades National
Park – a haven for many rare animals,
such as the Florida panther and
the manatee. Today, large areas of
the Everglades are threatened by
drainage schemes aimed at creating
more land for building and farming.
A state plan was launched in 1994 to
save the remaining wetlands and
create new areas of swamp.

Miami, Florida
☀ Jan 68°F (20°C)
July 82°F (28°C)
🌧 Jan 2.8 in (71 mm)
July 6.1 in (155 mm)

*The American alligator
lives in the swamps
and rivers of
Florida, Georgia,
and Alabama. It
can grow up to
12 ft (3.6 m) long.*

37

MEXICO

MEXICO

THE COLORFUL LAND OF MEXICO was once home to the golden civilizations of the Maya and Aztecs. These ancient empires were destroyed by the Spanish, who invaded in the 1500s and ruled the country until its independence in 1821. Descendants of the native peoples still live in Mexico, but most people are *mestizo*, of mixed Spanish and native Indian descent. Almost half of all Mexicans are under 19 years old, and the population is growing rapidly, leading to overcrowding in the cities. Mexico has limited farmland, and cannot produce enough food for the growing population.

MEXICO	
Capital city: Mexico City	
Area: 736,945 sq miles (1,908,690 sq km)	
Population: 98,900,000	
Official language: Spanish	
Major religions: Christian 96%, other 4%	
Government: Multiparty democracy	
Currency: Mexico new peso	
Adult literacy rate: 91%	
Life expectancy: 72 years	
People per doctor: 769	
Televisions: 261 per 1,000 people	

A LAND OF CONTRASTS
Mexico's landscape ranges from vast deserts in the north, through snowcapped mountains and a central plateau in the center, to tropical rain forests in the south. The Sonoran Desert, shown here, stretches across the border into the US. This desert is home to the giant saguaro cactus and to poisonous animals such as rattlesnakes and scorpions.

SIGHT-SEEING
Tourism is one of Mexico's biggest sources of income. Visitors from all over the world come to see Chichén Itzá, Tenochtitlán, Palenque, and other sites of the ancient Maya and Aztec civilizations. The warm sea and sandy beaches at coastal resorts, such as Acapulco and Cancun, also attract many tourists.

Mexico City's most famous street is the wide Paseo de la Reforma, with its tall buildings, cafés, and theaters.

These buildings at Teotihuacán, near Mexico City, are the remains of an ancient religious center

MEXICO CITY
With a population of almost 20 million, Mexico City is one of the world's largest cities. But its size and location create many problems. It lies at high altitude and is ringed by mountains, so pollution from cars and factories cannot escape and poisons the air. Children often wait to leave for school until after rush hour to avoid car fumes. Mexico City is very overcrowded, and the area is prone to earthquakes; the most recent one devastated the city center in 1985.

Most Mexicans are Roman Catholic and worship in churches often named after saints.

Women carry decorated baskets of flowers. They wear wraparound skirts, called enrados, and white blouses.

Men parade with large cotton globes on which the name of their town is written.

A dip called guacamole is made with avocados.

Beer with a slice of lime

Avocado

Chilies

Tortillas are eaten like bread or made into a snack called a taco.

VILLAGE FESTIVALS
Festivals, or *fiestas*, are a common part of Mexican village life. Each village has its own patron saint and on the saint's day there is a colorful celebration. There are 115 separate saints' days in Mexico. Here the people of a small town near Oaxaca celebrate their *fiesta* with a street procession. Although most people in Mexico are Roman Catholic, native Indian beliefs are also important, and many festivals are a mixture of Christian and Indian traditions.

MEXICAN FOOD
Mexicans eat a variety of spicy foods flavored with chilies. Most of the food is based on home-grown produce, such as avocados, beans, tomatoes, and corn. Pancakes, called tortillas, are made from corn flour and filled with meat or vegetables, and cheese. Cooks also mix chilies and chocolate to make a spicy sauce called mole, which is served on chicken.

A B C D E F G H I J K L
1 2 3 4 5 6 7 8 9 10

Monterrey
- Jan 58°F (14.5°C)
- July 80.5°F (27°C)
- Jan 0.6 in (15 mm)
- July 2.3 in (58 mm)

THINGS TO LOOK FOR ON THE MAP
Longest river: Rio Grande (Río Bravo del Norte), 1,883 miles (3,030 km) *Map G4*
Highest point: Citlaltépetl (Orizaba), 18,700 ft (5,700 m) *Map H8*
Largest lake: L. Chapala, 598 sq miles (1,550 sq km) *Map E7*
World's largest gulf: Gulf of Mexico, 700,000 sq miles (1,813,000 sq km) *Map I7*

MEXICO

Mexico City
- Jan 54°F (12.5°C)
- July 82.5°F (28°C)
- Jan 1.0 in (25 mm)
- July 4.8 in (122 mm)

Acapulco
- Jan 80°F (26.5°C)
- July 83.5°F (28.5°C)
- Jan 0.2 in (6 mm)
- July 10.1 in (256 mm)

OIL FROM THE GULF
Huge reserves of oil were found along the Gulf of Mexico coast in 1976, and today Mexico is the world's fifth largest oil producer. There are about 3,000 oil platforms in the gulf, extracting oil from the seabed. Mexico is also rich in other minerals, including iron, zinc, copper, and silver, of which it is the world's biggest producer.

TRADITIONAL CRAFTS
Weaving and embroidery are among the traditional crafts of Mexico's native Indian peoples. Images of gods, birds, and flowers are often used in their designs. Just like their ancestors, women bring brightly decorated clothes into the towns to sell in the markets.

Blue, red, and black are the main colors used in traditional Mexican designs.

MADE IN MEXICO
Clustered along Mexico's border with the US are some 2,000 factories, called *maquiladoras*. Here, huge numbers of cars, computers, shoes, and other manufactured goods are assembled from parts, ready to be exported. Most of the factories are owned by foreign companies that are attracted to Mexico by the cheap labor costs. The *maquiladoras* are an important source of income for Mexico and help prevent its economy from being too dependent on oil.

Find out more
OIL: *137, 152, 281*
POPULATION GROWTH: *16–17*
ROMAN CATHOLICS: *274*
TRADE (*MAQUILADORAS*): *280*

CENTRAL AND SOUTH AMERICA

CENTRAL AMERICA IS A NARROW BRIDGE of land linking Mexico in the north to South America in the south. A string of mountains runs down its length, capped by volcanoes. The beautiful, palm-fringed islands of the Caribbean Sea lie off its east coast. South America, the fourth largest continent, contains a range of very different landscapes. About 60 percent of the continent is covered in vast, grassy plains. The towering Andes mountains stretch along the west coast, with the long, thin Atacama Desert sandwiched between the mountains and the sea. Tropical rain forests spread in a lush green blanket across huge areas of the northeast.

The Andean condor has a wingspan of 10 ft (3 m). Its huge wings help it soar above mountain peaks.

THE ANDES

Stretching for 4,505 miles (7,250 km) along the entire length of South America, the Andes are the world's longest mountain range. Many peaks rise above 19,685 ft (6,000 m). The mountains were formed when two plates of the Earth's crust collided. The plates are still moving, causing numerous earthquakes and volcanoes along the range. An extinct volcano, Aconcagua, is the highest Andean peak and the highest mountain in South America at 22,835 ft (6,960 m). The world's highest navigable lake, Titicaca, lies in the Andes between Peru and Bolivia.

THE AMAZON RIVER

The world's largest rain forest grows in the vast basin of the mighty Amazon, the longest river in South America. The Amazon rises high in the snowcapped Andes in Peru, then flows 4,001 miles (6,439 km) across Peru and Brazil to its mouth in the Atlantic Ocean. The Amazon carries more water than any other river. At its mouth the Amazon is so wide that you cannot see from one bank to the other. The river discharges so much water into the ocean that the water is still brackish 112 miles (180 km) out to sea.

As the winds reach the Andes they cool, and rain starts to fall.

Fog bank

Pacific Ocean

Wet winds from the Atlantic

Rain forest

Very little rain falls on the west side of the Andes, which is mostly desert.

THE ANDES AND CLIMATE

The Andes have a major effect on the weather of South America. Warm, wet winds from the Atlantic rise up the eastern slopes. As they rise, they cool and the water in them falls as rain. On the dry, western slopes, the weather conditions are completely different. Here the winds pass over the cold Humboldt Current as they blow in off the sea. This causes them to cool and form a fog bank.

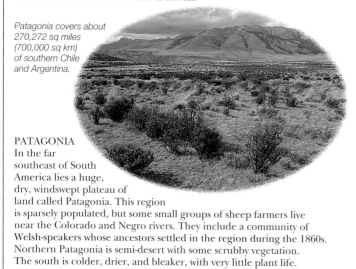

Patagonia covers about 270,272 sq miles (700,000 sq km) of southern Chile and Argentina.

PATAGONIA

In the far southeast of South America lies a huge, dry, windswept plateau of land called Patagonia. This region is sparsely populated, but some small groups of sheep farmers live near the Colorado and Negro rivers. They include a community of Welsh-speakers whose ancestors settled in the region during the 1860s. Northern Patagonia is semi-desert with some scrubby vegetation. The south is colder, drier, and bleaker, with very little plant life.

THE PAMPAS

Rolling grasslands cover the center of Argentina and extend into neighboring Paraguay. These are the pampas, vast open plains that stretch across an area of 250,967 sq miles (650,000 sq km). The western pampas are dry, semi-desert, but the eastern part has frequent rainfall. The pampas form the economic heartland of Argentina. Large herds of beef cattle are grazed on the plains. Other areas have been plowed up to grow huge amounts of wheat, corn, beans, and other crops.

A B C D E F G H I J K L

1 2 3 4 5 6 7 8 9 10 11 12 13 14 15 16

TROPIC OF CANCER

EQUATOR

TROPIC OF CAPRICORN

ANTARCTIC CIRCLE

Yucatan Channel

YUCATAN PENINSULA

Great Bahama Bank

Greater Antilles

Hispaniola

West Indies

ATLANTIC OCEAN

Gulf of Honduras

Coco

Mosquito Coast

CARIBBEAN SEA

Lesser Antilles

Mt. Pelée

Gulf of Tehuantepec

L. Izabel

L. Nicaragua

San Juan

Margarita I.

Trinidad

PACIFIC OCEAN

Panama Canal

ISTHMUS OF PANAMA

Coiba I.

Gulf of Panama

Malpelo I.

CORDILLERA OCCIDENTAL

CORDILLERA ORIENTAL

Magdalena

Meta

Guaviare

Orinoco

Angel Falls

GUIANA HIGHLANDS

Galapagos Is.

Caquetá

Napo

Rio Negro

Amazon

Marajó I.

Rocas I.

Fernando de Noronha I.

Marañón

Amazon

AMAZÔNIA

Amazon

Juruá

Purus

Madeira

Tapajós

Xingu

Ucayali

SELVAS

SERRA DO RONCADOR

Araguaia

Tocantins

São Francisco

C. St Antonio

PLATEAU OF MATO GROSSO

BRAZILIAN HIGHLANDS

ANDES

Paraguay

Paranaíba

SERRA DA MANTIQUEIRA

C. de São Tomé

L. Titicaca

C. Frio

ALTIPLANO

L. Poopó

Salar de Uyuni

N

Highest temperature:
Rivadavia, Argentina,
120°F (49°C)

Rivadavia

GRAN CHACO

Iguaçu Falls

San Félix I.

Paraná

Uruguay

San Ambrosio I.

Lagoa dos Patos

ATACAMA DESERT

SIERRAS DO CORDOBA

Aconcagua

Juan Fernández Is.

PAMPAS

ATLANTIC OCEAN

0 250 500 750 km

0 100 200 300 400 500 miles

Colorado

Rio de la Plata

FACTS ABOUT CENTRAL AND SOUTH AMERICA

Bahía Blanca

Gulf of San Matias

Chiloé I.

VALDÉZ PENINSULA

Los Chonos Archipelago

Sarmiento

Gulf of San Jorge

Lowest temperature:
Sarmiento, Argentina,
-27°F (-33°C)

L. Buenos Aires

L. General Carrera

PATAGONIA

Bahía Grande

Falkland Is.

I. Desolación

Strait of Magellan

Tierra del Fuego

Cape Horn

MONT PELÉE
On 8 May, 1902, Mont Pelée, a volcano on the Caribbean island of Martinique, erupted. A stream of lava, gas, and hot dust poured down the mountain toward the port of St. Pierre, engulfing the town and killing 30,000 people. Volcanoes are a constant hazard in the Caribbean. Fears of another eruption led to the evacuation of Plymouth, the capital city of Montserrat, in August 1995.

ISTHMUS OF PANAMA
The Isthmus of Panama is a narrow strip of land that separates the Caribbean Sea in the Atlantic Ocean from the Gulf of Panama in the Pacific. It forms the land bridge linking Central America to South America. The Isthmus is only 30–130 miles (48–210 km) wide. Its narrow shape and strategic location made it the ideal choice as the site for the Panama Canal.

FACTS ABOUT CENTRAL AND SOUTH AMERICA
Area: 7,177,259 sq miles (18,589,118 sq km)

Highest point: Mt. Aconcagua, Argentina, 22,835 ft (6,960 m) *Map F11*

Longest river: Amazon, Peru/Brazil, 4,001 miles (6,439 km) *Map I6*

Largest lake: L. Titicaca, Bolivia/Peru, 3,200 sq miles (8,287 sq km) *Map F8*

Largest island: Tierra del Fuego, 27,476 sq miles (71,163 sq km) *Map F16*

PEOPLES OF CENTRAL AND SOUTH AMERICA

Population: approximately 373,739,000 people

Number of countries: 32

THE LANGUAGE, HISTORY, and culture of Central and South America have been shaped by colonization. Until 1492, when Christopher Columbus first landed in the Bahamas, the continent was inhabited by native peoples. After that time, European settlers arrived from Spain and Portugal, and huge numbers of Africans were imported as slaves, especially to the Caribbean and Brazil. The Caribbean also became home to English, French, and Dutch settlers. As a result, the population of the continent today is a combination of these different ethnic groups. Spanish is the main language spoken throughout most of the continent, together with Portuguese in Brazil. English and French are more common in the Caribbean, while Dutch can still be heard in Suriname.

Most densely populated country: Barbados, 1,556 people per sq mile (601 per sq km)

Smallest country: Grenada, 131 sq miles (340 sq km)

Least densely populated country: Suriname, 7 per sq mile (3 people per sq km)

Largest country: Brazil, 3,286,472 sq miles (8,511,970 sq km)

Map labels: BAHAMAS, CUBA, DOMINICAN REPUBLIC, HAITI, JAMAICA, BELIZE, GUATEMALA, HONDURAS, EL SALVADOR, NICARAGUA, COSTA RICA, PANAMA, ANTIGUA & BARBUDA, ST. KITTS & NEVIS, DOMINICA, ST LUCIA, ST. VINCENT & THE GRENADINES, BARBADOS, GRENADA, TRINIDAD AND TOBAGO, VENEZUELA, COLOMBIA, GUYANA, SURINAME, FRENCH GUIANA (Fr), ECUADOR, Galapagos Is. (Ec), PERU, BRAZIL, BOLIVIA, PARAGUAY, San Felix I. (Ch), San Ambrosio I. (Ch), Juan Fernandez Is. (Ch), CHILE, ARGENTINA, URUGUAY, Falkland Is. (UK)

Magnificent Catholic churches, such as the Church of St. Francisco in Brazil, are a lasting reminder of colonial rule.

SPANISH INFLUENCE

From the 16th century on, Spain and Portugal colonized South America. Both countries also sent missionaries to spread the Roman Catholic religion. Spain colonized much of the continent, but Portuguese-ruled Brazil became the largest and most economically powerful country. Today, the majority of South Americans are still Roman Catholics.

ETHNIC GROUPS

Native Indians, who can trace their history back to people living in Central and South America before the Europeans arrived, make up just 2 percent of the continent's population today. The next largest group are people of African descent, the greatest number of whom are today found in Brazil and the Caribbean. In most countries, the largest group of people is of mixed European and native Indian descent, known as *mestizos*.

Ethnic groups

Key
- European
- Native Indian
- African/Mulatto
- Mestizo

Brazil / Ecuador / Guatemala / Uruguay

These young Brazilian men are a mix of ethnic groups.

The peoples of Central and South America can be divided into four distinct ethnic groups. This chart shows what proportion of the population makes up each of the four ethnic groups in four countries.

Key

■ 50% and more

▨ 10–49%

□ Less than 10%

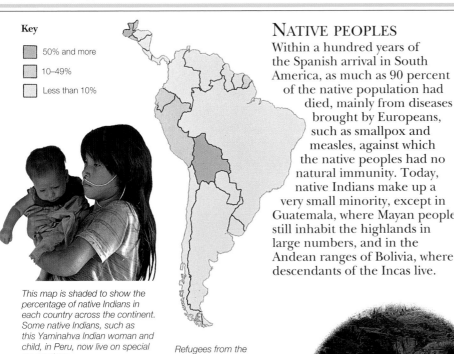

This map is shaded to show the percentage of native Indians in each country across the continent. Some native Indians, such as this Yaminahva Indian woman and child, in Peru, now live on special reservations.

NATIVE PEOPLES

Within a hundred years of the Spanish arrival in South America, as much as 90 percent of the native population had died, mainly from diseases brought by Europeans, such as smallpox and measles, against which the native peoples had no natural immunity. Today, native Indians make up a very small minority, except in Guatemala, where Mayan people still inhabit the highlands in large numbers, and in the Andean ranges of Bolivia, where descendants of the Incas live.

Nicaragua

$US6,986 million

$US2,012 million

□ Country earns in one year

▨ Country's foreign debt

Brazil

$US730,424 million

$US244,673 million

FOREIGN DEBT

All governments borrow money. The loans are paid back using the money that the country earns by exporting its goods. However, many countries in Central and South America have huge debts. Brazil has a very large foreign debt, but it is still relatively small compared to Brazil's earnings. Nicaragua has a much smaller debt, but it is more than three times the country's earnings.

Refugees from the countryside building a shack on the outskirts of Buenos Aires, Argentina

LARGE-SCALE FARMS

Across the region, ranches for cattle and sheep and plantations growing export crops, such as bananas and sugar, often extend over a vast area and are operated as profit-making businesses. These huge farms may be owned by foreign companies or by a handful of rich and powerful families. Cuba is different, for the government controls these large estates.

CROWDED CITIES

Nearly three-quarters of the continent's population lives in cities. In some countries, such as Chile and Uruguay, more than a third of the population lives in the capital. Many people have been forced to migrate from rural areas to escape widespread poverty, or have been drawn to the cities by the chance of work. They now live in crowded shantytowns that have grown up on the city outskirts.

SMALL-SCALE FARMS

Most of the continent's farmers have only enough land to support one or two people. People like this Bolivian family grow crops and keep a few animals, such as chickens or pigs, to eat rather than to sell. Since the farm often cannot provide enough food for the whole family, some family members are forced to move elsewhere in search of work.

Children per family

Kenya: 4.5

Bolivia: 4.0

Peru: 3.1

Argentina: 2.5

Germany: 1.4

POPULATION GROWTH

In the 20th century, population growth across the continent was rapid, particularly in Brazil and the northern countries. In most countries, birth rates are now beginning to fall. However, since so much of the population is young, and improvements in health allow more children to survive into adulthood, the population is still growing. By the year 2005, another 80 million people will be living here.

This chart shows the average number of children per woman in five countries. Birth rates in Central and South America are lower than in Africa, but higher than birth rates in Europe, where most families have 1 or 2 children.

CENTRAL AMERICA AND THE CARIBBEAN

THE SEVEN SMALL COUNTRIES OF CENTRAL AMERICA lie within a neck of land that joins North and South America. To the east, hundreds of Caribbean islands stretch from the US almost to Venezuela. When Christopher Columbus and his Spanish crew dropped anchor in the Caribbean in 1492, they thought it was Asia, and the islands became known as the West Indies. From that time on, Europeans competed for control of the region, bringing slaves from Africa to work on the land. Central America's greatest influence is still Spanish, while the Caribbean retains its African culture. The entire area is affected by natural hazards, with volcanoes, earthquakes, and hurricanes.

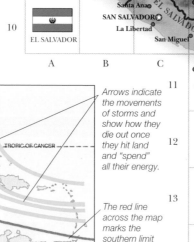

FARMING THE LAND
Even before the arrival of Europeans, Central America was an agricultural region. The land divides into three main zones: the fertile Pacific plain, ideal for growing crops such as bananas; the central highlands, with coffee plantations (above) and cattle ranches; and the forested northeast, where the soil is less suitable for farming. Intensive farming has damaged much of the environment.

Arrows indicate the movements of storms and show how they die out once they hit land and "spend" all their energy.

The red line across the map marks the southern limit of the area of hurricane activity.

HURRICANE STRENGTH
Powerful tropical storms known as hurricanes affect the Caribbean between May and October. A hurricane starts off as a normal storm over the ocean, but grows in force if the waters are particularly warm. Winds then blow the swirling mass of cloud, wind, and rain westward, toward the islands, where it can cause massive destruction when it hits land. The word hurricane comes from Huracan, the local name for the god of storms.

Havana, Cuba
Jan 72°F (22°C)
July 82°F (28°C)
Jan 2.8 in (71 mm)
July 4.9 in (125 mm)

San José, Costa Rica
Jan 66°F (19°C)
July 70°F (21°C)
Jan 0.6 in (15 mm)
July 8.3 in (211 mm)

ISLANDS LARGE AND SMALL

In the centuries after Columbus, Spanish influence remained strong on the mainland, although Spain, France, Britain, the Netherlands, and later the US laid claim to many of the islands. St. Lucia, for example, changed hands between Britain and France 14 times. Most of the larger islands are now independent countries, while others are still "dependencies." The island of Martinique, with its replica of the Sacré Coeur church in Paris, remains French, while the Netherlands Antilles are controlled by the Dutch.

PEOPLE OF THE CARIBBEAN

The original inhabitants of the Caribbean islands were the Carib and Arawak peoples. Most died from disease and slavery at the hands of the Spanish, although a few descendants of Caribs survive on the island of Dominica. Today, most people in the Caribbean are descendants of the African slaves brought over to work the plantations. Europeans, Asians, Syrians, and Lebanese also form a part of Caribbean culture.

BAHAMAS

JAMAICA

HAITI

DOMINICAN REPUBLIC

ST. KITTS & NEVIS

ANTIGUA & BARBUDA

DOMINICA

ST. LUCIA

ST. VINCENT & THE GRENADINES

GRENADA

BARBADOS

TRINIDAD & TOBAGO

THINGS TO LOOK FOR ON THE MAP

Longest river: Coco, Honduras/Nicaragua, 300 miles (483 km) *Map F10*

Highest point: Tajumulco, Guatemala, 13,845 ft (4,220 m) *Map A8*

Largest lake: L. Nicaragua, Nicaragua, 3,100 sq miles (8,029 sq km) *Map E12*

Port-of-Spain, Trinidad
Jan 78°F (26°C)
July 80°F (27°C)
Jan 2.7 in (69 mm)
July 8.6 in (218 mm)

0   50   100   150   200   250 km
0   50   100   150 miles

ATLANTIC OCEAN

Freeport
Little Abaco
Grand Bahama
Great Abaco
Berry Is.
Great Bahama Bank
NASSAU
New Providence
Eleuthera
Cat I.
San Salvador
Great Exuma
Rum Cay
Long I.
Andros I.
Crooked I.
Acklins I.
Mayaguana
ta Clara
BAHAMAS
Camagüey
Las Tunas
Holguín
Great Inagua
Caicos Is.
Turks Is.
TURKS & CAICOS ISLANDS (UK)
Gulf of Guacanayabo
Bayamo
Santiago de Cuba
Guantánamo
Guantánamo Bay (US)
Windward Passage
Port-de-Paix
Cap-Haitien
Montecristi
Gonaïves
Santiago
Puerto Plata
San Francisco de Macorís
anna-Mar
Montego Bay
JAMAICA
HAITI
DOMINICAN REPUBLIC
Spanish Town
KINGSTON
Jérémie
PORT-AU-PRINCE
Samaná
Les Cayes
Jacmel
L. Enriquillo
SANTO DOMINGO
La Romana
La Romana
Greater Antilles
Mona Passage
Puerto Rico (US)
Mayagüez
Virgin Islands (US)
British Virgin Islands (UK)
Leeward Islands
SAN JUAN
Ponce
St. Croix
Anguilla (UK)
St. Eustatius (Neth.)
St. Martin (France & Neth.)
Barbuda
ANTIGUA & BARBUDA
BASSETERRE
ST. KITTS & NEVIS
ST. JOHNS
Montserrat (UK)
Antigua
Basse Terre
Guadeloupe (France)
Grande Terre
Marie Galante
DOMINICA
ROSEAU
Martinique (France)
Lesser Antilles
Windward Islands
CARIBBEAN SEA
Aruba
Netherlands Antilles
Curaçao
Bonaire
Lesser Antilles
St. Vincent
KINGSTOWN
ST. LUCIA
CASTRIES
ST. VINCENT & THE GRENADINES
BRIDGETOWN
The Grenadines
BARBADOS
GRENADA
ST. GEORGE'S
Isla de Margarita
COLOMBIA
VENEZUELA
TRINIDAD & TOBAGO
Tobago
PORT OF SPAIN
Trinidad
San Fernando

K   L   M   N   O   P   Q   R   S   T   U   V   W

GUATEMALA

FROM THE RUINED CITIES of the ancient Mayan civilization to the Catholic churches of the Spanish, Guatemala represents a blend of cultures. Today, more than half the people are direct descendants of the Mayan Indians and live mainly in highland villages; the remainder of the population is part Indian and part Spanish. Many Mayans work for rich landowners who grow the coffee, sugar, and bananas that are the country's main cash crops. Guatemala also exports fresh cut flowers, mostly roses, which are grown in the valleys around Antigua.

Villagers carry a statue of the Virgin Mary.

HOLY WEEK
Most Guatemalans are Roman Catholic, the religion the Spanish brought with them in the 16th century. However, many people are now becoming Protestant. Guatemalans also practice their own form of worship based on traditional beliefs. This procession in Antigua forms part of their celebration of Holy Week.

MARKET DAY

Markets such as this one in Chichicastenango, in the highlands near Lake Atitlán, are a feature of daily life. Many native Guatemalans farm small plots of land where they grow corn, beans, and squash, as well as fruit. They regularly walk long distances from outlying villages to a market to sell crops, flowers, and handcrafted goods such as pottery and baskets.

People worship Catholic saints and ancient gods at the Church of Santo Tomas.

Lilies and roses, as well as carnations and gladioli, are grown in the valleys. Many are sold to North America.

Goods are weighed in a simple, handheld balance.

Village women wear brightly colored ankle-length skirts. Patterns date back hundreds of years.

Corn and other cereals are the main foods.

Mayan craft products, such as baskets and handwoven textiles, are popular with tourists.

A basket of papayas

Avocados have been cultivated in Central America for thousands of years.

GUATEMALA	
Capital city: Guatemala City	
Area: 41,846 sq miles (108,430 sq km)	
Population: 11,400,000	
Official language: Spanish	
Major religions: Christian 98%, other 2%	
Government: Multiparty democracy	
Currency: Quetzal	
Adult literacy rate: 69%	
Life expectancy: 64 years	
People per doctor: 3,333	
Televisions: 126 per 1,000 people	

BELIZE	
Capital city: Belmopan	
Area: 8,803 sq miles (22,800 sq km)	
Population: 190,792	
Official language: English	
Major religion: Christian 87%, other 13%	
Government: Multiparty democracy	
Currency: Belizean dollar	
Adult literacy rate: 93%	
Life expectancy: 75 years	
People per doctor: 2,128	
Televisions: 183 per 1,000 people	

WEAVING STYLES
Weaving is a traditional craft. Cloth is made from colored yarn, using patterns that have been handed down through the generations. There are more than 300 different styles, each with a special historical meaning.

Weavers use a backstrap loom that can be moved from place to place.

CITIES OF THE MAYA
Tourism is one of Guatemala's fastest growing industries. Each year almost one million tourists visit the country to see its ancient sites. Spectacular ruins mark the site of Tikal, one of the great Mayan cities. Tikal was mysteriously abandoned in about AD900. Today its ruined temples lie in a huge area of tropical forest.

REFUGEES

Life for the Mayans is a constant struggle for survival, and many have suffered hardship and death in their attempts to avoid being forced into mainstream society. Persecution was particularly bad in the early 1980s when the then military government set out to eliminate them. Some 60,000 Mayans fled to safety in refugee camps in Mexico. Today, they are returning to Guatemala, but their safety is uncertain and much of their land has been seized.

STREET CHILDREN
Guatemala City is home to growing numbers of so-called street children. Forced to leave home because of poverty and abuse, children live in small groups and survive through crime, by begging, and selling whatever they can find. Recently, human rights groups such as Amnesty International have drawn attention to their plight.

BELIZE

LYING ON THE CARIBBEAN COAST, Belize is both an old and a new country. Ancient ruins dot the landscape, reminders of its Mayan history, but the country itself only achieved full independence in 1981. For many years, Belize was a British colony, the only one in Central America. English is the official language, but Belizeans are descended from several ethnic groups – Caribs, Africans, Mayans, Asians, and Europeans – and many people speak a Creole or African dialect. Caribbean foods and music are popular, and the country is famous for its wildlife.

CORAL REEF

A chain of coral reefs, dotted with small sandy islands called cayes, runs 180 miles (290 km) along the coastline of Belize. It is the world's second largest barrier reef, after Australia's, and is home to turtles, sea anemones, and spiny lobsters, as well as a wonderful array of tropical fish. The clear, warm water attracts divers from around the world.

Flooding and hurricanes can cause serious problems along the coast of Belize, so a new capital, Belmopan, has been built farther inland than Belize City, the old capital.

[Map: MEXICO, GUATEMALA, BELIZE, Ambergris Cay, Belize City, Belmopan, Barrier Reef, CARIBBEAN SEA]

DEEP IN THE FOREST

Dense tropical rain forest covers half of Belize's land area. Rosewood, and other products from the forest, such as chicle, used to make chewing gum, and kapok, a silky cotton from the giant Ceiba tree, are important to the economy. So, too, are the increasing number of citrus groves. But cultivation is limited. Much of the rain forest is protected and provides a rich habitat for plants and animals.

BELMOPAN
In 1961, a massive hurricane and tidal wave devastated the coastal capital, Belize City. In 1970, a new capital, Belmopan, was built 50 miles (80 km) inland to protect it from tropical storms. Although people and businesses are gradually moving to the new capital, Belize City remains the country's most populated city.

FOREST WILDLIFE
The forests are filled with an amazing variety of wildlife. Jaguars, tapirs, howler monkeys, and coatimundi are just a few of the world's endangered species still thriving in the forests of Belize. Butterflies and tropical birds fly through the trees. And there are 250 different types of orchids, including the black orchid, Belize's national flower.

Toucans live in the treetops so they can fly around the open areas.

The howler monkey defends its part of the rain forest with a noisy howl.

Find out more
CORAL REEFS: *255, 258*
HURRICANES: *44*
RAIN FORESTS: *15, 69, 204*
RELIGION: *274–275*

HONDURAS

THE HOT, STEAMY CLIMATE of Honduras is ideal for growing fruit, and for many years the banana industry has dominated the life of the country. Today, Honduras has developed other exports, such as coffee, sugar, and beef. More than half of Hondurans live in the countryside, in small villages or isolated settlements. Many are poor farmers, growing corn, beans, or rice for their own use. Life is hard, and many people go hungry. Land is unevenly distributed – wealthy families and fruit companies own 60 percent of the land.

HONDURAN PEOPLE
Most Hondurans are *mestizos* – mixed descendants of native Indians and the Europeans who arrived in the 16th century. Some are descended from black Africans who were shipped to the Caribbean as slaves. Some are white (European) or Indian.

HONDURAS
Capital city: Tegucigalpa
Area: 43,201 sq miles (111,890 sq km)
Population: 6,500,000
Official language: Spanish
Major religion: Christian 100%
Government: Multiparty democracy
Currency: Lempira
Adult literacy rate: 72%
Life expectancy: 69 years
People per doctor: 2,500
Televisions: 90 per 1,000 people

EL SALVADOR
Capital city: San Salvador
Area: 8,000 sq miles (20,720 sq km)
Population: 5,057,925
Official language: Spanish
Major religion: Christian 98%, other 2%
Government: Multiparty democracy
Currency: Salvadorean colón, US Dollar
Adult literacy rate: 79%
Life expectancy: 69 years
People per doctor: 1,429
Televisions: 675 per 1,000 people

As the bananas grow, they begin to point upward.

The stalk has a flower on the end made of thick, purple petals.

Workers cover bananas with bags to protect them from insects and pesticide.

Bananas take between 9 and 13 weeks to ripen.

Workers cut the bananas down when they are still green.

Colored tags identify which bunches are ready for picking.

BANANA PLANTATIONS
Banana exports are important to the economy of Honduras. Many are grown on huge plantations, particularly around La Lima in northeastern Honduras. Laborers work long hours and the pay is low. Cutters regularly have to carry loads of bananas weighing about 88 lb (40 kg). Once cut down, the bananas are washed, inspected, and weighed into boxes, ready to be shipped abroad.

EL SALVADOR

THE SMALLEST COUNTRY in Central America, El Salvador has suffered a history of civil war and revolution. Historically, a handful of rich families have controlled the land and wealth, while most Salvadoreans have lived in poverty. A line of volcanoes, many still active, dominates the landscape. Forests, once rich with cedar, mahogany, and oak, have been cut down for farmland.

THE SOCCER WAR
In 1969, long-standing border disputes erupted when El Salvador played Honduras to qualify for the World Cup. The incident led to the Salvadoran army invading Honduras. More than 3,000 people were killed.

SAN SALVADOR
San Salvador was founded by Spanish colonists in 1525. Since then it has been damaged by earthquakes many times. Much of the original Spanish architecture has been replaced with modern buildings. Overcrowded slum areas have developed around the city as thousands of refugees have arrived in search of work.

PEACE ACCORD
Between 1979 and 1991, a bitter civil war raged between the US-backed government and left-wing guerilla forces. Some 75,000 Salvadoreans died. On January 16, 1992, the country celebrated a peace agreement signed by guerilla leader Chano Guevara (left).

Find out more
COFFEE: 50, 62, 66
PEOPLES OF THE CONTINENT: 42
SUGAR: 52
VOLANOES & EARTHQUAKES: 13

NICARAGUA

SOMETIMES CALLED "the land of lakes and volcanoes," Nicaragua is a beautiful country. It could also be one of the richest in Central America, but its recent history has been as violent as its earthquakes, and the economy has been thrown into chaos by past political events. The economy is mainly based on agriculture, with fishing along the coasts, but Nicaragua also has large deposits of minerals, including copper and gold, which are mined for export. The country has a young population, with more than half the people under the age of 15.

NICARAGUA

Capital city: Managua

Area: 45,849 sq miles (118,750 sq km)

Population: 5,100,000

Official language: Spanish

Major religions: Christian 97%, other 3%

Government: Multiparty democracy

Currency: Gold córdoba

Adult literacy rate: 64%

Life expectancy: 68 years

People per doctor: 1,429

Televisions: 190 per 1,000 people

SANDINISTA REVOLUTION

For over 40 years, the Somoza family ruled Nicaragua as a dictatorship. But in 1979, rebels took control and formed the left-wing Sandinista government. They provided better health care, and set up a program of taking land from the rich and giving it to peasants. However, they were opposed by the Contras, anti-Sandinista forces backed by the United States. Over the last decade the Contras' support has declined and the Sandinistas have regained popularity, though not enough to win back power.

FAMILY LIFE

Extended families are common in Nicaragua. Parents and children often live with their grandparents under one roof. Until 1979, more than half the population could not read or write. Under the Sandinistas, a literacy campaign was set up, and newly trained teachers, many of them women, were sent into rural areas to teach reading and writing. Within just a few months, literacy levels rose to 87 percent. However, when the Sandinistas lost power, the campaign faded and reading levels dropped again.

Overcrowding is a problem, and large families are often crammed into very small living spaces.

LIVING DANGEROUSLY

Most of the population of Nicaragua lives on the Pacific coast, where the major cities are located. Within this area, there are many active volcanoes, but the most serious danger comes from earthquakes. In 1972, the country's capital, Managua, was nearly destroyed by an earthquake that killed more than 6,000 people and left 300,000 homeless.

FARMING THE LAND

The fertile volcanic soil near the Pacific coast forms the main farming region of Nicaragua. Corn (shown growing here), beans, and sorghum are the main food crops, and are harvested twice a year. Coffee, cotton, and bananas are also important export crops.

The corn ear, or cob, needs plenty of sunshine to grow and ripen.

Corn kernels are ground into flour and used to make tortillas, a type of pancake.

Lake Nicaragua is named after Nicarao, an ancient Indian chief whose people lived by the lake.

LAKE NICARAGUA

The west of the country is dominated by Lake Nicaragua, the largest lake in Central America. It is also the only freshwater lake in the world to contain sea fish, including sharks and swordfish. Scientists now think that sharks find their way to the lake by swimming up the San Juan River from the Caribbean Sea.

Find out more

LITERACY: *277*
POLITICAL SYSTEMS: *270–271*
POPULATION GROWTH: *43*
VOLCANOES & EARTHQUAKES: *13*

COSTA RICA

BORDERED BY SEA on both sides, Costa Rica differs from its neighbors in many ways. It is a peaceful country with a democratically elected government and, since 1948, no army. The country is also relatively wealthy. Schools are free, and Costa Rica spends much of its budget on education. Life expectancy in Costa Rica is the highest in Central America. Exports include coffee, bananas, and sugar, which grow on the country's fertile volcanic soils. The main port is Limón on the Caribbean coast.

COSTA RICA	
Capital city: San José	
Area: 19,714 sq miles (51,060 sq km)	
Population: 4,000,000	
Official language: Spanish	
Major religions: Christian 95%, other 5%	
Government: Multiparty democracy	
Currency: Costa Rican colón	
Adult literacy rate: 96%	
Life expectancy: 76 years	
People per doctor: 1,111	
Televisions: 387 per 1,000 people	

THE WAY TO SAN JOSÉ
San José lies in the mountainous center of the country directly on the Pan-American Highway. It is the processing center for the crops that grow in the nearby valleys. The area developed as a tobacco growing center under Spanish rule and became the capital in 1823.

COFFEE BEANS

Costa Rica was the first country in Central America to grow coffee, and for more than 100 years this has been its leading export. From time to time this success is affected by falling international prices. Coffee is made from the fruit of the coffee tree, which grows best on well-drained soil. Trees need a warm, but not hot, climate, and are usually grown in areas partly shaded with larger trees. They can produce good crops for 15 years.

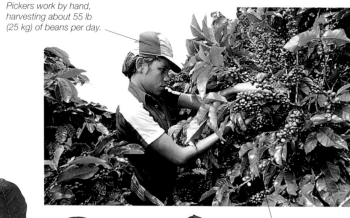

Pickers work by hand, harvesting about 55 lb (25 kg) of beans per day.

The coffee fruit is called a cherry.

The sweet-smelling flowers last about 3 to 4 days.

Coffee trees grow about 9.8 ft (3 m) tall.

Berries turn from dark green to yellow to ripe red.

Coffee is made from the two beans inside the cherry.

TRAIN TO THE COAST
The Atlantic Railway, completed in 1890, was built to take coffee from the plantations to the coast for export. The project was fraught with problems. Thousands of workers lost their lives due to terrible working conditions, and the cost plunged the government into debt.

SAVING THE FORESTS

Costa Rica was once covered with forests that included mahogany and tropical cedar trees. But its tree cover has been greatly reduced because forests have been cut down for timber and to make room for coffee plantations. However, the government is aware that loss of forest also means loss of valuable plant and animal life, and it is now working to conserve its forests. Today, much of the forest is protected in reserves and national parks.

This tiny violet-ear hummingbird is just 4.75 in (12 cm) long. It hovers in the air and takes nectar from flowers through its long beak.

The hummingbird's wings can beat 55 times per second.

Nectar is a sweet liquid.

Find out more
COFFEE: *62, 66*
DEMOCRACY: *270*
LOGGING: *69, 244*
TRADE : *281*

PANAMA

THE COUNTRY OF PANAMA forms a land link between the North and South American continents. The Panama Canal, which cuts through the country and joins the Atlantic and Pacific oceans, is a vital link in international sea trade. Panama has a hot, steamy climate with heavy rainfall, especially on its Caribbean coast. The interior is mountainous. The best farmland is in the lowlands on the Pacific coast, where the main cash crops, bananas, coffee, and sugar, are grown. Shrimps, caught in the coastal waters, are also an important export.

PANAMA

Capital city: Panama City

Area: 29,340 sq miles (75,990 sq km)

Population: 2,900,000

Official language: Spanish

Major religions: Christian 92%, Jewish and other 8%

Government: Multiparty democracy

Currency: Balboa

Adult literacy rate: 92%

Life expectancy: 74 years

People per doctor: 556

Televisions: 187 per 1,000 people

PANAMA CANAL

Every year some 14,000 ships negotiate the locks of the Panama Canal. First opened in 1914, the canal is 51 miles (82 km) long, with a minimum depth of 39 ft (12 m). Forty thousand workers, mostly from the Caribbean, worked on the canal, which took 10 years to build and cost $380 million. It also cost thousands of lives. After sharing the canal with the US for many years, Panama took complete control in 2000.

FROM OCEAN TO OCEAN
There is an 85-ft (26-m) difference in height between Gatun Lake and the two oceans. From the Atlantic, ships are raised up through the Gatun locks (1, 2, and 3). Then they are lowered via the Pedro Miguel locks (4) and, finally, through the Miraflores locks (5 and 6) into the Pacific.

Nine months of tropical rain each year keeps Gatun Lake full. Water from the lake feeds the locks.

Cross-section of canal

Atlantic Ocean · Gatun Lake · Pacific Ocean

Banks and business centers line the canal approach to Panama City.

CANAL AT THE CROSSROADS
The canal puts Panama at the crossroads of international trade. Revenue from the canal, and from the Free Trade Zone at its mouth in Colón, is vital to the economy. Since 1970, Panama has been one of the world's main financial centers, and its tax-free banking attracts investors from around the world.

Detail of lock chamber

A ship waits in a lock chamber while water is piped in to lift the ship to the next level.

Water is fed through huge pipes, called culverts, down the sides of the lock.

Trains, called mules, help pull the ship through the lock.

Ships travel in the opposite direction along this channel.

A series of smaller pipes feeds water into the lock from the culverts.

CUNA INDIANS
The original inhabitants of Panama were mostly Cuna, Guaymi, and Choco Indians, but their numbers were severely reduced after the arrival of European explorers in the 16th century. The Cuna once held considerable power in the area and traded, mainly by canoe, along the Caribbean coast. Important chiefs were carried by hammock. Today, the Cuna live in small villages and depend on agriculture for a living.

Hammocks are made of woven fiber from plants that grow on the coast.

Embroidered clothing designs, known as molas, are a feature of the Cuna culture.

THE GOOD SOIL
Panama has many rivers. The soil that develops from clays, sand, and silt deposited from these rivers is called alluvial soil, and is good for growing crops such as the vegetables shown here. With poorer soils the land is used for a few years and then left until its natural fertility returns. This system of land use is called *roza*.

Find out more

BANANAS: *48*

COFFEE: *50, 62, 66*

EXPORT DEPENDENCY: *281*

PEOPLES OF THE CONTINENT: *42*

CUBA

CUBA
Capital city: Havana
Area: 42,803 sq miles (110,860 sq km)
Population: 11,200,000
Official language: Spanish
Major religions: Christian 41%, other 59%
Government: One-party state
Currency: Cuban peso
Adult literacy rate: 96%
Life expectancy: 76 years
People per doctor: 278
Televisions: 239 per 1,000 people

MORE THAN 200 RIVERS WIND their way across Cuba, watering the lush green scenery of the Caribbean's largest island. The land is made up of mountains, rolling hills, and flat plains, all covered in a fertile soil that is ideal for growing sugar, tobacco, and a variety of tropical fruits and vegetables. Most Cubans are descended from the early Spanish settlers, or from Africans brought over later to work as slaves on the plantations. In recent decades, the socialist policies of the long-standing leader Fidel Castro have kept Cuba isolated from much of the world.

MUSIC AND DANCE
Cuba's lively music reflects its mix of Spanish and African influences. The Spanish brought distinctive melodies, along with the guitar and violin, and the Africans brought a very different style, as well as various drums and short wooden sticks called claves. The music has gradually fused to create rhythms such as the mambo and salsa. A thriving Afro-Cuban jazz scene has also developed.

CUBAN POLITICS

In 1959, Fidel Castro and a group of rebels overthrew the ruling dictator, Fulgencio Batista. Since then, Cuba has been a communist state, aided by the Soviet Union until its breakup in the early 1990s. Many of Castro's social policies have been successful. Housing and health care have greatly improved, and most people can now read and write. However, the US remains hostile to the communist government.

Cigars are stored in boxes made from cedar wood to keep them fresh.

CUBAN CIGARS
Cuba's warm days and cool nights are ideal for growing tobacco. Tobacco leaves are picked when pale green and hung up to dry for 40–45 days. They are then sorted and packed for the fermentation process, which mellows the flavor of the leaf before it is sent to one of Cuba's famous cigar factories. Cigars are rolled by hand by men and women working at long wooden tables.

A good cigar is made from at least five different types of tobacco.

Sugarcane is a giant grass that needs plenty of rain as well as sunshine.

Dark brown sugar has not been refined to remove all the syrup.

Light brown sugar has been partially refined.

Rum is made from the distilled juice of sugarcane.

Sugar is stored inside the stalk, in a firm pulp.

A dark syrup known as molasses is a by-product of cane juice.

HAVANA

The largest city in the Caribbean, Cuba's capital, Havana, has a population of more than 2 million. It was founded by the Spanish in 1515 and some areas of the city are extremely old, with cobbled streets and elegant colonial buildings. Today, parts of Havana have become run down and in need of improvement. However, housing policies mean there are no shantytowns around the city. Havana is a major port and exports most of Cuba's sugar, tobacco, and tropical fruit.

SUGAR INDUSTRY

Sugar has long been important to Cuba and still makes up 75 percent of the country's earnings from exports. By the 1800s, the sugar industry was already booming, fueled by African slaves who worked by hand on the vast colonial plantations. Today, the methods are more modern and the cane is usually cut down by machine or bulldozer. However, during the early 1990s, poor weather reduced the sugar harvests and there were also problems with obtaining fuel from the former Soviet Union. To overcome this oil crisis, many of the mills started to use *bagasse*, a by-product of sugarcane, to run their machinery.

Find out more
BREAKUP OF THE USSR: *136*
CITIES: *17, 43*
PEOPLES OF THE CONTINENT: *42*
POLITICAL SYSTEMS: *270–271*

JAMAICA

THE BEAUTIFUL ISLAND OF JAMAICA is a place of strong contrasts. On the one hand, there is the relaxed attitude of people enjoying the national passions – cricket and reggae music. On the other hand, there is tension between the few powerful families and the many poor living in violent slums. This side of life is rarely seen by the tourists who flock here each year. In addition to tourism, the mineral bauxite, used to make aluminum, is a valuable source of income. Sadly, the landscape is damaged by the bauxite mines, which leave red mud lakes with an acid content that kills vegetation.

JAMAICA

Capital city: Kingston

Area: 4,181 sq miles (10,830 sq km)

Population: 2,600,000

Official language: English

Major religions: Christian 56%, other 46%

Government: Multiparty democracy

Currency: Jamaican dollar

Adult literacy rate: 87%

Life expectancy: 75 years

People per doctor: 2,000

Televisions: 182 per 1,000 people

RASTAFARIANISM

The Rastafarian religion began among the poor of Kingston, Jamaica, in the 1930s. Members believe that Haile Selassie, the former Emperor of Ethiopia (Ras Tafari), was a god. They also believe that God (Jah) will lead black people back to Ethiopia, the promised land. Rastafarians do not usually eat pork, they are against violence, and wear their hair in long dreadlocks. Their clothes are often green, yellow, and red because these are the colors of the Ethiopian flag.

REGGAE MUSIC

The driving rhythms of reggae music can be heard everywhere across the island. Its songs often tell of hardship and political struggle, and are linked to Rastafarianism. Reggae developed in Jamaica from ska, which was a blend of African, European, and South American styles. Jamaican singer Bob Marley (1945–81) made reggae music popular around the world.

KINGSTON

Jamaica's capital city and chief port, Kingston, is one of the largest urban centers in the Caribbean. Founded by the British, the city first grew as a major port for shipping cane sugar to Europe. However, an earthquake in 1907 damaged the city. It has now been rebuilt with modern hotels, banks, and financial offices. Crowded shantytowns also exist on the western side of the city. Violence frequently breaks out here, connected either to political unrest or to the long-established trade in illegal drugs.

ISLAND INDUSTRIES

A variety of industries bring money to Jamaica, from oil refining to clothes manufacturing. Various minerals are mined, with bauxite being the most important. One rapidly growing industry is data processing, which involves typing data into computers and sending it to companies in the US. Unlike many other Caribbean countries, however, Jamaica's data processing companies are mostly owned by Jamaicans, and not by large foreign organizations.

FARMING THE LAND

Not everyone in Jamaica works in industry or tourism – agriculture is also important. Plantations growing sugar, bananas, coffee, and cocoa employ large numbers of people. Many Jamaicans also fish for a living or farm their own small plots of land, producing food for themselves, as shown here, with a little left over to sell at local markets.

The breadfruit tree produces fruit with a pulp that is eaten as a vegetable.

Dasheen is grown for its edible root and leaves.

Okra is used in soups and stews or eaten as a vegetable.

Find out more

ETHIOPIA: *218*
GROWTH OF CITIES: *17*
RELIGION: *274–275*
SUGAR: *52*

THE BAHAMAS

THIS LONG LINE OF ABOUT 700 coral islands snakes its way across the warm Caribbean Sea. It was on the island of San Salvador that Christopher Columbus first set foot when he arrived in the "New World" of the Americas in 1492. The Spanish, who called the islands *Bajamar*, meaning "shallow seas," were followed by British settlers, and the islands remained a British colony until 1973. Today, the islands are a paradise for vacationers of every nationality. They are also a major financial center, because tax laws make it profitable for banks and foreign businesses to have offices here.

THE BAHAMAS

Capital city: Nassau

Area: 3,864 sq miles (10,010 sq km)

Population: 307,000

Official language: English

Major religions: Christian 83%, other 17%

Government: Multiparty democracy

Currency: Bahamian dollar

Adult literacy rate: 96%

Life expectancy: 74 years

People per doctor: 709

Televisions: 230 per 1,000 people

PUERTO RICO*

Capital city: San Juan

Area: 3,459 sq miles (8,959 sq km)

Population: 3,800,000

Official language: Spanish

Major religions: Christian 85%, other 15%

Government: Multiparty democracy

Currency: US dollar

* Puerto Rico is not an independent country. It is a self-governing commonwealth state of the US.

JUNKANOO FESTIVAL
At the end of each year, the streets come alive with the dancing and music of the Junkanoo parades. This festival forms a link with the country's past. It is said that when an African chief, given the name John Canoe (Junkanoo), came here as a slave, he was granted the right to celebrate in true African style.

Main overseas tourists 2000

US	Canada	Europe	Others
1,293,140	78,850	126,160	78,850

TOURIST DESTINATION

People from all over the world come to play on the white sandy beaches and in the warm waters of the Bahamas. Tourism is vital to the economy and at least half the local people work in jobs linked to the tourist trade, in hotels, shops, and restaurants. The city of Freeport on Grand Bahama is the largest tourist resort, with a deep-water harbor for cruise ships. However, passengers often eat and sleep on their ship, which does not help the local economy.

PUERTO RICO

SPANISH IS THE MAIN language of Puerto Rico, but the country is strongly American in flavor. Colonized by Spain in the years after Columbus, the Spanish stayed in control until the 1890s, when the US took over. The cultivation of tobacco, sugar, and tropical fruits remains important despite the increasing number of factories set up by US manufacturers. Most people have a good standard of living with excellent education and health-care programs.

PEOPLE OF PUERTO RICO
Puerto Ricans are mainly of Spanish and African descent. Most live in cities, with one-third in the capital of San Juan. Overcrowding forces others into housing projects outside the main cities. Some people choose to move to the US.

OPERATION BOOTSTRAP

This plan, which began in 1948 with backing from the US, was set up to tackle the island's economic problems. Attracted by low taxes and cheap labor, many US companies moved here. Over the years, the plan has helped raise living standards on the island. The main industries include petrochemicals, textiles, and medicines.

Find out more

CORAL ISLANDS: *202*
EDUCATION: *277*
HEALTH: *276*
PEOPLES OF THE CONTINENT: *42*

HAITI

THE POOREST COUNTRY IN the western world, Haiti shares the island of Hispaniola with the Dominican Republic. A revolution by African slaves in 1791, led by Toussaint L'Ouverture, broke French rule, and Haiti became the first black republic. Recent politics have been turbulent. The long dictatorship of the Duvalier family ("Papa" and "Baby" Doc), gave way to a series of military coups. Political unrest continues and the country suffers from great poverty. Many Haitians practice the religious cult of voodoo, which blends traditional African beliefs with Roman Catholicism. Followers believe in powerful spirits, and dancing to the beat of sacred drums is part of the voodoo ritual.

ART AND CULTURE
Many Haitians try to make extra money by selling craft goods, such as straw hats and woodcarvings, and by acting as unofficial tourist guides. Since the 1930s, artists have been noted for producing simple, bold paintings in a style derived from the decorations in voodoo temples.

HAITI
Capital city: Port-au-Prince
Area: 10,641 sq miles (27,560 sq km)
Population: 8,200,000
Official languages: French, French Creole
Major religions: Christian 96%, other 4%
Government: Multiparty democracy
Currency: Gourde
Adult literacy rate: 49%
Life expectancy: 54 years
People per doctor: 10,000
Televisions: 5 per 1,000 people

DOMINICAN REPUBLIC
Capital city: Santo Domingo
Area: 18,815 sq miles (48,730 sq km)
Population: 8,500,000
Official language: Spanish
Major religions: Christian 92%, other 8%
Government: Multiparty democracy
Currency: Dominican Republic peso
Adult literacy rate: 84%
Life expectancy: 71 years
People per doctor: 909
Televisions: 95 per 1,000 people

SOIL EROSION
Farming is the main occupation here and most Haitians live on small plots of land, growing food and keeping goats. They make very little money and pressure for more land to farm means that trees are constantly being cut down. Some wood is turned into charcoal, shown here, and used as fuel in rural areas. Goats overgraze on the remaining woodland. The exposed soil has now become so severely eroded that crop yields are poor. It has been estimated that one-third of the land in Haiti is no longer arable.

DOMINICAN REPUBLIC

THE LANDSCAPE OF MOUNTAINS and forests in the Dominican Republic may be similar to that of its island neighbor, but other aspects of life are very different. Spain was the main colonial power here and US influences are also strong. The people and the culture are a mix of Spanish, African, and native peoples. The country is rich in natural resources, with deposits of silver, platinum, uranium, and nickel, and one of the world's largest gold mines. However, tourism is by far the most important source of foreign earnings.

Island of Hispaniola

HAITI

DOMINICAN REPUBLIC

	HAITI	DOMINICAN REP.
🚗	4 cars per 1,000 people	28 cars per 1,000 people
☎	9 telephones per 1,000 people	98 telephones per 1,000 people
📖	6,288 university students	176,995 university students

THE ECONOMY
People in the Dominican Republic have a better standard of living than those in Haiti, where most cannot even afford health-care. The economy is stronger in the Republic because it is boosted by earnings from tourism and mining and by a government that encourages new industries, such as textiles. In recent years vacation resorts have sprung up across the country, creating jobs. Many Haitians come here in search of work.

SANTO DOMINGO
The capital city of Santo Domingo was founded by Columbus's brother, Bartolomé, in 1496. The city became the main base from which Spain launched its conquest of the region. The city has many recently restored colonial buildings dating back to the 16th century.

Find out more
DICTATORSHIP: *271*
PEOPLES OF THE CONTINENT: *42*
RELIGION: *274–275*
SOIL EROSION: *55, 244*

LESSER ANTILLES

LESSER ANTILLES

THE ISLANDS OF the Lesser Antilles stretch in a gentle curve from the Greater Antilles island of Puerto Rico in the north, down to the coast of South America. Once European colonies, most of the islands are now independent. However, the background of African, European, and Asian influences has resulted in a vibrant and distinctive culture, highlighted in music and festivals. Bananas, which thrive in the heat and high rainfall, remain a major export, although some producers are at risk from hurricanes, which can devastate the land.

CRICKET
Cricket is the national game of the English-speaking islands. Children learn to play on sun-dried turf that allows the ball to be "bowled" at high speeds. As adults they can play for the West Indies team, drawn from the best players on each island. The team has included many great bowlers and batsmen.

Brian Lara from Trinidad has played for the West Indies cricket team since 1990.

ST. KITTS AND NEVIS
Capital city: Basseterre
Area: 139 sq miles (360 sq km)
Population: 41,000

ANTIGUA AND BARBUDA
Capital city: St. Johns
Area: 170 sq miles (440 sq km)
Population: 63,880

DOMINICA
Capital city: Roseau
Area: 290 sq miles (750 sq km)
Population: 66,422

ST. LUCIA
Capital city: Castries
Area: 236 sq miles (610 sq km)
Population: 155,461

ST. VINCENT AND THE GRENADINES
Capital city: Kingstown
Area: 131 sq miles (40 sq km)
Population: 115,461

BARBADOS
Capital city: Bridgetown
Area: 166 sq miles (430 sq km)
Population: 270,000

GRENADA
Capital city: St. George's
Area: 131 sq miles (340 sq km)
Population: 99,500

TRINIDAD AND TOBAGO
Capital city: Port-of-Spain
Area: 1,981 sq miles (5,130 sq km)
Population: 1,300,000

TOURISM
The main industry in the Caribbean is tourism, which provides work for local people in restaurants, hotels, shops, and beach stalls. However the work is mainly seasonal since most visitors only come to escape cold at home. Also many hotels are owned by foreign companies, and money does not always remain on the islands. Some local governments are trying to reduce their dependence on tourism.

TRANSPORTATION
In the past, people and goods were transported by boat between the islands. Today, ships are still the most economic way to move cargo, and ports, such as Castries in St. Lucia, handle the islands' exports. Many islands have no railroads and main roads are often confined to the coasts, making the interior difficult to reach. Antigua, Barbados, Martinique, and other islands now have large airports capable of handling jumbo jets.

SCARLET IBIS
The Caribbean is a haven for colorful bird life, notably the scarlet ibis of Trinidad and Tobago. The ibis lives in the islands' mangrove swamps, flying off during the day to feed on crabs and other small sea creatures that live in the coastal mudflats.

Curved beak for digging in mud

FOOD FROM THE LAND
Because of the shortage of land, most island farms are small. Farmers grow food for themselves, and sell a wide range of crops in local markets, including yams, sweet potatoes, okra, and salad crops, as well as fruits such as mangoes, limes, coconuts, and bananas. They also grow cash crops for export. The main crop varies from island to island, with nutmeg grown in Grenada, coffee in Trinidad, arrowroot in St. Vincent, and sugar and bananas almost everywhere.

INDUSTRY

The most industrialized country in the area is Trinidad and Tobago, which has petrochemical, iron, and steel industries based on its reserves of oil and natural gas. Apart from Barbados, the other islands have few mineral resources and rely on bananas, sugar, cotton, and cocoa for export. In recent years, all the islands have tried to produce a wider range of exports. St. Vincent now has a flour mill, and Martinique an oil refinery. Light industrial parks have been set up on a number of islands.

LESSER ANTILLES

LESSER ANTILLES

SOUTH AMERICA

PITCH LAKE
La Brea, in the south of Trinidad, boasts one of the world's most unusual sights. Near the town is a lake filled not with water, but with natural pitch, a black, sticky tar that is mainly used for surfacing roads. The lake, which is 200 ft (60 m) deep, is the world's largest single supply of natural pitch. It is thought to be linked to the underground rocks that supply nearby South America with oil.

LESSER ANTILLES INDUSTRIES
ANTIGUA AND BARBUDA
Tourism, cotton, rum
ST KITTS AND NEVIS
Sugar, cotton production, tourism
DOMINICA
Bananas, citrus fruits, essential oils
ST LUCIA
Bananas, tourism, electrical parts
ST VINCENT AND THE GRENADINES
Tourism, bananas, food processing, cement
BARBADOS
Sugar, tourism, petroleum products
GRENADA
Tourism, bananas, nutmeg
TRINIDAD AND TOBAGO
Oil refining, chemicals, sugar

ISLAND MUSIC
Almost every Caribbean island resounds with the beat of calypso music, which has its origins in the slave songs brought from West Africa. Calypso has a strong beat and lyrics about social and political problems. In recent years *soca*, a mixture of soul and calypso, has started to become popular with younger people.

Steel band music originated in Trinidad, using pans or drums made from large oil drums.

This steel band is playing music for tourists in Tobago.

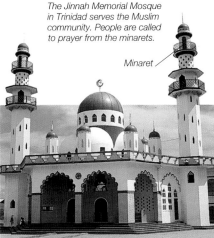

The Jinnah Memorial Mosque in Trinidad serves the Muslim community. People are called to prayer from the minarets.

Minaret

ISLAND SPICES

The island of Grenada is the world's second largest producer of nutmeg, after Indonesia, and grows almost one-quarter of the world's total crop. Nutmeg, a spice used to flavor food, originated in the East Indies, and was introduced to Grenada by the Dutch in the 19th century. The trees flourished in the fertile volcanic soil, warm temperatures, and high annual rainfall. Ginger, cinnamon, pepper, and cloves are also grown on the island.

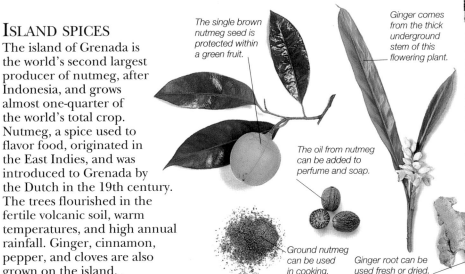

The single brown nutmeg seed is protected within a green fruit.

Ginger comes from the thick underground stem of this flowering plant.

The oil from nutmeg can be added to perfume and soap.

Ground nutmeg can be used in cooking.

Ginger root can be used fresh or dried.

PEOPLE OF THE CARIBBEAN
Most people who live on the islands are a mixture of descendants of African slaves, Europeans, and local Carib Indians. The exception are the people of Trinidad, where almost 40 percent of the population is originally from the Indian subcontinent. Shipped over to work in the plantations, the immigrants brought their religions with them, setting up Hindu temples and Muslim mosques and continuing to observe their own religious customs.

Find out more
BANANAS: *48*
HURRICANES: *44*
SPICES: *198, 264*
SUGAR: *52*

NORTHERN SOUTH AMERICA

ARCHING AROUND THE RAIN FORESTS of the great Amazon River, the countries in northern South America are dominated by the Andes Mountains. Running north to south from Venezuela to Ecuador, and then through Chile, the mountains were once home to the Inca Empire. In search of gold, the Spanish arrived in the 16th century and carved out a huge empire. British, French, and Dutch colonies were also established in the northeast. Except for French Guiana, these are now independent, although not without problems. Extremes of wealth and poverty, overcrowded cities, and the illegal drugs trade are features of most countries in this region.

ANIMALS OF THE ANDES

For centuries, the people of the Andes have relied on a group of versatile mammals for food and clothing. The wild guanaco and vicuña, as well as the domesticated llama and alpaca, are treasured for their wool and meat. Vicuña wool is as fine as silk, while coarse llama wool is used to make blankets, ropes, and other goods.

The llama is used to carry goods.

QUECHUA INDIANS

The Quechua have lived high in the Andes in Bolivia, Peru, and Ecuador for hundreds of years. The Quechua were once farmers, and shared common land equally between men and women. Today many Quechua have moved to the cities in search of work. Those who remain farm tiny plots of land.

The Andes is the longest unbroken mountain chain over 9,850 ft (3,000 m) tall in the world.

Lake Titicaca straddles the border between Peru and Bolivia.

The Altiplano, or high plain, is used for growing potatoes and grazing animals.

CULTIVATING THE ANDES

Fertile land is in such short supply in the Andes that every available scrap of soil must be used. Farmers often cut terraces into the hillsides to get the maximum use from their land. Crops are grown to suit the temperature, which is hot and humid on the lower slopes near the coast, but gets cooler as the mountains rise upward. On the high plains beyond the Andes only the potato will ripen successfully. This artwork shows a section of the Andes from Peru to Bolivia.

La Paz

9,850 ft (3,000 m)

Potatoes, wheat, and barley grow in the cool highland areas of the Andes.

6,550 ft (2,000 m)

Sugarcane

Sugarcane, coffee, tobacco, and corn flourish in the temperate zone.

Potato plant

3,280 ft (1,000 m)

Bananas, cocoa, cotton, and rice all grow well in the warm climate of the lowlands.

Sea level

Bananas

World drug routes

US

To eastern US

To Europe

To Mexico

To North Africa

To western US and Canada

SOUTH AMERICA

Main growing areas

Main traffic routes

THE DRUG TRADE

For many centuries, people in this region have chewed the leaves of the coca plant to reduce hunger. Today the leaves are processed to make cocaine, an illegal drug much in demand in North America and Europe. Coca bushes thrive on poor soil and need little attention, unlike food crops, which need tending. Growing coca is also more profitable than growing food. As a result, large quantities of coca are grown in isolated areas of the Andes. Once refined into cocaine, the drug is smuggled out of the region.

ANGEL FALLS

Angel Falls is the highest waterfall in the world. It was discovered in 1935 by Jimmy Angel, an American pilot who was flying across Venezuela in search of a river he had once prospected for gold. Instead he flew over a vast waterfall that plunges 3,215 ft (980 m) into the Churún River below.

A B C D E F G H I J K L

1 2 3 4 5 6 7 8 9 10 11 12

Bogóta, Colombia
☀ Jan 57°F (14°C)
July 57°F (14°C)
🌧 Jan 2.3 in (58 mm)
July 2 in (51 mm)

VENEZUELA

Georgetown, Guyana
☀ Jan 79°F (26°C)
July 80°F (26.5°C)
🌧 Jan 8 in (203 mm)
July 10 in (254 mm)

ECUADOR

GUYANA

SURINAME

COLOMBIA

PERU

THINGS TO LOOK FOR ON THE MAP

Longest river: Orinoco, Colombia/
Venezuela, 1,700 miles (2,736 km) *Map G3*

Highest peak: Huascarán, Peru, 22,205 ft
(6,768 m) *Map C8*

Largest lake: L.Titicaca, Bolivia/Peru,
3,200 sq miles (8,287 sq km) *Map F10*

World's highest waterfall: Angel Falls,
Venezuela, 3,215 ft (980 m) *Map H3*

N

0 100 200 300 400 500 km
0 100 200 300 miles

TROPIC OF CANCER

EQUATOR

TROPIC OF CAPRICORN

Lima, Peru
☀ Jan 74°F (24°C)
July 62°F (16°C)
🌧 Jan 0.1 in (3 mm)
July 0.3 in (8 mm)

BOLIVIA

LOST WORLDS
Towering above the rain forests
of Venezuela are more than 100
flat-topped sandstone hills, called
tepuis, some of them 3,300 ft
(1,000 m) high. These *tepuis* were
once part of a vast plateau that
has been eroded by wind and
rain over millions of years. Many
unique plants and animals have
evolved in these "lost worlds."

THE CARIBBEAN COASTLINE
In most of South America,
the population is made up
of a mixture of European
immigrants and the native
Indian peoples. But the
Caribbean coast and islands
are home to a largely black
population, like these
Colombians. They are the
descendants of slaves brought
over from Africa to work on
the sugar plantations. Many
have remained among the
poorest members of society.

BORDER DISPUTES
There is not a country in South
America that has not fought
with its neighbors over
its borders, and many
frontiers are still disputed
today. Wars between
Bolivia and Paraguay in
the 1930s, and Ecuador
and Peru in the 1940s,
resulted in thousands of
deaths. The checkpoint
shown here marks a border
crossing between Bolivia and Chile.

VENEZUELA

WHEN THE ITALIAN EXPLORER Amerigo Vespucci first visited the southern shores of the Caribbean Sea in 1499, he named the land Venezuela, or "Little Venice." The lake dwellings of the native Indians reminded him of the houses and canals of the Italian city of Venice. Part of the Spanish Empire for three centuries, Venezuela became independent in 1811. Today it is a country of huge contrasts: the oil industry produces immense wealth, yet many people live in shantytowns. Most people live in cities, yet the tribes of the interior are barely touched by modern life.

VENEZUELA	
Capital city: Caracas	
Area: 352,143 sq miles (912,050 sq km)	
Population: 24,200,000	
Official language: Spanish	
Major religions: Christian 99%, other 1%	
Government: Multiparty democracy	
Currency: Bolivar	
Adult literacy rate: 93%	
Life expectancy: 72 years	
People per doctor: 625	
Televisions: 185 per 1,000 people	

HIGH-RISE CARACAS
For most of its 400-year history, Caracas was a sleepy town 2,950 ft (900 m) up in the hills near the Caribbean coastline. With the discovery of oil, the population rapidly rose from a few thousand to more than 4 million. Today, Caracas is a modern city, with steel and glass architecture, an extensive highway, and a subway system.

SLASH AND BURN AGRICULTURE
In parts of the Amazon rainforest in Venezuela farmers practice a type of agriculture called slash and burn. This is where virgin rainforest is cut down and burned in order to provide farm land. The land cannot sustain being cultivated for long, so after a few years more forest must be destroyed for farmers to carry on growing crops.

Where people live

87% live in cities · 13% live in the country

RAIN FOREST TRIBES

The few native peoples who still survive in Venezuela live in the remote interior of the country near the border with Brazil. The main group is the Yanomami and numbers about 10,000 people. The Yanomami are hunters and gatherers who live in enormous thatched huts called *yanos*, built in clearings in the forest. Their way of life is threatened both by timber companies and mineral prospectors anxious to exploit the wealth of the region, and by measles and other diseases against which they have no defense.

Women tend the gardens as well as raise the children.

Circular yanos contain between 10 and 20 families, each living in their own section.

Yanos are made from wooden beams covered with palm branches and supported by tall poles; the central part is often open to the sky.

Yanomami men hunt wild animals for food. Boys are trained to hunt from an early age.

YOUNG VENEZUELA
Out of a total population in Venezuela of 20 million, more than 8 million people are under the age of 15. The majority of them live in the cities of the north. Many enjoy US activities such as playing baseball (introduced by workers in the oil industry), and listen to rock music.

OIL WEALTH

The discovery of oil in Lake Maracaibo, in 1917, transformed Venezuela from one of the poorest countries in South America to one of the richest. The reserves underneath Lake Maracaibo are the biggest outside the Middle East; oil-bearing beds of tar by the Orinoco River add to the country's wealth. Despite these reserves, many people remain poor. Public services and agriculture have been neglected, and the rise and fall in oil prices has affected the economy.

CABLE CAR
Far above the city of Mérida is the world's highest cable car system. It carries passengers from the city up to 15,600 ft (4,765 m) above sea level. The journey is in four stages and takes more than an hour.

Find out more
NATIVE PEOPLES: *43*
OIL: *137, 152, 281*
POPULATION GROWTH: *43*
RAIN FORESTS: *15, 69, 204*

GUYANA

O NLY ABOUT 800,000 PEOPLE live in Guyana, most of them on the coastal plain in and around the capital city of Georgetown. Guyana takes its name from a native Indian word meaning "Land of Many Waters," for the country is crossed by numerous rivers draining north into the Atlantic Ocean. Guyana was once a British colony, but gained independence in 1966. Today the country exports sugar and bauxite, and also possesses vast natural resources, including timber and minerals.

GUYANA

Capital city: Georgetown

Area: 76,004 sq miles (196,840 sq km)

Population: 861,000

Official language: English

Major religions: Christian 57%, Hindu 33%, Muslim 9%, other 1%

Government: Multiparty democracy

Currency: Guyana dollar

Adult literacy rate: 98%

Life expectancy: 64 years

People per doctor: 303

Televisions: 55 per 1,000 people

SURINAME

Capital city: Paramaribo

Area: 62,344 sq miles (161,470 sq km)

Population: 417,000

Official language: Dutch

Major religions: Christian 48%, Hindu 27%, Muslim 20%, other 5%

Government: Multiparty democracy

Currency: Suriname guilder

Adult literacy rate: 94%

Life expectancy: 70 years

People per doctor: 2,500

Televisions: 153 per 1,000 people

FRENCH GUIANA*

Capital city: Cayenne

Area: 35,135 sq miles (91,000 sq km)

Population: 114,808

Official language: French

Major religions: Christian 75%, other 25%

Government: Ruled from France as part of multi-party democracy

Currency: Euro

*French Guiana is not an independent country. It is a French overseas department.

THE POPULATION
Most people in Guyana are descendants of workers or slaves brought into the country to labor on the sugar plantations. African slaves were shipped over between the 17th and 19th centuries. After slavery was abolished in the British Empire in 1833, people from the Indian Subcontinent arrived to take their place. The Caribs, the original Indian inhabitants, now number no more than 50,000 people.

SUGAR PLANTATIONS
The Dutch were the first Europeans in Guyana, establishing a settlement on the Essequibo River in 1615. They planted sugar, cocoa, and other tropical crops, importing slaves from West Africa to help them run the plantations. The British took control of the country in 1814, and concentrated on growing sugar. Today sugar, rice, bauxite, and gold are the main exports.

SURINAME

F ORMERLY KNOWN AS DUTCH GUIANA, Suriname was originally owned by the British, who exchanged it for the Dutch island of Nieuw Amsterdam, now called Manhattan, in 1667. Suriname became independent from the Netherlands in 1975. Because the country is so poor, about 200,000 Surinamese live in the Netherlands, and send money back to support their families at home.

PARAMARIBO
The capital city of Suriname lies just inland from the Atlantic coastline. The Dutch origins of the city can be seen in the Dutch-style architecture and in street names such as Konigstraat. Most of the city is built of wood, including the 19th-century cathedral of St. Peter and St. Paul with its tall spires. Half the population of Suriname lives in Paramaribo.

FRENCH GUIANA

T HE ONLY REMAINING colony in South America is French Guiana. For years the colony was famous for its offshore prison on Devil's Island, but today it is better known for its role in the European space program. The colony is dependent on France for much of its income, and it now has one of the highest standards of living in South America.

The ocelot is an endangered animal.

FORESTS
Most people live on the coast and the interior is largely untouched tropical rain forest. Thousands of different species of flora and fauna, including ocelots, jaguars, and pumas, plus a variety of reptiles, inhabit the forests.

KOUROU
More than 15,000 people live and work at Kourou, the launch site for the European Space Agency. *Ariane* rockets put satellites and probes into space on behalf of European nations.

Find out more

DEPENDENT TERRITORIES: *271*
NATIVE PEOPLES: *43*
RAIN FORESTS: *15, 69, 204*
SUGAR: *52*

COLOMBIA

COLOMBIA

WHEN SPANISH CONQUERORS reached Colombia in 1499, they discovered a civilization that was rich in gold. They spread tales of a mysterious lost city called *El Dorado*, filled with wealth, but it has never been found. Since 1819, when Colombia became an independent country, it has suffered decades of violent political battles and, more recently, bloody rivalry between drug cartels. Today Colombia is the world's largest producer of cocaine. Large rivers, such as the Orinoco and Amazon, form an important means of transportation for goods across the country.

COLOMBIA	
Capital city: Bogotá	
Area: 401,042 sq miles (1,038,700 sq km)	
Population: 42,300,000	
Official language: Spanish	
Major religions: Christian 95%, other 5%	
Government: Multiparty democracy	
Currency: Colombian peso	
Adult literacy rate: 92%	
Life expectancy: 70 years	
People per doctor: 1,111	
Televisions: 217 per 1,000 people	

CARTAGENA

The bustling port of Cartagena was founded by the Spanish in the 1500s. Great Spanish galleons bound for home set off from here piled high with riches looted from the native peoples. The old city walls, enclosing beautiful mansions and churches, are still there today, along with the many fortifications built by the Spanish to ward off pirates and attacks from other countries.

The women's skirts look like those worn by Spanish flamenco dancers.

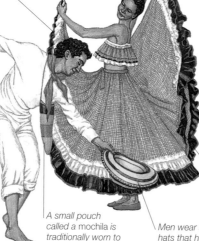

THE CUMBIA

All Colombians know how to dance the *cumbia*, even young children. The dance is a blend of traditions from the black slaves who were brought to Colombia from Africa in the 1800s, together with Spanish and native Indian influences. The men wear white, which was the color of slaves' clothes. Women's clothes are more Spanish in origin.

A small pouch called a mochila is traditionally worn to hold coca leaves or rum.

Men wear sombreros – hats that have wide brims to keep off the sun.

Skirts have weights in the hems to keep them from swirling too high.

BURIED TREASURE

Mining is becoming very important to the Colombian economy since large deposits of oil have been found northeast of Bogotá. Petrochemical plants, like this one at Barranquilla, convert oil into fuel for cars and planes. New sources of coal, the largest in Latin America, as well as deposits of nickel, are also helping boost the economy. The US, Germany, and Venezuela are Colombia's main trading partners.

EMERALDS

Many people consider Colombian emeralds to be the finest in the world. The earliest civilizations to live in this region made beautiful objects from gold and emeralds. Today, Colombia produces more than half of the world's emeralds.

Veins of natural emeralds are found in rocks such as calcite or pyrite.

AGRICULTURE

The variety of climate zones in Colombia means that a wide range of crops can be grown. For many years coffee was the country's main export and Colombia is still the world's third largest producer. Once picked, coffee beans are spread out in trays to dry naturally in the sun. Falling world coffee prices have forced Colombia's farmers to develop other products, such as sugar, bananas, cotton, and cut flowers, which are all grown for export.

SAN AGUSTIN

This small village near the southern mountains is famous for its ancient stone figures. The statues are at least 800 years old, but very little is known about the people who carved them. Some experts believe that the site was a ceremonial center where the Agustinians buried their dead, placing statues near the tombs.

About 500 statues have been found at San Agustin. Many are shaped like birds or animals.

Find out more
COFFEE: *50, 66*
DRUG TRADE: *58*
GEMSTONES: *172, 191*
OIL: *137, 152, 281*

ECUADOR

CUT THROUGH BY THE EQUATOR, after which it is named, Ecuador is a small country with a varied landscape. A journey of just 125 miles (200 km) takes you from humid coastal lowlands, up into the cold air of the Andes, and down into tropical rain forest. Ecuador also includes the Galápagos Islands, which lie about 620 miles (1,000 km) west in the Pacific Ocean. Ecuador has large reserves of oil and natural gas, and these products account for nearly half of the country's export earnings.

ECUADOR	
Capital city: Quito	
Area: 106,888 sq miles (276,840 sq km)	
Population: 12,600,000	
Official language: Spanish	
Major religions: Christian 95%, other 5%	
Government: Multiparty democracy	
Currency: Sucre	
Adult literacy rate: 92%	
Life expectancy: 70 years	
People per doctor: 667	
Televisions: 293 per 1,000 people	

COTOPAXI
Ecuador is home to the notorious "volcano boulevard" – four rows of volcanic mountains that form part of the Andes chain. At least 10 of them are still active. One of the most famous is Cotopaxi. At a towering 19,348 ft (5,897 m) in height, this is one of the world's tallest active volcanoes. It last erupted in the early 1900s.

MANGROVE SWAMPS
Along the coast are swamps filled with trees called mangroves, which can grow in salt water. This watery habitat is very important – the trees provide firewood and timber, while the fish, crustaceans, and shellfish that live here are an important source of food. Shrimps in particular have become a major export. Large shrimp farms have created thousands of much-needed jobs, but they are gradually destroying the coastal environment on which they depend.

The roots trap silt from the sea and help prevent erosion of the land.

Statice

Carnations

AGRICULTURE
Twenty years ago, Ecuador's economy was based on three crops: bananas, coffee, and cocoa. Today, agriculture is less dominant, but about a third of the workforce still makes a living from farming. Fishing is also important, with shrimps, sardines, and tuna among the main catches. A recently introduced crop is cut flowers, such as roses, carnations, and statice, which are exported to North America and Europe.

At high tide, the sea comes in and covers the roots.

Mudskippers are the only fish that can live on land and in the water.

Swamp water is usually very muddy.

Shrimps are washed in with the tide. They feed on plankton.

The mangroves' tangled roots spread far and wide, some even emerging above water to trap oxygen.

Panama hats are made from the leaves of the jipijapa plant.

Otavalo market is so popular with tourists that it now occupies all five squares in the center of town.

THE OTAVALO INDIANS
The town of Otavalo, high in the Andes, is home to one of the wealthiest groups of Indians in South America. The Otavalo make blankets, ponchos, rugs, and other woven goods, which they sell to tourists and export all over South America, the US, and Europe. Demand for Otavalo goods is so great that many of them are now mass-produced, using artificial dyes and fibers and machines for weaving. The money raised allows the Otavalo to continue their traditional way of life.

Otavalo rug, decorated with llamas

PANAMA HAT
Panama hats have never been made in Panama. They come from Ecuador, where they were originally made for export to Panama – hence the name. A good-quality hat takes three months to make and can be rolled up without being ruined.

Find out more
ANDES: *40, 58*
GALÁPAGOS ISLANDS: *265*
NATIVE PEOPLES: *43*
VOLCANOES: *13*

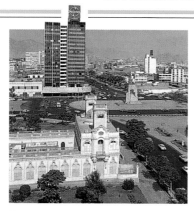

PERU

FOUR HUNDRED YEARS AGO, Peru was the center of the great Inca Empire, which stretched the length of South America. Descendants of the Incas still continue their traditional way of life in the Andes Mountains, and make up about half of Peru's population. In recent years, unemployment, poverty, and other social problems have led to much political violence in Peru. This has prevented foreign investment in Peru and kept it one of the poorest countries in South America.

PERU	
Capital city: Lima	
Area: 494,208 sq miles (1,280,000 sq km)	
Population: 25,700,000	
Official languages: Spanish, Quechua, and Aymará	
Major religions: Christian 95%, other 5%	
Government: Multiparty democracy	
Currency: New sol	
Adult literacy rate: 90%	
Life expectancy: 68 years	
People per doctor: 1,000	
Televisions: 144 per 1,000 people	

LIMA

Gray skies and damp mists hang over Lima for much of the year. But the population of Peru's capital city has grown rapidly to more than 6 million as people have flocked there in search of work. Although the rich live in new apartment buildings or suburban houses, the poor survive in *calampas*, huge, overcrowded shantytowns that have sprung up on the outskirts. Lima was founded in 1535 by the Spaniard Francisco Pizarro.

PACIFIC FISHING

Peru's coastal waters are teeming with plankton, which provide food for anchovies, sardines, pilchards, and mackerel. Anchovies, caught and processed into fish meal, are a major export. Every nine or 10 years a current of warm water, called *El Niño*, upsets the balance of plankton, and the fish move to better feeding areas. It struck throughout the 1990s, devastating the fishing industry.

Mackerel

Sardines

The islands are built from layers of reeds that rot away at the bottom and are replaced at the top.

New reeds are cut and stacked, ready for use.

Villagers grow potatoes in fields by the lake.

The Urus build their homes and boats from the totora reeds that grow at the edge of the lake.

Remains of the city of Machu Picchu

Women untangling fishing nets

LAKE TITICACA

Lying 12,500 ft (3,810 m) above sea level, Lake Titicaca is the world's highest navigable lake. It stretches across the border of Peru and into Bolivia. For thousands of years, native peoples have fished its waters. One group, the Urus, live on the lake in villages built on huge rafts made from reeds. They grow potatoes (one of the few crops that will ripen at such high altitudes), catch fish, and hunt birds that live by the lake.

Women wear their hair in a single braid, which they tuck into their hats.

THE LOST CITY OF THE INCAS

Perched high in the Andes, Machu Picchu was an important Inca city in the 15th and 16th centuries. This fortress city escaped the notice of the Spanish conquerors who arrived in 1532, and it remained a "lost city" until it was rediscovered by American archaeologist Hiram Bingham in 1911. The site includes the remains of ceremonial buildings, such as temples, and 143 homes.

SHINING PATH

During the 1980s a guerilla group called the Shining Path conducted a terrorist campaign in Peru. The group wanted to restore a communist government, and proceeded to terrorize the country. They were able to assassinate people and bomb targets in Peru's cities. Their leader, Abimael Guzman, was captured and imprisoned in 1993.

The Urus build boats from tightly bundled reeds. A well-built boat can last a family up to six months.

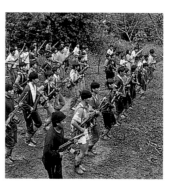

BOLIVIA

THE SMALL, MOUNTAINOUS country of Bolivia has no coastline. In 1883, its coastal region was lost to Chile in the Pacific Wars, and now its main means of export are roads and railroads through Peru and Chile. Bolivia has many resources, such as silver and tin, but its isolated position and many changes of government have kept it poor. About 70 percent of the population is made up of Aymará and Quechua Indians who live on the high windswept plains, called the *altiplano*, growing barely enough food to feed themselves and their families.

SIMÓN BOLÍVAR
Bolivia is named after Simón Bolívar (1783-1830), the Venezuelan freedom fighter known as "The Liberator." From 1812, Bolívar devoted his life to freeing South America from Spanish control. He liberated New Granada (Colombia), Venezuela, Ecuador, Panama, and finally Bolivia, then known as Upper Peru. Bolívar dreamed of a united South America, but his dream has not come true.

BOLIVIA

Capital cities: La Paz, Sucre

Area: 418,683 sq miles (1,084,390 sq km)

Population: 8,300,000

Official languages: Spanish, Quechua, and Aymará

Major religions: Christian 95%, other 5%

Government: Multiparty democracy

Currency: Boliviano

Adult literacy rate: 86%

Life expectancy: 61 years

People per doctor: 2,500

Televisions: 116 per 1,000 people

It is cold living on the high plains of Bolivia. The soil is poor. Villagers break up the ground to sow potatoes.

Tin

Silver

MINING
Bolivia is rich in tin, silver, lead, zinc, and other minerals. Tin mining is an important industry and, even though production has fallen, Bolivia still ranks among the world's top five tin producers. Thousands of people work in the mines, but conditions are dangerous and wages are low. Many miners believe that a spirit, called *El Tio*, lives in the mines, and they leave cigarettes as offerings for him.

LIFE ON THE HIGH PLAINS
Life is hard for the Aymará Indians, many of whom live in villages without electricity or plumbing. Most are poor farmers who grow potatoes as well as corn and barley stalks to feed their cows, sheep, and chickens. Sometimes they have to kill one of their animals for food. Llamas provide wool for warm clothing and llama droppings are used as fuel. Aymará women and girls wear dark green, black or brown hats.

This lamb will later provide milk for the family.

Many Aymará wear plastic shoes, called ojotas.

FESTIVAL IN THE SUN
Although Bolivia is Roman Catholic, many traditional beliefs still survive. The Isla del Sol (Island of the Sun) in Lake Titicaca is thought to be the birthplace of the Sun and is the location for the celebration shown here. Music is important at Bolivian festivals, when pan-pipes, drums, and brass instruments are played.

Traditional pan-pipes are made from reeds.

COCA GROWING
The leaf of the coca plant is used in the production of the illegal drug cocaine. Coca grows well in Bolivia's mountain valleys and provides a much-needed source of income for local people. The government has tried to stop coca production by offering farmers money to destroy their plantations and grow other crops, such as coffee, cocoa, or bananas, instead. However, this policy has not succeeded, and coca is still Bolivia's main crop.

Loose seeds inside the maracas make a noise when they are shaken.

Maracas are pairs of rattles made from dried gourds.

Find out more
DRUG TRADE: *58*
LLAMAS: *58*
NATIVE PEOPLES: *43*
ROMAN CATHOLICS: *274*

BRAZIL

THE LARGEST COUNTRY in South America, Brazil covers almost half the continent. From the 16th to 19th centuries it was ruled by the Portuguese, who named it after the brazilwood tree. The country contains deserts in the northeast, rain forests in the north and west, and rolling grasslands in the south. Because the climate is so varied, it is possible to grow almost any crop. Brazil has crowded modern cities – and areas that have never been explored. In the south, the forces of the Paraná and Paraguay rivers have been harnessed to form the one of the world's largest hydroelectric projects, the Itaipú Dam.

CITY LIFE

About 80 percent of Brazilians live in cities, most of which have developed near the coast. Over the years, many people have moved to the cities from the countryside in search of work and a better standard of living. For many years the cities grew rapidly, although this has now slowed down. The largest city, São Paulo, already has 17 million people – more than the populations of Paris and London put together.

TOP CITIES BY POPULATION	
São Paulo	17,750,000
Rio de Janeiro	10,500,000
Belo Horizonte	4,400,000
Porto Alegre	3,650,000
Recife	3,450,000

PEOPLE OF BRAZIL

The population of Brazil is a mixture of peoples. Some are descended from native Indians who have always lived in Brazil, others from the Portuguese who ruled there for 300 years. Many Brazilians have African ancestors who were brought over in the 17th century to work as slaves on the sugar plantations. At the beginning of the 20th century many Japanese sailed to Brazil to escape crop failures at home. Also during the 20th century, large numbers of European migrants settled in the south of the country.

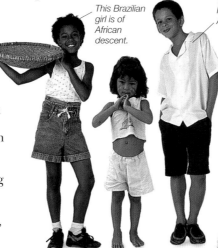

This Brazilian girl is of African descent.

This boy has both Portuguese and African ancestors.

The girl in the middle is a rain forest Indian from the Tembé tribe.

The homes in this shantytown in São Paulo are built from wood and corrugated metal.

World's top coffee producers
(Figures show percentage of world production)

8.7% 11.1% 25.1%

Colombia Vietnam Brazil

AGRICULTURE

Brazil is the world's major producer and exporter of coffee, which is grown on huge plantations, mostly in the states of Paraná and São Paulo. However, coffee is only one of the country's main crops; soy beans, sugarcane, and cotton are also produced on a large scale. Brazil is one of the world's main producers of oranges, bananas, and cocoa beans as well. About one-quarter of Brazilians work in agriculture, although the size of farms varies from tiny plots of land to vast estates. Many people work in the fields for little pay, while a few rich landowners benefit from huge profits.

SHANTYTOWNS

Housing shortages in Brazil mean that about 25 million people live in sprawling shantytowns called *favelas* that surround the cities. Most of the homes are built by the families themselves, sometimes from waste materials, but more often from wood, bricks, and cement bought from builder's merchants. Services such as running water and sanitation are poor.

Favela homes

No running water: 70%   No toilets or drains: 60%   No waste collection: 52%

SOCCER

Everyone in Brazil plays or watches soccer, and there is a stadium in every city. The huge Maracana Stadium in Rio de Janeiro was built for the 1950 World Cup, and holds 200,000 spectators. Brazil has won the World Cup more times than any other country, most recently in 1994. Many Brazilian stars play soccer abroad for teams in England, Spain, and Italy.

Manaus
- Jan 82°F (27°C)
- July 82°F (27°C)
- Jan 9.8 in (249 mm)
- July 2.3 in (58 mm)

BRAZIL

THINGS TO LOOK FOR ON THE MAP

Longest river: Amazon, Brazil/Peru, 4,001 miles (6,439 km) *Map G3*

Highest point: Pico da Neblina, 9,888 ft (3,014 m) *Map C3*

World's largest lagoon: Lagoa dos Patos, 3,917 sq miles (10,145 sq km) *Map G12*

VENEZUELA · GUYANA · SURINAME · FRENCH GUIANA (France)

COLOMBIA

Boa Vista

Pico da Neblina

Macapá

Belém

São Luís · Parnaíba

ATLANTIC OCEAN

Manaus · Santarém

Negro · Balbina Res. · Amazon · Jari

Amazon

Madeira · Tapajós · Xingu

A M A Z O N I A

Tucuruí Res.

SERRA GRANDE

Fortaleza

Teresina · Mossoró

Juruá · Purus · Teles Pires

Cruzeiro do Sul

Pôrto Velho

B R A Z I L

Carolina

Picos · Campina Grande · Natal · João Pessoa · Recife

Rio Branco

PERU

PLATEAU OF MATO GROSSO

SERRA DOS PARECIS

Palmas

Sobradinho Res.

Juàzeiro · Maceió

Aracaju

0 100 200 300 400 500 km
0 250 500 750 miles

SERRA DOS CARAJÁS

SERRA DO RONCADOR

Araguaia · Tocantins · Paranaíba

São Francisco

Barreiras · Ibotirama · Feira de Santana · Salvador

TROPIC OF CANCER

EQUATOR

TROPIC OF CAPRICORN

Cuiabá

BRASÍLIA

Goiânia

B R A Z I L I A N   H I G H L A N D S

N

BOLIVIA

Corumbá

Uberlândia

Ilha Solteira Res.

Furnas Res.

Belo Horizonte · Ouro Prêto · Vitória

Campo Grande

Ribeirão Prêto

Juiz de Fora

Paraná

PARAGUAY

Paraguay

Itaipú Res.

Campinas · São Paulo · Rio de Janeiro

Londrina · Santos

Iguaçu Falls · Iguaçu

Curitiba

Joinville

Porto Alegre
- Jan 77°F (25°C)
- July 57°F (14°C)
- Jan 3.5 in (89 mm)
- July 4.5 in (114 mm)

ARGENTINA

Uruguay · Passo Fundo · Florianópolis

ATLANTIC OCEAN

URUGUAY

Santa Maria · Pôrto Alegre

Lagoa dos Patos

Pelotas

Rio Grande

ATLANTIC OCEAN

PIRANHA FISH
These vicious fish live in the rivers of the rain forest. They have razor-sharp teeth and, when hundreds of them attack together, can kill and strip a large animal in minutes.

The Amazon and its tributaries, swamps, and lakes form a vast network of freshwater.

AMAZON
The Amazon River starts life in the Andes Mountains of Peru and flows for 4,001 miles (6,439 km) across South America until it gushes into the Atlantic Ocean. For more than half of its length, the Amazon flows through Brazil. It is the country's most important waterway, and large boats can travel inland as far as the modern city of Manaus, about 994 miles (1,600 km) from the sea. Every year the river floods and deposits fertile silt on the land.

FUN IN THE SUN
Brazil's eastern coastline stretches 4,598 miles (7,400 km) along the Atlantic Ocean. In Rio de Janeiro, local people and tourists flock to the wide, sandy beaches to meet friends and play volleyball. The most popular beach in Rio de Janeiro is Copacabana, which is overlooked by Sugarloaf Mountain. Only good swimmers brave the waves though, because of strong currents.

BRAZIL

BRAZIL

Capital city: Brasília

Area: 3,286,472 sq miles (8,511,970 sq km)

Population: 146,154,502

Official language: Portuguese

Major religions: Christian 90%, other 10%

Government: Multiparty democracy

Currency: Réal

Adult literacy rate: 82%

Life expectancy: 66 years

People per doctor: 670

Televisions: 215 per 1,000 people

BOOM AND BUST BEST DESCRIBES the pattern of the economy in Brazil. In the 1960s and 1970s the country enjoyed a period of massive industrial growth. Then the boom ended, Brazil went bust, and the country became the world's greatest debtor. Paying back the loans is now the government's biggest problem. But Brazil has a great supply of natural resources, including gold and iron ore, and mining is one of the country's most important industries. Brazil is both a rich and poor country. Some landowners and business people are extremely wealthy, but most of the rural population is very poor. Although there has been a democratic government since 1985, corruption is still a problem in Brazilian politics.

CARNIVAL

For four days and nights before Lent each year (February or March), it is carnival time in Brazil. People come from all over the world to join the celebration in Rio de Janeiro, where there are street parties, balls, and a contest for the best costume. Day and night the streets are crammed with people in wonderful costumes moving to the rhythm of music. A parade of brightly colored floats, organized by neighborhood samba schools, is the highlight of the carnival.

FOOD FROM BAHIA
The state of Bahia in northeastern Brazil was the first to be colonized by Europeans. Later, black slave cooks created lots of tasty dishes using fish mixed with spices from their native Africa. Along the beaches of Bahia, women still sell these dishes as well as snacks of coconut candies and delicious spicy fish patties.

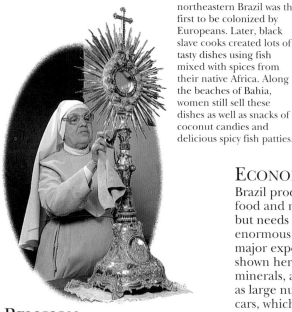

RELIGION

Almost all Brazilians are Roman Catholic, the religion the Portuguese brought with them, and every town and village has its own patron saint to protect it. Millions of Brazilians also exercise their right to freedom of belief, and worship gods and spirits from African religions. In December and January, for example, people leave gifts of flowers, soap, and fruit on the beaches in honor of *Iemanjá*, the African goddess of the sea, who they hope will grant their wishes for the new year. The goddess is linked with the Catholic Virgin Mary.

ECONOMY

Brazil produces most of its own food and manufactured goods, but needs money to pay off its enormous debts. The country's major exports, some of which are shown here, include coffee, minerals, and airplanes, as well as large numbers of Brazilian cars, which are sold in Argentina. Most of Brazil's manufacturing takes place in a rough triangle formed by the industrial cities of Rio de Janeiro, São Paulo, and Belo Horizonte.

Electrical goods such as refrigerators, washing machines, and food mixers

Leather goods such as bags, shoes, jackets, tennis shoes, and soccer balls

Textiles of cotton and silk, and finished goods including towels and sports clothes

Agricultural produce including oranges, tangerines, lemons, and limes

GREEN FUEL
In the 1970s, the rising cost of oil forced Brazil to look for an alternative fuel. Researchers came up with ethanol, a fuel made from fermented sugarcane. Ethanol is cheaper than ordinary gasoline and produces less carbon monoxide, which is much better for the environment. Today, about one-third of Brazil's cars run on this "green fuel."

AMAZON RAIN FOREST

Covering an area the size of Australia, the Amazon rain forest is the largest remaining tropical rain forest anywhere on Earth. It covers about one-third of South America, mostly growing around the Amazon River in Brazil. Many animals, birds, insects, and reptiles rely on the trees for food and shelter, as do the tribes of Amazonian Indians who have lived in the forest for thousands of years. But the rain forest is a fragile environment and both wildlife and people are under serious threat as vast areas of the forest are cut down.

Native Indian homelands

Brazilian rainforest

B R A Z I L

① Tikuna
② Yanomani
③ Guajajara
④ Xavante
⑤ Sateré Maué

This village chief is from the Tembé tribe.

INDIAN TRIBES

At one time there were about 5 million native Indians living in the rain forest; today, fewer than 200,000 remain. The largest of these tribes are located on the above map.
Most live as shifting cultivators, which means they settle for a while to hunt and grow basic food crops, and then move on. This way the forest soil can recover its fertility. Since the arrival of people from outside the forest, the Indians have been at risk from diseases, such as influenza and measles, to which they have no resistance.

MINING

In the last 20 years large deposits of gold and other minerals have been discovered in the Amazon rain forest. At Carajas, a huge iron mountain was accidentally discovered when a geologist crash-landed his helicopter. The rock contains massive amounts of iron ore, as well as manganese and copper. Mining is one of Brazil's major industries, despite the damage it does to the rain forest.

PLANT POWER

The forests contain plants that provide the basis for many valuable products, such as rubber, varnish, paint, cosmetics, and most importantly, medicines. The bark of *chinchona*, for example, supplies the quinine used to treat malaria. Other plants have properties that help fight cancer.

Quinine is obtained from the chinchona plant.

Brazil nuts contain vitamins.

Bark

Shelled nut

LOSS OF FOREST

Vital areas of forest are lost through logging, cattle ranching, and relocation (moving people). Building roads also opens up the interior to further destruction. If the present rate of deforestation continues, there will be no forest left by the end of the century.

RELOCATION

The Brazilian government recently cleared large areas of forest and encouraged landless people to buy small plots of land for farming. But the soil is shallow and rapidly loses its fertility.

CATTLE BREEDING

About 30 percent of Brazil's rain forest has been cut down for cattle ranches. But the land can only support cattle for a few years. Then the ranchers have to move on and clear another site.

LOGGING

Thousands of ebony, teak, and mahogany trees are cut down each year for export. People are now encouraged to buy furniture made of softwoods, such as pine, which take less time to regrow.

Plan of Brasília

Business districts

Government buildings

Residential areas

BRASÍLIA

The city of Brasília was built in the late 1950s as part of a government scheme to encourage people to move into the interior of the country. It became Brazil's capital in 1960, taking over from Rio de Janeiro. The city is laid out in the shape of an airplane, with the business district in the center, residential areas in the wings, and the government in the cockpit. Bold architecture, such as the glass cathedral shown here, is a feature of this modern city.

Find out more

CITIES: *17, 43*
COFFEE: *50, 62*
RAIN FORESTS: *15, 204*
ROMAN CATHOLICS: *274*

SOUTHERN SOUTH AMERICA

FROM THE TROPICAL INTERIOR OF Paraguay, through the warm Mediterranean climate of central Chile, to the freezing conditions around the glaciers of Argentina, southern South America is a region of great contrasts. Four countries – Chile, Argentina, Paraguay, and Uruguay – make up this half of the continent, often called the "southern cone" because of its shape. An important land resource is the pampas, a vast fertile plain that stretches across Argentina and Uruguay, where huge quantities of wheat are grown. During the 1970s, all four countries were known for their brutal military dictatorships. These have since been overturned, and the countries are now run as democracies.

ATACAMA DESERT
This desert in northern Chile is the driest place on Earth, often with no rain for years on end. When rain does fall, devastating flash floods are often the result. The Atacama is a barren wilderness of sun-baked rock and shifting sand dunes where the nighttime temperature can fall dramatically in just one hour. The only paved road across this desolate desert is the Pan-American Highway.

Main migration routes from 1860–1926

Mennonites to Paraguay 1926
Welsh to Argentina 1860s
Italians to Argentina 1870–1926
Spanish to Uruguay and Argentina 1870–1926

Uruguay
Paraguay
Argentina

MIGRANT GROUPS

Many people from Europe have settled in South America. During the 19th and early 20th centuries, poverty in Italy drove laborers to Argentina for the wheat harvest; many never went home. Workers also left Spain for Argentina and Uruguay. A German religious group, the Mennonites, moved to Paraguay from Canada to find freedom of worship, and the Welsh set up a community in Argentina to escape English rule and preserve their language.

INDIAN PEOPLES
Unlike northern South America, the countries in the south have only a few native Indian groups, with Paraguay home to the largest proportion. Uruguay has no Indian population at all. The main surviving groups include the Kolla of Argentina, shown here, the Mataco and Mapuche of central and southern Chile, and the Ache, who live in Paraguay.

WHERE PEOPLE LIVE

In the past 50 years there has been a great shift as people have moved from the country to the cities in search of work. In Argentina and Uruguay, city populations were already swollen by large numbers of immigrants. In each country, the capital city has grown very quickly while the population in other cities has remained fairly small. One-third of Argentinians, for example, live in the capital city of Buenos Aires, shown here. Since the 1970s, the move to the cities has begun to slow down.

About 11 million people now live in Buenos Aires.

Growth of cities

The chart shows the percentage of people living in cities in 1950, 1970, 1990, and 2000.

89%
86%
91%
89%
78%
82%
78%
37%
55%
65%
48%
35%

2000
1990
1970
1950

Paraguay   Argentina   Uruguay

CATTLE BREEDING

In Argentina and Uruguay, cattle breeding for beef exports is a major source of income. Vast herds of cattle graze the pampas, many feeding on alfalfa plants, which produce a leaner meat. The main breeds are Aberdeen Angus and Herefords, brought over from Europe during the last century. Sheep are grazed in the cooler area of Patagonia, and both Argentina and Uruguay are among the world's top wool-producing nations.

Asunción, Paraguay
Jan 83°F (28°C)
July 63°F (17°C)
Jan 5.5 in (140 mm)
July 2.2 in (56 mm)

PARAGUAY

Buenos Aires, Argentina
Jan 74°F (23°C)
July 50°F (10°C)
Jan 3.1 in (79 mm)
July 2.2 in (56 mm)

CHILE

URUGUAY

ARGENTINA

ITAIPU DAM
Huge amounts of earth were cleared to build the Itaipú Dam on the Paraná River in Paraguay. One of the world's largest hydroelectric projects, the dam was built jointly by Paraguay and Brazil, and can produce massive amounts of electricity. Unfortunately, the lake made by the dam drowned a set of waterfalls and created a breeding ground for malaria-carrying mosquitoes.

MORENO GLACIER
At the southern tip of Argentina lies one of the region's most dramatic natural spectacles, the vast Moreno Glacier. Every few years, the glacier advances across Lake Argentino, creating a dam of bluish-white ice that can be up to 197 ft (60 m) high. Eventually, the dammed water in the lake bursts through the icy barrier. The ice collapses and cracks while torrents of water gush over it.

GIANT ANTEATER
The giant anteater is one of South America's most striking animals. It spends the day roaming the pampas in search of ants and termites. If it finds a nest, the anteater breaks it open with its powerful claws and then laps up the insects with its long, sticky tongue.

THINGS TO LOOK FOR ON THE MAP
Longest river: Paraná, Argentina/Paraguay/Brazil, 1,827 miles (2,940 km) Map J7
Highest point: Mt. Aconcagua, Argentina, 22,835 ft (6,960 m) Map F7
Largest lake: L. Buenos Aires/L. General Carrera, Argentina/Chile, 865 sq miles (2,240 sq km) Map G13
World's driest place: Atacama Desert, Chile Map F4

URUGUAY

URUGUAY HAS BEEN DESCRIBED as a giant city with a ranch attached. Half the population of more than 3 million lives in the capital city of Montevideo, while the rest earn a living on the rich lowland pastures that spread out across the rest of the country. The rearing of livestock has brought great wealth to Uruguay, although recently tourism and banking have also contributed to the national income. Apart from a period of brutal military rule in the 1970s, the country has enjoyed a stable government that has built up an impressive welfare system for the people.

Silver straw, called a bombilla

Carved gourd for holding the maté tea

MATE TEA
The national drink of Uruguay and other South American nations is an herbal tea called *maté*. The hot drink, which is rich in caffeine, can be mixed with sugar and aromatic herbs. *Maté* is sipped by straw from a dried gourd, a type of fruit with a hard rind.

CATTLE AND SHEEP
Eleven million cattle and 15 million sheep live on the grassy plains of Uruguay, easily outnumbering the population. In the 1860s, the country's first meat-processing factory was set up in Fray Bentos. The town became the center of the national meat industry when a refrigeration plant opened in 1901. Today, Uruguay exports animal products all over the world and is the world's second biggest exporter of wool, after New Zealand.

PARAGUAY

TUCKED INLAND, LARGELY EMPTY, and with few natural resources, Paraguay is one of the forgotten countries of the world. Once part of the vast Spanish Empire, Paraguay gained its independence in 1811. For most of its history, it has been ruled by a series of military dictators. The most famous of these was General Alfredo Stroessner, who governed for 35 years until he was overthrown in a sudden coup in 1989. Today, Paraguay is struggling to modernize itself. The vast Itaipú Dam generates sufficient electricity to export supplies to neighboring Brazil. Efforts are also being made to lessen the economy's dependence on agricultural products.

JESUIT MISSIONS
Almost a century after the occupation of Paraguay by Spain, in 1536, Jesuit missionaries began to convert the local people to Christianity. The Jesuits, a Roman Catholic order of priests, set up missions and built huge stone churches, protecting the local Guaraní Indians from attack by their enemies. When the Jesuits were expelled in 1767, many of their buildings fell into disrepair, but are now being restored.

ASUNCIÓN
The capital, and almost only, city of Paraguay is Asunción, home to about 1.2 million people. Situated on the eastern bank of the Paraguay River, the city is laid out in a rectangular grid, with wide, tree-lined avenues and beautiful parks. Asunción still retains the atmosphere of the Spanish colonial town it once was.

PEOPLE OF THE CHACO
The north of Paraguay is dominated by the Gran Chaco, a vast stretch of grassland and forest. The only people who live there are the Guaraní and Macá Indians. The Macá sell woven bags to tourists.

Find out more
CATTLE FARMING: 75
NATIVE PEOPLES: 43
POLITICAL SYSTEMS: 270–271
ROMAN CATHOLICS: 274

CHILE

A NATIVE OF CHILE ONCE SAID that his country had a mad geography. It is the longest, thinnest country in the world. Protected by the Andes, it was the last country in the Americas to be occupied by the Spanish, but gained its independence in 1818. Since the end of a cruel military dictatorship that lasted from 1973-1990, the country has enjoyed a stable political life. Most people live in central Chile around the capital, Santiago, and the main port of Valparaiso. Fruit, cereals, and grapes are cultivated in the valleys, which are well watered by rivers from the Andes. Fishing off the long Pacific coast is also important.

CHILE	
Capital city: Santiago	
Area: 289,112 sq miles (748,800 sq km)	
Population: 15,200,000	
Official language: Spanish	
Major religions: Christian 80%, other 20%	
Government: Multiparty democracy	
Currency: Chilean peso	
Adult literacy rate: 96%	
Life expectancy: 75 years	
People per doctor: 909	
Televisions: 232 per 1,000 people	

CHILEAN WINE
Vines were first brought to Chile by the Spanish who grew grapes for their communion wine. Today, the valleys that surround Santiago contain some of the best vineyards on the American continent. Chilean red and white wines are exported around the world.

CHANGING SCENERY
From the dry, barren lands of the Atacama Desert in the north to the icy rocks of Cape Horn in the south, Chile includes almost every type of climate and landscape in the world. The northern desert is one of the driest places on Earth, while the central agricultural valley has a Mediterranean climate similar to California or southern Europe. In the cold and stormy south, 55 volcanoes are currently active, and huge glaciers block the valleys. More than 80 percent of the country is mountainous, and much of the rest is forested. Not much land is available for growing crops.

COPPER MINING
Chile is the world's largest exporter of copper, and also mines significant quantities of iron ore, coal, gold, silver, and other minerals. High up in the Atacama Desert, in the north of Chile, lies one of the world's largest deposits of copper. The mine at Chuquicamata is 13,500 ft (4,115 m) long and 2,200 ft (670 m) deep. Every week millions of tons of rock are blasted out of the ground and processed to produce copper.

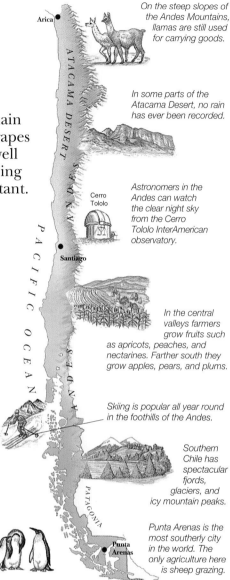

From north to south
Chile is 2,610 miles (4,200 km) long from north to south – the same as the distance from Norway to Nigeria. At no point is the country more than 112 miles (180 km) wide.

Arica

On the steep slopes of the Andes Mountains, llamas are still used for carrying goods.

In some parts of the Atacama Desert, no rain has ever been recorded.

Cerro Tololo

Astronomers in the Andes can watch the clear night sky from the Cerro Tololo InterAmerican observatory.

Santiago

In the central valleys farmers grow fruits such as apricots, peaches, and nectarines. Farther south they grow apples, pears, and plums.

Skiing is popular all year round in the foothills of the Andes.

Southern Chile has spectacular fjords, glaciers, and icy mountain peaks.

Punta Arenas is the most southerly city in the world. The only agriculture here is sheep grazing.

Punta Arenas

King penguins live on the ice caps of Chilean Patagonia.

Cape Horn

MAPUCHE INDIANS
For centuries, the Mapuche Indians have fought for their independence, first against the Incas of Peru, then against invading Spaniards, and most recently against the Chilean government. Today, most of the 800,000 Mapuche live on reservations in the south. One of Chile's main soccer teams, Colo-Colo, is named after an old Mapuche chief.

PUNTA ARENAS
The city of Punta Arenas lies on the Straits of Magellan, the route used by ships to avoid stormy Cape Horn. The port is filled with fishing and Antarctic research vessels and is a base for oil exploration. It lies under the hole in the ozone layer above Antarctica, and people are easily burned by the Sun's rays.

Find out more

ANDES: *40, 58*
COPPER MINING: *237, 245*
NATIVE PEOPLES: *43*
VEGETATION ZONES: *15*

ARGENTINA

ARGENTINA

STRETCHING FROM THE SUBTROPICAL forests of the north, down across the vast central plains of the Pampas, to the snowcapped mountains of Patagonia in the south, Argentina occupies most of southern South America. The country is bounded by the Andes Mountains in the west, and slopes gently downhill to the Atlantic Ocean in the east. Today's population is a mixture of native Indians, Spanish settlers, and immigrants from southern Europe who arrived during the past 100 years. The country is relatively wealthy, but has suffered from years of political instability, with periods of military rule alternating with elected governments.

ARGENTINA	
Capital city: Buenos Aires	
Area: 1,056,636 sq miles (2,736,690 sq km)	
Population: 37,000,000	
Official language: Spanish	
Major religions: Christian 92%, Jewish 2%, other 6%	
Government: Multiparty democracy	
Currency: Argentine peso	
Adult literacy rate: 97%	
Life expectancy: 73 years	
People per doctor: 370	
Televisions: 289 per 1,000 people	

DANCING THE TANGO
Tango, the national music of Argentina, began in the slums of Buenos Aires. The music, and the dramatic dance style that goes with it, reflects the hopes of working people and is sometimes happy, but often sad. Tango music is played on a *bandoneon*, a type of concertina, with a piano and violin accompaniment.

BUENOS AIRES

Almost 30 percent of Argentinians live in or near the capital city of Buenos Aires, making it one of the major cities in the southern half of the world. The city was founded by the Spanish in 1536 as a port on the Río de la Plata, and inhabitants are still called *porteños*, meaning "people of the port." Modern Buenos Aires is highly sophisticated, with grand avenues, a subway system, and expensive shops. It is the trading center of the country, and most of Argentina's exports are shipped through its docks.

MEDIA AND NEWSPAPERS

Argentinians can choose from a range of 180 daily newspapers, among them *El Crónista*, *La Nación*, and *Clarín*, which has the biggest circulation of any newspaper in South America. Most are published in Spanish, but German, English, and French language papers circulate widely. The constitution of Argentina guarantees freedom of the press, but during some military dictatorships, newspapers and television have been heavily censored.

Simple potato pasta is traditionally eaten at the end of the month, just before payday.

ITALIAN IMMIGRANTS
In the years leading up to World War I in 1914, about 2 million people fled the poverty of southern Europe to start a new life in Argentina. More than half came from Italy, finding work on the land or in the expanding cities of Buenos Aires and Rosario. Italian food, such as the potato pasta *ñoquis*, is still served in restaurants throughout Argentina.

FALKLAND ISLANDS
Some 300 miles (480 km) east of Argentina lie the disputed Islas Malvinas. Occupied by Spain in 1767, the islands were invaded by Britain in 1833 and renamed the Falkland Islands. Britain and Argentina have contested ownership ever since. In 1982 an Argentinian invasion was repelled by Britain, which now has a military garrison there.

TIERRA DEL FUEGO
When Ferdinand Magellan and his Spanish crew first saw the rocky islands at the tip of Argentina in 1520, they named them Tierra del Fuego, or Land of Fire, because they saw fires lit by the Fuegian Indians to keep warm. The islands, shared between Argentina and Chile, are wet and windswept, with glaciers carving out huge valleys in the mountains.

THE ECONOMY

With rich, productive farmland and plentiful mineral resources, Argentina is one of South America's wealthier countries. The major exports are the agricultural products from the Pampas: wheat, corn, meat, hides, and wool. Factories turn out steel, chemicals, plastics, and machinery. Argentina is also self-sufficient in energy supplies and has large reserves of oil and gas that have yet to be fully explored. Despite its natural resources, the country has not been well-run and has large overseas debts.

Argentine exports 2000

Agricultural products: 55%
Machinery and vehicles: 16%
Manufacturing: 15%
Fuels and minerals: 14%

STEAM TRAINS

In 1857, a steam train made its way slowly south from Buenos Aires to the inland town of Las Flores, opening the first railroad line in Argentina. Within 40 years, the country was linked by more than 21,000 miles (34,000 km) of track. Largely built by British engineers with rolling stock constructed in British factories, this vast railroad system still runs cars and freight wagons, although diesel locomotives are now taking over.

The car industry is important to Argentina, and many of the leading manufacturers have factories there. Cars are made in the industrial centers of Buenos Aires, Córdoba, and Rosario.

GOING TO SCHOOL

The literacy level of Argentina is one of the highest in South America. Primary education is compulsory up to the age of 12, although attendance is often low in country areas. In most state primary schools children wear white coats called *guarda polvo*, meaning "dust guard." The coats protect their clothes from chalk dust. About one-third of the students go on to attend one of the free state universities.

GAUCHOS OF THE PAMPAS

As famous as his northern cousin, the American cowboy, the Argentine gaucho has roamed the rolling plains of the Pampas for about 300 years. The name gaucho comes from a South American word for outcast, as gauchos have always chosen to live beyond the law of the cities. The men work on the vast *estancias*, or ranches, fixing fences and corrals (pens for animals), tending the horses, and looking after the large herds of cattle. Tough, self-reliant, and free, the gauchos have become legendary heroes and a national symbol of Argentina.

Gauchos ride criollos; a breed of wild horse that originally came from Mexico.

Beef cattle feed on pasture, or alfafa mixed with grains of sorghum grass, to produce a leaner meat.

Gauchos regularly have to "throw a steer" to check for ticks and fleas.

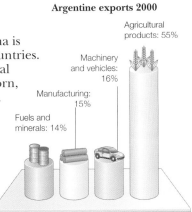

To throw a steer, one man holds the animal by the horns, while another two men hold on to the tail.

The gaucho wears a hat with a broad brim to protect him from the hot sun.

A cotton or wool cape called a poncho provides warmth at night.

The gaucho's broad leather belt has a silver buckle and is decorated with silver coins.

Bombachas, or baggy pants, are worn tucked into boots.

Boleadoras were whirled around and flung at the legs of a running animal to trip it up. Today, a gaucho would use a lasso.

The round stones of a boleadora are covered with horsehide.

Horse bridle of plaited raw horsehide

Boots are made of tough leather to withstand wear and tear in the stirrups.

Find out more

DEBT: *280*
EDUCATION: *277*
POLITICAL SYSTEMS: *270–271*
VEGETATION ZONES: *15*

THE ATLANTIC OCEAN

ICELAND	
Capital city: Reykjavik	
Area: 39,770 sq miles (100,250 sq km)	
Population: 281,000	
Official language: Icelandic	
Major religions: Christian 96%, other 4%	
Government: Multiparty democracy	
Currency: Icelandic krónur	
Adult literacy rate: 99%	
Life expectancy: 79 years	
People per doctor: 307	
Televisions: 320 per 1,000 people	

CAPE VERDE	
Capital city: Cidade de Praia	
Area: 1,556 sq miles (4,030 sq km)	
Population: 428,000	
Official language: Portuguese	
Major religions: Christian 98%, other 2%	
Government: Multiparty democracy	
Currency: Cape Verde escudo	
Adult literacy rate: 74%	
Life expectancy: 69 years	
People per doctor: 3,448	
Televisions: 4 per 1,000 people	

Key to currents

 Warm currents

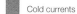 Cold currents

BORDERED BY THE AMERICAS to the west and Africa and Europe to the east, the Atlantic covers about 31.7 million sq miles (82 million sq km), one-fifth of the Earth's surface. Down the ocean's entire length runs the Mid-Atlantic Ridge, a great underwater mountain chain formed by lava that oozes up from the seabed, cools, and then hardens. Some peaks break the surface to form volcanic islands. The Atlantic contains some of the world's richest fishing grounds, but is also the most polluted ocean because of the industry around its shores.

ICELAND

The volcanic island of Iceland is part of the Mid-Atlantic Ridge. Intense heat generated deep underground creates bubbling hot springs and mud pools. Iceland has the most *solfataras* (volcanic vents) and hot springs in the world, and many of its towns are heated by underground hot water. Cape Verde, off the west coast of Africa, is also volcanic.

OCEAN CURRENTS

Water in the oceans is never still but moves in huge belts of water called currents. In the open ocean, surface winds drive these currents in vast, roughly circular patterns. The currents can be as warm as 86°F (30°C) or as cold as 30°F (-2°C), and affect the world's weather. Warm water from the Equator moves toward the cooler poles, helping spread warmth across the globe.

FISHING
About 90 percent of the world's fish live in the shallow waters of the continental shelves that surround land, feeding on the plankton that live there. Over the past 20 years, stocks of cod, herring, and other fish in the Atlantic have run low as the number and size of fishing fleets have grown.

ICEBERGS

Icebergs, which are made of frozen water, occur when warmer weather causes ice sheets and glaciers on icy coastlines to break up, or calve. At sea, icebergs are moved by the wind and ocean currents and can be a danger to ships. Icebergs vary in size from small Arctic growlers, which are about as big as a grand piano, to much larger Antarctic icebergs, which can be 5 miles (8 km) long.

Only about one-seventh of an iceberg shows above the surface of the ocean. The rest of the ice remains hidden below the waterline.

GULF STREAM
The Gulf Stream is a warm current only about 60 miles (100 km) wide that moves across the North Atlantic. It raises the temperature of northern Europe and helps keep its ports ice-free in winter. It also allows tropical plants to grow in normally cool places, such as the west coast of Scotland.

A B C D E F G H I J K L

1 2 3 4 5 6 7 8 9 10 11 12 13

Rio de Janeiro, Brazil
Jan 78°F (26°C)
July 69°F (20°C)
Jan 4.9 in (125 mm)
July 1.6 in (41 mm)

Reykjavik, Iceland
Jan 32°F (0°C)
July 52°F (11°C)
Jan 3.5 in (89 mm)
July 2 in (50 mm)

ICELAND

Praia, Cape Verde
Jan 72°F (22°C)
July 79°F (26°C)
Jan 0.1 in (3 mm)
July 0.2 in (5 mm)

CAPE VERDE

0 500 1000 1500 km
0 250 500 750 1000 miles

ARCTIC OCEAN

Greenland (Denmark)

GREENLAND SEA

Baffin Bay

Davis Strait

Hudson Bay

ICELAND

REYKJAVIK

Faeroe Is. (Denmark)

Murmansk

Bergen

NORTH SEA

BALTIC SEA

Rockall (UK)

British Isles

EUROPE

Rotterdam

C. Farewell

LABRADOR SEA

NORTH AMERICA

Newfoundland

St. John's

North Eastern Atlantic Basin

Marseille

Naples

BLACK SEA

St. Lawrence

Halifax

Bay of Fundy

Grand Banks

Newfoundland Basin

Azores (Portugal)

A Coruña

Porto

Gibraltar

Casablanca

ALGIERS

MEDITERRANEAN SEA

New York City

Baltimore

Mid-Atlantic Ridge

Madeira (Portugal)

Port Said

Mississippi

Bermuda (UK)

North American Basin

Nile

New Orleans

SARGASSO SEA

Canary Is. (Spain)

Canary Basin

AFRICA

Gulf of Mexico

Puerto Rico Trench

CENTRAL AMERICA

CARIBBEAN SEA

ATLANTIC

CAPE VERDE

PRAIA

C. Verde

Niger

PANAMA CITY

Lagos

Gulf of Guinea

São Tomé

Príncipe

LIBREVILLE

Georgetown

Cayenne

Guyana Basin

Amazon

Fortaleza

Fernando de Noronho I. (Brazil)

Ascension I. (UK)

Congo

Angola Basin

OCEAN

SOUTH AMERICA

Recife

Salvador

St. Helena (UK)

Brazil Basin

Rio de Janeiro

Trindade (Brazil)

Mid-Atlantic Ridge

Argentine Basin

Walvis Ridge

Cape Basin

CAPE TOWN

Cape of Good Hope

BUENOS AIRES

Tristan Da Cunha (UK)

Gough I. (UK)

Atlantic-Indian Ridge

Falkland Is. (UK)

C. Horn

SCOTIA SEA

South Georgia (UK)

South Sandwich Is. (UK)

Bouvet I. (Norway)

Atlantic-Indian-Antarctic Basin

South Shetland Is. (UK)

South Orkney Is. (UK)

WEDDELL SEA

ANTARCTICA

THINGS TO LOOK FOR ON THE MAP

World's largest island:
Greenland, 839,780 sq miles
(2,175,600 sq km) *Map F2*

Deepest Atlantic trench:
Puerto Rico Trench,
28,372 ft (8,648 m) *Map D6*

World's most remote island:
Bouvet Island, Norway,
1,056 miles (1,700 km) from
nearest land *Map I12*

TURTLE TURNAROUND
Green turtles live off the coast of
Brazil, but make their way across the
South Atlantic to Ascension Island to
lay their eggs. Once the young turtles
have hatched, they return to Brazil – a
round trip of 1,740 miles (2,800 km).

WHALE MIGRATION
Humpback whales
can be found in all
the world's seas. Many
spend a large part of the year
feeding on krill and fish in the cold
waters off the coasts of Canada, Greenland,
and Iceland. When it is time to breed,
however, they make their way south to the
tropical waters of the Caribbean Sea.

*An average humpback
whale needs about a
ton of food per day.*

Find out more
FISHING: *29, 203*
GEYSERS & MUD SPRINGS: *255*
MID-OCEAN RIDGES: *13*
OCEAN CURRENTS: *64*

EUROPE

A GREAT CURVE OF mountain ranges that includes the Pyrenees and the Alps roughly divides the cooler north of Europe from the warmer south. In the far north, treeless tundra merges into cool coniferous forests that extend across Scandinavia and into Russia. South of this lies the fertile North European Plain, which supports most of the continent's agriculture and mixed woodland. By contrast, the Mediterranean region to the south is hot and almost desertlike in places. Volcanic activity is confined to Iceland and southern Italy, where Mount Etna is constantly active. The Ural and Caucasus mountains form Europe's eastern borders.

Bird's Eye primrose

THE ALPS
The mountains that form the Alps run from southeastern France, through Switzerland and Italy, into Austria. In the last 2 million years, ice has moulded the scenery, carving pyramid-shaped peaks, like the Matterhorn, knife-edged ridges, dramatic waterfalls, and armchair-shaped basins filled with lakes. Alpine plants, such as the Bird's Eye primrose, have adapted to growing at high altitudes.

Highest temperature:
Seville, Spain, 122°F (50°C)

This is a river valley before the arrival of a glacier. Glaciers are huge masses of ice that grind away land as they move slowly forwards.

THE LAKE DISTRICT

The 15 lakes of the Lake District in northwestern England lie in U-shaped valleys extending outward like the spokes of a wheel from an uplifted dome of low mountains. Long ago, the valleys contained rivers, but during the Ice Age these were deepened by the movement of glaciers. Most were dammed by eroded rock left behind when the glaciers melted. The erosion of the main valleys has cut off tributary valleys and left them "hanging" above the main valleys, often with waterfalls cascading from them.

When glaciers retreat, at the end of an Ice Age for example, they leave behind U-shaped valleys.

A hanging valley on the side of the main valley

Ullswater is a lake that lies in a U-shaped valley.

NORTHERN FORESTS
A thick band of dense coniferous forest, known as taiga, covers northern Europe. Conifers (trees that have cones), such as spruce and pine, keep their leaves all year round and can withstand heavy snow. They also provide winter food and shelter for many animals.

NORTHERN PLAINS

The North European Plain stretches from southern England across France and Germany as far as Russia, ending at the Ural Mountains. Most of the Plain is low-lying, and in the Netherlands it even lies partly below sea level. Some of the world's most fertile farmland is found here, as well as important deposits of coal, oil, and natural gas. This is Europe's most densely populated area and contains many major cities.

Wheat, sugar beets, and apples are grown on the plains of northern France.

*KARA
SEA*

N

Novaya Zemlya

Kara Strait   Vaygach I.

Ust'Shchugor

URAL MOUNTAINS

Lowest temperature: Ust'Shchugor, Russian Federation, -67°F (-55°C)

Kama Res.

Ural

Foxes are often found in the fields and woodlands of Europe, although many now live in towns. They eat almost anything – from rabbits to apples or worms.

THINGS TO LOOK FOR ON THE MAP

Area: 4,000,000, sq miles (10,400,000 sq km)

Highest point: Mt. El'brus, Russian Federation, 18,510 ft (5,642 m) *Map K11*

Longest river: Volga, Russian Federation, 2,194 miles (3,530 km) *Map L8*

Largest lake: L. Ladoga, Russian Federation, 7,100 sq miles (18,389 sq km) *Map J7*

Largest island: Great Britain, 88,745 sq miles (229,850 sq km) *Map D9*

THE MEDITERRANEAN
The region around the Mediterranean Sea has a distinctive climate of hot, dry summers and mild, rainy winters. These conditions are perfect for growing crops such as citrus fruits, grapes, and olives, shown here in southern Spain. Many trees, such as cork oaks, develop thick bark as a protection against the heat.

THE DANUBE
The Danube, western Europe's longest river, flows eastward from its source in Germany to its mouth on the Black Sea. It serves as a trade route between the nine countries that lie along its course. The Danube delta, where the river divides into numerous channels, is an important wetland area. About 300 different bird species have been recorded in the delta, as well as boars, deer, and wild cats.

N   O   P

PEOPLES OF EUROPE

EUROPE IS A CROWDED CONTINENT. It is the second smallest of the continents by area, yet it has the third highest population. As a result, population densities are very high, and most Europeans live in cities. Europe is also crowded with countries – more than 40 different nations jostle for position on the continent. Conflicts between these countries have often erupted into war – two world wars have started on European soils in the last 100 years. Yet, despite these problems, Europe is by and large a rich continent, and many European countries are among the wealthiest in the world. Some pockets of poverty exist, but in general the population enjoys a high standard of living compared to most other parts of the world. Much of this wealth has come as a result of industrial growth, and because of the large colonial empires established by many European countries in Africa, Asia, and the Americas.

EUROPEAN CITIES
A large proportion of Europeans live in cities. The most densely populated part of Europe lies in the west and forms a belt that stretches more or less continuously from southeastern Britain, through northern France, Belgium, the Netherlands, and into Germany. In these densely populated areas, individual cities can merge into one another, forming what are known as conurbations. The largest of these is in the German industrial region known as the Ruhr. By contrast, in eastern Europe a greater proportion of the population lives in country areas.

Population: approximately 704,900,000 people

Number of countries: 43

Largest country: The Russian Federation straddles northern Europe and Asia (*see p. 138*) and its European part covers 1,527,349 sq miles (3,955,818 sq km)

Least densely populated country: Iceland, 7 people per sq mile (3 per sq km)

KEY
1 NETHERLANDS
2 BELGIUM
3 LUXEMBOURG
4 SWITZERLAND
5 LIECHTENSTEIN
6 MOLDOVA
7 ANDORRA
8 MONACO
9 SAN MARINO
10 VATICAN CITY
11 SLOVENIA
12 CROATIA
13 BOSNIA AND HERZEGOVINA
14 YUGOSLAVIA
15 ALBANIA
16 MACEDONIA

Most densely populated country: Monaco, 42,095 people per sq mile (16,253 per sq km)

Smallest country: Vatican City, 0.17 sq miles (0.44 sq km)

Netherlands: 1,206 (466)

Germany: 609 (235)

Poland: 230 (127)

USA: 79 (30)

World: 106 (41)

Population density chart

The figures on the chart show the number of people per sq mile (per sq km). Comparisons outside Europe are also included.

POPULATION DENSITY

Over 704 million Europeans are crammed into an area little more than the size of Australia. As a result, European countries have some of the highest population densities in the world. In the Netherlands, for example, there are 1,206 people per sq mile (466 per sq km). Population densities in eastern Europe are lower, but even these are above the world average.

Economically, Europe can be divided into two main sets of countries. Western Europe contains some very rich countries, such as Germany, Switzerland, and France, which have strong economies. By contrast, eastern Europe contains former communist countries such as Poland, Hungary, and Romania, which are much poorer. They are still struggling to adjust their economies in order to compete in world markets.

A market in the Russian Federation. Under communism all commerce was controlled by the State

THE CHANGING POPULATION

Compared to Asia and Africa, the populations of most European countries are stable – they are not increasing or decreasing to any great extent. Birth rates are low, and average life expectancy is very high – about 75 years in most countries, compared to less than 50 years in Afghanistan and most of Africa. As a result of these two factors, Europe's population is relatively elderly, with a large number of people aged over 65 years.

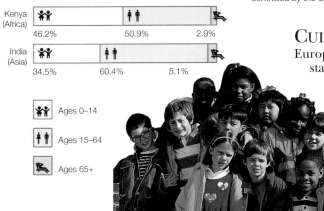

Age of population

Germany (Europe): 16.9% / 67.7% / 15.4%
Kenya (Africa): 46.2% / 50.9% / 2.9%
India (Asia): 34.5% / 60.4% / 5.1%

Ages 0–14
Ages 15–64
Ages 65+

CULTURAL MELTING POT

Europe's wealth and relative political stability have attracted large numbers of migrants to its shores, many from former colonies. As a result, most countries, particularly in western Europe, contain large numbers of people from ethnic minorities. In France, for example, north Africans from Algeria and other former colonies have settled in cities such as Marseilles and Paris.

The UK's population contains migrants from many countries, including the Caribbean, India, Pakistan, and Bangladesh.

New European countries

Former Czechoslovakia split apart peacefully in 1993, when the Czech Republic and Slovakia voted to separate.

Former Yugoslavia was shattered by war in the 1990s, as various regions declared themselves independent countries.

CZECH REPUBLIC
SLOVAKIA
CZECHOSLOVAKIA
SLOVENIA
CROATIA
BOSNIA AND HERZEGOVINA
YUGOSLAVIA
YUGOSLAVIA
MACEDONIA

The European Parliament, elected by the people of the EU, meets in this building in Strasbourg, France.

New European countries have also been formed from the former USSR – see page 136.

THE EUROPEAN UNION

In 1957, five European countries agreed to form the European Economic Community (EEC). They believed that economic cooperation would reduce the likelihood of war between the member countries and would bring prosperity to the peoples of Europe. Since that time, more countries have joined, and the EEC has been renamed the European Union (EU). Today it consists of 15 member states and in addition to closer economic cooperation, there are moves to encourage greater political union.

The stars on the flag of the European Union represent the member countries.

SPLITTING APART

Europe is a fragmented continent made up of more than 40 independent countries. Even within individual countries there are sometimes separate groups, such as the Basques in Spain, who claim some form of independence from the national government. New countries are still being formed. The former USSR, Yugoslavia, and Czechoslovakia are among the European countries that have split apart in recent years, sometimes violently.

SCANDINAVIA AND FINLAND

THE NORTHERN EUROPEAN countries of Norway, Sweden, and Denmark are together known as Scandinavia. Along with neighboring Finland, all four countries have small populations and enjoy a high standard of living with extensive social welfare systems that distribute wealth evenly among the people. Much of Norway, Sweden, and Finland is covered by forests of pine, spruce, and birch trees, riddled with lakes gouged out by glaciers during the last Ice Age. Norway and Sweden are mountainous, while Finland and fertile Denmark are low-lying.

Copenhagen, Denmark
- Jan 32°F (0°C)
- July 64°F (18°C)
- Jan 1.9 in (49 mm)
- July 2.8 in (71 mm)

NORWAY

Inari, Finland
- Jan 8°F (-13°C)
- July 56°F (13°C)
- Jan 0.9 in (22 mm)
- July 2.1 in (53 mm)

SWEDEN

FINLAND

DENMARK

THINGS TO LOOK FOR ON THE MAP

Longest river: Kemijoki, Finland, 340 miles (547 km) *Map J5*

Highest point: Mt. Galdhopiggen, Norway, 8,101 ft (2,469 m) *Map E7*

Largest lake: L. Vänern, Sweden, 2,154 sq miles (5,580 sq km) *Map G9*

THE MIDNIGHT SUN
Much of northern Norway, Sweden, and Finland lie in the Arctic Circle. Here the sun never sets at the height of summer – giving 24 hours of light – and never rises in the middle of winter – giving 24 hours of darkness. The periods of light or dark lengthen the farther north you go. In the far north the winter darkness lasts for almost two months.

Midnight sun in Senja, Norway

COASTLINE CITIES
Most people in the region live in towns and cities around the coast or on lakesides. These stretches of water provide the best form of transportation in an area where fast-flowing rivers are unsuitable and where much of the interior is rugged. The capitals of all four countries are on the coast, including Stockholm, the Swedish capital, which lies on the edge of the Baltic Sea.

NORWAY

NORWAY LIES ALONG the western coast of Scandinavia. It is a long country, narrow in its northern half and only 50 miles (80 km) wide at one point. Despite its northerly location, Norway's lengthy coastline is kept free of ice by the warm Gulf Stream. Most of the country is mountainous, with spectacular landscapes of thousands of lakes and offshore islands. Many people work in industry, including offshore oil and gas production, shipbuilding, and mining. Fishing, forestry, and agriculture employ only about five percent of the total workforce.

NORWAY
Capital city: Oslo
Area: 118,830 sq miles (306,830 sq km)
Population: 4,233,116
Official language: Norwegian
Major religions: Christian 90%, other 10%
Government: Multiparty democracy
Currency: Norwegian krone
Adult literacy rate: 99%
Life expectancy: 78 years
People per doctor: 303
Televisions: 579 per 1,000 people

OIL INDUSTRY

The discovery of oil and gas under the North Sea in 1969 transformed the Norwegian economy, turning the country into Europe's largest oil producer. Thousands of people work in the industry, constructing tankers and oil rigs and refining the crude oil. Today Norway is self-sufficient in energy, and exports most of its oil and natural gas to the rest of Europe.

Low-lying meadows are suitable for livestock.

Deep water allows cruise and other ships to sail far inland.

Rough upland grazing for herds of sheep and goats

Once-thriving coastal fishing communities are declining as fish stocks diminish, but fish farming is increasing.

South facing slopes are warm enough to support crops of soft fruit in the summer months.

FJORDS

Only 3 percent of Norway is suitable for farming because most of the country consists of rugged mountain ranges and deep lakes. Most farmland is situated at the head of fjords, the long inlets of sea that cut into Norway's coast. Fjords were created by glaciers gouging out valleys as they descended to the sea. The fjords are natural harbors, sheltering small communities of fishermen and farmers. Tourists visit the spectacular scenery in cruise ships.

Traditional stave church in Sogne Fjord

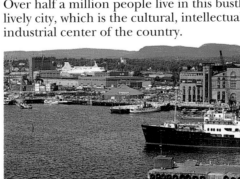

SHIPPING

Norway has one of the largest shipping fleets in the world. Many thousands of people are employed in shipyards and repair docks and on board the many merchant ships and ferries that supply the ports and islands of the west coast. The most important port is the capital city, Oslo. Over half a million people live in this bustling, lively city, which is the cultural, intellectual, and industrial center of the country.

WOODEN CHURCHES
Ancient stave churches are found throughout Norway. Unlike log cabins, which are made of horizontal logs, stave churches are built with vertical, curved strips of wood called staves. Not a single nail is used in the construction, which is powerful enough to withstand heavy winter snowfalls.

SKIING
Norway is the home of skiing. The earliest remains of skis were found in a glacier here, and the word "ski" is of Norwegian origin. During the snowy winter months, the most efficient way for many Norwegians to travel is on skis. A ski jump is a feature of most towns in Norway. Annual ski festivals are popular, as is the sport of cross-country skiing.

Find out more
GAS: *163, 198, 211*
GLACIERS: *79*
GULF STREAM: *76*
OIL: *152, 281*

DENMARK

THE LONG, NARROW Jutland Peninsula that makes up mainland Denmark extends from Germany toward Norway and Sweden. To the east of the peninsula more than a hundred islands make up the rest of the country. Denmark is the most southerly country in Scandinavia and is one of the flattest lands in the world. Like its neighbors, it enjoys political stability and a high standard of living. Industry has developed rapidly, and today a third of the people work in small factories.

DENMARK	
Capital city: Copenhagen	
Area: 16,629 sq miles (43,070 sq km)	
Population: 5,300,000	
Official language: Danish	
Major religions: Christian 90%, other 10%	
Government: Multiparty democracy	
Currency: Danish kroner	
Adult literacy rate: 99%	
Life expectancy: 76 years	
People per doctor: 345	
Televisions: 585 per 1,000 people	

COPENHAGEN

Denmark's capital, Copenhagen, is situated on the island of Sjælland. It is the biggest city in Scandinavia and the largest trading center in Denmark. Visitors wandering down old alleyways and pedestrianized streets will find historic churches, colorful marketplaces, and a network of canals. This is also a city of bicycles, with bike paths leading toward areas where many city-dwellers have summer homes.

ARCHITECTURE

Like the rest of the region, Denmark is famous for its architecture. Danish architects combine local materials such as cement, brick, and timber to create beautiful buildings that harmonize with the environment. Many housing developments have been built in which each house runs on a system of solar panels and insulation designed to keep energy waste to a minimum. Design is highly regarded in Denmark, especially for furniture, glassware, kitchenware, and porcelain.

Solar panels use the Sun's rays to heat the water.

The ventilation system ensures that fresh air is taken in and stale air is drawn out.

Sun rooms made almost entirely from glass attract the warmth of the Sun's rays.

Air trapped between the inner and outer walls of the house acts as insulation and keeps out the cold.

PIG AND DAIRY FARMING
Denmark is well known for its cooperative organizations. To keep up with modern agricultural development, the farmers have had to work together closely. Part of their strategy has been to establish cooperatively owned dairies and bacon factories and to concentrate their energies on promoting these foods abroad.

LEGOLAND
"Legos" – the colorful interlocking building blocks designed for children – were first produced by a carpenter in Jutland in the 1930s. Now Jutland is home to a massive Legoland theme park, where all the buildings are made of Legos. The name "Lego" comes from the two Danish words, *leg* and *godt*, meaning "play well."

FAMILY LIFE

Throughout much of the Western world (Europe and North America) many people are adopting more flexible attitudes to family life. This is particularly so in Denmark and the rest of Scandinavia. A high proportion of children in Denmark are brought up by one parent or by unmarried parents, who have the same legal rights as married couples. Men also play a large role in home life and child care, and the number of working women has soared.

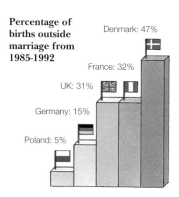

Percentage of births outside marriage from 1985-1992

Denmark: 47%
France: 32%
UK: 31%
Germany: 15%
Poland: 5%

Find out more
CYCLING: *92, 192*
EUROPEAN FAMILIES: *81*
INSULATED HOUSES: *143*
WORKING WOMEN: *137, 141*

SWEDEN

LYING BETWEEN NORWAY and Finland, Sweden stretches from the Arctic north to the fertile south, where most of its small population lives. Sweden's long industrial traditions and a highly skilled workforce have made it one of the world's most advanced manufacturing countries. Like its neighbors, Sweden is a prosperous place, where equal rights for all groups in society are taken very seriously.

SWEDEN	
Capital city: Stockholm	
Area: 173,730 sq miles (449,960 sq km)	
Population: 8,585,907	
Official language: Swedish	
Major religions: Christian 97%, other 3%	
Government: Multiparty democracy	
Currency: Swedish krona	
Adult literacy rate: 99%	
Life expectancy: 78 years	
People per doctor: 370	
Televisions: 470 per 1,000 people	

Recycling system

Customers return their empty aluminum cans to shops with machines that flatten the cans, allowing many more to be collected.

The flattened cans are taken away, melted down, and rolled into new sheets of aluminum.

Soon, brand new cans made from the sheets are rolling off the production line, ready to start the cycle all over again.

CONSERVATION

Swedes are very concerned about conserving their environment. This includes their historic buildings as well as the countryside. There are many nature reserves in Sweden and some of Europe's largest national parks in the mountainous north. Many people are worried about water pollution and Sweden is a leading campaigner in the movement to clean up the Baltic Sea. It has also restricted industrial development in some coastal areas. Conserving resources is part of everyday life and Sweden runs a highly successful recycling system (right).

SOCIAL WELFARE

Sweden has led the way in social welfare, and a small population has made it easy for the government to take care of everyone. Child care and facilities for the sick and the elderly are excellent. Unemployment figures have been relatively low (see chart below). However, to pay for these benefits the government must impose high taxes. Also, current economic problems have put some of the benefits under threat.

Germany: 12%
France 10%
Sweden: 6%
UK: 6%
Netherlands: 3%

Percentages of unemployed people

Lettuce
Prawn
Scrambled egg
Caviar (fish eggs)
Asparagus
Smoked salmon

DESIGN

Sweden is renowned for the simple lines of its design, which is copied all over the world. Swedish designers began to make an impact in the 1960s. Good design has helped sell cars, electrical equipment, textiles and furniture.

This Swedish office chair is designed to be comfortable and practical.

SMORGASBORD

Smörgas means a slice of bread and *bord* is the Swedish word for table, but this Scandinavian speciality is much more than a table of sandwiches. It usually refers to a vast buffet of tempting cold foods, such as herrings in mustard sauce, various cheeses, meats, and salads.

SUMMER HOMES

Vacation homes are common in this wealthy country. Pretty wooden houses, often painted red, are found along the coast, lakeshores, and in river valleys. They provide the perfect escape for city-dwellers on weekends or during the holidays. When they are not there themselves, families often rent these retreats out to friends or to the growing number of tourists to Sweden.

Find out more	
HEALTH, EDUCATION:	*276–277*
RECYCLING:	*94*
RICH AND POOR:	*278–279*
STOCKHOLM:	*82*

FINLAND

FINLAND

Capital city: Helsinki

Area: 117,610 sq miles
(304,610 sq km)

Population: 4,998,478

Official languages:
Finnish, Swedish

Major religions: Christian
91%, other 9%

Government: Multiparty
democracy

Currency: Euro

Adult literacy rate: 99%

Life expectancy: 77 years

People per doctor: 370

Televisions: 640 per 1,000
people

KNOWN AS "SUOMI" to its people, Finland is the most northerly independent country in the world. An aerial view of this land would show a spectacular pattern of forests, swampy peatland, massive lakes, and islands – scattered in the lakes and along the coastline. Most of it is covered with pine, spruce, and birch trees, and for up to half of the year it is carpeted with snow. After centuries of Swedish rule, Finland became part of Russia before independence in 1917. Finland has a distinctive language and culture that marks it apart from the rest of Scandinavia.

LOGGING INDUSTRY

Timber is a major industry in this forested country – Finland and Sweden are Europe's top producers of the softwoods pine and spruce. The timber is transported by truck to processing plants where the wood is boiled down to a pulp. The liquid produced, wood alcohol, is used in various chemicals, while the pulp is made into plywood, board, and paper. Sawdust, bark, and waste are burned to produce electricity.

What the land is used for

Forest: 76%

Other: 15%

Crops: 8%

Grassland: 1%

LAPLAND

The icy north of Norway, Sweden, and Finland is called Lapland. The people who live in the scattered villages of this region, the *Samer*, or Lapps, have their own language and customs. Some herd reindeer for their meat and milk. However, their traditional way of life is slowly changing. Lapland is also known as the home of Santa Claus, and thousands of children send letters to him there each year.

HELSINKI

Surrounded on three sides by water, Finland's capital, Helsinki, has an open, spacious feel. Its magnificent harbor boasts a colorful street market selling fish, fruit, vegetables, and flowers. The city is filled with exciting modern buildings that are designed to blend with the old, creating a distinctive national style.

SAUNAS

Finland is the home of the sauna. The Finns have used these steam baths for centuries, and today most houses in Finland have one. A sauna is a small, very warm room that people sit in to relax and cleanse their bodies. From time to time they throw water over hot stones and, as the water crackles and spits, the air fills with clouds of steam. Most families enjoy a shared sauna every week.

People beat themselves with birch twigs to stimulate their blood circulation and so refresh their bodies.

LAND OF LAKES

Well over 50,000 lakes take up about 10 percent of the country's area and are a major tourist attraction. Lake Saimaa is the largest lake and contains hundreds of islands. Ferries provide a vital link between the coastal islands. During the long, cold winters, lakes may freeze up and icebreakers keep coastal waters open for merchant shipping.

After a session in the sauna, it is time to cool off under a cold shower – or in the nearby lake!

Saunas are fueled by wooden logs in the country, and by electricity in towns and cities.

Find out more

ARCTIC PEOPLES: 25, 266
LOGGING: 26, 69, 244
NORTHERN FORESTS:
15, 132

THE BRITISH ISLES

TUCKED AWAY IN THE NORTHWESTERN corner of Europe, the British Isles consists of the United Kingdom (UK) and Ireland. The UK includes Scotland, England, Wales, and Northern Ireland. The rest of Ireland is an independent country. Once, the whole of Ireland was dominated by England, a Protestant nation. This caused resentment among the Catholic Irish and in 1922, the south broke away. Despite differences between the two countries – Ireland is mainly rural, while the UK is heavily urbanized – both share a strong sense of identity that comes from being island nations.

UNITED KINGDOM

Oban, UK
Jan 39°F (4°C)
July 57°F (14°C)
Jan 5.8 in (146 mm)
July 4.7 in (120 mm)

THINGS TO LOOK FOR ON THE MAP

Longest river: Shannon, Ireland, 240 miles (386 km) *Map F8*

Highest point: Ben Nevis, UK, 4,406 ft (1,343 m) *Map H5*

Largest lake: Lough Neagh, UK, 153 sq miles (396 sq km) *Map G7*

Deepest reservoir in Europe: Loch Morar, UK, 1,017 ft (310 m) *Map H4*

Cork, Ireland
Jan 42°F (6°C)
July 61°F (16°C)
Jan 4.7 in (119 mm)
July 2.8 in (70 mm)

IRELAND

London, UK
Jan 4°C (39°F)
July 18°C (64°F)
Jan 54 mm (2.1 in)
July 57 mm (2.2 in)

N

0   50   100   150 km
0   25   50   75   100 miles

THE EMERALD ISLE
Ireland gets its nickname, "The Emerald Isle," from the lush green grass that thrives in the island's mild and wet climate. This pasture makes excellent grazing land for cattle, and so dairy produce and beef are major products in a land where agriculture has always been the main industry. The beauty of the landscape, particularly its dramatic west coast, has also made Ireland a major tourist destination.

North Yorkshire coastline, England

LANDSCAPE
The landscape of the British Isles varies greatly within a small area. High, craggy mountains in northern England, Scotland, Wales, and Ireland contrast with the flat Fens (marshlands) of East Anglia, and the rolling green fields of southern England. Three-quarters of the land is used for farming, and the crops grown vary from region to region, depending on the climate and soil.

UNITED KINGDOM

FOR A SMALL COUNTRY, the United Kingdom (UK) has had a huge influence on world affairs. At one time it controlled a vast empire, which is why English is now spoken across the globe. The Industrial Revolution of the late 1700s, which brought large-scale factory production, began here, then spread worldwide. Today, many of the UK's traditional industries have declined. This highly urban society is now more reliant on service industries, such as banking and insurance, while huge reserves of oil in the North Sea meet much of its energy needs.

UNITED KINGDOM	
Capital city: London	
Area: 93,282 sq miles (241,600 sq km)	
Population: 58,800,000	
Official language: English	
Major religions: Christian 61%, Muslim 3%, other 36%	
Government: Multiparty democracy	
Currency: Pound sterling	
Adult literacy rate: 99%	
Life expectancy: 78 years	
People per doctor: 667	
Televisions: 645 per 1,000 people	

Red London buses rush past the Houses of Parliament, home of the United Kingdom's government.

Visitors to top 7 tourist sites charging admission

Alton Towers, Staffordshire: 2,650,000

Madame Tussaud's, London: 2,640,000

Tower of London: 2,422,181

Natural History Museum, London: 1,739,591

Science Museum, London: 1,480,000

Chessington World of Adventures: 1,550,000

Legoland, Windsor: 1,620,000

LONDON

Founded by the Romans in AD 43, London is now a city of 7 million people and is one of the largest cities in Europe. The capital is one of the world's leading centers of culture, finance, and tourism. Each year millions of people visit London to sample its theaters, museums, and historic buildings. Tourism is now a major industry throughout the whole of the UK. Places such as the west coast of Scotland and the ancient cities of Bath, York, and Stratford-upon-Avon attract thousands of tourists.

A MULTICULTURAL SOCIETY

Since the 1950s, the UK has become an increasingly multicultural society. Large numbers of people from the UK's former colonies in Africa, the West Indies, and the Indian Subcontinent have made their home here, establishing their own distinctive communities and enriching British life with their culture and traditions.

EDINBURGH
The beautiful city of Edinburgh lies on the chilly east coast of Scotland. Perched on a hill, Edinburgh Castle looks out over a city of winding medieval streets and splendid Georgian townhouses. The city is home to a major international arts festival held every summer.

Street performers at the Edinburgh Festival

HOMES

Many people in the UK live in suburbs on the outskirts of towns and cities. Suburbs offer a cleaner environment, more space, and transportation links, making commuting to jobs in city centers possible. British life is closely centered on the home. Houses tend to be more popular than apartments, and home improvement work and gardening are popular leisure activities.

Typical styles of housing in the UK

1960s apartment building, with communal garden at the front.

Semi-detached house, 1930s

Victorian terraced house, 1880s

Detached house, 1980s

Where people live

89% live in the city.   11% in the country.

WELSH MINING

Wales was until recently a major supplier of coal, and many towns and villages depended on the mines for their existence. But the coal industry has now been dismantled and large amounts of coal are imported, so that mines all over the UK have closed down. Wales especially has been badly hit, and there is high unemployment in many areas. Some towns, however, have succeeded in attracting new industries and the beautiful mountainous scenery brings increasing numbers of tourists.

SPORTS

Sports are close to the hearts of many British people. Soccer and rugby are generally played in the winter, and cricket and golf are popular in the summer months. Rugby, cricket, and golf – now played all over the world – originated in the UK, and the rules of soccer developed from games played in English boys' schools.

Hat made from Welsh wool

Scottish tartan scarf

Vest made from Irish linen

NATIONAL IDENTITY

The UK's government is based at Westminster in London, England, but a separate Scottish Parliament and Welsh Assembly – both with certain "devolved" powers – were approved by referendum and elected in May 1999. Strong national identities are also deeply-rooted through cultural and historic ties as well as by traditional arts, crafts and customs.

INDUSTRY

Heavy industry once supplied many jobs in the UK, but this pattern has changed. Now light engineering products, machinery, cars, and weapons are the major exports, and large numbers of people are employed in financial and service industries. These have helped an economy that was flagging, partly because the UK has to import so much of its food and raw materials. Many powerful multinational companies, with offices throughout the world, are also based here.

Banking and financial services in particular have helped boost the UK economy.

FINANCE

Each day more currency changes hands in London than in any other city in the world. The City of London, or the "square mile" as it is also known, contains more than 500 banks, attracted to the capital because of its leading role in world finance. This situation partly stems from the former importance of the British Empire, but today it has more to do with the city's location – midway between Tokyo and New York, the other main world financial centers – and the expertise in banking and financial services built up over many years.

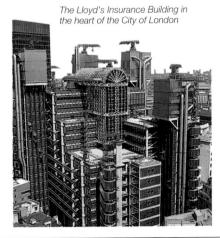

The Lloyd's Insurance Building in the heart of the City of London

NORTHERN IRELAND

Since the 1960s Northern Ireland and its capital, Belfast (above), have suffered violent conflict. The large Protestant community, descended from British settlers, wants to stay within the UK, while Irish Catholics, who have been discriminated against in jobs and housing, wish to join southern Ireland. Both sides have kept up terrorist campaigns, and the Catholic Irish Republican Army has also bombed the British mainland. The Irish and British governments are now trying to organize talks between all parties, but a solution is proving difficult to find.

Find out more

COAL MINING: *96, 114, 162*
ETHNIC MIX: *81*
EUROPEAN CITIES: *80*
SERVICE INDUSTRIES: *281*

IRELAND

IRELAND

THE GREEN PASTURES of Ireland are kept fertile by the country's mild, wet climate. Ireland was once ruled by Britain. In 1922, southern Ireland – which makes up about two-thirds of the island – became an independent republic, while Northern Ireland remained part of the United Kingdom. Natural resources are few and traditionally much of the population was employed in agriculture. However, a dramatic growth in tourism and light industry has radically altered people's lives and has turned Ireland into one of Europe's recent economic success stories.

IRELAND	
Capital city: Dublin	
Area: 26,598 sq miles (68,890 sq km)	
Population: 3,700,000	
Official languages: Irish, English	
Major religions: Christian 92%, other 8%	
Government: Multiparty democracy	
Currency: Euro	
Adult literacy rate: 99%	
Life expectancy: 76 years	
People per doctor: 500	
Televisions: 403 per 1,000 people	

RELIGIOUS LIFE

The Irish are a devout people and the Catholic Church plays an important role in daily life. Religious processions are held regularly, and shrines, many dedicated to the Virgin Mary (Jesus' mother), are dotted around the country. In addition to running schools and hospitals, the Church has an influence on the social life of the country and opposes abortion and birth control. Divorce was illegal in Ireland until 1997.

IRISH PUBS

Much social life in Ireland centers around the pub, or bar, where people meet to drink, chat, and exchange news. Stories from Irish history are told through songs, and bars are often alive with the sound of folk music. Irish stout – a strong, dark beer with a creamy, pale head – is the favorite drink. One of the largest breweries in Europe is found in Dublin, opened by the Guinness family 200 years ago.

Bustling O'Connell Street is Dublin's major roadway.

DUBLIN

The capital of Ireland, Dublin, is steeped in the country's history. This compact city was the focus for the revolt against British rule and it was here, in 1922, that the Irish state was born. In recent years, Dublin has attracted manufacturing and service industries, as well as many people from other parts of the country that have come here in search of work.

RACEHORSES

The lush pastures of Ireland provide excellent grazing land for racehorses. These fine Irish thoroughbreds are world famous and frequently win major international races. The animals, bred on stud farms, are valuable sources of income for the Irish economy. Buying and selling horses is also popular, and country horse fairs are a familiar sight.

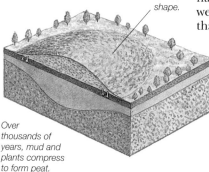

Many Irish peat bogs are a distinctive domed shape.

Over thousands of years, mud and plants compress to form peat.

PEAT

Ireland has few natural resources, such as coal or oil, that produce energy. What it does have are huge peat bogs. Peat consists of dead, rotted plants that have been compressed and can be burned as fuel. Some villages have their own peat supplies, and there are also vast government-owned areas that are dug out by mechanical cutters. These provide fuel for large power stations that generate electricity.

The peat is cut out in blocks and then stacked and left to dry.

Peat is still gathered by hand in many parts of Ireland.

Find out more

BEER BREWING: *117*
COAL AND OIL: *96, 152, 162*
NORTHERN IRELAND: *89*
RELIGIONS: *274–275*

THE LOW COUNTRIES

THE THREE COUNTRIES IN THIS REGION – Belgium, the Netherlands, and Luxembourg – are known as the Low Countries because much of their land is flat and low-lying. The Low Countries are also called "Benelux" after the economic union they formed in 1948. The Benelux union allows the free flow of goods between the three countries, although each keeps its own tax system. These are the most densely populated countries in Europe, yet their people generally enjoy a high standard of living. Although the region's traditional heavy industries, such as coal mining, are declining, they are being replaced by modern manufacturing industries and service activities, such as banking and administration.

THINGS TO LOOK FOR ON THE MAP
Longest river: Meuse, France/Belgium/Netherlands, 560 miles (901 km) *Map J8*

Highest point: Botrange, Belgium, 2,277 ft (694 m) *Map J10*

Largest lake: Ijsselmeer, Netherlands, 467 sq miles (1,210 sq km) *Map I5*

NETHERLANDS

BELGIUM

LUXEMBOURG

De Bilt, Netherlands
Jan 36°F (2°C)
July 64°F (18°C)
Jan 2.7 in (68 mm)
July 3 in (77 mm)

Luxembourg, Luxembourg
Jan 33°F (1°C)
July 64°F (18°C)
Jan 2.4 in (61 mm)
July 2.4 in (61 mm)

Rotterdam is Europe's busiest and largest port.

RIVERS
Some of Europe's most important rivers flow through these countries, linking the interior with the coast. The most useful rivers for transportation and trade are the Rhine, Mosel, and Meuse. At the mouth of the Rhine River stands the port of Rotterdam. Stretching for 12 miles (20 km) along the river, the port can handle 300 cargo ships at a time. Canals are also important for linking the ports with the rivers and inland areas.

FARMLAND
The region's flat plains are used for grazing dairy cattle and for growing flowers and vegetables. Much of the farmland has been reclaimed from the sea by enclosing areas with earth barriers, called dykes, and draining out the water. The only areas of high land are the forested Ardennes Mountains, which run across the south of Belgium and into Luxembourg.

NETHERLANDS

THIS SMALL, DENSELY POPULATED country is also referred to as Holland, the name of two of its provinces. In the 16th and 17th centuries, Dutch merchants and sailors traveled far and wide, trading in gold and spices. The empire they established stretched from Southeast Asia to the Caribbean. Trade is still of great importance to the Netherlands today, since several large international companies are Dutch, and exports make up about half the country's income. The Dutch are known for their tolerance and for their liberal social attitudes.

NETHERLANDS

Capital cities: Amsterdam, The Hague

Area: 13,097 sq miles (33,920 sq km)

Population: 15,800,000

Official language: Dutch

Major religions: Christian 63%, Muslim 3%, other 34%

Government: Multiparty democracy

Currency: Euro

Adult literacy rate: 99%

Life expectancy: 78 years

People per doctor: 400

Televisions: 543 per 1,000 people

AMSTERDAM

This historic city is the capital of the Netherlands and is much visited by tourists. In the 17th century, Amsterdam was a center of world trade. Merchants built the network of canals that crisscross the city and the tall, narrow houses that line the canals. Today, Amsterdam is a world center for diamond cutting and polishing.

CYCLING

The extreme flatness of the Dutch countryside makes cycling one of the easiest and most popular ways of getting around. Country areas have long-distance cycle routes, clearly posted and shown on maps. Town centers are planned for bicycles rather than cars. The lack of traffic means that more people can live in town centers, and so small, family-run shops are still thriving businesses.

More than half a million people in Amsterdam use bicycles to travel to school or work.

Tulips were first brought to the Netherlands from Turkey in the 1630s, as much for their edible bulbs as for their flowers.

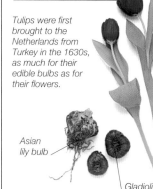

Asian lily bulb

Gladioli bulbs

AGRICULTURE

The Dutch have developed intensive farming methods to get the most from their limited but fertile land. Among the main crops grown are potatoes, barley, and salad vegetables, such as lettuce and tomatoes. Bulbs and flowers are probably the Netherlands' most famous export, particularly tulips. Other major exports are meat and dairy products, including cheeses, such as Gouda and Edam.

Making a polder

Earth dykes are built around a shallow area of water.

A mat of woven twigs is laid across the land surface.

A plane sows the seeds of reeds, which grow up through the twigs.

The reeds are burned down. Their ashes are dug into the soil.

Years 1–2
The water is gradually drained off the land and pumped away.

Years 3–6

Year 7

Year 8

Only eight years since it was beneath the sea, the land is ready to be used for farming and for building houses and roads.

LAND RECLAMATION

About a third of the Netherlands is land that has been reclaimed from the sea. These areas of land are called polders. Most of the reclaimed land is used for crop production and dairy farming, although about 25 percent is set aside for housing, roads, and open spaces. Since so much of the land lies at or below sea-level, flooding is a serious problem. Huge barrier dams are built to keep the sea at bay, and water levels are monitored.

ETHNIC MIX

Many people from the former Dutch colonies in Southeast Asia settled in the Netherlands in the 1940s and 1950s. They were followed in the 1960s by a flow of foreign workers from southern Europe, Turkey, and Morocco. Immigrants now make up about a fifth of the population of the Netherland's major cities. Most have full Dutch citizenship. The Dutch pride themselves on their policy of welcoming immigrants and refugees.

Find out more

CYCLING: *192*
ETHNIC MIX: *81*
POPULATION DENSITY: *80*
TRADE: *280-281*

BELGIUM

BELGIUM IS A FAIRLY NEW country that became independent from its Dutch rulers in 1830. Its current borders were only settled in 1919. The country is split in two by the valley of the Meuse River. To the north lie flat, fertile plains stretching to the coast. A thriving textile industry grew up here in the 16th century around cities such as Bruges, which is still known for its lacemaking. To the south lie the Ardennes Mountains, a region of poor soil and scattered farms.

The medieval Grand Place is at the heart of Brussels.

BRUSSELS

Brussels is the capital of Belgium and the center of government and trade. It is also an important international city. As a center of the Benelux union, Brussels has a long history of administering international relations. The city is now home to the administrative center of the European Union.

BELGIUM	
Capital city: Brussels	
Area: 12,672 sq miles (32,820 sq km)	
Population: 10,200,000	
Official languages: Dutch, French, and German	
Major religions: Christian 88%, Muslim 2%, other 10%	
Government: Multiparty democracy	
Currency: Euro	
Adult literacy rate: 99%	
Life expectancy: 78 years	
People per doctor: 270	
Televisions: 510 per 1,000 people	

LUXEMBOURG	
Capital city: Luxembourg	
Area: 998 sq miles (2,585 sq km)	
Population: 431,400	
Official language: Letzeburgish	
Major religions: Christian 99%, other 1%	
Government: Multiparty democracy	
Currency: Euro	
Adult literacy rate: 99%	
Life expectancy: 77 years	
People per doctor: 469	
Televisions: 391 per 1,000 people	

LANGUAGES
Three languages are spoken in Belgium. People in the southern part of the country, close to the border with France, speak French. North of Brussels, most people speak Flemish, a dialect of Dutch. In the far east, the official language is German. In Brussels, most people speak French, but Dutch is also widely spoken.

Main languages

BELGIUM

☐ Dutch

☐ French

☐ German

The three languages Dutch, French, and German are spoken in Belgium.

A Brussels newsstand sells newspapers in at least three languages.

Fries

Mussels

FOOD AND DRINK
Belgian food is a mixture of French and Flemish influences. Soup is very popular and many regions have their own local recipes. A specialty is mussels and fries, which can be eaten in an expensive restaurant or bought from a street stall.

INDUSTRY

Belgium's traditional heavy industries, such as coal mining and steel making, are now in decline. They are being replaced by newer industries such as the manufacture of chemicals and electrical equipment (shown here), and service industries, such as banking and administration. Two out of three Belgians now work in service industries.

LUXEMBOURG

SQUEEZED BETWEEN Germany, France, and Belgium, the Grand Duchy of Luxembourg is a tiny state. It has the highest standard of living in Europe and is famous as a center of international finance and a tax haven. Most of its wealth comes from heavy industry and services. Despite its small size, Luxembourg plays a vital part in the European Union as headquarters of the European Parliament and the European Court of Justice.

This tiny country has been at the crossroads of Europe for centuries. Walled towns and castles, built to offer protection from passing armies, are still dotted across the landscape.

TOURISM
As part of the Ardennes Mountain region, much of Luxembourg's countryside is hilly and forested. Tourism is a growing industry as visitors come to discover the unspoiled scenery, picturesque castles, and ancient walled towns.

Find out more
EUROPEAN PLAIN: *79*
EUROPEAN UNION: *81, 273*
RICH AND POOR: *278–279*
SERVICE INDUSTRIES: *281*

GERMANY

LYING AT THE HEART OF EUROPE, Germany is one of the world's wealthiest nations. In its present form, Germany is one of the newest countries in Europe. After World War II, it was divided into two separate countries – West Germany, a western-style democracy, and East Germany, a communist state. In 1990, the two parts of Germany were reunited as one country. The eastern part is now struggling to overcome the legacy of economic decay and pollution left by its communist past.

GERMANY

Capital city: Berlin

Area: 134,910 sq miles (349,910 sq km)

Population: 82,200,000

Official language: German

Major religions: Christian 71%, Muslim 2%, other 27%

Government: Multiparty democracy

Currency: Euro

Adult literacy rate: 99%

Life expectancy: 78 years

People per doctor: 303

Televisions: 580 per 1,000 people

EDUCATION
Young German children go to nursery school, then to primary school. At the age of 10, they move to either a *Gymnasium* (grammar school), a *Hauptschule* (secondary school) or a *Realschule* (middle school). These last two types of schools specialize in training students in technical skills.

RECENT HISTORY
The reunification of Germany took place on October 3, 1990. Growing protests in East Germany, and the collapse of communism in the USSR, finally led the government to make changes. The Berlin Wall, symbol of Germany's division, was demolished, and East Germans started to flood into West Berlin. The city has regained its status once more as the capital of Germany and the seat of government.

HAMBURG
SCHLESWIG-HOLSTEIN
BREMEN
MECKLENBURG-WEST POMMERANIA
BERLIN
LOWER SAXONY
BRANDENBURG
NORTH RHINE-WESTPHALIA
SAXONY-ANHALT
SAXONY
HESSE
THURINGIA
RHINELAND-PALATINATE
SAARLAND
BADEN-WURTTEMBERG
BAVARIA

FEDERAL STATES
Germany has only been a single country since 1871. Before that, it was divided into many independent states. Today, Germany is still made up of 16 states, or *Länder* (shown left), with a federal system of government, similar to the US. Each *Land* has its own state government and controls local issues such as education. Many Germans still have a strong sense of regional identity, thinking of themselves as Bavarians, for example, first, and Germans second.

Many provincial cities in Germany were formerly the capitals of independent states. Dresden, shown here, is now the capital of Saxony, a region that was once part of the former East Germany.

THE ENVIRONMENT
Thanks to the success of the Green Party, Germans are well aware of the need to protect the environment. There are very strict controls on pollution – Germany has led the way in fitting catalytic converters to cars and in using lead-free gasoline. Most houses have three separate trash cans for different types of waste, so that household garbage can be recycled.

Paper waste is collected separately from people's houses and taken to a refuse site like this one for recycling.

FOOD AND DRINK
The annual Munich *Oktoberfest* is the biggest of the many beer festivals held all over Germany. It lasts for two weeks and attracts millions of beer drinkers. Beer is Germany's national drink, with wine a close second. Popular types of food include bread, pastries, pretzels, cold meats, and cheese. *Wurst* (sausage) is another German specialty. Many regions make their own local sausages.

Wine from the Rhine Valley

Pretzels

Smoked cheese

Blue-veined cheese

A B C D E F G H I J K L
1
2
3
4
5
6
7
8
9
10
11
12

ARCTIC CIRCLE

N

DENMARK

North Frisian Is.

Sylt

Föhr

NORTH SEA

Nordstrand

Helgoland Bay

East Frisian Is.

BALTIC SEA

Fehmarn

Rügen

Mecklenburg Bay

Schleswig

Husum

Kiel

Neumünster

Kiel Canal

Stralsund

Greifswald

Rostock

Wismar

Lübeck

Neubrandenburg

L. Schwerin

Schwerin

L. Müritz

Berlin
☀ Jan 31°F (-0.5°C)
☀ July 66°F (19°C)
🌧 Jan 1.8 in (46 mm)
July 2.9 in (73 mm)

Cuxhaven

Wilhelmshaven

Bremerhaven

Emden

Hamburg

Elbe

Oldenburg

Bremen

Lüneburg

Cologne
☀ Jan 35°F (3°C)
☀ July 66°F (19°C)
🌧 Jan 2.4 in (60 mm)
July 2.7 in (69 mm)

NETHERLANDS

Ems

Dortmund-Ems Canal

Osnabrück

Weser

Celle

Hanover

Wolfsburg

Mittelland Canal

Stendal

BERLIN

POLAND

Oder

Brandenburg

Potsdam

Frankfurt an der Oder

Braunschweig

Salzgitter

Magdeburg

Bielefeld

Hildesheim

Münster

G E R M A N Y

Rhine

Hamm

Paderborn

Dessau

Wittenberg

Cottbus

Gelsenkirchen

Dortmund

Göttingen

Nordhausen

Halle

Leipzig

Riesa

Bautzen

Duisburg

Essen

Hagen

Krefeld

Wuppertal

Remscheid

Ruhr

Eder

Kassel

Mühlhausen

Saale

Elbe

Dresden

Görlitz

Düsseldorf

Leverkusen

Aachen

Cologne

Bonn

Siegen

Fulda

Gotha

Erfurt

Jena

Gera

Chemnitz

BELGIUM

RHINELAND

Giessen

Suhl

Zwickau

THURINGIAN FOREST

Plauen

ORE MTS.

THINGS TO LOOK FOR ON THE MAP
Longest river: Rhine, Switzerland/Germany/France/Netherlands 820 miles (1,320 km) *Map D6*
Highest point: Zugspitze, 9,718 ft (2,962 m) *Map H12*
Largest lake: L. Müritz, 45 sq miles (117 sq km) *Map J3*
World's busiest canal: Kiel, 61 miles (98 km) long *Map G2*

Koblenz

Mosel

Wiesbaden

Frankfurt am Main

Offenbach

Mainz

Darmstadt

Main

Würzburg

Schweinfurt

Bamberg

Bayreuth

Hof

CZECH REPUBLIC

LUXEMBOURG

Trier

Kaiserslautern

Mannheim

Heidelberg

Erlangen

Nuremberg

FRANCONIAN JURA

BOHEMIAN FOREST

Munich
☀ Jan 29°F (-2°C)
☀ July 65°F (18°C)
🌧 Jan 2.3 in (59 mm)
July 5.5 in (139 mm)

Saarbrücken

Heilbronn

FRANCE

Karlsruhe

Pforzheim

Stuttgart

Regensburg

Danube

Rhine

Tübingen

Ulm

SWABIAN JURA

Augsburg

Ingolstadt

Landshut

Passau

Inn

Nectar

BLACK FOREST

Danube

Munich

Freiburg im Breisgau

Ammersee

Rosenheim

Chiemsee

Starnberger See

Konstanz

Friedrichshafen

L. Constance

Zugspitze

BAVARIAN ALPS

GERMANY

SWITZERLAND

AUSTRIA

THE LANDSCAPE
From the flat, fertile plains of the north to the snowcapped peaks of the Bavarian Alps, shown here, the German landscape is extremely varied. One of the country's most famous and most picturesque regions is the Black Forest in the southwest, which gets its name from its dark coniferous trees.

INLAND WATERWAYS
Germany's extensive network of canals and rivers is vitally important for transporting cargo. Barges are a common sight along rivers, such as the Rhine, carrying goods around Germany and into other parts of Europe. In eastern Germany, the Oder River is an important waterway for taking goods into Poland. On land, Germany has excellent highways and a fast, efficient railroad system.

RELIGION

In the 16th century, a German monk, Martin Luther, attacked the teachings of the Roman Catholic Church in Germany, preaching his own brand of Christianity. The movement he started was called the Reformation, and his followers, Protestants. His movement gained most support in northern Germany, which is still largely Protestant. Most people in southern Germany are Catholic.

This Gutenberg Bible was printed in Germany.

SPORTS

Many of the world's top sports stars have come from Germany, including Borris Becker in tennis, brothers Michael and Ralf Schumacher in motor racing (shown here), and Katja Seizinger in skiing. Soccer is Germany's most popular spectator sport. The West German team was outstandingly successful, winning the World Cup several times. A single, unified German squad first entered competition for the 1992 European Cup.

NEW GERMANS

As the German economy grew, so did the need for labor. In the 1960s, thousands of people came from Turkey and former Yugoslavia to work in Germany. Life has not been easy for them. They have suffered discrimination and been refused citizenship, despite their contribution to German life. Since 1990, more than a million German-speaking immigrants have arrived from eastern Europe.

Foreign workers often took unskilled jobs that Germans were unwilling to do.

Around a third of German workers are employed in industry.

THE ECONOMY

Germany's industries were completely rebuilt and modernized after World War II. Today, Germany is one of the world's leading industrial nations. This success is largely due to its very strong manufacturing industry. Germany is one of the world's top producers of trucks, ships, electrical goods and cars, with such famous names as Volkswagen, Mercedes, and BMW. These are exported for sale all over the world.

Cross-section through a deep coal mine

Coal deposits, or seams, are removed from the Earth by mining.

Surface works of coal mine

Upper layers of rock are younger and do not contain coal.

Vertical shaft leads down to the coal seams.

Seam of coal

Horizontal shafts lead to the seams where the coal is mined.

Coalfields in the Ruhr Valley

- Current coalfields
- Exhausted surface coalfields
- Coal reserves less than than 3,000 ft (1,000 m) deep
- Coal reserves more than 3,000 ft (1,000 m) deep

Wesel

Recklinghausen

Oberhausen Essen Dortmund

Bochum

Hagen

THE RUHR VALLEY

The Ruhr Valley is the most heavily industrialized region in Germany, and also the most densely populated area, with many large towns and cities. In the 19th century, huge deposits of coal were discovered here. This led to the region's development as the center of iron and steel production, vital for Germany's car industry. At first, coal was mined in the south of the coalfield where it lay near the surface. These seams are now exhausted. Today, mining is concentrated in deeper mines in the north.

COAL MINING

The Ruhr coalfield is one of the largest in the world, producing both black coal and brown coal (lignite). Brown coal is found on the surface, but black coal has to be extracted from deep mines, like the one shown here. Today, the Ruhr region faces serious problems. Coal supplies are running out and other sources of fuel are being found, leaving many people without jobs.

Find out more

BREAKUP OF USSR: *136*
COAL MINING: *114, 162*
EUROPEAN IMMIGRANTS: *81*
PROTESTANTS: *274*

FRANCE

THE LARGEST COUNTRY IN western Europe, France includes the island of Corsica in the Mediterranean Sea. Two major mountain chains, the Pyrenees to the south and the Alps to the east, provide dramatic natural borders with neighboring countries. Several rivers, including the Loire, the Rhône, and the Seine, are important for transportation as well as irrigation of farmland. The states of Monaco and Andorra lie in the south.

LANDSCAPE
The landscape and climate of France varies from north to south. Northern France has gently rolling farmland with cool, wet weather, while the middle of the country is dominated by the rugged hills of the *Massif Central*. The south, with its Mediterranean climate, is dry and warm with lavender fields – a typical scene in the region of Provence.

FRANCE (flag)

MONACO (flag)

ANDORRA (flag)

THINGS TO LOOK FOR ON THE MAP

Longest river: Loire, 634 miles (1,020 km) *Map D5*

Highest point: Mont Blanc, 15,772 ft (4,807 m) *Map J6*

Largest lake: L. Geneva, 224 sq miles (580 sq km) *Map I6*

Marseille
☀ Jan 42°F (5°C)
☀ July 73°F (23°C)
☂ Jan 1.7 in (43 mm)
☂ July 0.4 in (11 mm)

Paris
☀ Jan 43°F (6°C)
☀ July 73°F (23°C)
☂ Jan 1.7 in (43 mm)
☂ July 0.4 in (11 mm)

Lyon
☀ Jan 36°F (2°C)
☀ July 70°F (21°C)
☂ Jan 2.1 in (52 mm)
☂ July 2.2 in (56 mm)

Map labels: ENGLISH CHANNEL, BELGIUM, LUXEMBOURG, GERMANY, SWITZERLAND, ITALY, SPAIN, ATLANTIC OCEAN, MEDITERRANEAN SEA, NORMANDY, BRITTANY, BURGUNDY, JURA, ALPS, PYRENEES, MASSIF CENTRAL, CEVENNES, PROVENCE, Côte d'Azur, Corsica

Dunkirk, Calais, Channel Tunnel, Boulogne-sur-Mer, Lille, Valenciennes, Arras, Dieppe, Amiens, St Quentin, Mézières, Cherbourg, Le Havre, Rouen, Beauvais, Laon, Rheims, Verdun, Thionville, Metz, Bar-le-Duc, Nancy, Strasbourg, Channel Islands (UK), St Lô, Caen, Évreux, PARIS, Versailles, Melun, Châlons-sur-Marne, Épinal, Colmar, Mulhouse, St Brieue, St Malo, Alençon, Chartres, Troyes, Chaumont, Belfort, Vesoul, Île d'Ouessant, Brest, Rennes, Laval, Le Mans, Orléans, Auxerre, Dijon, Besançon, Quimper, Lorient, Vannes, Angers, Tours, Blois, Bourges, Nevers, Doubs, Belle Île, St Nazaire, Nantes, Chenonceaux, Bourg-en-Bresse, L. Geneva, Mont Blanc, La Roche-sur-Yon, Châteauroux, Moulins, Mâcon, Annecy, Poitiers, Vichy, Lyon, Chambéry, Les Sables d'Olonne, La Rochelle, Limoges, Clermont-Ferrand, Charente, Saintes, Angoulême, Périgueux, Aurillac, Le Puy, St Étienne, Valence, Grenoble, Dordogne, Allier, Gap, Bordeaux, Lot, Mende, Digne, Arcachon, Garonne, Cahors, Rodez, Tarn, Nîmes, Avignon, Grasse, Nice, MONACO, Cannes, Agen, Montauban, Aix-en-Provence, Arles, Mont-de-Marsan, Albi, Marseille, Toulon, Auch, Toulouse, Montpellier, Bayonne, Pau, Tarbes, Foix, Carcassonne, Îles d'Hyères, Bastia, Perpignan, ANDORRA, ANDORRA LA VELLA, Ajaccio

Rivers: Somme, Seine, Marne, Meuse, Moselle, Rhine, Saône, Loire, Rhône, Durance

Scale: 0 50 100 150 km / 0 25 50 75 100 miles

FRENCH HISTORY
For hundreds of years, France was ruled by kings and queens. They built magnificent palaces and castles, such as Chenonceau, along the Loire River. All this was swept away in the revolution of 1789. The monarchy was overthrown and King Louis XVI and his queen, Marie Antoinette, were publicly beheaded. In 1792, France became a republic. Despite some efforts to restore the monarchy, France remains a republic.

FRANCE

THE INFLUENCE OF French culture, fashion, and food can be seen all over the world. As a leading industrialized nation and founding member of the European Union, France also plays a key role in world affairs. Since the end of World War II, the country has become Europe's major agricultural producer and exporter, with main crops of wheat, sugar beets, sunflower seeds, apples, and grapes used for wine. France boasts the world's fastest train, the TGV, which can travel at speeds up to 320 mph (515 km/h).

FRANCE	
Capital city: Paris	
Area: 212,394 sq miles (550,100 sq km)	
Population: 59,100,000	
Official language: French	
Major religions: Christian 90%, Jewish 1%, Muslim 1%, Buddhist, 1%, other 6%	
Government: Multiparty democracy	
Currency: Euro	
Adult literacy rate: 99%	
Life expectancy: 78 years	
People per doctor: 357	
Televisions: 601 per 1,000 people	

MONACO	
Capital city: Monaco	
Area: 0.75 sq miles (1.95 sq km)	
Population: 28,000	
Official language: French	
Major religions: Christian 95%, other 5%	
Government: Monarchy	
Currency: Euro	
Adult literacy rate: 99%	
Life expectancy: 79 years	
People per doctor: 333	
Televisions: 768 per 1,000 people	

ANDORRA	
Capital city: Andorra la Vella	
Area: 181 sq miles (468 sq km)	
Population: 66,824	
Official language: Catalan	
Major religions: Christian 94%, other 6%	
Government: Multiparty democracy	
Currency: Euro	
Adult literacy rate: 99%	
Life expectancy: 83 years	
People per doctor: 555	
Televisions: 391 per 1,000 people	

The Eiffel Tower is 984 ft (300 m) high and was built for the Paris World Exposition of 1889. The observation gallery can hold 800 people.

CITY OF CULTURE

Situated on the banks of the Seine River, Paris is the capital of France and its cultural and political center. One of the world's most visited cities, its famous landmarks include the Eiffel Tower, the Louvre, and the cathedral of Notre Dame. There are also many museums, shops, and restaurants. Each spring, the world's leading fashion designers arrive in Paris to present their latest collections.

The second level is reached by elevator or by climbing another 700 steps.

Visitors reach the first level by elevator or by climbing up 360 steps.

VILLAGE LIFE

Although many French people have moved from the countryside to live in the cities, village life is still important. Throughout France villages have kept a strong identity, with local festivals, fairs, and weekly food markets. Life centers around the village square, where people often gather to play *boules*, the national game of France.

INDUSTRY

One of the world's leading industrial nations, France has large manufacturing, steel, and chemical industries and competes at the front end of engineering and technology. The country is a major producer of cars and aircraft, such as this Airbus in its Toulouse factory. France has a large nuclear industry that generates over 75 percent of the country's electrical power. With millions of visitors a year, tourism is also important to the economy.

FOODS OF FRANCE

France has such a range of climates and landscapes that it can produce many different types of foods and fine wines. Each region has its own special dish. Central France, for example, is famous for boeuf bourguignon (beef in red wine), while Marseille on the Mediterranean coast specializes in bouillabaisse (fish soup with garlic). France is also known for its breads and pastries, such as croissants, and different types of cheeses.

Crottins de Chavignol cheese

Croissant

Garlic

French people relax with friends in a café or restaurant.

A FINE FRAGRANCE

Some of the world's finest perfumes come from France. Most perfume is made in Grasse in southern France where fields of lavender, roses, and jasmine are grown. Their essential oils are extracted and blended to make a variety of scents. As many as 300 oils may be used in one perfume.

Oil from lavender is an important ingredient in many perfumes, as well as in soaps and bath oils.

WINE MAKING

France produces about a fifth of the world's wine, and vineyards are a feature of the French landscape. Wine is made from the juice of black or white grapes (which are actually red or pale green in color). Although juice was once extracted by people trampling on the picked grapes, today's methods are generally more modern. There are several processes in the production of wine, including fermentation, which mixes a natural yeast on the grape skin with the sugar in the grape. Pressing grapes using a modern press is shown here.

A French vineyard

wind

The rows of vines are positioned so the sun warms the earth and also helps the grapes ripen.

Black or white grapes can be used to make white wine. It is the skins that give red wine its color.

Tall trees, such as poplars, protect young vines from wind damage.

Grape vines are planted in rows in vineyards.

Pneumatic press

Black grapes go through a crusher that tears off the stalks and pumps the grapes into the press.

Air pumped in here to inflate rubber bag

Pressed grapes

The press revolves to move the grapes around.

As the bag fills with air it gently pushes grapes against the cylinder to press out the juice.

Trough to collect grape juice before it is turned into wine

Wine is usually drunk from a tall glass that holds in the flavor.

IMMIGRATION

France has about 4 million immigrants, mainly Muslims from Morocco, Tunisia, and Algeria – France's former colonies in North Africa. People also arrive from Italy, Spain, and Poland in the hope of finding work. Immigrants often face problems such as discrimination, unemployment, and poor housing.

WORLD OF MOVIES

The film industry began in France in 1895 when the Lumiere brothers showed a film to an audience of 33. Today France is one of the leading makers of internationally acclaimed films. The crystal-shaped Kinemax in Poitiers has 10 different theaters and one of the biggest screens in Europe.

MONACO

A TINY COUNTRY ON THE Mediterranean coast, Monaco lies close to the Italian border. The heart of the country is the sophisticated city of Monte-Carlo, famous for its gambling casinos and car racing Grand Prix. Monaco is an independent principality, ruled for more than 800 years by the Grimaldi family. Only a small part of the population is originally from Monaco; more than half the people are citizens of France.

TOURISM

Monaco's warm climate and glamorous image attract thousands of tourists. Many rich people, with yachts moored in the old harbor, choose to live there because it has a low tax rate. Monaco is also a major international business center.

ANDORRA

HIGH IN THE PYRENEES MOUNTAINS, on the border between France and Spain, nestles the country of Andorra. The country is nominally ruled jointly by the President of France and the Bishop of Urgel in northeastern Spain. Catalan is the official language, although many people also speak French and Spanish. The country's only large town is the capital city, Andorra la Vella.

THE PYRENEES

The main source of income in Andorra is tourism. Many people come to ski in the Pyrenees, although the only road between France and Spain is often blocked by heavy snow in winter.

Find out more

ETHNIC GROUPS: *81*

EUROPEAN CITIES: *80*

EUROPEAN UNION: *81, 273*

FORMER COLONIES: *208–212*

SPAIN AND PORTUGAL

SPAIN AND PORTUGAL OCCUPY a peninsula of land in southwestern Europe called Iberia. For hundreds of years the area was ruled by the Moors, North African Muslims, who introduced orange trees to the region. Iberia is separated from the rest of Europe by the Pyrenees Mountains in the north, and from Africa by the Strait of Gibraltar to the south. Both countries share a warm Mediterranean climate and have economies based on tourism. Fishing off the Atlantic coast is also important.

LANDSCAPE

The landscape of Iberia is dominated by a vast, almost treeless, central plain called the *Meseta*. In summer, it is so hot here that nearly all the streams dry up. In winter, the temperature often falls below freezing and blizzards are common. Rain is so scarce that farmers have to rely on irrigation to water their crops.

Barcelona, Spain
- Jan 49°F (9°C)
- July 75°F (24°C)
- Jan 1.2 in (31 mm)
- July 1.1 in (27 mm)

PORTUGAL

Lisbon, Portugal
- Jan 52°F (11°C)
- July 72°F (22°C)
- Jan 4.3 in (111 mm)
- July 0.1 in (3 mm)

SPAIN

THINGS TO LOOK FOR ON THE MAP

Longest river: Tagus, Spain/Portugal, 1,007 km (626 miles) *Map E5*

Highest point: Mulhacén, Spain, 3,478 m (11,411 ft) *Map F8*

Most westerly point in mainland Europe: Cabo da Roca, Portugal *Map A6*

The Rock of Gibraltar lies at the entrance to the Mediterranean Sea.

GIBRALTAR

The tiny colony of Gibraltar stands on a rock just 3 miles (5 km) long. An important port for access to the Mediterranean, it was captured by Britain in 1704. Spain claims ownership of the colony, but, in 1967, the people of Gibraltar voted to remain British. After years of closure, the frontier between Spain and Gibraltar was reopened in 1985.

SPAIN

Fiestas and flamenco provide much of the flavor of Spain. Most Spaniards are Roman Catholic and fiestas, often to celebrate a local saint's day, include processions of people in traditional clothing, music, and dancing. After a bitter civil war in 1936–39, Spain was ruled by a dictator, Francisco Franco, until 1975. His successor, King Juan Carlos I, has restored democracy. Today, Spain is a major industrial nation with a large agricultural sector and a booming tourist trade. These activities are mainly based near the coasts, while central regions are less developed.

SPAIN

Capital city: Madrid	
Area: 192,834 sq miles (499,440 sq km)	
Population: 39,100,000	
Official language: Spanish	
Major religions: Christian 96%, other 4%	
Government: Multiparty democracy	
Currency: Euro	
Adult literacy rate: 98%	
Life expectancy: 78 years	
People per doctor: 244	
Televisions: 506 per 1,000 people	

CITIES OF SPAIN
Madrid, shown here, became Spain's capital in 1561 because King Philip II liked its climate and central location. Today, the city has a population of some 4 million people and is Spain's center of finance and government. Barcelona is Spain's second city and the capital of Catalonia. It lies at the heart of a large industrial area in the north and was the site of the 1992 Olympic Games.

Fan held by flamenco dancer

Wooden castanets played by dancers

FLAMENCO
Flamenco is the name given to the music and dance style developed by the gypsies of Andalusia in the 15th century. Dancers in traditional outfits, men in black and women in frilled dresses, stamp their heels and click castanets while flamenco music is played on a guitar.

The guitar originated in Spain in the 16th century. This model is a 19th-century court guitar.

PEOPLE OF SPAIN
The Spanish are divided into regional groups, some with their own language and culture. Local languages, include Catalan, Gallego, and Euskera from the Basque region, which stretches from northern Spain into France. The official dialect of Spain, Castilian, is taught in all schools, along with either English or French. Children in Spain tend to stay up late. They have a snack called *merienda* after school, then play outside, with a late family dinner held around 9 pm.

INDUSTRY

Farming and fishing used to be the basis of the Spanish economy. The country has now developed a large steel industry, centered in Barcelona in the north, and has also become an important center for making cars. In the 1980s, many new electronics and high-tech industries were set up, often supported by money from foreign investment. Major agricultural products include cereals, olives, grapes for wine, and citrus fruits, especially oranges from around Seville.

Top six exports
Figures show percentage of country's total exports

Vehicles: 23.7%

Heavy machinery: 9.8%

Electrical goods: 7%

Chemicals: 6.5%

Textiles: 4.6%

Fruit: 3.5%

SPANISH RESORTS
About 50 million tourists flock to Spain every year to enjoy the beaches and admire the architecture of cities such as Barcelona and Seville. Beaches on the Costa del Sol, as well as on the Balearic Island of Majorca, shown here, are popular with tourists from Britain and Germany. Bullfighting, held in arenas in most cities, either attracts or repels tourists.

Find out more

OLIVE GROWING: *130*
POLITICAL SYSTEMS: *270–271*
ROMAN CATHOLICS: *274*
SPANISH EMPIRE: *42*

PORTUGAL

A NATION OF GREAT SEAFARERS, Portuguese explorers sailed the world in the 15th and 16th centuries. They claimed territories as far apart as Africa and Asia, and they also colonized Brazil. From 1932–1968 Portugal was ruled by the dictator Oliveira Salazar, but after a military coup in 1974, the armed forces finally withdrew from politics. In 1986 Portugal joined the European Community, but it remains one of the poorest countries in western Europe. Tourism, particularly in the Algarve, is important to the economy.

LISBON
The capital of Portugal, Lisbon, lies at the mouth of the Tagus River. In the 15th century, Lisbon was a major port and world center for the spice and gold trade. The Tower of Belem, shown here, sits on the site where the explorer Vasco da Gama set sail. Today, many old palaces and mansions have been converted into elegant restaurants and bars, shops, and art galleries.

PORTUGAL	
Capital city: Lisbon	
Area: 35,502 sq miles (91,950 sq km)	
Population: 9,900,000	
Official language: Portuguese	
Major religions: Christian 98%, other 2%	
Government: Multiparty democracy	
Currency: Euro	
Adult literacy rate: 86%	
Life expectancy: 76 years	
People per doctor: 345	
Televisions: 452 per 1,000 people	

RURAL LIFE
Traditional farming methods, unchanged for centuries, are still used in many parts of Portugal. In some villages, oxen wearing carved wooden yokes still pull the plows. One of the country's main crops is corn, which was brought back from the Americas by Christopher Columbus in the 15th century. Other crops include olives and figs. Wine, cork, and tomatoes are exported abroad and fishing remains important along the Atlantic coast.

CRAFTS
Traditional Portuguese handicrafts include ceramic tiles, called *azulejos,* which are often used to decorate buildings. Street markets also display other local specialties, such as brightly colored pottery, painted furniture, glassware, and porcelain. Delicate silver filigree jewelry and richly embroidered cloth from the island of Madeira are exported all over the world.

The cork process

The cork oak tree grows to about 65 ft (20 m).

Workers strip cork away from the tree.

Bark has been removed from tree but will grow back over the years.

THE CORK INDUSTRY
Almost ten percent of Portugal is covered with cork oak trees, the bark of which is used to make cork products. The thick, spongy bark is stripped off and left to dry. It is then steamed or boiled to soften it and pressed into sheets ready for use. Portugal is the world's leading exporter of cork for products such as bottle stoppers, tiles, and the insides of shuttlecocks. By law, the bark is only removed every nine years so the trees can recover. Trees can provide cork for more than 100 years.

Cork bark

Cork tiles for home decoration

Cork used for shuttlecock

THE PORTUGUESE
Most Portuguese people are Roman Catholics. Family life is very important and girls often live at home until they marry, although more are now continuing their education and taking up careers. The *Queima das Fitas*, a festival held each May, celebrates university graduation. In recent years, as many as 3 million Portuguese have gone abroad in search of work. Some leave families behind, but send money home to support them.

Students celebrate graduation

Stoppers for bottles

Find out more	
EUROPEAN UNION:	*81, 273*
OLIVE GROWING:	*130*
POLITICAL SYSTEMS:	*270–271*
ROMAN CATHOLICS:	*274*

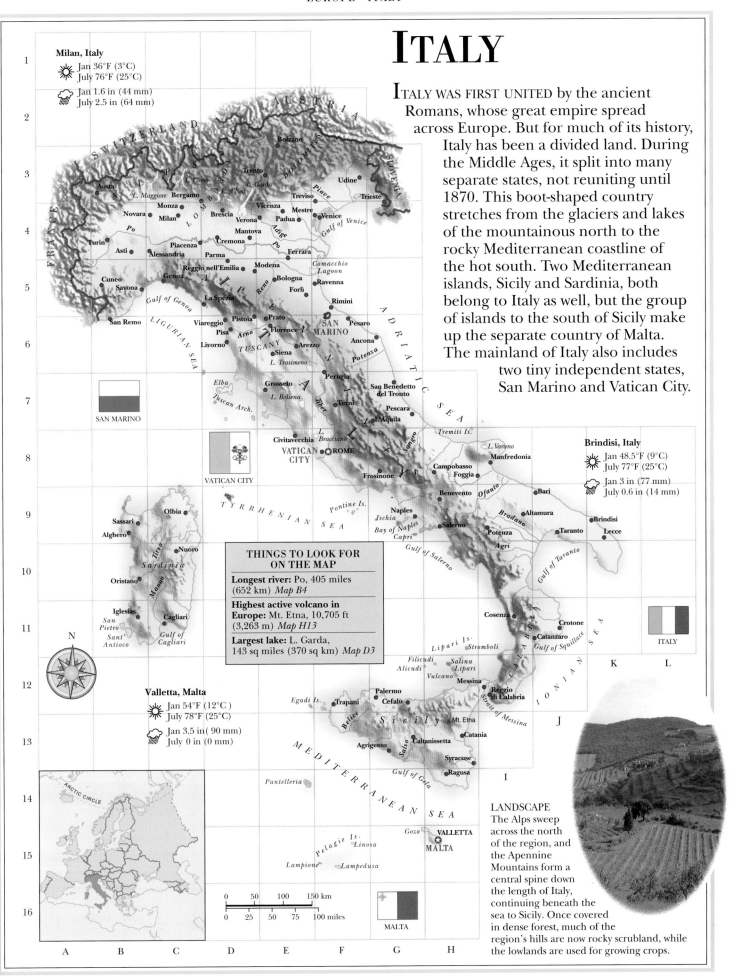

ITALY

ITALY WAS FIRST UNITED by the ancient Romans, whose great empire spread across Europe. But for much of its history, Italy has been a divided land. During the Middle Ages, it split into many separate states, not reuniting until 1870. This boot-shaped country stretches from the glaciers and lakes of the mountainous north to the rocky Mediterranean coastline of the hot south. Two Mediterranean islands, Sicily and Sardinia, both belong to Italy as well, but the group of islands to the south of Sicily make up the separate country of Malta. The mainland of Italy also includes two tiny independent states, San Marino and Vatican City.

Milan, Italy
Jan 36°F (3°C)
July 76°F (25°C)
Jan 1.6 in (44 mm)
July 2.5 in (64 mm)

Brindisi, Italy
Jan 48.5°F (9°C)
July 77°F (25°C)
Jan 3 in (77 mm)
July 0.6 in (14 mm)

Valletta, Malta
Jan 54°F (12°C)
July 78°F (25°C)
Jan 3.5 in (90 mm)
July 0 in (0 mm)

SAN MARINO

VATICAN CITY

ITALY

MALTA

THINGS TO LOOK FOR ON THE MAP

Longest river: Po, 405 miles (652 km) *Map B4*

Highest active volcano in Europe: Mt. Etna, 10,705 ft (3,263 m) *Map H13*

Largest lake: L. Garda, 143 sq miles (370 sq km) *Map D3*

LANDSCAPE
The Alps sweep across the north of the region, and the Apennine Mountains form a central spine down the length of Italy, continuing beneath the sea to Sicily. Once covered in dense forest, much of the region's hills are now rocky scrubland, while the lowlands are used for growing crops.

0   50   100   150 km
0   25   50   75   100 miles

ITALY

ANCIENT TRADITIONS and historic wealth have left Italy a rich legacy of art and architecture. Although Italy is one of the world's leading industrial powers today, there is a great divide between the wealthy, industrial north and the poorer, agricultural south. This economic division affects many aspects of Italian life and is one of the reasons behind the country's rapid turnover of governments. Most people throughout Italy follow the Roman Catholic religion.

TOURISM
Some of the world's most stunning sights can be found in Italy's cities. Tourists flock to the ancient ruins of Rome and to the palaces and churches of Florence, where the great revolution in art known as the Renaissance was born in the 15th century. The northern ski resorts and lakes are also popular. Tourism is vital to Italy's economy.

ITALY	
Capital city: Rome	
Area: 113,545 sq miles (294,060 sq km)	
Population: 57,300,000	
Official language: Italian	
Major religion: Christian 83%, other 17%	
Government: Multiparty democracy	
Currency: Euro	
Adult literacy rate: 97%	
Life expectancy: 78 years	
People per doctor: 588	
Televisions: 420 per 1,000 people	

Tall vines scramble up rows of posts and any available fruit trees.

An opera performance in Verona's Roman arena.

OPERA
The three great national passions are fast cars, soccer – and opera. Opera was virtually invented in Italy and performers such as Luciano Pavarotti are household names worldwide. Italian opera is unique in that it is a part of everyday life, and not just a pastime for the wealthy few, as it often is elsewhere.

A cereal crop such as corn is grown in a block between a row of vines and land left for grazing cattle.

AGRICULTURE
Small, family-run farms cover the Italian countryside, and many farmers work part-time. In the fertile northern plain surrounding the Po River, small-scale farmers get the most from their land by growing a variety of different crops close together. Cereals, fruit trees, grapes, and vegetables are widely grown, and there are olive groves in the south. Italy is a leading producer of fruit, wine, and olive oil.

On many small farms, a variety of different crops are grown mixed up together in what is known as polyculture. Grapes and fruits, vegetables, and cereals are main crops.

Crops such as potatoes are grown in the soil beneath vines.

Vine roots reach down to a deep layer of soil.

INDUSTRY
Once an agricultural nation, Italy is now a leading industrial country. Since it does not have many natural resources, Italy imports raw materials and uses its highly skilled workforce to turn them into manufactured goods, like the scooter shown here. Italy is a major player in industrial and product design.

The hard, strong-tasting Parmesan cheese is made from cow's milk in the north of Italy.

A popular meal is pasta with tomatoes, and often Parmesan cheese.

Tomatoes grow well in the warm sun around Naples.

Pasta comes in many shapes.

FAMILY MEALTIMES
To Italians, life revolves around the family, and large, extended networks of different generations usually live within close proximity. Meals are important family gatherings, and the food differs from region to region. In the north, pasta is often replaced by rice or polenta, made from corn flour. Olive oil and fresh vegetables are also important in Italian cooking.

A family enjoying a lunch together of pasta and fresh vegetables on the southern Italian island of Lipari.

Find out more
EUROPEAN CITIES: *80*
OLIVE GROWING: *131*
ROMAN CATHOLICS: *274*
WINE MAKING: *99*

MALTA

DUE TO ITS STRATEGIC POSITION on Mediterranean shipping routes, Malta has been ruled by many powers over the centuries. It finally became an independent country in the 1960s. Perhaps because of this history, the Maltese people cling to a strong sense of national identity, mostly following Roman Catholicism and speaking their own language. The country consists of two main islands, Malta and Gozo, and a smaller island called Comino.

MALTA

Capital city: Valletta

Area: 320 sq km (124 sq miles)

Population: 400,000

Official languages: Maltese and English

Major religion: Christian 98% Other 2%

Government: Multi-party democracy

Currency: Maltese lira

Adult literacy rate: 87%

Life expectancy: 78 years

People per doctor: 890

Televisions: 735 per 1,000 people

SHIPPING
The busy Grand Harbor of Malta's capital, Valletta, is a sign of how vital shipping is to the Maltese economy. This has been true for centuries due to Malta's position on the trade route between Europe and Africa. Many ships still come here to use the port and facilities for ship refitting.

TOURISM
A major source of Malta's income is provided by tourism. Visitors are drawn by its sheltered beaches and coves and its good climate. Another attraction is the country's imposing architecture, a legacy of its history as part of the Roman and Byzantine empires, and later as an Italian and British colony. Because of poor soil, farming produces little income. However, light industry, such as clothes manufacturing, is growing in importance.

VATICAN CITY

VATICAN CITY

Capital city: Vatican City

Area: 0.44 sq km (0.17 sq miles)

Population: 1000

Official languages: Italian and Latin

Major religion: Christian 100%

Government: Ruled by the Pope

Currency: Euro

No figures available for remaining statistics

THE WORLD'S SMALLEST independent state, Vatican City lies at the heart of Rome. This tiny state is the centre of the Roman Catholic Church and the home of the Pope. States ruled by the Pope once stretched right across Italy, and the Vatican is the last survivor. Many visitors are drawn by its religious significance and also its rich cultural legacy. The Vatican has its own flag, national anthem, and stamps, as well as a newspaper and radio station.

A spectacular view from St. Peter's Basilica
The Pope delivers his messages and blessings to packed crowds in this grand piazza.

SAN MARINO

Capital city: San Marino

Area: 61 sq km (24 sq miles)

Population: 26,937

Official language: Italian

Major religions: Christian 93%, other 7%

Government: Multi-party democracy

Currency: Euro

Life expectancy: 81 years

No figures available for remaining statistics

SAN MARINO

SITUATED IN ITALY'S MOUNTAINOUS NORTH, San Marino is Europe's smallest republic. It is also one of the oldest, possibly founded around AD 900. During the Middle Ages Italy was divided into powerful "city-states," such as Venice and Florence. These states gradually became absorbed into other, larger territories, but San Marino held on to its independence. The country consists of the capital, also called San Marino, and eight villages. The landscape is dominated by the three peaks of Mount Titano.

TOURISM
The fairy-tale fortress of Rocca Tower, perched high on a rocky outcrop, overlooks San Marino. With few resources, the republic relies heavily on a thriving tourist trade.

Find out more

POLITICAL SYSTEMS: *270–271*
ROMAN CATHOLICS: *274*
SMALL EUROPEAN STATES: *80–81*

SWITZERLAND AND AUSTRIA

HOME TO EUROPE'S TALLEST MOUNTAINS, the Alps, this region includes Switzerland, Austria, and the tiny state of Liechtenstein. The mountains have shaped the way Switzerland and Austria are organized politically, since communication has been difficult. Each is split up into individual districts with great control over their own affairs. With no direct access to the sea and few natural resources, all three countries have had to maintain good relations with their neighbors and develop specialized industries.

MOUNTAINS AND LAKES
Idyllic scenes of towns and villages next to peaceful lakes are just one of the sights that inspire so many tourists to visit this part of the world. Europe's largest lakes and its highest mountains are found in these two countries.

Innsbruck, Austria
- Jan 27°F (-3°C)
- July 66°F (19°C)
- Jan 2.1 in (54 mm)
- July 5.3 in (134 mm)

AUSTRIA

LIECHTENSTEIN

Zurich, Switzerland
- Jan 31°F (1°C)
- July 66°F (20°C)
- Jan 2.9 in (74 mm)
- July 5.4 in (136 mm)

SWITZERLAND

THINGS TO LOOK FOR ON THE MAP
Longest river: Rhine, Switzerland/France, 820 miles (1,320 km) *Map C7*

Highest point: Dufour Spitze, Switzerland/ Italy, 15,204 ft (4,634 m) *Map C9*

Largest lake: L. Constance, Switzerland/Austria/ Germany, 208 sq miles (540 sq km) *Map E7*

For centuries, narrow mountain passes have been the main links with surrounding countries.

COMMUNICATIONS
The towering Alps cut through these two countries, forming a massive wall separating northern Europe from the Mediterranean countries farther south. In the past, people had to cross the mountains via steep passes that were often blocked by snow. Today, tunnels and high bridges provide year-round access for road and rail transportation – Swiss engineering firms have become world experts in tunnel construction.

Ski resorts are built in the snowy peaks where few plants can grow.

On the higher slopes, patches of conifer trees are cleared for small farms.

The lower slopes are used as meadowland where cows can graze.

Vines and crops such as fruit are grown in the fertile valley bottom.

ALPINE VEGETATION
The different plants found at different levels on the Alps show how vegetation is affected by climate. On the upper, colder slopes only much hardier plants than those farther down can survive. Unlike the deciduous trees on the lower slopes, conifer trees have downward sloping branches so they can shed heavy snow. Above the tree line there is scrubland where only small, flowering plants and shrubs can thrive.

SWITZERLAND

SWITZERLAND HAS BEEN a neutral country since 1815, and has stayed out of all the wars that have affected Europe since that time. It is a country of isolated mountain communities in which people speak several different languages. Despite this, Switzerland is remarkably unified in many ways and has pooled its few resources to create a flourishing economy. Its neutrality and political stability have helped make it a major financial center.

SWITZERLAND

Capital city: Bern

Area: 15,355 sq miles (39,770 sq km)

Population: 6,873,687

Official languages: German, French, Italian, and Romansch

Major religions: Christian 86%, Muslim 2%, other 12%

Government: Multiparty democracy

Currency: Swiss franc

Adult literacy rate: 99%

Life expectancy: 79 years

People per doctor: 323

Televisions: 525 per 1,000 people

LIECHTENSTEIN

Capital city: Vaduz

Area: 62 sq miles (160 sq km)

Population: 32,207

Official language: German

Major religions: Christian 88%, other 12%

Government: Multiparty democracy

Currency: Swiss franc

No figures available for remaining statistics

MANUFACTURING
Even though it has virtually no raw materials, Switzerland has made itself a major industrial power. The Swiss have a skilled workforce specializing in producing high-value, lightweight products. Since Switzerland is a small country, Swiss companies have had to export goods in order to find large markets. Many businesses now have branches worldwide.

The pharmaceutical industry is important.

Switzerland is famous for making clocks and watches.

GENEVA
Many of Switzerland's banks and businesses are based in the beautiful lakeside city of Geneva. This city is also home to many international organizations, attracted here by Switzerland's political stability and its neutral status. These include the Red Cross, the World Health Organization, and the European headquarters of the United Nations.

AGRICULTURE
Farming is not easy in such mountainous terrain, but the fertile valleys are used extensively, and fruit and grape vines are grown on warmer, south-facing slopes. Dairy farming is a traditional way of life here. Cattle, sheep, and goats graze on the upland slopes in the warmer months, and are brought down to the valleys for the winter. Their milk is used to produce a variety of cheeses, such as Emmental, or Swiss chesse.

French-speaking Swiss people at a street market in Lausanne

LIECHTENSTEIN

NESTLING IN THE RHINE VALLEY between Switzerland and Austria, this tiny German-speaking principality is one of very few small European states to hold on to its independence. It is not totally independent, though, as Liechtenstein's Swiss neighbors provide its currency, as well as its postal and telephone services, and also direct the country's foreign policy.

SWISS LANGUAGES
Four different languages are spoken in Switzerland, Europe's most multi-lingual country. German, French, and Italian are the official languages, but a fourth, "Romansch," spoken in remote Alpine villages, has been given the status of a national language.

Liechtenstein produces highly decorative postage stamps that are much sought after by collectors. This one celebrates the anniversary of their prince and princess.

Stamp sales are still an important source of income for the state.

THE ECONOMY
Financial services are vital to the economy, and investors are drawn here by liberal banking laws and political stability. Intensive agriculture, a thriving small-scale manufacturing industry, and tourism bring in large amounts of revenue. Its varied economy makes this is an extremely wealthy state.

Find out more

INTERNATIONAL ORGANIZATIONS: *272–273*

RICH AND POOR: *278–279*

SERVICE INDUSTRIES: *281*

AUSTRIA

AUSTRIA

Capital city: Vienna

Area: 31,942 sq miles (82,730 sq km)

Population: 8,200,000

Official language: German

Major religions: Christian 83%, Muslim 2%, other 1%

Government: Multiparty democracy

Currency: Euro

Adult literacy rate: 99%

Life expectancy: 78 years

People per doctor: 385

Televisions: 516 per 1,000 people

THE SMALL, MOUNTAINOUS republic of Austria was once the center of the vast Austro-Hungarian Empire. Independent from 1918, it was encorporated into Nazi Germany in 1938–45. The Alps cover much of western Austria and fertile lowlands stretch across the east. Cattle graze on the mountain slopes, and crops, such as cereals and fruit, grow well in the north. Austria is a highly industrialized nation. Cities such as Linz produce iron, steel, heavy engineering products, and chemicals. Austria joined the European Union in 1995.

VIENNA

Austria's capital city was once the glittering capital of the Austro-Hungarian Empire. In the late 1700s and 1800s, Vienna was one of the most sophisticated cities in Europe. Today, the splendid architecture from that era attracts many visitors. Others come to soak up musical history – the imperial city was a magnet for composers, such as Mozart and Beethoven, who hoped to win commissions from the Austrian aristocracy or from the emperor himself.

HYDROELECTRIC POWER

Austria has little coal and no oil of its own, so other ways of producing power have been developed. Plentiful rivers and steep Alpine valleys provide an opportunity to harness the power of moving water to generate electricity. This is known as hydroelectric power. In the mountains, as water is released from an upper to a lower reservoir, it powers generators that produce electricity.

Water is collected in a reservoir high up in the mountains.

The water falls down to a motor called a turbine.

The energy of the falling water drives the turbine.

The movement of the turbine drives an electricity generator.

Steep roofs are built to shed heavy winter snowfalls.

MOUNTAIN HOUSES

In the past, Austrian farmers in the Alps built their steep-roofed houses from wood because trees were plentiful. Animals, hay, and humans were often housed in the same building. Hay was kept under the roof; cattle were kept in the basement; and the farmer's family lived in between. This kind of housing can still be seen in some farming villages, although tourism is changing the face of rural areas.

Tourism in the Austrian Alps

- 45% Winter 1997
- 55% Summer 1998
- 46% Winter 1998
- 54% Summer 1999

This chart shows the percentage of tourists visiting Austria in the winter or summer. Winter visitors go skiing; summer visitors go hiking.

TOURISM

Tourism accounts for nearly 20 percent of the country's income. In addition to exploring Austria's historic cities, visitors come to go skiing and hiking. Some of the world's best ski resorts are found here, and favorite summer haunts include the huge lakes nestling in the Alps. Conservation measures are being introduced to protect the land from damage by large numbers of visitors.

VARIED FOOD

Austrian food blends a range of influences – the result of all the different countries that once fell within the empire. For example, the famous *Wiener Schnitzel* (Viennese cutlet) is a breaded and fried piece of veal or pork that may have originated in Italy. Viennese coffee houses are famous worldwide for their vast selection of cakes and pastries.

Austrians drink coffee with milk, whipped cream, or strong and black.

Dobostorte is a rich, layered cake of sponge and chocolate cream, topped with caramel.

People enjoy a coffee break with lavish cakes mid-morning or afternoon.

Find out more

ALPINE LANDSCAPE: *106*
EUROPEAN UNION: *81, 273*
HYDROELECTRIC POWER: *262*
DANUBE RIVER: *78*

SLOVENIA and CROATIA

THE COUNTRIES of Slovenia and Croatia stretch from the snow-clad Alps in the north to the sunny Adriatic coast in the south. The area is crossed by the Sava River which flows past the capital cities of Ljubljana and Zagreb, across a fertile plain, eventually joining the Danube. In the west the Karst region of Slovenia has given its name to a type of scenery associated with limestone rock formations and deep caves. Some caves, such as those at Postojna, are as large as cathedrals. Ruled by Austria and Hungary for centuries, both countries retain strong cultural ties with Europe. At the end of World War I, Slovenia and Croatia were incorporated into the newly formed Yugoslavia but declared themselves independent in 1991.

WALLED CITY OF DUBROVNIK

This ancient Croatian port, with its narrow streets and massive walls, was founded by the Romans in the 7th century. Protected by its fortifications, Dubrovnik grew into a thriving city with trade links throughout the region. The wealth brought by trade encouraged a strong artistic tradition which persists today. Most of the damage from the war in the 1990s has now been repaired.

Dubrovnik, Croatia
Jan 46°F (8°C)
July 77°F (25°C)
Jan 5.5 in (139 mm)
July 1 in (26 mm)

Ljubljana, Slovenia
Jan 31°F (-1°C)
July 68°F (20°C)
Jan 3.5 in (88 mm)
July 4.5 in (113 mm)

SLOVENIA

CROATIA

THINGS TO LOOK FOR ON THE MAP

Longest river: Drava, Slovenia/Croatia, 450 miles (724 km) *Map F2*

Highest point: Triglav, Slovenia, 9,395 ft (2,864 m) *Map D2*

Largest lake: L. Vransko, Croatia, 13 sq miles (33 sq km) *Map F7*

0 25 50 75 100 125 km
0 25 50 75 miles

SOUTHERN ALPS

Much of northern Slovenia consists of the high mountains and steep-sided valleys of the southern Alps. Small towns and villages, many of which retain their winding streets and wooden buildings, nestle in the valleys on sheltered slopes. The rugged terrain and snow-covered mountains, which in previous centuries helped preserve the isolation of such places, now attract tourists to this part of Slovenia

SLOVENIA	
Capital city: Ljubljana	
Area: 7,820 sq miles (20,250 sq km)	
Population: 1,900,000	
Official language: Slovene	
Major religions: Christian 98%, other 2%	
Government: Multiparty democracy	
Currency: Tolar	

No figures available for remaining statistics

CROATIA	
Capital city: Zagreb	
Area: 21,829 sq miles (56,538 sq km)	
Population: 4,500,000	
Official language: Croatian	
Major religions: Christian 87%, Muslim 1%, other 12%	
Government: Multiparty democracy	
Currency: Kuna	

No figures available for remaining statistics

SLOVENIA

THE SMALL, alpine country of Slovenia lies at the northeastern end of the Adriatic Sea. Formerly ruled by Austria, and later part of Yugoslavia, Slovenia regained its independence in 1991 without involvement in the violence of the ensuing war. It maintains a strategic position in this corner of Europe, and its ports provide Austria with its main maritime outlet.

RIDING SCHOOLS
As long ago as 1580, a stud farm was set up in what is now Slovenia to supply horses to the Spanish Riding School in Vienna. The farm eventually bred the famous snow-white Lippizaner horse. Today they are considered the finest riding horses in the world.

ECONOMY
Widespread forests provide wood for sawmills, furniture, and papermaking industries in Slovenia. In recent years, license agreements with companies in western Europe have allowed local factories to produce a range of cars, trucks, motorcycles, and refrigerators.

SLOVENE PEOPLE
Despite being ruled for almost a thousand years by German-speaking Austrians, the Slovenes have kept their Slav language and folk culture. Colorful embroidery and distinctive headwear, as worn by women at this wedding, are part of that culture. Most people live in small towns or in one of the numerous villages scattered across the country. Only 300,000 people live in Ljubljana, making it one of Europe's smallest capitals.

Slovene women attend a village wedding.

The islands along the Adriatic coast are popular with tourists.

CROATIA

THE CRESCENT-SHAPED COUNTRY of Croatia was part of Hungary until it was joined to Yugoslavia in 1918. Along with Slovenia, it was the first country to declare its independence in 1991. War erupted almost immediately with Serbia. Until that time, the economy had prospered. Mineral wealth provided the basis for industry while vast areas of fertile land were used for crops. Although the war devastated much of the country, the economy was quick to recover.

TOURISM
A long coastline with hundreds of islands, bays, and secluded beaches, backed by the dramatic Dinaric Alps, has drawn tourists to Croatia for many years. Much of the damage the historic cities of Zagreb, Dubrovnik, and Split received during the war has been repaired, and tourist levels are returning to what they were before the conflict, with over 50% coming from Germany, Italy, and the United Kingdom.

The flax plant is harvested when the lower stalk starts to turn yellow.

Linen fiber is obtained by crushing the stalks of the flax plant.

CROATIAN CROPS
The fertile river valleys in the north have a warm climate that is ideal for growing fruits such as plums, apricots, and grapes. Flax is also grown, both for its fiber, which is made into linen clothing and canvas, and for its seeds, which are used for linseed oil.

___ *Find out more* ___

BREAKUP OF YUGOSLAVIA: *81, 124*
OIL AND COAL: *96, 152, 162*
TIMBER INDUSTRY: *26*

BELARUS AND THE BALTIC STATES

TUCKED AWAY in the northwestern corner of the vast landmass that was once the USSR, these four states are now independent countries. Three of the states – Estonia, Latvia, and Lithuania – border the chilly Baltic Sea. The fourth, Belarus, lies inland. The countries are low-lying, with hills, lakes, and marshes and a cool, moist climate. There are few natural resources in this thinly populated area. The peoples represent many different cultural groups and have suffered centuries of hardship from invasions and uprisings.

Tallinn, Estonia
- Jan 20°F (-7°C)
- July 61°F (16°C)
- Jan 1.5 in (39 mm)
- July 2.7 in (68 mm)

THINGS TO LOOK FOR ON THE MAP

Longest river: Western Dvina, Russian Federation/Belarus/Ukraine, 633 miles (1,018 km) *Map J8*

Highest point: Gaizin Kalns, Latvia, 1,024 ft (312 m) *Map H6*

Largest lake: L. Peipus, Estonia/Russian Federation, 1,400 sq miles (3,626 sq km) *Map I3*

ESTONIA

LATVIA

BELARUS

RUSSIAN FEDERATION

LITHUANIA

Vilnius, Lithuania
- Jan 18°F (-8°C)
- July 64°F (18°C)
- Jan 1.2 in (30 mm)
- July 2 in (51 mm)

FARMING AND FISHING
Lack of good farmland and a cold, damp climate limit the range of crops that can be grown in this region. The main crops are cereals, potatoes, and sugar beets. Cattle graze on the wet pastures. Fishing is an important industry in the Baltic States.

Tawny owls find shelter in the region's dense forests. At night they fly over farmland, hunting for prey.

INDEPENDENCE
The three Baltic States' struggle for independence during the 1980s played a large part in the USSR's breakup into many separate republics in 1991. At one point, as a form of protest, the people of these states formed a massive human chain across their lands. These Baltic peoples are now trying to forge closer links with neighboring countries, especially Finland and Poland.

BELARUS

THIS POOR, RURAL republic is sparsely populated and has few natural resources. However, living conditions have improved greatly since the 1960s when a drive began to develop industry and to provide better housing. In 1986, an explosion at the Chernobyl nuclear power station in Ukraine seriously affected people's health across the country. Two hundred years of Russian rule ended in 1991 with the breakup of the former USSR, and Belarus became an independent republic.

BELARUS

Capital city: Minsk

Area: 80,154 sq miles (207,600 sq km)

Population: 10,200,000

Official language: Belorussian

Major religions: Christian 68%, other 32%

Government: Multiparty democracy

Currency: Belarian rouble

Adult literacy rate: 98%

Life expectancy: 69 years

People per doctor: 244

Televisions: 314 per 1,000 people

PRIPET MARSHES

Huge areas of southern Belarus are covered in misty, marshy land. The Pripet Marshes form the largest expanse of marshland in Europe. Much of this area is forested with pine, alder, aspen, and oak trees, which supply a growing timber industry. Animals such as elk, lynx, wild boar, and grouse have made the marshes and forests their home.

LOCAL FOODS

Mushrooms and potatoes are staple foods. Potatoes cooked in different ways are eaten for breakfast, lunch, and dinner. Mushrooms and sour cream are served with meat dishes, such as baked rabbit or pork. In addition to being enjoyed fresh, mushrooms may be dried or salted and pickled.

Glassmaking
Glass is actually cooled liquid sand. It is made from sand, limestone, soda, and waste glass. These four ingredients are fed into a furnace where they are heated to produce molten glass.

Dried chanterelle mushrooms

Mushrooms flourish in the country's thick, damp forests, and mushroom-picking is so popular it has been called the national sport.

Boletus or cèpe mushrooms

INDUSTRY

Heavy industries such as oil-refining and machinery manufacturing are important to Belarus. Under the former USSR, large factories were located here to process raw materials from Russia and Ukraine. Reserves of useful minerals, such as oil, rock-salt, and types of sand have been discovered. The sands are used to make high-quality glassware.

The furnace is heated up to 2,550°F (1,400°C) to melt the raw ingredients.

As glass cools, it can be carefully shaped. To make sheets of glass, the liquid glass is floated on a river of molten tin. To make bottles, the glass is poured into bottle-shaped molds.

A lump of molten glass called a gob is dropped into a mold.

The liquid glass sinks to the far end.

Air is blown in to make the glass fill the mold.

The glass bottle is left to cool and set before being taken out of the mold.

MINSK

The centrally placed capital city has a history of changing fortunes. Although it was devastated by bombing in World War II, in peaceful times Minsk has blossomed as a center of government, education, culture, and communications. Recently, industrial growth has brought rapid expansion to the city. It is also the headquarters of the Commonwealth of Independent States (CIS), an organization that brings former Soviet states together.

EDUCATION

During the rule of the USSR, almost everyone in Belarus was taught to read and write. Education was free between the ages of 7 and 17. This firm educational foundation has led to the development of a strong literary and musical heritage within the republic.

Find out more

EDUCATION: *277*
EUROPEAN CITIES: *80*
FORMER USSR: *134*
OIL: *135, 152, 281*

ESTONIA	
Capital city: Tallinn	
Area: 17,423 sq miles (45,125 sq km)	
Population: 1,400,000	
Official language: Estonian	
Major religions: Christian 81%, other 19%	
Government: Multiparty democracy	
Currency: Kroon	
Adult literacy rate: 99%	
Life expectancy: 70 years	
People per doctor: 323	
Televisions: 480 per 1,000 people	

LATVIA	
Capital city: Riga	
Area: 24,938 sq miles (64,589 sq km)	
Population: 2,400,000	
Official language: Latvian	
Major religions: Christian 88%, other 12%	
Government: Multiparty democracy	
Currency: Lats	
Adult literacy rate: 99%	
Life expectancy: 70 years	
People per doctor: 333	
Televisions: 492 per 1,000 people	

LITHUANIA	
Capital city: Vilnius	
Area: 25,174 sq miles (65,200 sq km)	
Population: 3,700,000	
Official language: Lithuanian	
Major religions: Christian 88%, other 12%	
Government: Multiparty democracy	
Currency: Litas	
Adult literacy rate: 98%	
Life expectancy: 72 years	
People per doctor: 250	
Televisions: 459 per 1,000 people	

ESTONIA

A LAND OF FORESTS, low hills, and lakes, Estonia is the smallest of the Baltic States. Once a farming nation, the Soviets transformed Estonia into an urban, industrialized region. Today its industries include timber, shipbuilding, and food processing. Since becoming independent from the former USSR in 1991, tensions have sprung up between native Estonians and the third of the population that is Russian.

TALLINN
Roughly one-third of the people of Estonia live in or around the capital city of Tallinn. A regular flow of tourists comes to wander around the narrow, medieval streets of the city's old quarter.

LATVIA

SANDWICHED BETWEEN the other Baltic States, Latvia's central position, with easy access to the coast and three major ports, has done much to help trade. The cool, damp climate is well suited to dairy farming and meat production. Since becoming independent from the USSR in 1991, Latvia has concentrated on developing its farming, fishing, and timber industries, which had been overshadowed by large-scale factory production under the Soviets.

RIGA
The capital has been an important trading port since the Middle Ages. This is perhaps the most lively capital in the Baltic States and it is a vital cultural center. Latvia has strong historic links with Germany, and this can be seen at every turn in Riga – in the buildings, the fashions, and the many German visitors.

LITHUANIA

IN MANY WAYS, LITHUANIA stands apart from the other Baltic States. First, most of its people are native Lithuanians, whereas Estonia and Latvia have large Russian populations. Secondly, life here tends to be concentrated in the interior of the country, away from the coast. The third major difference lies in the fertile soil, which makes farming vital to the economy.

FOLK TRADITIONS
The songs, dances, music, and crafts of their folk history have great value for the people of the Baltic States. Keeping folk traditions alive became especially important as a way of maintaining a sense of identity under Soviet rule. Now, each country has annual folk festivals and parades.

Amber can be cut or polished to make jewelry.

A prehistoric fly has been caught in a tree's sticky resin, which then hardened into amber over time.

AMBER
Up to 90 percent of the world's amber comes from the shores of Lithuania, where it is found in sands dating back 50 million years. Amber is a fossilized tree resin, found in chunks of different shapes and sizes. Some is opaque and brown, but the most sought-after amber is yellow or gold. One small piece may contain the remains of insects or plants, trapped forever in the golden resin.

Find out more
EUROPEAN CITIES: *80*
FOLK TRADITIONS: *116, 118*
FORMER USSR: *134*
SHIPBUILDING: *183*

CENTRAL EUROPE

THE VERY HEART OF EUROPE consists of a compact block of four countries – Poland, the Czech Republic, Slovakia, and Hungary. Great plains and basins extend across this region, broken by low mountain ranges in the south. Over centuries, the country borders within Central Europe have been redrawn many times. This is partly because the flat landscape provides an easy target for invaders, and partly because four mighty empires have surrounded the area: Russia, Austro-Hungary, Prussia, and the Ottoman Turks. After World War II, Central Europe came under the communist control of the (now dissolved) Soviet Union, only gaining its independence since the late 1980s.

ROMAN CATHOLICISM
The celebration of saints' days and religious festivals is a regular feature of life in Central Europe, where Roman Catholicism is the main religion. This region was first converted to Christianity about 1,000 years ago. Repeated invasions have led its people to cling to their sense of national identity, and Roman Catholicism is an important part of this.

Each year, thousands of people visit the Black Madonna at Czestochowa, Poland's holiest shrine.

A Hungarian musician in traditional costume

FOLK MUSIC
Weddings, harvest festivals, Christmas, and other kinds of family and religious occasions are marked by music, song, and dance. Local styles vary widely, but traditions are particularly strong in rural areas. In Poland, for example, most musicians are amateurs, only picking up their instruments after a hard day's work in the fields. Slovakian folk music traditions survive mainly in the mountain villages, and are associated with brightly colored folk dress.

THE DANUBE RIVER
This major waterway links Slovakia and Hungary to Germany and the Rhine River in the west, and to the Black Sea in the southeast. In the past, the Danube has been a vital trading route for Central Europe, although river traffic has declined recently as trade with the former Soviet Union has fallen off sharply. However, the waters have been dammed to produce an important source of hydroelectric power – a dam at Gabcikovo now provides 15 percent of Slovakia's electricity.

How coal and lignite are formed

In swamps millions of years ago, plants died and were covered in mud.

The dead plant material was gradually compressed into peat.

Over centuries, layers of peat and rock sediment are laid down.

A chunk of lignite, also known as brown coal

Underlying bedrock

The weight of all the layers pushes downward.

The pressure turns the peat into lignite.

Over time, lignite may eventually become harder black coal.

Cabbage is very popular and is often eaten stuffed, or pickled as sauerkraut.

Potatoes are served with most main courses.

Root vegetables such as beets are used to make thick soups.

HEARTY FOOD
The more northerly areas of Central Europe tend to have warm summers but very cold winters. Plummeting temperatures have made heavy, warming foods popular here. Influences are strongly German, Austrian, and Russian, and potatoes, dumplings, soups, and meat stews are favorite dishes. To the south, Hungary has a more exotic tradition, featuring highly spiced foods such as goulash – its famous beef stew.

Meat, such as this Polish salt pork called oczek, is a central part of most meals.

LIGNITE
Brown coal, or lignite, is traditionally the main fuel in Central Europe. It is burned in power stations to produce much of the region's electricity. However, lignite is very rich in sulfur, and, when it is burned, its fumes join with moisture droplets in the air to produce a mild form of sulfuric acid, or "acid rain," which eats into stone buildings and destroys plant life. Air pollution in this region is made even worse by vehicle exhaust fumes – although car ownership is relatively unusual, the cars on the road are frequently old models running on inefficient engines.

A B C D E F G H I J K L

1 2 3 4 5 6 7 8 9 10 11 12

ARCTIC CIRCLE

POLAND

BALTIC SEA

Pomeranian Bay

Słupsk Gdynia *Gulf of Danzig* RUSSIAN FEDERATION LITHUANIA

Koszalin Gdańsk Elbląg L. Mamry Suwałki

Regu Słupia Wda Vistula L. Jeziorak Olsztyn Ełk L. Śniardwy

Szczecin Chojnice Grudziądz BELARUS

Drawa Piła Bydgoszcz Toruń Narew Ostrołęka Białystok

POMERANIA Noteć KUJAWY Włocławek Płońsk Bug PODLASIE

Gorzów Wielkopolski Odra L. Włocławskie Płock P O L A N D Krzna

Poznań Warta WARSAW Ursus

Zielona Góra Prosna Łódź Vistula

Bóbr Leszno Kalisz Piotrków Trybunalski Radom Lublin

Legnica Wrocław Odra Częstochowa Kielce Chełm

Wałbrzych SILESIA Opole Warta Bytom Vistula MAŁOPOLSKA San

Ústí nad Labem Liberec Sosnowiec Rzeszów

Karlovy Vary Hradec Králové Gliwice Katowice Tarnów Wisłoka

PRAGUE Pardubice Rybnik Kraków Dunajec GALICIA UKRAINE

Plzeň Ostrava Bielsko-Biała L. Solińskie

C Z E C H R E P U B L I C CARPATHIANS Gerlachovka

L. Vltava Tábor Jihlava Olomouc Žilina Poprad Prešov Ondava

Blanice Lužnice Brno Martin S L O V A K I A Košice Laborec

České Budějovice Jihlava MORAVIA Trenčín Váh Banská Bystrica Slaná Torysa

AUSTRIA Morava Nitra Banská Štiavnica Lučenec Tisza

Trnava Hron Miskolc Nyíregyháza

BRATISLAVA Ipeľ Debrecen

Gabčíkovo Danube BUDAPEST HUNGARIAN PLAIN

Győr Szombathely H U N G A R Y Szolnok Berettyó ROMANIA

Veszprém Székesfehérvár Kecskemét Körös

Zala L. Balaton Sárvíz Danube Tisza

Zalaegerszeg Kapos Szekszárd Szeged

SLOVENIA Nagykanizsa Baja

CROATIA Pécs YUGOSLAVIA

CZECH REPUBLIC

SLOVAKIA

HUNGARY

Warsaw, Poland
Jan 27°F (-3°C)
July 66.5°F (19.5°C)
Jan 1.1 in (27 mm)
July 3.8 in (96 mm)

50 100 150 km
25 50 75 100 miles

Brno, Czech Republic
Jan 29°F (-2°C)
July 67°F (19.5°C)
Jan 1.2 in (30 mm)
July 3.2 in (81 mm)

N

THINGS TO LOOK FOR ON THE MAP
Longest river: Vistula, Poland, 678 miles (1,091 km) *Map H2*
Highest point: Gerlachovka, Slovakia, 8,711 ft (2,655 m) *Map I8*
Largest lake: L. Balaton, Hungary, 231 sq miles (598 sq km) *Map G11*

Debrecen, Hungary
Jan 27°F (-3°C)
July 70°F (21°C)
Jan 1.3 in (34 mm)
July 2.2 in (56 mm)

WILD FOREST ANIMALS
Bialowieza National Park in Poland is northern Europe's largest area of woodland. Wild animals native to the forest include elk, deer, wolves, and bears, and conservation campaigns have done much to protect them. Special animal breeding programs have been set up here, and it is now the only natural breeding place for wild bison in Europe.

A bison cow feeding her calf in Bialowieza National Park, Poland

FOREST AREAS
Woodland covers a quarter of Central Europe. In some places, the forest dates back many thousands of years – there are centuries-old oaks near Poznan, in Poland. Acid rain has harmed trees across the region, but especially in Poland, where almost half the trees have been affected.

Ancient forest in Bialowieza National Park, Poland

POLAND

POLAND IS A MIX OF SCATTERED farming villages and magnificent medieval towns. This mainly flat country is larger than the other three countries of Central Europe put together. Once a land of many different peoples, warfare, migration, and border changes in 1945 have made the majority of people now Polish-speaking Roman Catholics. During the 1980s, Poland broke free from Soviet communist control and began the difficult journey toward a more democratic political system.

POLAND	
Capital city: Warsaw	
Area: 117,552 sq miles (312,680 sq km)	
Population: 38,800,000	
Official language: Polish	
Major religions: Christian 95%, other 5%	
Government: Multiparty democracy	
Currency: Zloty	
Adult literacy rate: 99%	
Life expectancy: 73 years	
People per doctor: 435	
Televisions: 413 per 1,000 people	

DEVELOPING INDUSTRIES

Poland is making the transition from a planned, Communist-style economy to a free market. It no longer relies on heavy industry such as shipbuilding and coalmining, but is starting to develop industries such as tourism (above) and electronics. A "shock therapy" program during the early 1990s helped the country transform its economy into one of the strongest in Central Europe, boosting hopes for acceptance to the EU. Poland joined the NATO alliance in 1999.

HEAVY INDUSTRY

Under the former Soviet Union, Poland was part of a vast centralized economy. For example, iron would be shipped into Poland, where it was then made into goods such as tractors for export to other parts of the Soviet Union. However, with the arrival of democracy, the country has attempted to find new markets for its goods in the West and Germany is now its main trading partner.

Market in Warsaw

Machinery: 30%
Manufacturing: 26%
Other: 21%
Textiles: 3%
Fuels: 5%
Chemicals: 6%
Food: 9%

Polish exports

Major exports include vehicles, machinery for industry and farming, and crops such as potatoes and other vegetables. Poland is also a major world exporter of coal and metals.

Painted wooden eggs are exchanged at Easter.

Wooden box carved with a traditional pattern

A TRADITIONAL WAY OF LIFE

This nation of small-scale farmers clung fiercely to its local traditions throughout the years of Soviet control. As a result, unlike other countries under Soviet rule, the many small farms were not merged into larger state-run farms. Today, traditions such as horse-drawn plowing are still common in parts of Poland. Local folk arts and crafts flourish, too. Embroidery and woodcarving are often used to decorate household objects, and wooden furniture may be colorfully painted.

MEDIEVAL KRAKOW

The superb medieval buildings found along the city streets of Krakow are a reminder that Poland was a major power during the 15th and 16th centuries, before it was divided up among other countries. Poland has some of the finest old churches, palaces, and public buildings in Europe. Many were lost or damaged during World War II, but Krakow's buildings escaped relatively unscathed. Unfortunately, this is also one of the most air-polluted cities in Europe, due mainly to the nearby Nowa Huta Steelworks.

The main market square in Krakow

AGRICULTURE

About a fifth of the nation's workforce is employed in agriculture. The most important products are potatoes, sugar beets, cereals, and livestock. Some farms specialize in commercial crops, but most grow some crops for selling and some for feeding the family. This is partly because most farms are still small and privately owned, often operated part-time, frequently by elderly or retired owners.

Find out more
AIR POLLUTION: *114*
POLITICAL SYSTEMS: *270–271*
ROMAN CATHOLICS: *274*
SOVIET UNION: *136*

CZECH REPUBLIC

As CENTRAL EUROPE'S most industrialized country, the Czech Republic has a modern economy and a good standard of living. From 1918 until 1993, the Republic was part of the union forming Czechoslovakia. By the 1950s, Czechoslovakia was under Soviet control, but democratic elections in 1990 led to its peaceful split into two countries – the Czech Republic and Slovakia. Much of the Republic lies on a high, mountain-ringed plateau, and its people have a strong national identity.

CZECH REPUBLIC

Capital city: Prague

Area: 30,449 sq miles (78,864 sq km)

Population: 10,200,000

Official language: Czech

Major religions: Christian 72%, other 28%

Government: Multiparty democracy

Currency: Czech koruna

Adult literacy rate: 99%

Life expectancy: 75 years

People per doctor: 345

Televisions: 447 per 1,000 people

Bridges over the Vltava River in Prague

PRAGUE
Not far from the historic core of this ancient city, one of the most beautiful capitals in Europe, a booming commercial center has sprung up. The capital is now host to ever-increasing numbers of visitors, coming for both pleasure and business. However, as elsewhere in Central Europe, air pollution is a major problem. It is caused mainly by factories in the commercial quarter, and in the extensive industrial suburbs beyond.

The main grain crops are wheat, and rye.

AGRICULTURE

In contrast to Poland, most of the agricultural land in the Czech Republic is worked by large farms owned by the state or by cooperatives. But, as in Poland, the changeover from a communist to a capitalist economy has proved difficult for farmers as they fight to compete in an open "market economy." Czech farms are very productive, with the highest grain yields in Central Europe. A large proportion of this grain is fed to livestock, since the Republic concentrates on meat and milk production.

THEATER
It is extremely appropriate that the Czech Republic's first president, Vaclav Havel, was also a playwright, since this region has a powerful theatrical tradition that stretches back to the 13th century. Contributions in other areas of the arts, notably music, literature, and film, have come from this region as well.

The Smetana Concert Hall, in Prague, was named after a Czech composer.

Intricate, highly decorated glassware

BOHEMIAN GLASS
For centuries, the fine sands found in this region, once known as Bohemia, have been used for glassmaking. Medieval craftsmen were praised for their breathtaking stained glass windows. Bohemian glass is renowned for its high quality and delicacy and is still made today.

The brewing process in the Czech Republic

Malted barley grains and water are fed into the mash tun.

When heated, the starch in the barley is converted into sugar.

Dried hops are added for flavor.

Yeast is added. It converts the sugar into alcohol.

The mixture is boiled with hops for 1–2 hours.

The beer stays in the fermenting tank for about a week.

The beer is bottled or stored in casks.

INDUSTRY

Beer is one of the best-known products to come out of this highly industrialized country. Its centuries-old brewing traditions have created such famous brands as Pilsner, made in Plzen since 1925, and Budweiss. Industry in general has a long history here. As long ago as the 1200s, mountains were excavated for their rich mineral deposits, and mining is still a major employer. Other important industries produce vehicles, explosives, plastics, and textiles.

Budweiser Budvar is a well-known export.

Find out more

AIR POLLUTION: *114*
GLASSMAKING: *112*
NEW EUROPEAN COUNTRIES: *81*
POLITICAL SYSTEMS: *270–271*

SLOVAKIA

ONCE THE EASTERN PART of Czechoslovakia, this small, beautiful country is much more rural than its highly industrialized neighbor, the Czech Republic. When Czechoslovakia broke free of Soviet control in 1990, the Slovaks felt they were being dominated by the wealthier Czechs and campaigned for independence, which came in 1993. The Slovakian economy was hit hard by the split because it relied on Czech money and resources. In this mountainous land, the Slovak population is divided between different valleys, and the country lacks a geographical focus. Most people speak Slovak, but various dialects are still spoken in the more isolated areas.

SLOVAKIA	
Capital city: Bratislava	
Area: 18,933 sq miles (49,036 sq km)	
Population: 5,400,000	
Official language: Slovak	
Major religions: Christian 72%, other 28%	
Government: Multiparty democracy	
Currency: Slovak koruna	
Adult literacy rate: 99%	
Life expectancy: 73 years	
People per doctor: 357	
Televisions: 402 per 1,000 people	

Distribution of timber and mining

Bratislava

⌐ Timber

Mining

BRATISLAVA

This city is one of the youngest capitals in the world – it became the new capital of its new country in 1993. This former residence of an archbishop has been made into a Presidential Palace. Bratislava is the only large city in Slovakia and historically has good links with Austria and Hungary. However, the city's good communications and modern industry have helped attract interest from foreign investors.

BANSKA STIAVNICA

As early as 1156, the term "terra banesium" (land of miners) was used to describe the region. Around 1237 Banská Štiavnica acheived legal status as a town, making it the oldest mining town in Slovakia. Then, in 1735, the first mining university in Europe was founded here. Ironically, economic stagnation in the 19th century, which halted the town's development, has led to a valuable tourist revenue in the 21st century, as the plan and architecture of the town have remained intact.

The castle used to control the mine revenues.

INDUSTRY

Today, one-third of the workforce has jobs in industry, as Slovakia fights for a place in the industrialized world. But the large industries set up by the former communist rulers have been difficult to break up. Some of the major Slovak industries include metallurgy and metalwork (which counts for 33% of all their industry), chemistry, and the alimentary industry, which is industrial production of food. Much of eastern Slovakia is still forested, so timber and papermaking are also important.

VILLAGE LIFE

This is a country of mountain villages and small towns. Slovakian farms are either tiny, family-run affairs, or they are large businesses run by the state or a group of people called cooperatives. As in the Czech Republic, the main crops are potatoes, sugar beets, and cereals, and many livestock are kept. Although Slovakia is traditionally rural, only a small proportion of the population is now employed in agriculture. There has been a great drive to develop industry, and many people are moving from the country to the towns.

Spis Castle is a national monument and is one of the largest castles in Central Europe.

Traditional wooden houses in Cicmany, Slovakia

UNSPOILED LANDSCAPE

The natural beauty of Slovakia's countryside gives it huge potential as a tourist destination as long as it remains unspoiled. Here are stunning mountain landscapes, castles perched on rocky outcrops, ancient walled towns, and mineral-rich spas. Great efforts are being made to develop the tourist trade, since there are as yet few facilities for visitors.

Find out more
CEREALS: *34, 122, 162*
NEW EUROPEAN COUNTRIES: *81*
POTATOES: *110*
SOVIET UNION: *136*

HUNGARY

A BROAD, FERTILE PLAIN sweeps across much of this country, while gentle hills and low mountains are found in the northern and western parts. The most southern country in Central Europe, Hungary has been home to many different peoples, including Germans, Slovaks, Serbs, Croats, Romanians, and Roma. Most Hungarians, however, are descended from the Magyars, who were fierce nomadic horsemen. After World War II, the communists established a harsh rule here, putting down a rebellion in 1956. A democratic government is now in place.

HUNGARY	
Capital city: Budapest	
Area: 35,652 sq miles (92,340 sq km)	
Population: 10,000,000	
Official language: Hungarian (Magyar)	
Major religions: Christian 93%, other 7%	
Government: Multiparty democracy	
Currency: Forint	
Adult literacy rate: 99%	
Life expectancy: 71 years	
People per doctor: 278	
Televisions: 437 per 1,000 people	

Flowers being gathered at a vast flower farm run by a cooperative

Paprika is used in many recipes, and Hungary grows over 40 percent of the world's paprika.

Paprika

Goulash was originally a basic dish eaten by shepherds.

A sauce of tomatoes, paprika, onions, and sour cream is served with fish, as well as on meat dishes such as goulash.

THERMAL SPRINGS AND SPAS
The grand architecture of Budapest's old Turkish baths is a distant echo of the country's past as part of the Ottoman Empire. There are baths and spas right across Hungary, centered on the hundreds of warm springs that gush naturally from the ground. Since ancient times, people have flocked to bathe in these mineral-rich waters, often seeking to cure their ailments.

AGRICULTURE
Since this fertile land is warmed by hot summers and short, mild winters, a wide variety of crops are found here. Cereals flourish, as in other parts of Central Europe, but Hungary also produces sunflowers, fruits, and vegetables, as well as olives, figs, and grapes – there is a thriving wine trade. However, the changeover from a communist to a capitalist economy has caused problems.

The parliament buildings on the Danube River in Budapest

CUISINE
The varied crops produced in Hungary mean that it has developed some distinctive dishes. Hungary's national dish is a famous beef and vegetable mix called goulash, served as a stew or a thick soup. A hot red pepper called paprika is added to give goulash its spicy flavor. Other examples of the rich and heavy cuisine include carp in paprika sauce, pastry filled with liver pâté, and grilled meats served with stuffed peppers.

BUDAPEST
If you were to take a cruise ship through Budapest along the great Danube River, you would discover that the capital is actually two cities. Buda, on one bank of the river, is the old royal capital, filled with ancient buildings. Across the water lies Pest, the heart of modern business and political life, where the government buildings are found. Budapest has more foreign visitors than any other Central European capital, and almost two-thirds of foreign money invested in Hungary is centered in the city.

The wine industry is modernizing with great speed and is continuing to expand its export markets.

INDUSTRY
Hungary's many industries produce metals, chemicals, and vehicles as well as textiles and electrical goods. Since a democratic government gained control in 1990, the country has had to compete in a worldwide market. Many firms have been privatized, and some industry has declined. However, Hungary's population has highly developed skills, especially in science and engineering, and it attracts more foreign investment per person than any other country in Central Europe.

Find out more
CEREALS: *34, 122, 162*
EUROPEAN PLAINS: *79*
POLITICAL SYSTEMS: *270–271*
WINE MAKING: *99*

UKRAINE, MOLDOVA, AND THE CAUCASIAN REPUBLICS

THE GRASSY STEPPE LOWLANDS of Ukraine and Moldova lie in the east of Europe. Farther east, the three mountainous Caucasian Republics of Georgia, Armenia, and Azerbaijan lie between the Black Sea and the Caspian Sea, cradled by the Caucasus Mountains. From the 17th century on, the Russian Empire dominated this region, and in the 20th century it became part of the USSR, regaining independence only in the 1990s. Fertile farmland and a wealth of natural resources have made this area one of the richest parts of the former USSR. The region's mountains give it protection from the extreme cold of the Russian winters, and this may help encourage a future tourist industry, particularly along the Black Sea coast.

Kiev, Ukraine
Jan 19°F (-7°C)
July 68°F (20°C)
Jan 2.3 in (58 mm)
July 3.6 in (91 mm)

These children at a wedding in Azerbaijan are from different ethnic groups.

MOLDOVA

Simferopol, Ukraine
Jan 31°F (-1°C)
July 71°F (22°C)
Jan 1.8 in (45 mm)
July 2.5 in (64 mm)

PEOPLES
The people of Ukraine and Moldova are mostly European, while more than 50 different ethnic groups exist in the Caucasian Republics. The USSR tried to wipe out differences between the peoples of its empire by forcing them to use the Russian language and by suppressing local culture. However, many of the people of this region have a proud and ancient history and have struggled to hold on to their own languages and culture.

NATURAL RESOURCES
Large deposits of coal, gas, and oil have made this region a leading producer of energy. In 1990, a quarter of all the energy used in the USSR came from this area. In addition to coal from the Donbass Basin in Ukraine, and oil and natural gas from the Caspian Sea off Azerbaijan, nuclear reactors, hydroelectric schemes, and wind-power plants have been built in the region. Metal ores such as iron, manganese, lead, zinc, copper, and uranium are also mined here.

Key
Coal mine
Gas field
Power station
Oil field

Azerbaijan's huge oil reserves are only now starting to be exploited.

THINGS TO LOOK FOR ON THE MAP

Longest river: Dnieper, Russian Federation/Belorussia/Ukraine, 2,285 km (1,420 miles) *Map G5*

Highest point: Shkhara, Georgia, 5,203 m (17,071 ft) *Map O12*

Largest lake: L. Sevan, Armenia, 1,414 sq km (546 sq miles) *Map Q14*

FARMING

The Caucasus Mountains protect the three republics from cold northerly winds and allow farmers to cultivate many exotic crops that cannot be grown elsewhere in the region. Crops such as tea, vines, nuts, tobacco, and cotton are sold to countries of the former USSR. Cattle and sheep are grazed on the high mountain pastures.

Figs

Tea

A variety of crops are grown in Armenia on the broad plain beneath Mount Ararat.

Crops such as tea, figs, almonds, and grapes flourish in the region's fertile soil and mild climate.

Fighting in Georgia has brought instability to the region.

CONFLICTS IN THE REGION

Since these countries gained their independence from the USSR, several conflicts have sprung up. Different ethnic groups are trying to stake their claim to territory, particularly in the Caucasian Republics. Tension exists in Ukraine and Moldova between the local ethnic groups and the large numbers of Russians who were brought into the area under Soviet rule.

Tbilisi, Georgia
Jan 37°F (3°C)
July 77°F (25°C)
Jan 0.7 in (17 mm)
July 1.8 in (46 mm)

Yerevan, Armenia
Jan -6°C (22°F)
July 26°C (78°F)
Jan 23 mm (0.9 in)
July 15 mm (0.6 in)

UKRAINE

GEORGIA

AZERBAIJAN

ARMENIA

0   50   100   150 km
0   25   50   75   100 miles

FERTILE PLAINS

Vast fields of cereal crops such as wheat, barley, oats, and corn cover the gently rolling, treeless steppes of Ukraine and Moldova. There is less rain here than in the Caucasian Republics, but broad, slow-flowing rivers, such as the Dnieper and the Dniester, provide plentiful water to irrigate the fertile, dark soil.

UKRAINE

WITH ITS VAST, FERTILE PLAINS and huge coal resources, Ukraine could be one of the most powerful countries of the former USSR. Following independence in 1991, relations with the Russian Federation were poor, because the two countries disagreed over ownership of weapons and ships belonging to the former USSR. Ethnic tension is a problem, too, as one in five of the population is Russian. In 1986, the world's worst nuclear accident, at the Chernobyl nuclear power plant, contaminated a huge area, affecting people, animals, and even the soil.

Kiev is situated on the Dnieper River, the Ukraine's main waterway.

HEAVY INDUSTRY
The Donbass Basin in eastern Ukraine is Europe's largest coalfield. It is also a major industrial area, with local coal and hydroelectricity powering one of the world's largest iron and steel industries. Factories process metals into finished products, including ships and machinery. However, many mines and factories are inefficient and new investment is needed.

CEREAL CROPS

Almost three-quarters of Ukraine is covered by fertile plains known as steppes. Much of this land is used to grow cereals. The huge quantities of wheat, corn, barley, oats, buckwheat, and rye Ukraine produces earned it the title "bread basket of the Soviet Union." However, farmers are not realizing the land's full potential due to a lack of new technology.

Oats

Rye

Wheat germ

Grains of cereal grow on the ears of each plant. This grain can be eaten whole or ground into flour.

KIEV
Ukraine's capital city has been overrun repeatedly by powerful invaders. In the 9th century, it was the center of a trading empire founded by the Vikings. It was invaded by the Mongols, and then by the Polish–Lithuanian Empire in the 14th century. In the 17th century, Kiev fell to the Russian Empire, later to become part of the USSR. Heavily bombed in World War II, Kiev was rebuilt in the 1950s–1960s and is now a center for communications, culture, and education.

Wholemeal bread

Caraway roll

Rye bread

Bread is the main food, eaten with every meal. Ukrainians bake a great variety of bread in all shapes, sizes, and textures.

Granary loaf

MOLDOVA

THIS SMALL, RURAL country was part of Romania before being taken over by the USSR in 1940. Although it is the most densely populated republic of the former USSR, native Moldovians make up fewer than two-thirds of the population. After independence ethnic unrest broke out and minority groups including Russians and Ukrainians wanted independence. Although there is now peace, tensions still remain.

Most of the population lives in country areas and makes a living from small-scale farming.

AGRICULTURE
Moldova's fertile soil and mild climate allow a variety of crops to be grown, such as corn, sunflower seeds, tobacco, and vines. Much of the produce is exported to countries of the former USSR to raise cash for vital imports such as oil – Moldova has few mineral resources of its own. Industries related to farming, such as food processing, are important, too.

Find out more
BREAKUP OF USSR: *136*
CEREALS: *34, 162*
COAL MINING: *96, 114, 162*
ROMANIA: *128*

GEORGIA

GEORGIA IS A LAND OF MOUNTAINS. The Caucasus range forms a barrier with Russia in the north, while snowy peaks overlook the Black Sea in the west. The country's sheltered fertile soil is suited to growing grapes, and Georgia is said to be the birthplace of wine. Its position between the Caspian and Black seas gives Georgia control over the movement of oil and other goods between countries in the region.

GEORGIA

Capital city: Tbilisi

Area: 26,911 sq miles (69,700 sq km)

Population: 5,000,000

Official language: Georgian

Major religions: Christian 83%, Muslim 11%, other 6%

Government: Multiparty democracy

Currency: Lari

Adult literacy rate: 99%

Life expectancy: 73 years

People per doctor: 238

Televisions: 473 per 1,000 people

TBILISI
The buildings of Georgia's capital rise steeply from the banks of the Kura River. Tbilisi is a uniquely multicultural city, with a synagogue, mosque, Georgian basilica, Armenian church, and a Zoroastrian fire-worshiper's temple within a few minutes walk of each other.

A LONG LIFE
Georgia holds a remarkable world record. More people here live to be over 100 years old than anywhere else in the world. Many centenarians continue to lead active lives, some up to the age of 120. Scientists cannot explain it, but they think that the combination of good climate, a healthy, balanced diet, a rural environment, and outdoor work are all part of the secret.

AZERBAIJAN

AZERBAIJAN

Capital city: Baku

Area: 33,436 sq miles (86,600 sq km)

Population: 7,000,000

Official language: Azerbaijani

Major religions: Muslim 87%, Christian 12%, other 1%

Government: Multiparty democracy

Currency: Manat

Adult literacy rate: 96%

Life expectancy: 71 years

People per doctor: 257

Televisions: 254 per 1,000 people

THIS HOT, DRY COUNTRY lies along the coast of the Caspian Sea. In the 8th century, the Persians named the area Azerbaijan, "the land of flames," when they saw burning natural gas seeping from the ground. The Azerbaijani people are Muslims who conquered the region in the 11th century. Tensions exist over the Nagorno Karabach region which is populated mainly by Armenians.

OIL PRODUCTION
Before oil was discovered in the Gulf states, Azerbaijan supplied half the world's oil output from oil fields near its capital, Baku. Today, villages on floating platforms house workers who drill for oil under the Caspian Sea. The transportation network and electricity supplies set up for the oil industry have helped the development of other industries, such as the manufacture of textiles.

ARMENIA

Capital city: Yerevan

Area: 11,506 sq miles (29,800 sq km)

Population: 3,500,000

Official language: Armenian

Major religions: Christian 94%, other 6%

Government: Multiparty democracy

Currency: Dram

Adult literacy rate: 99%

Life expectancy: 73 years

People per doctor: 298

Televisions: 218 per 1,000 people

ARMENIA

THIS TINY, MOUNTAINOUS state is the smallest of all the former republics of the USSR. Armenia was the first state in the world to adopt Christianity and is today bordered by three Islamic countries. With no access to the sea, Armenia relies on its neighbors for road and rail links to the outside world, but conflict with Azerbaijan has affected much-needed supplies of raw materials and fuel.

FARMING
Farming is the main source of employment in Armenia. Sheep and cattle graze on the high mountain slopes, while fruit trees and cereals are grown lower down.

Find out more

BREAKUP OF USSR: *136*
GAS: *163, 198, 211*
OIL: *135, 152, 281*
RELIGIONS: *274–275*

SOUTHEAST EUROPE

MUCH OF SOUTHEAST EUROPE consists of rugged mountains separated by deep river valleys. The area was called the Balkans, meaning "mountains" by the Turks, who ruled this area for 500 years until the early part of the 20th century. From 1918 until 1991, all these states, together with Croatia and Slovenia, were part of the newly created Yugoslavia; only Albania remained independent.Under the communist leader, General Tito, friction between the different cultures was kept under control. His death, and the fall of communism in Europe, allowed age-old rivalries to emerge. This led to the collapse of Yugoslavia and a vicious war that lasted from 1991–95.

CROSSROADS OF CULTURE

History has placed this area at the crossroads of many different empires and each has left its influence on the language, customs, and religions of the people. Here, in the Bosnian city of Mostar, church spires belonging to Orthodox Christian and Roman Catholic churches mingle with the mosque minarets of Islam, the religion introduced by the Turks in the 15th century. Today new cultural landscapes are being created as groups try to re-establish their national identity.

Belgrade, Yugoslavia
- Jan 32°F (0°C)
- July 73°F (23°C)
- Jan 1.9 in (47 mm)
- July 2.4 in (61 mm)

Sarajevo, Bosnia
- Jan 31°F (-1°C)
- July 68°F (20°C)
- Jan 2.6 in (66 mm)
- July 2.8 in (71 mm)

BOSNIA AND HERZEGOVINA

YUGOSLAVIA

THINGS TO LOOK FOR ON THE MAP

Longest river: Sava, Slovenia/Croatia/Bosnia and Herzegovina/Yugoslavia, 583 miles (938 km) *Map G4*

Highest point: Titov Vru, Macedonia, 9,013 ft (2,747 m) *Map J8*

Largest lake: L. Scutari, Yugoslavia/Albania, maximum size 205 sq miles (531 sq km) *Map H7*

ALBANIA

N

0   50   100   150 km
0   25   50   75   100 miles

Skopje, Macedonia
- Jan 34°F (1°C)
- July 73°F (23°C)
- Jan 1.5 in (39 mm)
- July 1.1 in (29 mm)

MACEDONIA

LANDSCAPE

Forests of deciduous and coniferous trees cloak the slopes of the mountains that dominate this area, as shown here in Montenegro. However, thin mountain soils are not well-suited to agriculture and only in the fertile plains surrounding the Danube, are crops grown in large quantities. A range of vegetables, such as cabbages, peppers, and beans, is grown there, while cattle graze on mountain pastures.

YUGOSLAVIA

WHEN THE FORMER YUGOSLAVIA broke up in 1991, the states of Serbia and Montenegro combined to form the new Federal Republic of Yugoslavia (from 2002 the official name is Serbia and Montenegro). Claiming to be the successor state of the former Yugoslavia, the new republic supported local Serbs in Croatia and Bosnia in the Bosnian War (1992–1995). Pressure from the United Nations and international armed forces have led to normal realtions being slowly resumed.

YUGOSLAVIA
Capital city: Belgrade

Area: 39,449 sq miles (102,173 sq km)

Population: 10,580,892

Official language: Serbian

Major religions: Christian 70%, Muslim 19%, other 11%

Government: Democracy

Currency: Dinar

Adult literacy rate: 93%

People per doctor: 500

Televisions: 259 per 1,000 people

BOSNIA AND HERZEGOVINA
Capital city: Sarajevo

Area: 19,741 sq miles (51,130 sq km)

Population: 4,200,000

Official language: Serbo-Croat

Major religions: Christian 50%, Muslim 40%, other 10%

Government: Democracy

People per doctor: 1167

Televisions: 41 per 1,000 people

Industry in Yugoslavia

- 🜁 Chemical
- △ Metallurgy
- ⚙ Light engineering
- ✿ Heavy engineering
- ⚡ Electronics
- ✳ Textiles
- ▯ Food processing
- ⚗ Pharmaceuticals

INDUSTRY
Serbia was once the industrial heartland of the former Yugoslavia, with extensive engineering, food, and textile industries. Reserves of coal, as well as hydroelectricity from the Danube and Drina rivers, provided power, while oil deposits in the north supplied one-third of oil needs. However, the pressure of sanctions has now severely damaged Serbian industry.

PEOPLE
More than 60 percent of people are Serbs, with Hungarians in Vojvodina, and Albanians in and around Kosovo. Yugoslavs speak a variety of languages. Serbs and Montenegrins speak a similar language and write in the Cyrillic script used in Russian. Hungarians and Albanians use the Latin alphabet, as used in English, and speak separate, unrelated languages. Voting papers, being handed in here, are printed in all languages.

Green and red peppers

Raznjici is made with skewers of grilled lamb.

Skewer

DISHES OF SERBIA
A wide variety of tasty dishes are eaten in Serbia. *Raznjici*, grilled lamb with sweet peppers, shown here, is usually served with a bowl of yogurt. Meatballs served with onions and cream, called *cevapcici*, and vegetables such as cabbage stuffed with meat, onions, herbs, and garlic, are all popular dishes.

BOSNIA AND HERZEGOVINA

BOSNIA AND HERZEGOVINA WAS THE LAST of the former republics of Yugoslavia to declare independence, in 1992. For centuries, the area contained a mixture of Muslim Bosnians, Catholic Croats and Orthodox Serbs. After independence, tensions led to a civil war. Many thousands of people were killed on all sides. The war ended in 1995 and the country was split into two separate halves – a Serb republic and a Muslim-Croat federation.

CITY OF SARAJEVO
By 1990, the ancient town of Sarajevo had grown into a large, modern city. But war exposed the city to Serb gunfire from the surrounding hills, and many citizens were killed. Those that remained led a primitive existence, often with no food, heat, or proper housing.

ETHNIC CLEANSING
Serbs fighting in Bosnia undertook a policy of ethnic cleansing. This involved removing, or "cleansing," Muslims and Croats from areas they inhabited alongside Serbs. Thousands of non-Serbs were murdered. Others were frightened into leaving their homes and seeking safety in more welcoming countries. Many Muslims sought refuge in Germany and Turkey.

Bosnian refugees in Europe

Germany: 330,000
Sweden: 86,445
Turkey: 36,800
Italy: 36,000

Muslim girls and women traditionally wear a headscarf to cover their hair.

Find out more
BREAKUP OF YUGOSLAVIA: *81, 124*

RELIGIONS: *274–275*

DANUBE RIVER: *79*

MACEDONIA

ALBANIA

MACEDONIA	
Capital city: Skopje	
Area: 9,929 sq miles (25,715 sq km)	
Population: 1,900,000	
Official language: Macedonian	
Major religions: Christian 64%, Muslim 26%, other 10%	
Government: Democracy	
Currency: Denar	
Adult literacy rate: 94%	
Life expectancy: 73 years	

ALBANIA	
Capital city: Tirana	
Area: 10,579 sq miles (27,400 sq km)	
Population: 3,100,000	
Official language: Albanian	
Major religions: Muslim 70%, Christian 30%	
Government: Democracy	
Currency: Lek	
Televisions: 109 per 1,000 people	

MACEDONIA

LANDLOCKED MACEDONIA has been controlled by its larger neighbors for many centuries. Historically linked to Greece, it has more recently been a part of Bulgaria and Yugoslavia. Since the country's independence however, the greatest threat has come from ethnic tensions between Macedonian Slavs and ethnic Albanians. In this part of the Balkans, the warm climate allows the cultivation of early fruit crops and industrial crops such as rice, cotton, and tobacco. However, its location also means that fuel, machinery, and manufactured goods have to be imported.

Freshwater carp

EARTHQUAKES

The capital city of Skopje is located where several geological fault lines meet, making it a likely place for earthquakes. In fact, earth tremors in Skopje are frequent, and the city has been destroyed four times in its history. In 1963 an earthquake registering 6.8 on the Richter scale destroyed much of the city. Fortunately, the Turkish area, parts of which date from 1392, survived the destruction.

LAKELAND AREAS

The mountainous area of southwestern Macedonia contains two of Europe's most beautiful freshwater lakes. When the country had more tourists, visitors flocked to Lake Ohrid, and to Lake Prespa, to enjoy the scenery and visit the ancient towns along the shores. Both lakes are teeming with fish, particularly carp, trout, and eels, which are used for local fish dishes. Colonies of pelicans and cormorants also feed on fish from Lake Prespa.

ALBANIA

ONE OF THE POOREST countries in Europe, Albania is mostly rugged mountains. For much of its history, the country was ruled by the Ottoman Turks, who withdrew in 1913 leaving no roads, railways, or industries. In the last century, Albania was ruled by a fascist king and a communist dictator. Democracy has been hindered by corruption and economic hardships. Violence erupted in 1997 after the collapse of an insurance scheme in which many Albanians had invested.

Employment

Jobs are scarce in Albania, and rates of pay are low. Over half of those with jobs work in agriculture, while the rest work in industry or services, such as education. Recently, thousands of people have moved to Greece or Italy to look for work.

Services: 21% Industry: 25% Agriculture: 54%

FAMILY LIFE

The family is an important part of Albanian life and, until recently, men were encouraged by the state to father large families. From an early age, Albanians are taught the importance of the promised word, known as *besa*. To break one's word, in a business deal for example, is considered a disgrace.

COMMUNISM

From 1944–1985, Albania was led by the communist leader Enver Hoxha. Under his rule, Albania was cut off from the rest of Europe. The borders with Yugoslavia and Greece were sealed, and no contact with Italy was permitted. All trade after 1960, through ports in Durres and Vlore, was with China. The Communists developed heavy industry at the expense of agriculture, leaving the country poor and undeveloped. This mural at Tirana Museum represents the people's struggle.

Find out more
EARTHQUAKES: *13*
HYDROELECTRIC POWER: *108*
MEDITERRANEAN CLIMATE: *15*
POLITICAL SYSTEMS: *270–271*

ROMANIA AND BULGARIA

DIVIDED BY THE MIGHTY Danube River, which flows eastward along most of the shared border to the Black Sea, Romania and Bulgaria have much in common. The most fertile land is found in the valley of the Danube, while forests of oak, pine, and fir grow on the sides of the Carpathian and the Balkan mountains. For hundreds of years, Black Sea ports, around areas such as Constanta and Burgas, have provided access to trade routes and they remain important for international shipping.

TOURIST ATTRACTIONS
Picturesque landscapes and colorful folk traditions make Romania popular with tourists. The legend of Count Dracula, from the forested region of Transylvania, shown here, attracts tourists who come to visit his castle. Black Sea beaches as well as mountain ski resorts cater to both summer and winter visitors.

ROMANIA

Bucharest, Romania
Jan 27°F (-3°C)
July 73°F (23°C)

Jan 1.8 in (46 mm)
July 2.1 in (53 mm)

THINGS TO LOOK FOR ON THE MAP
Longest river: Danube, Germany/Austria/Hungary/Yugoslavia/Romania/Bulgaria, 1,771 miles (2,850 km) *Map F10*
Highest point: Musala, Bulgaria, 9,597 ft (2,925 m) *Map F12*
Largest lake: L. Razim, Romania, 151 sq miles (390 sq km) *Map L8*

Sofia, Bulgaria
Jan 30°F (-1°C)
July 71°F (22°C)

Jan 1.4 in (36 mm)
July 2.7 in (68 mm)

Women hand sort the tobacco leaves, ready for making cigarettes and pipe tobacco.

AGRICULTURE
Much of Bulgaria's land is used for farming. In the south, around the Maritsa River valley, tobacco plants are grown and then dried into tobacco for export. In Romania, corn is the major crop, and it is used for food as well as fuel. The climate in parts of both countries is suitable for growing grapes to export as wine.

BULGARIA

UKRAINE
HUNGARY
MOLDOVA
CARPATHIAN MTS.
TRANSYLVANIA
ROMANIA
YUGOSLAVIA
CARPATHIAN MTS.
UKRAINE
BLACK SEA
BULGARIA
BALKAN MTS.
MACEDONIA
RHODOPE MTS.
GREECE
TURKEY

Satu Mare
Baia Mare
Botoşani
Suceava
Sângeorz-Băi
Bistriţa
Sireţ
Iaşi
Oradea
Somes
Cluj-Napoca
Piatra-Neamţ
Vaslui
Bistriţa
Târgu Mureş
Bacău
Bârlad
Arad
Alba Iulia
Copşa Mică
Mureş
Timişoara
Deva
Sibiu
Sfântu Gheorghe
Focşani
Galaţi
Prut
Timiş
Braşov
Brăila
Reşiţa
Tulcea
Danube Delta
Târgu Jiu
Râmnicu Vâlcea
Târgovişte
Buzău
Buzău
L. Razim
Băile Herculane
Pitești
Ploiești
L. Sinoe
Drobeta-Turnu-Severin
Ialomiţa
Slobozia
Danube
Slatina
BUCHAREST
Craiova
Călăraşi
Constanţa
Alexandria
Argeş
Danube-Black Sea Canal
Eforie Nord
Vidin
Jiu
Giurgiu
Mangalia
Danube
Corabia
Ruse
Olt
Dobrich
Mikhaylovgrad
Razgrad
Golden Sands
Pleven
Varna
Vratsa
Iskŭr
Lovech
Shumen
Kamchiya
Nesebŭr
Pravets
Gabrovo
Sliven
Burgas
SOFIA
Kazanlŭk
Yambol
Sozopol
Pernik
Stara Zagora
Tundzha
L. Iskŭr
Pazardzhik
Rila
Plovdiv
Musala
Velingrad
Khaskovo
Maritsa
Struma
Arda
Sandanski

0 25 50 75 100 125 km
0 25 50 75 miles

ROMANIA

ONCE THE FRONTIER OF THE ROMAN EMPIRE, Romania is one of the largest countries in Europe. The Carpathian Mountains form an arc across the country, curving around the region of Transylvania. Elsewhere the land is rich and fertile. Romania became independent from Turkey in 1878, but its borders have been redrawn several times as a result of war. A revolution in 1989 overthrew a harsh communist government and today Romania is struggling to improve the life of its people. Although Romanians can now travel and worship in freedom, there is high unemployment and food has become more expensive.

ROMANIA	
Capital city: Bucharest	
Area: 88,934 sq miles (230,340 sq km)	
Population: 22,300,000	
Official language: Romanian	
Major religions: Christian 85%, other 15%	
Government: Multiparty democracy	
Currency: Leu	
Adult literacy rate: 97%	
Life expectancy: 70 years	
People per doctor: 556	
Televisions: 223 per 1,000 people	

POLITICS
From 1965 until his overthrow and execution in 1989, communist leader Nicolae Ceausescu ruled Romania. During his brutal dictatorship, he tried to boost the population by encouraging women to have large families. Many people could not afford to keep their babies. The plight of Romanian orphans attracted internatonal attention and many were adopted abroad.

FOREIGN ORDERS
In order to modernize old industries and create new jobs, foreign companies are being encouraged to set up business in Romania. France, Spain, Italy, the US, and South Korea all now have manufacturing plants in or near Bucharest.

WOODEN BUILDINGS
The vast forests of Romania provide an ideal material for building, and wooden houses and churches are found throughout the country. Many are surrounded by wooden fences and elaborately carved gateways. The walls are constructed using horizontal planks of wood, unlike in the rest of Europe, where they are placed vertically. House styles vary from one region to another. The steep-roofed home shown here is from a snowy area in the Carpathian Mountains; homes in wine-growing areas would have large cellars to store wine and fruit from the orchards.

Homes in the mountains have steep roofs so that snow will slide off.

Wood from pine, beech, or spruce trees is used to build houses.

Columns may be hand-carved in a local design.

Houses are built on foundations of local stone to prevent the wood from rotting.

Rooms are decorated with carved wooden furniture and brightly painted plates.

Bedspreads are embroidered with traditional designs.

PEOPLE OF ROMANIA
Romania is home to many peoples, with Hungarians and Germans sharing the land with native Romanians. Ukrainians and Turks settled areas near the Black Sea coast, now popular as vacation destinations. In the past, people lived and worked on the land, but with the growth of industry the majority now live in Bucharest, the capital, and other towns and cities.

ROMA POPULATIONS
Despite their name, the 500,000 Roma who live in Romania belong to a different ethnic group from the rest of the population. Although they used to live as nomads, they are now mostly settled on the outskirts of towns.

Find out more

CITIES: *80*
COUNTRIES OF EASTERN EUROPE: *81*
POLITICAL SYSTEMS: *270–271*

BULGARIA

FOR MUCH OF ITS HISTORY, the area that is now Bulgaria has lived in the shadow of stronger neighbors. The Greeks, Romans, and Turks have all ruled here, and from 1944–1989 Bulgaria was part of the Russian communist bloc. Most of the population is made up of Bulgars, with sizeable minorities of Macedonians and Turks. Since the move to democracy, state-run farms have been reorganized, and western tourists are being encouraged to visit the old towns as well as lakes and resorts on the Black Sea.

BULGARIA	
Capital city: Sofia	
Area: 42,683 sq miles (110,550 sq km)	
Population: 8,200,000	
Official language: Bulgarian	
Major religions: Christian 85%, Muslim 13%, Jewish 1%, other 1%	
Government: Multiparty democracy	
Currency: Lev	
Adult literacy rate: 94%	
Life expectancy: 71 years	
People per doctor: 303	
Televisions: 398 per 1,000 people	

Women wear traditional costumes during the Festival of the Roses.

Roses are picked before fully open to avoid exposure to the sun.

Damask rose

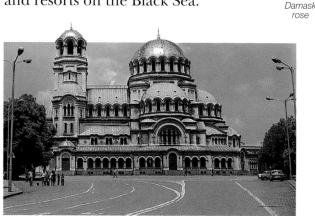

CITY OF SOFIA
The capital city of Sofia is home to more than a million people. Set in an area of mountains and lowland dairy farming, the city is a thriving industrial center. It is also a showcase for many fine Roman buildings, as well as the Alexander Nevsky Cathedral, shown here, which was built to honor Russian soldiers who liberated Sofia from Turkish rule in 1878. Bulgaria has a good transportation system. Many people in Sofia travel by trolleys that get their power from overhead electric cables.

ROSE GROWING
Situated in the foothills of the Balkan Mountains, near the town of Kazanluk, lies the Valley of the Roses. Fields of roses are grown here for their essential oil, called attar, which is used to make perfume. At dawn each day in May and June, before the sun has time to dry out their oil, blossoms of the damask rose are picked and the petals packed into sacks. These are taken by donkey cart to a distillery, where they are made into attar. Every June there is a festival to celebrate the rose harvest.

FESTIVAL MASKS
Folk customs play an important part in keeping Bulgarian traditions alive. Many towns have their own festival, featuring music and parades. People often make and paint their own masks, and decorate them with beads and ribbons.

Bulgarian industries

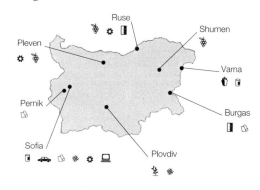

Ruse
Shumen
Pleven
Varna
Pernik
Burgas
Sofia
Plovdiv

NUCLEAR POWER
Bulgaria does not have enough coal or power from its hydroelectric plants to provide itself with energy. Forty percent of its electricity now comes from the Kozloduy nuclear power station. Because the station was built by the Soviet Union, and lies in an earthquake zone, there has been great concern about its safety. Since 1990, the European Union has helped make the plant safer.

ECONOMY
Bulgaria lacks the high-grade coal and iron necessary to support heavy industry. In the past, its factories relied on cheap supplies of coal and oil from the former USSR. Now they have to buy these on the open market. Bulgaria has been forced to arrange large loans from the West to finance development of new industries, such as computer technology. Textile mills and food processing are important.

🚗 Vehicle assembly	🗋 Steel
✿ Engineering	✼ Textiles
⚘ Tobacco	🍶 Shipbuilding
▮ Oil refining	🗐 Food processing
❦ Wine	🖥 Computers

Find out more

BREAKUP OF USSR: *136*
COUNTRIES OF EASTERN EUROPE: *80*
POLITICAL SYSTEMS: *270–271*

GREECE

GREECE HAS A RICH HISTORY stretching back thousands of years. Yet the modern nation state only won its independence from the Turks in 1832, and it took control of some islands as recently as 1947. With its mountainous terrain, more than 2,000 scattered islands, and lack of natural resources, Greece is one of the two poorest members of the European Union. However, its large shipping fleet and booming tourism industry have meant that the country was judged sufficiently financially reliable to become a member of the European Single Currency.

GREECE

Capital city: Athens

Area: 50,961 sq miles (130,850 sq km)

Population: 10,600,000

Official language: Greek

Major religions: Christian 98%, Muslim 1%, other 1%

Government: Multiparty democracy

Currency: Euro

Adult literacy rate: 97%

Life expectancy: 78 years

People per doctor: 250

Televisions: 477 per 1,000 people

Main tourist nationalities

The majority of tourists visiting Greece are European, although large numbers of people also travel to Greece from North America and Australasia.

Germany	UK	Italy	Netherlands	Other
20%	19%	6%	5%	50%

TOURISM

More than 12 million tourists a year come to Greece to enjoy the beautiful island scenery, the historic monuments, and the summer sun. Hotels, shops, and restaurants employ thousands of people to cater to the visitors, whose spending boosts the national economy enormously. The Greek government encourages tourism by giving grants for hotel building and the many Aegean islands are linked together by a comprehensive network of ferries. However, some islands are being developed too rapidly, and suffer from problems such as water shortages.

Vacationers enjoying the beach on the island of Samos

SHIPPING

The cheapest and easiest way to travel around Greece is still by boat. Fleets of merchant ships connect the many islands with the mainland, moving supplies and industrial products, while ferries carry vehicles, local people, and tourists. Ship owners have built up huge fleets of ships, with the result that Greece now has the largest merchant fleet in the world.

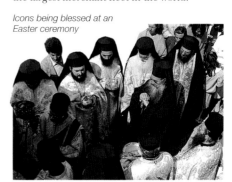

Icons being blessed at an Easter ceremony

GREEK ORTHODOX CHURCH

The state religion of Greece is Greek Orthodox, making it the only officially Orthodox Christian country in the world. Almost every Greek is a member of the church. Priests play an important part in national events and are recognized as leaders of their local communities. The churches are not allowed statues, but many contain holy pictures of saints known as icons.

Olives are treated, pickled, and fermented before being eaten whole.

Olives can be eaten when green or black, but must ripen to black when used for oil.

To make olive oil, the olives are ground to a thick paste before being pressed.

ATHENS

The ancient capital of Greece is dominated by the Acropolis and the dramatic ruins of the Parthenon temple. Much of the city, however, consists of modern buildings, for many people have left the countryside to seek employment in the city. As a result, Athens is one of Europe's most polluted cities; cars are banned from entering the city on certain days of the week in order to reduce the smog level.

Olive trees are usually quite small, but they can live for hundreds of years.

Olives are harvested in the fall. The trees are shaken by hand or by machine, and the olives are gathered up in large nets and sorted.

FARMING

Only a third of the mountainous terrain of Greece can be farmed, and much of the soil is poor. Many people are needed to work this land – nearly one-fifth of the Greek workforce is employed in agriculture, which is more than anywhere else in the European Union. The most important crop is olives, grown on hillsides across the country. Greece is the third biggest producer of olive oil after Italy and Spain, as well as a major producer of grapes and wine, citrus and other fruits, figs, cotton, tomatoes, and tobacco.

A B C D E F G H I J K L

1 2 3 4 5 6 7 8 9 10 11 12 13

Thessaloniki, Greece
Jan 42°F (5.5°C)
July 80°F (26.5°C)
Jan 1.7 in (44 mm)
July 0.9 in (22 mm)

BULGARIA

MACEDONIA

THRACE

TURKEY

Drama
Serres
Xanthi
Komotini
Kilkis
Kavala
Alexandroupoli
L. Prespa
Florina
Edessa
Vardar
Struma
Kastoria
L. Vegoritis
Veroia
Thessaloniki
Thasos
L. Kastorias
Kozani
Aliákmonas
Katerini
Polygyros
Samothraki
Grevena
Thermaic Gulf
Singitic Gulf
Gulf of Kassandra
Mt. Olympus
Pineios
GREECE
Ioannina
Larisa
Corfu
Corfu
Igoumenitsa
Trikala
PINDUS MOUNTAINS
Karditsa
AEGEAN
Ayios Evstratios
Limnos
Arta
Volos
Lesvos
Preveza
Sporades
Skiathos
Mytilini
Lefkada
Lamia
Stylis
Lefkada
Loutra Aidipsou
Skiros
Astakos
Acheloos
Amfissa
Kymi
Mesolongi
L. Trichonida
Itea
Delphi
Évvoia
Chios
Lixouri
Patrai
Gulf of Corinth
Chalkida
Chios
Argostoli
Kefallonia
Gulf of Patraï
Marathon
Andravida
Corinth
ATHENS
Karystos
Zakynthos
Kyllini
Corinth Canal
Piraeus
Andros
Samos
Pyrgos
PELOPONNESE
Mycenae
Epidauros
Lavrio
Tinos
Ikaria
Samos
Zakynthos
Katakolo
Olympia
Kea
Mykonos
Tripoli
Nafplio
Siros
GREECE
Kalamata
Sparti
Leonidi
Kithnos
Cyclades
Kos
Pilos
Gytheio
Serifos
Paros
Kos
Gulf of Messini
Sifnos
Naxos
Amorgos
Rhodes
Gulf of Laconia
Neapoli
Milos
Ios
Astipálaia
Monólithos
Kythira
Thira
Rhodes
Karpathos

Athens, Greece
Jan 49.5°F (9.5°C)
July 82.5°F (28°C)
Jan 2.4 in (62 mm)
July 0.2 in (6 mm)

Naxos, Greece
Jan 54°F (12.5°C)
July 76.5°F (24.5°C)
Jan 3.6 in (91 mm)
July 0.1 in (2 mm)

N

0 25 50 75 km
0 25 50 miles

SEA OF CRETE
Chania
Rethymno
Knossos
Irakleio
Crete
Agios Nikolaos
MEDITERRANEAN SEA

ARCTIC CIRCLE

THINGS TO LOOK FOR ON THE MAP

Longest river:
Aliákmonas, 195 miles (314 km) *Map D3*

Highest point:
Mt. Olympus, 9,570 ft (2,917 m) *Map D4*

Largest lake: L. Prespa, Greece/Albania/ Macedonia, 112 sq miles (290 sq km) *Map C2*

World's narrowest navigable strait:
between Évvoia and the mainland, 131 ft (40 m) wide *Map F7*

ALBANIA
IONIAN SEA
Ionian Islands

ANCIENT GREEK HISTORY
The remains of temples and other buildings from Greece's long and complex history can still be seen today. From about 2000 BC, advanced civilizations existed on Crete and on the mainland at Mycenae. By the 5th century BC, powerful city states emerged, including Athens and Sparta. Philosophers, mathematicians, architects, and dramatists contributed to a rich culture that spread around the Mediterranean.

Signs of Greece's rich classical past are revealed in its many ancient ruins, such as this temple of Apollo at Delphi.

Find out more
EUROPEAN UNION: *81, 273*
MEDITERRANEAN LANDSCAPE: *79*
ORTHODOX CHURCH: *274*
WINE MAKING: *99*

ASIA

STRETCHING FROM THE frozen Arctic to the hot Equator, Asia is by far the world's largest and most mountainous continent. Much of the land is barren, with vast, empty deserts in southwest and central Asia, and the remote, windswept plateau of Tibet to the north of the Himalayan mountains. Asia also has some of the world's most fertile plains and valleys beside rivers that include the Mekong, Indus, and Euphrates. In Southeast Asia, the land is mainly mountainous or covered in tropical rain forests that are teeming with wildlife. Away from the mainland, scattered on either side of the Equator, lie thousands of islands, many of them volcanic.

SIBERIA

Most of Siberia, the Asian part of Russia, is bitterly cold in winter. In the north lies the tundra, where part of the soil has been frozen since the end of the last Ice Age. Beneath its surface there are vast supplies of minerals. To the south lies the world's largest coniferous forest. This cold forest makes way for a dry grassland area, known as steppe, which forms Russia's main farming region.

Highest temperature: Tirat Zevi, Israel, 129°F (54°C)

THE YANGTZE RIVER

From its source in the Tanggula Mountains on the plateau of Tibet, the Yangtze River flows through mountainous land for most of its course. On its final stages, it follows the southern edge of the Great Plain of China until it reaches the East China Sea. In the flatter areas, the Yangtze supplies water for irrigation. In the past, flooding has caused thousands of deaths.

CENTRAL DESERTS

Unlike most deserts, the Takla Makan and Gobi in central Asia have hot summers, but extremely cold winters. Much of their landscape is made up of bare rock, with huge expanses of shifting sand. Vegetation is sparse, except in river valleys, as shown here in the Takla Makan. Some animals, including wild camels, can survive cold winters in the Gobi.

A Bactrian camels has two humps.

THE HIMALAYAS

The Himalayas, right, form a massive land barrier between the Indian Subcontinent and Tibet. The range is permanently snow-capped and contains the world's highest peak, Mount Everest. The mountains began to form about 50 million years ago when a moving plate, carrying the Subcontinent, began to push against the Eurasian plate. When the plates collided, the edge of the Indian plate was forced under the Eurasian plate, and the seabed in between was folded up to form the Himalayas.

HIMALAYAS
EURASIAN PLATE
INDIAN PLATE

Lowest temperature:
Verkhoyansk, Russian
Federation, -90°F (-68°C)

N

ARCTIC OCEAN

KARA SEA

Severnaya
Pioneer I. Zemlya
October
Revolution I.
Bolshevik I.
Vil'kitskiy Strait

LAPTEV SEA

New Siberian Is.

EAST SIBERIAN SEA

GYDA
PENINSULA

TAYMYR PENINSULA

L. Taymyr

CENTRAL
SIBERIAN
PLATEAU

Olenek

Khatanga

Wrangel I.

*CHUKCHI
SEA*

Yenisey

Taz

Lena

Yana

• Verkhoyansk

Indigirka

Kolyma

Omolon

OLOY
RANGE

C. Navarin

*BERIAN
LAIN*

Lower Tunguska

S I B E R I A

VERKHOYANSK RANGE

Vilyny

Aldan

KOLYMA RANGE

KORYAK RANGE

C. Olyutorskiy

Karaginskiy Is.

BERING SEA

Stony Tunguska

Ob'

Angara

Lena

Vitim

Olekma

STANOVOY RANGE

DZHUGDZHUR RANGE

Shantar Is.

*SEA OF
OKHOTSK*

KAMCHATKA

C. Sivuchiy

Irtysh

L. Baikal

Amur

Sakhalin

Kurile Is.

**THINGS TO LOOK FOR
ON THE MAP**

Area: 17,251,315 sq miles
(44,680,718 sq km)

Highest point: Mt. Everest,
China/Nepal, 29,029 ft
(8,848 m) *Map H11*

Longest river: Yangtze,
China, 3,430 miles
(5,520 km) *Map K10*

Largest lake: Caspian Sea,
Azerbaijan/Iran/
Turkmenistan/Kazakhstan/
Russian Federation,
146,101 sq miles
(378,400 sq km) *Map D8*

Largest island: Borneo,
286,969 sq miles
(743,250 sq km) *Map K14*

KAZAKH
UPLANDS

ALTAI MOUNTAINS

L. Uvs

Hulun
Nur

Songhua

MANCHURIAN
PLAIN

*SEA OF
JAPAN*

Balkhash

Issyk-Kul

TIEN SHAN

Tarim

GOBI DESERT

ALTUN MTS.

Hokkaido

Oki Is.

Honshu

O   P   Q   R   S

TAKLA MAKAN
DESERT

MIRS

KUNLUN SHAN

TANGGULA MTS

Yellow River (Huang He)

*YELLOW
SEA*

GREAT
PLAIN OF
CHINA

*EAST
CHINA
SEA*

Kyushu

KARAKORAM

PLATEAU
OF TIBET

RED
BASIN

Yangtze

Brahmaputra

▲ Mt. Everest

HIMALAYAS

Hongshui He

PACIFIC OCEAN

THAR
ESERT

Ganges

Irrawaddy

Mekong

Taiwan

*Bay of
Bengal*

Hainan

Luzon

Andaman
Is.

SOUTH
CHINA
SEA

Yap

Sri
Lanka

Nicobar
Is.

SULU
SEA

Mindanao

Palau

INDIAN

Sumatra

Borneo

CELEBES
SEA

JAVA SEA

Sulawesi

BANDA
SEA

New Guinea

15

Java

Timor

*ARAFURA
SEA*

16

OCEAN

H   I   J   K   L   M   N

THE RING OF FIRE

Volcanoes erupt so often on the rim of
land and islands around the Pacific that the
region is called the "Ring of Fire." The most
famous eruption took place in 1883, when
the volcanic island of Krakatoa, west of Java,
erupted. The explosion was so loud it was
heard in Australia. In 1928, a new volcano
burst into life on the island. It was named
Anak Krakatoa, meaning "son of Krakatoa."

PEOPLES OF ASIA I

OF ALL THE CONTINENTS, Asia has the largest population with the greatest variety of cultures. The history of civilization here stretches back for many thousands of years. Cities and writing, the development of which are closely connected, first appeared in Asia. More than 5,000 years ago the earliest cities, such as Babylon, emerged in the valley of the Tigris and Euphrates rivers, an area known as Mesopotamia (modern-day Iraq). Today, Asia contains over 60 percent of the world's population, much of which is concentrated in the southern and eastern regions of the continent. Although most of the people are farmers, city populations are growing very rapidly.

Stone reliefs in Persepolis, capital of the ancient Persian Empire

EARLY CIVILIZATIONS
The world's earliest civilizations grew up around river valleys in Asia in an area known as the fertile crescent, which stretches in an arc from the Persian Gulf to the Mediterranean Sea. Many cities here can trace their history back for several thousand years.

Population: approximately 3,719,000,000 people

Number of countries: 47

Largest country: Russian Federation – the Asian part covers 5,190,909 sq miles (13,444,468 sq km)

RUSSIAN FEDERATION

KAZAKHSTAN

MONGOLIA

UZBEKISTAN
KYRGYZSTAN
TURKMENISTAN
TAJIKISTAN

TURKEY

CYPRUS
LEBANON SYRIA
ISRAEL
JORDAN
IRAQ
IRAN
AFGHANISTAN
KUWAIT
PAKISTAN
BAHRAIN QATAR
U.A.E.
SAUDI ARABIA
OMAN
YEMEN

NEPAL BHUTAN
BANGLADESH

INDIA

CHINA

NORTH KOREA
SOUTH KOREA
JAPAN

TAIWAN

MYANMAR
LAOS
THAILAND
CAMBODIA
VIETNAM
PHILIPPINES

Andaman Is. (Ind)

Nicobar Is. (Ind)

SRI LANKA

MALAYSIA
BRUNEI
SINGAPORE

MALDIVES

INDONESIA

EAST TIMOR

Least densely populated country: Mongolia, 4 people per sq mile (2 per sq km)

Smallest country: Maldives 116 sq miles (300 sq km)

Most densely populated country: Singapore, 15,285 people per sq mile (5,902 per sq km)

EMPTY PLAINS
Although Asia has a huge population, many areas are hardly peopled at all. At just 4 people per sq mile (2 per sq km), Mongolia has the world's lowest population density.

GROWING CITIES

A large proportion of Asia's population still lives in the countryside as farmers, but the number living in cities is rising steeply. The largest cities in Asia now have populations of more than 10 million. These super-cities, along with many other cities in the continent, are destined to grow even faster as people move from the countryside to towns.

This crowded street scene is in India's capital, New Delhi. India is one of the world's most densely populated countries.

LARGEST CITIES IN ASIA	
Tokyo, Japan	26.4 million
Mumbai (Bombay), India	18.1 million
Shanghai, China	12.9 million
Calcutta (Kolkata), India	12.9 million
Delhi, India	11.7 million

Population density

The figures on the chart show the number of people per sq mile (per sq km). Countries outside Asia are included as a comparison.

Bangladesh: 2,499 (965)

China: 355 (135)

World average: 106 (41)

US: 79 (30)

Oman: 30 (12)

POPULATION DENSITY

Large areas of the Middle East and central Asia are empty wilderness, unsettled by people because of their extreme dryness or cold temperatures. Most of the population is concentrated in the fertile river valleys and coastal lowlands of south and east Asia. Apart from the island city-state of Singapore, Bangladesh is the most densely populated country in Asia with 2,499 people per sq mile (965 per sq km).

A Bedouin man in Jordan may have more than one wife and many children.

POPULATION GROWTH

Three out of every five people in the world live in Asia. Seven of the world's ten most populated countries are located here, with China and India heading the list. Between them these two countries account for about 40 percent of the world's population. In mainland China a strictly enforced government policy to restrict family size to just one child has slowed the rate of population growth, but elsewhere in the continent it is still very high. In 2000, India's population rose to over 1 billion and Indonesia's passed over 210 million.

In China, a family with just one child receives free education and a housing allowance.

RIVER VALLEYS

The first peoples settled in fertile river valleys where they could grow crops. They built irrigation systems to channel water from rivers to the crops. Today, rivers are still important to the people of southern and eastern Asia. In addition to irrigation, rivers are used for fishing and for drinking, and are dammed to produce hydroelectric power. Rivers often provide a country's main means of transportation, and some are the focus around which countries have developed.

World's top rice-growing countries

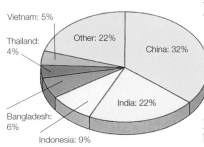

Vietnam: 5%

Thailand: 4%

Other: 22%

China: 32%

India: 22%

Bangladesh: 6%

Indonesia: 9%

RICE

Half the world's population depends on rice as a principal source of food, so a rice shortage can cause terrible famine. This plant, native to Southeast Asia, has been cultivated in the region for at least 7,000 years. In recent decades, new varieties of rice have been developed to help feed Asia's growing population. These new strains of rice are part of the "Green Revolution," which applies scientific knowledge to plant breeding and uses technology to increase productivity.

PEOPLES OF ASIA II

ALTHOUGH SOME ASIAN COUNTRIES, such as Japan and China, have been independent for a long time, others have only recently emerged from colonization. At the start of the 20th century, much of the Middle East, the whole Indian Subcontinent, and large areas of Southeast Asia were controlled by European powers. Nationalist movements grew up across Asia and the countries regained their independence. Many countries here have had very fast economic growth. Together with the recent pressures for change, this means that societies across the region are now evolving rapidly.

INDEPENDENCE
Each year, many countries in the region celebrate their freedom from colonial rule in independence day celebrations, like those in Pakistan shown above. Some countries, such as India, gained their independence through peaceful protest, while fierce fighting occurred in others, such as Myanmar. These countries are now struggling to forge a sense of national unity.

The former USSR
This map shows the former USSR and the 15 republics that it divided up into.

ESTONIA
LATVIA
LITHUANIA
BELARUS
UKRAINE
MOLDOVA

USSR
(Much of this area is now the Russian Federation.)

BREAKUP
The Soviet Union, or USSR, was the world's largest nation. However, in 1991, the USSR split up into 15 republics, which set up their own governments. Nine of the republics are in Europe and the other five are in Asia, while Russia straddles both. They are no longer part of a large, centralized economy, and so are struggling to compete in a world market. The USSR's collapse also freed some eastern European countries from Soviet control.

AZERBAIJAN
GEORGIA
ARMENIA

KAZAKHSTAN
KYRGYZSTAN
UZBEKISTAN
TURKMENISTAN
TAJIKISTAN

Most young men in Thailand live in a monastery as monks for a few months.

WORLD RELIGIONS
Asia was the birthplace of all the main world religions, including Hinduism, Buddhism, Judaism, Christianity, and Islam. Religious beliefs still have a strong influence on the people of the region today. Religions often emphasize modesty in wealth and the importance of donating to charity for spiritual reward rather than any personal gain.

This temple is in Thailand, where Buddhism is the main religion.

Chechnya's capital, Grozny, was heavily bombed by the Russian Federation in 1994.

ETHNIC GROUPS
Fighting between ethnic groups is still continuing in several parts of the former USSR. The Russian Federation, for example, includes some regions where the Russian population is in the minority and greater numbers of people belong to native ethnic groups. In Chechnya, only about a third of the population is Russian. Since the breakup of the USSR, the Chechens have been fighting for independence. However, the Russian Federation is not prepared to grant independence to any of these territories. It could lead to the breakup of Russia itself.

PRESSURES FOR CHANGE

In Asian societies today, the traditional rural ways of life and religious beliefs conflict with an increasingly money-oriented way of life, influenced by the West. As Asian societies become more open to western influences, so the pressures on traditional ways of life will intensify. Societies react to pressures for change in different ways. In Afghanistan, for example, religious leaders violently opposed western ideas, leading to the setting up of a hardline republic based on a strict interpretation of Islamic law.

Taliban supporters in Afghanistan burn video tapes, banned by the former hardline Islamic government.

OIL AND THE MIDDLE EAST

Before oil was discovered, many desert countries in the Middle East were very poor. Oil has transformed their fortunes. More than half the world's known reserves of crude oil and a third of all the natural gas occur here. Countries have become wealthy through the export of oil and natural gas throughout the world. New cities have sprung up, such as Dubai (shown above), and foreign workers have arrived in great numbers.

The influence of the US and capitalism can be seen on the streets of Tokyo, in Japan.

Shaded areas on the map show Southeast Asia's newly industrializing countries.

Asia's tiger economies

SOUTH KOREA

HONG KONG

TAIWAN

PHILIPPINES

THAILAND

MALAYSIA

SINGAPORE

WESTERN INFLUENCE

In some societies, change happens gradually and without violent demonstrations. In Japan, for example, economic development was seen by its rulers as a way of avoiding becoming dependent on European nations. Japan has therefore accepted Western capitalism while still managing to preserve many traditional Japanese values. Even China, so long closed to Western ideas, is now beginning to embrace capitalism.

LITTLE TIGERS

Following in the footsteps of Japan, a number of southeast Asian countries looked to make the most of their cheap and plentiful supply of workers to rapidly boost their economies. These "Little Tigers" achieved great success in the final decades of the 20th century. However, they are now having to deal with the side effects of rapid industrialization – pollution, unemployment, poverty in rural areas and new cheaper competition that has begun to emerge elsewhere.

Kazakh people in northern China outside a tent known as a yurt

NOMADIC EXISTENCE

The collapse of the USSR has led to a revival of traditional ways of life among the nomads of central Asia. Goods that were made in factories, such as felt, which is used to line the inside of nomads' tents, ceased to be available and now have to be made by hand using traditional methods. The same is true when it comes to moving. In recent years, many nomads have moved their belongings around in vehicles, but gasoline is now in very short supply, so nomads have returned to using camels and horses.

ROLE OF WOMEN

Women's lives differ hugely over such a large continent, influenced by each nation's culture, religion, and politics. In some areas, such as in India and the Islamic countries of the Middle East, the vast majority of the workforce is male. Yet Islamic women in Southeast Asian countries such as Indonesia often work outside the home. In other areas, such as communist China and North Korea and the former communist republics of the USSR, women make up a large proportion of the workforce and carry out most household chores.

Women in the workforce

This chart shows the percentage of men and women in the workforce in five countries.

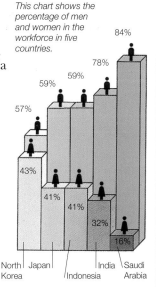

North Korea	Japan	Indonesia	India	Saudi Arabia
57%	59%	59%	78%	84%
43%	41%	41%	32%	16%

RUSSIAN FEDERATION

STRETCHING ACROSS two continents – Europe and Asia – and extending halfway around the globe, the Russian Federation is by far the largest country in the world. Because of the bitterly cold climate and harsh living conditions, this vast land is sparsely populated. However, Russia has areas of fertile land, rich mineral deposits, and abundant natural resources. The country was once the head of a powerful communist state, the Union of Soviet Socialist Republics (USSR). After the collapse of communism in 1991, many parts of the old Soviet Union declared independence. The government of the newly formed Russian Federation is now struggling to establish a Western-style democracy and economy.

Surrounded by high red-brick walls, the Kremlin (fortress) contains four gilt-domed cathedrals and the grand palace of the tsars.

RUSSIAN FEDERATION

St. Petersburg
☀ Jan 14°F (-10°C)
☀ July 63°F (17°C)
☔ Jan 1.4 in (35 mm)
☔ July 2.8 in (72 mm)

Perm
☀ Jan 2°F (-17°C)
☀ July 65°F (19°C)
☔ Jan1.6 in (40 mm
☔ July 3.5 in (89 mm

THINGS TO LOOK FOR ON THE MAP

Longest river: Lena, 2,648 miles (4,261 km) *Map N6*

Highest point: Klyuchevsk, 15,585 ft (4,750 m) *Map T5*

Largest lake: Baikal, 12,150 sq miles (31,468 sq km) *Map M10*

World's largest straits: Tatar Strait, 497 miles (800 km) long *Map S9*

POLITICAL CHANGE

The Moscow Kremlin reflects the changing political face of Russia. Once the home of the tsars (emperors), who ruled Russia for many centuries, it later became the headquarters of the world's first communist government in 1917. The government created the USSR, which became an industrial and military superpower, but at great cost to its people. The communist state collapsed in 1991, and the Kremlin is now the symbolic home of the new rulers of the Russian Federation.

VOLGA RIVER
The mighty Volga River rises northwest of Moscow and flows 2,193 miles (3,530 km) southward to the Caspian Sea. The Volga is the most important inland waterway in Russia. Hundreds of ships use it every day to transport goods to vast industrial sites that lie alongside the river. Huge dams have created a string of reservoirs providing water and electricity for the people who live on or near its banks.

J   K   L   M   N   O   P   Q   R   S   T   U

Verkhoyansk
Jan -59°F (-51°C)
July 57°F (14°C)
Jan 0.2 in (5 mm)
July 1.1 in (28 mm)

Franz Josef Land

Pioner I.
October Revolution I.
Severnaya Zemlya
Bolshevik I.
C. Chelyuskin

Wrangel I.
CHUKCHI SEA
EAST SIBERIAN SEA
Pevek
Ayon I.
C. Navarin
BERING SEA
Bear Is.
Ambarchik
OLOY RANGE
KORYAK RANGE
C. Olyutorskiy

Belyy I.
TAYMYR PENINSULA
LAPTEV SEA
L. Taymyr
Tiksi
Olenek
Indigirka
Kolyma
Korkodon
Ossora
Karaginskiy Is.

GYDA PENINSULA
Pyasina
Khatanga
CENTRAL SIBERIAN PLATEAU
Anabar
Lena
VERKHOYANSK RANGE
Yana
Byrantay
Verkhoyansk
Adycha
Suntang
KOLYMA RANGE
Ust'-Kamchatsk
Klyuchevsk
C. Sivuchiy

Nakhodka
Noril'sk
PUTORANA MTS.
Olenëk
Magadan
KAMCHATKA
Petropavlovsk-Kamchatskiy
Oktyabr'skiy

R U S S I A N
Lower Tunguska
Vilyuy
Yakutsk
Amga
Aldan
Okhotsk
DZHUGDZHUR RANGE
SEA OF OKHOTSK
C. Lopatka
Paramushir Is.

F E D E R A T I O N
Yenisey
Stony Tunguska
Suntar
Lena
Olëkma
Moya
C. Yelizavety
Okha
Sakhalin
The Kurile Islands are administered by the Russian Federation, but claimed by Japan.
Kurile Islands

Ket'
Angara
Vitim
Zeya Res.
Talar Strait
Poronaysk

Tomsk
Achinsk
Krasnoyarsk
Ust'-Ilimsk
STANOVOY RANGE
Skovorodino
Komsomol'sk-na-Amure
Soyetskaya Gavan
Yuzhno-Sakhalinsk

...vosibirsk
Kemerovo
Kansk
Bratsk
Svobodnyy
Khabarovsk

Novokuznetsk
...arnaul
Abakan
Oka
L. Baikal
Romanovka
Shilka
Chita
C H I N A
Amur
Blagoveshchensk

Biysk
Kyzyl
Irkutsk
Ulan-Ude
Olovyannaya
Ussuri
SEA OF JAPAN
PACIFIC OCEAN

M O N G O L I A
Vladivostok
NORTH KOREA

0   200   400   600 km
0 100 200 300 400 miles

1 2 3 4 5 6 7 8 9 10 11 12

SIBERIA

To the east of the Ural Mountains lies Siberia, a vast tract of largely uninhabited land that stretches across to the Pacific Ocean. Most of Siberia is covered with coniferous forest known as taiga, and which contains about a quarter of the world's wood reserves. In the north, the forest thins out as the climate gets colder and the land becomes a barren waste called tundra where the ground remains frozen throughout the year.

SIBERIAN WILDLIFE
The forests of Siberia provide a vital source of food for animals, such as reindeer, bears, and squirrels, especially during the long winter months. The region is also home to the largest tiger in the world, the Siberian tiger, which has thick fur to withstand the bitter winters.

Arctic ground squirrel

RUSSIAN FEDERATION

RUSSIAN FEDERATION	
Capital city: Moscow	
Area: 6,563,700 sq miles (17,000,000 sq km)	
Population: 146,900,000	
Official language: Russian	
Major religions: Russian Orthodox 75%, other 25%	
Government: Multiparty democracy	
Currency: Rouble	
Adult literacy rate: 99%	
Life expectancy: 66 years	
People per doctor: 219	
Televisions: 420 per 1,000 people	

THE URAL MOUNTAINS form the boundary between European and Asian Russia. European Russia lies to the west of the mountains. This vast stretch of land is home to more than 100 million people, two-thirds of the entire Russian population. Most people live in the big cities of Moscow – the capital of the country – and St. Petersburg, or along the Volga River valley. The land is rich in minerals. It is also intensively farmed, with wheat and other grains in the north giving way to tobacco, citrus fruit, and a variety of crops in the warmer south.

ST. PETERSBURG

With its network of canals and rivers, the elegant city of St. Petersburg is known as the "Venice of the North." It is a center for arts and culture and has many fine 18th-century buildings. It was the capital of Russia between 1713–1917. Under communist rule the city was renamed Leningrad to honor Lenin, the leader of the 1917 Russian revolution. With the collapse of communism in 1991, it reverted to its old name.

AGRICULTURE

Because of the harsh climate, only about 10 percent of Russian land is used for growing crops, mostly in an area known as the "fertile triangle" (see map right). The country is the world's leading producer of oats, and the second greatest producer of wheat, rye and potatoes. During the 1950s a vast area of barren land in south-central Russia was cultivated, the largest expansion of agriculture in the last 100 years. The new wheat fields freed up more fertile areas in the West to grow fodder for animals.

Potatoes are grown on a huge scale in Russia. The large, open fields are plowed into furrows and then the potatoes are planted in neat rows by machine.

At harvest time, the potatoes are dug out of the ground.

The potatoes are sorted and graded according to size and condition.

The fertile triangle

Most of Russia's crops are grown in "the fertile triangle," which stretches from St. Petersburg and the Ukraine in the west to southern Siberia in the east.

RUSSIAN BALLET
Ballet arrived in Russia from France in the 19th century thanks to close cultural and diplomatic ties between Paris and St. Petersburg, the old Russian capital. By the early 20th century, Russia had transformed traditional ballet, making it more creative and exciting. Today, the Bolshoi Ballet of Moscow and the Kirov Ballet of St. Petersburg are known throughout the world.

RELIGIOUS REVIVAL

The Russian Orthodox Church was suppressed for many years by the former Soviet government, but became legal once more with the ending of communism. Today churches and monasteries are reopening across the country, and many people regularly attend religious services. As Russian society continues to change rapidly, the unchanging traditions of the Orthodox Church are a great comfort to many people.

The head of the Russian Orthodox Church is known as the "Patriarch of Moscow and All Russia."

FOOD AND DRINK

The basic Russian diet, grain, potatoes, oil, and sugar, tends to be fattening. Fresh fruit, vegetables, and meat are regarded as luxuries. In the last few years, however, increased food production and a better system of supply has led to a wider range of foods on sale in the big cities.

Sour cream

Borscht, a soup made from beetroot

Vodka, a strong alcohol made from grain or potatoes, is the national drink. Alcoholism is a problem throughout Russia.

Black bread made from hard wheat

THE TATARS

The ancient town of Kazan, on the Volga, is the capital of Tatarstan, home to around two million Tatars. These Islamic peoples are descendants of the Mongols, who overran Russia in the 13th century. Under the Soviet Union, the Tatars were suppressed and their Islamic mosques closed. Today the Tatars – along with other non-Russian peoples – are asserting their independence within the Russian Federation. The Tatars are reviving their traditional customs and are taking steps to gain control of the local economy.

INDUSTRY

The former Soviet Union invested heavily in its industry. Vast industrial complexes were built in the iron-rich Ural Mountains and in the Kuzbass coalfield of southern Siberia. The production of coal, iron, and other minerals soared, and heavy industries, such as engineering, steel, iron, and chemical production, dominated the economy. However, Russia is now paying a price for this big advance. Many factories are old and inefficient, polluting the environment with harmful emissions.

Russian exports

Basic goods: 25%
Metals: 22%
Minerals: 19%
Oil: 18%
Other: 4%
Chemicals: 5%
Machinery: 7%

THE MOSCOW METRO

During the 1930s, the Soviet government built a huge underground railroad system beneath the streets of Moscow. The system is fast and efficient and is used daily by more than 7 million people. The stations were built deep down in the ground so that they could be used as air-raid shelters during wartime. Many are beautifully decorated with paintings, sculptures, and mosaics.

Well known Western brands were quick to sell their goods on the newly opened Russian market.

MARKET ECONOMY

When the USSR collapsed in 1991, the state-run, planned economy went with it. Switching abruptly to a liberal Western-style economy caused many problems for ordinary Russians, widening the gap between rich and poor. A severe crisis in 1998 wass largely overcome, but Russia is still struggling to achieve Western-style prosperity.

WOMEN WORKERS

Many more Russian men than women died during World War II and in the labor camps set up by the Soviet leader Stalin. As a result, there are far more women than men in Russia, and women make up around 50 percent of the workforce. Good child care and medical services enable women with children to go out to work. Many work on the railroads or drive buses and streetcars. Most factories have large female workforces and many professions, such as medicine, dentistry, and teaching, are dominated by women.

This woman worker is helping clear heavy snow in Moscow.

RUSSIAN FEDERATION

TO THE EAST of the Ural Mountains lies Asian Russia. This vast expanse of land, known as Siberia, is bigger than the combined size of the US and western Europe. Yet because of the harsh climate, only 40 million people live here. Parts of Siberia are colder in winter than the North Pole. To the north are frozen plains, or tundra, while farther south it is just warm enough to grow some hardy crops. For centuries, Siberia remained undeveloped, home only to peoples who trapped animals for their meat and fur and caught fish in the local rivers. But the discovery of minerals, such as gold and diamonds, has opened the region up to economic and industrial development.

KAMCHATKA

Hanging off the eastern end of Siberia, the Kamchatka Peninsula is one of the most isolated parts of Russia. Under the Soviet Union, Kamchatka bristled with military bases because of its closeness to both Japan and the US. Today, the military presence is reduced and people are returning to more traditional ways of making a living. Once more, people are fishing in the many rivers, herding reindeer, or hunting seals, sea otters, and bears for their skins.

Major mineral deposits

RAW MATERIALS

Siberia is rich in natural resources, with huge reserves of oil, gas, coal, metals, diamonds, and gold. The Trans-Siberian railroad transports vast amounts of minerals from Siberia to European Russia. Western Siberia contains one-third of the world's natural gas reserves, as well as a huge oilfield producing 8.4 million barrels of oil a day, more than two-thirds of the entire Russian output. Development of these resources, however, is difficult, for the climate is harsh and laying pipelines to carry fuel over such long distances is expensive.

- Coal
- Gas
- Oil
- Copper
- Diamonds
- Gold
- Iron

The elegant dining car of the Trans-Siberian Express

THE TRANS-SIBERIAN RAILROAD

The Trans-Siberian railroad is the world's longest continuous rail line. It begins at Moscow's Yaroslavl station in the west and stretches 5,866 miles (9,440 km) across to Vladivostok in the east. Trains cross eight time zones and take eight days to complete the journey. In recent years the line has become increasingly congested. New lines, including the Baikal-Amur Mainline, have been built alongside to relieve this problem.

CLOSED AND SECRET CITIES

Under Soviet Union rule, two types of cities were off limits to all but an authorized few. Closed cities, including Vladivostok (shown left), were sites of military or industrial importance. Secret cities were places of research in chemical and nuclear warfare. They did not appear on maps and were located in remote areas surrounded by restricted-access zones, patrolled by armed guards. Today, most closed cities are open to visitors, but secret cities remain out of bounds.

The boxes are often decorated with scenes from fairy tales.

ARTS AND CRAFTS

The rise in Russian nationalism has been accompanied by a return to traditional crafts, folk tales, and music and dance. Skilled craftworkers make boxes and other items from wood or *papier-mâché*. The lacquered boxes are decorated with miniature paintings.

Hand-painted Russian chess set

CHESS
The ancient game of chess became popular in Russia as a way of spending long, dark winter evenings by the fireside. Today, chess is still widely played here. Russian Grand Masters such as Karpov and Spassky have dominated world chess tournaments. During a big match, giant chessboards are displayed in big city squares so the public can follow the competitors' moves.

FORESTRY
The taïga forest of northern Russia and Siberia provides work in logging, paper production, chemicals, and furniture making. In the past, most forestry jobs were in the more accessible parts of northern Russia. But many of these forests have been cleared, and new seedlings take up to 80 years to produce mature wood. As a result, the center of the forestry industry has moved south and east into Siberia. Today, most timber production is located in southern Siberia near Lake Baikal or on the Amur River near the Pacific coast.

LIVING IN A COLD CLIMATE
The Yakut people of eastern Siberia are used to living in a cold climate – winter temperatures drop to −45°F (−43°C). Engines are kept running 24 hours a day to prevent them from freezing up. Drinking water is delivered as chunks of ice sawn out of the local river. Even during the brief summer, most ground remains frozen hard. Houses are often built on raised concrete platforms or wooden stilts to protect them from frost damage.

The Yakut survive the winter by wearing many layers of warm clothing made from animal skins and fur. People wear felt or reindeer-fur boots, rather than leather, which freezes and cracks quickly.

Window frames are often attractively decorated.

Food is stored in bags outside the windows and defrosted when needed.

Milk is sold in frozen brick form with wooden handles inserted so that it can be carried home easily.

Sleds pulled by dogs or reindeer are a traditional way of traveling through the snow.

The Yakut people make their living by herding reindeer in the north of the region and rearing cattle in the center.

Windows are triple-glazed to keep out the cold. The air between the three layers of glass acts as insulation.

Fur hats with ear-flaps protect their wearers from Russian winters.

FUR FARMS
For centuries, hunters and trappers have worked the Siberian forests to catch ermine, mink, sable, lynx, and fox. In order to protect some species from over-hunting, the Soviet government introduced fur farms, where breeders raise rare animals for their furs. Furs from Siberian animals are turned into hats, coats, and linings for boots and gloves.

LAKE BAIKAL
Known as the "blue eye of Siberia," Lake Baikal in southeastern Siberia covers 12,150 sq miles (31,468 sq km) and is up to 6,367 ft (1,940 m) deep. It is the deepest lake in the world and the largest freshwater lake, containing more than 20 percent of the world's entire supply of freshwater. In recent years, logging and chemical industries have polluted the water, prompting a major campaign to protect this unique environment.

Lake Baikal is home to the world's only freshwater seal, the nerpa, or Baikal seal. A wide variety of flora and fauna, unique to the area, are found in and around the lake.

Find out more

BREAKUP OF USSR: *136*
FORESTRY: *69, 86, 244*
ORTHODOX CHURCH: *274*
POLITICAL SYSTEMS: *270–271*

TURKEY

TURKEY LIES PARTLY IN EUROPE and partly in Asia and is divided by a narrow waterway. For more than 600 years, Turkey was part of the powerful Ottoman Empire. Today, Turkey is a republic and the country is a mix of Islamic and Western traditions. Most people are Turkish-speaking Muslims, although there is no official state religion. Turkey has a varied landscape and climate, and is a popular tourist destination. Many types of crops are grown, and the country is self-sufficient in food.

TURKEY

Capital city: Ankara

Area: 297,154 sq miles (769,630 sq km)

Population: 66,600,000

Official language: Turkish

Major religions: Muslim 99%, other 1%

Government: Multiparty democracy

Currency: Turkish lira

Adult literacy rate: 85%

Life expectancy: 70 years

People per doctor: 909

Televisions: 286 per 1,000 people

CYPRUS

Capital city: Nicosia

Area: 3,567 sq miles (9,240 sq km)

Population: 786,050

Official languages: Greek and Turkish

Major religions: Christian 77%, Muslim 23%

Government: Multiparty democracy

Currency: Cyprus pound and Turkish lira

Adult literacy rate: 94%

Life expectancy: 97 years

People per doctor: 433

Televisions: 325 per 1,000 people

KEMAL ATATURK
Kemal Ataturk was the founder and first president of the modern state of Turkey after the collapse of the Ottoman Empire in the early 20th century. He brought about many reforms in Turkish society, including greater freedom for women and better education for all.

This depiction of Kemal Ataturk towers over Antalya, in southern Turkey.

Kurdish children living in Harran in Turkey

THE KURDS
The Kurds, numbering about 25 million, are one of the largest groups of people in the world who have no homeland. They live in a mountainous area split between four countries: Turkey, Iran, Iraq, and Syria. The Kurds have sought to form their own state – Kurdistan.

AGRICULTURE
About half of the Turkish workforce is employed in agriculture – growing crops such as wheat, cotton, tobacco, sugar beet, and fruit. Tea is grown along the Black Sea coast and is a popular drink. Much of the work in the fields is done by women. With plenty of fertile farmland, Turkey can produce enough food not only for its own needs, but for export, too.

EPHESUS
Each year, millions of tourists visit Turkey for its sunny weather, sandy beaches, and ancient sites. These include the ruined city of Ephesus on the Aegean coast, famous for its huge, open-air theater, carved out of the hillside in the first century AD, with seating for 24,000 people. Tourism is one of Turkey's major industries.

MARKETS
Bustling street markets, or bazaars, are a common sight in many Turkish towns and cities. Turkey is famous for its arts and crafts, particularly for its fine carpets, pottery, beaten copperware, and leatherwork. Carpets are woven from silk, wool, and cotton and decorated with beautiful geometric and floral designs, often symbolizing the maker's family or area of origin.

This carpet stall is in the Grand Bazaar in Kusadasi, in western Turkey.

STREET CAFES
Street cafés are popular meeting places, especially with men. They visit them to drink tea or Turkish coffee, smoke pipes, and chat. Games, such as cards or backgammon, are often played.

Men smoke pipes called hubble-bubbles. Smoke is drawn into the mouth through a long tube.

Rich, dark Turkish coffee is a popular drink.

Men often play cards in street cafés.

0 50 100 150 200 250 km
0 50 100 150 miles

N

TURKEY

Istanbul, Turkey
☀ Jan 41.5°F (5.5°C)
July 73.5°F (23°C)
🌧 Jan 4 in (109 mm)
July 1.3 in (34 mm)

Kars, Turkey
☀ Jan 10°F (-12°C)
July 63°F (17°C)
🌧 Jan 1.1 in (28 mm)
July 2.1 in (53 mm)

THINGS TO LOOK FOR ON THE MAP
Longest river: Kizil Irmak, 715 miles (1,151 km) *Map F5*

Highest point: Mt. Ararat, 16,800 ft (5,123 m) *Map K6*

Largest lake: L. Van, 1,453 sq miles (3,763 sq km) *Map K6*

World's only city on two continents: Istanbul *Map C5*

Nicosia, Cyprus
☀ Jan 50.5°F (10°C)
July 84°F (29°C)
🌧 Jan 3.0 in (76 mm)
July 0 in (1 mm)

This house stands on Hermes Street in Nicosia, the capital of Cyprus. The street marks the division between the Greek south and Turkish north. Turkey is the only country to recognize Turkish Northern Cyprus officially.

ISTANBUL
Istanbul is the only city in the world to lie on two continents. It is split between Europe and Asia by a narrow channel of water called the Bosphorus. Bridges link the two parts of the city. Istanbul is a mixture of old and new, eastern and western, with elegant mosques side-by-side with sprawling slums. It is Turkey's largest city and main port. Until the move to Ankara in 1923, it was also Turkey's capital.

CYPRUS

CYPRUS IS A LARGE, picturesque island in the eastern Mediterranean, popular as a tourist destination. It was under Turkish, then British control, until its independence in 1959. The majority of the islanders are Greeks; about a fifth are Turkish. Conflict between the two groups led to a division of the island in 1974 into the Greek south and Turkish north.

Find out more
CARPET MAKING: *155, 165, 210*
ISLAM: *275*
TEA: *172, 238*

THE MIDDLE EAST I

At the eastern edge of the Mediterranean Sea, this region includes the countries of Israel, Lebanon, Jordan, and Syria. It is the birthplace of some of the world's oldest civilizations and has close ties with three major religions – Judaism, Christianity, and Islam. The land is mostly dry and barren, particularly to the east, but it is lusher and more fertile along the Mediterranean coast. After centuries of invasion by Arabs, Christian Crusaders, and Turks, the present-day countries took shape in the last 100 years. Since then, they have been plagued by civil wars and conflicts.

A LAND OF CONTRASTS
A range of mountains stretches from Lebanon in the north to Israel in the south, which contrasts with the deserts to the east and the coast to the west. In Lebanon, the mountains drop away to rich, fertile plains where cereal crops are grown. The mountaintops are covered in snow for most of the year and are popular with skiers.

The main mosque stands at the center of the city.

Streets are narrow and irregular.

Noisy or smelly market stalls, such as those belonging to metalsmiths (above) or leatherworkers, are placed at a distance from the main mosque.

A MIDDLE EASTERN CITY

Many traditional Muslim cities follow a distinctive pattern. At the heart of the city is the main mosque, which is usually the largest building. This is surrounded by other important buildings and market stalls. The narrow, irregular streets that radiate out toward the city walls provide shade and keep down wind and dust. Privacy is important, and doors opening onto narrow streets never face each other.

The market stalls selling religious goods, such as candles, incense, and books (above), are placed closest to the main mosque in the center of the city.

Many houses face courtyards.

PALESTINE

In 1948, the Jewish state of Israel was created from the country of Palestine, the ancient land of the Jews and the home of the Palestinian Arabs. Thousands of Palestinians were driven from their homes and land. Many went to live in the neighboring Arab territories of the West Bank and the Gaza Strip. In 1967, Israel captured and occupied these areas. After agreeing to peace accords in 1993, the Palestinians were given control over parts of these areas. However, violence between the two communities continues.

Yasser Arafat is the leader of the Palestine Liberation Organization (PLO), which represents the interests of Palestinian Arabs.

Gaza Strip **West Bank**

Dead Sea

▲ Israeli settlements
● Major cities

THE DEAD SEA
On the border between Israel and Jordan lies a large lake known as the Dead Sea. It is the lowest place on Earth – some 1,312 ft (400 m) below sea level. Salt deposits rise up like pillars out of the water. No fish can live there, which is how the lake got its name. Mud from the shore of the Dead Sea is said to have healing properties.

A B C D E F G H I J K L

1

Haifa, Israel
☀ Jan 57°F (14°C)
July 82°F (28°C)
🌧 Jan 6.9 in (175 mm)
July 0 in (0 mm)

ARCTIC CIRCLE

TROPIC OF CANCER

EQUATOR

T U R K E Y

Tigris

'Afrin

Halab

Al Hasakah

A L   J A Z I R A H

L. Assad

Ar Raqqah

Euphrates Dam

Dayr az Zawr

LEBANON

Al Ladhiqiyah

Hamah

S Y R I A

I R A Q

Euphrates

Tartus

THINGS TO LOOK FOR ON THE MAP

Longest river: Euphrates, Iraq/Syria/Turkey, 1,749 miles (2,815 km) *Map K4*

Highest point: Mt. Qornet es Saouda, Lebanon, 10,127 ft (3,087 m) *Map F5*

Largest lake: Dead Sea, Israel/Jordan/West Bank, 405 sq miles (1,049 sq km) *Map E8*

World's oldest walled town: Jericho, West Bank *Map E8*

ISRAEL

Hims

Tudmur

Tripoli

Mt Qornet es Saouda
Baalbek

SHAMIYAH DESERT

BEIRUT

Zahlé

Saïda

DAMASCUS

SYRIA

Sour

GOLAN HEIGHTS

S Y R I A N

Dayr az Zawr, Syria
☀ Jan 44°F (7°C)
July 92°F (34°C)
🌧 Jan 1.6 in (41 mm)
July 0 in (0 mm)

Haifa

L. Tiberias

Nazareth

Dar'ā

As Suwaydā'

D E S E R T

Irbid

Elat, Israel
☀ Jan 60°F (16°C)
July 91°F (33°C)
🌧 Jan 0 in (0 mm)
July 0 in (0 mm)

Petah Tiqwa

Al Mafraq

WEST BANK

Az Zarqā'

Tel Aviv-Yafo

Holon

Jericho

Beersheba

AMMAN

Al Azraq

N

JERUSALEM

Bethlehem

Gaza

GAZA STRIP

Dead Sea

J O R D A N

Rafah

Al Karak

I S R A E L

At Tafilah

E G Y P T

JORDAN

0   50   100   150 km
0   25   50   75   100 miles

NEGEV DESERT

Petra

Ma'ān

S I N A I

SAUDI ARABIA

Elat Al 'Aqabah

Gulf of Suez

Gulf of Aqaba

The Dome of the Rock

Jews praying at the Western Wall

JEWISH HOMELAND
Before the state of Israel was created, Jews were scattered throughout the world. Many suffered persecution. During World War II, six million Jews were killed by the Nazis in Europe. After the war, thousands of Jews from all over the world emigrated to Israel, the home of their ancestors.

THREE GREAT FAITHS
The history of three of the world's major religions is closely linked to this region. Judaism and Christianity began here, while Islam spread to the area from nearby Saudi Arabia. Jerusalem, in Israel, is a holy city for all three faiths. The Dome of the Rock, sacred to Muslims, and the Western Wall, sacred to Jews, stand on the same site.

SYRIA

SYRIA IS AN ANCIENT LAND. Its capital, Damascus, is one of the world's oldest cities. Because of its important position on major trade routes, Syria has been invaded and occupied many times – by the Romans, Arabs, Greeks, and Turks. After World War I, it came under French control, becoming independent in 1946. Since then Syria has been involved in several wars with Israel. Most Syrians are Muslim and speak Arabic. More than half of Syria is desert, but the river floodplains provide fertile land.

SYRIA	
Capital city: Damascus	
Area: 71,065 sq miles (184,060 sq km)	
Population: 16,100,000	
Official language: Arabic	
Major religions: Muslim 90%, Christian 10%	
Government: One-party dictatorship	
Currency: Syrian pound	
Adult literacy rate: 74%	
Life expectancy: 71 years	
People per doctor: 917	
Televisions: 70 per 1,000 people	

PALMYRA

The rich and varied history of Syria is reflected in the many ancient ruins from past civilizations found scattered throughout the country. In the 3rd century AD, Palmyra, with its palaces, temples, and theaters, was a flourishing city, but it was destroyed by the Romans for refusing to give up its independence. It lies in an oasis on the edge of the desert, and is one of the best preserved ancient cities in the world.

MARKETS

Markets, or *souks*, are held in villages and towns throughout Syria. The *souks* are lively, bustling places, with market stalls set out on winding alleyways selling anything from spices and vegetables, to carpets, jewelry, basketwork, and coffee pots. People come here to buy and sell, meet their friends, and haggle (bargain) over prices. *Souks* are more than just trading centers, they are a central feature of the Arab way of life.

Craftsmen and women are often seen working at their stalls in the souk: beating and engraving copper, carving wood, and weaving baskets.

The stalls selling fresh bread, fruit, and vegetables jostle for space with the craft stalls.

MUSLIM GROUPS

The majority of Syrians belong to the traditionally powerful Sunni Muslim group. But there are other Muslim sects, such as the Shi'as, Ismailis, and Alawis. The Alawis believe not only in Islam, but in some aspects of Christianity. For example, they celebrate Christmas and Easter. The Alawis were persecuted in the past, but many have now become rich and powerful. President Assad of Syria is an Alawi Muslim.

A minaret (tower) on a Muslim mosque, from which the faithful are called to prayer five times a day

THE EUPHRATES DAM

The Euphrates River flows through the northeast of Syria on its journey from Turkey to Iraq. A gigantic dam has been built across the river to harness the power of the water and produce hydro-electricity. Sharing the waters of the Euphrates is a big issue for Turkey, Syria, and Iraq. A huge lake, Lake Assad, was also created by the dam. Water from the lake is used to grow crops.

THE GOLAN HEIGHTS

The mountainous area known as the Golan Heights was seized from Syria by Israel in 1967. It is important to the Israelis because it overlooks the Hula Valley in Israel, offering a good strategic position. It has been a major issue in past peace talks between the two countries, but the renewed Israeli-Palestinian conflict since 2001 has left the issue unresolved.

Find out more

HYDROELECTRICITY: *108, 262*
ISLAM: *275*
ISRAELI TERRITORY: *146*
OASES: *213*

LEBANON

LEBANON IS A SMALL COUNTRY at the eastern end of the Mediterranean bordered by Syria and Israel. The people of Lebanon are mostly Arabs, belonging to a great variety of religious groups. Lebanon was once the cultural and business center of the region, but in 1975, tensions between Muslim and Christian groups led to the outbreak of a violent civil war that almost destroyed the country. Peace terms were agreed in 1989 and some stability was restored.

LEBANON

Capital city:	Beirut
Area:	3,949 sq miles (10,230 sq km)
Population:	3,700,000
Official language:	Arabic
Major religions:	Muslim 70%, Christian 30%
Government:	Multiparty democracy
Currency:	Lebanese pound
Adult literacy rate:	86%
Life expectancy:	73 years
People per doctor:	526
Televisions:	352 per 1,000 people

RELIGIOUS GROUPS

The Lebanese population is a jigsaw puzzle of religious groups, including different Christian and Muslim sects. The largest Christian group is the Maronites, who practice a form of Catholicism. Other Christian groups include the Greek Orthodox. The Muslims are mainly of the Shi'a sect, but there are also many Sunnis.

Although Beirut is no longer formally divided into Muslim West and Christian East, both groups have remained in their own area.

Beirut

- ▨ Greek Orthodox
- ☐ Maronite
- ▨ Sunni Muslim
- ▨ Shi'a Muslim
- ▨ Druze

DRUZES
The Druze faith is an offshoot of Islam that is now considered a religion in its own right. There are about 200,000 Druzes in Lebanon, mainly living in the southern mountains. They have many customs designed to protect their community. It is impossible to become a Druze unless you are born one, and you cannot give up your faith. Marriage is only allowed within the community to ensure that the Druze faith continues.

REBUILDING BEIRUT

Before its destruction in the civil war, Beirut was a cultural center. It was known as the "Paris of the East" and was one of the region's most important ports and business centers. For many years the city lay in ruins, but a government project to rebuild Beirut has managed to restore its financial center and has succeeded in attracting visitors back to the capital.

Where people live

89% live in cities   11% live in the country

CEDAR TREES
The cedars of Lebanon are the country's symbol and appear on the national flag. In biblical times, great forests of cedar trees covered the slopes of the Lebanese mountains. Today, they survive only in a few protected groves. Some of these trees are more than 1,500 years old.

LEBANESE FOOD

The national dish of Lebanon is *kibbe*, made of lamb, bulgur (cracked wheat), and onions, pounded together. The mixture is shaped into balls or patties and baked or fried. Sweet pastries, stuffed with nuts and dates and covered in honey, are also popular.

Vegetables such as rutabagas and spices such as chilies are often eaten with the main meal.

Baklava

Kibbe is the Lebanese national dish.

Rutabaga   *Chilies*

TYRE AND SIDON
The civil war ruined Lebanon's thriving tourist industry. Attempts are now being made to attract visitors back to the country's fine beaches and historical sites, such as the two cities of Tyre and Sidon. These were built by the Phoenicians some 3,000 years ago and were famous in Roman times for their glassware and purple dyes.

Find out more

LEBANESE FLAG: *147*
LEBANESE LANDSCAPE: *146*
RELIGION: *274–275*
WARS IN THE REGION: *146*

ISRAEL

ISRAEL IS A LONG, THIN STRIP of land running along the eastern coast of the Mediterranean Sea. Its landscape is varied, with fertile valleys, dry deserts, mountains, lakes, and rivers. It has a wide range of industries and a modern agricultural system. The state of Israel was created in 1948 as a homeland for Jews from all over the world. The country was previously called Palestine. Much of the Palestinian Arab population was forced to leave Israel, fleeing into Jordan and Lebanon. This has created conflict between Israel, the Palestinians, and neighboring Arab states ever since.

JERUSALEM
The city of Jerusalem is a holy place for Jews, Muslims, and Christians. Within the walls of the Old City is the Jewish Western Wall, the only remaining part of Herod's Temple, and the Temple Mount, from where the Muslim prophet Mohammed rose up to heaven. The major Christian shrine is the Church of the Holy Sepulchre, the traditional site of Christ's burial and resurrection.

ISRAEL*
Capital city: Jerusalem	
Area: 7,849 sq miles (20,330 sq km)	
Population: 6,200,000	
Official languages: Hebrew and Arabic	
Major religions: Jewish 82%, Muslim 14%, Christian 2%, other 2%	
Government: Multi-party democracy	
Currency: New shekel	
Adult literacy rate: 96%	
Life expectancy: 79 years	
People per doctor: 218	
Televisions: 318 per 1,000 people	

* Figures include the West Bank and Gaza Strip.

KIBBUTZ
Almost half of Israel's food is grown on large communal farms called kibbutzim, where many families live and work together. People share everyday tasks such as cleaning and cooking, as well as work on the farm. Use of computerized irrigation to water the land has made large areas of barren desert fertile.

Families live and work together on a kibbutz.

Some crops, such as tomatoes, are grown inside plastic greenhouses.

Water is pumped through pipes to irrigate the land.

Efficient irrigation is essential for farming in a hot, dry climate.

People from other countries, attracted by the way of life, come to stay and work on kibbutzim during busy periods.

Citrus fruits, such as oranges, lemons, and grapefruit, are grown.

AT PRAYER
Judaism is one of the world's oldest religions. Jews believe in one God and follow the teachings of the Torah, the first five books of the Bible. At prayer, many Jewish men wear blue-edged prayer shawls and small boxes called phylacteries, or *tephillin*, which contain verses from the Torah. Saturday is the Jewish holy day, or Sabbath.

DIAMOND CUTTING
About 25 percent of Israel's export earnings come from its diamond industry. The rough diamonds are imported, and then skillfully cut and polished for use in jewelry settings.

ISRAELI SOLDIERS
Because of the conflict between Israel and the Palestinians, and repeated wars with neighboring countries, the army plays a crucial part in Israeli life. From the age of 18, Israeli men and women must serve in the army for a number of years. Women receive the same training as men, but do not take part in direct combat.

Tephillin are worn on the head and left arm, near the heart, to show that God's teachings control a person's thoughts and feelings.

Knotted tassels serve to remind Jews of God's commandments.

Prayer shawl

Find out more
DIAMONDS: *226, 248*
IRRIGATION: *155, 156, 217*
JUDAISM: *275*
PALESTINE: *146*

JORDAN

JORDAN

JORDAN LIES TO THE NORTHWEST of the Arabian Peninsula. Apart from a short coastline along the Gulf of Aqaba, it is completely landlocked, or cut off from the sea. Much of eastern Jordan is desert, with mountains in the north and south. Most of its people are Muslim and speak Arabic. Jordan is a relatively new country (it became fully independent in 1946), but some of the world's oldest sites are found here. In recent years, the government has played a part in peace talks between the Israelis and their Arab neighbors.

JORDAN

Capital city: Amman	
Area: 34,335 sq miles (88,930 sq km)	
Population: 6,700,000	
Official language: Arabic	
Major religions: Muslim 92%, other 8%	
Government: Monarchy with democratic system	
Currency: Jordanian dinar	
Adult literacy rate: 90%	
Life expectancy: 70 years	
People per doctor: 625	
Televisions: 52 per 1,000 people	

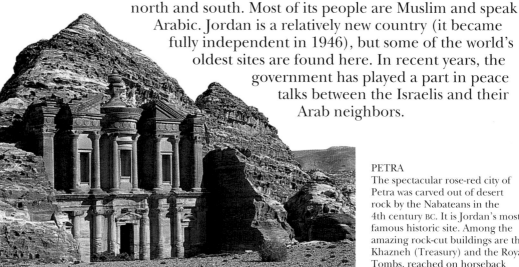

PETRA
The spectacular rose-red city of Petra was carved out of desert rock by the Nabateans in the 4th century BC. It is Jordan's most famous historic site. Among the amazing rock-cut buildings are the Khazneh (Treasury) and the Royal Tombs, reached on horseback through a narrow, winding gully.

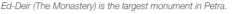
Ed-Deir (The Monastery) is the largest monument in Petra.

REFUGEE CAMPS

When Israel was formed in 1948, tens of thousands of Palestinians were forced to flee their homes and become refugees in Jordan and other Arab countries. More than 40 years later, they are still there. In Jordan alone, there are 1.6 million Palestinian refugees. Many have been born and brought up in refugee camps. This Palestinian refugee camp is near Amman.

Houses being built in Amman

POPULATION GROWTH

The population of Jordan, roughly equally divided between Jordanians and Palestinian refugees, is growing rapidly. Providing housing, jobs, schools, and health care for the growing number of people is one of the Jordanian government's most urgent problems.

In millions

Population growth in Jordan

1988	1993	1997	2000

6.5, 6.0, 5.5, 5.0, 4.5, 4.0, 3.5, 3.0, 2.5

GULF OF AQABA
The Gulf of Aqaba is the narrow, northeastern arm of the Red Sea between Saudi Arabia and the Sinai Peninsula. It is 99 miles (160 km) long and up to 17 miles (27 km) wide. At its head lies Jordan's one seaport, Aqaba. This short stretch of coastline is Jordan's only outlet to the sea. It is also popular with vacationers.

JORDAN RIVER

Water is in short supply throughout the Middle East. Control of the Jordan River, which forms the border between Jordan and Israel, has become an important issue in peace talks between the two countries. Jordan, a relatively poor country, has a particular need for a greater share of the water to irrigate its land so it can produce more crops.

Find out more
ANCIENT SITES: *134*
ISLAM: *275*
MIDDLE EAST HISTORY: *146–147*
POPULATION GROWTH: *16–17*

THE MIDDLE EAST II

THIS SECTION OF THE MIDDLE EAST is in southwestern Asia, and is covered primarily by dry, barren desert or rugged mountains. Ingenious irrigation techniques direct river water onto fields, and desalination plants are used to make seawater drinkable. Earlier this century, large deposits of oil were discovered around the Persian Gulf. Today, oil is the main source of income for many Middle Eastern countries. The majority of the population is Muslim and the most widely spoken language is Arabic. In recent years, the region has suffered a series of wars and conflicts between neighboring countries.

ROCKY DESERT
Part of the Middle East is rocky desert, where bare rock has been stripped clean by intense heat, drying winds, and occasional but heavy rainstorms.

Sand dunes are created by a buildup of sand carried along by strong winds.

Sandstorms arise when strong winds blow sand and dust across the desert, obscuring the sky.

Settlements may grow up around oases – these are often created by water coming to the surface through a fault (split) in the rock.

DESERT
Apart from fertile patches of land along the Tigris and Euphrates rivers, by the coast, and near isolated oases, much of this region is covered by hot, dry deserts, both rocky and sandy. These include the Rub'Al Khali, or Empty Quarter, a vast sandy desert in Saudi Arabia. Large areas of desert are uninhabited because of the lack of water for drinking and farming.

When the wind blows in one direction, it causes a ripple effect in the sand.

Some hardy plants can survive all year in the desert because their long roots collect water over a wide area.

Bedouin nomads face a constant fight for survival as they move from place to place with their animals in search of food and water.

OIL PRODUCTION
More than 65 percent of the world's oil is found in the Middle East, and the region supplies almost a third of the world's daily oil production. The discovery of oil has brought great wealth to the Middle East, leading to rapid industrial and social change in a formerly underdeveloped region. It has also greatly increased the region's international importance and influence on world affairs.

Drilling for oil

Drilling rig

Oil wells are drilled deep down into the ground to extract the oil trapped between layers of rock.

Distribution of oil production in the Middle East

Yemen: 2.1%
Qatar: 3.5.%
Oman: 4.3%
Kuwait: 9.6%
United Arab Emirates: 11.2%
Iraq: 11.7%
Iran: 16.8%
Saudi Arabia: 40.8%

WARFARE
In recent years, the Middle East has been frequently troubled by wars, in which thousands of people have lost their lives. In 1980, the long-standing rivalry and border dispute between Iran and Iraq erupted into a war that lasted until 1988. In 1991, an international force led by the US intervened when Iraq invaded Kuwait during the Gulf War.

A sign marks part of the border between Iran and Iraq.

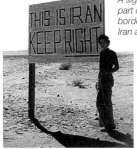

Rusting tanks in Iraq serve as a reminder of recent warfare.

DISPUTED BORDERS
Many Middle Eastern countries are relatively new, created earlier this century when the region was divided up by its Western rulers. These artificial divisions, sometimes poorly defined, have led to many border disputes, especially between Iraq and its six neighboring countries.

	A	B	C	D	E	F	G	H	I	J	K	L

ARCTIC CIRCLE
TROPIC OF CANCER
EQUATOR

0 100 200 300 400 500 km
0 100 200 300 miles

THINGS TO LOOK FOR ON THE MAP

Longest river: Euphrates, Iraq/Syria, 1,749 miles (2,815 km) *Map E5*

Highest point: Qolleh-ye-Damāvand, Iran, 18,605 ft (5,671 m) *Map H4*

World's largest oilfield: Ghawar, Saudi Arabia, 3,243 sq miles (8,400 sq km) *Map F8*

IRAN

Tehran, Iran
Jan 36°F (2°C)
July 86°F (30°C)
Jan 1.8 in (46 mm)
July 0.1 in (3 mm)

AZERBAIJAN

CASPIAN SEA

TURKMENISTAN

Urmia
Tabrīz
Orūmīyeh
Ardabīl
Rasht
Mosul
Irbil
Zanjān
Kirkuk
As Sulaymānīyah
Qazvīn
Sarī
Sanandaj
Karaj
Qolleh-ye-Damāvand
Mashhad
Hamadān
TEHRAN
Ar-Ramadi
Bakhtarān
Qom
Semnān
BAGHDAD
Karbala
Al-Hillah
Arāk
An-Najaf
Kāshān
Dezfūl
Esfahān
Al 'Amārah
An Nāsirīyah
Ahvāz
Yazd
Ur
Ābādān
Yāsūj
Al-Basrah
Shīrāz
Kermān
KUWAIT CITY
Bandar-e-Būshehr
Tabūk
Hā'il
Zāhedān

KUWAIT

BAHRAIN

QATAR

Buraydah
Medina
Ad Dammām
BAHRAIN
Bandar-e 'Abbās
Ghawar Oilfield
MANAMA
Khasab (to Oman)
RIYADH
Al Hufūf
DOHA
Sharjah
Jedda
Mecca
Harad
Dubai
Ta'if
ABU DHABI
UNITED ARAB EMIRATES
Al Khābūrah
MUSCAT
Abhā
Nazwā
Samā'il

UNITED ARAB EMIRATES

OMAN

Riyadh, Saudi Arabia
Jan 58°F (15°C)
July 93°F (34°C)
Jan 0.1 in (3 mm)
July 0 in (0 mm)

Jīzān
Hodeida
SAN'A
Salālah
Al Mukhā
Ta'izz
Dhamār
Aden
Al Mukallā

YEMEN

L. Tharthār
Babylon
Diyala
Wādī Hawran
Wādī 'Ar 'ar
Euphrates
Tigris
SYRIAN DESERT
JORDAN
EGYPT
Gulf of Aqaba
RED SEA
HEJAZ
AN NAFUD
NEJD
AD DAHNA
ASIR
SAUDI ARABIA
RUB 'AL KHALI (EMPTY QUARTER)
RAMLAT AS SAB'ATAYN
HADHRAMAUT
Wadi Bana
Bab el Mandeb
KUWAIT
Persian Gulf
QATAR
Strait of Hormuz
Gulf of Oman
Gulf of Masirah
Masirah I.
Kuria Muria Is.
ARABIAN SEA
IRAN
ZAGROS MTS.
DASHT-E KAVIR
DASHT-E LUT
ELBURZ MTS.
Jaz Mūriān Salt Lake
E. Sistan
AFGHANISTAN
PAKISTAN
OMAN
L. al Hammar

N

ISLAM

Islam originated in the Middle East in the 6th century AD and is still the dominant religion of the region. Muslims, the followers of Islam, believe in one God, Allah, and in Mohammed, his prophet. Mohammed was born in Mecca, in modern-day Saudi Arabia. The Muslims' holy book is the Koran, which contains Allah's teachings as revealed to Mohammed.

A devout Muslim reading the Koran

Dubai, United Arab Emirates

CITIES

The Middle East has some of the most rapidly growing cities in the world. This is because of the enormous wealth brought to the region by the discovery of oil and by the growth in population. These large cities are built along the lines of many modern cities in Western countries, with high-rise apartment and office buildings of glass, steel, and concrete.

IRAQ

IRAQ IS ONE OF THE LARGEST and most powerful countries in the Middle East. Most of its people are Muslim and Arabic speaking. There are also around 4 million Kurds living in the north. Apart from the fertile plains of the Tigris and Euphrates rivers, most of Iraq is mountainous or covered in desert. Only about a sixth of the country is suitable for farming and much of Iraq's food is imported. Since Iraq became a republic in 1958, it has experienced great political unrest. During the 1980s a bitter war was fought against Iran, and Iraq's invasion of Kuwait led to the Gulf War (1990–91) and to intervention by an international force.

IRAQ
Capital city: Baghdad
Area: 168,340 sq miles (437,340 sq km)
Population: 23,100,000
Official language: Arabic
Major religions: Muslim 95%, other 5%
Government: One-party dictatorship
Currency: Iraqi dinar
Adult literacy rate: 56%
Life expectancy: 59 years
People per doctor: 1,667
Televisions: 83 per 1,000 people

This ziggurat is in Ur, once a thriving city in Mesopotamia.

The fertile crescent extends through Iraq, Syria, Lebanon, Israel, and into northern Egypt.

MESOPOTAMIA
Many ancient peoples settled in Mesopotamia (part of which is now Iraq) because it lay in the fertile crescent of land formed by the Tigris and Euphrates rivers. The area has many ancient ruins, including stepped, pyramidlike structures called ziggurats, found at Babylon and Ur. The steps led to a temple at the top.

SADDAM HUSSEIN
Since 1979, Iraq has been ruled by Saddam Hussein. Under his dictatorship, many ordinary Iraqis, especially the Kurds, have suffered badly. The government is backed by the army and the secret service, which help prevent any political opposition. Saddam's invasion of Kuwait was condemned by the West and by some Arab countries, and led to Iraq's isolation in world affairs.

PIPING OIL
Iraq's most important natural resources are oil and natural gas. Oil production began on a large scale in 1945 and now dominates the economy. Because Iraq has only a short stretch of coastline along the Persian Gulf, it relies on pipelines through Turkey, Syria, and Saudi Arabia to export its oil.

BAGHDAD
Baghdad, the capital of Iraq, lies on the banks of the Tigris River. It is the largest city in Iraq and the country's center of business and government. A city of contrasts, it is a mixture of ancient mosques, modern high-rise buildings, and packed bazaars. Baghdad has been a center of Islamic culture for more than a thousand years.

MARSH ARABS
The Marsh Arabs have hunted and fished in the marshes of southern Iraq for more than 5,000 years. However, they are now under threat because of their opposition to Saddam Hussein in recent years. The government is draining the marshes to water crops elsewhere, endangering both the Marsh Arabs and the region's unique wildlife.

The huts, or mudhifs, are made of reeds bound tightly together.

The Marsh Arabs wind their way through the narrow reed-lined waterways in small wooden canoes, or mashhufs.

The white pelican is one rare species of bird that makes its home in the marshlands in winter.

The reed huts are built on platforms made of mud.

Find out more
ANCIENT SITES: *134*
DICTATORSHIP: *271*
KURDS: *144*
OIL: *137, 152, 281*

IRAN

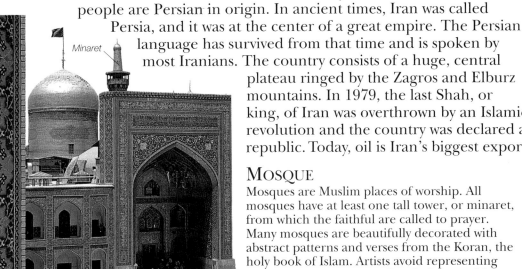

IRAN IS THE LARGEST NON-ARAB country in the Middle East; its people are Persian in origin. In ancient times, Iran was called Persia, and it was at the center of a great empire. The Persian language has survived from that time and is spoken by most Iranians. The country consists of a huge, central plateau ringed by the Zagros and Elburz mountains. In 1979, the last Shah, or king, of Iran was overthrown by an Islamic revolution and the country was declared a republic. Today, oil is Iran's biggest export.

Minaret

IRAN	
Capital city: Tehran	
Area: 631,659 sq miles (1,636,000 sq km)	
Population: 67,700,000	
Official language: Farsi	
Major religions: Muslim 99%, other 1%	
Government: Islamic republic	
Currency: Iranian rial	
Adult literacy rate: 77%	
Life expectancy: 69 years	
People per doctor: 3,333	
Televisions: 157 per 1,000 people	

MOSQUE
Mosques are Muslim places of worship. All mosques have at least one tall tower, or minaret, from which the faithful are called to prayer. Many mosques are beautifully decorated with abstract patterns and verses from the Koran, the holy book of Islam. Artists avoid representing living things because Muslims believe nothing should be worshiped apart from God, and that God is the only creator of life.

QANAT IRRIGATION
Less than half of the Iranian countryside is suitable for farming, and then only if it is well irrigated, or watered. Traditional irrigation methods include dams, wells, and *qanats*. A *qanat* is an underground channel that transports water from a source to an area that can be farmed. Some *qanats* are more than 25 miles (40 km) long.

Shepherds leading their flock of sheep through the Elburz Mountains

AGRICULTURE
In recent years, Iran has tried to become less dependent on food imports and has started growing more crops, such as cereals, tea, and cotton. Herds of cattle, sheep, and goats continue to be kept by many farming families.

The wells are used as ventilation and repair shafts, as well as to draw water.

Rainwater runs down and seeps into the ground.

The water flows along an underground channel that slopes gently downward.

A series of wells are used to dig the channel and then to draw water from it.

A settlement often grows up near the mouth of a qanat.

A class of girls in traditional dress. In Iran girls and boys are educated separately.

THE AYATOLLAH
Ayatollah Khomeini was a key figure in the Iranian revolution and remained Iran's political and religious leader until his death in 1989. The Shah had tried to introduce Western ideas to Iran, but Khomeini wanted the country to be governed by traditional Islamic laws and values. His ideas still dominate Iran.

PERSIAN CARPETS
Iran is famous for its handwoven Persian carpets. Each consists of thousands of pieces of wool knotted into elaborate patterns. The weavers always make a deliberate mistake in their work because, as Muslims, they believe that nothing is perfect except God. Carpets are Iran's second largest export, after oil.

This woman is weaving a carpet on a vertical loom.

Graceful patterns of flowers and leaves combined with abstract shapes are a feature of Persian carpets.

Find out more

CARPET MAKING: *144, 165, 210*
IRRIGATION: *156, 217*
ISLAM: *275*
POLITICAL SYSTEMS: *270*

SAUDI ARABIA

SAUDI ARABIA IS BY FAR the largest country in the Arabian Peninsula. Some 90 percent of this Muslim nation is covered by the hot, dry, sandy Arabian Desert, including the vast Rub'Al Khali, or Empty Quarter, in the south. There are no permanent rivers, and years may pass without any rainfall. The discovery of huge oil reserves has made Saudi Arabia extremely rich and powerful, and has enabled it to develop and improve its industry, agriculture, and standard of living.

SAUDI ARABIA	
Capital city: Riyadh	
Area: 829,995 sq miles (2,149,690 sq km)	
Population: 21,600,000	
Official language: Arabic	
Major religion: Muslim 100%	
Government: Absolute monarchy	
Currency: Saudi riyal	
Adult literacy rate: 77%	
Life expectancy: 71 years	
People per doctor: 769	
Televisions: 262 per 1,000 people	

Many Islamic women wear a veil, or burqa.

The Ka'ba stands on the remains of an ancient shrine, which, according to the Koran (the Muslim holy book), was built by Abraham.

OPEC
Saudi Arabia has the largest oil reserves in the world. Oil accounts for over 90 percent of the country's exports. Saudi Arabia is a key member of OPEC (Organization of Petroleum Exporting Countries). OPEC sets guidelines for the production and export of oil, and protects the interests of its member countries.

MECCA
Mecca, the birthplace of the prophet Mohammed and the holiest city of Islam, is in the west of Saudi Arabia. Each year, more than a million pilgrims from all over the world flock to Mecca to visit the sacred Ka'ba shrine in the Great Mosque. Muslims are expected to undertake the *hajj*, or pilgrimage to Mecca, at least once in their lives.

WOMEN'S ROLE
Women in Saudi Arabia and some other Muslim countries live restricted lives by Western standards. Many women wear traditional Muslim dress, with long robes and veils covering their heads and faces. In Saudi Arabia, women are not allowed to work with men nor to drive cars, although every girl has the right to a good education.

WATERING THE LAND
Much of Saudi Arabia's land is scrubby, barren, and unsuitable for growing food. Farmers rely on irrigation to water their fields. Recent projects have been so successful that farmers can now grow melons, tomatoes, wheat, and barley in the desert.

Disk-shaped fields are created by sprinklers that rotate to water the land.

THE BEDOUIN
For centuries, Bedouin nomads have roamed the deserts of Saudi Arabia in search of food and water for their animals. Some Bedouin are camel herders; others keep sheep and goats. The Bedouin traditionally live in tents that are light and easy to transport. Today, their way of life is endangered because the government is encouraging people to settle in towns and cities.

Camels are ideally suited to desert life and are highly valued by the Bedouin.

A Bedouin tent is made from long strips of tightly woven goat hair.

The tent is divided into male and female quarters.

Modern Bedouin use cars and trucks for transportation as well as camels and horses.

Bedouin women weave tent cloth, drapes, and cushion covers, and saddle bags for their camels and horses.

Long, loose-fitting robes protect the skin from sun, and keep the body cool during the day.

Find out more
DESERT NOMADS: 181, 209
DESERTS: 15, 132, 152
ISLAM: 275
OIL: 137, 152, 281

KUWAIT

KUWAIT LIES AT THE NORTHERN end of the Persian Gulf. It is a small country, largely covered by sandy desert. Huge oil reserves have made Kuwait rich, and oil refining has become its chief industry. In 1990, at the start of the Gulf War, Kuwait was occupied by Iraq. It was liberated in 1991 by an international force.

KUWAIT'S WEALTH

Until the discovery of oil in the 1940s, Kuwait was a poor, underdeveloped country. The wealth gained by selling oil has transformed it into one of the most prosperous nations in the world. Its people enjoy a high standard of living, with free education, free health care and social services, and no income tax.

POLLUTION
Kuwait suffered badly during its invasion by Iraq. Many of its oil wells were set on fire, causing enormous damage to the economy and the environment. A huge slick of oil spilled into the Gulf, poisoning the water and killing wildlife. Abandoned ammunition and unexploded mines litter the desert, and the cleaning up process continues today.

Kuwait's wealth is reflected in its impressive buildings, such as these water towers that dominate Kuwait City's skyline.

KUWAIT
Capital city: Kuwait	
Area: 6,880 sq miles (17,820 sq km)	
Population: 2,000,000	
Official language: Arabic	
Major religions: Muslim 85%, other 15%	
Government: Absolute monarchy with parliament	
Currency: Kuwaiti dinar	
Adult literacy rate: 83%	
Life expectancy: 76 years	
People per doctor: 690	
Televisions: 491 per 1,000 people	

BAHRAIN
Capital city: Manama	
Area: 263 sq miles (680 sq km)	
Population: 617,000	
Official language: Arabic	
Major religions: Muslim 99%, other 1%	
Government: Absolute monarchy	
Currency: Bahrain dinar	
Adult literacy rate: 88%	
Life expectancy: 73 years	
People per doctor: 930	
Televisions: 472 per 1,000 people	

QATAR
Capital city: Doha	
Area: 4,247 sq miles (11,000 sq km)	
Population: 699,000	
Official language: Arabic	
Major religions: Muslim 95%, other 5%	
Government: Absolute monarchy	
Currency: Qatar riyal	
Adult literacy rate: 81%	
Life expectancy: 69 years	
People per doctor: 699	
Televisions: 404 per 1,000 people	

BAHRAIN

BAHRAIN IS MADE UP OF A SMALL GROUP of islands in the Persian Gulf. Little rain falls, so farming is only possible on irrigated, or watered, land. Bahrain was one of the first Arab states to discover oil in the 1930s. Its oil reserves are now running out.

PEARLING
As Bahrain's oil runs low, traditional industries, such as pearling, are once again growing in importance. The pearl season lasts from June to September. Divers descend on weighted ropes, equipped only with nose-plugs, knives, and collecting bags. The most valuable pearls are bright white, tinged with pink.

A pearl taken from an oyster shell

LINKED ISLANDS
The main island of Bahrain is linked by a series of road causeways to the neighboring islands of Al Muharraq and Sitrah, and to the Saudi Arabian mainland, with which Bahrain has close relations. Bahrain island is only 30 miles (48 km) long, and the other islands are even smaller.

QATAR

QATAR IS A LONG PENINSULA of land jutting out into the Persian Gulf. It is mainly desert with a hot, dry climate. Oil production and refining form the basis of its economy. The government is trying to encourage the growth of fishing and agriculture to reduce the country's dependence on oil.

An Indian construction worker

WORKERS FROM ABROAD
In the 1940s, the smaller oil states such as Qatar and Kuwait encouraged workers from other parts of the Middle East, India, and Pakistan to work in their rapidly growing oil industries. Their own labor forces were simply too small to cope. Today, these migrant workers outnumber the local Qatari people.

Find out more
DESERTS: *15, 132, 152*
GULF WAR: *152, 154*
IRRIGATION: *155, 156, 217*
OIL: *137, 152, 281*

UNITED ARAB EMIRATES

THE UNITED ARAB EMIRATES (UAE) lies on the southern coast of the Persian Gulf. Three-quarters of this Islamic country is sandy desert, with a hot, dry climate all year round. Only a tiny proportion of the land is suitable for farming and most food has to be imported. Oil was discovered in 1958 and has turned the UAE into one of the world's most prosperous countries, with a high standard of living for most people. There are many huge oil refineries along the coast.

Abu Dhabi

UNITED ARAB EMIRATES

Capital city: Abu Dhabi

Area: 32,278 sq miles (83,600 sq km)

Population: 2,400,000

Official language: Arabic

Major religions: Muslim 96%, other 4%

Government: Federation of monarchies

Currency: UAE dirham

Adult literacy rate: 76%

Life expectancy: 75 years

People per doctor: 1,250

Televisions: 294 per 1,000 people

OMAN

Capital city: Muscat

Area: 82,030 sq miles (212,460 sq km)

Population: 2,500,000

Official language: Arabic

Major religions: Muslim 90%, other 10%

Government: Absolute monarchy

Currency: Omani rial

Adult literacy rate: 72%

Life expectancy: 71 years

People per doctor: 833

Televisions: 595 per 1,000 people

TOURISM
The UAE has a growing tourist industry. Some 2.5 million people arrive each year, mainly from Europe and Japan. Most visit in winter when it is warm, but not too hot. Attractions include luxury hotels and duty-free shops, traditional markets, fine beaches, and trips into the desert.

Al Mamza Beach Park, Dubai

SEVEN STATES
The United Arab Emirates is a federation of seven small states, or emirates, each ruled by an emir, or sheik. The emirs have absolute power over their own states, but they also meet regularly to make decisions affecting the whole federation. Abu Dhabi is the largest of the emirates and its capital is also that of the UAE.

ISLAMIC FESTIVALS
The two most important festivals of the Islamic year are *Id al-Fitr* and *Id al-Adha. Id al-Fitr* literally means "the breaking of the fast." It celebrates the end of the holy month of Ramadan, during which Muslims must fast from dawn to dusk. *Id al-Adha* is the festival of sacrifice. Prayers are followed by the sacrifice of a sheep, cow, or camel.

A Muslim family celebrating Id al-Fitr *(left) The feast consists of typical Middle Eastern foods, such as those shown on the right.*

Dates

Apricots and dates are often eaten as appetizers.

Dried apricots

Lentils are used to make soups.

Zucchini is often eaten with a main meat dish.

OMAN

THE SULTANATE (KINGDOM) OF OMAN lies on the southeastern coast of the Arabian Peninsula. Much of the land is desert, dotted with oases, but parts of the coastline are more fertile. Here farmers grow dates, pomegranates, limes, tobacco, and wheat. People also raise goats, sheep, and cattle. Oil is Oman's main export.

Omani fishermen

FISHING
The Oman coastline is 1,056 miles (1,700 km) long, and fishing is a valuable source of income and food. Omani fishermen catch large amounts of sardines, tuna, anchovies, cod, and cuttlefish. They use traditional dugout canoes fitted with outboard motors for greater speed.

LOST CITY OF THE SANDS
According to Arabian legend, a magnificent city called Ubar lies buried under the desolate sands of southern Oman. Archaeologists have excavated a watering hole and the remains of a city dating from about 3000BC near the Yemen border. Some experts believe that this is the lost city of Ubar.

Find out more
DESERTS: 15, 132, 152
ISLAM: 275
OIL: 137, 152, 281
OIL WEALTH: 137,278

YEMEN

THE COUNTRY OF YEMEN was formed in 1990 when North and South Yemen were reunited. Yemen lies at the southern tip of the Arabian Peninsula. It is more fertile than other Middle Eastern countries, with good farmland in the western highlands where there is regular rainfall. The coast and mountains of the east are hot, dry, and barren. Yemen is a poorer, less developed country than its neighbors. It is hoped that oil reserves, discovered in the 1980s, may help increase its prosperity in the future.

THE PORT OF ADEN
Aden is one of the biggest cities in Yemen and the country's main port. Because of its location on the Gulf of Aden, it has been the region's chief trading city since ancient times. Today, it is an important industrial center, with a huge oil refinery, factories, and an international airport.

YEMEN

Capital city: San'a	
Area: 203,850 sq miles (527,970 sq km)	
Population: 18,100,000	
Official language: Arabic	
Major religions: Muslim 97%, other 3%	
Government: Multiparty democracy	
Currency: Yemen riyal	
Adult literacy rate: 46%	
Life expectancy: 60 years	
People per doctor: 3,846	
Televisions: 29 per 1,000 people	

YEMENI TERRACES

In many places the mountain slopes of Yemen are terraced to provide extra space for crops. Some terraces are more than 1,300 years old. About half of Yemeni workers are farmers. They grow cereal crops, such as wheat and sorghum, along with citrus fruits and dates, and raise sheep, goats, and cattle. Coffee and cotton are grown mainly for export.

Traditional Yemeni tower houses are scattered throughout the terraced hills.

The upper floors are used as living quarters.

The terraces are built up into the mountains.

The first floor is often used for storage.

Animals, such as goats and sheep, are kept on the ground floor of a house.

A variety of crops, such as coffee and cotton, are grown on the Yemeni terraces.

Coffee is often served in traditional Bedouin pots.

COFFEE AND QAT
Coffee is thought to have originated as a drink in Yemen and the country produces some of the world's finest quality beans. Yemen is also famous for a plant called *qat*. Its leaves contain a mild drug and are often chewed. *Qat* parties are an important part of Yemeni social life.

Tribal men often wear a ceremonial dagger, or jambiya, strapped to the waist.

SAN'A

San'a, the capital of Yemen, is an ancient city famous for its traditional Yemeni-style architecture. In the old city you can still see clusters of 400-year-old multistory mud and brick tower houses, their outer walls often decorated with friezes. An international conservation effort has been launched to protect this unique city and preserve its buildings for the future.

TRIBAL SOCIETY

Most Yemeni people are Muslim Arabs belonging to various tribal groups. Each tribe elects a sheik as its leader and has its own customs, costumes, and folklore. Within a tribe, people live in large, closely knit, extended families. Several generations of the same family usually share the same house. The tribal tradition is particularly strong in northern Yemen.

CENTRAL ASIA

CENTRAL ASIA LIES FAR FROM the world's oceans. The winds are dry and there is little rainfall, so the area is generally arid. With cold, dry winters, and hot, dry summers, lack of water is a problem for farmers. The north consists of a flat, grass-covered plain, or steppe. In the center of the region are two vast deserts, the Kyzyl Kum ("Red Sands") and the Kara Kum ("Black Sands"). In the south are long chains of snowcapped mountain ranges that join the neighboring Himalayas. The entire region, apart from Afghanistan, used to be part of the Soviet Union. Industrialization and collective farms brought huge changes to a region once occupied mainly by nomads.

INDEPENDENCE
In 1991, the communist state of the Soviet Union fell apart and the central Asian countries became independent. While the countries were under Soviet rule, many Russian people settled there, and Russian replaced the local languages. Today, the peoples of central Asia have reestablished their own languages and national identities.

Nomadic herders in the hills of Afghanistan

This girl's hat from Uzbekistan is embroidered with gold thread.

Child's hat from Afghanistan

A LAND OF MANY PEOPLES
There is a great variety of people living in central Asia. The original inhabitants include the Kazakhs, Turkmens, and Uzbeks, related to the Turks, and the Tajiks and Afghans, related to the Iranians. Each group has its own distinctive style of hat, often woven in silk with brightly colored geometric patterns.

Silver ornaments adorn this Turkmen girl's hat.

NOMADIC LIFESTYLE
Many people living in central Asia are nomads, moving from place to place with their animals in search of new pastures. Nomads live in tents and have few belongings, making traveling easy and quick. They live by herding animals such as camels, goats, and sheep, which give them milk, meat, and wool, some of which they sell, but most of which they use themselves. Nomads mostly stay in the open country, but they visit the towns and cities occasionally to sell their products.

The Aral Sea in 1960

Fishing village on the coast

Fishing village stranded inland

DRILLING FOR OIL
The northern states of central Asia are sitting on huge reserves of oil and gas. Kazakhstan is slowly exploiting one of the world's biggest oil fields under the Caspian Sea, while Turkmenistan is beginning to make use of a vast reservoir of natural gas trapped beneath its land. Exploitation of these riches is hampered by lack of investment and a poorly skilled workforce.

Miners drilling for oil in the Tengiz oil field in Kazakhstan

The Aral Sea in 1995

The lake is about half its original size. By 2010, it may have almost disappeared.

SHRINKING SEA
The Aral Sea, once the fourth largest freshwater lake in the world, is shrinking. Fishing villages that once stood on the sea coast are now stranded inland, depriving villagers of their livelihood. This environmental disaster has been caused by water being drained for irrigation projects from the Amu Darya River, which flows into the Aral Sea. Huge areas of useless land have been laid bare. Wind storms are common, sweeping up polluted dust and dumping it on the surrounding countryside.

A B C D E F G H I J K L

1 2 3 4 5 6 7 8 9 10 11 12

RUSSIAN FEDERATION

KAZAKHSTAN

Almaty, Kazakhstan
Jan 15°F (-9°C)
July 71°F (22°C)
Jan 1.3 in (33 mm)
July 1.4 in (36 mm)

Petropavlovsk

Kustanay

Kokchetav

Pavlodar

Ural'sk
Aksay

Aktyubinsk
Alga

ASTANA

Semipalatinsk
Ust' Kamenogorsk

Zyryanovsk

Arkalyk
Temirtau
Karaganda

L. Tengiz

KAZAKH UPLANDS

RUSSIAN FEDERATION

Atyrau

Emba

KIRGHIZ STEPPE

K A Z A K H S T A N

L. Zaysan

Fort Shevchenko
Beyneu

Aktau

Novyy Uzen'

Aral'sk

Nikol'skiy
Zhezkazgan

Baykonur

Balkhash

L. Balkhash

KARA KUM

Taldykorgan

CHINA

Ili

USTYURT PLATEAU

ARAL SEA

Syr Darya
Kzyl-Orda

KYZYL KUM

TURAN LOWLAND

Chu

Kapchagay

Almaty

CASPIAN SEA

Zaliv Kara-Bogaz-Gol

UZBEKISTAN

Muynak

L. Sarykamysh
Dashkhovuz
Urgench

Nukus

Uchkuduk

Zhambyl

Shymkent

BISHKEK
Tokmak

L. Issyk-kul

Karakol

KYRGYZSTAN

TASHKENT

Naryn

TIEN SHAN

UZBEKISTAN

Krasnovodsk

Nebitdag

TURKMENISTAN

Kizyl-Arbat

L. Aydarkul'
Zeravshan
Navoi
Bukhara
Samarkand

Khujand
Andizhan
Fergana

Osh

Krasnovodsk, Turkmenistan
Jan 35°F (2°C)
July 83°F (28°C)
Jan 0.2 in (13 mm)
July 0.5 in (5 mm)

TURKMENISTAN

ASHGABAT

Chardzhev
Karshi

Kizyl-Atrek

Karakum Canal

Amu Darya

Mary

Teдžen

TAJIKISTAN

DUSHANBE

Communism Peak

Bartang

PAMIRS

0 100 200 300 400 km
0 50 100 150 200 250 miles

THINGS TO LOOK FOR ON THE MAP

Longest river: Amu Darya, Afghanistan/Tajikistan/Turkmenistan/Uzbekistan, 872 miles (1,403 km) Map F8

Highest point: Communism Peak, Tajikistan, 24,590 ft (7,495 m) Map H7

World's largest lake: Caspian Sea, Russian Federation/Kazakhstan/Turkmenistan/Iran/Azerbaijan, 146,111 sq miles (378,400 sq km) Map B6

World's longest irrigation canal: Karakum Canal, Turkmenistan, 683 miles (1,100 km) Map E8

KYRGYZSTAN

TAJIKISTAN

Mazār-e Sharif
Kurgan-Tyube
Khlyab
Pandj

Kunduz

IRAN

Morghab
Herāt
Harirūd

Kowl-e Namaksār

Qonduz

HINDU KUSH

KABUL
Jalālābād
Khyber Pass

TORKESTAN MTS.

AFGHANISTAN

Hāmūn-e Sāberī

Helmand
Arghandāb

Kandahār

Gowd-e Zereh

PAKISTAN

ARCTIC CIRCLE

TROPIC OF CANCER

EQUATOR

N

Kabul, Afghanistan
Jan 27°F (-3°C)
July 72°F (22°C)
Jan 1.2 in (31 mm)
July 0.1 in (3 mm)

AFGHANISTAN

CAVIAR
The largest inland lake in the world, the Caspian Sea covers 146,111 sq miles (378,400 sq km) and borders five countries. The lake is home to a variety of fish, such as sturgeon, from which a type of caviar (fish eggs) comes. However, pollution of the waters by industrial waste has led to a drop in the numbers of fish.

Caviar served on toast

ISLAM
Throughout central Asia, Islam is the main religion. It arrived in the region in the early 8th century. While central Asia was part of the Soviet Union, Islam was suppressed. Traditional Muslim wedding ceremonies were forbidden. Throughout this time, however, people continued to worship in secret. With the end of communism, Islam has gained strength in every country.

KAZAKHSTAN

KAZAKHSTAN

Capital city: Astana

Area: 1,049,150 sq miles (2,717,300 sq km)

Population: 16,200,000

Official language: Kazakh

Major religions: Muslim 50%, Christian 14%, other 36%

Government: Democracy

Currency: Tenge

Adult literacy rate: 99%

Life expectancy: 64 years

People per doctor: 265

Televisions: 231 per 1,000 people

STRETCHING FROM THE Caspian Sea to China, Kazakhstan is a vast country, almost the size of western Europe. It is also one of the most underpopulated countries in the world. With vast mineral reserves, fertile soil, and a stable government, Kazakhstan has the potential to be a wealthy country. However, industrial and agricultural pollution, particularly the use of pesticides and the way in which crops like cotton are grown, have caused considerable environmental problems.

At the processing plant, the coal is cleaned and dried and sorted into different sizes.

In the filter bed, any remaining pieces of rock and clay are removed.

Trucks transport the extracted coal along a hauling road.

RICH IN MINERALS

Mining is the most important industry in Kazakhstan. The country has huge coal and iron-ore reserves, the world's largest chrome mine, one of its biggest gold fields, and plentiful supplies of copper, zinc, lead, uranium, and other minerals. Most coal in Kazakhstan comes from open-pit mines, where coal is extracted near the surface of the ground, rather than from deep mine shafts.

Machines dig the coal out of the pit.

Steps are cut into the sides of the pit so that the coal can be reached safely.

Surface rock is loosened by explosives so that the digging machines can remove the rock and reach the coal.

THE VIRGIN LANDS

In the 1950s the Russian government increased grain production by cultivating the vast grassland steppes, or plains, of Kazakhstan. Huge farms were set up to grow corn and wheat on land that had been barren. Millions of Russians migrated or were forced to move to this empty region, known as the "Virgin Lands." The program met with mixed success. It left Kazakhstan self-sufficient in grain and other crops, but it led to enormous environmental damage.

THE KAZAKHS

Native Kazakhs make up only about 50 percent of the total population of their country and live mainly in the west and south. Many are farmers and have worked hard to preserve the natural beauty of the land, setting up reserves to protect the wildlife and environment. The rest of the population consists mainly of Russians, Germans, and Ukranians.

A government building in Almaty, the former capital of Kazakhstan.

SPACE RACE

History was made in Kazakhstan in 1957, when the world's first artificial satellite, *Sputnik I*, was launched from the Baykonur Cosmodrome, or space station, in the center of the country. The first person in space, Yuri Gagarin, was sent into orbit around the Earth from Baykonur in 1961. The site is still used today by the Russian government for its space program.

THE CITY OF APPLES

Almaty means "father of apple trees," and the former capital is known for its apple orchards. The city nestles at the foot of the Tien Shan mountains in the far south of the country. It has many parks and fountains, and narrow canals called *aryks* run along the sides of streets to cool the city during the hot summers. The capital was moved to Astana in the north in 1994.

Find out more

CEREALS: 34, 122
COAL MINING: 96, 114
POPULATION DENSITY: 135
STEPPE (GRASSLANDS): 15

UZBEKISTAN

UZBEKISTAN IS THE MOST DENSELY POPULATED country in central Asia. It also has a varied landscape. While two-thirds of the land is made up of desert and arid steppe land, there are also fertile areas, fast-flowing rivers, and snowy mountaintops. The ancient cities of the Silk Road are beginning to attract ever increasing numbers of tourists, and foreign investors are helping develop the country's huge mineral and energy resources. Uzbekistan is also the world's fourth largest producer of cotton, known locally as "white gold."

UZBEKISTAN

Capital city: Tashkent	
Area: 172,741 sq miles (447,400 sq km)	
Population: 24,300,000	
Official language: Uzbek	
Major religions: Muslim 91%, Christian 9%	
Government: Democracy	
Currency: Som	
Adult literacy rate: 90%	
Life expectancy: 69 years	
People per doctor: 301	
Televisions: 275 per 1,000 people	

TAJIKISTAN

Capital city: Dushanbe	
Area: 55,251 sq miles (143,100 sq km)	
Population: 6,200,000	
Official language: Tajik	
Major religions: Muslim 85%, other 15%	
Government: Democracy	
Currency: Rouble	
Adult literacy rate: 99%	
Life expectancy: 70 years	
People per doctor: 476	
Televisions: 285 per 1,000 people	

ISLAMIC CITIES

The Silk Road is an old trading route that linked China with central Asia, the Middle East, and Europe. Ancient Islamic cities, once major trading centers, are found along its route. These include Samarkand, which contains many fine examples of Islamic architecture, Bukhara, an important place of pilgrimage for Muslims, and Tashkent, the capital of Uzbekistan, known as the "city of fountains."

NATURAL GAS
Uzbekistan is rich in natural resources. It has plentiful supplies of oil, natural gas, coal, gold, and uranium. A huge pipeline used for exporting natural gas stretches from Bukhara to the Urals in Russia. Much of the local industry, producing machinery, chemicals, and aircraft, is based on energy from gas.

Registan Square in Samarkand dates back to the 14th century and contains many magnificent Islamic buildings.

TAJIKISTAN

THE POOREST OF THE FORMER SOVIET UNION states, Tajikistan is a mountainous country with only about six percent of its land available for farming. Most people work on the land, growing fruit, cotton, and tobacco and herding animals, or work in small factories producing textiles, silk, and carpets. From independence in 1991 until 1997, Tajikistan was split by armed conflict between the government and rebel groups.

In the Pamir mountain region, a different tribal group is found in almost every valley.

Peaches

Melon

Pistachios

FERTILE VALLEYS
In spring, melted snow from the Tien Shan and Pamir mountains flows down into the Fergana and other river valleys of Tajikistan, bringing with it rich, fertile mud. Irrigation channels direct this water into the surrounding fields, enabling farmers to grow a variety of crops, such as those above.

PAMIR VALLEY PEOPLES

Less than 100,000 people live in the Pamir mountain region, growing grain and fruit in the deep valleys, or herding sheep and yaks on the bleak high plains in the east. Because of the remoteness of the area and the isolation of the valleys from each other, there is a bewildering variety of peoples, languages, and dialects.

Find out more
COTTON: *36, 215, 216*
GAS: *198, 211*
ISLAM: *275*
ISLAMIC ARCHITECTURE: *155*

TURKMENISTAN

ALMOST 90 PERCENT of Turkmenistan consists of the vast Kara Kum ("Black Sands") Desert, where temperatures reach more than 122°F (50°C). A fertile strip of land stretches around the southern borders of the desert; here people grow cotton and other crops for export. Since Turkmenistan became independent in 1991, Turkmen has replaced Russian as the state language, and Islam is once again the major religion. The country is poor and isolated from the rest of the world, but possesses huge reserves of natural gas.

ASHGABAT
In 1948, the bustling market town of Ashgabat was totally destroyed by a huge earthquake. The town was completely replanned and rebuilt, and is now the capital city of Turkmenistan. Ashgabat is a center for food processing and silk, lace, and carpet manufacturing.

TURKMENISTAN

Capital city: Ashgabat

Area: 188,455 sq miles (488,100 sq km)

Population: 4,500,000

Official language: Turkmen

Major religions: Muslim 87%, Christian 11%, other 2%

Government: Democracy

Currency: Manat

Adult literacy rate: 98%

Life expectancy: 66 years

People per doctor: 313

Televisions: No figures available

KYRGYZSTAN

Capital city: Bishkek

Area: 76,640 sq miles (198,500 sq km)

Population: 4,700,000

Official language: Kyrgyz

Major religions: No figures available

Government: Democracy

Currency: Som

Adult literacy rate: 97%

Life expectancy: 67 years

People per doctor: 291

Televisions: No figures available

THE TURKMENS
The Turkmen people live in various parts of central Asia and many follow a nomadic lifestyle. In Turkmenistan, however, many Turkmens have settled as farmers and expert horse breeders. They visit local horse fairs and buy and sell horses for export to neighboring countries. The Turkmens are known for producing prized racehorses, such as the Akhal-Teke, a breed able to move quickly in desert conditions.

Ashgabat • Karakum Canal

● Main towns
⚓ Cotton

KARAKUM CANAL
The world's longest irrigation canal stretches from the Amu Darya River in the east to beyond Ashgabat in the west, a distance of 683 miles (1,100 km). Known as the "River of Life," the Karakum Canal provides water for a large area of arid land so that cotton and other crops can be grown.

KYRGYZSTAN

Gold nugget

KNOWN AS THE Switzerland of central Asia because of its mountainous landscape, over half of Kyrgyzstan is 8,200 ft (2,500 m) or more above sea level. The snowcapped Tien Shan Mountains dominate the countryside, but the river valleys are fertile and green. Most people are farmers. Animal breeding is particularly important because there is so little land to farm.

The Kyrgyz people practice Islam. They speak a Turkic language and live a nomadic life in the countryside.

MOUNTAIN RICHES
The mountains of Kyrgyzstan are rich in minerals. Gold and mercury are mined for export, while coal, oil, and gas are exploited for domestic use. The fast-flowing rivers are ideal for generating electricity, and new hydroelectric power stations have been built.

THE KYRGYZ PEOPLE
The population is more than half native Kyrgyz. These nomadic people are known for their skilled horsemanship. The largest minority group are Russians, who live in the towns and, until independence in 1991, ran the economy. As a result of rising nationalist feeling among the Kyrgyz, many Russian people have now returned to Russia.

Find out more
DESERTS: *15, 132, 152*
GAS: *163, 198, 211*
NOMADS: *160*
USSR BREAKUP: *136, 160*

AFGHANISTAN

AFGHANISTAN OCCUPIES AN IMPORTANT position between central Asia and the Indian Subcontinent. As a result the country has been fought over for centuries. It has few paved roads and no railroads, and three-quarters of the land is inaccessible. In 1979 Russian troops occupied the country, though they were forced out by the Islamic *mujahideen*. In 1996 the Taliban took control of Kabul and enforced a strict code of behavior, based on their interpretation of Islam. However their support for Osama bin Laden, wanted in connection with the destruction of the World Trade Center, led to bombing by the US and victory for the opposition Northern Alliance in 2001.

AFGHANISTAN

Capital city: Kabul

Area: 251,770 sq miles (652,090 sq km)

Population: 22,700,000

Official languages: Dari (Persian), Pashtu

Major religions: Muslim 99%, other 1%

Government: Islamic republic

Currency: Afghani

Adult literacy rate: 37%

Life expectancy: 46 years

People per doctor: 6,430

Televisions: 13 per 1,000 people

CULTURAL DESTRUCTION
In 2001 the Taliban destroyed two of the world's largest statues of Buddha at Bamiyan. Built in 5 AD, the tallest of the statues was over 174 ft (53 m) high. The Taliban justified this act by saying Islam forbids the depiction of the human form in art, but many Islamic nations disagreed with what they had done.

Some mujahideen *groups are based in the hills of Afghanistan.* Mujahideen *comes from the Arabic word for "fighter."*

The Turkmen nomads in the north of the country live in reddish-brown, dome-shaped tents.

The Pushtoon nomads of the south live in black tents spread low over the ground.

THE TALIBAN

In Pashtu, an Afghani language, Taliban means "religious student", and it was from religious schools in Pakistan and the south of Afghanistan that the Taliban developed their extreme ideology. The Taliban are an Islamic militia who promised Afghanis stability in return for one of the most repressive governments in the world. Their support of terrorist groups led to the US helping the Northern Alliance to overthrow them.

TENTS
Some Afghans are nomads, or *kochis* as they are known locally. The different groups can be distinguished by the unique designs of the felt or animal-skin tents they live in, each design having been passed down through countless generations.

OPPRESSION OF WOMEN

Under the Taliban, women were denied a full role in Afghan society and were subject to much discrimination. They were not allowed to go to work and girls were banned from school. They were not even allowed to go outside of the home without being accompanied by a male member of their family. When women were permitted outside they had to wear a *burka* – a traditional Afghani robe that covered them from head to toe.

CARPET WEAVING
The Turkmens of northern Afghanistan are skilled carpet makers, hand-knotting and weaving fine wool from the karakul sheep into geometric red, brown, and maroon patterns. The carpets are usually made by women and are used as saddlecloths, tent hangings, and prayer mats.

Major peoples in Afghanistan
1. Uzbek   4. Hazara
2. Tajik   5. Nuristani
3. Aimaq   6. Pushtoon

Find out more
CARPET MAKING: *144, 155, 210*
ISLAM: *275*
NOMADS: *160*
TENTS: *156, 181*

THE INDIAN SUBCONTINENT

FRINGED BY THE INDIAN OCEAN, the Arabian Sea, and the Bay of Bengal, and bordered to the north by the mighty Himalayas, the Indian Subcontinent covers a vast area. More than a fifth of the world's people live here. Dominated by India, the area also includes Pakistan, Bangladesh, Nepal, the island of Sri Lanka, and the tiny state of Bhutan. The Subcontinent has a long and turbulent history and has been invaded many times. In the 19th and early 20th centuries, most of the area, apart from Nepal and Bhutan, was ruled by Britain. The landscape and climate of the Subcontinent vary greatly, with snowcapped mountains in the north, dry, sandy desert in the northwest, and hot, tropical rain forest in the south.

INDEPENDENCE
India became independent in 1947. The country was divided into Hindu India and the new Muslim country of Pakistan, split into West and East. In 1971, East Pakistan became the independent country of Bangladesh.

Mahatma Gandhi, a central figure in India's struggle for independence, believed in using peaceful methods to achieve his country's aims.

Most villagers are farmers, but others follow a trade, such as weaving or pottery-making.

Most village people live in small houses with two or three rooms.

VILLAGE LIFE
Most people in the Subcontinent live in closely knit villages and make a living from farming. In India alone, more than 70 percent of the population lives in some 500,000 villages scattered across the country. Some consist of small clusters of houses, others have thousands of inhabitants. Most families have lived in the same village for many years, passing on their knowledge and skills from one generation to the next.

The houses of many villages are clustered around a village square. Here the village council (Panchayat) will meet to make decisions.

The well is one of the focal points of village life. Women collect water every day and meet to exchange news.

Because Bangladesh is flat and low-lying, it is particularly prone to flooding.

→ Southwest winds (June to October)
→ Northeast winds (November to February)

MONSOON
The climate of much of the Subcontinent is dominated by the monsoon winds, which bring rain to the area each summer. Farmers rely on this rainfall to water their crops. If the rains fail, they face ruin. Sometimes the rainfall is very heavy and causes terrible floods. Whole villages and fields of crops may be swept away.

SEASONAL WINDS
These winds blow from the southwest in summer and from the northeast in winter. As the summer winds sweep across the Indian Ocean, they pick up moisture, which turns into rain on reaching the hot, dry land.

TREKKING IN THE HIMALAYAS
Each year, thousands of tourists travel to Nepal to trek in the mountains. The Nepalese Himalayas include eight peaks more than 26,247 ft (8,000 m) high. The world's tallest mountain, Everest, stands on the border between Nepal and China. Many expeditions are accompanied by Sherpas. These Nepalese people are skilled climbers.

A B C D E F G H I J K L

Islamabad, Pakistan
☀ Jan 49°F (9°C)
July 87°F (31°C)
🌧 Jan 2.5 in (64 mm)
July 9.2 in (233 mm)

Kashmir: a "line of control" was established in 1972 by the Simla Agreement between Pakistan and India

Claimed by India

Aksai Chin is controlled by China but claimed by India

Demchok is claimed by both India and China

THINGS TO LOOK FOR ON THE MAP
Longest river: Ganges, India, 1,560 miles (2,510 km) *Map G5*
Highest point: Mt. Everest, China/Nepal, 29,029 ft (8,848 m) *Map J5*
Largest lake: L. Chilka, India, 351 sq miles (910 sq km) *Map H8*
World's largest delta: Ganges, India/Bangladesh, 28,957 sq miles (75,000 sq km) *Map J7*

AFGHANISTAN

TOBAKAKAR RANGE

CHAGAI HILLS

MAKRAN

PAKISTAN

Tarbela Res.
Peshawar
Srinagar
ISLAMABAD ✪
Rawalpindi
Jhelum
Gujrat
Gujranwala
Sargodha
Lahore
Amritsar
Faisalabad
Jalandhar
Okara
Ludhiana
Chandigarh
Quetta
Dera Ghazi Khan
Multan
Bahawalpur
Meerut
Shikarpur
Rahimyar Khan
NEW DELHI ✪
Bareilly
Larkana
Sukkur
Nawabshah
SINDH
THAR DESERT
Jaipur
Aligarh
Shahjahanpur
Agra
Lucknow
Jodhpur
Gwalior
Chambal
Yamuna
Kanpur
Varanasi
Kota
Allahabad
Patna
Gaya
Son
Karachi
Hyderabad
Indus

PUNJAB

HIMALAYA

KASHMIR

CHINA

NEPAL
KATHMANDU ✪
Nepalganj
Gorakhpur
Biratnagar
Mt. Everest
THIMPHU ✪
BHUTAN
Itanagar
Rangpur
Brahmaputra
Guwahati
Shillong
Jamalpur
Sylhet
Imphal
Ganges
Rajshahi
BANGLADESH
Aizawl
Dhanbad
Asansol
DACCA ✪
Chittagong

NEPAL

BHUTAN

RANN OF KUTCH
Gulf of Kutch
Ahmadabad
Bhopal
Jamnagar
Rajkot
Vadodara
Indore
Bhavnagar
Narmada
Jabalpur
Ranchi
Jamshedpur
Govind Ballash Pant Res.
Calcutta (Kolkata)
Khulna
Hirakud Res.
Surat
Dhule
Tapti
Nagpur
Raipur
Daman
Ganges Delta
Nasik
Thane
Nanded
Godavari
Mahanadi
Cuttack
Mumbai (Bombay)
Pune
DECCAN
Bhubaneswar
L. Chilka
Sholapur
Hyderabad
PLATEAU
Nagarjuna Res.
Vishakhapatnam
Krishna
Rajahmundry
Vijayawada
Panaji
Dharwad
Davangere
Nellore
Chenai (Madras)
Mangalore
Bangalore
Mysore
Salem
Coimbatore
Tiruchchirappalli
Cochin
Madurai
Jaffna
Mannar
Trivandrum
Nagercoil
SRI LANKA
Kandy
Trincomalee
COLOMBO ✪
Galle

INDIA

WESTERN GHATS
EASTERN GHATS
MALABAR COAST
COROMANDEL COAST
ARABIAN SEA
Gulf of Khambhat
Bay of Bengal
MYANMAR

PAKISTAN

BANGLADESH

INDIA

SRI LANKA

N

0 100 200 300 400 km
0 50 100 150 200 250 miles

Hyderabad, India
☀ Jan 72°F (23°C)
July 80°F (27°C)
🌧 Jan 0.3 in (8 mm)
July 6 in (152 mm)

ARCTIC CIRCLE
TROPIC OF CANCER
EQUATOR

Chittagong, Bangladesh
☀ Jan 67°F (20°C)
July 82°F (28°C)
🌧 Jan 0.2 in (5 mm)
July 23.5 in (597 mm)

SACRED RIVER
Followers of five of the world's major religions live in the Indian Subcontinent – Hindus, Muslims, Buddhists, Sikhs, and Christians. The majority of people are Hindu and their holiest city is Varanasi, in northern India. The city stands on the banks of the Ganges, the sacred river of the Hindus. Millions of pilgrims come to Varanasi each year to bathe in the river. This is believed to wash away their sins.

ENDANGERED WILDLIFE
The Subcontinent is rich in wildlife, from elephants and rhinoceros to monkeys and mongooses. Loss of habitat and poaching are serious threats to India's most famous animals, including tigers. Despite the establishment of protected reserves, illegal tiger-hunting continues. Only around 3,000 tigers are left in the wild.

PAKISTAN

PAKISTAN WAS CREATED IN 1947 as a home for Muslims in India. The country was originally divided into East and West, but in 1971 East Pakistan broke away to become Bangladesh, and West Pakistan became Pakistan. Today, most people make their living from farming, but industry, especially cotton and textiles, is growing steadily. Handicrafts, such as carpet-making and metalwork, are also important. Since Pakistan became independent, it has been in dispute with India over the largely Muslim state of Kashmir, which forms part of India, but is claimed by Pakistan.

PEOPLES OF PAKISTAN
There are many different groups of people living in Pakistan, all of whom have their own distinctive language and culture. The Pathan tribes of the Northwest Frontier are known for their fierce loyalty to family and tribe. The Sindhis (above) are a farming community living in the south of the country with a rich tradition in literature and music. The Punjabis live in the fertile plains of the Punjab.

PAKISTAN

Capital city: Islamabad

Area: 297,638 sq miles (770,880 sq km)

Population: 156,500,000

Official language: Urdu

Major religions: Muslim 97%, other 3%

Government: Military government

Currency: Pakistani rupee

Adult literacy rate: 46%

Life expectancy: 60 years

People per doctor: 1,915

Televisions: 88 per 1,000 people

BRIGHT BUSES
Many people in Pakistan travel on the brightly colored buses that run between the towns and cities. The buses often have flowers and patterns painted on them and are decorated with tinsel and lights. Trucks used to transport all sorts of goods are also often highly decorated.

● major cities
▨ irrigated land

WHERE PEOPLE LIVE
The population of Pakistan is unevenly distributed. More than 80 percent of the people live in the provinces of Punjab and Sind, on the fertile floodplains of the rivers.

WATERING THE LAND
The flat, fertile plains of the Punjab form the farming heartland of Pakistan. The rich soil is watered by the Indus River, which also provides water for drinking and for electricity. The river has five tributaries, the Jhelum, Chenab, Ravi, Sutlej, and Beas, which give the region its name — Punjab means "five waters." In other parts of the country, huge irrigation (watering) schemes have converted scrubland and semi-desert into fertile farmland.

WOMEN'S LIFE
Islamic law is very important in Pakistan. It determines how people worship and behave. It is Islamic custom for women to live in *purdah* (behind the veil). This means that when women appear in public, they cover themselves with a *burqa* (hooded gown) or a *chaddar* (veil) to ensure that men cannot see their faces. Traditional households are often divided into a men's section at the front and a women's section at the back.

ISLAMABAD
About a third of Pakistani people live in cities. The capital is Islamabad (right), a brand new city built in the early 1960s. The name Islamabad means the "place of Islam." The city is well planned, with lots of open spaces and wide, tree-lined avenues. Karachi is the major port and largest city, with around 10 million people.

Chaddar, or veil

Kamiz, or tunic

Find out more
COTTON: *36, 215, 216*
IRRIGATION: *155, 156, 217*
ISLAM: *275*
RIVER VALLEYS: *135*

BANGLADESH

BANGLADESH

IN 1971, EAST PAKISTAN broke away from West Pakistan to become the independent country of Bangladesh. Like Pakistan, it remains a largely Muslim country. The official language is Bengali. Bangladesh is one of the poorest and most crowded countries in the world, suffering from frequent cyclones and floods that cause devastation, especially along the coast. Efforts are being made to control the floods, to slow down the rate of population growth, and to modernize industry and farming.

BANGLADESH

Capital city: Dhaka

Area: 51,702 sq miles (133,910 sq km)

Population: 129,200,000

Official language: Bengali

Major religions: Muslim 87%, Hindu 12%, other 1%

Government: Multiparty democracy

Currency: Taka

Adult literacy rate: 41%

Life expectancy: 59 years

People per doctor: 5,000

Televisions: 6 per 1,000 people

GROWING JUTE

Known to Bangladeshis as "the golden fiber," jute is a tough, fibrous plant that has proved a valuable source of income for farmers. Jute is used to make sacking, rope, and carpet backing. It has traditionally been Bangladesh's most important export, but now faces competition from artificial fibers. Rice is a major food crop in Bangladesh, with tea and sugarcane grown for export.

Most Bangladeshi people make their living from fishing and farming. The annual floods provide plenty of fish and keep the land very fertile.

The flooded delta
The map shows the varying depths of water during the annual flood.

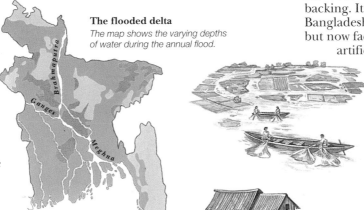

Depth of water
- up to 3 ft (1 m)
- 3-6 ft (1-2 m)
- more than 6 ft (2 m)

FLOODED LAND

Much of Bangladesh is made up of the delta (mouth) of three major rivers – the Ganges, Brahmaputra, and Meghna. During the monsoon season (June to October) the rivers flood, and huge amounts of rich silt are left behind, making the soil extremely fertile for farming. But the flooding can also cause devastation, killing many people and animals, and sweeping away homes and crops. Despite the risks, most Bangladeshis live in tiny villages scattered across the floodplains.

Houses are often raised up on stilts or embankments to protect them from the floods.

Boats are a vital means of transportation. People travel in all types of boats, which are often very crowded. Huge rafts are used to carry jute, bamboo, and other goods.

HEALTH CARE

Despite government health care programs, the death rate in Bangladesh is very high, especially among children in remote, rural areas. This is largely due to poor diet and to unclean water, which helps spread diseases such as cholera. Medical teams travel around the country immunizing people from disease and teaching them about diet and birth control.

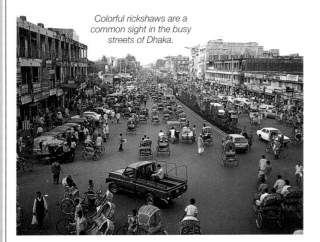

Colorful rickshaws are a common sight in the busy streets of Dhaka.

LIFE IN THE CITY

Only about a third of Bangladeshis live in cities, mainly in Dhaka, the capital, or the two ports of Chittagong and Khulna. City dwellers can enjoy a higher standard of living than people in the villages, with better homes and facilities such as piped water and electricity supplies. As the cities become more crowded with people looking for work, however, many new arrivals are being forced to live in slums and shantytowns.

Find out more
HEALTH: *276*
ISLAM: *275*
MONSOON: *166*
RIVER VALLEYS: *135*

INDIA

THE WORLD'S SEVENTH LARGEST and second most populated country, India is a vast, colorful land, full of variety in religion, language, and culture. Three of the world's major faiths, Hinduism, Buddhism, and Sikhism, originated here. More than 200 languages are spoken, although 40 percent of the population speaks Hindi. Despite much poverty, India is one of the world's top industrialized nations. Both agriculture and industry have expanded during the past 20 years and have attracted investment from international companies. India is also the world's largest democracy. Some 600 million people are eligible to vote.

INDIA

Capital city:	New Delhi
Area:	1,147,948 sq miles (2,973190 sq km)
Population:	1,013,700,000
Official languages:	Hindi, English
Major religions:	Hindu 83%, Muslim 11%, Christian 2%, Sikh 2%, other 2%
Government:	Multiparty democracy
Currency:	Rupee
Adult literacy rate:	57%
Life expectancy:	63 years
People per doctor:	2,500
Televisions:	69 per 1,000 people

BOLLYWOOD
More films are produced in India than anywhere else in the world, including the US. About 800 full-length feature films are shot each year, mainly in Mumbai (Bombay), nicknamed "Bollywood." Indian films are often packed with songs, dancing, romance, glamorous stars, and nonstop action. Going to the movies is a favorite pastime in India, and many films last for four or five hours.

These farm workers are winnowing, or sifting, grain after the harvest. Huge amounts of grain are kept in reserve in case the harvest fails.

GREEN REVOLUTION

One of India's most pressing problems has been to produce enough food for its ever-growing population. Today, it is self-sufficient in food. Production of rice and wheat has risen more than 200 percent since independence in 1947. This improvement is partly due to the "Green Revolution" of the 1960s, when farming methods were modernized and higher-yielding varieties of rice and wheat were planted.

FOOD PRODUCTION
India is the world's biggest producer of the crops shown below. Percentages indicate India's share in world production.

- sugar 11%
- bananas 13%
- tea 28%
- sesame seeds 33%
- jute 44%
- mangoes 60%

Cinnamon is used in both sweet and savory dishes.

Garlic is added to many spice mixtures.

Coriander is an essential ingredient in many Indian dishes.

Turmeric is used as a spice and a dye.

INDIAN FOOD

Many Indian people are vegetarians. They do not believe in killing animals to eat. Most Hindus never eat beef because they consider cows to be sacred, and Muslims do not eat pork. Food varies from place to place, but a typical meal might consist of several spicy vegetable dishes, *dhal* (lentils), *dahi* (yogurt), rice or *chappatis* (flat bread), and *poppadums.* The food is flavored with many spices, including turmeric, chili, coriander, cumin, and cardamom.

Rice

Vegetables in a spicy sauce

INDUSTRY

Since independence, industry has expanded in India. Factories produce and process goods such as cars, chemicals, food and drink, and computers. Jet airplanes and space rockets are now being made. Textiles and leather goods are major exports. Traditionally much of India's industrial output has come from small, family-run industries producing traditional handicrafts such as brasswork, mirror work, and tie-dye.

BUSY CITIES

India's cities are bustling, chaotic places where modern, high-rise office buildings stand next to ancient temples, mosques, and monuments. New Delhi is the capital, but the two largest cities are Calcutta (Kolkata) and Mumbai (Bombay). Both are major industrial centers. Overcrowding is a serious and growing problem in India's cities, as more and more people arrive from the countryside in search of work. Many people live in slums and shantytowns, or on the streets.

MEMORY IN MARBLE
The Taj Mahal, in Agra, was built in the 17th century by Shah Jahan, one of the Mughal emperors who ruled India from the 16th to 18th centuries. Built in white marble as a tomb for his beloved wife, it is a fine example of Islamic architecture and attracts many visitors. Tourism is an increasingly important industry in India, bringing millions of people every year.

HINDU WEDDING

Hindu weddings are elaborate affairs, with ceremonies and feasting lasting for several days. Most marriages take place among members of the same *caste*, or social group, and are arranged by the couple's parents. After the wedding, the bride lives with her husband's family. Family life is very important to Hindus. They often live as part of an extended family, with several generations sharing the same house.

The bride and groom wear garlands around their necks.

After the sheet has been lifted, the bride and groom take seven steps around the sacred fire. Each step represents an aspect of their future life together, such as happiness, children, and lifelong friendship.

At the beginning of the wedding ceremony, the bride and groom sit facing each other, holding hands through a silk sheet held as a screen between them.

Traditionally, a Hindu bride wears a red silk sari, embroidered with gold thread, together with special jewelry and makeup. Her hands and feet are decorated with mehndi (henna).

The henna lasts for weeks, reflecting the woman's new status as a wife.

A silk sari

SARI
The traditional dress for Indian women is the sari, a length of brightly colored silk or cotton, some 66 ft (20 m) long, which is wrapped around the body and draped over one shoulder. One end of the sari is left hanging or used to cover the head. Traditional dress for men is a *dhoti*, a length of cotton cloth usually wrapped around the waist and between the legs.

OTHER FAITHS
Most people in India are Hindu, but many other faiths are followed, such as Sikhism and Jainism. Sikhs believe in one god. Their holiest shrine is the Golden Temple, in Amritsar. Many male Sikhs wear turbans (left), a symbol of purity. Jainism is similar to Hinduism. Jains have respect for all life, and monks wear masks to prevent insects from entering their mouths.

Find out more

DEMOCRACY: *270*
GROWING CITIES: *17, 135*
RELIGION: *274–275*
SPICES: *57, 198, 264*

SRI LANKA

SRI LANKA IS A TEARDROP-SHAPED island that lies off the southeastern coast of India. It is known for its tropical, palm-fringed beaches, rugged mountains, and varied wildlife, which attract thousands of tourists. In recent years, Sri Lanka and its tourist trade have been badly hit by fighting between the Sinhalese people and the minority Tamil group, which wants an independent state. Agriculture is important to Sri Lanka. Tea, rubber, and coconuts are grown on large plantations and are the main export crops. Rice is the main food crop.

SRI LANKA

Capital city: Colombo

Area: 24,996 sq miles (64,740 sq km)

Population: 18,800,000

Official language: Sinhalese

Major religions: Buddhist 69%, Hindu 15%, Christian 8%, Muslim 8%

Government: Multiparty democracy

Currency: Sri Lanka rupee

Adult literacy rate: 92%

Life expectancy: 72 years

People per doctor: 10,000

Televisions: 92 per 1,000 people

THE SACRED TOOTH
The most important Buddhist festival in Sri Lanka takes place in Kandy in August. A beautifully decorated elephant parades through the streets, carrying a gold casket containing the sacred tooth of the Buddha. For the rest of the year, the tooth is kept in the Temple of the Tooth. It is said that the tooth was snatched from the Buddha's funeral pyre (fire) in 543BC.

Sapphire stone

Sapphire earrings

SAPPHIRE BLUE
Sri Lanka is known for its gemstones, particularly those from Ratnapura, the "City of Gems." Sapphires, rubies, topazes, amethysts, and garnets are all found in the rocks nearby. Many are made into superb jewelry or exported abroad.

Many Tamil women are employed as tea pickers.

THE TAMILS
Tensions between the Sinhalese government and the Tamils erupted into civil war in 1983 and have continued ever since. The Tamils object to the domination of the island by the Sinhalese and are demanding their own independent state in the north. Tamils, who are mostly Hindu, make up about 20 percent of the population. The mainly Buddhist Sinhalese form the majority, accounting for about 75 percent.

The women hang the baskets from their heads, so that both hands are free for picking.

BEAUTIFUL BEACHES
Tourism has become one of Sri Lanka's most important industries. The country is well known for its beautiful sandy beaches, especially on the south and southwest coasts, and its Buddhist temples and monuments further inland, particularly the ancient city of Kandy. However, intense fighting in the civil war has recently scared tourists away, seriously affecting the ecomomy.

Tea seeds are first sown in a nursery bed and then the young plants are transplanted to a field.

The leaves are then fermented and dried to produce the final product.

TEA GROWING
Tea is grown mainly on large plantations in the central highlands. The cooler climate makes the tea grow slowly, adding to its flavor. Only the youngest, tenderest leaves are harvested, and then processed quickly to retain quality. Tea makes up about a third of the island's exports. Recently, the tea industry has suffered fierce competition from countries producing cheaper, lower quality tea.

The tea plants are plucked once a week. Picking is still done by hand as machines would bruise the leaves and spoil their flavor.

When the tea picker's basket is full, it is taken for weighing. The picker is paid by the basket.

Find out more

BUDDHISM: *275*
GEMSTONES: *62, 191*
RUBBER: *194, 226*
TEA GROWING: *238*

NEPAL

THE SMALL, ISOLATED country of Nepal lies in the Himalayan mountains and is cut off from the sea (landlocked). It is a Hindu state, although many people practice a mixture of Hinduism and Buddhism. Until 1991, the king was the absolute ruler. In that year, democratic elections were held for the first time. Nepal is now ruled by an elected government. Trekkers and tourists flock to Nepal every year, bringing valuable income to this very poor country.

NEPAL	
Capital city: Kathmandu	
Area: 52,818 sq miles (136,800 sq km)	
Population: 23,900,000	
Official language: Nepali	
Major religions: Hindu 90%, Buddhist 5%, Muslim 3%, other 2%	
Government: Multiparty democracy	
Currency: Nepalese rupee	
Adult literacy rate: 42%	
Life expectancy: 58 years	
People per doctor: 12,500	
Televisions: 6 per 1,000 people	

BHUTAN	
Capital city: Thimpu	
Area: 47,147 sq miles (47,000 sq km)	
Population: 2,100,000	
Official language: Dzongkha	
Major religions: Buddhist 70%, Hindu 24%, other 6%	
Government: Absolute monarchy	
Currency: Ngultrum	
Adult literacy rate: 47%	
Life expectancy: 62 years	
People per doctor: 5,825	
Televisions: 6 per 1,000 people	

KATHMANDU
Kathmandu is the capital and largest city in Nepal. In the old part of the city there are many narrow streets and squares lined with ancient temples and monuments. In one temple lives the Kumari Devi, or living goddess. She is a young girl chosen to represent the Hindu goddess Parvati until she reaches puberty.

MOUNTAIN TERRACES
About 90 percent of Nepalese people work on the land. Crops such as rice are grown on immaculately kept terraces cut into the mountainsides. This allows farmers to grow crops on land that would otherwise be inaccessible. Farmers depend on the monsoon rains for a good harvest.

These Sherpa women are carrying heavy loads as they trek through the mountains.

NEPALESE PEOPLES

There are many different groups of people living in Nepal. The Sherpas of the eastern mountains are known for their climbing skill. The Gurkha people are famous for their courage and military skills. Their reputation has spread all over the world. The Newars of Kathmandu Valley are known for their magnificent wood carvings, which decorate many Nepali temples and houses. More than half of the people are Nepalese, of Indian descent.

Bhutanese people eat yak meat, use yak milk to make butter and cheese, and use yak dung as fuel.

Yak hair is used for tents and clothes, and yak tails are used as fans or dusters.

USEFUL YAKS
For many people living in the mountains of Bhutan, life revolves around their herds of yaks. These tough, hardy animals can carry heavy loads and survive freezing temperatures.

BHUTAN

THE HIMALAYAN KINGDOM of Bhutan is a mysterious, isolated place because of its location in the mountains and its restrictions on tourism. With limited natural resources, Bhutan has been trying to exploit the fast-flowing mountain rivers to produce hydroelectricity. Bhutan is a Buddhist country, ruled by a monarch, a government, and an assembly.

Drukpas speak Dzonghkha, the national language of Bhutan, which is closely related to Tibetan.

DRUKPAS

About 70 percent of the Bhutanese are Drukpas of Tibetan origin. Clashes between the Drukpas and the Nepali-speaking Lhotsampa people of the south led to violent demonstrations against the government in 1990. Further immigration into Bhutan is banned.

Find out more

HIMALAYAS: *132, 166*
HINDUISM & BUDDHISM: *275*
POLITICAL SYSTEMS: *270–271*
TERRACE FARMING: *159, 201*

EAST ASIA

EAST ASIA IS DOMINATED by the vast country of China, but it also includes the windswept plains of Mongolia, North and South Korea and the fertile island of Taiwan. China itself is full of contrasts. In the west, high ranges of mountains tower over rocky valleys and semidesert plains. Tibet, a previously independent country occupied by China since 1950, is known as the "roof of the world" because it is so high above sea level. In the north of the country is the harsh and empty Gobi Desert. In eastern China and North and South Korea, river valleys and flood plains are farmed intensively, providing food for the millions of people who live in the cities on or near the coast.

Urumqi, China

Jan 3°F (-17°C)
July 70°F (21°C)

Jan 0.6 in (15 mm)
July 0.7 in (18 mm)

THE YELLOW RIVER

The Yellow River, or Huang He, is one of the world's most destructive rivers. It has flooded the surrounding land many times, causing enormous loss of life. For this reason, the river is known as "China's Sorrow." As it slowly glides eastward through central China, it erodes huge amounts of fertile loess (fine soil) from the land, which stains the river yellow.

THE GREAT WALL

Snaking across northern China, from the Yellow Sea in the east to the deserts of central Asia in the west, is one of the technological wonders of the ancient world. Much of the Great Wall was built in the 1400s to protect Chinese farmers from invasion by nomads from Mongolia. At almost 4,000 miles (6,400 km) long, it is the world's longest structure, and can be seen by astronauts in outer space.

ANCESTOR WORSHIP

One of the main ideas of Confucianism, the ancient religion of China, is the importance of family loyalties and the honoring of ancestors. Because of this, traditional funerals in East Asia follow a set ritual to ensure that the soul of the dead person is well provided for. At the graveside, mourners make food offerings and burn paper money and paper models of cars, bikes, and other goods to accompany the soul to heaven.

Buddhist priests often lead the funeral procession. They chant prayers and play musical instruments.

People throw paper money to pacify spirits that are thought to haunt the road.

Mourners often wear over-garments made of sackcloth and white headdresses.

Effigies (models) of Confucius, the founder of Confucianism, are carried along the way.

The richer the family, the more ornate the coffin.

THINGS TO LOOK FOR ON THE MAP

Longest river: Yangtze, China 3,430 miles (5,520 km) *Map L11*

Highest point: Mt. Everest, on border of China/Nepal/Tibet, 29,029 ft (8,848 m) *Map D12*

Largest lake: Qinghai Hu, China 1,722 sq miles (4,460 sq km) *Map H9*

World's largest square: Tiananmen Square, Beijing, China 4,269,027 sq ft (396,606 sq m) *Map M8*

MONGOLIA

NORTH KOREA

SOUTH KOREA

TAIWAN

CHINA

0 100 200 300 400 km
0 50 100 150 200 250 miles

N

Beijing, China
Jan 24°F (-4°C)
July 79°F (26°C)
Jan 0.2 in (4 mm)
July 9.6 in (243 mm)

Lhasa, China
Jan 29°F (-1°C)
July 62°F (16°C)
Jan 0 in (0 mm)
July 4.8 in (122 mm)

Taipei, Taiwan
Jan 60°F (16°C)
July 84°F (29°C)
Jan 3.4 in (86 mm)
July 9.1 in (231 mm)

RUSSIAN FEDERATION

MONGOLIA

INNER MONGOLIA

GOBI DESERT

BAIDAN JARAN DESERT

ORDOS DESERT

C H I N A

QINGHAI

BAYAN HAR MTS.

QIN LING

GREATER KHINGAN RANGE

LESSER KHINGAN MTS.

MANCHURIA

NORTH KOREA

SOUTH KOREA

SEA OF JAPAN

YELLOW SEA

SHANDONG PENINSULA

Bo Hai

Korea Bay

Korea Strait

EAST CHINA SEA

Taiwan Strait

TAIWAN

SOUTH CHINA SEA

GUANGXI ZHUANG AUTONOMOUS REGION

LEIZHOU PENINSULA

Gulf of Tongking

Hainan

MYANMAR

VIETNAM

LAOS

INDIA

HANGAYN NURUU

ALTAI MTS.

L. Uvs
Ulaangom
Ólgiy
L. Hyargas
Hovd
Har Us L.
Uliastay
Altay
Tsetserleg
Arvayheer
Hami
Lenghu
Yumen
Da Qaidam
Delingha
Golmud
Yushu
Litang
Nyingchi
Qamdo
Panzhihua
Dali
Kunming
Gejiu

Móron
Erdenet
Darhan
Sühbaatar
ULAN BATOR
Öndörhaan
Choybalsan
Saynshand
Erenhot

Manzhouli
Hailar
Hulun Nur
Yakeshi
Zalantun
Qiqihar
Ulanhot
Bei'an
Yichun
Jiamusi
L. Khanka
Harbin
Jixi
Changchun
Jilin
Liaoyuan
Tongliao
Chifeng
Shenyang
Fushun
Anshan
Ch'ŏngjin
Hamhŭng
Wŏnsan
Sinŭiju
Namp'o
PYONGYANG
Kangnŭng
Haeju
Inch'ŏn
SEOUL
SOUTH KOREA
Taejŏn
Taegu
Pusan
Kwangju
Cheju

Xilinhot
Jining
Great Wall
Hohhot
Baotou
Linhe
Wuhai
Dongsheng
Datong
BEIJING
Tianjin
Tangshan
Dalian
Yantai
Qingdao
Shijiazhuang
Taiyuan
Handan
Jinan
Zibo
Tai'an
Zaozhuang
Lianyungang
Changzhi
Yellow R.
Xining
Wuwei
Yinchuan
Lanzhou
Baoji
Xi'an
Luoyang
Zhengzhou
Xuzhou
Grand Canal
Hongze Hu
Huainan
Nanjing
Hefei
Wuxi
Shanghai
Suzhou
Hangzhou
Shaoxing
Ningbo
Xiangfan
Xinyang
Jingmen
Wuhan
Jingdezhen
Wenzhou
Ankang
Mianyang
Wanxian
Yichang
Yangtze
Chengdu
Leshan
Zigong
Chongqing
Dongting Hu
Yueyang
Poyang Hu
Nanchang
Nanping
Fuzhou
Chi-lung
TAIPEI
Changsha
Pingxiang
Shaoyang
Ganzhou
Xiamen
Kao-hsiung
Xichang
Zunyi
Guiyang
Dongchuan
Guilin
Shaoguan
Shantou
Liuzhou
Wuzhou
Canton
Dongguang
Kowloon
Hong Kong
Macao
Nanning
Pingxiang
Zhanjiang
Xuwen
Haikou
Sanya
Hongshui He

Kerulen
Orhon
Uldz
Argun
Amur
Amur

Yellow R.
Yangtze
Mekong
Salween
Yalong
Dadu He
Jinsha
Yuan
Min

175

CHINA

ONE IN EVERY FIVE PEOPLE in the world live in just one country – China. This vast country is almost the same size as Europe. It is the third largest country in the world after Russia and Canada. It has also one of the world's oldest civilizations, with a history stretching back more than 7,000 years. Ruled by a succession of emperors, China became a republic in 1911 and a communist state in 1949. Under the communists, every aspect of life is controlled by the state and China has become a major industrial and military power. In recent years it has begun to move toward a more competitive economy that encourages investment from other countries.

CHINA

Capital city: Beijing	
Area: 3,600,927 sq miles (9,326,410 sq km)	
Population: 1,277,600,000	
Official language: Mandarin	
Major religions: Traditional religions 20%, Buddhist 6%, Muslim 2%, other 72%	
Government: One-party state	
Currency: Yuan	
Adult literacy rate: 82%	
Life expectancy: 70 years	
People per doctor: 629	
Televisions: 272 per 1,000 people	

THE FORBIDDEN CITY
When the emperor Zhu Di rebuilt China's capital, Beijing, in the 15th century, he created a vast imperial palace in the center of the city. The palace became known as the Forbidden City because only the emperor's family and closest advisers could enter it. Encircled by walls, it contains nearly 1,000 buildings, including temples, stables, and a library.

The art of handwriting, or calligraphy, is highly prized in China because great care is required to draw each character correctly.

CHINESE WRITING
Unlike English or French, which use an alphabet of 26 letters, Chinese writing uses more than 50,000 characters, or symbols. Each character depicts a different word or idea. Simple words, such as "sky," or "rain," use one character. Complex words use two or more – "telephone" uses the characters for "electric" and for "talk."

CHINESE COMMUNISM
The Communist Party took control of China in 1949. Led by Mao Zedong, the party believed in a society in which everyone would be equal and property would be owned by the whole community. Land was taken from wealthy landowners and given to groups of peasant farmers who worked on large, collective farms. Industry was put under state control. These attempts to transform China met with mixed success. Since Mao's death in 1976, private ownership has begun to develop again.

Portraits of Mao Zedong still hang in Tiananmen Square in Beijing, the largest public square in the world.

RICE GROWING
Two-thirds of China's large population lives and works on the land. The most fertile areas are found in the south. The main crop is rice, though tea, cotton, fruit, and vegetables are also grown. The rice is planted in flooded paddy fields (shown below). Two crops of rice and one of vegetables or cereal grains are harvested in a good year. In the north and west of the country, which is drier and hillier, farmers grow a single crop of cereal grains and tend sheep and cattle.

Plowing
Water buffaloes are used to plow, rake, and flatten the muddy paddy fields, ready for planting.

Low earth barriers known as bunds separate the paddy fields.

Planting
Women do the back-breaking work of planting out the rice shoots.

Sowing

While the paddy fields are being prepared, rice seeds are sown in a separate flooded field, or seedbed.

After a month, the tightly packed rice shoots are ready for transplanting into the paddy fields.

Some farms in China have tractors, but most use water buffaloes or oxen.

Water in the paddy fields keeps down weeds.

FOOD

Chinese people take great pleasure in their food, which varies from region to region. Western cuisine from Sichuan province uses spices, while northern cuisine from Beijing is famous for its tasty roast duck. Cantonese food from the south is renowned across the world for its fish dishes and delicate flavors. Meals are cooked by steaming or stir-frying in a large pan called a wok. Rice is served in the south of the country, wheat buns or noodles in the north. The food is held in small bowls and chopsticks are used for eating.

Bean sprouts

Green mung beans are eaten as a dessert or candy.

Native to China, star anise is a spice that has a similar flavor to aniseed.

Ginger root adds a fresh, spicy taste to many dishes in western China.

Chili peppers are added to make hot, spicy dishes.

Rice, whether boiled, steamed, or fried, forms the basis of many Chinese dishes.

China bowl

Tea is served in handleless cups.

Tea, made without milk or sugar, is the most popular drink in China.

Jasmine tea is a light refreshing drink made from green leaves. Black and Oolong are other types of Chinese tea.

Chopsticks are used for eating.

Knives are not needed because food is sliced before cooking.

Harvesting
Farmers cut the stalks with sickles and tie them into bundles.

The rice stalks are beaten to shake off the grain.

Piles of rice grains are left in the sun to dry.

When the rice is dry, the outer shells, or husks, are removed, and the rice is sifted.

CITY LIFE

More than 400 million Chinese people live in towns and cities, many of which are overcrowded. Accommodations are scarce, and families usually live in one or two rooms rented from the company they work for. The city streets are full of bicycles, and public transportation, while cheap and frequent, is always packed. The main industrial and commercial city is Shanghai, home to 12 million people.

ONE-CHILD FAMILIES

The Chinese population is growing by about 9 million people a year, which is around the total population of Sweden. In order to reduce this rapid growth, the government introduced a policy in 1979 to limit each family to one child only. The single children are known as "Little Emperors" because they are often spoiled. The one-child policy has succeeded in the towns, but not in the country, where large families are needed to provide labor in the fields.

FOOD PRODUCTION

Every patch of fertile soil in China is used for agriculture. Crops are planted alongside roads and railroad tracks, and one type of crop is often planted between rows of another. China is the world's biggest producer of the crops shown below. Percentages indicate China's share in world production.

- carrots — 26%
- rice — 32%
- pears — 52%
- cucumbers — 56%
- water-melons — 61%
- sweet potatoes — 85%

THE NEW YEAR

Every year, in late January or early February, Chinese people prepare to celebrate the New Year. They spring-clean their houses, put up red decorations to bring them luck, and give new clothes and toys to their children. The New Year festival itself lasts for several days. Every shop and office is closed, and people take to the streets, letting off firecrackers and joining in the displays of lion and dragon dances.

THE BUDDHISTS OF TIBET

Tibet, once an independent country, has been part of China since 1950. Tibetans are devout Buddhists and their religion has been suppressed by the Communist Party, which discourages any religious practice. However, the Buddhist faith remains strong in Tibet. Buddhists devote their lives to prayer. They hang up flags with prayers printed on them to bring fortune and good luck.

Tibetan Buddhists hang prayer flags from their houses, across bridges, or on mountainsides.

THE GRAND CANAL

The world's longest waterway, the Grand Canal, stretches for 1,790 km (1,110 miles) across China. It was begun in the 5th century BC to connect the cities of the north with the rice growing valleys of the south. Near its southern end, the canal passes through Suzhou, a picturesque city known as the "Venice of the East" because it is crisscrossed by rivers and canals.

LIFE IN THE PARK

Because most city people live in flats with no gardens, parks play an important part in everyone's life. Exercise is encouraged in China, and people go regularly to the park to keep fit. Early in the morning, many people practise *tai chi* or the more vigorous *kung-fu.* Children fly kites on windy days, and adults play table tennis, cards, or chess, or just sit and chat with their friends.

Table tennis is very popular in China; tables are set up in parks for people to enjoy a game out in the open air.

Kites are made by pasting brightly coloured paper on to simple bamboo frames, often in the shape of animals or birds.

People often play Chinese chess and cards.

Cycling is popular, as a means of transport and as a way of keeping fit.

Tai chi is a form of gentle exercise with slow movements, which resembles shadow boxing.

Chinese parks are beautifully kept and contain rockeries and trees that blossom in the spring.

INDUSTRY

Over the last 20 years China has transformed itself from one of the world's poorest nations to a rapidly expanding economy. It is a leading producer of textiles, clothing and electronics. Western-style market reforms have led to a surge in growth and the rise of cities such as Shanghai with its new, futuristic economic quarter, Pudong (pictured). However, in spite of this, much of the population remains very poor.

CHINESE MEDICINE

The Chinese believe that a person falls ill because the opposing forces of *yin* and *yang* in the body become unbalanced. Doctors rebalance the body with herbal remedies and acupuncture, which involves sticking thin needles into various parts of the body to relieve pain. Many people are treated by "barefoot doctors", or locally trained healers.

Bugbane rhizome (sheng ma) is used to treat headaches, colds, and measles.

Wolfberry (guo qi zi) is used for diabetes and is said to improve eyesight.

Senn leaf (fan xie ye) is a herb used to cleanse the system.

Chain fern bark (gou ji) helps ease back pain.

HONG KONG SHANGHAI BANK
In the central business district of Hong Kong stands the impressive Hong Kong Shanghai Bank. This masterpiece of technological engineering was completed in 1985. At every stage of its construction, experts in *feng shui*, the ancient Chinese belief in the natural forces of wind and water, were consulted to ensure that the building would bring health, prosperity, and good fortune to its many occupants.

HONG KONG

Tucked into a corner of southeast China, Hong Kong occupies only a small area, yet almost 6 million people live squashed on its rocky islands and mountainous mainland. It is one of the world's most important finance centres and has one of its most prosperous economies. In 1898, the New Territories of Hong Kong were leased by China to Britain for 99 years. On 1st July, 1997, the British government returned Hong Kong to China.

HAPPY VALLEY
Surrounded by the towering skyscrapers of Hong Kong, the Happy Valley racecourse is one of Hong Kong's most famous landmarks. Betting money on horse races is hugely popular and is the only legal form of gambling allowed. A season's takings at the race course can amount to over US$11 billion

TEXTILES
For over one hundred years Hong Kong has had a flourishing textiles industry, exporting its products all over the world. Across Hong Kong, thousands of people are still employed in workshops making T-shirts, suits, and shirts though there is now fierce competition from countries such as India.

FLOATING HOMES

Many people in Hong Kong live not on the land but on boats. Families are squashed on to wooden junks and sampans, mostly making their living by fishing. Floating schools, shops, and restaurants serve their needs, while doctors, dentists, and hairdressers do their rounds by boat. Thousands of people still live in these floating villages, but, increasingly, deep sea trawlers are replacing the traditional boats and forcing the fisherfolk to look for work on land.

TECHNOLOGY
As traditional industries have declined, Hong Kong's economy has diversified into producing "high tech" products such as computers, digital cameras, watches and mobile phones.

digital camera

MACAO

Overshadowed by Hong Kong, its richer and bigger neighbour, Macao consists of a mainland and two islands linked by a bridge and causeway. Macao was returned to China in 1999. When its Portuguese rulers gave up power – after almost 450 years – it was the end of the longest surviving European settlement in Asia.

INDUSTRY
Macao produces a variety of goods for export, ranging from textiles and electronic goods to fireworks (shown above), and toys. Every day, low-paid workers from mainland China come to work in the many factories of Macao.

TOURISM

Macao's skyline is dominated by casinos and hotels. The casinos are a big tourist attraction because gambling is very popular with the Chinese and casinos are outlawed in Hong Kong and China. Gambling is a major industry in Macao, and provides about one-third of the territory's income.

Find out more
BUDDHISM: *275*
POLITICAL SYSTEMS: *270–271*
POPULATION GROWTH: *16–17*
RICE GROWING: *135, 185, 197*

TAIWAN

WHEN PORTUGUESE SAILORS first visited this island in 1590, they named it *Ilha Formosa* – "Beautiful Island" – because of its lush, mountainous scenery. In 1949 at the end of civil war in China, the defeated Nationalist government fled here and established itself as a rival to the communists on the mainland. Taiwan still officially calls itself the Republic of China. Since then, both Taiwan and China have tried to seek international recognition as the official Chinese government. However, few nations recognize Taiwan and it does not have a seat at the United Nations. Despite this, Taiwan has a thriving economy based on mass production and high tech industries.

TAIWAN

Capital city: Taipei

Area: 12,455 sq miles (32,260 sq km)

Population: 20,800,000

Official language: Mandarin

Major religions: Buddhist, Confucian, and Taoist 93%, Christian 5%, other 2%

Government: Multiparty democracy

Currency: New Taiwan dollar

Adult literacy rate: 94%

Life expectancy: 76 years

People per doctor: 824

Televisions: 237 per 1,000 people

INDUSTRY

Once a poor agricultural island, Taiwan has succeeded in developing one of the world's most successful industrial economies. It is a world exporter of electronic and electrical goods, machinery, textiles, shoes, sports equipment, TV sets, and watches. This huge export trade pays for the oil and other raw materials the economy needs, for Taiwan has few natural resources of its own.

TAIPEI

For most of its history, Taipei has been a city of low-rise buildings. But during the last few decades the city has been transformed into the modern hi-tech capital of the island, with many new high-rises, public buildings, and landscaped gardens. Almost 3 million people live in Taipei, and the capital has problems with congestion and pollution. Most people travel to work on motorcycles, contributing to the smog that covers the city for most of the year.

OPERA

Traditional Chinese opera is popular in Taiwan. The basic stories are simple, concerning good against evil, or boy meets girl, and there are few props on stage. Instead, the actor's movements, elaborate costumes, and facial makeup all convey character and plot.

The largest surviving tribe are the Ami, who are expert potters and farmers. The Ami live in large villages, with women holding power in the family home.

TRIBAL GROUPS

Long before the Chinese first came to Taiwan, the island was home to a variety of peoples. Each tribe had its own distinct language, but all had many customs and skills in common. In the 1600s, the Chinese came to the island and fought the tribes for control. Today the surviving tribes make up only 2 percent of the total population.

TAOISM

The major religions practiced in Taiwan are Buddhism, Taoism, and Confucianism. These faiths are closely linked, and many people follow aspects of all three. Taoism, which began in China around 300BC, teaches how people can follow the *tao* (path) to a life of simplicity and freedom from desire. Taoists aim to live in harmony with nature, balancing the calm, feminine side of the body (*yin*) with the active, male side (*yang*).

Temples are used as social centers and playgrounds as well as places of worship.

Major tribes in Taiwan

- ☐ Tsou
- ☐ Paiwan
- ☐ Ami
- ☐ Atayal
- ☐ Bunun

Find out more

GROWTH OF CITIES: *17*
PACIFIC RIM ECONOMIES: *137*
RELIGION: *274–275*
TRADE: *280-281*

MONGOLIA

THE REMOTE, SPARSELY POPULATED country of
Mongolia was once the center of a vast empire.
For most of the 20th century, however, Mongolia
was a communist country linked to Soviet Russia until
democratic rule was introduced in 1990. Many people
live on the grassy plains in the center of the country,
tending their flocks as they move in search of new
pasture. The climate is harsh – summers are short,
winters are long and cold. Mountain ranges ring the
country to the north and west, while the south is
bordered by the Gobi Desert. The country is rich in
natural resources, with huge deposits of coal and oil,
but it is only recently that these have been developed.

MONGOLIA

Capital city: Ulan Bator

Area: 604,247 sq miles
(1,565,000 sq km)

Population: 2,700,000

Official language: Khalkh
Mongol

Major religions: Buddhist
96%, Muslim 4%

Government: Multiparty
democracy

Currency: Tughrik

Adult literacy rate: 99%

Life expectancy: 63 years

People per doctor:
370

Televisions: 63 per 1,000
people

GENGHIS KHAN
During the 13th century, the
Mongol leader Genghis Khan
carved out a huge empire that
stretched across much of central
Asia and China. By the time of
his death, it was said that it took
almost a year to ride from one side
of his empire to the other. He was
succeeded by his grandson, Kublai
Khan, but in the 1300s the empire
was conquered by China.

The framework of a yurt
consists of a circular
latticework frame with a
central ring to support the
roof. The frame is covered
with felt lashed together
with rope.

Smoke from the iron stove
escapes through a chimney
in the roof of the yurt.

NOMADIC LIFE

The nomadic farmers
of Mongolia move with
their yaks, sheep, goats, camels, and cattle
from the summertime pastures high in the
mountains down to the grassy lowland steppes
during the winter months. Yaks are ideally
suited to the harsh Mongolian climate, and
provide milk, butter, meat, and wool. As the
nomads move with their flocks, they take their
portable dome-shaped yurts with them.

A yurt may have as many as eight layers
of felt to keep out the winter cold.

Flaps may be drawn over the
single wooden or felt door.

The scroll is
carved in the
shape of a
horse's head.

ULAN BATOR

The capital city of Mongolia lies at the center of
road and rail networks in the country. Until the
1920s Ulan Bator was a small country town, but
development by its communist rulers has turned
it into a major city. The influence of Soviet Russia
is reflected in the style of many of the city's
major buildings.

Traditional
wooden
Mongolian
fiddle

Bow

MAKING
MUSIC
Mongol nomads
like to entertain
themselves in
the evening with
music. Stringed
instruments, such
as the Mongolian
fiddle, are popular.

HORSE RIDERS
Many Mongols are accomplished horse
riders. From a very early age, Mongolian
children learn to ride horses, becoming
jockeys at the age of as little as three. Every
July 11 they get the chance to show off their
skills at the Nadam Festival, a nationwide
sporting event that includes horse-racing,
archery, and wrestling competitions.

Find out more

NOMADS: *156, 160, 209*
POLITICAL SYSTEMS: *270–271*
STEPPE (GRASSLANDS): *15*
YAKS: *173*

NORTH KOREA

WITH ITS RUGGED, HILLY INTERIOR and limited fertile land, North Korea is a harsh country. Winds from central Asia produce extreme winter temperatures, and snow covers the ground for many months. Politically, North Korea is equally harsh. The communist government maintains a tight grip on its people. It limits contact with the outside world and forbids all foreign newspapers. Its health and education services have been badly affected by a lack of money, and many people face starvation every year. Recently there have been attempts to break the country's long isolation.

NORTH KOREA	
Capital city: Pyongyang	
Area: 46,490 sq miles (120,410 sq km)	
Population: 24,000,000	
Official language: Korean	
Major religion: No figures available	
Government: One-party state	
Currency: Won	
Adult literacy rate: 95%	
Life expectancy: 63 years	
People per doctor: 370	
Televisions: 53 per 1,000 people	

A DIVIDED LAND

At the end of World War II, Korea was occupied by Russian and American armies. In 1948, the country became divided in two. A communist government ruled the North and an American-backed, democratic government ruled the South. Today, the two sides face each other along one of the most heavily armed borders in the world.

Most farm houses are built of brick with tile or slate roofs.

Both men and women work on the land, growing rice, vegetables, grain, and fruit.

COLLECTIVE FARMING

Under the communist government, thousands of small, family-owned farms were abolished, replaced by 3,800 enormous state-controlled farms. These collective farms are run by people who work together to produce enough food to supply the country's needs. Because North Korea is so mountainous, every piece of available land is farmed intensively, with irrigation (watering) systems, advanced machinery, and fertilizers used to improve the annual harvest.

Health services are free for everyone, with doctors and nurses employed on each collective farm.

Every farm has its own day-care center and nursery school for babies and young children stay whose parents work on the land.

KOREAN FOOD

In North and South Korea, a whole meal is served at once, rather than in separate courses. Rice is always the main dish, often combined with barley and red beans and eaten with a range of spicy vegetables, herbs, and meats. Steamed rice-cakes are prepared for important celebrations.

Ginseng is exported around the world.

Kimchi, made from pickled cabbage and radishes mixed with garlic, salt, red pepper, and other spices, is a popular dish.

In jeolme, a type of rice-cake powdered with soya flour, is served as a dessert.

GINSENG

The root of the ginseng plant is grown in both North and South Korea. It is believed to promote good health and energy. After being washed, steamed, and dried, it can be ground into pills or made into lotion.

KIM IL SUNG

Kim Il Sung, dominated North Korea from 1948 until his death in 1994. He established an image as the father of working people. His portrait was hung in every office and huge statues were erected to him in public places. Under his rule, North Korea became increasingly isolated politically and economically from the rest of the world. He was succeeded by his son, Kim Jong Il, but is still referred to as the "eternal president."

Find out more

FARM "SHARING": *115, 140, 150*
HEALTH, EDUCATION: *276, 277*
IRRIGATION: *155, 156, 217*
POLITICAL SYSTEMS: *270–271*

SOUTH KOREA

LIKE NORTH KOREA, much of South Korea is mountainous and forested. Compared with its northern neighbor, however, it has a strong economy that trades with many other countries, such as Japan and the US. After becoming independent in 1948, South Korea was invaded by North Korea. By the end of the Korean War (1950–53), the cities and factories of South Korea were devastated and thousands of refugees had arrived in the country from the North. Within 20 years, a remarkable turnaround had taken place. New factories began to produce world-class products, and new cities sprang up. Today, South Korea has a well-educated workforce producing high-technology goods for export.

SOUTH KOREA	
Capital city: Seoul	
Area: 38,119 sq miles (98,930 sq km)	
Population: 46,800,000	
Official language: Korean	
Major religions: Christian 49%, Buddhist 47%, Confucianist 3%, other 1%	
Government: Multiparty democracy	
Currency: Won	
Adult literacy rate: 98%	
Life expectancy: 75 years	
People per doctor: 784	
Televisions: 346 per 1,000 people	

SEOUL
More than 10 million people live in the capital, Seoul. Most of this modern city has been built in the decades since the end of the Korean War. As more people have moved here from the countryside, the city has become very crowded. To cope with this, Seoul has an excellent public transportation system, linking buses, trains, boats, and planes into one timetable.

Shipbuilding has expanded rapidly in South Korea, which is now the second biggest shipbuilder, after Japan, in the world.

A Korean shaman is usually a woman, called a mundang.

People bring offerings of money and food to the mundang.

Burned offerings are made to pacify the spirits.

SHAMANISM
People in South Korea belong to a number of religions. About half are Buddhists, the rest are Christian or Confucianist. Many people in rural areas still believe in shamanism – that an invisible spirit world lives alongside the visible human world. When the spirits interfere in the lives of humans, a shaman (priest) acts as a link between the two worlds.

Apart from obtaining blessings from spirits, a mundang will try to cure people's diseases and help with personal problems.

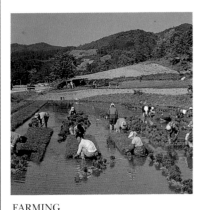

The traditional Korean fan dance is performed by women only. As the women dance, they move faster and faster around each other while making patterns with their fans.

Women wear long, brilliantly colored, high-waisted dresses.

INDUSTRY
After the devastation of the Korean War, South Korea had to rebuild its industry from scratch. It concentrated on producing and exporting manufactured goods, setting up huge industrial companies, known as *chaebol*, to make shoes, clothes, ships, cars, and more recently, computers and video sets. Large iron and steel plants were built to supply the factories with raw materials. South Korea now has one of the most successful economies in the world.

Figures show South Korea's share in world production.

25%

12%

4%

Ship production in South Korea

1980 1990 2000

FARMING
Unlike North Korea, most farms in South Korea are small and family owned. Rice is the main crop, but barley, wheat, fruit, vegetables, and spices are also grown. Because much of the land is mountainous, farms can be found clustered along the river valleys and lowlands near the coast.

KOREAN DANCE
Korean dancing is popular in both the South and North. Dancers dress up in traditional clothes called *hanbok*. The aim of Korean dancing is to create a mood rather than to tell a story.

Find out more
PACIFIC RIM ECONOMIES: *137*
POLITICAL SYSTEMS: *270–271*
RELIGION: *274–275*
TRADE: *280–281*

JAPAN

JAPAN IS A CHAIN OF SOME 4,000 ISLANDS stretching for more than 1,553 miles (2,500 km) off the east coast of mainland Asia. Most people live on the four largest islands – Honshu, Hokkaido, Shikoku, and Kyushu. Flat land is in short supply. More than three-quarters of the country is hilly, leaving less than a quarter suitable for building and farming. To create more level ground, hillsides are being cut back and land is being reclaimed from the sea. Japan's climate is a varied one. The islands in the south are warm all year round, while in the north it is cooler, with snowfall on the mountains in winter. The Japanese call their country *Nippon*, "the land of the rising Sun," as the Sun can be seen rising above the Pacific Ocean.

ISLAND LINKS
Travel between the islands is made easier by a network of bridges and tunnels linking them together. The Seto Ohashi bridge (above) connects several of the smaller islands. The Akashi Kaikyo Road Bridge, linking Honshu and Shikoku, opened in 1998. It is the world's longest suspension bridge, with an overall span of 6,529 ft (1,990 m).

THE EMPEROR
Japan has the oldest hereditary monarchy in the world, dating back to before the 6th century. In the past, the emperor was very powerful and many Japanese people believed he was a god. But the emperor's status changed after Japan's defeat in World War II, and his role was reduced to a symbolic one.

The present emperor, Akihito, is the 125th in the imperial line. He is highly respected by Japanese people, but he has no political power.

Mount Fuji is a huge, cone-shaped volcano. It last erupted in 1707.

SACRED MOUNTAIN
At 12,388 ft (3,776 m), Mount Fuji, on Honshu, is Japan's highest mountain. For the followers of Shinto, one of Japan's major religions, Mount Fuji is a sacred mountain. Each year, thousands of pilgrims make the long climb to visit the Shinto shrine on the summit. Many Japanese consider Mount Fuji to be a symbol of their country and keep a photograph or painting of the mountain on display in their homes.

Children are taught to duck under desks to protect themselves from falling objects.

UNSTABLE LAND
Japan suffers from hundreds of earthquakes a year. Slight shakes are recorded almost every day, while larger tremors causing minor damage can be felt several times a year. Strong earthquakes occur more rarely, causing damage, injury, and death. Buildings and bridges topple, roads and railroads are destroyed, and devastating fires break out. In 1995, a massive earthquake struck the port of Kobe and killed more than 5,000 people. Regular earthquake drills are held in schools, homes, and workplaces.

Modern skyscraper

Pagoda

Strong central column

BUILT TO LAST
Both new and old buildings in Japan have been designed with earthquakes in mind. A pagoda has a strong central column sunk into the ground to give it added stability. A modern skyscraper has a regular shape and thick walls reinforced by steel columns, which help make the building more secure.

Skyscrapers are often built on pads made of steel and rubber that absorb earthquake tremors.

PEACEFUL PLACES

Japanese gardens are carefully designed places of peace and beauty. They contain sand, rocks and pebbles, trees, ponds, and streams. The elements are arranged in a particular way to create a balanced, harmonious setting in which people can relax and meditate. Many gardens are influenced by Zen Buddhism, a branch of Buddhism that emphasizes the need for meditation.

A Japanese garden represents the world in a miniature form.

Trees represent forests.

Rocks symbolize mountains.

Ponds represent oceans, rivers, and streams.

JAPAN

The Kurile Islands are administered by the Russian Federation, but claimed by Japan.

SEA OF OKHOTSK

Rebun-tō
Wakkanai
Reshiri-tō
Hokkaidō
Abashiri
Asahikawa
Kitami
ISHIKARI MTS.
Nemuro
Ishikari Bay
Obihiro
Otaru
Sapporo
Kushiro
Tomakomai
HIDAKA MTS.
Uchiura Bay
Hakodate
Okushiri-tō
Hakodate
Fukushima
Tsugaru Strait
Seikan Tunnel
Aomori
OU MTS.
Morioka
Akita
Mogami
Yamagata
Sendai
Niigata
Fukushima
Sado
Kōriyama
Shinano
Iwaki
Honshū
Hitachi
Toyama
Utsunomiya
Kanazawa
Maebashi
Kasumi Lagoon
Fukui
TOKYO
Kawasaki
Yokohama
Oki Is.
Mt. Fuji
Tottori
Nagoya
L. Biwa
Okazaki
Matsue
Kōbe
Kyōto
Shizuoka
Hamada
CHUGOKU MTS.
Osaka
Hamamatsu
Kurashiki
Okayama
Izu Is.
Hiroshima
Tokushima
Wakayama
Tsushima
Matsuyama
Iki
Kitakyūshū
Shimonoseki
Shikoku
Kōchi
Fukuoka
Ōita
Kyūshū
Gotō Is.
Saesebo
Nakamura
Nagasaki
Kumamoto
Amakusa Is.
Miyazaki
Kagoshima
Osumi Strait
Osumi Is.
Tanega-shima
Yaku-shima
Tokara Is.
Amami Is.
Amami-ōshima
Okinoerabu-jima
Tokuno-shima
Okinawa
Ryukyu Islands

SEA OF JAPAN
Toyama Bay
JAPANESE ALPS
EAST CHINA SEA

PACIFIC OCEAN
Iturup
Kurile Islands
Kunashir
Habomai Is.
Shikotan

THINGS TO LOOK FOR ON THE MAP

Longest river: Shinano, 230 miles (370 km) *Map G8*

Highest point: Mt. Fuji, 12,388 ft (3,776 m) *Map H9*

Largest lake: L. Biwa, 260 sq miles (673 sq km) *Map F9*

World's longest undersea rail tunnel: Seikan Tunnel between Hokkaido and Honshu, 33.46 miles (53.85 km) *Map H4*

Hakodate
☀ Jan 26°F (-4°C)
July 67°F (20°C)
🌧 Jan 2.6 in (66 mm)
July 5.4 in (137 mm)

Tokyo
☀ Jan 38°F (3°C)
July 77°F (25°C)
🌧 Jan 1.9 in (48 mm)
July 5.6 in (142 mm)

Nagasaki
☀ Jan 43°F (6°C)
July 79°F (26°C)
🌧 Jan 2.8 in (71 mm)
July 10.1 in (257 mm)

0 50 100 150 km
60 50 100 miles

ARCTIC CIRCLE
TROPIC OF CANCER
EQUATOR

N

E F G H I J K L

RICE GROWING

Although only about a tenth of the land is suitable for farming, Japan has traditionally produced all the rice it needs. Rice is Japan's main food crop, and it is eaten almost every day. It is intensively cultivated on small farms, using sophisticated farm machinery such as rice planters and harvesters. The work is done very quickly, so fewer workers are needed, and farmers often have a second job.

JAPAN

FOR MANY CENTURIES, Japan was closed to foreigners and wary of the outside world. Today, it is a leading industrial and technological power and one of the world's richest countries. This transformation is even more remarkable given Japan's mountainous landscape and lack of natural resources. Most raw materials have to be imported from abroad. Japanese people enjoy a high standard of living, with good health and education systems. Average life expectancy in Japan is among the highest in the world. Western influence is strong, but people remain proud of their culture and traditions.

JAPAN	
Capital city: Tokyo	
Area: 145,374 sq miles (376,520 sq km)	
Population: 126,700,000	
Official language: Japanese	
Major religions: Shinto and Buddhist 92%, other 8%	
Government: Multiparty democracy	
Currency: Yen	
Adult literacy rate: 99%	
Life expectancy: 81 years	
People per doctor: 556	
Televisions: 707 per 1,000 people	

MAKING MONEY

Japan is a huge economic power. It invests in land and property around the world. A lot of the world's largest commercial banks are Japanese. Japan's economic and industrial heart is the capital, Tokyo, where the world's second largest stock exchange and the headquarters of many banks and corporations can be found in the Central Business District. It is said that if an earthquake hit this area, the world would suffer economic chaos.

Electronic goods produced in Japan

Electronic components: 34%

Computers: 24%

Other 5%

Consumer goods: 18%

Industrial equipment: 19%

The Japanese excel at making electronic goods, such as televisions, cameras, digital watches, and computers, which are sold worldwide. Many Japanese companies are world leaders in the research and development of new technology.

The Rainbow Bridge connects the port with the city.

ECONOMIC STRENGTH

Japan has a highly developed infrastructure and industrial base. One of the main reasons why the country's industries have grown so quickly is that the Japanese are very hardworking. Many of the larger companies are like families, providing housing and health care for their employees. However, society is slowly changing. Young people are starting to question this working culture, especially as the economy began to slow down in the 1990s and unemployment rose.

Traditional folding fans made of bamboo and covered with paper are carried by both men and women.

TRADITIONAL DRESS

People in Japan wear kimonos for religious festivals and other special occasions. A kimono (which means "clothing") is a long-sleeved, wrap-around robe, tied with a broad sash. It may be made of silk, cotton, or wool. Many formal silk kimonos are richly colored and beautifully embroidered.

Black silk kimono

CHERRY BLOSSOM

Japanese people share a love of nature and pay close attention to the changing seasons. The blossoming of cherry trees is a reminder that spring has arrived. The first blossoms appear in southern Kyushu. Their progress is plotted on maps shown on television news. The blossoms last for a few days, and people celebrate by picnicking under the cherry trees.

Wooden clogs, or geta

RELIGION
Shinto and Buddhism, the two major religions of Japan, have always existed side by side and even merge together to a certain extent. Most Japanese people consider themselves Buddhist, Shintoist, or Shinto-Buddhist. There is also a significant Christian community, making it the third most popular religion in Japan.

A Japanese woman praying to a statue of Buddha.

OVERCROWDING
With a large population and a lack of flat land for settlement, Japan is a crowded country. Land is expensive, especially in the cities, and many people commute long distances to work. During rush hour, subway trains are so crowded that guards have to push commuters on board. The uncomfortable journeys that people endure inspired Japanese technicians to invent personal stereos so people could listen to music while traveling.

FESTIVALS
There are plenty of festivals in Japan, each with their own emphasis and tradition. The parade shown here is from the Hakata Dontaku Festival in Kyushu, which is steeped in over 820 years of history. In the festival, Fukujin, Ebisu, and Daikoku, the three gods of good fortune, make the rounds of the city.

CHILDREN'S LIVES
Children are well taken care of in Japan. There is even a national holiday, Children's Day, dedicated to them. In another festival, "seven-five-three day," children are dressed in traditional clothing and taken to religious shrines. Japanese children are expected to study hard at school. In addition to a long school day, many pupils attend extra classes on Saturdays and in the evenings.

SPORTING LIFE
Whether watching or taking part, Japanese people love sports. The national team sport is baseball, which came to Japan from the US. An ancient sport unique to Japan is sumo wrestling. Success in the ring depends on weight and strength, so wrestlers follow high-protein diets.

Golf is popular in Japan. Practice ranges are often built on several levels to save space.

FISHING FOR FOOD
As a nation of islands, Japan depends heavily on the surrounding seas for food. The Japanese catch and eat more fish than any other country, and have the largest fishing fleet in the world. There are hundreds of villages dotted along the coast from which small fishing boats venture out, while deep-sea fish are caught by larger trawlers. Some trawlers are floating fish factories that process the catch on board. Millions of fish are also bred each year on fish farms.

Deep-sea trawlers may stay at sea for months at a time.

Fish are cleaned and filleted on board.

Many types of fish and seafood are eaten raw, as sushi, and artistically presented on lacquered dishes or trays.

After filleting, the fish are frozen or canned.

Fish are stored in the hold.

Find out more
EARTHQUAKES: *13*
GROWING CITIES: *17, 136*
LIFE EXPECTANCY: *276*
PACIFIC RIM ECONOMIES: *137*

MAINLAND SOUTHEAST ASIA

STRETCHING FROM THE FOOTHILLS of the Himalayas in the north almost to the Equator in the south, the seven countries of mainland southeast Asia are largely mountainous. About half the region is covered with forest. Most people live in the river valleys that cut through the fertile countryside. Myanmar is isolated, poor, and underdeveloped. In comparison, Thailand, Malaysia, and above all, the island of Singapore are rich countries with modern industrial economies. Vietnam, Cambodia, and Laos have had to recover from years of war. The region has a monsoon climate, with a dry season from November to March and a wet season from May to October.

THE COMING OF THE RAIN
As the wet season starts in May, the people of Laos and northeast Thailand celebrate *bun bang fai*, the skyrocket festival. They build huge rockets up to 13 ft (4 m) long from steel or plastic pipes and pack them with up to 1,100 lb (500 kg) of gunpowder. The rockets are launched into the sky to prompt the rain god, Vassakarn, to send the annual rains.

In the uplands, the river picks up silt, which it carries down to the valleys.

During the monsoon season, the river bursts its banks and floods the surrounding fields.

THE MEKONG DELTA
The delta of the Mekong River in Vietnam is one of the world's great rice-growing areas, producing much of the surplus that has made Vietnam the world's fifth largest rice exporter. Farmers in the delta also grow fruit and catch the many breeds of fish that thrive in the muddy river waters.

RIVER VALLEYS
From ancient times, people have settled in the valleys of the great rivers, such as the Irrawaddy, Mekong, and Salween, because the land there is suitable for growing rice. All the major cities in the region are situated on a river. In the valleys, farmers cultivate every corner of the land, often constructing terraces on the hillsides to grow rice and other crops. They use the river waters to irrigate (water) their crops.

Silt from the uplands helps fertilize the paddy fields.

This Akha village on the border of Thailand and Myanmar is surrounded by land that is cleared for slash-and-burn farming.

Rice is grown near the river, where the paddy fields can be easily watered.

1 and 2: in January an area of forest is cut down and left to dry. During the dry season in April, the area is burned.

SLASH-AND-BURN FARMING
In the uplands, where there is a lot of land but few people to work it, farmers use a technique called slash-and-burn. An area of forest is cleared and cultivated for a few years, then the farmer moves on to another patch, leaving the original land to recover. In this way, the land is never exhausted, and the forest is not destroyed to create permanent fields.

3 and 4: crops are planted during the monsoon rains in May, and harvested in October.

THE UPLANDS
In contrast to the crowded river valleys, the uplands are sparsely populated and largely covered by forest. Here the hill peoples live in villages, farming small plots of land and gathering fruit and other food from the forest. This traditional way of life is now threatened by the region's growing population, and by logging companies, which are cutting down the forest.

Stages 3 and 4 are repeated for 2–4 years, until the soil becomes less fertile.

①
②
③
④
⑤
⑥

5 and 6: the area is left fallow for 15–25 years, and the forest grows back.

Mandalay, Myanmar
☀ Jan 68.5°F (20.5°C)
July 85.5°F (30°C)
🌧 Jan 0.1 in (3 mm)
July 2.7 in (69 mm)

Hanoi, Vietnam
☀ Jan 62°F (16.5°C)
July 84.5°F (29.5°C)
🌧 Jan 0.7 in (18 mm)
July 127 in (323 mm)

LAOS

Bangkok, Thailand
☀ Jan 78.5°F (26°C)
July 83°F (28°C)
🌧 Jan 0.3 in (8 mm)
July 6.3 in (160 mm)

Kuala Lumpur, Malaysia
☀ Jan 81°F (27°C)
July 81.5°F (27.5°C)
🌧 Jan 6.2 in (158 mm)
July 3.9 in (99 mm)

MYANMAR

CAMBODIA

THAILAND

MALAYSIA

SINGAPORE

VIETNAM

HA LONG BAY
A Vietnamese legend tells of a gigantic dragon that thrashed its way into the sea, smashing the limestone coastline into thousands of islands and rocky outcrops. Today, Ha Long Bay, which means "where the dragon descends into the sea," has some of the most dramatic scenery in this region. It has inspired many poets and painters.

PINEAPPLES
Thailand is the world's leading producer of pineapples, but this fruit is grown in many parts of Southeast Asia. Much of the crop is canned and exported.

BIRDS' NEST SOUP
The brown-rumped swift builds its nest high in the roofs of caves throughout southeast Asia. Local men risk death climbing flimsy ladders to collect these nests, which form the main ingredient of birds' nest soup. The nests are made from the birds' saliva, but when they are plunged in boiling water they look like noodles.

THINGS TO LOOK FOR ON THE MAP

Longest river: Mekong, Thailand/Laos/Cambodia/Vietnam, 2,600 miles (4,184 km) *Map F6, H8*

Highest point: Hkakabo Razi, Burma, 19,294 ft (5,881 m) *Map D1*

Largest lake: Tônlé Sap, Cambodia, maximum size in wet season 2,500 sq miles (6,475 sq km) *Map G10*

Ha Long Bay: Vietnam *Map I5*

THAILAND

THE KINGDOM OF THAILAND was established in the 13th century, and the country has remained independent for most of its history. It was the only country in mainland southeast Asia not to be colonized by Britain or France. Modern Thailand is an economically successful nation, with rapid economic growth and a huge tourist industry. The north, west, and south are mountainous and fairly empty. About a third of the people live in the fertile and densely populated center of the country. Thailand was once covered in forest, but so much of it has been cut down for timber that logging is now banned.

THE KING OF THAILAND
King Bhumibol Adulyadej has ruled Thailand since 1946, making him the longest serving head of state in the world. The king is a powerful unifying force in the country and has often intervened in politics to restore order. He is highly respected by Thais and any criticism of him or his family is frowned upon.

These young men's orange robes and shaved heads show that they are monks.

BANGKOK
Officially 6 million people live in Bangkok, but the true figure is probably closer to 10 million. Originally built on a network of canals, the city still has relatively few major roads and a limited public transportation system. As a result, Bangkok has some of the worst traffic jams in the world. In July 1992, after a monsoon storm, it took 11 hours for one jam to clear. Some commuters have converted their cars into mobile offices, even installing chemical toilets, so they can work while they are driven in.

A MODERN ECONOMY
Thailand is the world's biggest producer of pineapples, and also exports large quantities of rubber and rice. However, in recent years manufacturing has overtaken agriculture in economic importance. American and Japanese companies have set up factories in Thailand, which is now a leading producer of electronic goods, such as integrated circuits for computers. Many of the workers in these new factories are women.

Women are often employed in the electronics industry because they earn lower wages than men and because smaller hands can handle the tiny components best.

BUDDHISM
Monks from Sri Lanka introduced Theravada Buddhism to this region in the 12th century and it soon became Thailand's main religion. Theravada Buddhism – the "Way of the Elders" – encourages its followers to obey the Law of Karma and do all they can to reduce suffering in the world. Traditionally young men are expected to become monks for a period of their lives, and many still follow this custom today.

The Emerald Temple in Bangkok is named after the green jade statue of the Buddha that it contains.

TOURISM
The thousands of ornate Buddhist temples and monasteries in Thailand have always drawn tourists from around the world to admire their beautiful architecture. Today, visitors also come to lay on the long, unspoiled beaches, trek in the wild hills of the north, or play on one of the new golf courses that are being constructed to attract businessmen from Japan.

MYANMAR

OVERSHADOWED BY THE POWERFUL neighboring countries of India, China, and Thailand, Myanmar (also known as Burma) is little known to the outside world. When the country became independent in 1948, it adopted a policy of political and economic isolation that reduced this once rich nation to one of the poorest on Earth. Revolts by the hill peoples and, in recent years, political repression by a military government have kept nearly all foreign influences away. Yet Myanmar is rich in natural resources, is well watered by the great Irrawaddy River, and is fertile enough to support intensive farming.

MYANMAR

Capital city: Rangoon	
Area: 253,876 sq miles (657,540 sq km)	
Population: 45,600,000	
Official language: Burmese	
Major religions: Buddhist 87%, Muslim 4%, Christian 6%, Hindu 1%, other 2%	
Government: Military government	
Currency: Kyat	
Adult literacy rate: 85%	
Life expectancy: 56 years	
People per doctor: 3,521	
Televisions: 7 per 1,000 people	

The Akha people value silver highly. This chief and his family wear silver neck-rings, bracelets, and ornaments on their clothes to show their wealth and status.

THE HILL PEOPLES

In the upland areas of the east, north, and west of Myanmar live the hill peoples. They include the Shan, Akha, Karen, and Kachin tribes, and make up more than a quarter of the total population. Most hill peoples live in small villages and make their living from slash-and-burn farming on the land around their villages. They are fiercely independent and resent interference from outside. As a result, more than 200,000 Karen and others have lost their lives fighting the Myanmar government for independence.

TEAK

Hard, easily carved, and containing an oil that resists water and stops iron from rusting, teak is a highly desirable wood for furniture, flooring, and other building uses. About 70 percent of the world's teak trees grow on the hills of Myanmar, but intensive felling means that soon few trees will be left standing unless action is taken to replant the forests.

Rubies

Poppy-growing area

The opium poppy has white, pink, or purple flowers and can grow to a height of 4 ft (1.2 m).

Seed head

NATURAL WEALTH

Rubies and sapphires are among the many gemstones produced in northern Myanmar. Many people consider Myanmar rubies to be the finest in the world because of their deep red color. Myanmar is also rich in silver, copper, jade, lead, zinc, and tin, and has extensive reserves of oil and natural gas.

Ruby crystals are often found in calcite rock.

Ruby crystal

THE GOLDEN TRIANGLE

The area where Myanmar, Thailand, and Laos meet is known as the Golden Triangle. Here the hill peoples grow opium poppies as one of their few sources of income. Opium is a useful painkiller, but it can also be used to make narcotics. Two-thirds of the world's heroin comes from this region. In order to combat this lethal trade, the government is encouraging the local people to plant other crops for export, such as tobacco or flowers.

Opium is made from the sap that oozes out of cuts scored in the seed head.

RANGOON

Situated in the delta of the great Irrawaddy River, the capital city of Myanmar was established in 1852 by the British, who laid out the streets in a grid pattern. Since then, Rangoon has grown to be the country's major port and industrial center. Dominating the city is a Buddhist temple called the Shwe Dagon Pagoda. Situated on a hill just north of the city center, the gold-covered pagoda towers 325 ft (99 m) above the city streets.

Find out more

BUDDHISM: *275*
DRUG TRADE: *58*
GEMSTONES: *62, 172*
LOGGING: *69, 227, 244*

VIETNAM

VIETNAM

Capital city: Hanoi

Area: 125,621 sq miles
(325,360 sq km)

Population: 79,800,000

Official language:
Vietnamese

Major religions: Buddhist
55%, Christian 7%, other
38%

Government: One-party
state

Currency: New dong

Adult literacy rate: 93%

Life expectancy: 68 years

People per doctor: 2,417

Televisions: 47 per 1,000
people

EVERY DAY FOR 13 YEARS Vietnam appeared on television sets and in newspapers around the world as the communist-led north of the country fought the American-backed south in a vicious war. When the war ended in 1975, with victory for the north, Vietnam had been devastated by the years of fighting and many of its people wanted to leave. Although the communist government struggled for years to recover, its policy of allowing foreign firms to invest in new industries slowly strengthened the economy. Today tourists are beginning to visit this beautiful country in ever greater numbers. Despite this success, most people in Vietnam remain very poor.

RUSH HOUR ON A BICYCLE
Cars dominate most large cities in the world, but in Vietnam the bicycle rules the road. Everyone has a bicycle that they use to get to work or for shopping, because few people are rich enough to afford a car. In the morning and evening rush hours, streets like this one in Ho Chi Minh City are packed with cyclists, ringing their bells and shouting out loud to warn pedestrians and other cyclists to get out of the way.

THE BIRTH OF A CHILD
In the past, many Vietnamese babies did not live for long, so families did not celebrate the birth of a child, but rather its survival for a month. This ritual continues today. Later, when the child is a year old, the family celebrates *Thoi Noi*. The child is shown a tray with objects on it. Whichever one the child chooses shows which career he or she will follow – for example a pen for a teacher, scissors for a tailor.

Many of the boat people died at sea from disease or because their boats were not strong enough for the hazardous voyage.

THE BOAT PEOPLE

After the end of the war, many Vietnamese people tried to leave in search of jobs abroad or out of fear of persecution. They took to the sea in boats, hoping to reach the West via Hong Kong, Malaysia, or Singapore. By 1980 about half a million people had set sail. The flood of refugees stopped when neighboring countries began to send them home.

RICE GROWING

Two-thirds of the farmland in Vietnam is under water for part of the year, but deliberately so, because the fields are flooded to grow rice. During the rainy season, the fields slowly fill with rainwater, which is kept in place by low earth dikes. Soon a series of shallow, muddy paddy fields appears. Women plant the rice by hand. It takes two to three months to grow to full strength, and is then harvested.

Most villages have an electricity supply, and some families own a television set.

House made of concrete

Plot for growing vegetables and corn

Outdoor shower

VILLAGE LIFE

Four out of every five people in Vietnam live in the countryside. Because cars are rare, and there are few railroad lines, most of them will never visit the great cities of Hanoi or Ho Chi Minh. The vast majority live in small villages and earn their living as farmers or laborers. Here they live in simple houses made of concrete, brick, or, more traditionally, wood, straw, and palm leaves. A typical house has two rooms – one for eating and living, the other for sleeping – but no running water. Water comes from a well outside.

Families live on the fruits and vegetables they grow on their farm. They eat meat only on special occasions.

Find out more
CYCLING: *92*
PACIFIC RIM ECONOMIES: *137*
POLITICAL SYSTEMS: *270–271*
RICE GROWING: *135, 176, 197*

CAMBODIA

Angkor Wat consists of a central temple building surrounded by smaller temples and palaces and huge moats and reservoirs.

CAMBODIA

FEW COUNTRIES HAVE SUFFERED as much as Cambodia. In 1970 it was drawn into the fighting in neighboring Vietnam. Then, from 1975–79, the country was ruled by Pol Pot and the Khmer Rouge, a revolutionary group that killed more than a million Cambodians. In 1979 the Vietnamese invaded to overthrow Pol Pot, and the country fell into civil war, which lasted until 1991. Today Cambodia is slowly rebuilding its shattered society.

CAMBODIA

Capital city: Phnom Penh	

Area: 68,154 sq miles (176,520 sq km)

Population: 11,200,000

Official language: Khmer

Major religions: Buddhist 95%, other 5%

Government: Multiparty democracy

Currency: Riel

Adult literacy rate: 37%

Life expectancy: 56 years

People per doctor: 7,600

Televisions: 15 per 1,000 people

LAOS

Capital city: Vientiane

Area: 89,111 sq miles (230,800 sq km)

Population: 5,400,000

Official language: Lao

Major religions: Buddhist 85%, other 15%

Government: One-party state

Currency: Kip

Adult literacy rate: 49%

Life expectancy: 53 years

People per doctor: 5,000

Televisions: 4 per 1,000 people

ANGKOR WAT
For centuries the vast temple complex of Angkor Wat lay hidden in the jungles of northern Cambodia. It was built in the 12th century by the Khmer King Suryavarman II, in honor of the Hindu god Vishnu, and was once the center of a huge empire. When the Khmers fell from power, Angkor Wat was abandoned, and the jungle gradually grew over the buildings. The site has been uncovered in the last 100 years.

CLASSICAL DANCE
In the temple of Angkor Wat, royal dancers performed religious dances based on the Indian epic tales of the Ramayana and the Mahabharata. This type of classical dance is highly stylized, with graceful movements requiring years of training to perfect. The dancers wear richly embroidered costumes so tight that they have to be sewn into them before each performance.

THE WORLD'S BIGGEST MINEFIELD
The lengthy wars in Cambodia have left the country in a desperate state. The road and rail systems have collapsed, and industry barely exists. Up to 3 million mines are thought to lie buried in the ground. Despite the efforts of mine clearers, like the man in this picture, many mines are discovered only when someone steps on one. As a result, some 20,000 people have been disabled.

Hmong men often have more than one wife. Each wife is responsible for bringing up her children, and tends her own poultry and vegetable garden.

LAOS

LAOS IS A COMMUNIST STATE and one of the poorest and most isolated countries in the world. Three-quarters of its people are farmers; many of them grow only enough food to feed their families. Apart from the fertile Mekong Valley, the land is rugged and unsuitable for farming. Yet Laos is rich in gold and other minerals, and also produces timber and coffee.

THE HILL PEOPLES
Peoples such as these Hmong have lived in the isolated hill areas of Laos for many years. They grow corn and rice to eat, and opium poppies to sell. But this traditional way of life has been badly affected by the wars in this region and many Hmong have left the country and settled in Thailand or the US.

THE FRIENDSHIP BRIDGE
Spanning the Mekong River near the capital city of Vientiane is the Friendship Bridge, which opened in 1994. Laos is landlocked (it has no coastline), and the bridge provides the only direct route to Thailand and its seaports.

Find out more

HILL PEOPLES: *188, 191*
HINDUISM: *275*
OPIUM: *191*
POLITICAL SYSTEMS: *270–271*

MALAYSIA

SPREAD ACROSS THE SOUTH CHINA SEA is the divided land of Malaysia. Part of the country lies on the Malay Peninsula, which hangs off the corner of mainland southeast Asia, but the states of Sarawak and Sabah are on the island of Borneo to the east. More than 22 million people live in the country, most of them in the rapidly growing cities on the peninsula. Every five years Malaysia gets a new head of state: nine sultans, who each rule one of the states that make up the country, take turns acting as king.

THE PEOPLE OF MALAYSIA
Almost half the population of Malaysia are Malays, like this family. About one-third are Chinese; the rest are either descendants of settlers from the Indian Subcontinent, or local tribespeople. This mix of peoples has led to racial conflict in the past.

MALAYSIA	
Capital city: Kuala Lumpur	
Area: 126,853 sq miles (328,550 sq km)	
Population: 22,200,000	
Official language: Malay	
Major religions: Muslim 53%, Buddhist 19%, Chinese faiths 12%, Hindu 7%, Christian 7%, traditional beliefs 2%	
Government: Multiparty democracy	
Currency: Ringgit	
Adult literacy rate: 87%	
Life expectancy: 72 years	
People per doctor: 2,076	
Televisions: 166 per 1,000 people	

SINGAPORE	
Capital city: Singapore City	
Area: 235 sq miles (610 sq km)	
Population: 2,705,100	
Official languages: Malay, Chinese, Tamil, and English	
Major religions: Buddhist 55%, Taoist 22%, Muslim 16%, other 7%	
Government: Multiparty democracy	
Currency: Singapore dollar	
Adult literacy rate: 92%	
Life expectancy: 77 years	
People per doctor: 664	
Televisions: 348 per 1,000 people	

NATURAL RESOURCES

Malaysia is rich in natural resources, with large oil and gas reserves off the coast of Sarawak. The country is the world's top producer of palm oil, used to make soap and for cooking, and the third biggest producer of natural rubber. The rain forests of Sarawak are rich in hardwood trees, but experts are worried that the timber industry is cutting down trees faster than the forest can renew itself.

Peas, beans, and other vegetables are often grown between the rows of trees.

Strips of bark are cut away to let the latex run down the trunk and into a collecting cup.

RUBBER
Hidden inside the bark of the rubber tree is a white liquid, called latex, that is used to make natural rubber. Rubber trees grow in hot, wet climates and flourish on the lower slopes of the mountains that run down the length of the Malay Peninsula. Collected latex is sent to a local factory. There it is mixed with water and acid in a large pan to make a sheet of rubber that is then smoked or hung on a line to dry.

Rubber tappers go out before dawn to collect the latex before the high daytime temperatures stop its flow.

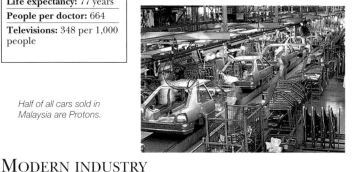

Half of all cars sold in Malaysia are Protons.

MODERN INDUSTRY

The first car to be manufactured in Malaysia – the Proton – rolled off the production line outside Kuala Lumpur in 1985. Today more than 90,000 Protons are produced every year, many for export to Indonesia, Singapore, and the UK. The Proton has been so successful that it has been followed by a second car project, the Perodua. Malaysia is also an international center for the electronics industry and is the world's biggest producer of disk drives for computers.

THE CHANGING ECONOMY
1970s: in 1970, Malaysia had few factories, and most of its raw materials, such as rubber and tin, were exported to be manufactured into finished goods abroad.

2000s: today, Malaysia's economy is one of the most successful in the world. Malaysia continues to produce large amounts of raw materials, and its manufacturing sector has grown dramatically. Three-quarters of all exports are now finished goods, such as cars, electronics, textiles, and foods.

Exports in 1970
42.5%
15%
25%
12.5%
5%

Manufactured goods: 76%

Other: 16.5%

Exports in 1998
Oil and gas: 6.2%
Rubber: 1.1%
Tin: 0.2%

ISLAM

In 1414, the people of Malacca (modern-day Melaka) converted to Islam when their ruler married a Muslim princess from Sumatra. The new faith spread rapidly throughout the country. Today, more than half the population of Malaysia is Muslim. Islamic law is widely obeyed and many women wear a headdress in the street.

Modern-day Kuala Lumpur is a mixture of skyscrapers and old colonial buildings.

KUALA LUMPUR

In 1857, a group of miners in search of tin set up a camp where the Kelang and Gombak rivers join. They called their settlement Kuala Lumpur, which is Malay for "muddy meeting place." The camp soon grew in size and importance as a center of the tin mining and rubber industries. Today it is Malaysia's biggest city and home to more than 1.3 million people.

LIFE ON STILTS

Faced with the problem of building on the banks of rivers or next to the sea, villagers developed an ingenious solution – they built their houses on stilts. Villages of these houses, called *kampungs*, are found throughout southeast Asia. The wooden houses stand high enough above the water to protect them from flooding, while the raised floors and many windows help keep the houses well ventilated.

A high, steep roof protects the inhabitants from the heavy monsoon rains.

Animals are often kept under the raised floor.

Many kampung villagers make their living from fishing.

Fish are laid out to dry in the sun so that they can be stored.

SINGAPORE

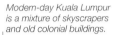

Off the tip of Malaysia lies the tiny island state of Singapore, one of the most densely populated countries on Earth. Singapore was originally a trading settlement on the shipping route between India and China. It was founded in 1819 by Sir Stamford Raffles, an official of the British East India Company. Today rapid economic growth has turned the island into one of the world's most successful economies.

THE PORT OF SINGAPORE

Every three minutes a ship enters or leaves the bustling harbor of Singapore, making it the busiest port in the world. Tankers from the Persian Gulf bring crude oil to be refined into fuel and other products, which are then shipped out to ports throughout eastern Asia. Cargo ships on the way to and from China and Japan stop to use the harbor's facilities, and most of Malaysia's large export trade goes out through this port.

SINGAPORE SOCIETY

Three-quarters of the people of Singapore are Chinese; the rest are Malays and descendants of people from the Indian Subcontinent. Because Singapore is so wealthy, most people lead comfortable lives. The government keeps tight control over the country: it regulates the press, owns the television and radio services, and limits car ownership to prevent congestion on the roads. It is illegal to drop litter in the street, eat in the subway, or chew gum in public.

Singapore's banks and stock exchange, based in this part of the city, generate about a quarter of the country's income.

Singapore's skyline is dominated by modern high-rise buildings, built because land is in such short supply.

Find out more
ISLAM: *275*
OIL: *137, 152, 281*
PACIFIC RIM ECONOMIES: *137*
RUBBER: *226*

MARITIME SOUTHEAST ASIA

MARITIME MEANS "CONNECTED WITH THE SEA," and maritime southeast Asia is a belt of thousands of islands strung out across a vast expanse of ocean. Here, sandwiched between mainland southeast Asia and Australia, are four countries: the eastern part of Malaysia, Brunei, Indonesia, and the Philippines. This is one of the world's most volcanic regions, and the monsoon climate makes some areas among the wettest places on Earth. A huge variety of animals and plants live here, because the environment is slightly different on each island. There are many different peoples, too. More than 250 languages are spoken on the islands of Indonesia alone.

WATER TRANSPORTATION
In this island region, boats have traditionally provided the main method of getting from place to place. Small boats, such as this outrigger canoe, are ideal for navigating the waterways between clusters of islands.

TYPHOON CLIMATE
Each year, about 20 tropical storms called typhoons batter the islands of the Philippines. They bring flooding and winds traveling over 62 mph (100 km/h). Many people are killed in storms, and thousands of homes are destroyed. Low-lying coastal areas are most at risk, but people are forced to live there because land is in short supply, and these areas are cheap.

Manila, Philippines
Jan 77.5°F (25.5°C)
July 81.5°F (27.5°C)
Jan 0.9 in (23 mm)
July 17 in (432 mm)

Medan, Sumatra
Jan 78°F (25.5°C)
July 80.5°F (27°C)
Jan 5.4 in (137 mm)
July 5.3 in (135 mm)

Jakarta, Java
Jan 79°F (26°C)
July 80°F (27°C)
Jan 11.8 in (300 mm)
July 2.5 in (64 mm)

VOLCANOES

Volcanic eruptions and earthquakes are a frequent part of life in this region. They are caused by the movement of huge pieces of the Earth's crust, called tectonic plates. Much of maritime southeast Asia lies over a massive arc-shaped join between two of these plates. Despite the terrible destruction that eruptions cause, the islanders risk growing crops on the slopes of active volcanoes because their ash makes the soil fertile.

NATURAL VARIETY

This Australasian Komodo dragon lives on an island to the east of Wallace's Line.

During the 1850s the British naturalist Alfred Russel Wallace journeyed through these islands. He noticed that most of the animals on the island of Bali were Asian in origin, but those on neighboring Lombok were mainly Australasian. "Wallace's Line" is an imaginary line drawn across the region to divide the islands with Asian animals from those with Australasian animals.

Scientists studying the rain forests in this region have discovered that they contain one-sixth of all the world's bird species.

THE TROPICAL RAIN FORESTS

Individual islands provide different natural habitats, so the animals and plants that have evolved on one island may be very different from those on the next. This means that the region's dense rain forests contain the greatest variety of species in the world. This is why it is so vital that these forests be protected and not cut down or cleared.

Islands to the west of Wallace's Line are filled with Asian animals, such as this orangutan.

THINGS TO LOOK FOR ON THE MAP

Longest river: Kapuas, Indonesia, 710 miles (1,142 km) *Map G9*

Highest point: Puncak Jaya, Indonesia, 16,502 ft (5,030 m) *Map R10*

World's largest volcano crater: Toba, Indonesia, 685 sq miles (1,775 sq km) *Map B8*

World's largest cave: Sarawak Chamber, Malaysia, 2,296 ft (700 m) long *Map I7*

THE RAFFLESIA FLOWER

This rare plant, found deep in the rain forests, is named after Sir Stamford Raffles, a British governor in this region during the 19th century. It has the world's largest flowers, measuring up to 3 ft (91 cm) across. *Rafflesia* is famous for its foul smell, which attracts insects.

USING THE PADDY FIELDS

Rice is the main, or staple, food for most people in this region, and much of it is grown in specially flooded paddy fields. All kinds of plants and animals are raised in and around these fields, including vegetables, fruit trees, fish, shellfish, crabs, and frogs. They provide food and income for the people, give nutrients to the waters, and the animals eat pests that could otherwise do great damage to this finely balanced underwater world.

Ambon, Moluccas

Jan 82°F (27.5°C)
July 77.5°F (25°C)

Jan 5 in (127 mm)
July 23.7 in (602 mm)

EAST TIMOR (under UN Transitional Authority from Feb 2000)

Trees grown by the paddy fields supply fruit and firewood.

Local people eat and sell fish that are raised in the paddy fields.

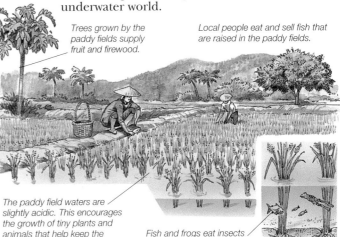

The paddy field waters are slightly acidic. This encourages the growth of tiny plants and animals that help keep the waters full of nutrients.

Fish and frogs eat insects that live on the rice plants.

INDONESIA

Capital city: Jakarta

Area: 699,447 sq miles (1,811,570 sq km)

Population: 212,100,000

Official language: Bahasa Indonesia

Major religions: Muslim 87%, Christian 9%, other 4%

Government: Military government

Currency: Rupiah

Adult literacy rate: 87%

Life expectancy: 66 years

People per doctor: 6,423

Televisions: 136 per 1,000 people

BRUNEI

Capital city: Bandar Seri Begawan

Area: 2,228 sq miles (5,770 sq km)

Population: 260,482

Official language: Malay

Major religions: Muslim 66%, Buddhist 14%, Christian 10%, other 10%

Government: Absolute monarchy

Currency: Brunei dollar

Adult literacy rate: 85%

Life expectancy: 74 years

People per doctor: 1,460

Televisions: 241 per 1,000 people

EAST TIMOR

Capital city: Dili

Area: 11,880 sq miles (153,870 sq km)

Population: 750,000

Official languages: Portuguese, Tetum, Bahasa Indonesia

Major religions: Roman Catholic 91%, Protestant 3%, Muslim 2%, other 4%

Government: Independent republican government

Currency: US Dollar (transitional currency)

Adult literacy rate: 84%

Life expectancy: 54

People per doctor: 62 per 1,000

Televisions: 56 per 1,000

INDONESIA

EVERYTHING ABOUT INDONESIA IS BIG. It is the world's largest archipelago, made up of 13,677 islands, of which only about 1,500 are inhabited. It stretches for 3,169 miles (5,100 km) and is spread across 3 million sq miles (8 million sq km) of sea and three time zones. The population contains 362 different ethnic groups, speaking over 250 languages and dialects. More than 180 million Indonesians are Muslims, making it the world's biggest Muslim country. It is also a land of contrasts: along with its modern cities and industries, Indonesia contains peoples whose lifestyles have not altered for centuries.

THE SPICE ISLANDS
For centuries, the Moluccas islands in eastern Indonesia were Europe's main source of cloves, nutmeg, cinnamon, and other spices. While Indonesia was a Dutch colony, the merchants of the Dutch East India Company had total control of this trade and grew fabulously rich. Indonesia became an independent country in 1949.

Pepper

Nutmeg

Cloves

Cinnamon

The temple of Borobudur is the world's largest Buddhist monument.

BOROBUDUR
Situated in the heart of Java is one of the architectural wonders of the world. The vast Buddhist temple of Borobudur – which means "monastery on the hill" in Javanese – was built between AD778-856. The temple consists of a series of platforms, each one representing a different stage in the Buddhist's spiritual journey from ignorance, through enlightenment, to nirvana, or heavenly bliss.

JAKARTA
Indonesia's capital is home to more than 11 million people, making it the largest city in Southeast Asia. It was originally a small trading port at the mouth of the Ciliwung River, shipping spices throughout eastern Asia. In 1618, the Dutch made Jayakarta, as it was then called, the capital of their East Indies empire. They renamed the town Batavia and rebuilt it around canals to look like Amsterdam.

OIL AND GAS
The first oil well was drilled in Sumatra in 1871, and oil has dominated the Indonesian economy ever since. By 1981 oil and gas products made up more than 80 percent of exports, but this figure is now dropping as the oil reserves begin to run out. To reduce dependence on oil, Indonesia is exploiting its reserves of natural gas. The gas is exported in a liquid form, called liquefied natural gas.

BALI
With lush plants covering the island in a carpet of green and sandy beaches stretching along the coast, Bali is one of the world's most beautiful places. It is a favorite destination for tourists, who come to enjoy the scenery and to watch local groups of musicians perform ancient dances. Most Balinese are Hindu, and processions, like these women taking offerings to the temple, are part of everyday life.

PEOPLES OF INDONESIA

More than 212 million people live in Indonesia, 60 percent of them packed onto the island of Java. Yet this island occupies just 7 percent of the country's total land area. Many of the other islands are barely occupied, despite their vast size. In 1950 the government began to resettle people from Java on other islands. More than 6 million people have been resettled in this way, despite opposition from local people who are sometimes moved to make way for the new settlers.

THE DANI

The people who live in Indonesia's easternmost province of Irian Jaya are related to the dark-skinned peoples of the Pacific Ocean rather than the lighter-skinned inhabitants of the rest of Southeast Asia. Among the many tribes who live in this isolated area are the Dani, whose agricultural way of life has changed little in thousands of years.

Field of crops

The Dani barter for goods, such as pigs.

Dani houses are made of wood and thatch.

A longhouse is usually constructed of timber and bamboo.

Covered gallery

Loft storage area, where rice is kept in large baskets.

Women separating rice grains from the chaff

THE DAYAKS

The native inhabitants of Borneo, the Dayaks, are expert builders who construct elaborate longhouses on stilts. Several families live in a longhouse, each with their own cooking and sleeping quarters. Meetings are held in the covered gallery that runs along the length of the building, and rice, fish, and other foods are dried on the open verandah in front.

THE BUGIS

The Bugis people of southern Sulawesi are famous for their seafaring skills and, in previous centuries, for their ferocity in battle. They built elegant wooden ships in which they terrorized the inhabitants of neighboring islands. It is thought that the English word "bogeyman" comes from Bugis.

The Bugis still build their wooden ships, but they now have diesel engines.

BRUNEI

SANDWICHED BETWEEN THE Malaysian state of Sarawak and the South China Sea lies Brunei. It consists of a humid tropical rain forest with a swampy plain along the coast. Once an outpost of the British Empire and a haven for pirates, this country was transformed by the discovery of oil in 1929. Today Brunei is one of the world's wealthiest nations, with huge resources of oil and natural gas.

THE SULTAN OF BRUNEI

Brunei is ruled by one of the wealthiest people on Earth. Thanks to the country's vast oil and gas reserves, Sultan Hassanal Bolkiah is worth about US$25 billion, although he denies this figure. In recent years the Sultan has spent more than US$450 million building one of the world's largest mosques in Brunei's capital city, Bandar Seri Begawan.

Brunei women dressed in the Muslim veil (hijab) greet the sultan.

EAST TIMOR

BEING A PORTUGUESE COLONY for 400 years, gave East Timor a very different identity to its neighbors. Most people are Roman Catholic and the country is full of Portuguese architecture. It became independent in 1975 but was taken over by its giant neighbor, Indonesia, the same year. After 26 years of war and famine, that saw the death of 200,000 East Timorese, the tiny nation finally gained independence in 2002.

STRUGGLE FOR INDEPENDENCE

East Timor's fight to rule itself followed a long guerrilla war with Indonesia in which over 200,000 East Timorese were killed. The Revolutionary Front for an Independent East Timor (known in Portuguese as Fretelin) consists of many of these former fighters and will have a big say in the running of the country's affairs.

Find out more
ISLAM & BUDDHISM: *275*
OIL & GAS: *137, 152, 163, 211*
POPULATION DENSITY: *16, 135*
SPICES: *57, 264*

THE PHILIPPINES

THE PHILIPPINES

LOCATED ON THE "RING OF FIRE" – the arc of volcanoes running through Maritime Southeast Asia – and in the path of violent tropical storms, the Philippines suffers from earthquakes and volcanic eruptions. The country consists of 7,107 islands, of which only about 1,000 are inhabited. Most of the people live on the northern island of Luzon, which contains the capital, Manila. For almost 400 years the Philippines was governed by Spain; in fact the country is named after the Spanish king Philip II. In 1898 control passed to the US, then in 1946 the Philippines became an independent nation. Most Filipinos are of Malay origin, but there are some Chinese immigrants and mixed-blood *mestizos*.

THE PHILIPPINES

Capital city: Manila

Area: 115,123 sq miles (298,170 sq km)

Population: 76,000,800

Official languages: Filipino and English

Major religions: Christian 92%, Muslim 5%, other 3%

Government: Multiparty democracy

Currency: Philippine peso

Adult literacy rate: 95%

Life expectancy: 69 years

People per doctor: 10,000

Televisions: 108 per 1,000 people

MANILA

Much of the capital city of the Philippines lies below sea level, and it suffers from floods during the rainy summer season. The Spanish captured Manila in 1571, fortifying its walls and making it the center of their Asian empire. Over the centuries, Manila has been an important trading port, with merchants arriving from as far afield as Arabia, India, and Japan. Today, it is a bustling modern city with more than 10 million inhabitants.

April 2, 1991: the growth of a lava dome shows that Mt. Pinatubo is about to erupt.

June 14, 1991: the mountain begins to spew deadly clouds of gas and ash.

June 15, 1991: a huge blast blows out the mountainside, and molten lava floods down the slopes.

MOUNT PINATUBO

In June 1991, Mount Pinatubo, a volcano north of Manila on the island of Luzon, burst into life. For 10 days, it spewed out volcanic ash and rocks in one of the biggest volcanic eruptions ever recorded. The landscape was soon covered with a layer of debris some 23 ft (7 m) deep. Heavy rainfall turned much of this to sludge, blocking rivers, and filling up valleys. The local Aeta tribespeople lost their land and houses overnight.

SMOKY MOUNTAIN
On the edge of Manila lies a vast mountain. Unlike other mountains, this one is not made of rock, but of garbage. Every day the garbage trucks of Manila arrive there to dump their loads of household waste. Many people, some of them children as young as four, live on the mountain, searching the refuse daily for bottles, cans, plastics, and cardboard that they can sell for recycling.

Filipinos working abroad in 2000

Europe: 3.8%

Asia: 47.8%

Middle East: 44.3%

The Americas: 2.1%

Africa: 1.2%

Australasia: 0.8%

About 2% of the workforce are working abroad at any one time, sending money home to support their families. Each year, more than US$1 billion flows into the country's economy in this way.

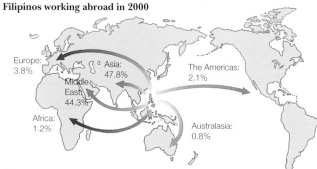

THE ECONOMY

Once one of the richer nations in Asia, in the last few decades the Philippines has fallen behind its economically powerful neighbors. Half the population lives in poverty, and many Filipinos can only support their families by working abroad. The Philippines is rich in natural resources, with reserves of gold, copper, and chrome. The main export crops are tobacco, sugar, and a wide range of tropical fruits.

AMAZING JEEPS
At the end of World War II, the US Army left thousands of unwanted jeeps in the Philippines. Local people soon converted these for their own use, decorating them in amazing colors and patterns. The jeep can cope with the rugged conditions and poor roads of the countryside and is now one of the main forms of transportation in the Philippines.

POLITICS

The presidential system of government in the Philippines has caused problems over the last few decades. In 1965, Ferdinand Marcos became president, but governed the country harshly, cheated in elections, and used his position to make a personal fortune. He was finally forced to leave when thousands of people took to the streets in protests known as "People Power," organized by the Catholic Church. In 2001 another corrupt president, Joseph Estrada, a former film star, was also forced to step down after more mass protests from Filipinos.

ANCIENT TERRACES, MODERN METHODS

The Ifugao people have farmed the mountainous landscape in the north of Luzon island for thousands of years, laboriously constructing terraces on the steep hillsides to grow rice. These ancient terraces are now a major tourist attraction. But not all rice-growers in the Philippines use such traditional methods. The country is also home to the International Rice Research Institute, where scientists have bred new species of rice that yield more grains per plant, and are also developing rice-planting and harvesting machines.

RELIGION

Roman Catholicism was introduced to the Philippines by the explorer Magellan, who visited the island of Cebu in 1521 during his voyage around the world. Under Spanish rule, many Filipinos converted to Catholicism. It became the major religion in all but the southern, Muslim island of Mindanao. Today, the Philippines is the only Christian country in Asia, and the Catholic Church continues to exert a powerful influence on everyday life.

Farmers here sow rice in the ground like any other cereal crop, rather than in a flooded paddy field.

The terraces are held in place by stone walls built entirely by hand.

COCONUTS

The coconut palm flourishes in the warm, damp climate of the Philippines, producing nuts for up to 70 years. The nuts ripen in bunches of 15 to 20, and are harvested by farmers who knock them out of the trees with long bamboo poles. After Indonesia, the Philippines is the world's second largest producer of coconuts and the world's biggest producer of copra, the fleshy meat inside the nut, exporting the products around the world.

Reaching a height of up to 100 ft (30 m), the coconut is one of the most beautiful palm trees in the world. Long leaves form on top of the slender trunk, and cream flowers grow on long spikes.

Inside the nut is a refreshing milk drink that, as the nut ripens, slowly turns into coconut meat, or copra.

Copra

Copra
Coconut milk

Coconut

Outer husk

Basket woven from palm leaves

101 USES OF THE COCONUT

Every part of the coconut tree has a use. The roots are turned into dyes and medicines, the trunk into timber and charcoal, and the leaves into thatch for roofs and woven material. The nut is used for matting, food, and cosmetics.

Mat made from the outer husk of the coconut

Copra is used to make soap, cosmetics, and detergents.

HUNTER-GATHERERS

On some of the more remote islands of the Philippines groups of hunter-gatherers live, roaming the countryside fishing, hunting animals, and gathering vegetables, fruit, and berries. These people are among the last in the world to continue this ancient way of life, but their lifestyle is under attack as the forests in which they live are felled for timber.

Find out more
RICE GROWING: *135, 176, 197*
ROMAN CATHOLICS: *274*
TERRACE FARMING: *159, 173*
VOLCANOES: *13, 197*

THE INDIAN OCEAN

THE THIRD LARGEST of the world's oceans, the Indian Ocean covers 28 million sq miles (73 million sq km) and contains some 5,000 islands, many of them surrounded by coral reefs. This ocean is unique because, unlike the Atlantic and Pacific, it has no outlet to the north. It contains both the saltiest sea (the Red Sea), and the warmest sea (the Persian Gulf) on Earth. The Indian Ocean is at risk from pollution, especially from oil tankers leaving the Persian Gulf. Monsoon rains and tropical storms can bring disastrous flooding to its northern coasts.

ISLAND PARADISE
The islands of the Indian Ocean include coral atolls, like the Maldives and Seychelles, which attract thousands of tourists every year. Although this brings money to the islands, it also threatens to damage the environment. Gradual erosion of the coral reefs also leaves the islands exposed to ocean tides and flooding. This Maldive island has a barrier to protect it from sea damage.

CORAL ISLANDS

Coral is formed in warm waters by tiny creatures known as polyps. These marine creatures build limestone skeletons around themselves. Over many thousands of years, these skeletons gradually grow up toward the surface of the ocean to form a coral island. An atoll, shown right, is a form of circular coral reef that grows around an underwater volcano. As the volcano sinks, the coral forms an atoll. The water in the center is called a lagoon.

1. Corals grow in shallow waters around volcanic island.

2. Coral reef builds up as movements in the Earth's surface make the island sin

3. Island finally disappears, leaving a coral atoll.

MADAGASCAR

Madagascar lies off the east coast of Africa and, because of its isolation, is home to many unique plants and animals. Most people in Madagascar scratch out a living by farming, clearing a new patch of land each year to plant their crops. One of the island's main crops is vanilla, grown for use as flavoring in food and drinks. Women traditionally have elaborate hairstyles that indicate the village they are from.

THE SALTY SEA
Oceans are salty because minerals dissolved from rocks by rivers are washed into them. Around the shores of the Indian Ocean, people extract the salt by channeling water into shallow pans. The sun's heat evaporates the water, leaving salt behind, as shown here in Mauritius.

This port in Fremantle, Australia, handles freight from across the world.

SHIPPING ROUTES
More than 200 large ships a day sail around the Cape of Good Hope at the southern tip of Africa as they enter or leave the Indian Ocean. Many are vast tankers laden with oil from the Persian Gulf. Smaller ships are able to pass through the Suez Canal. On the other side of the Indian Ocean, ships pass through the Strait of Malacca carrying cargo to ports in eastern Asia.

MALDIVES
Capital city: Male
Area: 116 sq miles (300 sq km)
Population: 286,000
Official language: Dhivehi
Major religion: Muslim 100%
Government: One-party state
Currency: Rufiyaa

COMOROS
Capital city: Moroni
Area: 861 sq miles (2,230 sq km)
Population: 694,000
Official languages: Arabic and French
Major religions: Muslim 99%, other 1%
Government: Multiparty democracy
Currency: Comoros franc

MAURITIUS
Capital city: Port Louis
Area: 718 sq miles (1,860 sq km)
Population: 1,200,000
Official language: English
Major religions: Hindu 52%, Christian 28%, Muslim 17%, other 3%
Government: Multiparty democracy
Currency: Mauritian rupee

MADAGASCAR
Capital city: Antananarivo
Area: 224,532 sq miles (581,540 sq km)
Population: 15,900,000
Official languages: Malagasy and French
Major religions: Christian 41%, traditional beliefs 52%, Muslim 7%
Government: Multiparty democracy
Currency: Malagasy franc

SEYCHELLES
Capital city: Victoria
Area: 104 sq miles (270 sq km)
Population: 79,326
Official language: Creole
Major religions: Christian 98%, other 2%
Government: Multiparty democracy
Currency: Seychelles rupee

The dried salt is stored in baskets. Workers then carry the heavy baskets on theirheads to a waiting truck.

N

Maldives

☀ Jan 79°F (26°C)
July 80°F (27°C)

🌧 Jan 1.8 in (46 mm)
July 8.9 in (226 mm)

SEYCHELLES

COMOROS

Antananarivo, Madagascar

☀ Jan 70°F (21°C)
July 58°F (14°C)

🌧 Jan 11.8 in (300 mm)
July 0.3 in (9 mm)

MADAGASCAR

MAURITIUS

MALDIVES

THINGS TO LOOK FOR ON THE MAP

World's longest archipelago: Indonesian Islands, 3,480 miles (5,600 km) *Map J5*

Deepest trench: Java Trench, 23,376 ft (7,125 m) *Map J6*

World's highest rainfall: Réunion, 73.62 in (1,870 mm) in 24 hours *Map E7*

Mauritius

☀ Jan 79°F (26°C)
July 68°F (20°C)

🌧 Jan 8.5 in (216 mm)
July 2.3 in (58 mm)

Parson's chameleon

WILDLIFE

Half of all the chameleons – a type of lizard – in the world are found on Madagascar. Although harmless, they are feared by local people who believe the animals represent human spirits not yet at rest. The chameleon is best known for its ability to change color when angry or frightened.

FISHING

Large-scale fishing is less developed in the Indian Ocean than in the Atlantic or Pacific because there are not as many areas of shallow sea. Most of the fish are caught by shore-based fishermen for family use or to sell in a local market.

Fishermen bring in the catch in the Maldives

These men are following a traditional method of fishing with a square net raised and lowered by wooden poles.

AFRICA

THE SECOND LARGEST CONTINENT, Africa is a land of contrasts. To the north lies the great Sahara, the largest desert in the world, yet the central equatorial area is covered by dense tropical rain forests, while farther south a series of grassy plateaus (areas of flat highland) give way to narrow coastal plains. Major mountain ranges include the Atlas in the north and the Ruwenzori range on the Uganda-Democratic Republic of Congo (Zaire) border. Africa's highest mountain is Kilimanjaro, a dormant volcano, in Tanzania. To the east is the Great Rift Valley, which contains several huge lakes. Some of the world's longest rivers drain the continent, including the Nile, Niger, Congo, and Zambezi.

DESERTS

Africa has three huge deserts. The vast Sahara is the world's largest desert and dominates the northern third of the continent. Thousands of years ago the Sahara had a moist climate. Today, the path of wet winds blowing in from the sea is blocked by other winds blowing outward from the desert. The Namib and Kalahari deserts cover vast areas of southwestern Africa. Although it lies along the coast, the Namib Desert (shown here) is particularly barren and dry.

GREAT RIFT VALLEY

The Great Rift Valley stretches from Mozambique in the south, through eastern Africa and the Red Sea, into Syria. In most places the valley is 19–62 miles (30–100 km) wide, with steep sides rising up to 6,562 ft (2,000 m). The valley was formed as blocks of land sank between faults in the Earth's crust. In eastern Africa, the valley has two main branches. The Rift Valley is marked by volcanoes, hot springs, and a long chain of lakes.

Formation of a rift valley

Movements deep within the Earth's crust cause stretching, and cracks appear on the surface.

Surface cracks

Block mountains

Lake

Volcano

The cracking creates long faults. Some blocks of land slip down between parallel faults to create a rift valley.

RAIN FORESTS

The world's second largest rain forest, after the Amazon, lies in central Africa. The Congo teems with plant and animal life, including rare creatures such as okapis. It was also the home of groups of pygmies, but many now live in settled villages, because vast areas of forest have been destroyed for logging and farming. One group, the Bambuti, still live in the northeastern forests of Democratic Republic of Congo (Zaire).

Millions of flamingos flock to Lake Turkana and other Rift Valley lakes to nest and feed on tiny water plants.

LAKE VICTORIA

Lake Victoria is Africa's largest lake and the second largest freshwater lake in the world. Lying on the Equator, between Kenya, Tanzania, and Uganda, it covers about 26,828 sq miles (69,484 sq km) and reaches 269 ft (82 m) at its deepest point. The Nile River flows out of the northern end of the lake. Lake Victoria is rich in fish, which provide an important source of income for the large numbers of people living along the lake shores.

DRAKENSBERG MOUNTAINS

The highest mountains in southern Africa are the Drakensberg. They form part of the rim of a saucer-shaped plateau of high land called the Great Escarpment. In the local Zulu language, the mountains are known as *Quathlamba*, which means the "barrier of pointed spears." The highest peak, Thabana Ntlenyana, rises 11,424 ft (3,482 m) above sea level and is capped with snow in winter.

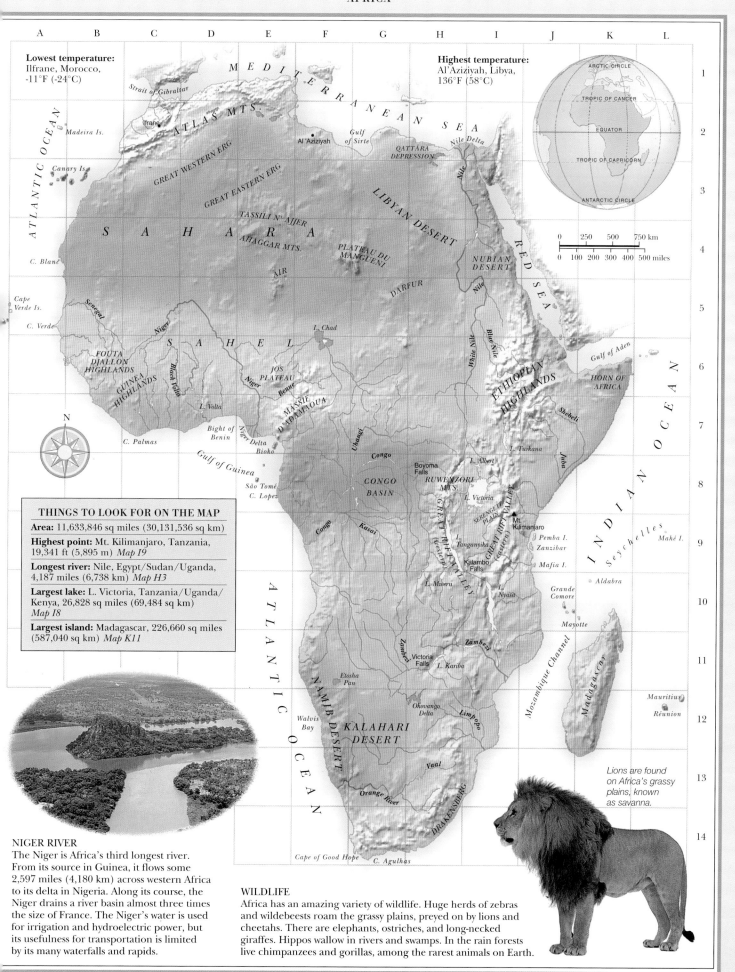

Lowest temperature:
Ilfrane, Morocco,
-11°F (-24°C)

Highest temperature:
Al'Aziziyah, Libya,
136°F (58°C)

ARCTIC CIRCLE
TROPIC OF CANCER
EQUATOR
TROPIC OF CAPRICORN
ANTARCTIC CIRCLE

MEDITERRANEAN SEA

Strait of Gibraltar

ATLAS MTS.

Madeira Is.

Ifrane

Al'Aziziyah

Gulf of Sirte

QATTĀRA DEPRESSION

Nile Delta

Canary Is.

GREAT WESTERN ERG

GREAT EASTERN ERG

TASSILI N'AJJER

AHAGGAR MTS.

PLATEAU DU MANGUENI

LIBYAN DESERT

RED SEA

NUBIAN DESERT

0   250   500   750 km
0 100 200 300 400 500 miles

C. Blanc

S A H A R A

AIR

DARFUR

Nile

Cape Verde Is.

C. Verde

Senegal

Niger

S A H E L

L. Chad

White Nile

Blue Nile

Gulf of Aden

HORN OF AFRICA

FOUTA DJALLON HIGHLANDS

Black Volta

JOS PLATEAU

Niger

Benue

ETHIOPIAN HIGHLANDS

Shebeli

GUINEA HIGHLANDS

L. Volta

MASSIF D'ADAMAOUA

Juba

N

C. Palmas

Bight of Benin

Niger Delta

Bioko

Ubangi

Congo

RUWENZORI MTS.

L. Albert

L. Turkana

Gulf of Guinea

São Tomé

C. Lopez

CONGO BASIN

Boyoma Falls

L. Victoria

SERENGETI PLAIN

Mt. Kilimanjaro

Pemba I.

Zanzibar

Mahé I.

Seychelles

INDIAN OCEAN

THINGS TO LOOK FOR ON THE MAP

Area: 11,633,846 sq miles (30,131,536 sq km)

Highest point: Mt. Kilimanjaro, Tanzania, 19,341 ft (5,895 m) *Map I9*

Longest river: Nile, Egypt/Sudan/Uganda, 4,187 miles (6,738 km) *Map H3*

Largest lake: L. Victoria, Tanzania/Uganda/Kenya, 26,828 sq miles (69,484 sq km) *Map I8*

Largest island: Madagascar, 226,660 sq miles (587,040 sq km) *Map K11*

Congo

Kasai

L. Tanganyika

Kalambo Falls

Mafia I.

L. Mweru

L. Nyasa

Grande Comore

Aldabra

Mayotte

GREAT RIFT VALLEY (western)

GREAT RIFT VALLEY (eastern)

Zambezi

Victoria Falls

Zambezi

L. Kariba

Mozambique Channel

Madagascar

Mauritius

Réunion

ATLANTIC OCEAN

Etosha Pan

Okovango Delta

Limpopo

NAMIB DESERT

Walvis Bay

KALAHARI DESERT

Vaal

DRAKENSBERG

Lions are found
on Africa's grassy
plains, known
as savanna.

Orange River

Cape of Good Hope   *C. Agulhas*

NIGER RIVER
The Niger is Africa's third longest river.
From its source in Guinea, it flows some
2,597 miles (4,180 km) across western Africa
to its delta in Nigeria. Along its course, the
Niger drains a river basin almost three times
the size of France. The Niger's water is used
for irrigation and hydroelectric power, but
its usefulness for transportation is limited
by its many waterfalls and rapids.

WILDLIFE
Africa has an amazing variety of wildlife. Huge herds of zebras
and wildebeests roam the grassy plains, preyed on by lions and
cheetahs. There are elephants, ostriches, and long-necked
giraffes. Hippos wallow in rivers and swamps. In the rain forests
live chimpanzees and gorillas, among the rarest animals on Earth.

PEOPLES OF AFRICA

Population: approximately 783,800,000 people

Number of countries: 53

AFRICA IS HOME TO about 784 million people – one in eight of the world's population. The most densely populated areas are along the northern and western coasts, especially in the fertile valleys of the Nile, Niger, Congo, and Senegal rivers. The population of Africa is growing rapidly, as birth rates in many African countries are extremely high. Families are often large, and about half the population is young, below the age of 15. Although most Africans live in the countryside, a growing number are now found in towns and cities. Many people have moved because of poverty and lack of work in country areas; others have gone to escape civil wars, droughts, and famines.

Largest country: Sudan, 967,493 sq miles (2,505,810 sq km)

Smallest country: Seychelles 108 sq miles (280 sq km)

Least densely populated country: Namibia, 5 people per sq mile (2 per sq km)

Most densely populated country: Mauritius, 1,671 people per sq mile (645 per sq km)

THE FIRST PEOPLE
The history of human beings would seem to have begun in Africa. The skeletons of people who walked upright and lived up to 2 million years ago have been found in the Rift Valley that runs through Tanzania and Ethiopia. Archaeologists now believe that this region was the birthplace of our human ancestors. From here, these early human beings, known as *Homo Erectus*, soon moved into other parts of the continent and rapidly spread even farther afield.

Richard Leakey discovered some of the earliest known human remains in Africa's Rift Valley.

Percentage of population under 15 years of age

Egypt: 37%   Ghana: 46%   Ethiopia: 46%   Tanzania: 47%

YOUNG POPULATION
The population of Africa is growing rapidly. Improved medicine has generally decreased death rates, while birth rates remain very high. Women in countries such as Angola and Burkina have six children each on average, whereas in North America and Europe they have only one or two. However, HIV infection is fast becoming widespread among young people and is set to kill many in the near future.

TOWN AND COUNTRY
Most African people live as farmers or herders in the countryside. However, about one in five people now live in towns. The most heavily urbanized region is northern Africa, and Cairo, in Egypt, is the largest city on the continent with a population of more than 10 million. Several other cities have more than a million inhabitants, including Addis Ababa in Ethiopia, Kinshasa in Zaire, and Johannesburg in South Africa. The poor often live on the outskirts of the cities, in shantytowns.

BIGGEST URBAN POPULATION	
Libya	87%
Djibouti	83%
Gabon	80%
Tunisia	65%
Dem. Rep. of Congo (Zaire)	62%

SMALLEST URBAN POPULATION	
Rwanda	6%
Burundi	9%
Uganda	14%
Malawi	15%
Ethiopia	17%

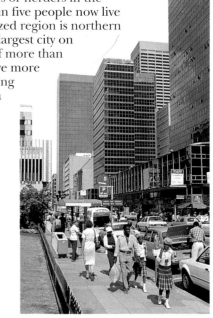

Many people go to the cities on a temporary basis in search of work. In Johannesburg, shown here, migrants seek work in the gold and diamond mines.

THE PEOPLE

The vast Sahara Desert separates the peoples of northern Africa, who are mostly Berbers and Arabs, like these Tunisian men, from those to the south, who are mostly Negroid. Northern Africa is predominantly Islamic, but south of the Sahara people follow a variety of religions, including Christianity and traditional animist beliefs. Two other groups are also important: there are about 8 million people of European descent, who live mainly in southern Africa, as well as a large number of Indians, who live along the eastern coast and in South Africa.

ART

Africa has produced a great variety of art from prehistoric times to the present. Often, art was related to ritual or tribal ceremonies, as well as being used for decoration. In many tribes the artist was given high status and art was often regarded as an essential part of religion. It is possible to isolate different areas and different practices of African art. From around 7000 BC rock drawings include representations of animals and hunters. Tribal art has become a way of distinguishing one tribe from another and can take many forms, including body painting and sculptural masks.

Bronze head of the Queen Mother of Benin, made by taking a clay mold from a wax sculpture.

PEOPLES AND COUNTRIES

There are more than 600 ethnic or tribal groups in Africa, and only 53 countries. Many of today's national boundaries were created in the late 19th century by colonial rulers. Borders sometimes follow natural features, such as rivers, but often they just follow straight lines on a map. As a result, tribes are often split between different countries. The Ewe people, for example, are divided between Ghana and Togo. After independence, it has often proved difficult to create unity among the different peoples in one country.

Groups of nomadic Fulani people are found throughout the area shaded brown on this map of western Africa. They roam across many countries.

WEST AFRICA

These refugees at a camp in Rwanda are Hutu people from neighboring Burundi. War between the Hutu and Tutsi peoples has forced thousands of people in this region to leave their homes.

Peanuts (groudnuts) are one of the main export crops in western Africa.

ECONOMIC PROBLEMS

Most African countries rely on exporting raw materials, such as coffee, cocoa, or oil. In recent years, the prices of these products have fallen. In contrast, the cost of importing machinery and other manufactured goods has risen. Thus the amount that African countries can earn from their exports is often less than what they have to spend on imports. These factors, along with the growing population and the effects of drought and war, mean that the economies of many African countries are in difficulty.

FRESH WATER

Only around 62% of Africans have access to decent sources of water. Often people must make long journeys to collect it and millions are forced to drink water that is contaminated by dangerous bacteria. The situation is worst across central Africa where the hot climate and lack of investment makes clean water scarce. Aid agencies have made access to clean water a key issue and have used funding to build safe water wells and educate people about the importance of hygiene.

Percentage of people with access to safe water

Other: Europe: 90% 91%
Asia: 82%
Africa: 62%

NORTHWESTERN AFRICA

MOROCCO, ALGERIA, TUNISIA, LIBYA, and Western Sahara make up the northwestern corner of Africa. Most of the region's peoples are Arabic-speaking Muslims whose ancestors came to the area from the Middle East. From the 1530s to the 1830s, the region was part of the Turkish Ottoman Empire. It was then ruled by the colonial powers of France, Italy, and Spain, until the various countries gained independence in the mid-1900s. These countries are described as "middle income," thanks largely to their rich supplies of oil and gas.

ALONG THE COAST
The vast majority of northwestern Africa's 75 million people live along the narrow coastal plain that borders the Mediterranean Sea and the Atlantic Ocean. Here, the climate is warm and wet in winter and hot and dry in summer, making it more suitable for farming than the arid desert farther inland. Citrus fruits, dates, olives, tomatoes, and flowers are grown. The major towns and cities are located here, too.

A GROWING POPULATION
One of the most serious problems facing northwestern Africa is the rapid growth of its population. In Algeria alone, the population increased 31 million between 1966 and 2000. Millions of people have moved from the countryside to the cities in search of work. This has led to severe housing shortages in the city centers and to the rise of overcrowded shantytowns on the outskirts.

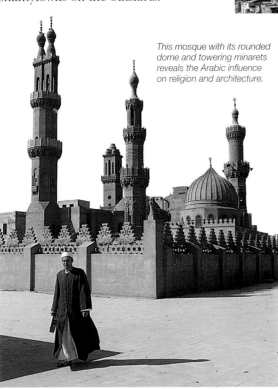

This mosque with its rounded dome and towering minarets reveals the Arabic influence on religion and architecture.

Marrakesh, Morocco
Jan 53°F (11°C)
July 84°F (29°C)
Jan 1 in (25 mm)
July 0.1 in (3 mm)

MOROCCO

Tangier
Tétouan
Kénitra
RABAT
Casablanca
Meknès
Safi
MOROCCO
Khouribga
Essaouira
Beni Mellal
Er Rach
Marrakesh
Djebel Toubkal ▲ Boumalne
Dadès
Agadir
Tiznit
Tan-Tan
ATLANTIC OCEAN
EL AAIUN
WESTERN SAHARA
Semara
Tindouf
Ad Dakhla
WESTERN SAHARA
MAURITANIA

Morocco occupied the whole of Western Sahara in 1979.

Lagouira

0   100   200   300   400 km
0   50   100 150 200 250 miles

TROPIC OF CANCER
EQUATOR
TROPIC OF CAPRICORN

N

In Salah, Algeria
Jan 56°F (14°C)
July 98°F (37°C)
Jan 0.1 in (3 mm)
July 0 in (0 mm)

ARAB INFLUENCE
The Arab invasions of the 7th and 11th centuries have had a long-lasting effect on northwestern Africa. The Arabs soon outnumbered the local Berber people who rebelled against their rule. They quickly established their own language, Arabic, and their own religion, Islam, throughout the region. Despite the later arrival of European colonists, northwestern Africa today, in its language, culture, religion, and architecture, remains firmly part of the Arab world.

A   B   C   D   E   F   G

The Tuareg ride on camelback, although motorcycles and four-wheel-drive trucks are increasingly used.

SAHARA DESERT

Much of northwestern Africa is covered by the scorching sand and rocks of the Sahara Desert. The world's largest desert, the Sahara is expanding at an alarming rate as the land at its edges is overgrazed and gradually turned to dust. Despite daytime temperatures of up to 122°F (50°C), freezing nights, and years on end without rain, the desert is home to some amazing animals, adapted to survive the conditions.

The fennec fox's huge ears let heat escape from its body, cooling it down.

DESERT PEOPLES

Few people can survive in the harsh environment of the Sahara Desert. The hardy Tuareg are desert nomads who may travel vast distances a day, carrying salt to trade in markets. Traditionally, the Tuareg use camels for transport and also to provide milk, meat, and hides. However, many Tuareg are now abandoning their centuries-old nomadic lifestyle and settling in cities.

TUNISIA

Tunis, Tunisia
☀ Jan 51°F (10°C)
　July 79°F (26°C)
🌧 Jan 2.5 in (64 mm)
　July 0.1 in (3 mm)

THINGS TO LOOK FOR ON THE MAP

Longest river: Oued Chelif, Algeria, 435 miles (700 km) *Map K2*

Highest point: Djebel Toubkal, Morocco, 13,665 ft (4,165 m) *Map G4*

World's highest sand dune: is in the Erg Tifernine, Algeria, 1,411 ft (430 m) *Map M7*

World's highest recorded temperature: Al' Aziziyah, Libya, 136.4°F (58°C) *Map O4*

Benghazi, Libya
☀ Jan 14°C (57°F)
　July 26°C (78°F)
🌧 Jan 66 mm (2.6 in)
　July 0 mm (0 in)

ALGERIA

LIBYA

MOROCCO

MOROCCO'S WARM CLIMATE, sandy beaches, and stunning mountain scenery make it a popular destination for vacationers. Tourism, along with agriculture and phosphate production, is vital to the country's economy. In 1956, Morocco gained its independence from the French, who had governed it since 1912. It is one of the few Arab countries to be ruled by a king, Mohammed VI. Since coming to the throne in 1999, King Mohammed has won international recognition for his moderate leadership. The main issues facing Morocco today are Islamic fundamentalism and the undecided fate of the Western Sahara region in the south.

MOROCCO*	
Capital city: Rabat	
Area: 172,316 sq miles (446,300 sq km)	
Population: 28,400,000	
Official language: Arabic	
Major religions: Muslim 99%, Christian 1%	
Government: Monarchy with democratic system	
Currency: Moroccan dirham	
Adult literacy rate: 50%	
Life expectancy: 67 years	
People per doctor: 2,500	
Televisions: 160 per 1,000 people	

* Figures include Western Sahara

Berber wedding ceremony

BERBERS

Since the Arab invasions of the 11th century, the local Berber people have lived in villages high up in the Atlas Mountains. Most Berbers converted to Islam, but kept their own culture and way of life. They call themselves *Imazighen*, or "people of the land." Today, about a third of Moroccans are Berber-speaking, although most also speak Arabic and French.

AN ISLAMIC CITY

The ancient Moroccan city of Fez is a good example of a traditional Islamic town. Each part has been designed with a purpose, as set out in the Koran, the Muslim holy book. The streets are narrow to provide shade, but wide enough to let a pair of fully laden camels pass through. Houses have small, high windows on street walls to guard their owners' privacy. In the city center stands the largest mosque, surrounded by the *souks*, or markets.

The numerous, carefully planned streets in the old city of Fez look chaotic from a distance.

Carpets with symbolic patterns and ornate metalwork lanterns are made by local people.

ARTS AND CRAFTS

Millions of tourists visit Morocco each year to relax on the beaches along the Atlantic coast or to explore the historical cities of Fez and Marrakesh. The cities' colorful *souks*, or markets, are a treasure chest of traditional goods and handicrafts, such as Moroccan leather, silver jewelry, and handwoven carpets.

WESTERN SAHARA

This is a desert region south of Morocco with a population of some 200,000 people. It was formerly ruled by Spain. Since 1975, Morocco has been fighting a war for control of the region and its valuable mineral resources. Opposing the Moroccans are the Polisario, a guerilla force of desert tribesmen who want complete independence for the Western Sahara.

A supporter of the Polisario in the Western Sahara

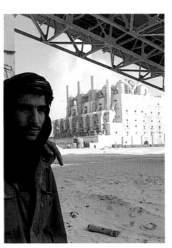

A phosphate-processing factory in the south of Morocco

ECONOMY

Morocco's economy depends on three major industries – tourism, agriculture, and phosphates. Farm products make up about a third of exports. The main crops are cereals, vegetables, citrus fruits, and dates. Irrigation systems pipe water to many dry areas for farming. Morocco is the world's third largest producer of phosphates, which are used to make chemicals and fertilizers. Large factories process the phosphates for export.

Find out more

CARPET MAKING: 144, 155, 165
IRRIGATION: 155, 156, 217
ISLAM: 275
MONARCHY: 270–271

ALGERIA

STRETCHING FROM THE MEDITERRANEAN coast deep into the heart of the Sahara Desert, Algeria is the second largest country in Africa. It won independence from France in 1962, after a bitter, eight-year struggle that claimed one million lives. During French rule, tens of thousands of Europeans arrived, many of them later leaving after independence. Since then, Algeria has played an important part in world affairs as a member of the United Nations and the Arab League. The main challenge facing the democratic government today comes from Islamic fundamentalists who support the setting up of an Islamic government.

ALGERIA	
Capital city: Algiers	
Area: 919,590 sq miles (2,381,740 sq km)	
Population: 31,500,000	
Official language: Arabic	
Major religions: Muslim 99%, other 1%	
Government: Democratic government	
Currency: Algerian dinar	
Adult literacy rate: 68%	
Life expectancy: 69 years	
People per doctor: 1,250	
Televisions: 105 per 1,000 people	

The leaves of date palms are used for thatching.

Arabs selling local produce at a market in Ghardaia, Algeria

Dates can be eaten in many ways.

Wood is used for timber.

Date palms are grown at desert oases, where water comes up to the surface.

ALGIERS
Algiers, the capital of Algeria, is the country's largest city and most important port. The city was founded in the 10th century by Muslims from Arabia. It was seized by the Turks in 1518 and by the French in 1830. The French influence can still be seen in these buildings in the modern part of the city along the Bay of Algiers. The old city, with its narrow streets, mosques, and markets, stands on the slopes of the Sahel Hills.

Algerian exports

Oil and oil products: 57%

Gas and gas products: 40%

Other: 3%

ETHNIC MIX
About 27 million people live in Algeria. Although the vast majority of Algerians are Arabs, about a fifth of the population is descended from the earlier Berber settlers. Arabic is the official language and Islam the main religion. Of the million or so Europeans who settled in Algeria before independence, only a few thousand remain. These include people of French, Spanish, and Italian descent.

ECONOMY
Algeria's economy is dependent on its oil and gas reserves. These come from large deposits in the Sahara Desert. Oil production began in 1958. By 1979, it had reached 1.2 million barrels a day. Although falling world oil prices in the 1980s and 1990s caused a drop in oil production, the exploitation of natural gas has since increased. Algeria supplies both France and Italy with gas.

FARMING
Algeria cannot grow enough crops to feed its rapidly increasing population and has to import about three-quarters of the food it needs. However, about a quarter of the workforce is employed in farming. Major crops include cereals, citrus fruits, grapes, olives, and tobacco. Figs and dates are important, too. Algeria is one of the world's leading producers of dates and of cork, which is made from cork oak bark. Dates are eaten fresh, dried, or ground into flour. Roasted and ground date stones are made into date coffee.

TERRORIST ATTACKS
Islamic fundamentalists, like these members of the Islamic Salvation Front (FIS), are in open revolt against Algeria's government. Thousands of Algerians have died in recent years as a result of terrorist violence. Westerners have also been attacked and bombs have been planted in Paris and other French cities.

Find out more
COLONIAL PERIOD: *207*
ISLAM: *275*
OIL & GAS: *137, 152, 163, 211*
SAHARA: *204, 209*

TUNISIA

NORTHWESTERN AFRICA'S SMALLEST country, Tunisia lies between Libya to the south and Algeria to the west. Throughout its history, Tunisia has had close links with Europe. It was at the heart of the ancient empire of Carthage in the 4th century BC, and later became part of the mighty Roman Empire. In the 7th century AD, Tunisia was colonized by Muslim Arabs, and in the early 1880s by French forces. It became independent in 1956. The government has since been restructured and a multi-party system introduced.

TUNISIA	
Capital city: Tunis	
Area: 59,984 sq miles (155,360 sq km)	
Population: 9,600,000	
Official language: Arabic	
Major religions: Muslim 98%, Christian 1%, Jewish 1%	
Government: Multiparty democracy	
Currency: Tunisian dinar	
Adult literacy rate: 71%	
Life expectancy: 70 years	
People per doctor: 1,492	
Televisions: 334 per 1,000 people	

A heap of steamed couscous served with roast chicken and sausages

Brightly dyed wool will soon be woven into carpets.

TUNISIAN FOOD
Traditional food is influenced by Arabic, Turkish, and French cooking. The national dish is couscous, a mix of semolina, meat, and vegetables. Spicy stews cooked in clay pots, called *tajines*, are also popular. For dessert, people eat fruit, dates stuffed with almond paste, or *baklava*, a sweet nut and honey pastry. To drink, there is strong black coffee or mint tea. Many Tunisian men go to cafés in the evening to meet friends and drink coffee.

A glass of strong, sweet mint tea

TOURISM
Tunisia's warm winter climate and historic sites attract numerous tourists each year. Until 1976, tourism was Tunisia's highest earner of foreign currency. Numbers fell in the early 1980s, but have now risen again to over five million tourists per year. The government has encouraged the building of new hotels and the development of resorts to meet the growing demand. Hundreds of thousands of Tunisians work in the tourist industry.

Libya: 18%

Germany: 19%

France: 15%

Algeria: 15%

Other: 33%

Most tourists come from neighboring Algeria and Libya, and from Europe. Cheaper air travel and the search for an exotic vacation location have made Tunisia a favorite destination for Europeans.

INDUSTRY
Until the collapse of world oil prices in the 1980s, Tunisia's major exports were oil and gas. Today, textiles and agricultural products have become much more important. Tunisia is also one of the world's leading producers of calcium phosphates, used to make chemicals and fertilizers. Most of the country's industries are located in and around the capital city, Tunis.

ARTS AND CRAFTS
One of the liveliest parts of a Tunisian city is the *souk*, or market. The *souk* is a maze of narrow, winding streets, each crowded with traders and craftsmen selling their wares. Here, you can buy a wide range of traditional arts and crafts, including copper pots and pans, carpets, leather goods, jewelry, and embroidered cloth. Other stalls sell fish, meat, fruit, and vegetables.

Grapes grow well in Tunisia's light soil and strong sunshine.

Oranges and limes come from groves along the fertile coast.

Dates are grown in the desert oases in the dry south.

AGRICULTURE
About two-thirds of Tunisia is suitable for farming. Many areas suffer from a lack of rainfall and rely on irrigation to water crops. The main crops include cereals, such as wheat and barley, citrus fruits, grapes, figs, dates, and olives. Tunisia is the world's fourth largest producer of olive oil. Despite efforts to improve output, however, Tunisia still has to import many basic foods.

Find out more
OIL & GAS: *137, 152, 163, 211*
OLIVES: *130*
POLITICAL SYSTEMS: *270–271*

LIBYA

SITUATED ON THE MEDITERRANEAN COAST between Egypt and Algeria, Libya is the fourth largest country in Africa. It has been part of the Roman, Byzantine, Arab, and Ottoman empires, and from 1911 to 1943 was an Italian colony. The Sahara Desert covers about 90 percent of the country, so farming is only possible along the coastal strip, where many people work as sheep or goat herders. The discovery of oil in 1959 very quickly transformed Libya from a poor to a wealthy country. Many foreigners have since arrived to work in the oil industry.

LIBYA

Capital city: Tripoli

Area: 679,358 sq miles (1,759,540 sq km)

Population: 5,600,000

Official language: Arabic

Major religions: Muslim 97%, other 3%

Government: Dictatorship

Currency: Libyan dinar

Adult literacy rate: 80%

Life expectancy: 70 years

People per doctor: 909

Televisions: 126 per 1,000 people

OIL AND GAS

The production of oil and gas dominates the Libyan economy, with oil making up 98 percent of the country's exports. Before oil was discovered, Libya's major exports were rushes (river plants) and scrap metal. Most of the oil is produced in western Libya, but there are also some offshore oil reserves. As the oil industry has grown, so have Libya's cities, providing more houses, jobs, and services. Some 87 percent of the population now resides in cities. Before this, many people lived as farmers or nomads.

Where people live

87% live in cities   13% live in the country

FAMILY GROUPS
Most Libyans are Arabs, with some Berbers and Tuaregs in the south. Almost all are Muslim. They belong to large, extended family groups called tribes or clans. The clan is an important part of society and also has an influence on politics. Many of Colonel Gadhafi's government ministers are members of his clan. People's names often reveal which clan they belong to.

COLONEL GADHAFI
Since 1969, Libya has been ruled by Colonel Muammar Gadhafi, who overthrew the king to become president. Gadhafi rules through military committees. His politics are a very personal mix of socialism, Islam, and Arab nationalism. Since all political parties were banned in 1971, any opposition to Gadhafi's rule has to come from outside Libya. Colonel Gadhafi's support in the past for terrorist organizations has sometimes brought him into conflict with Western governments.

OASIS TOWN

In the vast, arid desert, small towns and villages have grown up around oases. Here, underground water rises to create rare patches of fertile land where crops are grown. The communities that live around oases rely on farming, receiving money from relations working in the cities, and dealing with passing traders. In the past, oasis towns were important stopping places for camel caravans transporting goods across the desert. Today, many of these journeys are made by truck instead.

A small village grows up at the edge of the oasis.

People grow crops such as date palms, grapes, figs, and peaches.

Rain falls in the mountains and sinks into the porous rock.

Impermeable rock stops the water from sinking farther.

Rainfall is stored in porous rock called an aquifer.

Water seeps up through a split in the rock layers.

ROMAN RUINS
Signs of Libya's rich classical past can still be seen in its many historical ruins. It has some of the finest Roman ruins in North Africa, such as the impressive site of Leptis Magna, which has a forum, aqueduct, and amphitheater (shown left). This port was founded by the Phoenicians in about 800BC and became a major center for trade with Africa. It was then part of the Roman Empire, before the Arab invasions of the 7th century AD led to the city's downfall.

Find out more

ISLAM: *275*

OIL: *137, 152, 281*

OIL WEALTH: *137, 278*

SAHARA: *204, 209*

NORTHEASTERN AFRICA

NORTHEASTERN AFRICA CONTAINS EGYPT and Sudan, two desert lands watered by the Nile River, and the region known as the Horn of Africa, shaped like an animal horn, which consists of Somalia, Djibouti, Ethiopia, and Eritrea, which are among the poorest countries in the world. The boundaries that divide these countries date from the last 100 years and follow borders drawn up by the old colonial rulers of the area. However, many people that live here are nomadic herders and take little notice of the borders as they travel over vast areas in search of pasture for their animals.

BASIC TOOLS
Farming methods in the area are often inefficient, and simple tools, such as hoes, digging sticks, and sickles, are widely used. The ox-drawn scratch plow (above) is light and can be carried to scattered fields. But it only turns over the surface layer of the soil and does not allow nutrients to spread deeper, so after a few years, the soil is no longer fertile.

TROUBLED LANDS
In recent years the countries of Somalia, Sudan, Ethiopia, and Eritrea have been devastated by war. In 1993, Eritrea gained independence from Ethiopia after a civil war that lasted 20 years. Somalia has been torn apart by civil war between its rival groups, or clans. Conflict continues in Sudan between the Arabic-speaking Muslims in the north and the African, non-Muslim peoples in the south.

Thousands of Eritrean women fought alongside men in the war against Ethiopia, and many held positions of command.

INTERNATIONAL AID
Many parts of northeastern Africa have suffered from drought and famine in recent years. In 1984–85, a terrible famine swept through Ethiopia. It was caused by a combination of drought, warfare, and population growth. The famine drew the world's attention to the region and a huge international aid effort was launched, helped by the pop charity Band Aid.

The White Nile meanders slowly through the Sudd, a vast region of dense reed swamps in Sudan.

The White Nile and the Blue Nile meet at Khartoum in Sudan to form the Nile River.

As the Nile reaches the border of Sudan and Egypt, it flows into Lake Nasser, one of the world's largest artificial lakes. The lake was created by the building of the Aswan High Dam.

Many birds, including storks, herons, and pelicans, make their home in the Sudd.

The Blue Nile begins at Lake Tana. It flows through the mountains of Ethiopia, collecting rainfall along the way.

Fertile farmland

THE NILE RIVER
The world's longest river, the Nile River, flows northward from Lake Victoria in Kenya, through the Sahara Desert, to the Mediterranean Sea. It passes through Ethiopia, Sudan, and Egypt, providing precious water for drinking, farming, and fishing. The river is also a major tourist attraction. People travel along the Nile on cruise liners and traditional sailing boats called *feluccas* to see the ancient sites of Egypt.

North of the Aswan Dam, the Nile is surrounded by desert, but rich, fertile land lies along the banks of the river.

Feluccas are now mainly used by tourists.

MEDITERRANEAN SEA

Marsa Matrûh
El Mansûra
Alexandria
Port Said
Suez Canal
Tanta
Ismâ'iliya
CAIRO
Suez
Giza
Helwân
QATTARA DEPRESSION
El Faiyûm
SINAI
El Minya
EGYPT
Gulf of Suez
Gulf of Aqaba
Asyût
Bûr Safâga
Sohâg
Qena
Luxor
RED SEA
LIBYA
LIBYAN DESERT
Aswân High Dam
Aswân
L. Nasser
Administration Border
Wadi Halfa
NUBIAN DESERT

N

Cairo, Egypt
Jan 56°F (13°C)
July 83°F (29°C)
Jan 0.2 in (5 mm)
July 0 in (0 mm)

TROPIC OF CANCER
EQUATOR
TROPIC OF CAPRICORN

EGYPT

ERITREA

THINGS TO LOOK FOR ON THE MAP
World's longest river: Nile, Egypt/Sudan/Uganda, 4,187 miles (6,738 km) *Map E5*
Highest point: Ras Dashen Terara, Ethiopia, 15,157 ft (4,620 m) *Map G7*
Largest lake: L. Tana, Ethiopia, 1,100 sq miles (2,849 sq km) *Map G8*
World's longest shipping canal: Suez Canal, Egypt, 101 miles (163 km) *Map E1*

CHAD
SUDAN
Nile
Port Sudan
Atbara
Atbara
Khartoum North
Omdurman
KHARTOUM
Kassala
ASMARA
Wad Medani
Adwa
El Fasher
Mekele
Ras Dashen Terara
Assab
El Obeid
White Nile
Blue Nile
Gonder
En Nahud
DJIBOUTI
Nyala
Ed Damazin
L. Tana
Dese
Awash
DJIBOUTI
Kaduqli
Bahir Dar
DJIBOUTI
Debre Markos
Gulf of Aden
Boosaaso
ERITREA
Dahlak Archipelago
HORN OF AFRICA
Berbera

Addis Ababa, Ethiopia
Jan 59°F (15°C)
July 60°F (16°C)
Jan 0.5 in (13 mm)
July 11 in (279 mm)

DJIBOUTI

Malakal
ETHIOPIAN
Nekemte
ADDIS ABABA
Dire Dawa
Hargeysa
Garoowe
SUDD
HIGHLANDS
Harer
Gore
ETHIOPIA
Wau
Jima
Jonglei Canal
Rumbek
Omo
Awasa
Gaalkacyo
CENTRAL AFRICAN REPUBLIC
Elemi Triangle is administered by Kenya
L. Abaya
Genale
Shebeli
SOMALIA
Beledweyne
INDIAN OCEAN
DEM. REP. CONGO (ZAIRE)
Juba
L. Rudolf
Juba
Baydhabo
UGANDA
KENYA
MOGADISHU
Marka

SOMALIA

Mogadishu, Somalia
Jan 80°F (27°C)
July 78°F (26°C)
Jan 0 in (0 mm)
July 2.5 in (64 mm)

Jilib
Kismaayo

SUDAN

ETHIOPIA

0 100 200 300 400 500 km
0 100 200 300 miles

Pyramids

Cairo

Many people live on the banks and delta of the Nile.

New land has been formed in the delta by mud and rock deposited by the river.

As the river nears the Mediterranean Sea, it separates into many tributaries and forms a fertile triangle of land called a delta.

COTTON FIELDS
Largely as a result of European colonization in the 19th and 20th centuries, cotton growing and processing are important industries in Egypt and Sudan. Production was begun in these areas by the British to provide cotton for their textile mills. The cotton is grown on large, highly mechanized farms that lie along the fertile banks of the Nile River.

EGYPT

IT IS SAID THAT EGYPT is the gift of the Nile River. The site of one of the world's first great civilizations, Egypt grew up under the rule of the pharaohs along the banks of the Nile more than 5,000 years ago. Most of the country is dry, sandy desert with a narrow, fertile strip that follows the river valley and widens into the delta. This is where the vast majority of Egypt's population lives. Most of the people are Arab and follow the Muslim faith. The economy is dominated by farming, oil, tourism, income from ships passing through the Suez Canal, and money earned by Egyptians working abroad.

EGYPT	
Capital city: Cairo	
Area: 384,343 sq miles 995,450 sq km)	
Population: 56,100,000	
Official language: Arabic	
Major religions: Muslim 94%, other 6%	
Government: Multiparty democracy	
Currency: Egyptian pound	
Adult literacy rate: 55%	
Life expectancy: 67 years	
People per doctor: 495	
Televisions: 122 per 1,000 people	

CAIRO

With a population of some 10.5 million, Cairo is the second largest city in Africa and one of the fastest growing. The city faces terrible housing problems. New arrivals often have to live in dirty, overcrowded slums. Some live among the graves of the City of the Dead, a huge cemetery on the outskirts of the city. People also live on the roofs of the many high-rise buildings in Cairo.

The Suez Canal is used by more than 20,000 ships every year.

SUEZ CANAL

The Suez Canal runs from the Red Sea to the Mediterranean Sea. It is the one of the world's largest and most important artificial waterways, providing a shortcut from Europe to India and East Asia. The canal was built with French and British help and was completed in 1869. It has since been made deeper and wider to allow for the increasing size of ships and tankers. In 1956 the canal came under Egyptian control. Today, the tolls taken from the ships that use the canal are an important source of income for the Egyptian government.

→ Route before Suez Canal
→ Route after Suez was built

The Suez Canal offered a shortcut from Europe to India and East Asia. Earlier, ships from Europe had sailed around Africa.

FUL MEDAMES
This Egyptian dish is made by boiling fava beans with onions, vegetables, and spices. This may be eaten with an egg for breakfast. A similar mixture is used to stuff *aysh* (flat bread), making sandwiches.

THE NILE RIVER
Some 99 percent of Egyptians live in the valley or delta of the Nile River. The river is Egypt's lifeline, providing water for farming, industry, and home use. When the Aswan High Dam was built on the Nile, it created the world's largest reservoir, Lake Nasser.

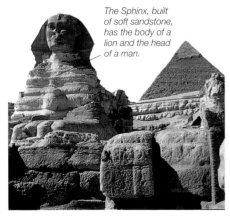

The Sphinx, built of soft sandstone, has the body of a lion and the head of a man.

FARMING IN EGYPT

Many Egyptian farmers, or *felahin*, use traditional farming methods to grow cotton, wheat, rice, sugar, fruit, and vegetables. Egypt is the world's second largest producer of dates. Another important crop is *berseem*, a type of clover grown for animal feed. Egypt is also one of the world's biggest cotton growers. Many people are employed in the textile industry, spinning, weaving, and dyeing the fine quality cotton to make clothes and other goods.

ANCIENT SITES
Egypt is littered with ancient monuments. Every year, millions of tourists flock to Egypt to see the pyramids and other sites, or to take a boat trip on the Nile River. The pyramids, built more than 4,000 years ago as tombs for the pharaohs, are one of the seven wonders of the ancient world, and the only one to survive.

Cool and comfortable cotton tunics, called jellabas, are often worn by Egyptian men.

Find out more

CITIES: *17, 206*
COTTON: *36, 215*
ISLAM: *275*
NILE: *214*

SUDAN

SUDAN, THE LARGEST COUNTRY in Africa, is one of
the poorest and least developed countries in the
world. The Nile River flows from south to north,
and most people live along its fertile banks. The
landscape ranges from rocky desert in the north
to swampland in the south. Sudan is also divided
culturally. The people of the north are mainly
Arabic-speaking Muslims, while in the center and
south, African languages and religions, together
with Christianity, dominate. Clashes between the
two sides have led to decades of civil war.

SUDAN	
Capital city: Khartoum	
Area: 917,373 sq miles (2,376,000 sq km)	
Population: 29,500,000	
Official language: Arabic	
Major religions: Muslim 70%, traditional beliefs 20%, Christian 9%, other 1%	
Government: Military government	
Currency: Sudanese dinar	
Adult literacy rate: 58%	
Life expectancy: 56 years	
People per doctor: 10,000	
Televisions: 87 per 1,000 people	

WATERING THE LAND
Much of Sudan is too dry to live or
farm in, and large areas of suitable
farmland have been destroyed by
war. The majority of people live by
the Nile River and use its water to
irrigate their fields. Two-thirds of
workers make their living from the
land, growing crops such as cotton,
peanuts, gum arabic, millet, and
dates. A large-scale irrigation
scheme set up by the government
has helped farmers to grow more
crops for export.

NOMADIC LIFE
Many of Sudan's tribal people live
by herding cattle, moving from
place to place in search of fresh
pasture. The more cattle a person
owns, the greater his importance
in the tribe. The civil war has
disrupted the lives of many
herders, destroying their pastures
and their herding routes.

*The Dinka tribe are nomadic cattle herders who
live on the plains east of the Nile.*

TRIBES

The people of Sudan are divided into
more than 500 different tribes and
groups speaking more than 100
languages and dialects. Each tribe
shares a common ancestor. Many,
such as the Dinka and Juhaynah
tribes, are nomadic. Others have
settled in particular areas, such as the
Shilluk tribe, a farming group living
on the west bank of the Nile. The
people shown left are from the Beni
Amer tribe, a Muslim group.

HOUSING

Life in the Arab north of
Sudan is very different from
that of the African south.
There are differences in
language, religion, customs,
and style of housing. The
Nubian people of the north (an African
people who adopted Islam as their religion)
build rectangular, flat-roofed houses of sun-dried
bricks. The Nubans of central Sudan (a tribe of hill
farmers) build round huts with conical roofs made
of grass, wooden poles, and millet stalks.

*Flat-roofed houses
built of mud brick
are common in
northern Sudan.*

*Conical-roofed huts are common in central and
southern Sudan. Each hut has its own purpose.*

Storeroom

*Living
quarters*

*A small "keyhole"
doorway helps
keep the hut warm
and dry inside.*

*Wrestling is a
popular sport
among the
Nuban people.*

KHARTOUM

Since Sudan became independent in
1956, the Muslim government in the
capital, Khartoum, has tried to impose
Islam on the rest of the population,
leading to civil war and famine. Millions
of refugees have poured into Khartoum
from the south and west to
escape the fighting and to
find food and work. Many
now live in shantytowns on
the outskirts of the city.

Find out more

IRRIGATION: *155, 156*
PEOPLES OF AFRICA: *206–207*
REFUGEES: *207*
RELIGION: *274–275*

ETHIOPIA

A LAND RICH in its own unique traditions, Ethiopia has in recent years suffered from drought, famine, and warfare. In 1984–85, a terrible famine, caused by a combination of civil war, drought, overpopulation, and overfarming, struck the northern highlands. During this time, Ethiopia was involved in a long, bitter war with the Eritreans, which only ended in 2000. Four out of five Ethiopians live off the land, growing crops such as *teff* (a type of grass) or herding cattle. Coffee is Ethiopia's major export crop. It is mostly grown in the mountains of Kaffa province, from which it gets its name.

ETHIOPIA
Capital city: Addis Ababa

Area: 349,490 sq miles (905,450 sq km)

Population: 62,600,000

Official language: Amharic

Major religions: Muslim 40%, Christian 40%, indigenous beliefs 15%, other 5%

Government: Provisional government

Currency: Ethiopian birr

Adult literacy rate: 38%

Life expectancy: 44 years

People per doctor: 24,135

Televisions: 5 per 1,000 people

ADDIS ABABA
The capital, Addis Ababa, is the biggest city in Ethiopia, with some 2.5 million inhabitants. It is a rapidly growing city, home to many refugees from the north and Eritrea. Housing is in short supply and there are about 20,000 children living on the streets. Many people live in crowded slums without toilets or running water. It is not unknown for a family of eight to ten people to share one room.

MUSIC AND DANCE
There are many groups of Ethiopians, each with their own language and traditions in storytelling, music, and dance. Traditional dances tell stories from everyday life. The music and songs that accompany them are an important means of passing on information about local cultures and customs.

Traditional instruments include the kra (a type of lyre).

Traditional Ethiopian dancers shake their shoulders as they dance.

Coffee-making ceremonies are elaborate. The coffee is brewed with added spices, incense is burned, and grass spread over the floor.

Traditional dress consists of an embroidered white dress and shawl for women, and white shirts and pants for men.

Ethiopian Orthodox priests at a religious festival in Addis Ababa

ETHIOPIAN CHURCH
The Ethiopian Orthodox Church can be traced back to the 4th century AD. Its most impressive monuments are the 12th-century churches in the village of Lalibela, which are carved out of solid rock. The Ethiopian Church has similarities with other Eastern churches and some Jewish customs have been retained, but its colorful ceremonies and festivals have their own distinctive flavor.

A typical vegetable dish made from cabbage, carrots, garlic, and red lentils

Wot, made from red onions, chilies, garlic, ginger, and other herbs and spices, is added to meat and vegetable dishes.

Hard-boiled eggs are often eaten with the meal.

FIREWOOD
Women are responsible for cutting, carrying, and selling firewood, a major source of fuel and income. Much of Ethiopia's forests have now been destroyed, however. This has led to the soil, no longer protected by trees, being blown or washed away and to the loss of valuable farmland.

Chicken stew, made from chicken, egg, and red peppers

Enjera

Beef stew, made from beef, cinnamon, peppers, red chili, and tomatoes

FOOD
The national dish of Ethiopia is *enjera*, a type of soft, flat bread made from *teff*, eaten with a mixture of meat and vegetables. These are cooked in a hot, spicy sauce, called *wot*. Traditionally, the sauce is served on top of the *enjera*. Raw beef, served with hot spices and melted butter, is eaten at festival times.

Find out more
CHRISTIANITY: *274*
CITIES: *17, 206*
COFFEE: *50, 62, 66*
SOIL EROSION: *55, 244*

SOMALIA

SOMALIA GAINED INDEPENDENCE from Italy in 1960. However, this diverse country with a rich history did not achieve peace. Since 1991, Somalia has been torn apart by civil war, resulting in widespread famine. Many Somalians are nomadic herders, wandering through the dry, barren countryside with their camels, sheep, and goats in search of food and water.

SOMALIA

Capital city: Mogadishu

Area: 242,215 sq miles (627,340 sq km)

Population: 10,100,000

Official languages: Somali, Arabic.

Major religion: Muslim 98%, Christian 2%

Government: None at present

Currency: Somali shilling

Adult literacy rate: 24%

Life expectancy: 48 years

People per doctor: 25,000

Televisions: 15 per 1,000 people

DJIBOUTI

Capital city: Djibouti

Area: 8,950 sq miles (23,180 sq km)

Population: 638,000

Official languages: Arabic, French

Major religions: Muslim 94%, other 6%

Government: Multiparty democracy

Currency: Djibouti franc

Adult literacy rate: 65%

Life expectancy: 44 years

People per doctor: 5,000

Televisions: 45 per 1,000 people

ERITREA

Capital city: Asmara

Area: 43,405 sq miles (117,600 sq km)

Population: 3,900,000

Official languages: Tigrinya, Arabic

Major religions: Christian 45%, Muslim 45%, other 10%

Government: Provisional government

Currency: Nakfa

Adult literacy rate: 56%

Life expectancy: 52 years

People per doctor: 5,000

Televisions: 14 per 1,000 people

RELIEF CAMPS

Since war broke out, many thousands of Somalis have moved into relief camps for food, safety, and shelter. The troubles, however, have made it difficult for international aid to be distributed. Up to one million Somalis sought refuge in neighboring countries, although many began to return as the fighting decreased in 2000 and 2001.

MOGADISHU
Mogadishu is the capital of Somalia and its major port and commercial center. The various styles of the buildings reflect the history of the country. Arabs settled there in the 9th century, and it became a European colony in the 20th century.

WOMEN'S DRESS
Many Somali women wear a cotton, sarilike garment called a *guntimo*, and a shawl, called a *garbasaar*. Unlike many Muslims in other countries, Somali women do not wear veils that cover the face.

DJIBOUTI

THE SMALL, MAINLY DESERT country of Djibouti became independent in 1977. Many of its people are nomads. Djibouti is of great importance to this part of Africa because of its port and capital city, also called Djibouti. The country's economy relies almost entirely on income from the port.

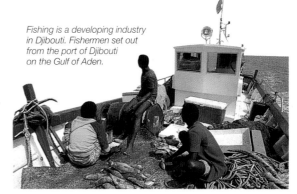

Fishing is a developing industry in Djibouti. Fishermen set out from the port of Djibouti on the Gulf of Aden.

ERITREA

AFTER 20 YEARS OF WAR, the mountainous land of Eritrea effectively became independent of Ethiopia in 1991. However relations remained tense and a new war broke out in 1998. Ethiopian troops finally left the country in 2001, leaving the Eritrean people to rebuild their shattered economy.

This theater in Asmara, the capital of Eritrea, is an example of the fine Italian-style architecture found in parts of the city. Eritrea was once an Italian colony.

Find out more
COLONIAL PERIOD: *207*
DESERTS: *15, 204, 209*
ISLAM: *275*
REFUGEES: *207*

WEST AFRICA

MANY CENTURIES AGO, great civilizations such as the Ashanti and Mali were thriving in the region now known as West Africa. Word of rich gold deposits brought Europeans flocking here, and by the 1880s they had colonized nearly all of this vast region. West Africa did not win back its independence until the 1960s. Although this region is rich in oil, gold, timber, and other natural resources, most of the 15 countries in West Africa are very poor. There are large numbers of ethnic groups here – more than 200 different peoples in Nigeria alone. The combination of poverty and clashes between different peoples has made political turmoil another all-too-familiar feature of the region.

RELIGION
West Africa divides roughly into northern and southern regions where the landscape and climate are concerned, and this also applies to its religions. Islam is dominant in the north, while there are more Christians in the south. Throughout the region, many people follow ancient traditional religions such as voodoo, which is especially strong in Benin.

Climate zones in West Africa

Desert
Sahel
Savanna
Tropical forest

THE CLIMATE
If you set out on a journey from north to south across this huge region, you would pass through a fascinating variety of hot, tropical landscapes. The vegetation of each zone has developed because of the amount of rain that falls there. Plenty of rain falls in the far south, whereas the arid northerly region is prone to serious drought. In some parts, there is a distinct wet season that lasts about 4–6 months, but no rain at all falls for much of the rest of the year.

Desert
The burning Sahara Desert forms the northern "lid" of West Africa. Very little grows here. The border of the desert advances or retreats, depending on how dry it becomes in neighboring areas.

Sahel
The arid northern grasslands that border the desert are called sahel – the word means "shore" of the desert in Arabic. Few trees can survive in this region.

Savanna
Moving south, a little more rain falls in the vast expanses of savanna – grassland scattered with acacias, baobabs, and other trees. Much of West Africa consists of savanna.

Tropical forest
Moist forests flourish under the heavy rains of the far south. Many animals and plants exist here, although there are not as many different species as in the rain forests of central Africa.

Freetown, Sierra Leone
Jan 80°F (26.5°C)
July 78.5°F (25.5°C)
Jan 0.5 in (13 mm)
July 35.2 in (894 mm)

SENEGAL
GAMBIA
GUINEA-BISSAU
GUINEA
SIERRA LEONE
LIBERIA

There are many nomadic cattle herders in Burkina, which lies in the dry sahel region.

WEST AFRICAN FARMERS
This region is home to two very different types of farmers – settled and nomadic. Settled farmers live near small plots of land on which they grow enough to feed their families, and perhaps grow some cash crops, such as cocoa or oil palms. Nomadic cattle herders, such as the Fulani, roam constantly across the region in search of good grazing land. They are more common toward the drier north, where the land is not as fertile for agriculture.

F G H I J K L M N O P Q

MAURITANIA

MALI

Timbuktu, Mali
Jan 71°F (22°C)
July 90°F (32°C)
Jan 0 in (0 mm)
July 3.1 in (79 mm)

BURKINA   NIGER

THINGS TO LOOK FOR ON THE MAP

Longest river: Niger, Guinea/Mali/Niger/Benin/Nigeria/
Sierra Leone, 2,548 miles (4,100 km) *Map E9, M11*

Highest point: Dimlang, Nigeria, 6,400 ft (2,042 m) *Map O11*

Largest lake: L. Volta, Ghana, formed by the Akosombo
Dam, 3,275 sq miles (8,482 sq km) *Map I11*

Westernmost point in Africa: Cape Verde, Senegal, *Map A8*

ALGERIA

LIBYA

ERG CHECH

PLATEAU DU MANGUENI

PLATEAU DU DJADO

MALI

AZAOUAD

ADRAR DES IFOGHAS

TALAK

TÉNÉRÉ

AIR

NIGER

NIA

MAURITANIA

Néma

Timbuktu   *Niger*   Gao

L. Faguibine

L. Niangay

Niger inland delta

Agadez

Mopti

BANDIAGARA ESCARPMENT

Niger

Bani

Ouahigouya

Tillabéri

Tahoua

Birni n'Konni

Maradi

Zinder

Nguigmi

Diffa

Hadejia

L. Chad

BAMAKO

Bougouni

Sikasso

Bobo-Dioulasso

Koudougou

BURKINA

OUAGADOUGOU

NIAMEY

Dosso

Sokoto

Sokoto

Gusau

Katsina

Kano

Zaria

Maiduguri

NIGERIA

Fada-Ngourma

Kainji Res.

ankan

Odienné

MONTS DU TOURA

Korhogo

GUINEA HIGHLANDS

ama

Man

nga

YAMOUSSOUKRO

Dimbokro

Gagnoa

Buyo Res.

IVORY COAST
(CÔTE D'IVOIRE)

Bouaké

L. de Kossou

Abengourou

Bolgatanga

Wa

Tamale

GHANA

Sunyani

Kumasi

Akosombo Dam

L. Volta

Black Volta

Red Volta

White Volta

Komoé

Dapaong

Kara

TOGO

Natitingou

Parakou

BENIN

Kandi

Ouémé

Abomey

Ogbomosho

Ilorin

Oshogbo

Ibadan

Abeokuta

Lagos

Benin City

Enugu

Onitsha

Aba

Kaduna

Minna

Jos

JOS PLATEAU

ABUJA

Niger

Lokoja

Makurdi

Benue

Bauchi

Dimlang

Taraba

Gongola

CAMEROON

CHAD

NIGERIA

BENIN

PORTO-NOVO

LOMÉ

Bight of Benin

Niger Delta

Port Harcourt

Calabar

Kano, Nigeria
Jan 81°F (27°C)
July 78.5°F (25.5°C)
Jan 1.1 in (28 mm)
July 11 in (279 mm)

ERIA

Harper

Cavally

ATLANTIC OCEAN

Ivory Coast

Abidjan

Cape Coast

Sekondi-Takoradi

Tema

ACCRA

IVORY COAST   GHANA

TOGO

FOOD CROPS

The cereals millet and rice are grown widely across West
Africa. Millet is common in the drier north, but where
there is more rainfall, rice and root vegetables such as
yams and cassava can be grown. Among the region's
popular dishes are peanut stew and Jollof Rice, a
Senegalese recipe that mixes rice with tomatoes,
onions, and spices and is served with fried meat.
Cassava and yams are also favorites, boiled and
eaten with goat, chicken, or fish.

Cassava

Rice

Millet grains

Peanuts (groundnuts)

Yams

MAURITANIA

COVERING AN AREA TWICE THE SIZE of Spain, but with a population smaller than Madrid's, Mauritania is one of the emptiest countries in the world. In recent years, many of the people have left the countryside to live and work in the towns, and Nouakchott, the capital, has grown from 20,000 people in 1960 to 800,000 today. The country is dominated by the Arab Maures (Moors) from the north, but their political control is resented by the black peoples from the south. Mining is an important industry – Mauritania is rich in phosphates, copper, gold, and other minerals. Drought is a major problem in this region.

MAURITANIA

Capital city: Nouakchott

Area: 395,953 sq miles (1,025,520 sq km)

Population: 2,700,000

Official language: French

Major religion: Muslim 100%

Government: Multiparty democracy

Currency: Ouguiya

Adult literacy rate: 42%

Life expectancy: 51 years

People per doctor: 10,000

Televisions: 91 per 1,000 people

NIGER

Capital city: Niamey

Area: 489,188 sq miles (1,267,000 sq km)

Population: 10,700,000

Official language: French

Major religions: Muslim 85%, traditional beliefs 14%, other 1%

Government: Multiparty democracy

Currency: CFA franc

Adult literacy rate: 16%

Life expectancy: 45 years

People per doctor: 33,333

Televisions: 27 per 1,000 people

FISHING
Fleets from all over the world come to fish off the coast of Mauritania, where some of the richest fish stocks in West Africa are found. By law, all fish caught here must be landed and processed in Mauritania before they are exported to overseas markets. However, overfishing of the seas by fleets of trawlers has led to concern about the future of the industry.

Projects like this one for planting trees and grass to hold the soil in place are helping stop erosion.

Areas at risk of desertification

This map shows the areas of West Africa that are at risk of turning into desert.

Very high risk
High risk
Medium risk

THE SAHEL
Two-thirds of Mauritania is covered by the Sahara, and only the land along the Senegal River is suitable for farming. The semi-desert land in between, known as the Sahel, is the grazing land for nomadic farmers. This area suffers from frequent droughts and from soil erosion, made worse by people cutting down the few trees for firewood and by overgrazing cattle. For these reasons – both natural and human – the Sahel is gradually becoming more desertlike.

NIGER

THE VAST STATE OF NIGER is completely surrounded by other countries. Its main link to the sea is the Niger River, the only major river in the country. Most of Niger's 11 million people live in the semi-desert Sahel region, which stretches in a narrow ribbon across the south of the country. North of the Sahel lies the vast and inhospitable Sahara, home to the nomadic Tuareg peoples. Niger has few natural resources apart from uranium, which brought in considerable wealth during the 1980s. Most of the people, however, remain poor, earning their living herding flocks or growing crops in the few fertile parts of the country.

FARMING
Every year, the Niger River floods. As the floodwaters retreat, local farmers quickly plant crops of cereals, rice, vegetables, peanuts, and cotton in the fertile soils left behind. The banks of the Niger also provide pasture for cattle and other livestock reared for meat and milk.

THE TUAREG
As a result of frequent droughts in northern Niger, many Tuareg lost all their animals and were forced to give up their nomadic lifestyle. Many moved south to the towns in search of food and work. In reaction to this enforced move, some Tuareg have campaigned for a country of their own.

Find out more

NIGER RIVER: 205
SAHEL: 220
SOIL EROSION: 55, 244
TUAREG: 209

MALI

THE LANDSCAPE OF MALI ranges from the vast desert plains of the Sahara in the north, through the semi-desert Sahel region in the center, to wetter savanna in the south. A thin belt of fertile land stretches on either side of the Niger and Senegal rivers. The country gets its name from the great Muslim empire of the Malinke people, which flourished in this region in the 13th and 14th centuries. Today, Mali is a poor country where most people make their living from farming or herding cattle.

MALI

Capital city: Bamako

Area: 478,837 sq miles (1,240,190 sq km)

Population: 11,200,000

Official language: French

Major religions: Muslim 80%, traditional beliefs 18%, Christian 1%, other 1%

Government: Democracy

Currency: CFA franc

Adult literacy rate: 41%

Life expectancy: 51 years

People per doctor: 26,138

Televisions: 12 per 1,000 people

MOSQUES

Islam arrived in Mali with merchants traveling across the Sahara from the Arab north. By the 13th century, Mali was entirely Muslim, with mosques built in most towns. Mosques like this one at Mopti are constructed of clay around a wooden framework that sticks out in turrets above the roof. The wooden beams jutting out through the walls allow villagers to climb all over the building to carry out its annual repairs.

TIMBUKTU
Founded by Tuareg nomads in 1100, Timbuktu became one of the most famous cities in Africa. Because of its position on the trade route across the Sahara, it soon developed into a major town. Arab traders from the north brought salt, cloth, and horses to exchange for gold and slaves from the south. By 1400, Timbuktu had become a major center of Islamic learning.

The Niger River at Bamako, in southern Mali

THE NIGER

The Niger River is the lifeline of Mali, flowing through the country from west to east before turning south to pour into the Atlantic Ocean. Most people in the country live along its banks, using the river as a source of water and food and as a main means of transportation. The capital of Mali, Bamako, on the upper reaches of the river, is a major port, shipping cement and fuel downriver, and receiving rice and peanuts for export in exchange.

Granaries are built of thick clay to keep the grain cool and free of rats.

Dogon houses are made of clay, often with terraces above the main living area.

The flat rooftops are used to dry onions and to store pots and baskets.

Compound

Outer wall

Entrance

The Dogon live in walled compounds built on steep hillsides for protection against attack from their enemies.

RICE GROWING
In the center of Mali, the Niger River splits into several branches. This area is called the river's inland delta, and is one of the most fertile regions of the country. Here, as the river begins to flood, farmers plant a special "floating" rice that grows up to 12 in (30 cm) a day to keep pace with the rising waters. When the crop is ready, the farmers harvest it from boats.

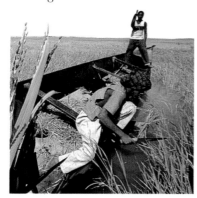

THE DOGON
South of Timbuktu, the flat river plain gives way to sandstone cliffs surrounding the Bandiagara plateau. Living in the cliffs are the Dogon people, who first settled in the area in the 1500s. The Dogon worship their own gods, and have many legends about the creation of the world. Because of the harsh conditions in which they live, the Dogon are expert farmers, using every available strip of land to grow crops of rice, millet, and corn.

Find out more

ISLAM: *275*
MALINKE PEOPLE: *225*
NIGER RIVER: *205*
RICE GROWING: *135, 176, 197*

SENEGAL

THE MIGHTY SENEGAL RIVER dominates large areas of this country. Every year the river floods, and seasonal crops are grown on the fertile land that the floodwaters leave behind. Senegal is wealthy compared to other countries in this region. It was once an important part of French West Africa, and still maintains close links with France. Among the mix of ethnic groups, such as the Wolof and Mandinke, there are still many French inhabitants. There is a similar mix of religions – Islam exists side-by-side with traditional beliefs. Senegal's beautiful, palm-fringed coastline makes tourism an important economic force here.

SENEGAL	
Capital city: Dakar	
Area: 74,335 sq miles (192,530 sq km)	
Population: 7,900,000	
Official language: French	
Major religions: Muslim 90%, traditional beliefs 5%, Christian 5%	
Government: Multiparty democracy	
Currency: CFA franc	
Adult literacy rate: 37%	
Life expectancy: 53 years	
People per doctor: 10,000	
Televisions: 41 per 1,000 people	

GAMBIA	
Capital city: Banjul	
Area: 3,861 sq miles (10,000 sq km)	
Population: 1,305,000	
Official language: English	
Major religions: Muslim 90%, Christian 9%, traditional beliefs 1%	
Government: Multiparty democracy	
Currency: Dalasi	
Adult literacy rate: 37%	
Life expectancy: 46 years	
People per doctor: 5,000	
Televisions: 3 per 1,000 people	

MUSICAL STORYTELLING

History is a living thing in West Africa. For centuries, history and other information has been passed on by word of mouth, from one generation to the next, through stories, poems, and songs. In Senegal, storytellers called *griots* travel from village to village. They play a variety of traditional instruments, such as the *kora*.

The kora has 21 strings.

Front view of kora

The soundbox is made from a hollowed-out gourd.

GAMBIA

THE TINY COUNTRY of Gambia is a long, thin sliver of land carved out of Senegal, which surrounds it on three sides. At its widest point, Gambia measures no more than 50 miles (80 km) from north to south. Like Senegal, Gambia has a wide ethnic mix and Islam is very important. Most of the people work in agriculture, relying heavily on the peanut crop. Women play a major role in agricultural life. Rice growing is their main occupation, but near the coast, large areas of swampy rice land have been ruined by the buildup of salt in the soil. Many women now grow vegetables to sell in local markets.

DAKAR
The lively city of Dakar, Senegal's capital, perches on a rocky peninsula that forms the westernmost point of Africa. This major port was once the capital of French West Africa, as can be seen from its grand colonial buildings. Today great poverty is found alongside the expensive restaurants and modern hotels on the streets of Dakar.

FARMING AND FISHING

Nearly three-quarters of Senegal's people work in agriculture. In the north, cereals such as millet and sorghum are the main food crops, and peanuts are a vital cash crop. Rice is common in the wetter southern areas. Peanuts were once grown on nearly half the farmland, but fish is now taking over as the country's main export. A common sight is fishermen setting out in dugout canoes called *pirogues*, made from local trees.

Tourists come for the beaches, but many take trips inland to see the crocodiles, monkeys, and many species of birds that live along the Gambia River.

TOURISM
The tourist trade is the fastest growing part of the Gambian economy. More and more Europeans are coming here to escape cold winters, attracted by the magnificent beaches. Gambia is particularly popular with visitors from the UK, because English is widely spoken in this former British colony. But fears are already mounting that the easy-going local lifestyle will soon be ruined by advancing tourism.

Find out more	
AFRICAN CITIES: *206*	
COLONIAL PERIOD: *207*	
RELIGION: *274–275*	
RICE GROWING: *135, 176, 197*	

GUINEA

ONCE A FRENCH COLONY, this fertile, hilly country is rich in minerals and has perfect weather conditions for growing many crops, including bananas, citrus fruits, and rice. These factors could make Guinea a rich country, but it is one of the poorest in the world, with a life expectancy of just 47 years and only very basic medical and educational facilities. This is largely the result of the French leaving Guinea without financial support, poor management of the economy, and years of harsh political rule under Sekou Touré, who was president from 1958–84.

GUINEA	
Capital city: Conakry	
Area: 94,926 sq miles (245,860 sq km)	
Population: 7,400,000	
Official language: French	
Major religions: Muslim 65%, traditional beliefs 4%, Christian 1%	
Government: Provisional government	
Currency: Guinea franc	
Adult literacy rate: 27%	
Life expectancy: 44 years	
People per doctor: 50,000	
Televisions: 7 per 1,000 people	

GUINEA BISSAU	
Capital city: Bissau	
Area: 13,940 sq miles (36,120 sq km)	
Population: 1,000,000	
Official language: Portuguese	
Major religions: Traditional beliefs 54%, Muslim 38%, Christian 8%	
Government: One-party state	
Currency: Guinea peso	
Adult literacy rate: 39%	
Life expectancy: 43 years	
People per doctor: 7,260	
Televisions: no figures available	

THE GUINEA HIGHLANDS
Thick forest covers the mountainous Guinea Highlands in the south of the country. In addition to providing timber products, conditions in this highly fertile area are ideal for growing various crops, including coffee. Three of the region's major rivers – the Niger, the Gambia, and the Senegal – have their sources here. Rich iron deposits exist here, and the whole area is nourished by abundant rainfall.

About two-thirds of Guinea's population lives in small villages like this one.

PEOPLE OF GUINEA

A varied mix of peoples, including the Malinke, Fulani, and Soussou, live in Guinea. Most of them are Muslim. The Malinke make up about a third of the population and are named after a mountainous area on the Mali border. This was once part of the great Mali Empire, which dominated West Africa in medieval times. Today, the Malinke are famous for their centuries-old storytelling and musical skills.

MINING
The mountainous areas of Guinea are rich in a mineral ore called bauxite. Ores are substances from which metals can be obtained, and bauxite is used to make aluminum. Guinea is the world's second largest producer of bauxite, after Australia, and it accounts for around 60 percent of the country's earnings from exports. Guinea's mountain regions yield other valuable minerals, including iron, gold, and diamonds.

GUINEA BISSAU

SANDWICHED BETWEEN SENEGAL and Guinea, this low-lying, swampy country is a particularly unspoiled place. Once ruled by Portugal, Guinea Bissau was the first Portuguese colony to gain independence, in 1974. Today it is very poor, and heavily dependent on financial aid from other countries. The people are a mix of ethnic groups, the largest of which is the Balante, from the south. Most people scrape a living by growing coconuts, cotton, peanuts, or cashew nuts. Timber and fishing are also important.

ALONG THE COAST
Like its neighbors, Guinea Bissau has spectacular beaches. Its coastline is edged with mangrove swamps, mud flats, and estuaries leading to a maze of inland waterways. A huge variety of fish are found off the coast, and many people in this coastal region make their living from fishing.

Peanuts

PEANUTS
As the name suggests, the actual nuts of the peanut, or groundnut, plant grow underground. The nut pods are pulled out of the ground and left to dry before being shelled and skinned. Some of the nuts are sold in local markets, but most are used to extract peanut oil, used in food production, or crushed to make peanut butter.

Cashew nuts

Find out more
COLONIAL PERIOD: *207*
ISLAM: *275*
LIFE EXPECTANCY: *276*
RICH AND POOR: *298–299*

SIERRA LEONE

IN 1787, THE BRITISH colonized this region and created a settlement for freed African slaves. This is how Sierra Leone's capital, Freetown, got its name. Today, there are still a few descendants of the freed slaves, known as Creoles, living here. The main peoples, however, are the Mende in the south and the Temne in the north. In recent years, conflicts between the various ethnic groups have led to civil war. Sierra Leone is one of the poorest countries in the world, and two-thirds of its workforce make their living from small-scale farming.

Diamonds

MINING
Sierra Leone's rich mineral deposits have made mining a vital industry, with diamonds among the main products. Diamond mining methods vary from using fully mechanized diggers, to chipping gemstones out of rock by hand, or panning for them in rivers. Other mineral exports include gold, iron ore, bauxite (from which aluminum is made), and rutile (from which titanium is made).

Rice grains

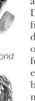

Diamonds found among the gravel in rivers are called alluvial diamonds.

Cut diamond

FARMING
Sierra Leone's main cash crops are cocoa, coffee, nuts, and palm kernels (seeds from which oil is extracted). The main food crop is rice, which is grown in the river valleys. "Dry" rice is grown in the soil on the valley sides, and "wet" rice is grown in flooded fields on the valley floor. Attempts have been made to raise production – for example, clearing mangrove swamps to make way for extra rice fields.

LIBERIA

LIBERIA BECAME AN INDEPENDENT country in 1847 and has never been colonized, making it the oldest independent republic in Africa. In the 19th century, the American Colonization Society helped thousands of freed African slaves return from the US and settle here. They gave Liberia its name, which means "freed land." Links between the US and Liberia still exist today. Since 1990, Liberia has suffered from civil war, and the economy has virtually collapsed.

THE RUBBER TRADE
One of Liberia's strongest links with the US is its extensive, American-owned rubber plantations. Over the years, these have employed huge numbers of people and have accounted for a very large slice of the country's income from exports. The American Firestone company, which makes world-famous tires, has been at the forefront of this rubber production. Rubber is made from a sticky substance called latex, which can be "tapped" from rubber trees by cutting slits in the bark.

CIVIL WAR
In recent years there have been clashes between Liberia's different ethnic groups, which include the Kpelle, Bassa, and Kru peoples. These problems erupted into civil war in the early 1990s, which did a great deal of damage to an already weakened economy. The war has forced about half the population to leave their homes, and many people have starved because of food shortages.

Children as young as 8 have been forced to fight in the war.

Find out more
DIAMONDS: *150, 248*
REFUGEES: *207*
RICE GROWING: *135, 176, 197*
RUBBER: *194*

IVORY COAST

These hardwoods all come from Ivory Coast.

BEING RULED BY ONE MAN, Félix Houphouët-Boigny for 33 years until his death in 1993, gave Ivory Coast a reputation as one of the most politically and economically stable countries in Africa. Many different ethnic groups lived largely in peace. However, some tenisons between the Muslim north and the Christian south led to violence in 2000. The economy is based on a wide range of products, and coffee and cocoa are the main cash crops. Other products include cotton, fruit, tobacco, and timber. Ivory Coast was a French colony until 1960 and is often known as Côte d'Ivoire.

Mahogany

Iroko

Idigbo

IVORY COAST

Capital city: Yamoussoukro

Area: 122,780 sq miles (318,000 sq km)

Population: 14,800,000

Official language: French

Major religions: Traditional beliefs 63%, Muslim 25%, Christian 12%

Government: Multiparty democracy

Currency: CFA franc

Adult literacy rate: 47%

Life expectancy: 48 years

People per doctor: 10,000

Televisions: 70 per 1,000 people

TIMBER INDUSTRY
Ivory Coast once had vast areas of forest, containing ebony, mahogany, and other hardwood trees. Today hardly any is left. For years the country's economy was heavily dependent on the timber industry. Timber exports were seen as vital for paying off foreign debts, and large areas of forest were cleared to make way for coffee and cocoa plantations. A program was recently started to help save the forests and plant new ones.

ETHNIC GROUPS
More than 60 ethnic groups live side-by-side in Ivory Coast, with relatively few clashes. The Dan people, for example, live deep in the heart of the western forests and are famous for their carving skills. They make wooden masks that are worn by the members of special secret societies to keep their identities hidden. Only members of these societies are allowed to take part in the Dan stilt dances.

YAMOUSSOUKRO
The dome of the world's largest church rises up above the rooftops of Yamoussoukro, a small town in the center of the country that recently became Ivory Coast's capital city in 1983. Personally overseen by former president Boigny, the cathedral was completed in 1989 at huge cost. It seats 7,000 people and has an open-air area for another 350,000 – three times the city's population. There has been much controversy about undertaking such an extravagant project in a country with widespread poverty.

Pineapple

Bananas

Coffee beans

Many of Abidjan's banks and businesses are based in the skyscrapers of the Plateau district.

THE ECONOMY
Compared to much of West Africa, Ivory Coast is a fairly prosperous country. This is partly the result of a policy of growing a variety of crops. Ivory Coast is the world's leading cocoa grower – in some years, it produces about a third of the world's cocoa exports. However, competition from elsewhere may change this. It is also Africa's biggest coffee producer and grows vast numbers of pineapples and bananas.

World's top five cocoa producers

Figures show the share of total world cocoa production.

Nigeria 7% | Brazil 7% | Indonesia 11% | Ghana 12.5% | Ivory Coast 41%

ABIDJAN
This modern port, with its glittering glass skyscrapers, is the country's largest city. Abidjan is filled with smart shops and restaurants that show a powerful French influence, reminding visitors of Ivory Coast's historical ties with France. It was also the country's capital until the 1990s, when Yamoussoukro took over that role.

Find out more

CHRISTIANITY: *274*
COCOA: *228, 234*
COFFEE: *50, 62, 66*
LOGGING: *69, 244*

GHANA

GHANA SHOULD BE A RELATIVELY wealthy country. Its many riches include fertile farmland, reserves of gold, bauxite, and oil, and a young population that is among the best educated in Africa. However, years of unstable government, low earnings from exports, and bad management of the economy have hindered Ghana's development. More than 50 different ethnic groups live in Ghana, each with its own language and traditions. Among the largest groups are the Akan peoples, who include the Ashanti in the south of the country, the Dagomba in the north, and the Ewe in the southeast.

GHANA	
Capital city: Accra	
Area: 88,811 sq miles (230,020 sq km)	
Population: 20,200,000	
Official language: English	
Major religions: Traditional beliefs 38%, Christian 43%, Muslim 11%, other 8%	
Government: Multiparty democracy	
Currency: Cedi	
Adult literacy rate: 71%	
Life expectancy: 57 years	
People per doctor: 22,685	
Televisions: 99 per 1,000 people	

GHANA

SLAVERY
Between 1500 and 1800 over 10 million Africans were sold into slavery. Many were shipped from Ghana to work on plantations in America and the Caribbean. Elmina Castle (above) was built by the Portuguese to hold slaves before they crossed the Atlantic. Once onboard the slaves were kept in terrible conditions and many died before they reached land.

THE AKOSOMBO DAM
One of the world's largest artificial lakes, Lake Volta, is formed by the Akosombo Dam on the Volta River. When the dam was built in the 1960s, about 85,000 people had to be moved from areas flooded by the lake. The dam's power station generates electricity for factories in the city of Tema and for domestic use. Some power is exported to Togo and Benin.

Ashanti gold head showing a defeated enemy general.

THE ASHANTI
When Europeans first visited Ghana in the 15th century, they named it the Gold Coast because of the gold offered to them in trade by the local people. The main gold workers were the Ashanti. The symbol of Ashanti unity was a golden stool, which they believed had come down from the sky. Gold from the Ashanti mines is still an important export for Ghana.

MARKETS
Every Ghanaian town has a bustling market, drawing people in from the surrounding area. Here they can buy and sell a wide range of goods, from food and animals to household supplies and even false teeth. Many of the market traders are women, often involved because "marketing" is part-time and leaves the rest of the day free for other work. Many traders are financially very successful.

Women traders at the market in Accra

Cocoa pods grow directly from the trunk. They are harvested once they have ripened to a yellow color.

A mature cocoa tree produces 20–30 fruit pods a year.

COCOA
Cocoa trees need plenty of shade when they are young and water when they are mature. This is why they grow so well in the humid forests of southern Ghana. Here young cocoa plants are grown between rows of other food crops, which provide the necessary shade. The trees only begin to produce fruit after about seven years. Cocoa production is a major industry, accounting for up to 34 percent of the country's exports, but Ghana now faces stiff competition from neighboring Ivory Coast and from Southeast Asia.

Each pod contains up to 40 pale pink beans covered in a pink pulp.

Roasted cocoa beans

Cocoa pod

Cocoa beans are fermented, roasted, and ground to produce a chocolate liquid. This is used to make cocoa butter for cosmetics, or is reheated and molded to make blocks of chocolate.

Find out more
COCOA: *227, 234*
COLONIAL PERIOD: *207*
GOLD MINING: *253*
TRADE DEPENDENCY: *281*

BURKINA

LANDLOCKED BURKINA (formerly known as Upper Volta) is one of the world's poorest countries. Like the other countries in the Sahel region, Burkina is at constant risk from drought, and in recent years large amounts of grazing land have turned to desert as the Sahara has expanded southward. Burkina has few cities, and most of the people live in villages, making a living from farming and herding. Burkina's economy has suffered badly from political unrest. Because the country is so poor, millions of people from Burkina must go abroad to find jobs.

BURKINA	
Capital city: Ouagadougou	
Area: 105,714 sq miles (273,000 sq km)	
Population: 11,900,000	
Official language: French	
Major religions: Traditional beliefs 55%, Muslim 35%, Christian 10%	
Government: Multiparty democracy	
Currency: CFA franc	
Adult literacy rate: 24%	
Life expectancy: 46 years	
People per doctor: 57,300	
Televisions: 9 per 1,000 people	

TOGO	
Capital city: Lomé	
Area: 21,000 sq miles (54,390 sq km)	
Population: 4,600,000	
Official languages: French, Kabye, and Ewe	
Major religions: Traditional beliefs 70%, Christian 20%, Muslim 10%	
Government: Multiparty democracy	
Currency: CFA franc	
Adult literacy rate: 57%	
Life expectancy: 52 years	
People per doctor: 10,000	
Televisions: 18 per 1,000 people	

FOREIGN AID

Burkina is very dependent on foreign aid. Each year around $US400 million of aid comes into the country, much of it from Burkina's former colonial ruler, France, and from the European Union. The money is used for both large-scale projects, such as dams to generate hydroelectric power, and smaller schemes, like this well that provides clean water for a village.

Many farmers have a vegetable garden where they grow food for their families.

AGRICULTURE

Lack of water and poor soil cause huge problems for Burkina's farmers. Before any crops can be planted, a farmer has to clear the land, burning the scrub and plowing the ash into the ground to act as a fertilizer. The new field can only be used for four to five years before it is exhausted. Then it has to be left for at least another five years to recover.

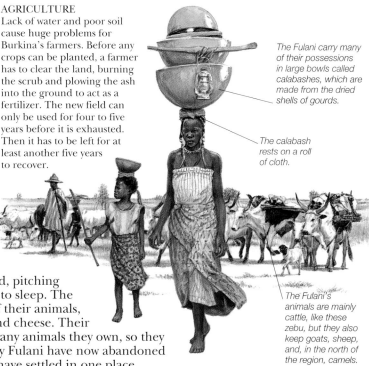

The Fulani carry many of their possessions in large bowls called calabashes, which are made from the dried shells of gourds.

The calabash rests on a roll of cloth.

The Fulani's animals are mainly cattle, like these zebu, but they also keep goats, sheep, and, in the north of the region, camels.

THE FULANI

The Fulani are nomadic cattle herders. They travel wherever there is grazing land, pitching huts or tents when they want to sleep. The Fulani live off the produce of their animals, eating mainly milk, butter, and cheese. Their wealth is measured by how many animals they own, so they rarely kill and eat them. Many Fulani have now abandoned this nomadic way of life and have settled in one place.

TOGO

SANDWICHED BETWEEN GHANA and Benin, Togo is a former French colony that gained its independence in 1960. The population is a mix of about 30 different ethnic groups; the two largest are the Ewe in the south of the country and the Dagomba in the north. Phosphates – minerals used to make fertilizers – account for half of Togo's exports, but the economy has been badly affected by changes in world phosphate prices. Togo's capital city, Lomé, is one of the major ports in West Africa.

FARMING AND FISHING

Although Togo is a very poor country, it produces nearly all its own food. About two-thirds of the population lives in the countryside and work there as farmers. Corn, yams, rice, and cassava are grown to eat, and cocoa, coffee, and cotton to sell and export. Along the coast, many people make a living from fishing.

Find out more

FULANI: *207*
PHOSPHATES: *210*
RICH AND POOR: *278–279*
SAHEL: *220, 222*

NIGERIA

NIGERIA IS HOME TO AN AMAZING mix of more than 250 different peoples. The largest groups are the Hausa-Fulani, in the north, the Yoruba in the west, and the Ibo in the east. Nigeria could be one of Africa's most successful economies. It has large reserves of oil, gas, and minerals, and abundant farmland. The population of 112 million is the largest of any African country, and one of the best educated. It has had a troubled history with a civil war in 1967, and a series of military coups. Today, Nigeria is struggling to pay off huge debts and to modernize its industry and agriculture.

NIGERIA

Capital city: Abuja

Area: 351,648 sq miles (910,770 sq km)

Population: 111,500,800

Official language: English

Major religions: Muslim 50%, Christian 40%, traditional beliefs 10%

Government: Military government

Currency: Naira

Adult literacy rate: 64%

Life expectancy: 52 years

People per doctor: 5,000

Televisions: 66 per 1,000 people

BENIN

Capital city: Porto-Novo

Area: 43,480 sq miles (112,620 sq km)

Population: 6,100,000

Official language: French

Major religions: Traditional beliefs 70%, Christian 15%, Muslim 15%

Government: Multiparty democracy

Currency: CFA franc

Adult literacy rate: 40%

Life expectancy: 54 years

People per doctor: 10,000

Televisions: 10 per 1,000 people

LAGOS

The city of Lagos is situated on a coastal island in the southwestern corner of Nigeria. The island was first settled in the 15th century by local Yoruba people. The town grew rapidly as a trading port used by European merchants, and became the capital of independent Nigeria in 1960. In 1992, the capital was moved to Abuja, in central Nigeria, but Lagos is still the largest city.

OIL

Oil was first produced in Nigeria in 1956, and within 20 years, the new industry dominated the economy. Today, it makes up about 97 percent of the country's exports. Nigerian oil is high quality with a low sulfur content, making it ideal as aircraft fuel. However, it is dangerous for a country to rely on just one product. When world oil prices fell in the 1980s, Nigeria suffered badly. Efforts are now being made to develop other products and lessen the country's dependence on oil.

The Niger Delta in the south of the country contains huge oil reserves, enough to last for at least another 25 years. Four huge refineries prepare the crude oil for export.

Main exports

Oil: 97%

Others: 3%

PLANTATIONS

In recent years huge plantations have been set up throughout Nigeria to produce crops in large quantities, mainly for export. Plantations make use of modern machinery to plant, grow, and process the crops, which include cotton, coffee, sugar, cocoa, and oil palms. Today, Nigeria is one of the world's largest producers of palm oil. Oil from the fleshy fiber of the palm nut is used in cooking oil, margarine, soap, candles, and paint.

Farmers clear and plow the land ready to plant crops.

SMALL FARMS

Most Nigerian farmers work on their own small farms. They use hoes, plows, and other simple tools to grow food crops such as cassava, rice, yams, and corn to feed their families. They also grow crops such as cocoa, oil palms, rubber, and peanuts (groundnuts) to sell. These are known as cash crops. Despite the recent investment in plantations, most of Nigeria's cash crops are still grown on these small farms.

Oil palm tree

Palm nuts grow in large bunches. When they are ripe, they are cut down and taken to factories where the oil is extracted.

Fleshy fiber

Kernel

Cross-section of a palm nut

VILLAGE LIFE

Most Nigerians are born and die in the same village, and think of it as home even if they move to a big city. Most of the villagers work as farmers, although each village usually has a traditional doctor, blacksmith, and carpenter. Villagers are almost self-sufficient, growing much of their own food, building their own houses, weaving cloth for clothes, and making pots for cooking. Anything they cannot make, they buy with money earned by selling goods in the local market.

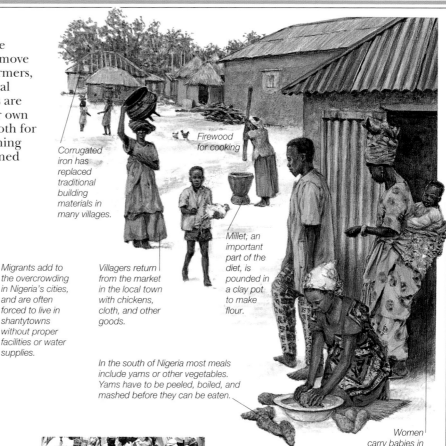

Corrugated iron has replaced traditional building materials in many villages.

Firewood for cooking

Millet, an important part of the diet, is pounded in a clay pot to make flour.

Villagers return from the market in the local town with chickens, cloth, and other goods.

Migrants add to the overcrowding in Nigeria's cities, and are often forced to live in shantytowns without proper facilities or water supplies.

In the south of Nigeria most meals include yams or other vegetables. Yams have to be peeled, boiled, and mashed before they can be eaten.

Women carry babies in slings made of cloth.

MOVING TO THE CITY

Many young Nigerians leave their villages for a few years and move to a city. They go to study, or to earn money that they can send back to their families when profits from farming are low. This money may be used to buy food or books for a child going to school. Once the "migrants" have finished their studies or saved up enough money, they return home to their villages.

One of the main dyes is indigo, a blue color produced by pulping the leaves of the indigo vine.

DYEING

The Yoruba people of southwestern Nigeria are skilled cloth dyers, making intricate patterns from a range of natural dyes. The cloth is usually dyed in earthenware pots, although the Hausa people in the northern city of Kano use large pits in the ground lined with a local cement.

RELIGION

Nigeria is divided in its religious beliefs. In the north, people follow Islam, which was introduced by Arab traders from across the Sahara Desert during the 11th century. Religious festivals, such as this Sallah procession to mark the end of Ramadan (the Islamic month of fasting), are important local events. Five hundred years later, European merchants brought Christianity into the south. Many Nigerians, however, still follow traditional African religions.

BENIN

SQUASHED UP AGAINST THE WESTERN border of Nigeria, Benin is a long, thin country that stretches north from its narrow Atlantic Ocean coastline to the Niger River. Originally called Dahomey (it was renamed Benin in 1975), the country gained its independence from France in 1960. Since then Benin has had a series of military governments and been a one-party state. In 1991 it became the first African nation to move from one-party rule to a multiparty democracy. Although it is a poor country, Benin has a growing economy based on agricultural products such as cotton, cocoa, and coffee.

COASTAL REGIONS

For centuries, the inhabitants of stilt houses like these along the shores of Lake Ganvie have made their living from fishing. But many former lakes and lagoons have become partly silted up, and many of the fishermen have had to take up sea fishing or move to the towns to find work.

Find out more

AFRICAN CITIES: *206*
COCOA: *227, 228, 234*
OIL: *137, 152, 281*
RELIGION: *274–275*

CENTRAL AFRICA

IN FERTILE CENTRAL AFRICA, steaming rain forests cluster around the Equator, and the mighty Congo River snakes its way through Congo and the Democratic Republic of Congo (Zaire). In the 1400s, Europeans began a cruel slave trade here; by the late 19th century, the region was colonized. Independence came in the 1960s, but democracy has been slow to arrive. The area has met with mixed fortunes. Countries range from stable, prosperous Cameroon to the Central African Republic, which has been crushed by poverty and harsh dictatorships.

Faya, Chad
- Jan 69°F (21°C)
- July 93°F (34°C)
- Jan 0 in (0 mm)
- July 0 in (0 mm)

CHAD

THINGS TO LOOK FOR ON THE MAP

Longest river: Congo (Zaire), Zaire/Congo, 2,900 miles (4,666 km) *Map G10*

Highest point: Mt. Stanley Democratic Rep. of Congo (Zaire), 16,765 ft (5,110 m) *Map K11*

Largest lake: L. Tanganyika, Dem. Rep. of Congo (Zaire), 12,700 sq miles (32,893 sq km) *Map K12*

N

CAMEROON

0 100 200 300 400 500 km
0 100 200 300 miles

EQUATORIAL GUINEA

SÃO TOMÉ & PRÍNCIPE

GABON

CENTRAL AFRICAN REPUBLIC

RAIN FOREST

Various landscapes exist here. Close to the Equator, dense rain forests flourish in the hot, humid climate with its year-round rains, although vast areas have been cleared for timber. Farther away from the Equator, rain is seasonal, producing scrub vegetation and grassland. Burning desert land lies in the far north of the region, in Chad.

Lubumbashi, Democratic Republic of Congo (Zaire)
- Jan 72°F (22°C)
- July 31°F (16°C)
- Jan 10.5 in (267 mm)
- July 0 in (0 mm)

DEMOCRATIC REPUBLIC OF CONGO (ZAIRE)

CONGO

CAMEROON

IN AN AREA THAT HAS SEEN many troubles since independence, Cameroon is a relatively prosperous and stable success story thanks to sensible government policies. Along with its southern neighbors, Gabon and Congo, the country has earned money from oil, and has used this to develop its economy. Many different peoples live in Cameroon, and its geography is just as varied. The humid coastal plain in the south gives way to a drier central plateau, while a finger of land points up to the marshes around Lake Chad.

CAMEROON

Capital city: Yaoundé

Area: 179,691 sq miles (465,400 sq km)

Population: 15,100,000

Official languages: French, English

Major religions: traditional beliefs 51%, Christian 33%, Muslim 16%

Government: Multiparty democracy

Currency: CFA franc

Adult literacy rate: 76%

Life expectancy: 50 years

People per doctor: 10,000

Televisions: 32 per 1,000 people

Pearl millet grows to a height of 5–10 ft (1.5–3 m).

PEOPLES

With more than 130 ethnic groups, Cameroon has one of the richest mixes of peoples in Africa. These range from the Fulani cattle herders, who live in the north and follow Islamic beliefs, to forest dwellers farther south, who practice traditional religions. Most people are settled farmers producing enough for their own needs, like this Hausa farmer tending his cattle.

Women grind and sieve the millet grains to make a coarse flour.

Millet can also be used to make beer. It is dried, pounded, and then brewed in large pots.

GROWING MILLET

Most farmers in Cameroon grow some crops, such as millet, for their own use (subsistence farming), but also produce crops to sell. Millet is cultivated widely in northern Cameroon, where there is less rainfall, because it grows well in poorer, drier soils. There has also been great investment in the production of commercial "cash" crops such as cocoa and coffee, oil palms, and bananas.

A stiff white porridge made from millet flour is a popular breakfast dish.

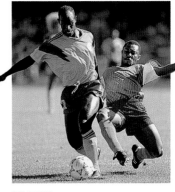

SOCCER

Cameroon has one of Africa's most celebrated soccer teams, known for some spectacular displays of skill on home territory and in the World Cup. The people of Cameroon love soccer – at lunchtime and in the evenings informal games spring up on any spare piece of open ground.

This bow is basically a wooden stick with strings stretched down its length and dried, hollowed-out gourds placed at intervals.

The gourds vibrate when the strings are plucked or a piece of wood is drawn across them.

MUSIC

Traditional musical instruments of all shapes and sizes, such as this bow, can be heard in villages up and down the country. The most popular style of folk music in Cameroon is *makossa*, which mixes African sounds and soul music, and its lively rhythms are perfect to dance to. *Makossa* is widely enjoyed by people all over central Africa.

INDUSTRY

Cameroon has an expanding timber industry. The country has extensive forests, and mahogany, ebony, and teak are all exported abroad. However, the industry is hampered by roads that are impassable during the rainy season. Much of the country's wealth is based on its reserves of oil, and other natural resources include bauxite, iron, and gold.

Find out more
COCOA: *227, 228, 234*
LOGGING: *69, 227, 244*
OIL: *152, 230, 281*
OIL PALMS: *230*

CENTRAL AFRICAN REPUBLIC

CENTRAL AFRICAN REPUBLIC	
Capital city: Bangui	
Area: 240,530 sq miles (622,980 sq km)	
Population: 3,600,000	
Official language: French	
Major religions: traditional beliefs 60%, Christian 35%, Muslim 5%	
Government: Multiparty democracy	
Currency: CFA franc	
Adult literacy rate: 47%	
Life expectancy: 44 years	
People per doctor: 5,000	
Televisions: 5 per 1,000 people	

EQUATORIAL GUINEA	
Capital city: Malabo	
Area: 10,830 sq miles (28,050 sq km)	
Population: 453,000	
Official language: Spanish	
Major religions: Christian 90%, other 10%	
Government: Multiparty democracy	
Currency: CFA franc	
Adult literacy rate: 83%	
Life expectancy: 51 years	
People per doctor: 4,819	
Televisions: 10 per 1,000 people	

SITUATED AT THE CORE OF AFRICA, the north of the Central African Republic (CAR) is arid, while lush rain forest covers the south. Drought and political unrest have caused great problems here. In 1965, Emperor Bokassa began a 14-year reign of terror, which was followed by military dictatorship. The first multiparty elections were held in 1993, but the economy is still unstable, and this is one of the poorest places in the world.

This woman is sifting diamonds from a riverbed.

INDUSTRY
A large part of the country's income comes from diamonds. There is potential for developing other industries, too, since gold, iron ore, copper, and uranium are also found here. Flooding caused by heavy seasonal rains, however, is a constant threat to any kind of mining.

RIVER ROUTES
The CAR is surrounded by land and has no railroad system and few well surfaced roads, so its rivers are vital for transportation and trade. Nearly three-quarters of trading goods are shipped down the 4,350 miles (7,000 km) of inland waterways. Many goods travel to Brazzaville in Congo. Here they are loaded onto trains and taken to the Atlantic coast.

PYGMIES
Small huts made from banana leaves are found deep in the country's rain forests. These are the homes of a people known as pygmies, called this because they rarely grow taller than about 5 ft (1.5 m). Pygmies are "hunter-gatherers," living on food collected from the rain forest. They are a shining example of people living in harmony with the natural world, not damaging the environment.

EQUATORIAL GUINEA

THE ECONOMY AND PEOPLE of Equatorial Guinea have suffered badly because of brutal leadership. Macias Nguema ruled as a cruel dictator during the 1970s, but a more moderate government came to power in the 1990s. This tiny, beautiful country, which includes five islands, is now working hard to build its economy.

Hippopotamus tooth

Animal bone

Cowrie shell

Tree root

TRADITIONAL MEDICINE
Traditional medicine is still widely practiced in Africa. Animal bones, shells, and wooden sticks are used in public healing ceremonies. The healer will often sing and dance around the patient, using chants to cry out to the spirits for help.

FARMING
Although the hot climate and fertile volcanic soil of the largest island, Bioko, are perfect for growing crops, there are few good roads and the workforce is unskilled. Concentrating on growing cocoa for export has left little land for people to grow food for themselves.

CHAD

MUCH OF CHAD falls inside a wide belt of hot, dry grassland called the Sahel, which extends across the African continent. Drought is a frequent occurence in the Sahel. This has proved a disaster for the country because its economy is heavily dependent on agriculture. Politically, Chad is an unstable place, and recent decades have seen a series of military coups and civil wars.

CHAD

Capital city: N'Djamena

Area: 486,177 sq miles (1,259,200 sq km)

Population: 7,700,000

Official language: French

Major religions: Muslim 50%, Christian 7%, traditional beliefs 43%

Government: Multiparty democracy

Currency: CFA franc

Adult literacy rate: 43%

Life expectancy: 46 years

People per doctor: 49,938

Televisions: 1 per 1,000 people

SAO TOME AND PRINCIPE

Capital city: São Tomé

Area: 370 sq miles (960 sq km)

Population: 159,884

Official language: Portuguese

Major religions: Christian 84%, other 16%

Government: Multiparty democracy

Currency: Dobra

Adult literacy rate: 75%

Life expectancy: 65 years

People per doctor: 3,125

Televisions: 163 per 1,000 population

THE KANIMBO
Chad's northern deserts stretch up into the Arab lands of North Africa, so the country is a mixture of Arabic and black African influences. More than 100 languages are spoken. One of Chad's many peoples is the Arabic and Muslim group made up of the Kanimbo nomads in the arid north.

Camels being brought to drink at the waters of Lake Chad

DISAPPEARING WATERS

Lake Chad was once a huge expanse of water that formed the meeting point of Chad, Cameroon, Niger, and Nigeria. In the past, water poured into Lake Chad from surrounding rivers, but as the climate has become drier (over the past 10,000 years), the lake has dried up. The shrinking lake poses a serious problem for the local people, who rely on its fish for food.

Original size of the lake, more than one million years ago

Areas of damp, fertile land are left behind as the waters of the lake retreat.

Lake Chad today

Gourds are one of the crops grown on the fertile land surrounding Lake Chad. When cut and dried, gourds can be carved and decorated.

SAO TOME AND PRINCIPE

THE VOLCANIC ISLANDS of São Tomé and Príncipe lie off the coast of Equatorial Guinea and Gabon. Dense tropical forest cloaks the upper slopes while lower down farms and large plantations growing cocoa and sugar can be found. The islands were ruled by Portugal until 1975. Today, the people make a living from farming and fishing, and cocoa remains a vital crop.

The creole people of São Tomé and Príncipe are called filhos de terra, *which is Portuguese for "sons of the earth."*

CREOLE CULTURE

No one was living on these islands when the Portuguese first landed in the 1400s. Soon a population was built of slaves imported from the mainland. Today, one of the main groups of people combine both African and Portuguese ancestry, and have created a "creole" culture with a distinctive language and style of building.

VOLCANIC LANDSCAPE
This part of Africa lies on a fault line – a crack in the Earth's crust. Molten rock can seep through this crack and cool to form volcanoes. These islands are the peaks of such volcanoes. Their soil is enriched by volcanic ash, which makes it extremely fertile.

Find out more
COCOA: *227, 228, 234*
PEOPLES OF AFRICA: *206–207*
SAHEL: *220, 222*
VOLCANOES: *13*

GABON

SITTING ASTRIDE THE EQUATOR, with plentiful rain all year round, three-quarters of Gabon is covered with tropical rain forest. Timber is an increasingly valuable resource, although Gabon's biggest earner is oil. This should have made Gabon a wealthy country, but most people are very poor. This is partly because after independence in 1960, a one-party state was created that wasted much of the wealth. In 1990 Gabon became a multiparty democracy.

LIBREVILLE
The capital city, Libreville, means "free town" in French, and was founded in 1849 as a haven for freed slaves. French influence is strong because Gabon was colonized by France during the 1800s. Libreville is a bustling modern city, where some people enjoy great wealth, in contrast to the poverty suffered by most people on the city streets.

GABON

Capital city: Libreville

Area: 99,486 sq miles (257,670 sq km)

Population: 1,200,000

Official language: French

Major religions: Christian 55%, traditional beliefs 40%, other 5%

Government: Multiparty democracy

Currency: CFA franc

Adult literacy rate: 70%

Life expectancy: 53 years

People per doctor: 2,000

Televisions: 55 per 1,000 people

CONGO

Capital city: Brazzaville

Area: 131,853 sq miles (341,500 sq km)

Population: 2,900,000

Official language: French

Major religions: Traditional beliefs 50%, Christian 48%, Muslim 2%

Government: Multiparty democracy

Currency: CFA franc

Adult literacy rate: 81%

Life expectancy: 51 years

People per doctor: 3,765

Televisions: 12 per 1,000 people

PEOPLE
Although just over 1 million people live in Gabon, there are about 40 different ethnic groups here, each speaking their own dialect. The largest group is the Fang, known for its warriors and skilled wood-carvers. Many people in Gabon moved here from other African countries in search of work.

MINERAL RICH

Oil and manganese became important exports in the 1960s. This manganese mine is in southeastern Gabon. The country is one of the world's biggest producers of the mineral, which is used to make paints, batteries, and steel. There are also plentiful reserves of iron ore and other metals, but these have yet to be developed to their full potential.

CONGO

Oil is of vital importance to Congo, bringing in 90 percent of the country's export income.

CONGO'S EASTERN BORDER follows the course of the Congo River and the Ubangi, its main tributary, or offshoot. Oil reserves have boosted Congo's economy considerably in recent years. Although ordinary people have benefited from this – more than those in Gabon – many still scratch out a living from farming, producing just enough to feed themselves. Cassava, a starchy root vegetable, is the major food crop.

Animal skin stretched across the top and secured with pegs

DRUMBEAT
As in other parts of Africa, music is a vital part of life, and drumbeats form the backbone of this music. Many drums are wooden, and the one shown here is almost as tall as its players. One popular style in the region is called Congo Music, which is similar to soul music.

OIL WEALTH

The government has wisely invested the money that comes from oil in the economy, in projects such as dams, paper mills, transportation systems, and reforestation. Although industry is limited, there is a skilled workforce. Most industries are found around the towns and cities, especially Congo's capital, Brazzaville.

Find out more

CASSAVA: 221, 240
OIL: 152, 230, 281
POLITICAL SYSTEMS: 270–271
RAIN FORESTS: 15, 69, 204

DEMOCRATIC REPUBLIC OF CONGO (ZAIRE)

APART FROM A TINY FINGER of land that
stretches to the coast, the vast country of the
Democratic Republic of Congo is landlocked.
The Congo, or Zaire, River snakes its way
through the country, providing a watery
lifeline for its people. The climate is warm
and wet, and most people are farmers. Since
independence from Belgium in 1960, the
Democratic Republic of Congo has suffered
from civil war, a harsh dictator, and falling
prices for its products. These problems have
made it one of the world's poorest countries.

Shells sewn onto
material made from
vegetable fibers

AFRICAN ART
The Democratic Republic of Congo is famous
for its distinctive art. The Kuba people of the
country's central region, whose ancestors date
back many centuries, use shells, beads, and
raffia (fibers from palm leaves) to create
geometric patterns. A Kuba chief would have
worn the haunting mask shown above in order
to take on some of the power of a great spirit.

DEM. REP. OF CONGO	
Capital city: Kinshasa	
Area: 875,520 sq miles (2,267,600 sq km)	
Population: 51,700,000	
Official language: French	
Major religions: Christian 50%, traditional beliefs 50%	
Government: Multiparty democracy	
Currency: Congolese franc	
Adult literacy rate: 61%	
Life expectancy: 51 years	
People per doctor: 10,000	
Televisions: 135 per 1,000 people	

A hydroelectric dam has
been built on the Congo at
Inga. The dam harnesses
the power of the water to
create electricity.

Boats stop at river ports for repair
work and to refuel.

Tugboat pushing
logs along the river

CONGO (ZAIRE) RIVER
The people here call the Congo River
the Zaire. One of the largest rivers in the
world, this wide ribbon of water forms the
nation's transportation system, cutting a
great upside-down "U" through miles of
forest. People traveling from place to
place crowd into motorized boats and
dugout canoes. Some large boats are
even floating health clinics or bars. The
river's fish provide vital food, while crops
are grown on the fertile riverbanks.

**The course of
the Congo River**

Kisangani

Mbandaka

EQUATOR

Kinshasa

Traders taking
their produce to
a river market

People travel
downstream in dugout
canoes produced by
local craftsmen or in
passenger boats with
outboard motors.

The curving Congo
River crosses the
Equator twice.

MINING WEALTH
The Democratic Rep. of Congo's mining
industry seems to hold the key to greater wealth
in the future. There are vast seams of copper,
cobalt, gold, uranium, silver, and diamonds
here, and reserves of oil lie just off the coast.
Copper mining, shown below, is very important,
but when the price of copper fell in the 1970s,
the economy virtually collapsed.

**Diamond
production
in Dem. Rep.
of Congo**

x 1,000
carats

24,500

20,000

15,000

10,000

5,000

1948 1970 1980 1990 2000

The Democratic Rep. of Congo is one
of the biggest producers of diamonds
in the world. Together with copper
and cobalt, they provide over 30% of
the country's export earnings.

MARKETS
Colorful, bustling river ports are meeting
points for trade and travel along the Congo
River. Stores selling travel provisions or farming
tools nestle alongside markets where people
from riverside villages come to sell their goods.
Markets are not only based on land. Traders
often sell their fresh vegetables and fish directly
from their dugout canoes.

Find out more

COPPER MINING: *73, 245*
DIAMONDS: *150, 226, 248*
HYDROELECTRICITY: *108, 262*
POLITICAL SYSTEMS: *270–271*

CENTRAL EAST AFRICA

A LINE OF DRAMATIC HIGHLANDS, volcanic mountains, gorges, and vast lakes runs through this region from Uganda in the north to Malawi in the south. This is part of a huge split in the Earth's crust known as the Great Rift Valley. Much of the rest of the landscape is flat grassland, called savanna – the perfect environment for big game animals, which draw thousands of tourists to countries such as Kenya and Tanzania. Growing tea and coffee provides another important source of income for the seven countries of the region. Mining and small-scale farming have always been important, and other industries are now increasing.

SAVANNA LANDSCAPE

Golden grasses that can grow up to 13 ft (4 m) tall cover the flat savanna. Rains come only once a year, so the grasses make the most of whatever water is available by spreading long roots deep into the soil. Needlelike leaves on acacia trees minimize water loss, while baobab trees can store water in their swollen trunks. To protect this landscape and its wildlife, vast areas have been turned into game parks, such as the Serengeti in Tanzania and the Masai Mara in Kenya.

ANIMALS OF THE SAVANNA
Rhinoceri, giraffes, elephants, antelopes, and zebras wander across the savanna in search of pasture and water. They are closely watched by cheetahs, lions, and leopards, waiting to kill any weak animals. Finally, jackals and vultures will move in to finish off the carcasses.

Masai warriors and women wear jewelry – usually bead necklaces, large earrings, and copper bracelets.

Most Masai men have more than one wife. Each wife lives in a separate hut with her children.

FARMING IN THE HIGHLANDS

Most farmers in this region produce only enough food to feed their own families, either from small plots of land or from cattle herding. In the highland areas, which have a cool, moist climate, the volcanic soils are particularly fertile and companies own large farms where tea and coffee are grown for export. However, as the population has grown, farms have been divided up into impossibly small units. The soil has begun to erode, too, since farmers cultivate even the steepest slopes.

Tea is made from the leaves of the tea bush. Pickers have to push their way into the bushes to reach the freshest shoots, so they wear rubber aprons to protect themselves.

THE RIFT VALLEY

The Great Rift Valley stretches 4,350 miles (7,000 km) from Syria in Asia to Mozambique. Over millions of years, movement between two of the plates that form the Earth's crust has created this dramatic landscape. In some places, this movement has formed steep-sided valleys such as Kenya's Mau Escarpment. Elsewhere, volcanic peaks have erupted and wide plateaus, such as the Athi Plains in Kenya, have formed where lava has seeped through the Earth's surface.

Africa's tallest mountain is Mount Kilimanjaro, a dormant volcano in the Tanzanian part of the Rift Valley.

NOMADIC CATTLE FARMERS
In the lowland areas of central east Africa, where lack of rainfall makes growing crops difficult, nomadic people travel with herds of cattle, sheep, goats, and sometimes donkeys and camels in search of water and grazing. In Kenya, the Masai people herd humpbacked zebu cattle in the area south of Nairobi straddling the Tanzanian border. The Masai keep their cattle for milk and for blood, which they draw off from a vein through a thin reed to drink.

Kampala, Uganda
☀ Jan 74°F (23°C)
July 70°F (21°C)
🌧 Jan 1.8 in (46 mm)
July 1.8 in (46 mm)

UGANDA   KENYA

Nairobi, Kenya
☀ Jan 66°F (19°C)
July 60°F (16°C)
🌧 Jan 1.5 in (38 mm)
July 0.6 in (15 mm)

Elemi Triangle
is administered
by Kenya

RIFT VALLEY FISHING

A chain of large fresh- and
saltwater lakes runs along the Rift
Valley. Many of the lakes are home
to vast numbers of fish, and along the
shores of Lake Albert (Mobutu Sese
Seko), Lake Nyasa (Lake Malawi),
and Lake Tanganyika many people
make a living by fishing with
small nets or spears.

TROPIC OF CANCER

RWANDA

EQUATOR

TROPIC OF CAPRICORN

BURUNDI

0   100   200   300   400 km
0   50   100   150   200   250 miles

N

ZAMBIA

TANZANIA

Dar es Salaam, Tanzania
☀ Jan 82°F (28°C)
July 75°F (24°C)
🌧 Jan 2.6 in (66 mm)
July 1.2 in (31 mm)

**THINGS TO LOOK FOR
ON THE MAP**

Longest river: Luangwa,
Zambia/Mozambique,
500 miles (804 km) *Map G11*

Highest point:
Mt. Kilimanjaro, Tanzania,
19,341 ft (5,895 m) *Map J6*

Largest lake: L. Victoria,
Tanzania/Uganda/Kenya,
26,828 sq miles
(69,484 sq km) *Map G6*

Lusaka, Zambia
☀ Jan 71°F (22°C)
July 61°F (16°C)
🌧 Jan 9.1 in (231 mm)
July 0 in (0 mm)

MALAWI

Map labels

SUDAN
ETHIOPIA
SOMALIA
Lokichokio
Mandera
Moyale
CHALBI DESERT
Arua
Gulu
Moroto
Pakwach
Albert Nile
Victoria Nile
L. Albert
L. Kyoga
Mbale
Kitale
Wajir
UGANDA
Eldoret
KENYA
Fort Portal
Kasese
KAMPALA
Jinja
Kakamega
Meru
Mt. Kenya
Tana
L. Edward
Masaka
Entebbe
Nakuru
Kisumu
Nyeri
Garissa
Mbarara
Thika
Bukoba
Lake Victoria
Musoma
NAIROBI
Machakos
L. Kivu
KIGALI
RWANDA
Butare
Mwanza
Mt. Kilimanjaro
BUJUMBURA
Olduvai Gorge
Arusha
Malindi
BURUNDI
Shinyanga
L. Eyasi
Moshi
Galana
Kigoma
L. Manyara
Mombasa
Wembere
Singida
MASAI STEPPE
Tanga
Tabora
Pangani
Pemba I.
GREAT RIFT VALLEY
TANZANIA
DODOMA
Zanzibar
INDIAN OCEAN
Great Ruaha
Morogoro
Dar es Salaam
L. Rukwa
Iringa
Sumbawanga
Rufiji
Mafia I.
Mbala
Mbeya
Kilwa Masoko
L. Mweru
Njombe
Lindi
Kasama
Songea
Mtwara
DEM. REP. CONGO (ZAIRE)
Mansa
L. Bangweulu
Ruvuma
Mzuzu
Mpika
Luangwa
Solwezi
Lundazi
MUCHINGA MTS
L. Nyasa
MOZAMBIQUE
Chingola
Nkhotakota
Mufulira
Kitwe
Ndola
Bua
Luanshya
Chipata
LILONGWE
Zambezi
Salima
ZAMBIA
Kabwe
MALAWI
Mongu
Kafue
LUSAKA
Zomba
Kafue
Blantyre
KAFUE FLATS
MOZAMBIQUE
Kariba Dam
L. Kariba
Choma
ANGOLA
Zambezi
Nsanje
Victoria Falls
Livingstone
NAMIBIA
BOTSWANA
ZIMBABWE
RUWENZORI
Tanganyika
DEMOCRATIC REPUBLIC OF CONGO (ZAIRE)
ABERDARE RANGE
L. Turkana

1
2
3
4
5
6
7
8
9
10
11
12
13
14
15

A   B   C   D   E   F   G   H   I   J   K   L

UGANDA

BEFORE INDEPENDENCE IN 1962, Uganda was a prosperous country – Winston Churchill called it the "Pearl of Africa." But by 1986, the country lay shattered and bankrupt. From 1971–79, President Idi Amin ruled Uganda as a dictator. Thousands of people were persecuted or murdered. Europeans and Asians were expelled and their property seized. International aid was cut off when other countries realized how corrupt Amin's government was. In 1979, Amin was deposed, but the disruption continued until 1986, when President Yoweri Museveni came to power. His government restored peace and has begun to rebuild the economy.

UGANDA	
Capital city: Kampala	
Area: 77,046 sq miles (199,550 sq km)	
Population: 21,800,000	
Official language: English	
Major religions: Christian 71%, traditional beliefs 13%, Muslim 5%, other 11%	
Government: One-party state	
Currency: Uganda Shilling	
Adult literacy rate: 67%	
Life expectancy: 43 years	
People per doctor: 25,000	
Televisions: 27 per 1,000 people	

FISHING IN LAKE VICTORIA
Vast, shallow Lake Victoria is shared by Uganda, Tanzania, and Kenya. Huge Nile perch fish were introduced to the lake 30 years ago to increase fish production and provide sport fishing for tourists. Since then the perch have spread to every corner of Lake Victoria and have devoured most of its original species.

FARMING

Fertile, volcanic soil and high levels of rainfall make more than four-fifths of Uganda's land suitable for farming. Large plantations produce the coffee, cotton, and tea that make up 90 percent of the country's exports. Although 90 percent of Ugandans work on farms, most are involved in small-scale farming, growing crops such as corn, millet, cassava, and sweet potatoes for their own use or to sell in local markets.

The cassava plant grows up to 3 ft (90 cm) tall. It is grown for its roots, which can be eaten as a vegetable or ground to make flour.

Sweet potato (left) and cassava (right) are common vegetables in this region.

Kampala is said to be built on seven hills. The city center lies on just one of them – Nakasero Hill.

KAMPALA
People in Uganda's capital, Kampala, rarely go out without an umbrella, since most days see a heavy downpour in the afternoon. Kampala has an average of 242 days a year with violent thunderstorms. By evening, the rain has stopped and the air is cool. Kampala suffered much destruction during and immediately after Amin's period in power, but is now being restored with the help of foreign investment.

What Have You Heard About AIDS?

What Does It Mean?

What Can We Do For People Who Have It?

How Does It Harm Us?

How Can It Be Cured?

Who Can Get It?

What Does It Look Like?

What Causes It?

How Can We Stop It?

Which Of Us Has It?

Don't GUESS the Answers! LEARN THE TRUTH ABOUT AIDS!

AIDS AWARENESS

Uganda has one of the highest numbers of AIDS sufferers in the world. In some parts of the country about 20 percent of the population is infected. AIDS is a sexually transmitted disease, and as yet there is no cure for it, so doctors are trying to teach people how to avoid catching it. Special campaigns, like this poster produced by UNICEF, are aimed at educating children of the risk of AIDS.

WILDLIFE
In Ruwenzori National Park, tourists can take a boat trip down the Kazinga Channel to see thousands of hippos and pelicans. Much of Uganda's wildlife was wiped out during the years of conflict, and today there are not many places in Africa where you are likely to see so many hippos.

Find out more
COFFEE: *50, 62, 66*
LAKE VICTORIA: *204*
POLITICAL SYSTEMS: *270–271*
TEA: *172, 238*

RWANDA

SINCE 1994, RWANDA HAS rarely been out of the news. War between the two main ethnic groups – the Tutsi and Hutu – has torn Rwanda apart and wrecked its economy, leaving it one of the poorest countries in the world. Before the war, Rwanda's main export was coffee. Today, although 95 percent of the people still live off the land, few crops are grown for export. The country's instability has also hindered attempts to develop manufacturing and mining industries.

RWANDA	
Capital city: Kigali	
Area: 9,633 sq miles (24,950 sq km)	
Population: 7,700,000	
Official languages: French and Kinyarwanda	
Major religions: Traditional beliefs 50%, Christian 45%, other 5%	
Government: One-party state	
Currency: Rwanda franc	
Adult literacy rate: 67%	
Life expectancy: 40 years	
People per doctor: 40,600	
Televisions: No figures available	

BURUNDI	
Capital city: Bujumbura	
Area: 9,903 sq miles (25,650 sq km)	
Population: 6,700,000	
Official languages: French and Kirundi	
Major religions: Christian 60%, traditional beliefs 39%, Muslim 1%	
Government: Multiparty democracy	
Currency: Burundi franc	
Adult literacy rate: 48%	
Life expectancy: 41 years	
People per doctor: 17,210	
Televisions: 4 per 1,000 people	

GENOCIDE

In 1994, centuries-old tensions between the majority Hutu and minority Tutsi populations boiled over into one of the world's worst acts of genocide (the murder of one ethnic group). Around 500,000 of the previously dominant Tutsi were massacred alongside some of their Hutu supporters. Over one million Rwandans fled the country. Although peace has been restored, few people have been put on trial and tensions remain high.

HEALTH
Rwanda is one of Africa's most densely populated countries and the population continues to grow. Most Rwandan women have at least six children, compared to an average of only one or two in developed countries. However, few Rwandans live to be over 50. Diseases such as malaria and AIDS are common, and medical facilities are in short supply and are rarely free, so few people can afford them.

There are only about 650 gorillas left in the world. The mountain gorilla is found only in this region of Africa.

MOUNTAIN GORILLAS
One of the last known refuges for the mountain gorilla is the Volcanoes National Park in Rwanda. Even though the gorilla is protected here, it is still in danger of extinction by poachers, and its habitat is threatened by farming.

BURUNDI

UNTIL INDEPENDENCE IN 1962, Burundi and neighboring Rwanda formed one country. Like Rwanda, Burundi is home to both Tutsi and Hutu people, and the wars between these tribes have been part of Burundi's history, too. In 1972, about 10,000 Hutu were killed by Tutsis. Warfare continues today, although a peace agreement was reached in 2001. Burundi's problems are made worse by fighting in neighbouring Democratic Republic of Congo (Zaire).

POPULATION PRESSURE
Most people in Burundi make a living from farming. So many people live in the most fertile areas that land is very scarce. Plots of land are usually just large enough to support a family in good years, but bad weather or disease can lead to widespread famine. In some areas, the land is so over-used that the soil has begun to erode.

DRUMMING GROUPS
In Burundi, stories, songs, and music are passed down from generation to generation rather than written down in a formal way. Tutsi folk dancing is one of the highlights of traditional culture, as are the groups of 12 to 15 drummers who play together with no other instruments.

Find out more
HEALTH: *276*
POPULATION: *16–17, 206*
REFUGEES: *207*
SOIL EROSION: *55, 244*

KENYA

UNLIKE MANY AFRICAN countries, Kenya has been stable and relatively democratic since it gained its independence from Britain in 1963. Under British rule, large farms were created in many areas to produce cash crops, and a network of roads and railroads was built to link ports and towns. Today, Kenya is one of Africa's richest countries, producing crops such as coffee and tea for export, and welcoming tourists to its vast game reserves. Side-by-side with this, many people still make their living from small farms or cattle herding. Kenya has one of the world's fastest growing populations, which has led to increasing poverty, rivalry over land, and some ethnic violence.

KENYA

Capital city: Nairobi

Area: 218,907 sq miles (566,970 sq km)

Population: 30,100,000

Official language: Swahili

Major religions: Christian 60%, traditional beliefs 25%, Muslim 6%, other 9%

Government: Multiparty democracy

Currency: Kenya shilling

Adult literacy rate: 82%

Life expectancy: 51 years

People per doctor: 6,667

Televisions: 21 per 1,000 people

NAIROBI

Lions, giraffes, and cheetahs roam the plains that surround Kenya's capital, Nairobi, with the skyscrapers of the modern city as a backdrop. This is the largest city in eastern Africa, with a population of about two million people. It developed after European colonization as a convenient stopping place on the railroad from Uganda to Kenya's main port of Mombassa.

Kenya's main crops

The main farming area, shown enlarged on the map below, is in the southwest of the country.

KENYA

On game reserves such as Kenya's Masai Mara and Amboseli National Park, tourists can photograph wild animals close up.

☐ Coffee
☐ Tea
☐ Sisal
☐ Sugarcane
☐ Rice
☐ Forest
☐ Other

Tea

Coffee beans

TOURISM

Tropical beaches and some of Africa's best game reserves attract thousands of tourists to Kenya. Tourism is vital to the country's economy, and the government has invested in roads, airports, and hotels to make Kenya one of the easiest and most comfortable African countries for tourists to visit. Because most people come to see the animals on game reserves, the government has placed a high priority on protecting wildlife and stamping out poaching.

FARMING
AND THE ECONOMY

Farming is Kenya's chief export earner, but much of the country is far too dry to grow crops. In the highlands – where there is more rain – tea, coffee, wheat, corn, sisal, and sugarcane are grown. Where less water is available, dairy and meat cattle are farmed on large ranches. Dams and lakes provide water to irrigate land for growing market garden crops, such as green beans, which are exported by air to foreign supermarkets.

Green beans

KENYAN PEOPLES

These villagers belong to Kenya's largest tribe, the Kikuyu, who live around Mount Kenya. The Kikuyu god, Ngai, is believed to live on the mountain, so the Kikuyu traditionally built their houses with the doors facing the mountain. Like two-thirds of the country's 70 tribal groups, the Kikuyu speak Bantu. Small numbers of Asians, Arabs, and Europeans also live in Kenya.

KENYAN ATHLETES

Athletes from Kenya's Rift Valley area excel at running long distances. They have won the gold medal in the Olympic 3,000 m steeplechase events at the last five Olympic Games, and Kenyan Moses Kiptanui was the first man to run the 3,000 m steeplechase in under eight minutes. The runners' skill may stem from the high altitude they live and train in, or from years of running long distances to school.

Find out more

AFRICAN CITIES: *206*
HIGHLAND FARMING: *238*
POPULATION: *16–17, 206*
RIFT VALLEY: *204*

TANZANIA

TANZANIA WAS CREATED in 1964, when the mainland country of Tanganyika and the island of Zanzibar united. For its first 21 years Tanzania had a socialist government that tried to encourage people to work together on programs such as state-run plantations. Although it is now expanding its range of exports, Tanzania is much poorer than neighboring Kenya, and only a fifth of people live in towns and cites. About 120 different peoples live here, most of whom speak Swahili, a language developed as a means of communication between Africans and foreign traders.

TANZANIA	
Capital city: Dodoma	
Area: 342,100 sq miles (886,040 sq km)	
Population: 33,500,000	
Official languages: English and Swahili	
Major religions: Traditional beliefs 30%, Christian 33%, Muslim 33%, other 4%	
Government: Multiparty democracy	
Currency: Tanzanian shilling	
Adult literacy rate: 76%	
Life expectancy: 51 years	
People per doctor: 23,939	
Televisions: 21 per 1,000 people	

DAR ES SALAAM
Although Tanzania's capital is now the inland city of Dodoma, the old capital, Dar es Salaam, remains the country's biggest city and port. It is also the end of the TanZam railroad, which carries goods from land-locked Zambia to the sea.

The name Dar es Salaam means "Haven of Peace." The city is still fairly small, with few high-rise buildings and many low, red-tiled roofs.

OLDUVAI GORGE
The steep sides of Olduvai Gorge in northern Tanzania were carved out of the flat Serengeti Plain by the flow of water over millions of years. Here, archaeologists have unearthed fossils of the earliest humans, dating back 2 million years. Yet more ancient footprints of humanlike creatures have been discovered, too, left by two adults and a child walking across the still-soft lava that formed the plain 3.5 million years ago.

Making sisal fiber
The outer leaves of the sisal plant are cut off close to the stalk when they reach their full length.

The sisal fiber is usually obtained by crushing the leaves between rollers. The pulp is removed, leaving strands of white fiber over 3 ft (1 m) long.

The strands of fiber are washed and then hung out to dry.

SISAL
One of Tanzania's main crops is sisal, a plant with leaves that are used to make rope and twine, and also mats, brushes, hats, and baskets. Sisal ropes are particularly useful on board ships since they do not rot in seawater. However, Tanzania's sisal trade is now under threat because many products made with sisal in the past can now be made with synthetic substitutes.

String made from sisal

TANZANIAN VILLAGES
The country's population used to be scattered in small villages. Then, in 1970, the government started a program to resettle the population in larger villages of about 250 households. By grouping people together in this way, it is easier and more economic to provide schools, water, and other services, and to distribute fertilizers and seeds. Today, 73 percent of Tanzanians live in villages in the countryside.

The buildings and style of clothes reflect Zanzibar's continuing Arabic flavor.

ZANZIBAR
Off Tanzania's coast lies the island of Zanzibar. In the 18th and 19th centuries, the port of Zanzibar, on the island's western side, was used as an Arab trading post. African slaves passed though here, en route to the Arab world. The island's main crop, cloves, was also shipped out of the port. The clove tree was only introduced to the island in 1818, but today Zanzibar is the world's third largest producer.

Find out more
EARLY PEOPLE: *206*
POLITICAL SYSTEMS: *270–271*
POPULATION DISTRIBUTION: *206*
TANZAM RAILROAD: *245*

MALAWI

LYING ON A PLATEAU at the southern end of the Great Rift Valley, Malawi's six major tribal groups have lived together in relative peace. This was in part due to the harsh rule of the dictator Hastings Banda. Since democracy was introduced in 1994, however, there have been some open political tensions. Malawi's economy is based on agriculture, but the government is trying to encourage the growth of agricultural processing industries, such as food canning and cooking oil manufacture, as well as mining and other heavy industries. New mineral deposits were discovered in 2000.

MALAWI	
Capital city: Lilongwe	
Area: 36,324 sq miles (94,080 sq km)	
Population: 10,900,000	
Official languages: Chewa and English	
Major religions: Christian 75%, Muslim 20%, traditional beliefs 5%	
Government: Multiparty democracy	
Currency: Malawian kwacha	
Adult literacy rate: 60%	
Life expectancy: 40 years	
People per doctor: 50,000	
Televisions: 2 per 1,000 people	

LAKE NYASA
Over one-fifth of Malawi's total area is taken up by Lake Nyasa, one of the largest and deepest lakes in the world.

Fishermen collect these brightly colored fish, called cichlids, for export to aquariums around the world.

A huge fishing industry has developed around the lake, which is home to more than 500 species of fish. A sardinelike fish called the usipa is one of the main catches. The fish are dried on the shore and sold throughout Malawi. However, overfishing has meant that there are not enough fish left over for export.

Many people grow just enough food to feed themselves and their family. If there is any extra produce, they sell it in local markets like this one.

FARMING
Farming is the most important business in Malawi. Tobacco, tea, and sugar make up 85 percent of exports, and more than 80 percent of Malawi's population makes a living by farming. To increase the land available to farm, swamps have been drained and woodland has been cleared. Rivers have been dammed and wells dug to water dry grasslands. Poor harvests can lead to extreme hardship among Malawi's people.

Soil erosion

Wind blows away soil on exposed areas.

Water runs down the hillside, washing the soil away to form gulleys.

Tree roots help bind the soil together.

If the trees are cut down, wind and rain wear away the soil.

FORESTS
Forest and woodland cover nearly half the country, but huge areas have been cut down for fuel and to clear land for farming. Malawi has no oil and little coal, so the most popular fuel is charcoal, made by partially burning wood so that it becomes smokeless and slow-burning. Where more land is needed for farming, trees are cut down and burned, and crops are grown in the ashes. Such land is fertile for only a short time because the forest soil is quickly eroded.

PEOPLE OF MALAWI
Malawi is one of the least urbanized countries in the world, with 85 percent of its population living in villages in the countryside, mostly near seasonal wetlands called *dambos*. Villages are small and are usually made up of people who are closely related. Unlike many other African countries, Malawi's main ethnic groups, the Chewas, Nyanja, Tumbuka, Tonga, Ngonis, and Yao, live together peacefully.

HASTINGS BANDA
For 30 years after achieving independence in 1964, Dr. Hastings Banda was president of Malawi, ruling the country virtually alone. His government helped the country become strong and self-reliant, but other political opinions were not tolerated and many people were tortured or imprisoned. In 1994, demorcatic elections led to Banda's downfall.

Find out more

DEFORESTATION: *69, 227, 233*
PEOPLES OF AFRICA: *206–207*
POLITICAL SYSTEMS: *270–271*
REFUGEES: *207*

ZAMBIA

ZAMBIA OCCUPIES A BROAD plateau scattered with mountains and deep valleys. After independence from Britain in 1963, political violence based on tribal differences rocked the country until 1972, when President Kenneth Kaunda declared a one-party state. In 1991, Kaunda was defeated in the first democratic elections in 19 years. Today, the country is less affected by ethnic conflict than many African states, even though there are 14 main tribal groups. Zambia is the world's fourth largest producer of copper, and the country's economy depends almost entirely on the fortunes of this industry.

ZAMBIA	
Capital city: Lusaka	
Area: 285,992 sq miles (74,720 sq km)	
Population: 9,200,000	
Official languages: English, Bemba, and Nyanja	
Major religions: Christian 63%, traditional beliefs 36%, other 1%	
Government: Multiparty democracy	
Currency: Zambian kwacha	
Adult literacy rate: 78%	
Life expectancy: 41 years	
People per doctor: 10,000	
Televisions: 137 per 1,000 people	

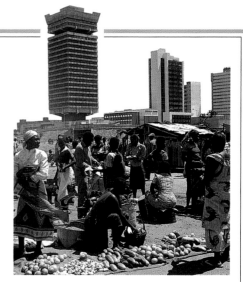

CITIES

A chain of shantytowns lies along the railroad linking Zambia's copper belt with the capital, Lusaka. The makeshift shacks have no water, power, or drains, and disease is widespread. Most people here have jobs in the copper industry. In fact, 44 percent of Zambians live in the towns, making it the most urbanized country in the region. Many Zambian families have been city-dwellers for three or four generations, which is rare in Africa.

Mineral deposits in Zambia

- Copper
- Cobalt

Zambia's exports

Copper: 49%

Other: 33%

Cobalt: 18%

Copper ore

TanZam railroad

Kasama

ZAMBIA

Lusaka

Livingstone

TANZAM RAILROAD
Landlocked Zambia has to rely on roads and railroads through other countries to export copper and other products to ports, so good relations with its neighbors are important. Until the 1960s, most goods went through Rhodesia (now Zimbabwe), but relations between the two countries broke down. Today, the main trade route is the TanZam railroad through Tanzania.

The TanZam railroad links Zambia to the port of Dar es Salaam in neighboring Tanzania.

COPPER MINING

Seams of copper run through an area more than 200 miles (320 km) long and 30 miles (50 km) wide in central Zambia called the copper belt. First developed commercially in the 1930s, copper mining has funded much of Zambia's development. Copper accounts for 50 percent of the country's exports, and if the world price of copper were to fall, Zambia's economy could be wrecked. To add to this problem, the copper reserves are beginning to run out.

ZAMBEZI RIVER

Forming Zambia's southern border, the Zambezi River is one of the country's main tourist attractions. Visitors can go white-water rafting on the river, take a wildlife safari in one of the area's game parks, and visit the magnificent Victoria Falls. A huge dam at Kariba provides power in the form of hydroelectricity for Zambia's copper belt and for neighboring Zimbabwe. Lake Kariba, the artificial lake formed by the dam, is a popular fishing destination for tourists.

FISH EAGLE
National parks, set up to protect wildlife, take up more than one-third of the country's area. The fish eagle is Zambia's national symbol, and appears on the country's flag. It is common around open stretches of water, where it swoops down to snatch fish from the surface and rises up with a fish in its talons.

Find out more

EXPORT DEPENDENCY: *281*
HYDROELECTRICITY: *108, 262*
POLITICAL SYSTEMS: *270–271*
VICTORIA FALLS: *250*

SOUTHERN AFRICA

THE EIGHT COUNTRIES THAT MAKE UP southern Africa have much in common. Once governed by European settlers, almost all of them had to struggle to achieve independence. Many endured years of vicious warfare. Today, all eight countries are independent, multiracial democracies. Their climates range from warm and mild in the south to tropical in the north, while the landscape includes both deserts and rain forests, vast plains, and towering mountain ranges. The population varies in wealth from extremely rich industrialists and landowners in South Africa to hunter-gatherer Bushmen in the Kalahari Desert.

Before 1994, demonstrations against apartheid were held throughout South Africa.

Magnificent Table Mountain towers above Cape Town in the Cape Peninsula, South Africa. The Cape is home to many unique species of plants and flowers.

POLITICS

Southern Africa is dominated by the politics of South Africa. After 1948, South Africa pursued a policy of separate development for white and black people known as apartheid. South Africa tried to weaken the neighboring countries that opposed it. It supported rebels fighting the Angolan and Mozambique governments, and helped those resisting black rule in Zimbabwe and Namibia. The ending of white rule in 1994 led to better relations between South Africa and its neighbors.

A LAND OF CONTRASTS

The landscape of southern Africa varies from the Namib and Kalahari deserts in the west and center to lush vegetation and tropical forests in the north. Inland, vast grassy savannas and woodlands are home to much of the region's wildlife, from the minute *dik-dik* (the world's smallest antelope) to the African elephant. Game reserves and national parks have been set up to protect endangered species. Tourists come from all over the world to visit the reserves and enjoy the dramatic scenery.

OKAVANGO DELTA
Unlike most rivers, which run out to the sea, the Okavango River runs inland into a desert. The river begins in Angola, then flows southeast through Namibia into a delta in the Kalahari Desert in Botswana. The vast swamps and waterways of the river and its delta cover an area of more than 8,500 sq miles (22,000 sq km). This provides a haven for a wide variety of plants and animals. People travel into the swamps in dugout canoes, called *mokoros*.

KALAHARI BUSHMEN
The Bushmen, or San, of the Kalahari Desert are one of the few groups of hunter-gatherers left in Africa. These people live and work together in small, tightly knit communities. Traditionally they moved from place to place, searching for insects and edible plants and hunting small animals with poisonous arrows. Today, however, many of the San live a more settled existence.

MINERAL RICHES

Southern Africa is rich in mineral resources. Much of the world's gold, diamonds, uranium, and copper come from the region, and have transformed the local economies. Botswana is the most dependent upon its minerals. Almost 80 percent of the country's export earnings come from diamonds. South Africa is the world's leading producer of gold, and Namibia has one of the world's largest uranium mines. Coal is southern Africa's major source of energy. South Africa, Zimbabwe, Botswana, and Mozambique all have large coal reserves.

Major mineral deposits

- Uranium
- Coal
- Iron
- Diamonds
- Copper
- Oil
- Gold

A B C D E F G H I J K L

1
2
3
4
5
6
7
8
9
10
11
12

CONGO
CABINDA
(Angola)
Cabinda
ATLANTIC OCEAN
Ambriz
Uíge
LUANDA
Caxito
N'Dalatando
Cuanza
Malanje
Lucapa
Saurimo
DEM. REP. CONGO (ZAIRE)
Cuango
Congo

ANGOLA
Sumbe
Lobito
Benguela
Kuito
Huambo
Luena
Zambezi
Lumbala N'guimbo

Namibe
Lubango
Cuito Cuanavale
Menongue
Okavango
Cuito

N'Giva
Kunene
Ondangwa
Rundu
Etosha Pan
Chobe
Okavango Delta
Maun

NAMIB DESERT
Tsumeb
Grootfontein
Otjiwarongo
Okahandja
Ghanzi
Orapa
Francistown
Makgadikgadi Pans
Shashe

NAMIBIA
Gobabis
WINDHOEK
Rehoboth
Mariental
Maltahöhe
Olifants
BOTSWANA
KALAHARI DESERT
Selebi-Phikwe
Serowe
Mahalapye

Walvis Bay

Lüderitz
Keetmanshoop
Karasburg
Fish
Orange R.
Ghanzi
GABORONE
Jwaneng
Lobatse
Sun City
Mmabatho
Soweto
Vryburg
Klerksdorp
Vereeniging

SOUTH AFRICA
Upington
Kimberley
BLOEMFONTEIN
De Aar
Orange
Vaal

Calvinia
Beaufort West
Umtata

Saldanha
Oudtshoorn
Grahamstown
East London
CAPE TOWN
Table Mt.
Cape of Good Hope
C. Agulhas
Port Elizabeth

ZAMBIA
Zambezi
Cabora Bassa L.
Tete
Chinhoyi
Bindura
L. Kariba
Victoria Falls
HARARE
Hwange
Chitungwiza
Gweru
Mutare
Chimoio
ZIMBABWE
Bulawayo
Masvingo
Beira
Thohoyandou
Limpopo
Save
Pietersburg
Inhambane
PRETORIA
Johannesburg
Xai-Xai
MAPUTO
MBABANE
SWAZILAND
Tugela
MASERU
LESOTHO
Mafeteng
Pietermaritzburg
Durban
Mt. Thabana-Ntlenyana
DRAKENSBERG

TANZANIA
Rovuma
Lugenda
L. Nyasa
MALAWI
Mocimboa da Praia
Pemba
Nacala
Moçambique
Nampula
Quelimane
MOZAMBIQUE
INDIAN OCEAN

N

THINGS TO LOOK FOR ON THE MAP
Longest river: Zambezi, Mozambique/Zimbabwe/Zambia/Namibia/Angola, 1,678 miles (2,700 km) Map J5
Highest point: Mt. Thabana-Ntlenyana, Lesotho, 11,424 ft (3,482 m) Map H10
Largest lake: L. Nyasa, Mozambique/Malawi/Tanzania 11,000 sq miles (28,490 sq km) Map J4

0 100 200 300 400 500 km
0 100 200 300 miles

ZIMBABWE
MOZAMBIQUE
ANGOLA
NAMIBIA
SWAZILAND
LESOTHO
SOUTH AFRICA
BOTSWANA

Francistown, Botswana
Jan 77°F (25°C)
July 58°F (15°C)
Jan 4.2 in (107 mm)
July 0 in (0 mm)

Port Elizabeth, South Africa
Jan 70°F (21°C)
July 56°F (13°C)
Jan 1.2 in (31 mm)
July 1.9 in (48 mm)

TROPIC OF CANCER
EQUATOR
TROPIC OF CAPRICORN

CITY GROWTH

Across southern Africa, people are leaving the countryside and moving to the cities in search of work. The outlying areas surrounding such cities as Johannesburg in South Africa are crammed with shanty towns which are now a permanent feature of the landscape. Maputo, the capital of Mozambique (right), doubled in size between 1975 and 1983, and now contains more than 1.5 million people.

WOMEN'S ROLE

In traditional African society, women generally acted as wives and mothers and were responsible for routine household tasks and growing crops. Today, many African men work away from home in the mines and cities for one or two years at a time, leaving women to form a majority in their villages. This means that women are now taking on more responsibility in the communities.

ANGOLA

ANGOLA SHOULD BE ONE of the most successful countries in Africa. The land is largely fertile, with dense tropical forests in the north giving way to drier grasslands in the south. Farmers produce enough food to support the small population, while huge oil and mineral reserves bring wealth to the economy. However, Angola has been torn apart by a civil war that began in 1975. Few parts of the country have been left unaffected by the fighting, which has killed or injured thousands of people and reduced this potentially rich country to poverty.

ANGOLA	
Capital city: Luanda	
Area: 481,351 sq miles (1,246,700 sq km)	
Population: 12,900,000	
Official language: Portuguese	
Major religions: Christian 70%, other 30%	
Government: Multiparty democracy	
Currency: New kwanza	
Adult literacy rate: 40%	
Life expectancy: 45 years	
People per doctor: 14,300	
Televisions: 14 per 1,000 people	

 Major towns
••••••• Benguela railroad

The Benguela railroad runs from the coastal ports of Benguela and Lobito in Angola eastward until reaching Zaire.

CIVIL WAR
In 1975, Portuguese rule in Angola ended and civil war broke out. The conflict was between the Angolan People's Liberation Movement (MPLA), supported by the Soviet Union and Cuba, and the National Union for Total Angolan Independence (UNITA), supported by South Africa and the US. After a ceasefire in 1991, the MPLA was elected to power, but fighting broke out again and continues today despite a peace agreement made in 1994–5.

BENGUELA RAILROAD
Opened in 1931, the Benguela railroad was built to transport copper and other minerals from the mines of landlocked Zambia and Zaire to the coastal ports of Lobito and Benguela for export around the world. The railroad and ports provided work for many Angolans, who lost their jobs when the railroad was destroyed in the civil war. After the ceasefire of 1991, engineers began to rebuild sections of the track, and plans have been made to reopen the railroad.

LUANDA
The port of Luanda is Angola's capital and biggest city. Founded by the Portuguese in 1576, for centuries it was a center for shipping slaves to the Portuguese colony of Brazil. The Portuguese built a fort and many other fine buildings, which stand alongside modern skyscrapers. On the hills surrounding the city vast shantytowns house thousands of people.

INDUSTRY
The tiny Angolan territory of Cabinda, to the north of the main part of the country, is one of the richest oil-producing regions in Africa. Offshore oil fields contain reserves of 1.5 billion barrels of oil and vast quantities of natural gas. Some of the richest diamond deposits in the world are found in the northeast of the country, while iron and other minerals are mined farther south. However, constant fighting has destroyed some mines and factories.

A brace divides the bow string into two unequal lengths.

MUSICAL BOW
The Humbi people of southwestern Angola use an ordinary hunting bow as a musical instrument. The musician supports the bow with one hand and holds it in his mouth. As he hits the string with a stick held in his other hand, he produces different notes by altering the shape of his lips.

Find out more
AFRICAN CITIES: *206*
DIAMONDS: *150, 226, 248*
OIL: *152, 230, 281*
RAILROADS: *245*

BOTSWANA

WITH ONE OF THE WORLD'S FASTEST growing economies, based on rich diamond supplies and large cattle ranches, Botswana was one of Africa's few real economic success stories. In recent years, however, it has become the most powerful symbol of Africa's greatest modern threat – HIV and AIDS. It has the highest proportion of sufferers in the world – 36 percent of all adults are infected.

GABORONE
When Botswana became independent, the country had no capital city, as it had previously been governed from Mafikeng in South Africa. The new country therefore built a new capital, called Gaborone. Today, more than 200,000 people live in the city, which houses the national government and is the center of communications and industry.

BOTSWANA	
Capital city: Gaborone	
Area: 224,600 sq miles (581,730 sq km)	
Population: 1,600,000	
Official language: English	
Major religions: traditional beliefs 50%, Christian 30%, other 20%	
Government: Multiparty democracy	
Currency: Pula	
Adult literacy rate: 77%	
Life expectancy: 42 years	
People per doctor: 5,000	
Televisions: 20 per 1,000 people	

NAMIBIA	
Capital city: Windhoek	
Area: 318,260 sq miles (824,290 sq km)	
Population: 1,700,000	
Official language: English	
Major religions: Christian 90%, traditional beliefs 10%	
Government: Multiparty democracy	
Currency: Namibian dollar	
Adult literacy rate: 82%	
Life expectancy: 45 years	
People per doctor: 5,000	
Televisions: 37 per 1,000 people	

Parents and young children live in the main sleeping hut.

People cook, eat, and receive guests in the lolwapa.

Trees are valued for their shade.

Women are responsible for building and maintaining the huts.

TSWANA HOMES
The Tswana people, who make up most of the Botswana population, traditionally organize themselves into chiefdoms. Each chiefdom consists of a capital town, around which are a number of satellite villages. Families live in dwellings made up of three or four huts, each hut serving a particular purpose. The huts are arranged around a central courtyard, or *lolwapa*.

The lolwapa is surrounded by a low wall.

The thatched roof is supported on poles that circle the wall of the hut. The space between the wall and the roof gives ventilation.

The huts are decorated with finger markings in earth shades of brown, red, and orange.

NAMIBIA

Copper

ORIGINALLY A GERMAN COLONY, Namibia was governed by its neighbor, South Africa, from 1915 until independence in 1990. Rich in minerals and other natural resources, the country is dominated by the Namib Desert, which runs in a thin strip down the west of the country near the Atlantic Ocean, and the vast Kalahari Desert, which lies in the south.

MINING
Namibia is one of the four biggest mineral producers in Africa, with large deposits of copper, diamonds, tin, and other minerals. One of the world's largest uranium mines is located at Rössing, in the Namib Desert, in the center of the country. Namibia is the largest producer of salt in Africa.

To show that she is married, a Himba woman will lengthen her hair by adding hair cut from her brother's head.

RURAL LIFE
Most Namibian people live on the high plains in the north of the country. Here the Ovambo people build fenced-in enclosures known as *kraals*. The Himba people live farther west in the rugged land bordering Angola. These semi-nomadic people make their living from tending cattle, which provide them with meat, milk, and clothing. The number of cattle owned is a reflection of wealth and status.

| ___ *Find out more* ___ |
| COPPER MINING: *73, 237, 245* |
| DEMOCRACY: *270* |
| DESERTS: *15, 204* |
| DIAMONDS: *150, 226, 248* |

ZIMBABWE

ZIMBABWE

Capital city: Harare

Area: 149,293 sq miles (386,670 sq km)

Population: 11,700,000

Official language: English

Major religions: Syncretic (part Christian, part traditional beliefs) 50%, Christian 25%, traditional beliefs 24%, other 1%

Government: Multiparty democracy

Currency: Zimbabwe dollar

Adult literacy rate: 89%

Life expectancy: 43 years

People per doctor: 6,900

Televisions: 30 per 1,000 people

ZIMBABWE WAS ONCE PART OF a great trading empire. Many centuries ago, central African merchants exported gold and copper to India and China. The center of this empire was Great Zimbabwe ("house of the chief"), a huge palace, from which Zimbabwe took its name when it became independent in 1980. Today the country's economic potential has been ruined by the corrupt rule of the president, Robert Mugabe. He has oppressed opposition parties and his policy of encouraging illegal occupation of white-owned farmland by black settlers has led to a breakdown in law and order.

FIGHTING OPPRESSION
Robert Mugabe's Zanu-PF party has been in power since the country's independence in 1980. The harsh rule imposed by him and widespread corruption of his party led to the formation of the Movement for Democratic Change (MDC) in September 1999. This party campaigns for an end to political oppression, but supporters risk violent attacks by Mugabe supporters.

VICTORIA FALLS
As the Zambezi River flows eastward along the border between Zambia and Zimbabwe, it drops 420 ft (128 m) down into a narrow chasm. The thick mist and loud noise produced by the waterfall can be seen and heard up to 25 miles (40 km) away. Local people call the falls *Mosi-oa-tunya* ("the smoke that thunders"), but internationally they are known as the Victoria Falls.

ECONOMIC CRISIS

A few years ago Zimbabwe had one of the most successful economies in Africa. During the Ethiopian drought in the 1980s it was the only country in the region to export food there. However political uncertainty has had a destabilizing effect on the economy and jobs have been lost in all sectors. The country no longer has regular supplies of oil, as it does not have the foreign currency required to pay for them, and this has led to gas shortages.

THE SHONA PEOPLES
The majority of Zimbabweans are Shona (or Mashona) peoples, who live in the center and east of the country. Many make a living from farming or, increasingly, work in industry. Many Shona people are Christians, but they also believe in animism, that is that natural objects such as lakes and trees have spirits. The Shona are known for their pottery and sculpture.

FARMING THE LAND

The center of Zimbabwe is rich in fertile farmland, producing tobacco and other crops for selling (commercial farming). Until recently the best land was owned white landowners, leaving the poorer areas to be farmed by 5 million blacks, who grow enough to live on (subsistence farming). Mugabe's policy of seizing land from the whites has meant many thousands of black farm workers have lost their jobs, while Mugabe supporters were given the best land.

Tobacco plant

How the land is farmed

- Commercial farming
- Subsistence farming
- Land unsuitable for farming
- Tobacco
- Cattle

Find out more

AFRICAN CITIES: *206*
PEOPLES OF AFRICA: *206–207*
RELIGION: *274–275*
TOBACCO: *52*

MOZAMBIQUE

WHEN MOZAMBIQUE BECAME independent from Portugal in 1975, its former rulers fled the country, destroying roads and machinery as they left. Years of civil war, drought, and flooding have since reduced the country to one of the poorest in the world. Mines left over from the war still litter the countryside, and few bridges remain standing. But Mozambique has the potential to overcome its disastrous recent history. The land is rich and fertile, and its mineral resources are largely untouched.

MOZAMBIQUE

Capital city: Maputo	
Area: 302,737 sq miles (801,590 sq km)	
Population: 19,700,000	
Official language: Portuguese	
Major religions: traditional beliefs 60%, Christian 30%, Muslim 10%	
Government: Provisional government	
Currency: Metical	
Adult literacy rate: 24%	
Life expectancy: 40 years	
People per doctor: 50,000	
Televisions: 5 per 1,000 people	

BEIRA
The Indian Ocean port of Beira is the second city of Mozambique, and its major port. Most of neighboring Zimbabwe's imports and exports pass through the port, using the rail, road, and pipeline links that run between Beira and the Zimbabwean capital of Harare. During the civil war, up to 10,000 Zimbabwean soldiers guarded this vital lifeline.

During the civil war, milions of refugees fled the country or left villages to find safety in the towns.

Workers taking a health-care class in Mozambique

HEALTH CARE
After independence, the Mozambique government brought all health services under national ownership and provided free health care for all. However, years of civil war have destroyed most rural hospitals and clinics, and diseases such as tuberculosis, malaria, and pneumonia continue to kill many people. Today, almost the entire population lives in poverty, and more than half relies on food aid supplied from abroad. Each year Mozambique receives millions of dollars worth of aid, mainly from European nations and the US.

Where the aid comes from

Japan: 6.5% Portugal: 7.1% Italy: 7.6% Germany: 8.5% US: 8.8%

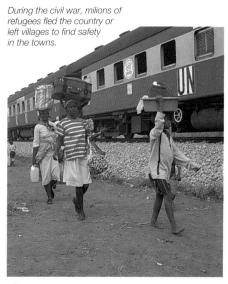

CIVIL WAR
After independence in 1975, civil war broke out between the communist Frelimo government and the Mozambique National Resistance (Renamo) rebels, supported by South Africa. The war led to the deaths of 900,000 people and to widespread starvation. Withdrawal of international support for Renamo and the decision of the Frelimo government to hold multiparty elections resulted in a peace treaty being signed between the two sides in 1992.

FARMING
More than 85 percent of Mozambique's people work on the land. Farmers grow crops such as sugar, cotton, tea, cashew nuts, and citrus fruits on the fertile coastal plains, and grow tobacco and herd cattle on the inland pastures. The seas are rich in fish, and the export of shrimp, lobster, and other seafoods provides much-needed income for the national economy.

Workers carrying bundles of sugarcane after the harvest

LOCAL MUSIC
The coastal Chopi people produce music based on the sound of the *timbila*, a type of xylophone. *Timbila* orchestras provide the music for poetic songs and elaborate *migodo* (dance suites) reflecting village life. *Timbila* music is the national music of Mozambique.

Find out more

HEALTH CARE: *276*
REFUGEES: *207*
RICH & POOR: *278–279*
SUGAR: *52*

SOUTH AFRICA

IN 1994 SOUTH AFRICA moved from minority rule by its white population to majority government under the multiracial control of the African National Congress (ANC). Since 1948, the South African government had practiced apartheid, keeping the different races apart and restricting power to white people. South Africa became isolated from the rest of the world and violence between the races grew. After the election of the ANC leader Nelson Mandela as president, the apartheid system was dismantled and South Africa has resumed full international relations.

NELSON MANDELA
Jailed in 1964 as a senior member of the ANC, Nelson Mandela (shown above with F. W. de Klerk) spent 26 years in prison until he was released in 1990. This was a result of President de Klerk's decision to legalize black freedom groups, with a view to ending apartheid. Under Nelson Mandela's leadership, the ANC won political power in 1994, and Mandela became the first black president of South Africa.

SOUTH AFRICA

Capital cities: Pretoria, Cape Town, Bloemfontein

Area: 471,443 sq miles (1,221,040 sq km)

Population: 40,400,000

Official languages: 9 African languages, English, Afrikaans

Major religions: Christian 47%, other 53%

Government: Multiparty democracy

Currency: Rand

Adult literacy rate: 85%

Life expectancy: 54 years

People per doctor: 1,695

Televisions: 125 per 1,000 people

SWAZILAND

Capital city: Mbabane

Area: 6,641 sq miles (17,200 sq km)

Population: 1,008,000

Official languages: Siswati, English

Major religions: Christian 60%, traditional beliefs 40%

Government: Absolute monarchy

Currency: Lilangeni

Adult literacy rate: 78%

Life expectancy: 47 years

People per doctor: 18,800

Televisions: 23 per 1,000 people

LESOTHO

Capital city: Maseru

Area: 11,718 sq miles (30,350 sq km)

Population: 2,200,000

Official languages: English, Sesotho

Major religions: Christian 90%, traditional beliefs 10%

Government: Military government

Currency: Loti

Adult literacy rate: 83%

Life expectancy: 48 years

People per doctor: 20,000

Televisions: 25 per 1,000 people

THE TOWNSHIPS

As part of South Africa's apartheid policies, black workers and their families were excluded from the main towns and forced to live in specially built townships a great distance from their work. The biggest and most famous of these townships is Soweto, home to more than 1 million people. Every day, black workers leave Soweto and commute for many hours on overcrowded buses and trains to work in the mines and factories of neighboring Johannesburg.

THE NDEBELE
South Africa is a multiracial country, with many different ethnic groups and 11 official languages. One group, the Ndebele, are known for their distinctive houses, which are brightly decorated in strong, geometric shapes. Women are responsible for the upkeep of the huts, and repaint the outer walls each spring.

Grapefruit

Lime *Lemon*

FRUIT GROWING
South Africa is a major exporter of food, thanks to its warm, dry climate and fertile soil. Citrus fruits, apples, and grapes are grown and then exported around the world. South Africa is also known for its fine wines.

THE GOLDEN CITY

South Africa has three capital cities, with the administration in Pretoria, the law courts in Bloemfontein, and the parliament in Cape Town. However, the financial and industrial heart of South Africa is Johannesburg (shown right), known as "the golden city." Gold mines deep beneath the surface have created enormous wealth, encouraging the development of a sprawling industrial area manufacturing cars, textiles, and high-tech and heavy engineering products.

DIGGING FOR GOLD

Over the last 100 years, the Witwatersrand gold field around Johannesburg has produced almost half the world's gold, and still accounts for more than 30 percent of the world's total output each year. Diamonds and other minerals are also mined in huge quantities, and the country has a large manufacturing industry and financial sector. As a result, South Africa has the strongest and most advanced economy in Africa. However, population growth and rising unemployment are putting the economy under pressure.

Huge underground rooms known as stoped-out areas are created by drilling and blasting the surrounding rock.

In the reduction plant, gold ore is removed from its surrounding rock.

A ventilation shaft lets air into the mine.

Tunnels lead from the main shaft to the reef – the thin, slanting layer of rock that contains the gold.

Reef

Diesel trains take the gold ore to large containers called ore skips that carry the gold up to the surface.

Ore skip

Shafts may be more than 2 miles (3 km) deep.

The main shaft takes workers and supplies down into the mine.

What the gold is used for

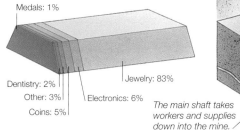

Medals: 1%
Dentistry: 2%
Other: 3%
Coins: 5%
Jewelry: 83%
Electronics: 6%

SPORTS

Under apartheid, sporting facilities were segregated and black and white players belonged to different teams. As a result, South Africa was banned from international sports competitions. With the ending of apartheid, sports became multiracial and South African teams were allowed once more to compete in world sports events. The national rugby team, the Springboks became the first team to win the Rugby World Cup twice in 1995 and 1999.

SWAZILAND

THE KINGDOM OF SWAZILAND is dominated by its powerful neighbor, South Africa, relying on it for much of its wealth and energy supplies. Swaziland's main export is sugarcane, although it also exports wood pulp, coal, and asbestos. The king of Swaziland holds great power, running its affairs as head of government and appointing many members of its parliament. His power is reflected in his title, *Ngwenyama*, meaning "lion."

The coronation of King Mswati III in 1986

LESOTHO

ENTIRELY SURROUNDED BY South Africa, the mountainous kingdom of Lesotho is the only country in Africa where all the land is above 3,300 ft (1,000 m). Its main natural resource is water. A huge hydroelectric plant currently being built will eventually supply all of Lesotho's energy needs as well as vast quantities of water for South Africa. Until then, Lesotho is economically dependent on its wealthy neighbor.

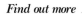

MOHAIR SPINNING

The mountainous terrain of Lesotho is ideal for rearing goats, whose mohair wool is much prized. Using foot-powered treadle wheels, women spin the mohair into yarn to make finely woven material for clothes and other products.

Find out more

AFRICAN CITIES: *206*
HYDROELECTRICITY: *108, 262*
POLITICAL SYSTEMS: *270–271*
SUGARCANE: *52*

AUSTRALASIA AND OCEANIA

THIS VAST ISLAND REGION is spread over a huge area of the Pacific Ocean to the south of Southeast Asia. Australasia is made up of Australia, New Zealand, Papua New Guinea, and several nearby islands. Australia is the only country that is also a continent in its own right, the smallest of the seven. Australasia is often linked with three groups of Pacific islands – Melanesia, Micronesia, and Polynesia – which form an even wider region, called Oceania. The climate and geography of Australasia and Oceania are as diverse as the region itself, ranging from the rain forests of northern Australia and the glaciers of southern New Zealand, to the coral atolls and volcanoes that form many of the Pacific islands.

PAPUA NEW GUINEA

Papua New Guinea is the eastern end of the island of New Guinea. The western end is Irian Jaya, part of Indonesia. Papua is a country of high mountains and thick forests. The highest peak, Mount Wilhelm, reaches 14,107 ft (4,300 m) and is often snow-capped, despite lying close to the Equator. Lower down, the climate is hot and humid, ideal for the growth of the rich, tropical rain forests that cover two-thirds of the island.

The frilled lizard lives in the deserts of the outback.

THE AUSTRALIAN OUTBACK

Australia has four major deserts – the Simpson, Gibson, Great Sandy, and Great Victoria. Together they cover most of the heart of the continent in a vast, barren area known as the outback. Very few people live in the outback, although the dry conditions are good for raising sheep and cattle.

Highest temperature:
Bourke, Australia,
128°F (53°C)

Lowest temperature:
Canberra, Australia,
-8°F (-22°C)

THINGS TO LOOK FOR ON THE MAP

Area: 3,285,048 sq miles (8,508,238 sq km)

Highest point: Mt. Wilhelm, Papua New Guinea, 14,107 ft (4,300 m) *Map F7*

Longest river: Murray-Darling, Australia, 2,376 miles (3,824 km) *Map F12*

Largest lake: L. Eyre, Australia, maximum size 3,742 sq miles (9,690 sq km) *Map E11*

Largest island: New Guinea, 304,200 sq miles (787,878 sq km) *Map E7*

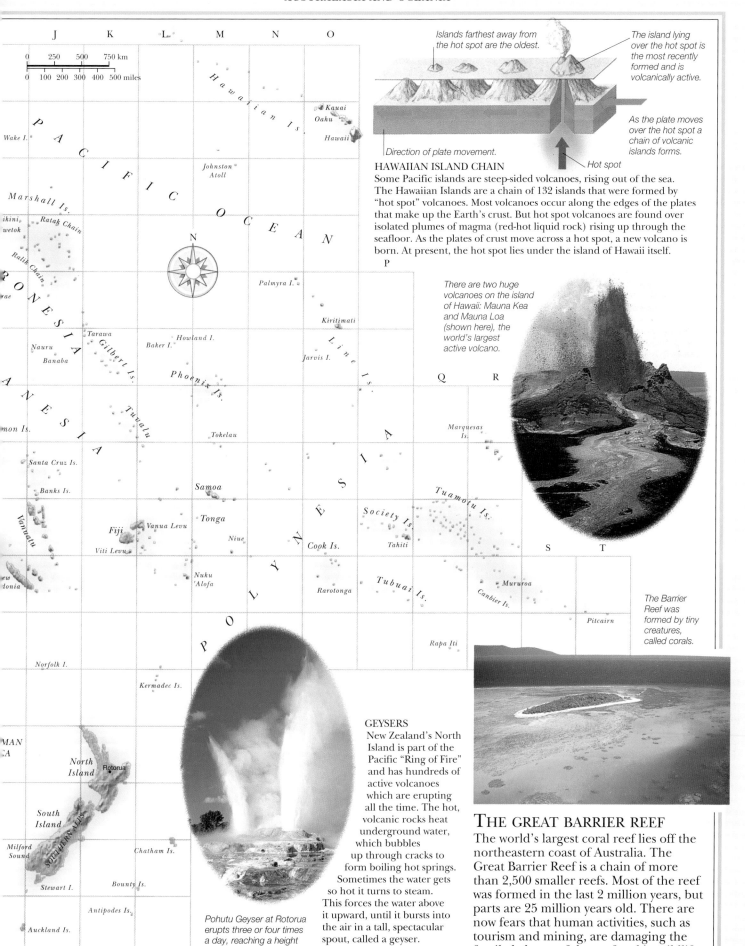

HAWAIIAN ISLAND CHAIN
Some Pacific islands are steep-sided volcanoes, rising out of the sea. The Hawaiian Islands are a chain of 132 islands that were formed by "hot spot" volcanoes. Most volcanoes occur along the edges of the plates that make up the Earth's crust. But hot spot volcanoes are found over isolated plumes of magma (red-hot liquid rock) rising up through the seafloor. As the plates of crust move across a hot spot, a new volcano is born. At present, the hot spot lies under the island of Hawaii itself.

Islands farthest away from the hot spot are the oldest.

The island lying over the hot spot is the most recently formed and is volcanically active.

Direction of plate movement.

As the plate moves over the hot spot a chain of volcanic islands forms.

Hot spot

There are two huge volcanoes on the island of Hawaii: Mauna Kea and Mauna Loa (shown here), the world's largest active volcano.

The Barrier Reef was formed by tiny creatures, called corals.

GEYSERS
New Zealand's North Island is part of the Pacific "Ring of Fire" and has hundreds of active volcanoes which are erupting all the time. The hot, volcanic rocks heat underground water, which bubbles up through cracks to form boiling hot springs. Sometimes the water gets so hot it turns to steam. This forces the water above it upward, until it bursts into the air in a tall, spectacular spout, called a geyser.

Pohutu Geyser at Rotorua erupts three or four times a day, reaching a height of about 98 ft (30 m).

THE GREAT BARRIER REEF
The world's largest coral reef lies off the northeastern coast of Australia. The Great Barrier Reef is a chain of more than 2,500 smaller reefs. Most of the reef was formed in the last 2 million years, but parts are 25 million years old. There are now fears that human activities, such as tourism and mining, are damaging the fragile balance of the reef and its wildlife.

PEOPLES OF AUSTRALASIA AND OCEANIA

ISOLATED FROM THE REST OF THE WORLD, parts of this region were among the last places on Earth to be settled. The first inhabitants came from Asia, and include the Aboriginals of Australia, the Maoris of New Zealand, and the peoples of the Pacific Islands. In the 18th century, settlers started to arrive from Europe, and both Australia and New Zealand became British colonies. Many Pacific Islands were European colonies. Today, links with the European colonizers are no longer so strong. In recent decades, people have migrated to Australia and New Zealand from the Middle East and Southeast Asia, and both countries now have multicultural societies and successful modern economies.

About 60 percent of Australians live in or near the country's five biggest cities – Sydney (shown here), Melbourne, Brisbane, Perth, and Adelaide.

Population density chart

UK: 630 (243)

Samoa: 165 (64)

World: 106 (41)

New Zealand: 38 (15)

Australia: 6 (2)

The figures show the number of people per sq mile, with per sq km in brackets.

POPULATION DENSITY

With a population density of only six people per sq mile (two per sq km), Australia is the most sparsely populated continent. Most Australians live in the cities around the coasts, away from the harsh climate of the interior. Many of the Pacific Islands are more densely populated, as relatively large numbers of people live on very small areas of land.

Population: approximately 29,700,000 people

Number of countries: 14

Smallest country: Nauru, 8 sq miles (21 sq km)

Most densely populated country: Nauru, 1,461 people per sq mile (564 per sq km)

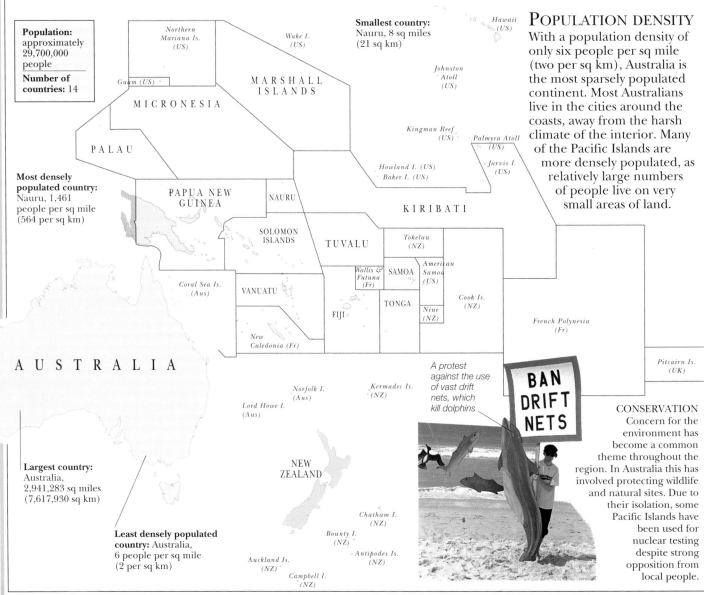

Midway Is. (US)

Hawaii (US)

Northern Mariana Is. (US)

Wake I. (US)

Johnston Atoll (US)

Guam (US)

MARSHALL ISLANDS

MICRONESIA

Kingman Reef (US)

Palmyra Atoll (US)

PALAU

Jarvis I. (US)

PAPUA NEW GUINEA

NAURU

Howland I. (US)
Baker I. (US)

KIRIBATI

SOLOMON ISLANDS

TUVALU

Tokelau (NZ)

Coral Sea Is. (Aus)

Wallis & Futuna (Fr)

SAMOA

American Samoa (US)

VANUATU

TONGA

Cook Is. (NZ)

FIJI

Niue (NZ)

New Caledonia (Fr)

French Polynesia (Fr)

Pitcairn Is. (UK)

AUSTRALIA

Norfolk I. (Aus)

Kermadec Is. (NZ)

Lord Howe I. (Aus)

A protest against the use of vast drift nets, which kill dolphins

BAN DRIFT NETS

NEW ZEALAND

Largest country: Australia, 2,941,283 sq miles (7,617,930 sq km)

Chatham I. (NZ)

Bounty I. (NZ)

Least densely populated country: Australia, 6 people per sq mile (2 per sq km)

Auckland Is. (NZ)

Campbell I. (NZ)

Antipodes Is. (NZ)

CONSERVATION Concern for the environment has become a common theme throughout the region. In Australia this has involved protecting wildlife and natural sites. Due to their isolation, some Pacific Islands have been used for nuclear testing despite strong opposition from local people.

Key to arrows

→ 50,000–70,000 years ago
→ 5,000–1,000BC
→ AD100–200
→ AD700–950

Early peoples sailed from New Guinea to the nearest islands, known as Melanesia. Over the next few thousand years they settled other islands. To the north they arrived in the region known today as Micronesia.

The early settlers sailed in outrigger canoes. Today, similar canoes are still used by islanders for fishing.

NEW GUINEA

Toward Hawaii

EARLY SETTLERS

The first settlers were the Aboriginals, who arrived in Australia between 50,000 and 70,000 years ago, when the continent was still connected by a land bridge to New Guinea. The inhabitants of the Pacific Islands arrived next, when, about 7,000 years ago, people from Southeast Asia began to settle the islands. Parts of this region have been settled for little more than 1,000 years – the Maoris, for example, arrived in New Zealand in about AD 950.

AUSTRALIA

Toward Easter Island

The Maoris sailed to New Zealand around AD 950.

NEW ZEALAND

Australia's history as a British colony is reflected in its flag, which features the British flag, the Commonwealth Star, and the Southern Cross constellation.

AUSTRALIA'S EXPORT MARKETS	
1 Japan	19% of exports
2 US	10% of exports
3 South Korea	7% of exports
4 New Zealand	7% of exports
5 Taiwan	5% of exports

TRADING PARTNERS

Traditionally the UK was the main trading partner for both Australia and New Zealand. However, since the UK joined the European Union in 1973, Australia and New Zealand have had to look for new export markets. Both countries are now concentrating on the growing Asian market. In 1960, Asia accounted for only 25 percent of Australia's exports. Today over 40 percent of Australia's trade is with Asia, and Japan is its most important market.

POPULATION TODAY

As a legacy of their colonial past, most people in New Zealand and Australia today are of British descent. In the last few decades, however, new settlers have arrived in the region from throughout the world. For more than two million Australians, English is not their first language. The various groups of migrants have brought their own customs, traditions, festivals, and food, making Australia and New Zealand multicultural societies.

Today, Aboriginals make up between one and two percent of Australia's population.

The England-Australia Test Matches are played every four years.

SPORTS

In both Australia and New Zealand, sports have played an important role in creating a sense of national identity. Rugby is the national sport of New Zealand, while Australia's main sports are Australian rules football, rugby and cricket. Success in these sports is a great source of national pride.

ABORIGINAL RIGHTS

For many years, Aboriginal children in Australia and Maoris in New Zealand were taught only in English and were discouraged from learning their own languages. Today the situation is very different. The Maori language is officially recognized in New Zealand, and in Australia schoolchildren learn about Aboriginal culture and traditions. But many people feel that the future also depends on reclaiming the land and resources taken from the original peoples when European settlers first arrived.

AUSTRALIA AND PAPUA NEW GUINEA

SURROUNDED BY THE INDIAN and Pacific Oceans, Australia is the world's smallest continent. It is vast, nearly the size of the United States of America, and very dry. There is little rain, and arid desert stretches across about two-thirds of the land. Most of the people live in the big cities along the coasts. To the north, only 93 miles (150 km) across the Torres Strait, lies Papua New Guinea. An Australian colony until 1975, it consists of the eastern end of the island of New Guinea and more than 600 surrounding islands.

Raggiana's bird of paradise – two-thirds of all birds of paradise live in the forests of Papua New Guinea.

ISLAND OF MOUNTAINS AND FORESTS

Papua New Guinea lies entirely in the tropics and has a hot, wet climate. Running from west to east along the island is a range of high rugged mountains covered with dense rain forest. These remote forests are home to a vast range of plants and animals, many of which are found nowhere else in the world. Mangrove swamps grow along many of the island's coasts.

When rains do come, there are flash floods, and plants like this Sturt's Desert Pea flower from seeds that have lain dormant for years.

THE OUTBACK

Most of Australia is a flat plain without mountains, forests, or rivers. The huge central region, known as the outback, is one of the hottest and driest places on Earth. It has sandy or stony deserts, which can be baked by intense heat during the day and frozen by extreme cold at night. In places where there is some vegetation, or the land has been irrigated, farmers raise cattle and sheep.

ULURU

This massive block of sandstone stands almost in the middle of Australia. It measures 5.8 miles (9.4 km) around the base, and rises to 1,142 ft (348 m). To the Aboriginals, the first people of Australia, the rock is known as Uluru. It is a sacred site and features in their beliefs about the creation of the world. Once called Ayers Rock after a former premier of South Australia, the rock regained its Aboriginal name in 1985.

GREAT BARRIER REEF

The Great Barrier Reef, the largest living thing on Earth, stretches for 1,243 miles (2,000 km) along the northeastern coast of Australia. It is the world's largest coral reef and home to more than 2,000 species of fish. Its coral is made of layer upon layer of tiny anemonelike creatures called polyps. The Great Barrier Reef is a major tourist attraction, but swimmers and divers can easily pollute and damage it. To protect it, the reef has been made a World Heritage Area.

EQUATOR

TROPIC OF CAPRICORN

AUSTRALIA

INDIAN OCEAN

Broome

GREAT SANDY DESERT

North West C.

Port Hedland
Dampier

HAMERSLEY RANGE
Ashburton

L. Disappoin

L. Macleod

Carnarvon
Shark Bay

A

Murchison

U

WESTER
GIBSON DESERT

L. Carnegie
Meekatharra

AUSTRAL
Mount Magnet
GRE

Geraldton

L. Moore   L. Barlee

Kalgoorlie

PERTH
Fremantle
Rockingham

Bunbury
Augusta

Esperance

C. Leeuwin

Albany

Perth, Australia
Jan 74°F (23°C)
July 55.5°F (13°C)
Jan 0.3 in (8 mm)
July 6.7 in (170 mm)

THINGS TO LOOK FOR ON THE MAP

Longest river: Murray-Darling, Australia, 2,376 miles (3,824 km) *Map I10, K9*

Highest point: Mt. Wilhelm, Papua New Guinea 14,107 ft (4,300 m) *Map K2*

Largest lake: L. Eyre, Australia, maximum size 3,742 sq miles (9,690 sq km) *Map I9*

A   B   C   D

PAPUA NEW GUINEA

FEWER THAN FIVE MILLION PEOPLE live in Papua New Guinea, most of them in small, isolated villages. By western standards, many people are poor. Papua is rich in natural resources, especially minerals, such as copper and gold. The island of Bougainville now looks after its own affairs after a long war ended in 2001. Timber from the rain forests is another major export. The challenge is to develop these resources without damaging the environment.

PAPUA NEW GUINEA

Capital city: Port Moresby

Area: 174,849 sq miles (452,860 sq km)

Population: 4,800,000

Official language: English

Major religions: Christian 62%, traditional beliefs 34%, other 4%

Government: Multiparty democracy

Currency: Kina

Adult literacy rate: 64%

Life expectancy: 56 years

People per doctor: 10,000

Televisions: 24 per 1,000 people

Port Moresby, Papua New Guinea

☀ Jan 82.5°F (28°C)
July 78°F (25.5°C)

🌧 Jan 7 in (178 mm)
July 1.1 in (28 mm)

PAPUA NEW GUINEA

Alice Springs, Australia

☀ Jan 83.5°F (28.5°C)
July 53°F (11.5°C)

🌧 Jan 1.7 in (43 mm)
July 0.3 in (8 mm)

0 100 200 300 400 500 km
0 100 200 300 miles

Sydney, Australia

☀ Jan 71.5°F (22°C)
July 53°F (12°C)

🌧 Jan 3.5 in (89 mm)
July 4.6 in (117 mm)

BIG BUTTERFLY
Queen Alexandra's Birdwing butterfly, with a wingspan of 10 in (25 cm), is the world's largest butterfly.

Tribespeople from Mendi, wearing headdresses made from bird of paradise feathers

TRIBAL PEOPLE

The mountains and forests of Papua New Guinea have always restricted contact between the various groups of people who live there. As a result, the country is now home to about 1,000 tribes speaking more than 700 different languages. Most of these people live off the land they farm.

PORT MORESBY
The capital, Port Moresby, is a sprawling city built around a natural harbor on the island's southern coast. Unlike the rest of the country, it is dry for much of the year. Port Moresby has grown rapidly in recent years, as people from remote regions have moved there to find work.

AUSTRALIA

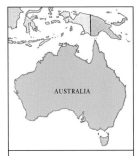

UNTIL ABOUT 200 YEARS AGO, the land that is now Australia was occupied only by Aboriginals. Then, in 1770, the British explorer James Cook arrived in Botany Bay and claimed it for Britain. In 1901, Australia became an independent commonwealth. Over the years, settlers from overseas, first from Britain and Europe, but more recently from Asia, have shaped the culture of this huge country. Wool and wheat, as well as mineral resources of iron ore, coal, and copper, have made Australia wealthy, and most people benefit from a high standard of living.

SETTLERS
In the 18th century, British prisons were overcrowded and criminals were often sent overseas. In 1778 the first ship to Australia arrived from Britain with 757 convicts, forming a settlement in what is now Sydney. By 1860 more than 160,000 convicts had been transported.

AUSTRALIA

Capital city: Canberra

Area: 2,941,283 sq miles (7,617,930 sq km)

Population: 18,900,000

Official language: English

Major religion: Christian 64%, other 36%

Government: Multiparty democracy

Currency: Australian dollar

Adult literacy rate: 99%

Life expectancy: 79 years

People per doctor: 455

Televisions: 639 per 1,000 people

LIVING ON THE COAST

About 85 percent of Australians live in or around cities along the coast. Most of the schools, hospitals, offices, and factories are located there, and life is easier than in the remote towns and farms of the outback. Homes in the city are built of wood or brick, often with verandas or "sleepouts," as well as a backyard for a barbecue. The five largest cities contain 60 percent of the population. One of these is Sydney, shown left, with its Opera House overlooking the harbor.

ABORIGINAL BELIEFS

The word Aboriginal means "from the beginning," and Aboriginals believe they have occupied Australia since the beginning of time. They have a detailed knowledge of the land; women gathered fruits, nuts, and grubs, and men hunted animals such as kangaroos and possums. The Dreamtime, long ago when the land and all living things were made, is the basis of Aboriginal culture.

MAIN CITIES BY POPULATION	
Sydney	3,986,700
Melbourne	3,371,300
Brisbane	1,574,600
Perth	1,341,900
Adelaide	1,088,400

Aboriginals act out their beliefs in their songs, ceremonies, and art. This group is from Queensland.

People in Sydney demonstrate for land rights. On the Aboriginal flag, black represents the people, yellow the Sun, and red the land.

VAST DISTANCES
Away from the coasts, much of Australia is dry and hot, with very few towns or settlements. Alice Springs, in the center of the country, began as a station linking the telegraph line between Darwin and Adelaide. Separated by such large distances, many children cannot get to schools. They study through the special School of the Air learning program.

The journey from Darwin to Sydney, via Adelaide, is 2,996 miles (4,822 km). This would take about 2.5 days and nights of nonstop driving.

LAND RIGHTS
The arrival of the British changed life for the Aboriginals. Many lost their land and thousands died of European diseases. Today, they no longer live off the land in the traditional way, but work in factories or farms. Many suffer poor health and bad housing. In 1967, they were granted the right to vote. Since then a series of laws have given Aboriginals control over some of the land.

Major roads
Route shown below

| Darwin | Uluru (Ayers Rock) | Alice Springs | Lake Eyre | Adelaide | Sydney |

Darwin to Alice Springs 937 miles (1,508 km)

Alice Springs to Adelaide 950 miles (1,529 km)

Adelaide to Sydney 1,109 miles (1,785 km)

SHEEP FARMING

Australia is the world's chief wool-producing country, with New South Wales the leading area. Most of Australia's sheep are Merinos, which were brought from South Africa and England in the 1790s. Today, there are about 120 million sheep in Australia, most of them on farms called stations. Some stations are huge, and cover up to 5,792 sq miles (15,000 sq km), which is half the size of Belgium. Motorcycles and four-wheel-drive vehicles are used to control the livestock over such wide areas.

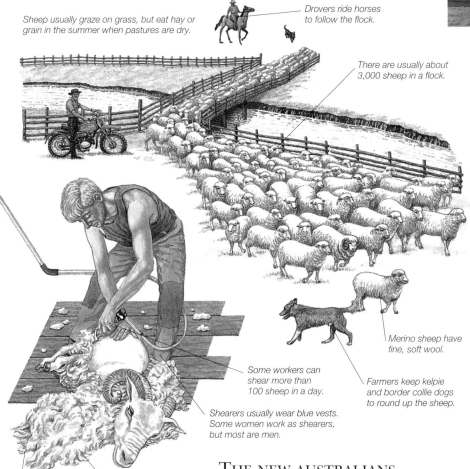

Sheep usually graze on grass, but eat hay or grain in the summer when pastures are dry.

Drovers ride horses to follow the flock.

There are usually about 3,000 sheep in a flock.

Some workers can shear more than 100 sheep in a day.

Merino sheep have fine, soft wool.

Shearers usually wear blue vests. Some women work as shearers, but most are men.

Farmers keep kelpie and border collie dogs to round up the sheep.

Merino sheep can survive the heat and still produce a heavy fleece of good wool.

Wool is graded and stored in bins.

RICHES FROM THE EARTH

In the 1850s, the discovery of gold in Victoria and New South Wales attracted people to Australia and helped boost the economy. Today, mining for coal, copper, and iron ore, shown above, is still big business. Australia is the world's largest coal exporter and also has the world's most productive diamond mine, near Lake Argyle. However, modern mining relies more on machinery than on labor, and does not employ many people.

LOOKING EAST

For many years, Australia traded mainly with Britain. However, since Britain joined the European Union in 1973, Australia has strengthened its trading links with the United States as well as with countries that are closer, such as Japan. Today, many foreign companies, such as car manufacturers and computer businesses, have set up factories in Australia.

THE NEW AUSTRALIANS

For many years, Australia allowed only white people to settle; mostly people from Britain, Italy, and Greece. In 1972, this policy was changed, and since then immigrants have arrived from all over the world. The "New Australians" include Vietnamese, Japanese, and Chinese. These groups have brought their own languages, festivals, and types of food.

Many Italians moved to Australia after World War II.

Many Australians have relatives in Britain.

This boy has parents who came from Vietnam.

Many Greek people live in the city of Melbourne.

This girl has parents who came from China.

In Australian Rules football, players can kick or punch the ball, but they must not throw it.

SPORTING LIFE

Australians love the outdoors, and sports are a major part of their lifestyle. Sandy beaches, warm water, and good surf make swimming, sailing, waterskiing, and surfing extremely popular. Australians are also experts at cricket, tennis, and their own brand of football, called Australian Rules. In the year 2000, Sydney hosted the Olympic Games.

NEW ZEALAND

SITUATED ABOUT 932 MILES (1,500 KM) from Australia, New Zealand consists of two large islands – North and South Island – and several smaller ones. The North Island has a warm, mild climate and is volcanically active. The South Island is colder, with glaciers, high mountain peaks, and forests. From 1840 to 1907 New Zealand was a British colony, but it gained full independence in 1947. The original inhabitants, the Maoris, still make up about 12 percent of the population. New Zealand is a wealthy and progressive country, and was the first in the world to give women the right to vote.

PEOPLE AND CITIES
There are only about 3.9 million people in New Zealand – just over half the population of London or Paris. Nearly three-quarters of New Zealanders live on the North Island, and most of them live in the cities. Wellington, shown here, is New Zealand's capital city.

NEW ZEALAND

Capital city: Wellington	
Area: 103,733 sq miles (268,670 sq km)	
Population: 3,900,000	
Official language: English	
Major religions: Christian 62%, other 38%	
Government: Multiparty democracy	
Currency: New Zealand dollar	
Adult literacy rate: 99%	
Life expectancy: 77 years	
People per doctor: 476	
Televisions: 508 per 1,000 people	

FARMING
Large areas of grass and a warm, damp climate make New Zealand ideal for farming, especially raising sheep and cattle. There are around 45 million sheep (about 12 for every one person)and 9 million cattle. Around half of New Zealand's exports are agricultural products. The country is one of the world's leading exporters of wool, frozen meat, and dairy products, such as butter and cheese.

ENERGY
More than 60 percent of New Zealand's electricity comes from hydroelectric plants, like the Clyde Dam on the South Island, which harness the power of its rushing rivers. New Zealand does not use nuclear power. This, together with its small population and lack of heavy industry, make it one of the world's least polluted countries. New Zealand is very proud of its "clean green" image.

Auckland, North Island
Jan 66.5°F (19.5°C)
July 51°F (10.5°C)
Jan 3.1 in (79 mm)
July 5.7 in (145 mm)

Great Exhibition Bay
Waipapakauri
Waitangi
Whangarei
Kaipara Harbour
Great Barrier I.
Auckland
Coromandel
Thames
Bay of Plenty
Waikato
Tauranga
Hamilton
Roturua
L. Taupo
Taupo
Gisborne
New Plymouth
NORTH ISLAND
Napier
Hawke Bay
Wanganui
Hastings
Palmerston North
Cook Strait
Levin
Tasman Bay
Masterton
Nelson
Picton
WELLINGTON
Blenheim
Westport
Waiau
NEW ZEALAND
Greymouth
Kaikoura
Hurunui
SOUTHERN ALPS
Pegasus Bay
Mt. Cook
Rakaia
Christchurch
Timaru
Waitaki
Canterbury Bight
Milford Sound
Taieri
L. Te Anau
Queenstown
L. Wakatipu
SOUTH ISLAND
Dunedin
Invercargill
Foveaux Strait
Stewart I.
TASMAN SEA
PACIFIC OCEAN

EQUATOR
TROPIC OF CAPRICORN

NEW ZEALAND

N

| 0 | 50 | 100 | 150 km |
| 0 | 50 | | 100 miles |

Dunedin, South Island
Jan 58°F (14.5°C)
July 3.1°F (6°C)
Jan 3.4 in (86 mm)
July 3.1 in (79 mm)

THINGS TO LOOK FOR ON THE MAP

Longest river: Waikato, North Island, 264 miles (425 km) *Map F4*

Highest point: Mt. Cook, South Island, 12,316 ft (3,754 m) *Map C9*

Largest lake: L. Taupo, North Island, 234 sq miles (606 sq km) *Map G5*

THE FIRST NEW ZEALANDERS

New Zealand was one of the last places on Earth to be inhabited by people. The first settlers, the Maori, arrived from Polynesia in about AD950. Today, although most Maoris have adopted western lifestyles, their culture lives on in their language, art, and extended family groups. Maoris are represented in the government, and there are moves to ensure that they receive equal opportunities in health, education, and employment, which have been lacking in the past.

MAORI ART
This neck pendant represents Tiki, one of the Maori gods, and is worn to bring good luck. It is carved from greenstone, a kind of hard jade found on the South Island.

OUTDOOR LIFE
New Zealand's pleasant climate and beautiful countryside make it ideal for outdoor activities. New Zealanders enjoy sports of all kinds, from hiking and mountain climbing to canoeing, yachting, and rugby. The country's rugby team, the All Blacks, are shown in action above. Many tourists visit New Zealand for its outdoor lifestyle, and tourism is now a major source of income.

KIWI FRUIT

The Chinese gooseberry was introduced into New Zealand in about 1900 and was later renamed the kiwi fruit after the country's famous bird. New Zealand is now the world's principal producer and exports kiwi fruit worldwide. This subtropical fruit needs a warm, sunny climate. It is grown in special orchards divided into sections by fences or hedges.

The orchards are divided into sections about 492 ft x 131 ft (150 m x 40 m).

Home of the orchard manager.

Strong supports hold the vines steady while the kiwi fruit grows.

Tall trees, or hedges, protect the vines from gusts of wind.

Pickers, wearing gloves to protect the fruit, pluck the kiwi fruit from the branch.

The fruit is placed in a special apron while the picker moves along the rows.

The kiwi fruit has a fuzzy, greenish-brown skin a little like the feathers of the bird after which it is named.

Pickers sort the fruit by size, then pack it in boxes.

ORCHARD FRUITS

Because New Zealand lies in the southern hemisphere, it can grow crops when its customers in the north are in the middle of their winter. The main types of fruit, with examples from each group shown below, are pip fruit (apple), berry fruit (strawberry), stone fruit (peach), citrus fruit (orange), and subtropical fruit (tamarillo).

Orange

Apple

Strawberry

Peach

Tamarillo

FLIGHTLESS BIRDS

New Zealand's isolated position has allowed many unique plants and animals to develop there. The most famous are the flightless birds, such as the kakapo and kiwi. These birds lost the ability to fly because they had no enemies and did not need to be able to fly away.

The long-beaked kiwi is New Zealand's national emblem.

The rare kakapo, or owl parrot, nests under tree roots.

Find out more

HYDROELECTRICITY: *108*
SETTLING PACIFIC ISLANDS: *257*
SHEEP FARMING: *261*
VOLCANIC ACTIVITY: *13, 255*

THE PACIFIC OCEAN

MICRONESIA
Capital city: Kolonia
Area: 271 sq miles (702 sq km)
Population: 133,144

NAURU
Capital city: None
Area: 8.2 sq miles (21.2 sq km)
Population: 18,845

PALAU
Capital city: Koro
Area: 196 sq miles (508 sq km)
Population: 18,766

SOLOMON ISLANDS
Capital city: Honiara
Area: 11,158 sq miles (289,000 sq km)
Population: 300,000

VANUATU
Capital city: Port-Vila
Area: 4,707 sq miles (12,190 sq km)
Population: 200,000

FIJI
Capital city: Suva
Area: 7,054 sq miles (18,270 sq km)
Population: 817,000

TUVALU
Capital city: Fingafale
Area: 10 sq miles (26 sq km)
Population: 10,838

TONGA
Capital city: Nuku'alofa
Area: 278 sq miles (720 sq km)
Population: 102,231

SAMOA
Capital city: Apia
Area: 1,093 sq miles (2,830 sq km)
Population: 180,000

KIRIBATI
Capital city: Bairiki
Area: 274 sq miles (710 sq km)
Population: 91,985

MARSHALL ISLANDS
Capital city: Majuro
Area: 70 sq miles (181 sq km)
Population: 68,126

THE WORLD'S LARGEST, DEEPEST OCEAN, the Pacific covers one-third of the Earth's surface, stretching from the shores of Asia and Australia to America and Antarctica. About 20,000 volcanic and coral islands lie scattered over its vast expanse, many covered with lush vegetation. Over much of the Pacific the climate is hot and moist. The native island peoples, who originally came from southeast Asia, fall into three main groups: Polynesians, Melanesians, and Micronesians. Europeans began to arrive in the 1500s, and by the 1800s many islands were colonies of powerful countries overseas. Today, some of the islands are self-governing; in others foreign control is still strong.

Coconut palms provide the islanders with food, milk, and fiber to make rope.

Large families of 10 or more live together under one roof.

PACIFIC PEOPLES
Some islanders live in towns, but many people continue the traditional farming way of life, growing crops such as yams and sweet potatoes, or fishing from the sea. The shape of homes varies from island to island but most, like this Fijian *bure*, are simply built using a large wooden frame topped with a thatch of plant fronds. Today, corrugated iron is often used as roofing because it lasts longer than thatch. Community life on the islands is important, with large extended families ruled by tribal chiefs. Property and personal objects belong to everybody.

People often keep chickens and pigs.

Men wear a cloth skirt called a sulu.

A special meal might include fish, chicken, yams, vegetables, coconut, and bananas.

Boys learn to weave using green coconut leaves.

This area of the house is used for guests.

The green fruit of the black pepper plant is dried to make black peppercorns.

Ground pepper

EXPORTS
Rich, volcanic soil and regular rainfall make these hot, sunny islands especially fertile. Some farmers produce surplus crops that they export. Sugar, ginger, black pepper, and copra (dried coconut) are among the main export crops. Fish, timber, livestock, and minerals are also important sources of income on certain islands.

THE EFFECT OF TOURISM
Many of the "island paradises" are fast becoming major tourist destinations – especially around Fiji, Tonga, and Samoa. Tourism brings in valuable income, but it can also damage the environment and affect the life of local people. For example, already limited water supplies may be diverted away from villages to hotel pools and showers.

NUCLEAR TESTING
Since the first experiments at Bikini Atoll in 1946, the US, Britain, and France have used the Pacific to test nuclear weapons. The islanders and groups such as Greenpeace campaigned to stop the testing. France carried out the last explosions in 1996. A treaty banning tests was signed in 1998, but some islands are still not safe to live on due to high radiation levels.

B C D E F G H I J K L

Marshall Islands
- ☀ Jan 81°F (27°C)
  July 83°F (28°C)
- ☁ Jan 2.1 in (53 mm)
  July 8.4 in (213 mm)

NAURU

ARCTIC OCEAN

ASIA

SEA OF OKHOTSK

Bering Strait

BERING SEA

SEA OF JAPAN

Gulf of Alaska

Aleutian Is.

NORTH AMERICA

International Date Line

Kurile Islands

Vancouver

Shanghai

EAST CHINA SEA

●TOKYO

San Francisco

Canton

Hong Kong

Emperor Seamounts

PHILIPPINE SEA

Guam (USA)

●MANILA

SOUTH EAST ASIA

PALAU

Mariana Trench

Northern Mariana Is. (USA)

Wake I. (USA)

Enewetak

Bikini

Kwajalein

MARSHALL ISLANDS

Mid-Pacific Seamounts

Midway Is. (USA)

Hawaiian Islands

Honolulu

PACIFIC

Johnston Atoll (USA)

Kingman Reef (USA)

Palmyra Atoll (USA)

Howland I. (USA)

Baker I. (USA)

Islas Revillagigedo (Mexico)

CENTRAL AMERICA

Clipperton I. (France)

●PANAMA CITY

MICRONESIA

FEDERATED STATES OF MICRONESIA

Gilbert Is.

NAURU

Phoenix Is.

KIRIBATI

Line Islands

Galápagos Is. (Ecuador)

Cocos Ridge

OCEAN

MELANESIA

TUVALU

New Guinea

CORAL SEA

SOLOMON ISLANDS

SAMOA

Tokelau (N.Z.)

American Samoa (USA)

Cook Is.

Marquesas Is.

French Polynesia (France)

East Pacific Rise

●LIMA

SOUTH AMERICA

ARAFURA SEA

VANUATU

Wallis and Futuna (Fr.)

Niue

Tahiti

Society Is.

Isla San Félix (Chile)

Isla San Ambrosio (Chile)

New Caledonia (France)

FIJI

TONGA

POLYNESIA

Muroroa Atoll

Pitcairn Is. (UK)

Easter I. (Chile)

Islas Juan Fernández (Chile)

AUSTRALIA

Coral Sea Is. (Aus.)

Brisbane

Norfolk I. (Aus.)

Kermadec Is. (N.Z.)

SANTIAGO

Sydney

●CANBERRA

Lord Howe I. (Aus.)

Chiloé I.

PALAU

TASMAN SEA

NEW ZEALAND

●WELLINGTON

Chatham Is.

Bounty Is.

C. Horn

SOLOMON ISLANDS

Auckland Is.

Antipodes Is.

Pacific Antarctic Ridge

VANUATU FIJI

Campbell I.

Macquarie I. (Aus.)

Fiji
- ☀ Jan 80°F (26°C)
  July 74°F (23°C)
- ☁ Jan 11.4 in (290 mm)
  July 4.9 in (125 mm)

SOUTHERN OCEAN

ANTARCTICA

MARSHALL ISLANDS

KIRIBATI

Scale:
0 500 1000 1500 2000 km
0 250 500 750 1000 1250 miles

N

TUVALU

TONGA

WESTERN SAMOA

Giant tortoise found only on the Galápagos Islands

GALÁPAGOS ISLANDS

When British naturalist Charles Darwin (1809-1882) went to the Galápagos Islands, off the west coast of South America, he found many unusual creatures, including giant tortoises. He also noticed differences between animals of the same kind living on different islands. This led him to believe that, over many generations, animals change, or evolve, to suit their habitat.

As a person travels west, he or she moves into different time zones, losing one hour for every 15° traveled around the Earth.

At the International Date Line, where the date changes, you lose or gain a day, depending on which way you are traveling.

Since 1884, time has been measured from Greenwich, in Britain. Originally known as Greenwich Mean Time (GMT), it is now referred to as Universal Time.

180° 12 +11 +10
-10 -11 +9
-9 +8
-8 +7
90° 90°
-7 +6
-6 +5
-5 +4
-4 +3
-3 +2
-2 +1
0°
GMT

As a person travels east, he or she moves into different time zones, gaining one hour for every 15° traveled around the Earth.

INTERNATIONAL DATE LINE

The world is divided into 24 imaginary time zones, shown left, and the time of day changes by one hour from one zone to the next. At a halfway point – the International Date Line – the date changes. The line dissects the Pacific Ocean, although in some places it winds its way between the islands – life would be difficult if it was two different days on one island.

THE ARCTIC

THE MOST NORTHERLY CONSTELLATION of stars, Arktos, or the Great Bear, gives its name to the icy ocean beneath it, which surrounds the North Pole. One of the coldest places on Earth, the Arctic Ocean is bordered by the northernmost parts of Europe, Asia, and North America, including Greenland, the world's largest island. Most of the Arctic Ocean is covered by ice, although warmer currents from the Atlantic and Pacific flow northward into it, warming the sea and air and clearing ice from the coasts in summer. Few people live in the Arctic, although the region is rich in minerals and wildlife.

CLIMATE

During the long winter months, the Sun never rises over the horizon, and temperatures drop as low as -94°F (-70°C). In the summer, the Sun never sets, bathing the region in constant daylight and raising temperatures considerably. This is because the Earth rotates at an angle to the Sun, plunging the Arctic from total light to total darkness as the North Pole moves toward and away from the Sun. The dark polar skies are lit by the Aurora, wispy curtains of red and green light caused by electricity in the upper atmosphere.

The polar bear is well adapted to Arctic life. It has acute senses, runs fast, swims well, and is camouflaged against the snow and ice by its white fur. Polar bears feed on seals and other animals, ranging far across the ice in search of prey.

Arctic terns breed in large colonies during the Arctic summer. When winter comes, they fly halfway around the world to take advantage of the daylight and rich food supply of the Antarctic summer.

NATURAL RESOURCES

The lands that surround the Arctic Ocean are rich in minerals. Vast oil and gas reserves lie under Alaska, while Norwegian and Russian companies are mining coal on the island of Svalbard (shown here). Smaller quantities of gold, iron, silver, tin, and other minerals are found throughout the region. Extracting these resources is expensive, but as supplies elsewhere begin to run out, oil and mining companies are turning their attention to the untapped wealth of the Arctic region.

ARCTIC WILDLIFE

The Arctic Ocean teems with wildlife. Seals, walrus, and many species of whales thrive in the icy water, protected from the cold by layers of thick blubber beneath their skins. On land, reindeer, musk ox, hares, foxes, and wolves scavenge for food, migrating south to avoid the worst of the winter. In the brief summer hardy plants bloom, providing food for millions of insects. Birds such as the Arctic tern and Brent goose take advantage of this insect food supply to breed and raise their young.

PEOPLE OF THE ARCTIC

The cold, inhospitable Arctic region is home to few people. The Sami of northern Scandinavia, the Yugyts and Nenets of Siberia, and the Inuit of Canada have traditionally survived by hunting and trapping wild animals. Large herds of reindeer provide them with all their basic needs, such as food, clothing, tents, tools, and items to trade. Some native peoples still follow this nomadic lifestyle, but most now live in settled communities, like this one at Iqaluit in Canada.

Traditional Inuit clothing is often lined with fur to keep out the cold.

TRAVEL IN THE ARCTIC

Travel on land has always been difficult in the Arctic. In the winter, thick snow covers the ground, while the summer thaw turns much of the land into a boggy marsh. Snowshoes and skis stop people from sinking into the soft snow, while boots with rough or spiky soles grip well on icy ground. In the past, teams of huskies pulled sleds with supplies over great distances, but now the dogs have largely been replaced by snowmobiles. These small, motorized sleds on skis are easy to maneuver and can pull very heavy loads.

A B C D E F G H I J K L

1 Cape Deshnev
KEY
• Research stations

CHUKCHI SEA
RUSSIAN FEDERATION

2 ALASKA (US)
Wrangel
Wrangel I. (Russian Fed.)
Pevek
Ambarchik
EAST SIBERIAN SEA
Barrow
Prudhoe Bay
BEAUFORT SEA

THINGS TO LOOK FOR ON THE MAP

Highest point: Mt. Gunnbjørn, Greenland 12,139 ft (3,700 m) *Map D9*

Most northerly land on Earth: Oodaaq Island, *Map F7*

Lowest temperature in the Arctic: -94°F (-70°C) recorded at Nord station, Greenland *Map F7*

North Pole: *Map F5*

3 Approximate Limit of Permanent Pack Ice
New Siberian Is. (Russian Fed.)
Tiksi
Kotelniy
C. Kellett

Barrow, Alaska
☀ Jan -15.5°F (-26.5°C)
July 39.5°F (4.5°C)
❄ Jan 0.2 in (5 mm)
July 0.9 in (23 mm)

4 Banks I. (Canada)
Prince Patrick I. (Canada)
Mould Bay
Melville I. (Canada)
CANADA
ARCTIC OCEAN
LAPTEV SEA
Nordvik
TAYMYR PENINSULA

0 250 500 750 km
0 100 200 300 400 500 miles

5 Resolute
Queen Elizabeth Is. (Canada)
Axel Heiberg I. (Canada)
North Pole
Approximate Limit of Permanent Pack Ice
Cape Chelyuskin
Severnaya Zemlya (Russian Fed.)
Mys Arktiskogo
Dikson
KARA SEA

Godthåb, Greenland
☀ Jan 14.5°F (-9.5°C)
July 45°F (7°C)
❄ Jan 1.4 in (36 mm)
July 2.2 in (56 mm)

6 Devon I. (Canada)
Ellesmere Island (Canada)
Alert
North Pole
☀ Jan -49°F (-45°C)
July 32°F (0°C)
Qaanaaq
Savissivik
PEARY LAND
Franz Josef Land (Russian Fed.)
Krenkel
Novaya Zemlya (Russian Fed)

7 Baffin Island (Canada)
Baffin Bay
KNUD RASMUSSEN LAND
Oodaaq Island
Nord
BARENTS SEA
SVALBARD (Norway)
B

8 Panguirtung
GREENLAND (Denmark)
Upernavik
Davis Strait
Qeqertarsuaq
Søndre Strømfjord
Ny Ålesund
LONGYEARBYEN
GREENLAND SEA
Spitsbergen

9 **NUUK (GODTHÅB)**
Frederikshåb
Narsarsuaq
Mt. Gunnbjørn Ittoqqortoormiit
Ammassalik
Denmark Strait
Jan Mayen (Norway)

10 Nanortalik
Nunap Isua (C. Farvel)
ATLANTIC OCEAN
REYKJAVIK
ICELAND

Nils Nordenskjöld discovered the northeast passage in the Vega in 1879.

ICE-BREAKERS

The Arctic sea ice is usually about 6 ft (2 m) thick. Ships called ice-breakers are specially constructed with reinforced hulls and bows shaped for ploughing through this icy obstacle. Their powerful engines push the bow on top of the ice until the weight of the ship breaks it, clearing a passage for other sea vessels.

ARCTIC EXPLORATION

In the 16th century, European sailors first explored the Arctic seas in search of a new trade route to Asia. English sailors began to map the northwest passage around the top of Canada, while the Dutch explored the northeast passage around Siberia. By 1906, both routes had been successfully navigated. Three years later, an American, Robert Peary, claimed to have reached the North Pole itself. However, the speed of his journey has led some explorers to doubt his achievement.

Roald Amundsen sailed through the northwest passage in the Gjöa in 1906.

This cross-section follows the line A–B on the map above.

CROSS-SECTION THROUGH THE ARCTIC

For centuries, some Arctic explorers believed that the polar ice lay on top of a vast continent. In 1958, an American atomic-powered submarine, the USS *Nautilus*, demonstrated that this was untrue by sailing from Alaska to Svalbard underneath the ice. Subsequent exploration beneath the ice has revealed the ridges and basins of the seabed below.

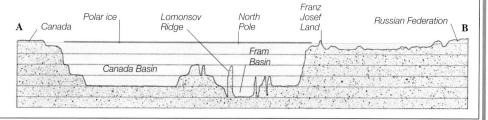

A Canada
Polar ice
Lomonsov Ridge
North Pole
Franz Josef Land
Russian Federation B
Fram Basin
Canada Basin

THE ANTARCTIC

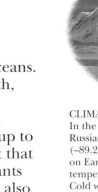

UNLIKE THE ARCTIC, which is an ocean surrounded by continents, the Antarctic is a continent surrounded by oceans. Antarctica is the most remote, inhospitable place on Earth, and consists of a large land mass and numerous offshore islands. Most of the mainland is covered by a vast ice cap, which breaks up at the coastline, forming huge icebergs up to 125 miles (200 km) long. Antarctica is the only continent that has no permanent human population – the only inhabitants are visiting scientists studying the local environment. It is also unique in being governed by an international treaty that forbids countries from owning or exploiting the land.

CLIMATE
In the winter of 1983, the temperature at the Russian research station, Vostok, reached –128.6°F (–89.2°C), the lowest temperature ever recorded on Earth. Even at the height of summer, temperatures rarely rise above the freezing point. Cold winds blow down from the central plateau toward the coasts, causing intense blizzards. The high winds and low temperatures make it dangerous for an unprotected person to be outside.

The American-owned Amundsen-Scott base is situated at the South Pole.

Territorial claims in the Antarctic
These claims have been suspended under the Antarctic Treaty. Stations can be set up for research, but military activities are forbidden.

By taking samples of ice from deep inside the ice cap, scientists are able to study changes in the climate.

STUDYING ANTARCTICA
Scientists from all over the world come to Antarctica to study its unique climate, weather, geology, and wildlife. The age-old rocks tell them much about the development of the Earth, while analysis of the many meteorites that hit the ice cap provides valuable information about the Universe.

THE ANTARCTIC TREATY
In the first half of the 20th century, many countries claimed territory in Antarctica. In order to prevent future conflict, 12 countries signed the Antarctic Treaty in 1959, which suspended all national claims to the land. The treaty designated Antarctica as "a continent for science," and stated that it should be used for peaceful purposes only. Today, 44 countries have signed the treaty, which is one of the most successful examples of international cooperation.

RESEARCH STATIONS
Barely 1,000 people live in Antarctica in the winter, with another 3,000 joining them during the summer months. All are involved in scientific research and live on one of the 46 or so bases dotted around the continent. Each base is specially insulated against the intense cold and some have been constructed below the surface in order to conserve heat. Diesel fuel is used for heating and generating electricity, and enough fuel, food, and other supplies are kept to last 12 months, in case weather prevents new supplies from being brought in.

Captain Roald Amundsen taking sights at the South Pole in 1911.

ANTARCTIC EXPLORATION
It wasn't until 1820 that the shores of Antarctica were first sighted. From the 1840s onward, explorers began to map the continent, but the South Pole remained unknown. In the summer of 1911–12, two expeditions – one from Norway led by Roald Amundsen, the other from Britain led by Robert Scott – set out to reach the Pole. Amundsen arrived on December 14, followed by Scott a month later.

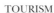

TOURISM
Each year, a few intrepid tourists visit Antarctica, exploring the dramatic coastline in cruise ships or flying inland over the ice to land at the South Pole. So far, the small number of tourists has had little effect on the environment. However, the environment is threatened by the garbage slowly accumulating around the older scientific bases.

Cruise liners have been bringing tourists to Antarctica since the 1950s, and now bring about 10,000 people each year.

Map of The Antarctic with grid coordinates A–L (columns) and 1–10 (rows).

A T L A N T I C   O C E A N

Drake Passage

Orcadas (Argentina)
South Orkney Is. (UK)
South Shetland Is. (UK)

SANAE (S. Africa)
Eimbul Ice Shelf
Neumayer (Germany)

SCOTIA SEA

King George I. (UK)
2,3,4,5,6
Esperanza (Argentina)

Rüser-Larsen Ice Shelf

QUEEN MAUD LAND

Lützow-Holm Bay

Syowa (Japan)
Molodezhnaya (Russian Fed.)

ENDERBY LAND

Anvers I. (US)
7
8

Larsen Ice Shelf

Halley (UK)

WEDDELL SEA

Belgrano II (Argentina)

Mawson (Australia)

Heard I. (Australia)

Stonington I. (UK)
9
Adelaide I. (UK)

ANTARCTIC PENINSULA

Filchner Ice Shelf

Ronne Ice Shelf

A N T A R C T I C A

C. Darnley

Amery Ice Shelf

BELLINGSHAUSEN SEA

SOUTH POLAR PLATEAU

Lambert Glacier
Prydz Bay

South Pole
Jan -9.5°F (-23°C)
July -105°F (-76°C)

Peter the First I. (Norway)

A

Vinson Massif ▲

ELLSWORTH MTS.

TRANSANTARCTIC

Amundsen-Scott (US)
South Pole

West Ice Shelf

DAVIS SEA

MARIE BYRD LAND

Mirnyy (Russian Fed.)
Shackleton Ice Shelf

AMUNDSEN SEA

Getz Ice Shelf

Ross Ice Shelf

Vostok (Russian Fed.)

WILKES LAND

Casey (Australia)
B C. Poinsett

C. Colbeck

McMurdo (US)
Scott Base (New Zealand)

VICTORIA LAND
M T S.

Deepest point of ice ★

Porpoise Bay

PACIFIC OCEAN

ROSS SEA

C. Adare

Dumont d'Urville (France)

Balleny Is.

INDIAN OCEAN

KEY
● Numbered Research stations
1 Signy (UK)
2 Comandante Ferraz (Brazil)
3 Teniente Rodolfo Marsh Martin (Chile)
4 Chang Cheng (China)
5 King Sejong (Korea)
6 Henryk Arctowsky (Poland)
7 Palmer (US)
8 Faraday (UK)
9 Rothera (UK)

Scale: 0 200 400 600 800 1000 km / 0 200 400 600 miles

EQUATOR
TROPIC OF CAPRICORN
ANTARCTIC CIRCLE

Stonington Island
☀ Jan 32°F (0°C)
☀ July 10.5°F (-12°C)
❄ Jan 0.4 in (10 mm)
❄ July 1.3 in (33 mm)

THINGS TO LOOK FOR ON THE MAP

Highest point: Vinson Massif, 16,063 ft (4,896 m) *Map D5*

Lowest temperature on Earth: -128.6°F (-89.2°C) recorded at Vostok Station, *Map H6*

Deepest point of ice: 15,669 ft (4,776 m) *Map H8*

South Pole: *Map F5*

CROSS-SECTION THROUGH THE ANTARCTIC

Antarctica is buried beneath an enormous ice cap that covers 99.6 percent of the land area. It has formed from the buildup of snow compacted over 100,000 years. The ice cap contains most of the freshwater on Earth, and 90 percent of all the ice. If the ice were to melt, the oceans would rise by up to 210 ft (64 m). The ice weighs so much that it pushes much of Antarctica below sea level.

This cross-section follows the line A–B on the map above.

Sea level
A
Ross Ice Shelf
Transantarctic Mountains
Deepest point of ice
B

ANTARCTIC WILDLIFE

Antarctica's severe climate and isolated position have greatly reduced the variety of its wildlife. The largest animal that lives on land all year round is a tiny insect. During the brief summer, however, seals, penguins, and many birds visit the continent to take advantage of the safe breeding sites and plentiful food supply to raise their young. At sea, a dozen species of whales feed off the many seals, fish, and krill that live in the icy waters.

KRILL

Krill are shrimplike crustaceans up to 2 in (5 cm) in length. They feed on plankton and other crustaceans and occur in such large numbers that they sometimes turn the oceans around Antarctica pink.

EMPEROR PENGUINS

The majestic emperor penguin stands up to 4 ft (1.15 m) tall and can weigh 66 lb (30 kg). After spending most of the year at sea, the emperors come ashore in April to breed. The male alone then incubates the single egg during the icy winter, holding it on his feet to keep it warm. The female returns in July to feed the newborn chick.

POLITICAL SYSTEMS

NO TWO COUNTRIES have identical political systems, as over the years each country has evolved a form that suits its history, culture, people, and rulers. However, it is possible to group the political systems of the world into a few main categories. Within each category there can be many variations. Some countries have a system that is in transition from one category to another, such as when East Timor was moving from colonial rule to multiparty democracy, or Zimbabwe, which is being moved from democracy to dictatorship by its leader, Robert Mugabe.

Woman voting in elections in India – the world's most populous democracy.

POLITICAL TERMS

Alliance A formal agreement between nations for economic, political, or military reasons.

Apartheid A policy of separating people by race.

Capitalism A system in which wealth and profit in the hands of a few people drives the country's economy.

Communism A system in which property and land are owned by the whole community and each person is paid according to their needs and abilities.

Democracy A system in which people vote for the government of their choice.

Economy The organization of a country's finances, exports, imports, industries, and services.

Multiparty elections More than one party standing for election.

Nationalized Industries or services owned by the state.

Privatization State-owned organizations taken over by private companies.

Republic A state where people elect the head of state and the government.

Socialism A system in which the economy is controlled by the whole community.

Trade union An organized group of workers united to protect their rights and interests.

West, the Countries in Europe and North America with capitalist economies and democratic governments that share similar cultural values.

MULTIPARTY DEMOCRACY

In a multiparty democracy, people are given a choice between several parties to elect. Because this allows different points of view to be expressed in public, and opposition to form against the elected government, not every country can make a multiparty democracy work. Some countries claim to be multiparty democracies, but real power is actually held by the president.

CONSTITUTIONAL MONARCHY
In a constitutional monarchy, the head of the ruling royal family is head of state and is succeeded by his or her closest relative in hereditary succession. Japan, for example, is a constitutional monarchy whose head of state is the emperor. The monarch has no real power, but acts as a figurehead for the country. This is in the hands of the democratically elected government, led by the prime minister, the ruler of the largest party in parliament. Over the years, many countries have evolved from absolute to constitutional monarchies.

FEDERAL REPUBLIC
Some nations, including Germany, are federal republics, with each state in the republic having considerable power and electing its own prime minister. In Germany, the federal assembly acts as an umbrella over the states and elects a chancellor (prime minister) to rule the republic as a whole. The president is chosen by the states and assembly together.

Pro-democracy protesters are confronted by riot police in Indonesia.

PRESIDENTIAL REPUBLIC
A presidential republic is a true democracy where voters choose both the head of state – the president – and elect representatives to parliament. It is the most common form of government in the world. In countries such as the US and South Africa, the president is both the head of state and of government. In France and Russia, the president is elected head of state and chooses the prime minister to run the government, but retains considerable power in the running of the nation. In many countries, such as Ireland, India, and Israel, the president is a symbolic figurehead and real power is held by the prime minister and government.

Voters → *Candidates* →

Candidates from several parties are elected into office.

ONE-PARTY STATE

In a one-party state, only one political party is allowed to exist. All other parties are forbidden. All power in the state is held by the one party. The former communist states of eastern Europe and many of the African nations are now moving from being one-party states to establishing a multiparty democracy.

Soldiers on the streets in Indonesia

In an election, the party decides who its candidate will be and voters are only required to endorse that choice.

Voters ↓

One candidate →

One party in office.

THEOCRACY
In a theocracy, power is held by religious leaders who rule according to their scriptures. In Iran, the *mullahs* – Muslim scholars and priests – hold the real power, though the government is in non-religious hands. The Vatican City, the world's smallest state, is a mixture of a theocracy and an elected monarchy. The head of state is the Pope, who is leader of the world's Roman Catholics. He is elected for life by cardinals, who are senior clergy.

ONE-PARTY DOMINATED STATES
Some countries, such as Egypt and Tunisia, claim to be multiparty democracies, but are run by a single party that keeps a firm hold on power, often with the support of the army, as in Syria.

ABSOLUTE MONARCHY

In an absolute monarchy, power is held by the ruling monarch of the country and is handed down through the royal family to his or her successor. In the past, absolute monarchs kept all power to themselves, but today most appoint a small advisory council to help them rule.

MONARCHY WITH A PARTIAL DEMOCRATIC SYSTEM

In some countries, the ruling monarch retains a strong grip on the government but allows some limited democracy. In Jordan, King Abdullah allows direct elections to the lower House of Representatives, but keeps strong control by appointing all 40 members of the upper house, or Senate.

MILITARY GOVERNMENT

Military governments are usually set up after the army has seized leadership from a weak or unpopular government. An example of a military government is Pakistan, where the military under Pervez Musharraf seized power. All power is held by senior military officers, usually drawn from the army. Elections and parliament are abolished and political parties are declared illegal. Military governments have often held power in South and Central America, Africa, and Asia.

DICTATORSHIP

A number of countries around the world are ruled by single rulers, called dictators, who have absolute authority. Most dictators gain power either through military coups (an army takeover), by seizing leadership from an existing ruler, as in Iraq, or through direct elections and then banning opposition parties. Once in office, dictators rule in a personal, often brutal, fashion, eliminating all opposition to themselves.

Dictator of the Central African Republic from 1965 to 1975, Jean-Bédel Boukassa crowned himself "emperor" in 1977.

EMPIRE

Empire is when one country controls a number of other countries, usually under the control of one ruler or emperor. Empires have existed since ancient times, though the 19th century is often called "the Age of Empire" as this was when the European powers expanded their rule throughout the continents of South America, Africa and Asia. Today, only small pockets of these European empires remain.

Hong Kong was handed back to the Chinese after 157 years of British rule in 1997.

DEPENDENT TERRITORIES

Not every country rules itself. About 10 million people around the world live under the protection of either the UK, Denmark, Norway, France, Portugal, the US, New Zealand, or Australia. Most dependent territories are relics of the colonial era that have remained attached to their former colonial rulers. Some territories have recently changed status. Hong Kong, for example, reverted from British to Chinese rule in 1997. Some territories are retained because of their strategic or economic importance, while others remain colonies because they are too small, remote, or weak to survive on their own.

Gibraltar is a self-governing British colony, captured from the Spanish in 1704.

Examples of dependent territories

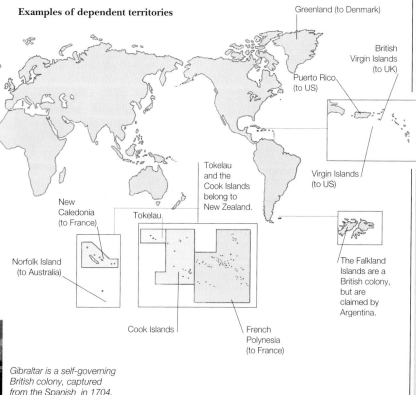

Greenland (to Denmark)

British Virgin Islands (to UK)

Puerto Rico (to US)

Virgin Islands (to US)

New Caledonia (to France)

Norfolk Island (to Australia)

Tokelau

Tokelau and the Cook Islands belong to New Zealand.

Cook Islands

French Polynesia (to France)

The Falkland Islands are a British colony, but are claimed by Argentina.

NATURAL DISASTERS

NATURAL DISASTERS SHAPE both our landscape and human history. Since civilization began, mankind has had to cope with the the power unleashed by nature in the form of volcanoes, earthquakes, floods, and fires. The immense forces nature unleashes affect all our lives and influence everything from the way we construct buildings, to where we situate towns and cities. Though we can prepare in a limited way for natural disasters, no one knows when the next will strike and with what force. Mankind's polluting of the atmosphere also means that our climate and its destructive power is changing in ever more extreme and unpredictable ways.

Kiribati in the Pacific will be one of the first countries to be totally submerged.

TROPICAL CYCLONES

Tropical cyclones, known as hurricanes in the the Caribbean and the US, and typhoons in the west of the Pacific Ocean are powerful, seasonal storms with high winds of over 70 mph (113 km/h). They originate in oceans over the equator and there are around 100 worldwide each year. Sometimes they do not reach land, but when they do, vast destruction is usual. Tropical cyclones are given names, such as Hurricane Mitch, to allow people to identify them easily in forecasters' warnings. The thunder storms they generate can produce 10 in (25 cm) of rain each day and thus make huge amounts of energy, often equivalent in one day to as much power as the US uses in one year.

EL NINO
The satellite image of Earth shows the temperature of the land and sea around Indonesia, the red and white colors indicating higher than average readings. Later sea temperatures dropped dramatically. The departure of the large mass of warm water affects where rain clouds come from, and brought drought to Indonesia. This is the weather disrupting phenomenon known as El Niño.

GLOBAL WARMING

An ever increasing amount of so-called "natural disasters" are, in fact, the results of global warming, a heating up of the Earth's climate that scientists now believe is probably caused by atmospheric pollution. As countries' climates change, people must prepare for new weather situations they had not previously encountered, such as flooding and drought. The warmer temperatures are also melting polar ice caps, thus increasing sea levels. The result of this is that low lying areas of some countries will revert back to the sea and some whole islands may be lost.

A bush fire rages in Kakadu National Park, Australia.

FIRE

Bush, or forest fires can be one of the most terrifying of all natural disasters. They destroy vast tracts of vegetation, kill large numbers of animals, and can do great damage to crops and property. A forest fire usually starts after a particularly dry season, and while fires may be set off spontaneously or through a strike of lightning, often they are caused by people. Once burning, the fire quickly grows in scale becoming a huge wall of flame. Strong winds can drive the flames spreading them at huge speed and across vast distances.

Hurricane Mitch sustained winds of over 180 miles per hour (290 km/h) and caused huge destruction.

VOLCANOES

A volcano is a vent in the Earth's surface through which molten rock and hot gases escape. Volcanoes can lie dormant for many years before erupting suddenly, causing tremendous destruction as the poisonous gases are discharged and lava (molten rock) flows out. The word volcano comes from an island in the Mediterranean that the Romans called Volcano. This volcanic island had a crater that blew out smokelike vapor, making the Romans believe that it was the home of Vulcan, their god of fire.

A mud slide in Nicaragua which killed over 1,000 people.

LANDSLIDES

When a hillside collapses, it is called a landslide. It can be both a natural or a man-made disaster. It can be caused by the ground becoming saturated with rain water and giving way, earthquakes, or volcanic eruptions, but can also be by human activity weakening the hillside through deforestation, machinery vibration, or the weight of buildings.

Mount Ruapehu in New Zealand lights up the night sky as it erupts.

TORNADOES

Tornadoes, sometimes called twisters, are powerful whirling winds, accompanied by funnel-shaped clouds. The winds blow clockwise north of the equator and counterclockwise south of the equator. It is thought they form when cold polar air meets warm tropical air. These winds have tremendous power and can rip up everything in their path, including whole buildings. Tornadoes are most common in Australia and the Midwestern and Southern USA.

A tornado approaches a corn field in Kansas, USA.

RED CROSS

The Red Cross (or Red Crescent as it is known in Muslim countries) was founded in 1864 in Switzerland to help sick and wounded soldiers in war. Since then it has extended its role to help people whenever there is a major accident or natural disaster. The society distributes medicine and food, such as at this refugee camp in Mekkele, Ethiopia (above) and helps alleviate people's suffering in times of crisis.

MAJOR INTERNATIONAL AID ORGANIZATIONS

CARE
One of the world's largest private international relief and development organizations, it works in over 60 countries around the world. CARE reaches out to people whose lives are devastated by humanitarian emergencies, or who are struggling each day in poor communities to survive and improve their lives.

CARITIS INTERNATIONALIS
A worldwide network of Catholic relief and development organizations, such as CAFOD in the United Kingdom, which spreads solidarity

and social justice, without regard to creed, race, gender, or ethnicity.

INTERNATIONAL RED CROSS AND RED CRESCENT
See above, Red Cross.

MEDECINS SANS FRONTIERS (DOCTORS WITHOUT BORDERS)
Medecins Sans Frontiers (MSF) is an international humanitarian aid organization that provides emergency medical assistance to populations in danger in more than 80 countries. It provides medical aid wherever it is needed, regardless of race, religion, politics, or sex, and also raises

awareness of the plight of the people in the developing world.

MUSLIM AID
Founded in 1985, it tries to improve the lives of people in the 44 poorest countries in the world through long-term development programs such as the provision of clean water, healthcare, shelter, education, and income generation.

OXFAM INTERNATIONAL
Working for an end to the waste and injustice of poverty, both in long-term development work and times of urgent need. A group of independent

nongovernmental organizations that work together to achieve greater impact by collective efforts.

SAVE THE CHILDREN
Founded in the United Kingdom in 1919 by Egtantyne Jebb, it works to create opportunities for the world's children to live safe, healthy lives.

UNITED NATIONS CHILDREN'S FUND (UNICEF)
Founded in 1946, UNICEF works for the protection of children's rights, to help them meet their basic needs and to expand their opportunities to reach their full potential.

WORLD RELIGIONS

THROUGHOUT HISTORY, people have asked about the meaning of life and death and have sought answers through religion. There are many faiths throughout the world, each with its own practice and belief. Some religions, such as Christianity, have spread over the world; others, such as traditional African beliefs, have stayed in one place. The world's major faiths roughly divide into two groups – the Western tradition and the Eastern tradition. The Western tradition originated in the Near and Middle East and includes Judaism, Christianity, and Islam. The Eastern tradition began in India and includes Hinduism and Buddhism.

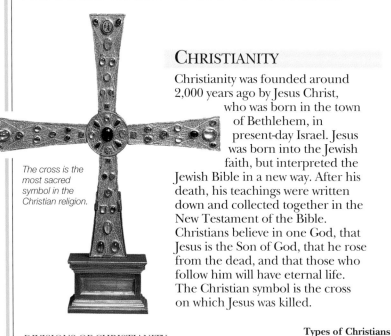

The Ka'bah in Mecca is Islam's holiest site and the focus for the annual hadj (pilgrimage) made by millions of Muslims.

CHRISTIANITY

Christianity was founded around 2,000 years ago by Jesus Christ, who was born in the town of Bethlehem, in present-day Israel. Jesus was born into the Jewish faith, but interpreted the Jewish Bible in a new way. After his death, his teachings were written down and collected together in the New Testament of the Bible. Christians believe in one God, that Jesus is the Son of God, that he rose from the dead, and that those who follow him will have eternal life. The Christian symbol is the cross on which Jesus was killed.

The cross is the most sacred symbol in the Christian religion.

ISLAM

Muslims follow the Islamic faith, based on a belief in one God, Allah. Islam shares the same roots as Judaism and Christianity, all three recognizing certain prophets, such as Abraham. Followers believe the last and greatest of the Islamic prophets was Mohammed, who was born in Mecca, Saudi Arabia, in AD570. The words revealed to Mohammed by Allah were later written down in the Koran. After Mohammed's death, Islam split into two branches: the traditional Sunnis, who follow Mohammed's original successors (the Caliphs), and the radical Shi'ites, who followed Mohammed's cousin and son-in-law, Ali. Shi'ites are the majority in Iran and Iraq, Sunnis the majority elsewhere.

DIVISIONS OF CHRISTIANITY
More than half of all Christians are Roman Catholics, who follow the leadership of the Pope in Rome. There are large numbers of Catholics in southern Europe, Central and South America, and Philippines. One quarter of Christians are Protestants, who split from the Catholic Church 500 years ago, and belong to a number of self-governing churches. The main areas of Protestantism are in northern Europe and North America. About one in 10 Christians belong to one of the Eastern Orthodox Churches of Eastern Europe and Russia; each national church has its own Patriarch, or leader.

Types of Christians

Eastern Orthodox: 9.3%

Others: 10.2%

Roman Catholics: 56%

Protestants: 24.5%

The Western Wall in Jerusalem is Judaism's most holy place.

JUDAISM

Judaism, the religion of the Jews, began in about 2000BC when the ancient Hebrew people settled in what is now mainly Israel. Judaism is the parent of the other two major monotheist (one-god) religions, Christianity and Islam. There is no single founder, but Abraham was the first leader. The scripture is the Jewish Bible, of which the Torah (the first five books) is the most important part. After persecution in Europe, the Jewish people established a homeland in Israel in 1948, although Jews are found in most countries of the world. The Jewish symbol is the six-pointed Star of David.

The Torah is a Jewish sacred scroll and is made up of the first five books of the Old Testament.

BUDDHISM

Buddhism is based on the teachings of Buddha, the "Enlightened One," a prince who was born in India in about 563BC. Buddha taught that suffering is always present in daily life and is caused by desiring things. Freedom from desire leads to the end of suffering and the attainment of perfect peace, or *nirvana*. Although Buddhism began in India, most Buddhists today are found elsewhere, in China, Sri Lanka, Tibet, and Southeast Asia.

Buddhist monks in Thailand in their traditional saffron colored robes – Buddhism came to Thailand from India in around the first century BC.

ANGKOR WAT

Between 880 AD and 1228, a city called Angkor was built by the Khmer people in what is now northwestern Cambodia. One of the most impressive buildings was a temple called Angkor Wat (pictured). Originally dedicated to the Hindu god Vishnu, it is a fusion of Hindu and Khmer art, and is spread over 200 acres (81 hectares). It consists of five towers, each thought to represent Mount Meru, the home of the gods and center of the Hindu universe. With the decline of the Khmer empire and the rise of Buddhism in Cambodia, Angkor Wat became a Buddhist temple. Today it is a World Heritage site, though rising numbers of tourists are causing increasing amounts of damage to it.

HINDUISM

The world's third largest religion with approximately 762 million followers, Hinduism originated in India in about 1750BC. The word "Hindu" comes from the Persian for "India". Today it is the dominant faith in India, Nepal and among the Tamils of Sri Lanka. It has no single founder or scripture, though the earliest beliefs were written down in the *Vedas*, a collection of hymns and chants. Most Hindus believe in many gods but in one underlying reality (*Brahman*). They believe that when a person dies their soul is reborn in another body. People who live good lives are born again in a higher life; bad lives lead to a lower life. Devout Hindus aim to be free from the cycle of rebirth and become one with *Brahman*.

A statue of the Hindu god Shiva, the destroyer. Shiva, along with Brahma and Vishnu are three of the most important gods in Hinduism.

SIKHISM

This faith began in the Punjab region of India in the 1400s. Its founder was Guru Nanak. He was succeeded by nine other Gurus who all helped to develop Sikhism. The *Guru Granth Sahib* is the Sikh holy book. The religion is based on the worship of one God and on the cycle of human rebirth. Sikhs believe that God is found in all things, and that all people are equal in the eyes of God. Sikhism is mainly practiced in India, but followers are also found throughout the world.

Varanasi in India stands on the banks of the Ganges River, a holy place for Hindus.

The golden Palace in Amritar, Punjab, is a site sacred to Sikhs.

OTHER FAITHS

CONFUCIANISM Often thought to be more like a philosophy than a religion, Confucianism was founded by Confucius, or K'ung Fu Tze, in around 500BC. It is not based on the worship of a god but on following a moral code. Confucianism is practiced in China and other parts of east Asia.

TAOISM This faith was founded in China by Lao Tzu around 300BC. Taoists believe in many gods and aim to live in harmony with nature. Their symbol, *Yin Yang*, stands for balance and harmony. Taoism is followed in China and other parts of east Asia.

SHINTOISM The ancient religion of Japan is based on the worship of gods of nature and ancestor worship. Most Shinto shrines are in parks, gardens, and on mountains.

JAINISM Jains do not believe in a god; their faith is based on non-violence to all living things and a belief in rebirth. Most of its followers live in India.

ZEN BUDDHISM Very important in Japan, this branch of Buddhism originated in China. It aims at harmony in living and stresses the need for meditation.

TRADITIONAL BELIEFS Around the world, there are numerous local religions handed down by word of mouth from generation to generation. Many share a belief that there are spirits living in the world – in the sky, stars, trees, lakes, and rivers. Many traditional faiths are found in Africa, where beliefs vary widely depending on the individual tribe. The ancient faith of Shamanism, found in parts of Asia, centers on a priest, or *shaman*, who goes into trances in order to enable people to leave their bodies and visit the spiritual world.

HEALTH

THE WORLD HAS BECOME A HEALTHIER PLACE
to live in over the last 100 years. Advances in
medical science, improved diet, higher living
standards, and better health education have
all helped people live longer and healthier
lives. However, many problems remain,
especially in the poorer countries of Africa
and Asia. While immunization has protected
millions of children against disease, many
illnesses remain common. Tuberculosis and
malaria are widespread, AIDS is decimating
some countries' populations in Africa, and
thousands of babies die each year of tetanus.
In the world's richer areas, which include
North America, Oceania, and Europe, cancer
and heart disease affect many people.

*The Japanese generally live longer as
they often have a high standard of living
and a low fat diet.*

LOW LIFE EXPECTANCY	
Uganda	43
Guinea Bissau	45
Afghanistan	46
Gambia	46

LIFE EXPECTANCY

Life expectancy is a measure
of how long a person is likely
to live. In 1950, the average
person expected to live 40
years, now most live till at
least 63. But this hides the
differences between rich
and poor countries, and
the social groups within
them. Wealthier people
are generally healthier
than poor, and rich
countries, like Japan, with
the world's highest life
expectancy, are usually
healthier places to live.

HIGH LIFE EXPECTANCY	
Andorra	83
San Marino	81
Japan	81
Switzerland	79

*In wealthy countries many premature babies survive
because of good health facilities such as incubators.*

PEOPLE PER DOCTOR

One way of measuring the provision
of healthcare in a country is to count
the number of people cared for by
each doctor. Countries that are
rich or have good welfare systems
provide easy access to health
services, and on average have one
doctor for every 390 people. In
contrast, there is only one doctor to
every 50,000 people in the world's
poorer African countries, and over half
the population live more than 6 miles
(10 km) from a doctor or medical center.

CHILD MORTALITY

The child mortality rate is the number
of deaths of children under five years
of age per 1,000 births. In some areas
of the world, such as Afghanistan and
parts of Africa, poor medical care and
lack of nourishment lead to a high
number of child deaths. The story is
much better in Europe and North
America where less than 10 out of
every 1,000 under-fives die.

HIGHEST CHILD MORTALITY	
Country	*per 1,000 births*
Afghanistan	270
Sierra Leone	250
Guinea Bissau	240
Mozambique	240
Gambia	230
Malawi	230

PREVENTIVE MEDICINE

There are many ways of safeguarding
against illness. Immunization
protects people from catching
diseases such as measles and tetanus.
In rich countries most children are
immunized, but in some poor
countries only 30 percent of children
receive this care. Across the world,
adults are warned of the dangers
of smoking, alcohol, and drugs.
Governments also try to promote the
idea of regular exercise to keep the
population fit and healthy. Attention
to water quality, food hygiene,
sanitation, and good housing all
play their part in keeping people
well. In the countries that can
afford it, campaigns in the media,
schools, and clinics help to educate
people in basic healthcare and
issues such as hygene.

CONTROLLING DISEASE

War has a devastating effect upon every country, but
apart from the carnage and destruction it causes, the
humanitarian crisis can be enormous. People fleeing
from areas of conflict to live in refugee camps often
have little food and fresh water and serious diseases
spread quickly. Organizations such as the Red Cross
(shown here at a refugee camp for Cambodians in
Thailand) try to minimize suffering by providing
food and medical supplies at the camps.

HEALTHY EATING

People generally live longer if they eat a
healthy diet that includes lots of fruit
and fresh vegetables and is low in
saturated fat. The "Mediterranean Diet"
eaten by people in countries such as
Italy and Spain, which includes a wide
variety of healthy, low-fat food, olive
oil, fish, and pulses, is one of the
most healthy balanced diets in
the world.

*Typical food eaten in many
Mediterranean
countries.*

EDUCATION

EDUCATION IS ONE OF the most important ways of creating a better world, for it enables people to improve their own lives. Most children receive a primary education up to the age of 11, which gives them the basic skills of reading, writing, and mathematics. About half the world's children also receive a secondary education up to the age of 16 or 18, and some go on to higher education. But education provision varies greatly. Children in rich countries generally receive a better education than those in poorer areas. One of the biggest problems for poor countries is that having fewer educated people, they are less capable of coping with the demands of the modern world.

ADULT LITERACY

The adult literacy rate of a country shows how many adults over the age of 15 can read and write. The test involves asking a person to read and write a short, simple statement about their everyday life. In the US, for example, the literacy rate is 99 percent, which means that only one adult in 100 cannot read or write. In the poor country of Djibouti in east Africa the adult literacy rate is only 19 percent, which shows a low level of national education.

US: 99%
Brazil: 82%
China: 80%
Kuwait: 74%
India: 50%
Djibouti: 19%

Adult literacy rates

EDUCATION LEVELS

A country's education level is related to its wealth, as mostly richer countries have the money to provide adequate schools, teachers, and books. In turn, education adds to the national wealth as it provides well-educated young people to work in the factories, offices, and farms. Better education helps farmers produce more crops, and office workers become better managers.

In the US over a quarter of all young people go on to higher education.

Children in Japan work hard to pass their exams. Many attend special classes on Saturdays or in the evenings.

RURAL AND URBAN SCHOOLING

In the poorer countries of Africa and Asia, children who live in towns usually receive a better education than those who live in the countryside. This is because many country children are needed to stay at home to work the land and help in the family, and would have to travel long distances to get to school. However, educating rural children can bring great advantages, because they can develop skills to increase productivity in agriculture and local industry.

Children being taught in a rural school in Bangladesh.

EFFICIENT EDUCATION

Japan has one of the most efficient education systems in the world. Nearly all children attend a nursery school before they are old enough to go to primary school, and one-third of children stay on for higher education. Japanese children do well in science and math, which are subjects much in demand by industries.

MALE AND FEMALE DIFFERENCES

In many poorer countries, girls are not educated as well as boys. Girls often have to help in the home and have little time left for education. But the situation is improving, as educating women has great benefits – it improves healthcare and hygiene, and helps reduce infant deaths.

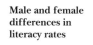

In some countries girls are forced to leave school early to help in the home.

Male and female differences in literacy rates

In each case the female figure is a percentage of the male average, which is given as 100. The closer the figure to 100, the smaller the gap in literacy rates.

Male average: 100

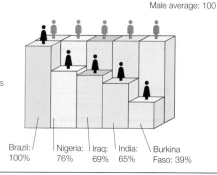

Brazil: 100%
Nigeria: 76%
Iraq: 69%
India: 65%
Burkina Faso: 39%

RICH AND POOR

THE DIFFERENCE IN WEALTH between the richest and poorest countries is vast. The average person in Mozambique earns one six-hundredth of the average person in Switzerland. How wealthy a country is depends on its natural resources, industrial strength, population size, and political stability. Libya is much richer than its neighbor, Chad. Both are desert countries with small populations, but Libya has oil while Chad has few natural resources. Many poor countries borrow money from richer countries. Debt repayment is expensive, with the result that poor countries stay poor, while rich countries continue to grow richer.

POOREST COUNTRIES (Based on real GDP per person)	
Country	*US$*
Ethiopia	370
Chad	447
Zaire	469
Mali	480
Guinea	500

RICHEST COUNTRIES (Based on real GDP per person)	
Country	*US$*
US	22,130
Switzerland	21,780
Luxembourg	20,800
Germany	19,770
Japan	19,390

NATIONAL WEALTH
There are two official measures of national wealth. The Gross Domestic Product (GDP) measures the total value of finished goods and services produced by a national economy. The Gross National Product (GNP) measures GDP and the income from abroad that flows into the country. Both figures are usually expressed in US dollars. When the figures are divided by the total population of the country, they give an indication of how rich or poor that country is. The tables on the left show that whereas the five richest countries span three continents, the five poorest countries are all in Africa.

World distribution of wealth

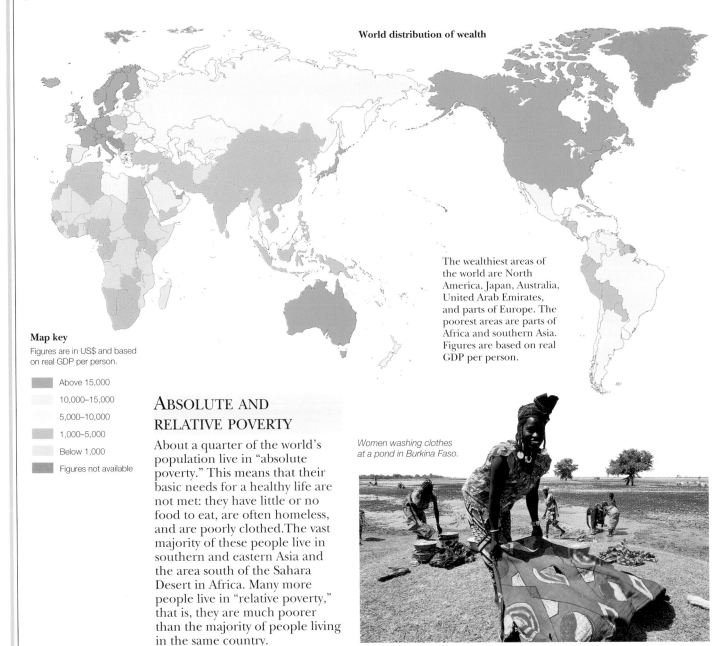

The wealthiest areas of the world are North America, Japan, Australia, United Arab Emirates, and parts of Europe. The poorest areas are parts of Africa and southern Asia. Figures are based on real GDP per person.

Map key

Figures are in US$ and based on real GDP per person.

▮	Above 15,000
▮	10,000–15,000
▮	5,000–10,000
▮	1,000–5,000
▮	Below 1,000
▮	Figures not available

ABSOLUTE AND RELATIVE POVERTY

About a quarter of the world's population live in "absolute poverty." This means that their basic needs for a healthy life are not met: they have little or no food to eat, are often homeless, and are poorly clothed.The vast majority of these people live in southern and eastern Asia and the area south of the Sahara Desert in Africa. Many more people live in "relative poverty," that is, they are much poorer than the majority of people living in the same country.

Women washing clothes at a pond in Burkina Faso.

SOCIAL POVERTY

In most countries, there are groups of people who are poorer than others. Women are usually poorer than men – they are often paid less (see chart right) or are housewives with no income. Also, women often have a lower standard of education, which means they do not have the qualifications to obtain higher-paid jobs. Single mothers and elderly single women are particularly at risk from poverty. Older people on low pensions and the sick are also poorer than average. In some places, such as São Paulo in Brazil (shown left), children are forced to live on the streets because they have no families to support them or homes to live in. They often beg or turn to crime to survive.

Favelas (slums) in Rio de Janeiro, Brazil, stand next to luxurious apartment blocks.

Male and female wages

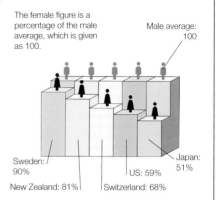

The female figure is a percentage of the male average, which is given as 100.

Male average: 100

Sweden: 90%
New Zealand: 81%
US: 59%
Switzerland: 68%
Japan: 51%

WOMEN'S EQUALITY

In September 1893, New Zealand became the first country in the world to give women the right to vote. This marked the beginning of a long, worldwide struggle by women in many countries for equal rights in all aspects of life, including education, divorce, and equal opportunities at work.

THE NEWLY RICH

Historically, the wealthy countries of the world have been in Europe and North America. With the discovery of oil reserves in the Middle East in the past 60 years, the desert states of the Arabian Peninsula are now among the richest nations in the world. Also, the spectacular growth of the southeast Asian economies, such as Hong Kong, Taiwan, South Korea, and Singapore – which have all followed in the footsteps of Japan – means that these countries will soon join the world's wealthiest nations.

Oil wealth has seen Dubai grow from a small trading post 50 years ago to a rich city with modern buildings today.

EQUAL WEALTH DISTRIBUTION

Some countries strive for a more equal distribution of wealth among their citizens, so that there are few, if any, very rich or very poor people. Some governments spend a large proportion of national wealth on education, healthcare, social welfare, and job creation to help all people in society. New Zealand was the first country in the world to introduce a full welfare state, while Scandinavian countries such as Sweden concentrated on providing jobs for everyone. Today they are among the most equal societies in the world.

The Big Issue is one of 35 street papers sold round the world by the homeless.

DIFFERENCES IN WEALTH

Within many countries there are great differences in income between rich and poor. In Europe and North America there are many homeless people on the streets or seeking shelter in cardboard boxes. In some poor countries, such as India, rich landowners and industrial managers flourish. In Brazil, the poorest 20 percent of the people earn only 2.1 percent of the total income, while the richest 20 percent earn 67.5 percent, a difference of 32 times. In comparison, the poorest 20 percent in Hungary earn 10.9 percent, and the richest 20 per cent earn 34.3 percent, a difference of only 3.2 times.

Rodeo Drive, Beverley Hills, is one of the richest shopping streets in the world.

AID

In order to help the world's poorest countries, the richer nations give them aid in the form of grants, loans, or, when a natural disaster such as an earthquake occurs, food, tents, and clothing. Some African countries, such as Mozambique, are dependent on aid for much of their income. The largest source of aid is the US, which provides more than $11 billion a year, though this is only 0.8 percent of its total government spending.

WORLD TRADE

TRADE BETWEEN THE COUNTRIES of the world allows each nation to specialize in the goods it produces best. A country will sell its products abroad to buy goods that are produced more cheaply elsewhere. Trade creates wealth and jobs by encouraging countries to produce goods that can be sold abroad, or exported. However, the benefits of trade are not evenly spread across all countries – some produce a range of goods much more cheaply than others, and these gain the most from trading. Today, much of world trade is controlled by about 200 multinational companies, which have offices and factories across the globe.

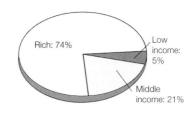

SHARE OF WORLD TRADE
The 23 richest countries in the world control 74 percent of all world trade. The 40 poorest countries, such as Ethiopia and Laos, control only 5 percent. The remaining 128 countries, such as the nations of eastern Europe and much of South America, control 21 percent.

Rich: 74%
Low income: 5%
Middle income: 21%

NORTH AND SOUTH

As shown on the map, there is a clear divide in the share of world trade between the rich economies of the "North" and the poor economies of the "South". In order to prosper, a country needs to have a positive balance of trade, that is, earn more from exports than it spends on imports. Many nations have a negative balance of trade – importing more than they export. In order to improve their trade balance, many have grouped together to form regional trading blocs, such as the European Union (EU).

Percentages of world exports and imports by region

Western Europe
40.4% 42.2%

Eastern Europe and the former USSR
4.9% 4.6%

North America
25.4% 19.5%

Asia
19.6% 24%

Africa
2.4% 2.2%

Near and Middle East
2.6% 3%

Oceania
1.5% 1.4%

South America
3.2% 3.1%

The countries above this line control about 70% of world trade, while the countries below control about 30%. This is known as the "North" and "South" divide.

In each case, the exports figure is on the left and the imports figure is on the right.

THE PACIFIC RIM
Over the last 20 years, the center of world trade has begun to shift from the US and Europe to the US and Asia, in particular those countries found around the edge of the Pacific Ocean, an area known as the Pacific Rim. Countries such as South Korea and Thailand, as well as the island states of Singapore and Taiwan, and the Chinese province of Hong Kong (above), have developed hi-tech electronic industries, exporting their low-cost products around the world. Secure government and encouragement of foreign investment have helped generate trade.

TRADING BLOCS

Some countries form trading alliances, or trading blocs, which give companies easier access to foreign markets, and make it more profitable for them to trade with the countries that are members of the bloc. Countries may try and harmonize the rules which govern buying and selling so that foreign firms can trade on an equal footing with local companies. Some trading blocs, such as the European Union (EU), also have political functions, while others, such as the North American Free Trade Agreement (NAFTA), are concerned solely with the buying and selling of goods.

NORTH AMERICAN FREE TRADE AGREEMENT
The North American Free Trade Agreement (NAFTA) was created in 1994 and is an agreement between the US, Mexico (pictured), and Canada that removes many barriers to trade and investment between these countries. It is the largest free trade zone in the world, and there are plans to extend it to other countries on the American continent.

OIL TRADE

Without oil, the world would grind to a halt. Industry and transportation would stop. This is why oil is the most important product traded in the world today. Oil is produced and exported by a few countries, mostly in the Middle East, north and west Africa, and Central and South America. Because oil is not a renewable source of energy, and its use causes a lot of pollution, alternative sources of energy are being developed.

All oil products start life as crude oil, a dark sticky liquid.

WHAT IS TRADED

World trade is dominated by manufactured goods, such as cars, televisions, and computers. Most of these products are made by rich countries. Poorer countries generally produce food and raw materials, known as primary products. This means that rich countries are growing richer, because at present bigger profits are to be made by exporting expensive manufactured goods rather than cheaper primary products.

Other: 2.1%
Mining: 9.3%
Agriculture: 9.4%
Manufacturing: 57.3%
Services: 21.9%

Figures show percentage of types of products traded worldwide

INVISIBLE EXPORTS

As well as goods, companies may also trade internationally in services. This trade is often referred to as "invisible exports." The term Invisible exports cover a wide range of services, and can include anything from banking and insurance to tourism and even modeling. France (pictured above), for example, is the world's most popular tourist destination, while the United Kingdom is one of the world's most important financial centers.

TRADE DEPENDENCY

Some countries rely almost entirely on one product to sell abroad. For example, many smaller countries in Central America and the Caribbean depend on bananas for a large percentage of their income. This dependency on one product can leave a country at the mercy of events beyond its control. If the price of a commodity rises around the world, the country will benefit, but if the price drops, or a natural disaster such as a hurricane destroys the harvest, the country can be plunged into economic hardship.

Workers sort and pack the bananas in warehouses for distribution.

FINANCIAL EXCHANGES

When money, stocks and shares and other financial assets are traded, this is called a financial market. Stock exchanges are the best known type of financial market – here people buy and sell shares in companies. For example if you own 500 shares in a firm which has issued 5 million shares, you would own a 1,000th part of the company. Share prices can go up and down. Futures markets, such as the London International Financial Futures and Options Exchange (above) is a financial market where dealers speculate on what the price of stocks, shares, and commodities will be in the future.

CHILD LABOR

In many countries in the developing world, children are forced to work, often for very little money. It is estimated that in some countries up to 20 percent of children who are forced to work are under the age of 10. In Pakistan, for example, it is estimated that there are over 11 million children working in the country's factories, including 1 million working in the carpet weaving industry, such as these boys in Lahore, Punjab. Children are usually employed because factory owners do not have to pay them as much money as adults and sometimes because their fingers are more dextrous than those of an adult.

GLOSSARY

Aboriginals: the earliest known original inhabitants of a country; most often used to refer to the native peoples of Australia.

Acid rain: rain that has been polluted by gases from factories and traffic; when the rain falls it can damage crops, forests, and lakes.

Apartheid: the policy, developed in South Africa, of separating people according to their race.

Archipelago: a large group of islands

Arid: dry; with little rainfall.

Barren: lacking in vegetation; not able to produce fruit or crops.

Bauxite: the mineral ore from which aluminum is obtained.

By-product: a substance produced as a result of making something else.

Capitalism: an economic system based on private ownership of property, and on free and competitive conditions for business.

Cash crops: crops that are grown specifically to be sold for a profit.

Cattle ranch: a large farm where cattle are reared.

Civil war: a war between rival groups that live in the same country or region.

Collective farm: a farm owned and run by a group of people working together.

Colonize: to send a group of people to settle in another land and establish a colony.

Colony: a region or country that is controlled by another country; a group of people settled in a land outside their homeland, but still ruled by its laws.

Commercial farming: raising crops or animals for sale and profit.

Communism: an economic and political system in which farms and factories and the goods they produce are owned by the state.

Consumer goods: goods such as cars, computers, and televisions, purchased by people for personal use.

Cooperative farm: see Collective farm

Crude oil: petroleum in its natural state, before it has been treated in any way.

Culture: the values, beliefs, and way of life of the people of a country or region.

Deforestation: the large-scale clearing of healthy trees, often to make room for cash crops or for cattle ranching.

Delta: the flat area (often triangular in shape) formed by material deposited at the mouth of some rivers where they enter the sea or a large lake; deltas usually have highly fertile soil.

Democracy: a form of government based on the rule of the people, usually through representatives who have been voted into office by the people.

Dependency: a land run by another, usually more powerful, country.

Deposit: a natural grouping of minerals, such as oil or coal, within the Earth.

Dictatorship: a system of government where the ruler, or dictator, has absolute power.

Economy: the system by which a society manages its resources, and makes and distributes goods and services.

Emigrant: a person who leaves their native country to settle in another.

Empire: a country and the conquered lands that it rules.

Environment: the natural world around us.

Ethnic group: a group of people sharing a common racial, religious, or cultural background.

Ethnic mix: the mix of ethnic groups in a country or region.

Export earnings: the money a country earns from selling goods or services to other countries.

Exports: goods or services sold to another country.

Extended family: a family that may include grandparents and other relatives as well as their children.

Favela: name used in Brazil for a shantytown.

Fertility, or birthrate: the average number of children born to a woman of childbearing age.

Fundamentalism: the belief that all the teachings of a particular religion must be strictly obeyed.

Guerilla: a member of a small military group fighting a stronger, official army, usually through surprise attacks.

Gulf: a large area of sea partly enclosed by land, such as the Persian Gulf or the Gulf of Mexico.

Hardwood: wood from broad-leaved trees, such as beech, oak, and mahogany.

Health care: medical services that diagnose and treat illness and provide care for pregnant women, the elderly, and disabled.

High-tech industries: industries that use or make the most recently invented and technologically advanced products, such as computers.

Hunter-gatherers: people who feed themselves by hunting wild animals and gathering fruits, nuts, and berries.

Hydroelectric power: electricity created by capturing the power of running water.

Immigrant: a person who has come from another country to settle.

Imports: goods or services bought from another country.

Indigenous people: the first, or native, people of an area or country.

Industry: economic activity that is concerned with manufacturing goods or processing raw materials.

Investment: the provision of resources, usually money, for a business venture, with the goal of later making a profit from it.

Irrigation: supplying dry land with water through a system of canals or pipes so that crops will grow.

Landlocked: surrounded by land; with no access to the sea.

Latin America: those parts of the American continent where the official language is Spanish or Portuguese; often used to mean Mexico, and Central and South America.

Life expectancy: the average number of years a person can expect to live.

Literacy rate: the percentage of people over the age of 15 who can read and write a simple sentence.

Manufactured goods: products made from raw materials using machines, or made by hand.

Mestizo: a person of mixed race, with one parent European and the other native Indian.

Migrant: a person moving from one place or country to settle in another.

Mineral: a natural substance found in rocks of the Earth, such as a metal; removed by mining.

Missionary: a person who goes abroad trying to convert others to his or her particular religion.

Monarchy: a country ruled by a king or queen who has usually inherited the position rather than been elected by the people.

Monsoon: a wind that changes direction with the change of seasons; it causes a rainy season from April to October in southern Asia.

Multicultural: a group of people or a society made up of various different ethnic groups.

Native peoples: the people who belong by birth or origin to a place.

Natural resources: materials that occur naturally in an area, such as wood, coal, oil, or gas.

Nomads: people who move from place to place in search of food, water, and land to graze their animals.

Northern hemisphere: the half of the Earth that lies north of the equator.

Oasis: a fertile place in the desert, where water lies near or on the surface.

Ore: a mineral or rock from which a valuable metal, such as iron, gold, or copper, can be mined or extracted.

Overfarming: exhausting the soil by growing too many crops.

Overgrazing: exhausting the land by not moving animals around to graze in different places.

Overpopulation: when population growth exceeds economic growth and results in food shortages and lack of housing.

Paddy field: a flooded field where rice is grown.

Peninsula: a strip of land surrounded on three sides by water.

Petrochemicals: chemicals obtained from natural gas or oil.

Phosphate: a chemical compound used in fertilizers and detergents.

Pilgrim: a person who goes on a journey, or pilgrimage, to a sacred place.

Plantation: a large farm using hired workers to grow and harvest one main crop, such as coffee, sugarcane, rubber, or cotton.

Plateau: a high, flat area of land.

Population density: the number of people living in a given area of land.

Racism: the belief that one's own racial group is superior to others.

Raw materials: the basic materials, such as minerals or wood, used to make a product.

Refined oil: oil that has been treated to remove water and other impurities to separate out fuels such as gasolene and diesel.

Refugee: a person who has fled to another country in search of safety because of war, or political or religious oppression.

Regime: a particular government, or system of government.

Republic: a country ruled by elected representatives of its people, with an elected president rather than a king or queen.

Reserves: the amount of a resource, such as copper, known to exist, and not yet used.

Revolution: the overthrow of a government.

Ring of Fire: the zone around the Pacific Ocean where there are many volcanoes and frequent earthquakes.

Rural: relating to the countryside.

Sahel, the: zone of semi-desert and dry grassland to the south of the Sahara Desert in Africa.

Sanctions: penalties imposed by one or more countries on another to persuade that country to follow a certain course of action.

Savanna: open grassland in a tropical or sub-tropical region.

Shantytown: an area in or around a city where people live in temporary shacks, often without basic services such as running water.

Silt: very small particles deposited by a river or lake.

Slash-and-burn agriculture: a method of clearing land to create fields, by cutting down trees or bushes and then burning away any remaining roots.

Social services: welfare services provided by a state or local authority.

Socialism: a system of society in which goods are owned collectively and the whole community exercises political power.

Softwood: wood from cone-bearing trees, such as pine or cedar.

Soil erosion: the natural wearing away of the soil by wind or rain.

Southern hemisphere: the half of the Earth that lies south of the equator.

Standard of living: the quality of life in a country, usually measured by income, possessions, and levels of health care and education.

Staple crop or food: a crop that provides the main food of a region, such as rice, potatoes, or wheat.

Steppe: vast grass-covered plains, that stretch from eastern Europe across central Asia.

Stock exchange: an international market for buying and selling the stocks or shares of a public company.

Subsistence farming: raising just enough crops or animals to feed the farmer's family.

Technology: the development of methods, materials, and tools used in doing work.

Terrorist: a person who uses violence to win demands or influence the policies of a government.

Third world: the poorer, less-developed parts of the world in Asia, Africa, and Central and South America.

Urban: relating to a town or city.

Vegetation: the plant life of a region.

Welfare system: the way a government organizes assistance to its people, particularly the young, the elderly, the sick, and the unemployed.

West, the: the Western, industrially advanced countries of the world, specifically North America and western Europe.

Workforce: all the people available to work in a country; all the workers employed by a particular factory or place of work.

GAZETTEER

HOW TO USE THE GAZETTEER

This gazetteer helps you find places on the maps. For identification most places are followed by a brief description. Town has been used to describe all communities from villages to cities. For example, to find the city of Paris in France, look up its name in the gazetteer. The entry reads:

Paris *Town* France 97 F3

The first number, 97, tells you that Paris appears on the map on page 97. The second number, F3, shows that it is in square F3 of the grid printed over the map. Turn to page 97. Trace down from the letter F along the top of the grid and then across from the number 3 along the side of the grid. You will find Paris in the square where the letter and the number meet.

A

Aachen *Town* Germany 95 D7
Abadan *Town* Iran 153 F6
Abeokuta *Town* Nigeria 221 K12
Aberdeen *Town* UK 87 J5
Abha *Town* Saudi Arabia 153 C10
Abidjan *Town* Ivory Coast 21 H12
Abilene *Town* Texas, USA 35 H10
Abu Dhabi *Town* United Arab Emirates 153 H9
Abuja *Town* Nigeria 221 M11
Acapulco *Town* Mexico 39 G9
Accra *Town* Ghana 221 I12
Aconcagua, Mt. Argentina 41 F11, 71 F7
Ad Dammam *Town* Saudi Arabia 153 F8
Adamaoua, Massif d' *Region* Cameroon 205 E7
Adana *Town* Turkey 145 F8
Adapazari *Town* Turkey 145 C5
Addis Ababa *Town* Ethiopia 215 G9
Adelaide *Town* South Australia, Australia 259 I11
Aden *Town* Yemen 153 C12, 203 D3
Aden, Gulf of 10 F8, 132 C13, 203 D3, 215 J8
Adriatic Sea S. Europe 78 G11, 103 G6
Aegean Sea 78 H12, 131 H6
Afghanistan *Country* Central Asia 18 G6, 161 F9
Africa *Continent* 10 C7, 205
Agadir *Town* Morocco 208 F4
Agalega Islands Indian Ocean 10 F10, 18 F10
Agra *Town* India 167 F5
Aguascalientes *Town* Mexico 39 F7
Ahaggar Mts. Algeria 205 E4, 209 L8
Ahmadabad *Town* India 167 D6

Ahvaz *Town* Iran 153 F5
Ajaccio *Town* Corsica 97 L10
Akosombo Dam Ghana 221 J12
Akron *Town* Ohio, USA 37 F5
Al 'Amarah *Town* Iraq 153 F5
Al Hufuf *Town* Saudi Arabia 153 F8
Al Ladhiqiyah *Town* Syria 147 F3
Al Mukha *Town* Yemen 153 C12
Al' Aziziyah *Town* Libya 205 F2, 209 O4
Al-Basrah *Town* Iraq 153 F6
Al-Hillah *Town* Iraq 153 E5
Alabama *State* USA 37 D10
Åland *Island group* Finland 82 I8
Alaska *State* USA 19 Q3, 33 C2, 267 E2
Alaska, Gulf of USA 11 Q4, 20 E6, 265 G2
Alaska Range *Mountain range* Alaska, USA 20 D4, 33 C2
Albania *Country* S.E. Europe 124 I10, 18 D5
Albany *Town* New York, USA 37 I5
Albany *Town* Western Australia, Australia 258 D11
Albert Canal Belgium 91 H9
Albert, Lake Uganda/Zaire 205 I8, 239 F4
Alberta *Province* Canada 27 E12
Ålborg *Town* Denmark 82 E10
Albuquerque *Town* New Mexico, USA 35 E9
Aldabra Islands Indian Ocean 203 D6, 205 K10
Ålesund *Town* Norway 82 E7
Aleutian Islands Alaska, USA 11 O4, 20 B7, 33 B3, 265 E2
Alexandria *Town* Egypt 215 D1
Algeciras *Town* Spain 100 D9
Algeria *Country* N.W. Africa 18 B6, 209 J6
Algiers *Town* Algeria 209 K2
Aliákmonas *River* Greece 131 D3
Alicante *Town* Spain 100 I6
Alice Springs *Town* Northern Territory, Australia 259 H7
Allahabad *Town* India 167 G6
Allentown *Town* Pennsylvania, USA 37 H5
Alps *Mountain range* C. Europe 10 C5, 78 E11, 97 I7, 103 B3, 106 D8
Altai Mts. N. Asia 10 I5, 133 H7, 175 F5
Altiplano *Region* Bolivia 41 G9
Altun Mts. China 133 H9, 174 D9
Amarapura *Town* Burma 189 C4
Amarillo *Town* Texas, USA 35 G9
Amazon *River* Brazil/Peru 11 W9, 41 G6, 59 E5, 67 C4, G3
Amazonia *Region* S. America 11 W9, 41 G6, 59 E5, 67 E4
Ambato *Town* Ecuador 59 C5
Ambon *Town* Moluccas, Indonesia 197 O10
American Samoa *Dependent territory* Polynesia, Pacific Ocean 11 O10, 19 P10, 265 F6
Amherst *Town* Burma 189 D8
Amicante Islands Indian Ocean 203 E5
Amiens *Town* France 97 F2
Amman *Town* Jordan 147 F8
Amritsar *Town* India 167 E3
Amsterdam *Town* Netherlands 91 H6
Amsterdam Island Indian Ocean 18 H12, 203 G9
Amu Darya *River* Central Asia 132 E9, 161 F8

Amundsen Sea Pacific Ocean 269 B7
Amundsen-Scott *Research station* Antarctica 269 F5
Amur *River* China/Russian Federation 10 L4, 133 M7, 139 R10, 175 N2, Q3
An Nasiriyah *Town* Iraq 153 E5
An-Najaf *Town* Iraq 153 E5
Anchorage *Town* Alaska, USA 33 D2
Andalusia *Region* Spain 100 F8
Andaman Islands Indian Ocean 10 H8, 18 I8, 133 I13, 203 H3
Andaman Sea 189 C9, 203 I3
Andes *Mountain range* S. America 11 V9, W11, 41 E7, 59 D3, D9, 71 F6, G13
Andizhan *Town* Uzbekistan 161 H7
Andorra *Country* Europe 18 B5, 97 F10, 100 J2
Andorra la Vella *Town* Andorra 97 F10
Angel Falls *Waterfall* Venezuela 41 G4, 59 H4
Angkor Wat *Ancient site* Cambodia 189 G9
Anglesey *Island* UK 87 H9
Angola *Country* Southern Africa 18 D10, 247 D3
Angola Basin Atlantic Ocean 77 I9
Ankara *Town* Turkey 145 E6
Annaba *Town* Algeria 209 M2
Annapolis *Town* Maryland, USA 37 H6
Ann Arbor *Town* Michigan, USA 37 E5
Anshan *Town* China 175 O7
Antakya *Town* Turkey 145 G9
Antalya *Town* Turkey 145 D8
Antananarivo *Town* Madagascar 203 D7
Antarctic Peninsula Antarctic 269 B4
Antarctica *Continent* 265 I11, 269
Antigua and Barbuda *Country* West Indies 19 W7, 45 V11
Antipodes Islands New Zealand, Pacific Ocean 11 O13, 19 O13, 255 K16, 265 E9
Antofagasta *Town* Chile 41 E4
Antwerp *Town* Belgium 91 G9
Anvers Island Pacific Ocean 269 A3
Apeldoorn *Town* Netherlands 91 J6
Apennines *Mountain range* Italy 78 F11, 103 F6
Appalachian Mts. USA 11 V6, 21 M10, 37 G7
Apure *River* Venezuela 59 F2
Aqaba, Gulf of S.W. Asia 147 E11, 215 F2
Ar-Ramadi *Town* Iraq 153 E4
Arabian Peninsula S.W. Asia 10 E7
Arabian Sea 10 G7, 132 E12, 153 G12, 203 F3
Arad *Town* Romania 127 D6
Arafura Sea S.E. Asia 10 L9, 133 M16, 197 Q10, 265 B6
Arak *Town* Iran 153 G5
Aral Sea *Lake* Kazakhstan/Uzbekistan 10 G5, 132 E8, 161 D5, 258 E8
Ararat, Mt. Turkey 145 K6
Arauca *River* Colombia/Venezuela 59 E2
Arctic Bay *Town* Northwest Territories, Canada 27 H5
Arctic Circle 11 Z2
Arctic Ocean 10 K1, 267 F4
Ardabil *Town* Iran 153 G3
Ardennes *Region* Belgium 91 I11
Arequipa *Town* Peru 59 E10
Argentina *Country* S. America 19 W12,

71 G8
Argentine Basin Atlantic Ocean 77 F11
Århus *Town* Denmark 82 E11
Arica *Town* Chile 71 E2
Arizona *State* USA 33 K11
Arkansas *State* USA 35 K9
Arkhangel'sk *Town* Russian Federation 138 F4
Arlon *Town* Belgium 91 J12
Armenia *Country* S.W. Asia 18 E5, 121 P14
Armenia *Town* Colombia 59 D3
Arnhem *Town* Netherlands 91 J7
Arnhem Land *Region* Northern Territory, Australia 254 D8, 259 G4
Arno *River* Italy 103 D6
As Sulaymaniyah *Town* Iraq 153 E4
Ascension Island *Dependent territory* Atlantic Ocean 10 A9, 18 A9, 77 H8
Ashgabat *Town* Turkmenistan 161 D7
Ashmore and Cartier Islands Indian Ocean 18 K10, 203 K6
Asia *Continent* 10 I4, 132
Asmara *Town* Eritrea 215 G7
Assad, Lake Syria 147 H3
Assen *Town* Netherlands 91 K4
Astana *Town* Kazakhstan 161 G3
Astrakhan' *Town* Russian Federation 138 B8
Asunción *Town* Paraguay 71 J4
Aswân *Town* Egypt 215 E4
Aswân High Dam Egypt 215 E4
Asyût *Town* Egypt 215 D2
Atacama Desert Chile 11 V11, 41 F10, 71 F4
Athabasca, Lake Alberta/Saskatchewan, Canada 21 J6, 27 F11
Athens *Town* Greece 131 F7
Atlanta *Town* Georgia, USA 37 E9
Atlantic Ocean 10 B10, 11 X5, 77
Atlantic-Indian Ridge 77 J12
Atlas Mts. *Mountain range* Morocco 10 B6, 205 D2, 208 H4
Auckland *Town* New Zealand 262 F3
Auckland Islands New Zealand, Pacific Ocean 11 N13, 19 N13, 255 I16, 265 D9
Augsburg *Town* Germany 95 H10
Augusta *Town* Maine 37 K4
Austin *Town* Texas, USA 35 I12
Australasia and Oceania 254-255
Australia *Country and continent* 10 K10, 18 K11, 259 G8
Australian Capital Territory *Territory* Australia 259 L11
Austria *Country* Europe 18 C5, 106 J6
Ayacucho *Town* Peru 59 D9
Ayers Rock *see* Uluru
Ayutthaya *Town* Thailand 189 E9
Az Zarqa' *Town* Jordan 147 F7
Azerbaijan *Country* S.W. Asia 18 F5, 121 P15
Azores *Island group* Atlantic Ocean 11 Z5, 19 Y5, 77 G4
Azov, Sea of Russian Federation/ Ukraine 78 J10, 121 J9, 138 A7

B

Babruysk *Town* Belarus 111 J10
Babylon *Ancient site* Iraq 153 E4
Bacau *Town* Romania 127 I6

Bacolod *Town* Philippines 196 L4
Badgastein *Town* Austria 106 H7
Baden *Town* Austria 106 K5
Badlands *Region* North/South Dakota, USA 35 F3
Baffin Bay Canada/Greenland 11 W2, 21 O3, 27 I4, 267 C7
Baffin Island Northwest Territories, Canada 11 V2, 21 N4, 27 J6, 267 B7
Bafoussam *Town* Cameroon 232 D8
Baghdad *Town* Iraq 153 E4
Baguio *Town* Philippines 196 K2
Bahamas *Country* West Indies 11 V7, 19 V7, 45 M5
Bahía Blanca *Town* Argentina 71 I9
Bahrain *Country* S.W. Asia 18 F7, 153 F8
Baia Mare *Town* Romania 127 F4
Baikal, Lake Russian Federation 10 J4, 133 J6, 139 M10
Baja California *Peninsula* Mexico 39 B3
Baker Island *Dependent territory* Pacific Ocean 19 P9, 255 L6, 265 E5
Bakersfield *Town* California, USA 33 H11
Bakhtaran *Town* Iran 153 F4
Baku *Town* Azerbaijan 121 T13
Balaton, Lake Hungary 115 G11
Balearic Islands Spain 78 E12, 100 J5
Bali *Island* Indonesia 196 I12
Balikesir *Town* Turkey 145 B6
Balikpapan *Town* Borneo, Indonesia 196 J9
Balkan Mts. S.E. Europe 78 H11, 124 K7, 127 F11
Balkhash, Lake Kazakhstan 10 HS, 133 G8, 161 I5
Ballarat *Town* Victoria, Australia 259 J12
Baltic Sea N. Europe 10 D4, 78 G8, 82 I10, 111 E5
Baltimore *Town* Maryland, USA 37 H6
Bamako *Town* Mali 221 F9
Banda Sea S.E. Asia 133 M15, 196 M10
Bandar Seri Begawan *Town* Brunei 196 I7
Bandar-e 'Abbas *Town* Iran 153 H8
Bandar-e-Bushehr *Town* Iran 153 G7
Bandundu *Town* Zaire 232 G11
Bandung *Town* Java, Indonesia 196 F12
Bangalore *Town* India 187 E11
Bangkok *Town* Thailand 189 E9
Bangladesh *Country* S. Asia 18 H7, 167 J6
Bangui *Town* Central African Republic 232 G9
Banja Luka *Town* Bosnia and Herzegovina 124 F4
Banjarmasin *Town* Borneo, Indonesia 196 I10
Banjul *Town* Gambia 220 B8
Banks Island Northwest Territories, Canada 11 S2, 21 H3, 29 E5, 267 C4
Baotou *Town* China 178 K8
Baranavichy *Town* Belarus 109 H10
Barbados *Country* Caribbean Sea 19 W8, 45 W14
Barbuda *Island* Antigua and Barbuda 45 V11
Barcelona *Town* Spain 100 K3
Barcelona *Town* Venezuela 59 G1
Bareilly *Town* India 167 G4
Barents Sea Arctic Ocean 10 E2, 78 K4, 138 G3, 267 H7
Bari *Town* Italy 103 J9
Barinas *Town* Venezuela 59 F2
Barisian Mts. Sumatra, Indonesia 196 C10
Barnaul *Town* Russian Federation 139 I10
Barquisemeto *Town* Venezuela 59 F1
Barranquilla *Town* Colombia 59 D1

Barysaw *Town* Belarus 111 J9
Basque Provinces Spain 100 F2
Bassein *Town* Burma 189 B7
Basseterre *Town* St. Kitts and Nevis 45 U11
Batangas *Town* Philippines 196 K3
Batdâmbâng *Town* Cambodia 189 G10
Baton Rouge *Town* Louisiana, USA 35 K11
Bavarian Alps *Mountain range* Austria/Germany 95 I11
Baykonur *Space center* Kazakhstan 161 F5
Beagle Channel Argentina 71 I16
Bear Island *Island group* Russian Federation 139 Q3
Beaufort Sea Arctic Ocean 11 Q2, 20 F4, 27 C6, 33 C1, 267 D3
Beaumont *Town* Texas, USA 35 J12
Beersheba *Town* Israel 147 E8
Beijing *Town* China 175 M8
Beira *Town* Mozambique 247 J6
Beirut *Town* Lebanon 147 F5
Bejaia *Town* Algeria 209 L2
Belarus *Country* E. Europe 18 D4, 111 I10
Belém *Town* Brazil 67 H3
Belfast *Town* UK 87 G7
Belgium *Country* Europe 18 C4, 91 G10
Belgrade *Town* Serbia, Yugoslavia 124 I4
Belize *Country* Central America 19 U7, 44 D8
Belle Île *Island* France 97 B5
Bellevue *Town* Washington, USA 33 G4
Bellinghausen Sea Pacific Ocean 269 B5
Bello *Town* Colombia 59 D2
Belmopan *Town* Belize 44 D8
Belo Horizonte *Town* Brazil 67 I9
Ben Nevis *Mountain* UK 87 H5
Bengal, Bay of India 10 H7, 133 H12, 167 H9, 203 I3
Benghazi *Town* Libya 209 R4
Benidorm *Town* Spain 100 I6
Benin *Country* W. Africa 18 C8, 221 K10
Berbera *Town* Somalia 215 I8
Berbérati *Town* Central African Republic 232 F9
Bergen *Town* Norway 82 D8
Bergen op Zoom *Town* Netherlands 91 G8
Bering Sea Pacific Ocean 11 O3, 20 B6, 33 A3, 139 T3, 265 E2
Bering Strait Arctic Ocean/Pacific Ocean 11 P3, 20 C5, 33 B2, 265 F1
Berlin *Town* Germany 95 J5
Bermuda *Dependent territory* Atlantic Ocean 11 W6, 19 I8
Bern *Town* Switzerland 106 C8
Bethlehem *Town* West Bank 147 E8
Bhopal *Town* India 167 F6
Bhutan *Country* S. Asia 18 I6, 167 J5
Bialystok *Town* Poland 115 K3
Bielefeld *Town* Germany 95 F5
Bien Hoa *Town* Vietnam 189 I11
Bihac *Town* Bosnia and Herzegovina 124 E4
Bikini Island Marshall Islands, Pacific Ocean 265 D5
Bila Tserkva *Town* Ukraine 120 F5
Bilbao *Town* Spain 100 G1
Birmingham *Town* Alabama, USA 37 D9
Birmingham *Town* UK 87 J10
Biscay, Bay of 10 B5, 78 D11, 100 G1
Bishkek *Town* Kyrgyzstan 161 I6
Bismarck *Town* North Dakota, USA 35 H3
Bismarck Archipelago *Island group* Papua New Guinea 10 L9, 254 G6, 259 L1

Bissau *Town* Guinea-Bissau 220 B9
Bitola *Town* Macedonia 124 J9
Biwa, Lake Japan 185 F9
Black Forest *Region* Germany 78 F10, 95 E10
Black Hills South Dakota, USA 35 G4
Black Rock Desert Nevada, USA 33 H8
Black Sea Asia/Europe 10 E5, 78 J11, 127 L10, 132 B8, 138 A7
Black Volta *River* W. Africa 205 C6, 221 H10
Blackpool *Town* UK 87 I8
Blantyre *Town* Malawi 239 H14
Blenheim *Town* New Zealand 262 E7
Blida *Town* Algeria 209 K2
Bloemfontein *Town* South Africa 247 G10
Blue Mts. Oregon/Washington, USA 33 H6
Blue Nile *River* E. Africa 205 I5, 215 E7
Bobo Dioulasso *Town* Burkina 221 G10
Bogor *Town* Java, Indonesia 196 F12
Bogota *Town* Colombia 59 D3
Bohemia *Region* Czech Republic 115 C8
Bohemian Forest *Region* Germany 95 J9
Boise *Town* Idaho, USA 33 H6
Bolivia *Country* S. America 19 W10, 59 G10
Bologna *Town* Italy 103 E5
Bombay *Town* India 167 D8, 203 G3
Bonin Islands Pacific Ocean 10 L6
Bonn *Town* Germany 95 E7
Borås *Town* Sweden 82 F10
Bordeaux *Town* France 97 D8
Borneo *Island* S.E. Asia 10 J9, 133 K14, 196 I8
Bornholm *Island* Denmark 78 G8, 82 G12
Borobudur *Ancient site* Java, Indonesia 196 G12
Bosnia and Herzegovina *Country* S.E. Europe 18 D5, 124 F4
Bosporus Channel Turkey 145 C5
Boston *Town* Massachusetts, USA 37 J5
Bothnia, Gulf of Finland/Sweden 78 H6, 82 I6
Botosani *Town* Romania 127 I4
Botrange *Mountain* Belgium 91 J10
Botswana *Country* Southern Africa 18 D11, 247 F7
Bounty Islands New Zealand, Pacific Ocean 11 O13, 19 N13, 255 L15, 265 E9
Bourke *Town* New South Wales, Australia 254 G12
Bournemouth *Town* UK 87 J12
Bouvet Island *Dependent territory* Atlantic Ocean 77 I12
Boyoma Falls *Waterfall* Zaire 205 H8, 232 J10
Bradford *Town* UK 87 J8
Brahmaputra (Yarlung Zangbo) *River* India/China 133 H10, 167 K5, 174 C11
Braila *Town* Romania 127 K7
Brasília *Town* Brazil 67 H8
Brasov *Town* Romania 127 H7
Bratislava *Town* Slovakia 115 F10
Braunschweig *Town* Germany 95 H5
Bravo del Norte *River* Mexico 39 E2
Brazil *Country* S. America 19 W9, 67 F5
Brazil Basin Atlantic Ocean 77 G8
Brazilian Highlands *Mountain range* Brazil 41 J9, 67 I8
Brazzaville *Town* Congo 232 F12
Breda *Town* Netherlands 91 H8
Bremen *Town* Germany 95 F4
Brest *Town* Belarus 111 F11
Bridgeport *Town* Connecticut, USA 37 I5
Bridgetown *Town* Barbados 45 W14

Brighton *Town* UK 87 K12
Brindisi *Town* Italy 103 K9
Brisbane *Town* Queensland, Australia 259 M8, 265 C7
Bristol *Town* UK 87 I11
British Columbia *Province* Canada 27 B12
British Indian Ocean Territory *Dependent territory* Indian Ocean 18 H9, 203 G5
British Isles *Country* Europe 10 B4, 78 C8, 87
British Virgin Islands *Dependent Territory* Caribbean Sea 45 T10
Brittany *Region* France 97 B4
Brno *Town* Czech Republic 115 F8
Broken Hill *Town* New South Wales, Australia 259 J10
Broken Ridge Indian Ocean 203 I9
Brooks Range *Mountain range* Alaska, USA 20 D4, 33 C1
Broome *Town* Western Australia, Australia 258 D6
Bruges *Town* Belgium 91 F9
Brunei *Country* Borneo, S.E. Asia 18 J8, 196 H7
Brussels *Town* Belgium 91 G9
Bucaramanga *Town* Colombia 59 D2
Bucharest *Town* Romania 127 I9
Budapest *Town* Hungary 115 H10
Buenaventura *Town* Colombia 59 C3
Buenos Aires *Town* Argentina 71 J8, 77 E10
Buenos Aires, Lake (Lake General Carrera) Argentina/Chile 41 F15, 71 G13
Buffalo *Town* New York, USA 37 G4
Bujumbura *Town* Burundi 239 E7
Bukavu *Town* Zaire 232 K11
Bukhara *Town* Uzbekistan 161 F7
Bulawayo *Town* Zimbabwe 247 H7
Bulgaria *Country* E. Europe 18 D5, 127 H11
Buon Me Thuot *Town* Vietnam 189 I10
Buraydah *Town* Saudi Arabia 153 D7
Burgas *Town* Bulgaria 127 J11
Burgundy *Region* France 97 H5
Burkina *Country* W. Africa 18 B8, 221 I9
Bursa *Town* Turkey 145 C6
Burundi *Country* Africa 18 E9, 239 E7
Butuan *Town* Philippines 196 M5
Buzau *Town* Romania 127 I8
Bydgoszcz *Town* Poland 115 G3

C

Cabanatuan *Town* Philippines 196 K2
Cabimas *Town* Venezuela 59 E1
Cabinda *Region* Angola 18 C9, 232 E12, 247 B1
Cabo da Roca *Cape* Portugal 78 C11, 100 A6
Cabot Strait Canada 29 J5
Cacak *Town* Serbia, Yugoslavia 124 I5
Cadiz *Town* Philippines 196 L4
Cádiz *Town* Spain 100 D8
Caen *Town* France 97 D3
Caernarfon *Town* UK 87 H9
Cagayan de Oro *Town* Philippines 196 M5
Cagliari *Town* Sardinia 103 C11
Cairns *Town* Queensland, Australia 259 K5
Cairo *Town* Egypt 215 D1
Calabria *Region* Italy 103 I12
Calais *Town* France 97 F1
Calama *Town* Chile 71 F4
Calbayog *Town* Philippines 196 M4

Calcutta *Town* India 167 J7
Calgary *Town* Alberta, Canada 27 E13
Cali *Town* Colombia 59 C3
California *State* USA 33 H10
Callao *Town* Peru 59 C8
Camaguey *Town* Cuba 45 L6
Cambodia *Country* S.E. Asia 18 I8, 189 H10
Cambrian Mts. UK 87 H10
Cambridge *Town* UK 87 K10
Cameron Highlands *Mountain range* Malaysia 189 E14
Cameroon *Country* Central Africa 18 C8, 232 D8
Cameroon, Mt. *Volcano* Cameroon 232 D9
Campbell Island New Zealand, Pacific Ocean 19 N13, 265 E9
Campeche *Town* Mexico 39 K8
Campinas *Town* Brazil 67 H10
Can Tho *Town* Vietnam 189 H11
Canada *Country* N. America 19 S3, 26–27, 28–29
Canary Basin Atlantic Ocean 77 G6
Canary Islands Atlantic Ocean 10 A6, 18 A6, 77 H5, 205 A3
Canberra *Town* Australian Capital Territory, Australia 254 G13, 259 L11, 265 C8
Cancún *Town* Mexico 39 L7
Cannes *Town* France 97 J9
Canterbury *Town* UK 87 L11
Canton *Town* China 175 N14
Cape Basin Atlantic Ocean 77 I10
Cape Canaveral *Peninsula* Florida, USA 37 G12
Cape Cod *Peninsula* Massachusetts, USA 21 N9, 37 K5
Cape Horn *Peninsula* Chile 11 off W13, 41 off G16, 71 I16, 77 D12
Cape of Good Hope *Peninsula* South Africa 10 D12, 77 J10, 203 B9, 205 G14, 247 E12
Cape Town *Town* South Africa 203 B9, 247 E11
Cape Verde *Peninsula* Senegal 205 A5, 220 A8
Cape Verde Islands Atlantic Ocean 10 A7, 18 A7, 77 G6, 205 A5
Cape York *Peninsula* Queensland, Australia 254 F9, 259 J4
Cappadocia *Region* Turkey 145 G7
Capri *Island* Italy 103 G9
Caracas *Town* Venezuela 59 G1
Cardiff *Town* UK 87 I11
Caribbean Sea 11 V8, 41 F2, 44 J10, 77 C6
Caroline Islands Federated States of Micronesia, Pacific Ocean 10 L8, 254 G5
Carpathians *Mountain range* Central Europe 10 C4, 78 H10, 115 I8, 120 B6, 127 F10, H8
Carpentaria, Gulf of Northern Territory/Queensland, Australia 254 E8, 259 I5
Carson City *Town* Nevada, USA 33 H9
Cartagena *Town* Colombia 59 D1
Cartagena *Town* Spain 100 H7
Casablanca *Town* Morocco 208 G3
Cascade Range *Mountain range* USA 21 H7, 33 G6
Caspian Sea *Lake* Central Asia 10 F5, 78 M11, 132 D8, 138 B9, 161 B6
Castries *Town* St. Lucia 45 V14
Catalonia *Region* Spain 100 J3
Catania *Town* Sicily 103 H13
Caucasus Mts. Europe/Asia 10 E5, 78 L11, 121 O12, 132 C8
Cayenne *Town* French Guiana 59 L3

Cayman Islands *Dependent territory* Caribbean Sea 44 I7
Cebu *Town* Philippines 196 M4
Cedar Rapids *Town* Iowa, USA 35 K5
Celebes Sea S.E. Asia 133 L14, 196 K8
Central African Republic *Country* Central Africa 18 D8, 232 H8
Central America *Region* 11 U7, 41, 44
Central Siberian Plateau Russian Federation 10 I2, 133 K3, 139 M5
Ceuta *Spanish enclave* Morocco 208 H2
Cevennes *Mountain range* France 97 G8
Chad *Country* Central Africa 18 D7, 232 G4
Chad, Lake Central Africa 205 F5, 221 P9, 232 F5
Chagos Archipelago *Island group* Indian Ocean 10 H9
Chalbi Desert Kenya 239 J3
Chandigarh *Town* India 167 F3
Changchun *Town* China 175 O5
Changsha *Town* China 175 M12
Channel Islands UK 18 B4, 78 D10, 87 I13, 97 C3
Channel Tunnel UK/France 87 L11, 97 F1
Chapala, Lake Mexico 39 E7
Chardzhev *Town* Turkmenistan 161 E7
Charleroi *Town* Belgium 91 G11
Charleston *Town* South Carolina, USA 37 G10
Charleston *Town* West Virginia, USA 37 F7
Charlotte *Town* North Carolina, USA 37 F8
Charlottetown *Town* Prince Edward Island, Canada 29 J6
Chatham Islands New Zealand, Pacific Ocean 11 O13, 19 O13, 255 L15, 265 E8
Chattanooga *Town* Tennessee, USA 37 E8
Cheju *Town* South Korea 175 Q9
Chelyabinsk *Town* Russian Federation 138 F8
Chemnitz *Town* Germany 95 J7
Chengdu *Town* China 175 J11
Chenonceaux *Town* France 97 E5
Cherbourg *Town* France 97 C2
Cherkasy *Town* Ukraine 120 G6
Chernihiv *Town* Ukraine 120 G4
Chernivtski *Town* Ukraine 120 C6
Chernobyl *Town* Ukraine 120 F4
Cheyenne *Town* Wyoming, USA 35 F6
Chiang Mai *Town* Thailand 189 E6
Chicago *Town* Illinois, USA 35 L5
Chichén Itzá *Ancient site* Mexico 39 L7
Chiclayo *Town* Peru 59 B7
Chihuahua *Town* Mexico 39 E3
Chile *Country* S. America 19 V12, 71 F6,F14
Chilka, Lake India 167 H8
Chillán *Town* Chile 71 F9
Chimbote *Town* Peru 59 C7
China *Country* E. Asia 18 I6, 175 G8
Chingola *Town* Zambia 239 D12
Chios *Island* Greece 131 I7
Chisinau *Town* Moldova 120 E8
Chittagong *Town* India 167 K7
Chitungwiza *Town* Zimbabwe 247 I6
Chon Buri *Town* Thailand 189 E9
Ch'ongjin *Town* North Korea 175 Q6
Chongqing *Town* China 175 K12
Christchurch *Town* New Zealand 262 E9
Christmas Island Indian Ocean 18 J10, 203 J6
Chugoku Mts. Japan 185 D10
Chukchi Sea Arctic Ocean 11 O2, 20 B4, 139 R1, 267 F1
Churchill *Town* Manitoba, Canada

27 I10
Cincinnati *Town* Ohio, USA 37 E6
Citlaltépetl (Orizaba) *Volcano* Mexico 39 H8
Ciudad Bolívar *Town* Venezuela 59 H2
Ciudad Guayana *Town* Venezuela 59 H2
Ciudad Juárez *Town* Mexico 39 E2
Clermont-Ferrand *Town* France 97 G6
Cleveland *Town* Ohio, USA 37 F5
Clipperton Island *Dependent territory* Pacific Ocean 19 T8, 265 I5
Cluj-Napoca *Town* Romania 127 F5
Coast Mts. Canada 11 R3, 20 G6
Coast Ranges *Mountain range* N. America 11 S5, 21 H9, 33 F8
Cobán *Town* Guatemala 44 C8
Cochabamba *Town* Bolivia 59 G10
Cochin *Town* India 167 E12
Coco *River* Honduras/Nicaragua 44 F10
Cocos Islands Indian Ocean 10 I10, 18 I10, 203 J6
Coihaique *Town* Chile 71 G13
Coimbatore *Town* India 167 E11
Coimbra *Town* Portugal 100 B4
Cologne *Town* Germany 95 E7
Colombia *Country* S. America 19 V8, 59 E3
Colombo *Town* Sri Lanka 167 F13, 203 H4
Colón *Town* Panama 44 H14
Colorado *River* Argentina 41 G13, 71 I10
Colorado *River* Mexico/USA 21 J9, 33 I12, 35 E6
Colorado *State* USA 35 E6
Colorado Springs *Town* Colorado, USA 35 F7
Columbia *River* Canada/USA 27 D13, 33 G5
Columbia *Town* South Carolina, USA 37 F9
Columbus *Town* Georgia, USA 37 E10
Columbus *Town* Ohio, USA 37 F6
Communism Peak *Mountain* Tajikistan 161 H7
Como, Lake Italy 103 C3
Comodoro Rivadavia *see* Rivadavia
Comoros *Country* Indian Ocean 10 E10, 18 E10, 203 D6
Conakry *Town* Guinea 220 C10
Concepción *Town* Chile 71 F9
Concord *Town* California, USA 33 G10
Concord *Town* New Hampshire, USA 37 J4
Congo *Country* Central Africa 18 C9, 232 F10
Congo (Zaire) *River* Central Africa 10 C9, 205 F9, G8, 232 F11, G10
Congo Basin *Region* Congo/Zaire 205 G8
Connecticut *State* USA 37 J6
Constance, Lake Switzerland/Austria/Germany 95 G12, 106 E7
Constanta *Town* Romania 127 K9
Constantine *Town* Algeria 209 M2
Cook Islands *Dependent territory* Polynesia, Pacific Ocean 11 P10, 19 P10, 255 O9, 265 F6
Cook Strait New Zealand 262 F7
Cook, Mt. New Zealand 262 C9
Copenhagen *Town* Denmark 82 F11
Copiapó *Town* Chile 71 F5
Coral Sea Islands *Dependent territory* Pacific Ocean 18 M10, 265 C7
Coral Sea Pacific Ocean 10 M10, 254 G8, 259 L4, 265 C6
Córdoba *Town* Argentina 71 H7
Córdoba *Town* Spain 100 E7
Corfu *Island* Greece 131 A5
Corinth *Town* Greece 131 E8

Cork *Town* Ireland 87 E10
Coromandel *Town* New Zealand 262 G3
Coromandel Coast India 167 G11
Corpus Christi *Town* Texas, USA 35 I13
Corrib, Lough *Lake* Ireland 87 E8
Corrientes *Town* Argentina 71 J5
Corsica *Island* France 78 E11, 97 L10
Costa Blanca *Coast* Spain 100 I7
Costa Brava *Coast* Spain 100 K3
Costa del Sol *Coast* Spain 100 F8
Costa Rica *Country* Central America 19 U8, 44 E13
Côte d'Azur *Coast* France 97 J9
Coventry *Town* UK 87 J10
Craiova *Town* Romania 127 F9
Crete *Island* Greece 78 H13, 131 H12
Crimea *Peninsula* Ukraine 121 H9
Croatia *Country* S.E. Europe 18 C5, 109 H4
Crozet Islands Indian Ocean 10 F13, 18 F13, 203 E10
Cuba *Country* Caribbean Sea 19 V7, 45 K6
Cúcuta *Town* Colombia 59 E2
Cuenca *Town* Ecuador 59 C5
Culiacán *Town* Mexico 39 D5
Cumaná *Town* Venezuela 59 H1
Curitiba *Town* Brazil 67 H10
Cusco *Town* Peru 59 E9
Cyclades *Island group* Greece 131 H9
Cyprus *Country* Europe 18 E6, 132 B10, 145 F10
Czech Republic *Country* Central Europe 18 C4, 115 E7

D

Da Lat *Town* Vietnam 189 J10
Da Nang *Town* Vietnam 189 I8
Dacca *Town* Bangladesh 167 J7
Dagupan *Town* Philippines 196 K2
Dakar *Town* Senegal 220 A8
Dalian *Town* China 178 O8
Dallas *Town* Texas, USA 35 I10
Dalmatia *Region* Croatia 109 G7
Damascus *Town* Syria 147 F6
Dampier *Town* Western Australia, Australia 258 C7
Danube *River* Central Europe 10 D5, 78 G10, H11, 95 G11, J10, 106 K5, 109 K4, 115 G10, J5, 127 F10, K8
Danube Delta Romania 127 L7
Danzig, Gulf of Poland/Russian Federation 115 H14
Dar es Salaam *Town* 239 K9
Dardanelles *Channel* Turkey 145 A5
Darling *River* New South Wales, Australia 10 L11, 254 F12, 259 K9
Dartmoor *Region* UK 87 H12
Darwin *Town* Northern Territory, Australia 259 G4
Dashkhovuz *Town* Turkmenistan 161 D6
Datong *Town* China 175 L8
Daugavpils *Town* Latvia 111 H7
Davao *Town* Philippines 196 M6
David *Town* Panama 44 G15
Davis Sea Antarctica 269 K5
Davis Strait Canada/Greenland 11 W2, 21 O4, 27 L5, 267 B8
Dayr az Zawr *Town* Syria 147 J3
Dayton *Town* Ohio, USA 37 E6
De Bilt *Town* Netherlands 91 I6
Dead Sea *Lake* Israel/Jordan/West Bank 132 B10, 147 E8
Death Valley California, USA 21 I10
Debrecen *Town* Hungary 115 J10
Deccan Plateau *Region* India 10 H7,

167 E8
Delaware *State* USA 37 I7
Delphi *Ancient site* Greece 131 D7
Democratic Republic of Congo (Zaire) *Country* Central Africa 18 D9, 232 H11
Denali (Mt. McKinley) *Mountain* Alaska, USA 20 E5, 33 C2
Denizli *Town* Turkey 145 C7
Denmark *Country* Europe 18 C4, 82 E10
Denmark Strait Greenland/Iceland 10 A2, 267 E9
Denver *Town* Colorado, USA 35 F7
Derby *Town* UK 87 J9
Des Moines *Town* Iowa, USA 35 J6
Detroit *Town* Michigan, USA 37 E5
Devon Island Northwest Territories, Canada 11 U1, 27 H4, 267 C6
Dezful *Town* Iran 153 F5
Dhanbad *Town* India 167 I6
Dharwad *Town* India 167 D10
Dieppe *Town* France 97 E2
Dijon *Town* France 97 H5
Dimlang *Mountain* Nigeria 221 O11
Dinaric Alps Bosnia and Herzegovina/Croatia 109 F6
Dire Dawa *Town* Ethiopia 215 H9
Diyarbakir *Town* Turkey 145 I7
Djebel Toubkal *Mountain* Morocco 208 G4
Djibouti *Country* E. Africa 18 F8 215 H8
Djibouti *Town* Djibouti 203 D3, 215 I8
Dnieper *River* E. Europe 10 E4, 78 I9, J10, 111 K12, 120 G5, I7
Dniester *River* Ukraine 78 I10, 120 C6
Dnipropetrovs'k *Town* Ukraine 121 I7
Dobrich *Town* Bulgaria 127 K10
Dodecanese *Island group* Greece 131 J9
Dodoma *Town* Tanzania 239 I8
Doha *Town* Qatar 153 G8
Dolomites *Mountain range* Alps, Italy 103 E3
Dominica *Country* Caribbean Sea 19 W7, 45 U13
Dominican Republic *Country* Caribbean Sea 19 W7, 45 P9
Don *River* Russian Federation 10 E4, 78 K9, K10
Donbass *Region* Ukraine 121 K7
Donegal Bay Ireland 87 E7
Donets'k *Town* Ukraine 121 K7
Dongguang *Town* China 175 N14
Dordogne *River* France 97 E7
Dordrecht *Town* Netherlands 91 H7
Dortmund *Town* Germany 95 E6
Douglas *Town* Isle of Man, UK 87 H8
Douro (Duero) *River* Portugal/Spain 78 C12, 100 D3, F3
Dovala *Town* Cameroon 232 D9
Dover *Town* Delaware, USA 37 H6
Dover *Town* UK 87 L11
Drake Passage *Channel* Atlantic Ocean/Pacific Ocean 269 A1
Drakensberg *Mountain range* South Africa 205 H14, 247 G11
Drava *River* S.E. Europe 78 G10, 109 F2, G4
Dresden *Town* Germany 95 K7
Drobeta-Turnu-Severin *Town* Romania 127 E8
Dubai *Town* United Arab Emirates 153 H8
Dublin *Town* Ireland 87 G8
Dubrovnik *Town* Yugoslavia 109 J9
Dufourspitze, Mt. Switzerland 106 C9
Duisburg *Town* Germany 95 D6
Duluth *Town* Minnesota, USA 35 K3
Dumont d'Urville *Research station* Antarctica 269 H9
Dundee *Town* UK 87 J5
Dunedin *Town* New Zealand 262 C11

Dunkirk *Town* France 97 F1
Durango *Town* Mexico 39 E5
Durban *Town* South Africa 247 I10
Dushanbe *Town* Tajikistan 161 G8
Düsseldorf *Town* Germany 95 D6
Dvina (Northern, Western) *River* Russian Federation 78 I8, L6, 111 G6, J8, 138 E5
Dzhugdzhur Range *Mountain range* Russian Federation 133 O6, 139 Q8

E

East China Sea China 10 K6, 133 L10, 265 A3
East Frisian Islands Germany 95 E3
East London *Town* South Africa 247 H11
East Siberian Sea, Arctic Ocean 11 N2, 133 P3, 139 P3, 267 H2
Easter Island *Dependent territory* Polynesia, Pacific Ocean 265 I7
Eastern Ghats *Mountain range* 167 G9
Ebro *River* Spain 78 D11, 100 H3
Ecuador *Country* S. America 19 V9, 59 C5
Edinburgh *Town* UK 87 I6
Edmonton *Town* Alberta, Canada 27 E13
Egypt *Country* N.E. Africa 18 D7, 147 D10, 215 D2
Eindhoven *Town* Netherlands 91 I8
El Aaiun *Town* Western Sahara 208 D5
El Faiyûm *Town* Egypt 215 D2
El Mansûra *Town* Egypt 215 D1
El Minya *Town* Egypt 215 D2
El Obeid *Town* Sudan 215 D7
El Paso *Town* Texas, USA 35 E11
El Salvador *Country* Central America 19 U8, 44 C10
El'bruz, Mts. Russian Federation 78 K11
Elat *Town* Israel 147 E10
Elâzig *Town* Turkey 145 I7
Elba *Island* Italy 103 D7
Elbe *River* Germany 78 F9, 95 H3, J6
Elbert, Mt. Colorado, USA 35 E7
Elburz Mts. Iran 132 D9, 153 G4
Ellesmere Island Northwest Territories, Canada 21 N1, 27 H2
Ellsworth Mts. Antarctica 269 D5
Emperor Seamounts Pacific Ocean 265 D3
Enderby Land *Region* Antarctica 269 H3
England *Region* UK 87 K10
English Channel France/UK 78 D9, 87 J12
Enschede *Town* Netherlands 91 J6
Entebbe *Town* Uganda 239 G5
Ephesus *Ancient site* Turkey 145 A7
Epidaurus *Ancient site* Greece 131 E8
Equator 11 Z9
Equatorial Guinea *Country* Africa 18 C9, 232 C9
Erfurt *Town* Germany 95 H7
Erg Tifernine *Desert region* Algeria 209 M7
Erie *Town* Pennsylvania, USA 37 G4
Erie, Lake Canada/USA 21 M9, 29 F9, 37 F5
Eritrea *Country* E. Africa 215 G6
Erzurum *Town* Turkey 145 J6
Esequibo *River* Guyana 59 I3
Esfahan *Town* Iran 153 G5
Eskisehir *Town* Turkey 145 C6
Esmeraldas *Town* Ecuador 59 B4
Essen *Town* Germany 95 E6
Estonia *Country* E. Europe 18 D3, 111 H4

Ethiopia *Country* E. Africa 18 E8, 215 H9
Ethiopian Highlands *Mountain range* Ethiopia 10 E8, 205 I6, 215 G9
Etna, Mt. *Volcano* Sicily 78 G12, 103 H13
Eugene *Town* Washington, USA 33 F6
Euphrates *River* S.W. Asia 132 C9, 145 H8, 147 K4, 153 E5
Europe *Continent* 10 D4, 78–79
Evansville *Town* Indiana, USA 37 D7
Everest, Mt. China/Nepal 10 H6, 133 H11, 167 J5, 174 D12
Everett *Town* Washington, USA 33 G4
Everglades Swamp *Region* Florida, USA 21 M11, 37 F13
Evvoia *Island* Greece 131 F6
Exeter *Town* UK 87 H11
Eyre, Lake South Australia, Australia 10 L11, 254 E11, 259 I9

F

Faeroe Islands *Dependent territory* Atlantic Ocean 10 B3, 18 B3, 77 H3, 78 C6
Fairbanks *Town* Alaska, USA 33 D2
Faisalabad *Town* Pakistan 167 D3
Falkland Islands *Dependent Territory* Atlantic Ocean 11 W13, 19 W13, 41 H16, 71 K15, 77 E11
Famagusta *Town* Cyprus 145 F9
Faro *Town* Portugal 100 B8
Fens, The *Region* UK 87 K10
Fergana *Town* Uzbekistan 161 H7
Fernando de Noronho *Island* Atlantic Ocean 19 J9, 77 G8
Fez *Town* Morocco 208 H3
Fianarantsoa *Town* Madagascar 203 D7
Fiji *Country* Melanesia, Pacific Ocean 11 O10, 19 O10, 255 K9, 265 E7
Finland *Country* Europe 18 D3, 82 K6
Finland, Gulf of 78 H7, 82 K9, 111 I3
Fitzroy *River* Western Australia, Australia 258 E6
Flinders *River* Queensland, Australia 259 J6
Flinders Ranges *Mountain range* South Australia, Australia 259 I10
Flint *Town* Michigan, USA 37 E4
Florence *Town* Italy 103 E6
Flores *Island* Indonesia 196 L12
Florida *State* USA 37 F11
Focsani *Town* Romania 127 J7
Formentera *Island* Balearic Islands, Spain 100 J6
Formosa *Town* Argentina 71 J4
Fort Lauderdale *Town* Florida, USA 37 G13
Fort Wayne *Town* Indiana, USA 37 E5
Fort Worth *Town* Texas, USA 35 I10
Fortaleza *Town* Brazil 67 K4
Forth *River* UK 87 I5
Foxe Basin Northwest Territories, Canada 21 M5, 27 J7
France *Country* Europe 18 B4, 97
Francistown *Town* Botswana 247 H7
Franconian Jura *Mountain range* Germany 95 I9
Frankfort *Town* Kentucky, USA 37 E7
Frankfurt am Main *Town* Germany 95 F8
Franz Josef Land *Island group* Russian Federation 10 F1, 139 J1, 267 H6
Fray Bentos *Town* Uruguay 71 J7
Fredericton *Town* New Brunswick, Canada 29 I6
Frederikshavn *Town* Denmark 82 E10
Freeport *Town* Bahamas 45 L3

Freetown *Town* Sierra Leone 220 C11
Fremantle *Town* Western Australia, Australia 203 K9, 258 C10
French Guiana *Country* S. America 19 X8, 59 K3
French Polynesia *Dependent territory* Pacific Ocean 19 Q10, 265 G6
Fresno *Town* California, USA 33 G10
Fribourg *Town* Switzerland 106 B8
Frobisher Bay Baffin Island, Northwest Territories, Canada 27 L7
Fuji, Mt. *Volcano* Japan 185 H9
Fundy, Bay of Canada 29 I7, 77 D4
Fushun *Town* China 175 O6
Fuzhou *Town* China 175 O12

G

Gabon *Country* Central Africa 18 C9, 232 F10
Gaborone *Town* Botswana 247 H8
Gaizin Kalns *Mountain* Latvia 111 H6
Galápagos Islands Pacific Ocean 11 V9, 19 V9, 265 J5
Galati *Town* Romania 127 K7
Galdhøppigen, Mt. Norway 82 E7
Galicia *Region* Poland 113 I8
Galicia *Region* Spain 100 C2
Galway Bay Ireland 78 B9
Gambia *Country* W. Africa 18 A8, 220 B8
Gäncä *Town* Azerbaijan 121 Q13
Gander *Town* Newfoundland, Canada 29 K4
Ganges *River* India 10 H7, 133 H11, 167 G5, I6, J7
Ganges Delta *River mouth* Bangladesh 167 J7
Garda, Lake Italy 103 D3
Garova *Town* Cameroon 232 E7
Gary *Town* Indiana, USA 37 D5
Gaza Strip *Region* Middle East 147 D8
Gaziantep *Town* Turkey 145 H8
Gdansk *Town* Poland 115 G2
Geelong *Town* Victoria, Australia 259 J12
Gelsenkirchen *Town* Germany 95 E6
General Santos *Town* Philippines 196 M6
Geneva *Town* Switzerland 106 A9
Geneva, Lake France/Switzerland 97 I6, 106 B9
Genoa *Town* Italy 103 C5
George Town *Town* Malaysia 189 E14
Georgetown *Town* Guyana 59 J1
Georgia *Country* S.W. Asia 18 E5, 121 O12
Georgia *State* USA 37 E9
Gerlachovka *Mountain* Slovakia 115 I8
Germany *Country* Europe 18 C4, 95
Ghana *Country* W. Africa 18 B8, 221 I11
Gharyan *Town* Libya 209 O4
Ghawar Oilfield Saudi Arabia 153 F8
Ghent *Town* Belgium 91 F9
Gibraltar *Dependent territory* Mediterranean Sea 18 B6 100 E9
Gibraltar, Strait of 78 C13, 100 D9
Gibson Desert Western Australia, Australia 10 K11, 254 C11, 258 D8
Gilbert Islands Kiribati, Pacific Ocean 11 N9, 255 K6, 265 D6
Gisborne *Town* New Zealand 262 H5
Giza *Town* Egypt 215 D1
Glana *River* Norway 82 F7
Glasgow *Town* UK 87 I6
Gobi Desert Central Asia 10 IS, 133 I8, 175 I7
Godavari *River* India 167 F8

Godoy Cruz *Town* Argentina 71 G8
Godthab (Nuuk) *Town* Greenland 267 B9
Goiânia *Town* Brazil 67 H8
Golan Heights *Region occupied by Israel* Syria 147 F6
Gold Coast *Town* Queensland, Australia 259 M9
Gonder *Town* Ethiopia 215 G8
Goose Lake California/Oregon, USA 33 G7
Gostivar *Town* Macedonia 124 J8
Göteborg *Town* Sweden 82 F10
Gotland *Island* Sweden 82 H11
Gough Island Atlantic Ocean 10 B12, 18 B12, 77 H10
Gozo *Island* Malta 103 G15
Grampian Mts. UK 87 I5
Gran Chaco *Region* Argentina 41 G11, 71 H4
Granada *Town* Spain 100 F8
Grand Banks *Sea shelf* Atlantic Ocean 29 L4, 77 E4
Grand Canal China 178 O10
Grand Canyon Arizona, USA 21 I10, 33 J10
Grand Cayman *Island* Cayman Islands 44 F7
Grand Forks *Town* North Dakota, USA 35 I2
Grand Junction *Town* Colorado, USA 35 D7
Grand Rapids *Town* Michigan, USA 37 D4
Grasse *Town* France 97 J8
Graz *Town* Austria 106 K7
Great Australian Bight Australia 10 K12, 254 D13, 259 G10
Great Barrier Reef Australia 254 G9, 259 L6
Great Basin *Region* USA 21 I9
Great Bear Lake *Northwest Territories*, Canada 11 S2, 21 H5, 27 D8
Great Dividing Range *Mountain range* Queensland, Australia 10 M11, 254 G11, 259 L8
Great Eastern Erg *Desert region* Algeria 205 D3, 209 L5
Great Lakes Canada/USA 11 V4, 21 M8, 37 E2
Great Plain of China 10 J6, 133 K10
Great Plains USA 11 T5, 21 J8, 35 G6
Great Rift Valley E. Africa 10 D9, 205 H9, I9, 239 F9, I6
Great Salt Lake Utah, USA 21 I9, 33 J8
Great Salt Lake Desert Utah, USA 33 J8
Great Sandy Desert Western Australia, Australia 10 K11, 254 C10, 258 E7
Great Slave Lake Northwest Territories, Canada 11 S3, 21 I6, 27 E10
Great Victoria Desert Western/South Australia, Australia 10 K11, 254 C11, 258 F9
Great Wall *Ancient site* China 175 H8, I8, J9, K9, M7
Great Western Erg *Desert region* Algeria 205 C3, 209 J5
Greater Antilles *Island group* Caribbean Sea 11 V7, 41 E1, 45 M10
Greater Khingan Range *Mountain range* China 175 N5
Greece *Country* Europe 18 D5, 131
Green River W. USA 33 K9
Greenland *Dependent territory* Arctic Ocean 11 X1, 19 X1, 21 R3, 77 F2, 267 D3
Greenland Sea Arctic Ocean 11 Z2, 77 H2, 267 F8
Greensboro *Town* North Carolina, USA 37 G8

Grenada *Country* Caribbean Sea 19 W8, 45 U15
Greymouth *Town* New Zealand 262 D8
Groningen *Town* Netherlands 91 K4
Groznyy *Town* Russian Federation 138 B9
Guadalajara *Town* Mexico 39 E7
Guadalquivir *River* Spain 100 D7
Guadeloupe *Dependent territory* Caribbean Sea 45 V12
Guadiana *River* Portugal/Spain 100 C6, E6
Guam *Dependent territory* Micronesia, Pacific Ocean 18 L8, 254 F3, 265 B5
Guantánamo *Town* Cuba 45 M8
Guatemala *Country* Central America 19 U8, 44 B8
Guatemala City *Town* Guatemala 44 B9
Guayaquil *Town* Ecuador 59 B5
Guernsey *Island/Dependent territory* UK 87 I13
Guiana Highlands *Mountain range* S. America 41 G4
Guinea *Country* W. Africa 18 B8, 220 C10
Guinea Highlands *Region* W. Africa 205 C6, 221 E11
Guinea, Gulf of Atlantic Ocean 10 B8, 77 I7
Guinea-Bissau *Country* W. Africa 18 A8, 220 B9
Guiyang *Town* China 175 K13
Gujranwala *Town* Pakistan 167 E3
Gulf, The S.W. Asia 10 F6
Gunnbjørn, Mt. Greenland 267 D9
Guri *Reservoir* Venezuela 59 H2
Guwahati *Town* India 167 K5
Guyana *Country* S. America 19 W8, 59 I4
Guyana Basin Atlantic Ocean 77 F7
Gwalior *Town* India 167 F5
Gyda Peninsula Russian Federation 133 G3, 139 J5
Gyumri *Town* Armenia 121 P14

H

Ha Long Bay Vietnam 189 I5
Haarlem *Town* Netherlands 91 H6
Hagen *Town* Germany 95 E6
Hai Phong *Town* Vietnam 189 I5
Haifa *Town* Israel 147 E6
Haikou *Town* China 175 M15
Hainan *Island* China 175 L16
Haiti *Country* Caribbean Sea 19 V7, 45 O9
Hakodate *Town* Japan 185 H4
Halab *Town* Syria 147 G2
Halifax *Town* Nova Scotia, Canada 29 J6
Halle *Town* Germany 95 F6
Hälsingborg *Town* Sweden 82 F11
Hamada *Town* Japan 185 D10
Hamadan *Town* Iran 153 F4
Hamah *Town* Syria 147 G4
Hamburg *Town* Germany 95 G3
Hamersley Range *Mountain range* Australia 254 B10, 258 C7
Hamilton *Town* New Zealand 262 F4
Hamilton *Town* Ontario, Canada 29 F6
Hammar, Lake al- Iraq 153 E4
Handan *Town* China 175 M9
Hangzhou *Town* China 175 O11
Hanoi *Town* Vietnam 189 H9
Hanover *Town* Germany 95 G5
Harad *Town* Saudi Arabia 153 F8
Harare *Town* Zimbabwe 247 I6
Harbin *Town* China 175 P5
Hardanger Fjord Norway 82 D8

Hargeysa *Town* Somalia 215 I9
Harrisburg *Town* Pennsylvania, USA 37 H6
Hartford *Town* Connecticut 37 J5
Hasselt *Town* Belgium 91 I9
Hastings *Town* New Zealand 262 G6
Hat Yai *Town* Thailand 189 E13
Havana *Town* Cuba 44 I5
Hawaii *Island* USA 33 H15, 255 O2
Hawaii *State* USA 19 P7, 33 G14
Hawaiian Islands Polynesia, Pacific Ocean 11 P7, 255 M1, 265 F4
Heard Island Indian Ocean 203 G11
Hefei *Town* China 175 N10
Helena *Town* Montana, USA 35 C3
Helsinki *Town* Finland 82 J9
Helwân *Town* Egypt 215 D2
Henzada *Town* Burma 189 C7
Herat *Town* Afghanistan 161 E9
Hilo *Town* Hawaii, USA 33 H14
Himalayas *Mountain range* S. Asia 10 H6, 133 G10, 167 H4, 174 D12
Hims *Town* Syria 147 G4
Hindu Kush *Mountain range* Central Asia 10 G6, 132 F9, 161 G9
Hiroshima *Town* Japan 185 D10
Hispaniola *Island* Caribbean Sea 41 F1
Hitachi *Town* Japan 185 I8
Hkakabo Razi *Mountain* Burma 189 D1
Ho Chi Minh City *Town* Vietnam 189 I11
Hobart *Town* Tasmania, Australia 259 K13
Hodeida *Town* Yemen 153 C11
Hohhot *Town* China 175 L7
Hokkaido *Island* Japan 10 L5, 133 N8, 185 I2
Holguín *Town* Cuba 45 M7
Holon *Town* Israel 147 E7
Holyhead *Town* UK 87 H9
Homyel' *Town* Belarus 111 K11
Honduras *Country* Central America 19 U7, 44 E9
Hong Gai *Town* Vietnam 189 I5
Hong Kong China E. Asia 18 J7, 175 N14, 285 A4
Honolulu *Town* Hawaii, USA 33 G14, 265 F4
Honshu *Island* Japan 10 L6, 133 N9, 185 H8
Horlivka *Town* Ukraine 121 K7
Hormus, Strait of Iran/Oman 153 I8
Horn of Africa *Region* Somalia 205 K6, 215 K8
Houston *Town* Texas, USA 35 J12
Howland Island *Dependent territory* Polynesia, Pacific Ocean 19 P9, 255 L6, 265 E5
Hrodna *Town* Belorussia 111 F9
Huainan *Town* China 175 N10
Huancayo *Town* Peru 59 D8
Huang He, see Yellow River
Huascarán *Volcano* Peru 59 C7
Hudson *River* New York, USA 37 I5
Hudson Bay Canada 11 U3, 21 L6, 27 I10, 29 D4
Hudson Strait Northwest Territories, Canada 27 K8
Hue *Town* Vietnam 189 I8
Hungary *Country* Central Europe 18 D5, 115 G11
Huntsville *Town* Alabama, USA 37 D9
Huron, Lake Canada/USA 21 M8, 29 F8, 37 E3
Hyderabad *Town* India 167 F9
Hyderabad *Town* Pakistan 167 C5

I

Iasi *Town* Romania 127 J5
Ibadan *Town* Nigeria 221 K11
Ibiza *Island* Balearic Islands, Spain 100 J6
Ica *Town* Peru 59 D9
Iceland *Country* Atlantic Ocean 10 A3, 18 B44, 77 H2, 78 A5, 267 E10
Idaho *State* USA 33 H6
Iguaçu Falls *Waterfall* Brazil 41 I10, 67 F10
Ijsselmeer *Lake* Netherlands 91 C5
Île d'Ouessant *Island* France 97 A4
Ilebo *Town* Zaire 232 N12
Îles d'Hyères *Islands* France 97 J9
Iligan *Town* Philippines 196 M5
Illinois *State* USA 37 C6
Iloilo *Town* Philippines 196 L4
Ilorin *Town* Nigeria 221 L11
In Salah *Town* Algeria 209 K6
Inari *Lake* Finland 78 I4, 82 K3
Inch'on *Town* South Korea 175 Q8
Independence *Town* Missouri, USA 35 J7
India *Country* S. Asia 18 H7, 167 F6
Indian Ocean 10 H10, 203
Indiana *State* USA 37 D6
Indianapolis *Town* Indiana, USA 37 D6
Indonesia *Country* S.E. Asia 18 J9, 196 K11, 203 J5
Indore *Town* India 167 E7
Indus *River* Pakistan 132 F11, 167 B6, C4
Inner Hebrides *Island group* UK 78 C7, 87 G5
Innsbruck *Town* Austria 106 G7
Insein *Town* Burma 189 C7
International Date Line 265 E3
Invercargill *Town* New Zealand 262 B11
Ionian Islands Greece 131 A6
Ionian Sea Greece/Italy 103 J12, 131 A6
Ios *Island* Greece 131 H10
Iowa *State* USA 35 J5
Ipoh *Town* Malaysia 189 E14
Ipswich *Town* UK 87 L10
Iquique *Town* Chile 71 E3
Iquitos *Town* Peru 59 D5
Irakleio *Town* Crete 131 H12
Iran *Country* S.W. Asia 18 F6, 153 H5
Iranian Plateau S.W. Asia 10 G6, 132 D10
Iraq *Country* S.W. Asia 18 E6, 153 E4
Irbid *Town* Jordan 147 F7
Irbil *Town* Iraq 153 E3
Ireland *Country* Europe 18 34, 87 F8
Irian Jaya *Region* Indonesia 197 R10
Irish Sea Ireland/UK 87 H8
Irkutsk *Town* Russian Federation 139 M10
Irrawaddy *River* Myanmar 133 I12, 189 C4
Irtysh *River* N./Central Asia 10 H4, 133 G7, 138 H7, H8, 161 I2, 174 E5
Ischia *Island* Italy 103 G9
Ishim *River* Kazakhstan/Russian Federation 161 F2
Iskenderun *Town* Turkey 145 G8
Islamabad *Town* Pakistan 167 D2
Ismâ'iliya *Town* Egypt 215 E1
Isparta *Town* Turkey 145 D7
Israel *Country* S.W. Asia 18 E6, 147 E9
Istanbul *Town* Turkey 145 C5
Itaipú Dam Paraguay 71 K4
Italy *Country* Europe 18 C5, 103 E7
Ivano-Frankivs'k *Town* Ukraine 120 C6
Ivory Coast *Country* W. Africa 18 B8, 221 G11
Izabal, Lake Guatemala 44 C9

Izhersk *Town* Russian Federation 138 E7
Izmir *Town* Turkey 145 A7
Izmit *Town* Turkey 145 C5

J

Jabalpur *Town* India 167 G7
Jackson *Town* Mississippi, USA 37 C10
Jacksonville *Town* Florida, USA 37 F11
Jacques Cartier, Mt. Quebec, Canada 29 I5
Jaipur *Town* India 167 E5
Jakarta *Town* Java, Indonesia 196 F11
Jalandhar *Town* India 167 E3
Jamaica *Country* Caribbean Sea 18 V7, 46 K9
Jambi *Town* Sumatra, Indonesia 196 D9
Jan Mayen *Island* Norway 18 B2, 267 F9
Japan *Country* E. Asia 18 L6, 185
Japan, Sea of E. Asia 10 L5, 133 M9, 139 S11, 185 G7, 265 B3
Japanese Alps *Mountain range* Japan 185 G9
Jarris *Island* Pacific Ocean 19 Q9
Java *Island* Indonesia 133 K16, 196 G12
Java Sea Indonesia 10 J9, 196 F11
Jayapura *Town* Irian Jaya, Indonesia 197 T9
Jaz Murian *Salt Lake* Iran 153 J8
Jedda *Town* Saudi Arabia 153 B8
Jefferson City *Town* Missouri, USA 35 K7
Jember *Town* Java, Indonesia 196 I12
Jerez de la Frontera *Town* Spain 100 D8
Jericho *Town* Israel 147 E8
Jersey *Island/Dependent territory* UK 87 I13
Jerusalem *Town* Israel 147 E8
Jilin *Town* China 175 P5
Jinan *Town* China 175 N9
Jingdezhen *Town* China 175 N11
Jingmen *Town* China 175 M11
Jodhpur *Town* India 167 D5
Johannesburg *Town* South Africa 247 H9
John Day *River* Oregon/Washington, USA 33 H6
Johnston Atoll *Dependent territory* Polynesia, Pacific Ocean 19 P8, 255 M3, 265 F4
Johor Baharu *Town* Malaysia 189 G16
Jönköping *Town* Sweden 82 G10
Jordan *Country* S.W. Asia 18 E6, 147 G8
Jordan *River* S.W. Asia 147 E7
Juan Fernández, Islas *Island group* Pacific Ocean 11 U12, 19 V12, 265 K8
Juliaca *Town* Peru 59 E10
Juneau *Town* Alaska, USA 33 E3
Jura *Mountain range* Switzerland/France 97 I5, 106 B8
Jutland *Peninsula* Denmark 78 F8, 82 E11

K

K'ut'aisi *Town* Georgia 121 O12
Kabalebo Reservoir Suriname 59 J3
Kabul *Town* Afghanistan 161 G9
Kabwe *Town* Zambia 239 E13
Kaduna *Town* Nigeria 221 M10
Kafue Flats *Region* Zambia 239 C13
Kagoshima *Town* Japan 185 C12
Kahramanmaras *Town* Turkey 145 G8
Kaikoura *Town* New Zealand 262 E8
Kalahari Desert Botswana 10 D11, 205 G12, 247 F8

Kalemie *Town* Zaire 232 K12
Kalgoorlie *Town* Western Australia, Australia 258 E10
Kaliningrad *Town* Russian Federation 111 D8
Kamchatka Peninsula Russian Federation 10 M4, 133 P6, 139 T6
Kampala *Town* Uganda 239 G5
Kâmpóng Cham *Town* Cambodia 189 H10
Kananga *Town* Zaire 232 I12
Kandahar *Town* Afghanistan 161 E10
Kandi *Town* Benin 221 K10
Kano *Town* Nigeria 221 N9
Kanpur *Town* India 167 G5
Kansas *State* USA 35 H7
Kansas City *Town* Kansas, USA 35 J7
Kao-hsiung *Town* Taiwan 175 P14
Kapuas *River* Borneo, Indonesia 196 G9
Kara Kum *Desert* Kazakhstan 10 F5, 132 F9, 161 J4
Kara *Sea* Russian Federation 10 G2, 79 O3, 133 G2, 138 H4
Kara *Town* Togo 221 J10
Karachi *Town* Pakistan 167 B5, 203 F2
Karaganda *Town* Kazakhstan 161 H3
Karaj *Town* Iran 153 G4
Karakoram Mts. Central Asia 133 G10, 174 A8
Karakum Canal Turkmenistan 161 E8
Karbala *Town* Iraq 153 E5
Kariba Dam Zambia/Zimbabwe 239 E14
Karlsruhe *Town* Germany 95 F10
Karpathos *Island* Greece 131 K12
Karshi *Town* Uzbekistan 161 F7
Kashmir *Region* India/Pakistan 167 F2
Kathmandu *Town* Nepal 167 I5
Katowice *Town* Poland 115 H7
Kattegat *Channel* Denmark/Sweden 82 F10
Kauai *Island* Hawaii, USA 33 G14, 255 O2
Kaunas *Town* Lithuania 111 G8
Kawasaki *Town* Japan 185 H9
Kayseri *Town* Turkey 145 G7
Kazakh Uplands *Region* Kazakhstan 133 G7, 161 H3
Kazakhstan *Country* Central Asia 18 G4, 161 F4
Kazan' *Town* Russian Federation 138 E7
Kefallonia *Island* Greece 131 B7
Kelang *Town* Malaysia 189 E15
Kemerovo *Town* Russian Federation 139 J9
Kemijoki *River* Finland 82 J5, K4
Kendari *Town* Celebes, Indonesia 196 L10
Kénitra *Town* Morocco 208 G3
Kentucky *State* USA 37 E7
Kenya *Country* Africa 18 E9, 239 J4
Kenya, Mt. Kenya 239 J5
Kerguelen *Island group* Indian Ocean 18 G13, 203 G11
Kermadec Islands Polynesia, Pacific Ocean 19 O11, 255 L12, 265 E7
Kerman *Town* Iran 153 I7
Kerulen *River* Mongolia/China 175 L5
Khabarovsk *Town* Russian Federation 139 R10
Kharkiv *Town* Ukraine 121 J5
Khartoum *Town* Sudan 215 E7
Kherson *Town* Ukraine 121 H8
Khmel'nyts'kyy *Town* Ukraine 120 D5
Khon Kaen *Town* Thailand 189 G8
Khujand *Town* Tajikistan 161 G7
Khulna *Town* Bangladesh 167 J7
Khyber Pass *Mountain pass* Afghanistan/Pakistan 161 G9
Kiel *Town* Germany 95 G2
Kiel Canal Germany 95 G2

Kiev *Town* Ukraine 120 F5
Kigali *Town* Rwanda 239 F6
Kigoma *Town* Tanzania 239 E8
Kikwit *Town* Zaire 232 G12
Kilimanjaro, Mt. Tanzania 205 I9, 239 J6
Kimberley *Town* South Africa 247 G10
Kimberley Plateau *Region* Western Australia, Australia 254 C9, 259 F5
Kingman Reef *Dependent territory* Polynesia, Pacific Ocean 19 P8, 265 F5
Kingston *Town* Jamaica 45 L9
Kingston *Town* St. Vincent and the Grenadines 45 V14
Kingston upon Hull *Town* UK 87 K8
Kinshasa *Town* Zaire 232 F12
Kirghiz Steppe *Region* Kazakhstan 10 F4, 132 D7, 161 D3
Kiribati *Country* Micronesia/Polynesia, Pacific Ocean 19 P9, 265 F6
Kirkuk *Town* Iraq 153 E4
Kirov *Town* Russian Federation 138 E6
Kirovohrad *Town* Ukraine 120 G7
Kisangani *Town* Zaire 232 I10
Kismaayo *Town* Somalia 215 I12
Kisumu *Town* Kenya 239 H5
Kitwe *Town* Zambia 239 E12
Kitzbühel *Town* Austria 106 G7
Kizil Irmak *River* Turkey 145 F5, G6
Kjølen Mts. Norway/Sweden 78 G5, 82 G5
Klagenfurt *Town* Austria 106 I8
Klaipeda *Town* Lithuania 111 E7
Klerksdorp *Town* South Africa 247 G9
Klyuchevsk *Volcano* Russian Federation 139 T5
Knossos *Ancient site* Crete 131 H12
Knoxville *Town* Tennessee, USA 37 E8
Knud Rasmussen Land *Region* Greenland 21 O2, 267 E7
Kobe *Town* Japan 185 F10
Kodiak Island Alaska, USA 20 E7, 33 C3
Kola Peninsula Russian Federation 78 J5, 138 F3
Kolyma Range *Mountain range* Russian Federation 133 P5, 139 S5
Konya *Town* Turkey 145 E7
Koryak Range *Mountain range* Russian Federation 133 Q5, 139 T3
Kos *Island* Greece 131 K9
Kosciusko, Mt. Queensland, Australia 259 K11
Kosovo *Province* Serbia, Yugoslavia 124 I7
Kosovska Mitrovica *Town* Serbia, Yugoslavia 123 I9
Kota Baharu *Town* Malaysia 189 F13
Kota Kinabalu *Town* Borneo, Malaysia 196 J6
Kota *Town* India 167 E6
Kowloon *Town* Hong Kong China 175 N14
Kragujevac *Town* Serbia, Yugoslavia 124 J5
Kraljevo *Town* Serbia, Yugoslavia 124 J5
Kramators'k *Town* Ukraine 121 K6
Krasnodar *Town* Russian Federation 138 A7
Krasnovodsk *Town* Turkmenistan 161 B6
Krasnoyarsk *Town* Russian Federation 139 K9
Krefeld *Town* Germany 95 D6
Kremenchuk *Town* Ukraine 121 H6
Krusevac *Town* Serbia, Yugoslavia 121 J7
Kryvyy Rih *Town* Ukraine 121 H7
Kuala Lumpur *Town* Malaysia 189 F15
Kuala Terengganu *Town* Malaysia 189 F14
Kuantan *Town* Malaysia 189 F15
Kuching *Town* Borneo, Malaysia 196 G8
Kujawy *Region* Poland 115 G4

Kumamoto *Town* Japan 185 C12
Kumanovo *Town* Macedonia 124 K8
Kumasi *Town* Ghana 221 I12
Kunlun Mts. China 10 H6, 133 H9, 174 D9
Kunming *Town* China 175 J14
Kupang *Town* Timor, Indonesia 196 M13
Kurile Islands *Disputed territory* E. Asia 10 M5, 133 O8, 139 U9, 185 K1, 265 C2
Kütahya *Town* Turkey 145 C6
Kuwait *Country* S.W. Asia 18 F6, 153 F6
Kuwait City *Town* Kuwait 153 F6, 203 E1
Kwajalein Atoll Marshall Islands, Pacific Ocean 265 D5
Kyoto *Town* Japan 185 F10
Kyrgyzstan *Country* Central Asia 18 G5, 161 H6
Kythira *Island* Greece 131 E11
Kyushu *Island* Japan 133 M10, 185 C11

L

L'viv *Town* Ukraine 120 B5
La Paz *Town* Bolivia 59 F10
La Plata *Town* Argentina 71 J8
La Serena *Town* Chile 71 F7
Labrador *Region* Newfoundland, Canada 29 I3
Labrador Sea Canada/Greenland 11 W3, 21 P6, 29 H2, 77 E3
Laccadive Islands Indian Ocean 203 G3
Laccadive Sea Indian Ocean 10 G8
Ladoga, Lake Russian Federation 10 E3, 78 J7
Lagos dos Patos *Lagoon* Brazil 67 G12
Lagos *Town* Nigeria 221 K12
Lahore *Town* Pakistan 167 E3
Lake District *Region* UK 78 D8, 87 I7
Lakshadweep *Island group* Indian Ocean 18 G8, 132 E13
Lambert Glacier Antarctica 269 I4
Lanai *Island* Hawaii, USA 33 G14
Land's End *Cape* UK 87 G12
Lansing *Town* Michigan, USA 37 E4
Lanzhou *Town* China 175 J9
Laos *Country* S.W. Asia 18 I7, 189 F6
Lapland *Region* N. Europe 78 H4, 82 I4
Laptev Sea Arctic Ocean 10 K1, 133 L2, 139 M4, 267 I4
Laredo *Town* Texas, USA 35 H13
Larisa *Town* Greece 131 D5
Larnaca *Town* Cyprus 145 E10
Larsen Ice Shelf Antarctica 269 B3
Las Vegas *Town* Nevada, USA 33 I11
Latvia *Country* E. Europe 18 D4, 111 G6
Lausanne *Town* Switzerland 106 B9
Laval *Town* Québec, Canada 29 H7
Le Havre *Town* France 97 E2
Le Mans *Town* France 97 E4
Lebanon *Country* S.W. Asia 18 E6, 147 F5
Leeds *Town* UK 87 J8
Leeward Islands Caribbean Sea 45 U10
Lefkada *Island* Greece 131 B6
Legaspi *Town* Philippines 196 L3
Leicester *Town* UK 87 J10
Leiden *Town* Netherlands 91 H6
Leipzig *Town* Germany 95 I6
Leiria *Town* Portugal 100 B5
Lelystad *Town* Netherlands 91 I5
Lena *River* Russian Federation 10 K2, 133 K5, L4, 139 N6, N8
León *Town* Nicaragua 44 D11
Léon *Town* Mexico 39 F7
Leskovac *Town* Serbia, Yugoslavia 124 K6
Lesotho *Country* Southern Africa

18 D11, 247 H10
Lesser Antilles *Island group* Caribbean Sea 11 W8, 41 G3, 45 R14, T12
Lesser Khingan Mts. N.E. Asia 175 O3
Lesvos *Island* Greece 131 I5
Leuuwarden *Town* Netherlands 91 J4
Levin *Town* New Zealand 262 F6
Lexington *Town* Kentucky, USA 37 E7
Lhasa *Town* China 175 F12
Liberia *Country* W. Africa 18 B8, 221 E12
Libreville *Town* Gabon 232 D10
Libya *Country* N. Africa 18 D6, 209 Q6
Libyan Desert Egypt/Libya/Sudan 10 D6, 205 G3, 209 T7, 215 C3
Liechtenstein *Country* Europe 18 C5, 106 E7
Liège *Town* Belgium 91 I10
Liepaja *Town* Latvia 111 E6
Ligurian Sea Italy 103 C6
Likasi *Town* Zaire 232 J14
Lille *Town* France 97 F1
Lillehammer *Town* Norway 82 F8
Lilongwe *Town* Malawi 239 H13
Lima *Town* Peru 59 C8, 265 L6
Limassol *Town* Cyprus 145 E10
Limoges *Town* France 97 E6
Limpopo *River* Southern Africa 205 I12, 247 I8
Lincoln *Town* Nebraska, USA 35 I6
Lincoln Sea Arctic Ocean 21 O1
Line Islands Kiribati, Pacific Ocean 11 P8, 255 O6, 265 F5
Linz *Town* Austria 106 I5
Lisbon *Town* Portugal 100 B6
Lithuania *Country* E. Europe 18 D4, 111 F7
Little Rock *Town* Arkansas, USA 35 K9
Liverpool *Town* UK 87 I9
Ljubljana *Town* Slovenia 109 E3
Llanos *Region* Colombia/Venezuela 11 V8
Locarno *Town* Switzerland 106 D9
Lódz *Town* Poland 115 H5
Lofoten *Island group* Norway 78 G4, 82 G3
Logan, Mt. Yukon Territory, Canada 27 A9
Logroño *Town* Spain 100 G2
Loire *River* France 78 D10, 97 D5, H6
Lombardy *Region* Italy 103 D4
Lombok *Island* Indonesia 196 J12
Lomé *Town* Togo 221 J12
Lomond, Loch *Lake* UK 87 H5
London *Town* Ontario, Canada 29 F6
London *Town* UK 87 K11
Londonderry *Town* UK 87 G6
Long Beach *Town* California, USA 33 H12
Long Island New York, USA 37 I5
Long Xuyen *Town* Vietnam 189 H11
Longyearbyen *Town* Svalbard 267 G8
Lop Nur *Lake* China 175 F8
Lord Howe Island *Dependent territory* Pacific Ocean 19 N11, 265 D8
Los Angeles *Town* California, USA 33 H12
Los Ángeles *Town* Chile 71 F10
Louang Phrabang *Town* Laos 189 F6
Louise, Lake Alberta, Canada 27 E13
Louisiana *State* USA 35 K11
Louisville *Town* Kentucky, USA 37 D7
Lowell *Town* Massachusetts, USA 37 J4
Loyalty Islands Pacific Ocean 11 N10
Luanda *Town* Angola 247 B2
Luanshya *Town* Zambia 239 E12
Lubbock *Town* Texas, USA 35 G10
Lübeck *Town* Germany 95 H3
Lublin *Town* Poland 115 K6
Lubumbashi *Town* Zaire 232 J14

Lucena *Town* Philippines 196 L3
Lucerne *Town* Switzerland 106 C8
Lucknow *Town* India 167 G5
Ludhiana *Town* India 167 E3
Lugano *Town* Switzerland 106 D9
Luhans'k *Town* Ukraine 121 L6
Lundy *Island* UK 87 H11
Luoyang *Town* China 175 L10
Lusaka *Town* Zambia 239 E13
Luts'k *Town* Ukraine 120 C4
Luxembourg *Country* Europe 18 C4, 91 J12
Luxembourg *Town* Luxembourg 91 J13
Luxor *Town* Egypt 215 E3
Luzon *Island* Philippines 133 L12, 196 L2
Lyon *Town* France 97 H6

M

Maastricht *Town* Netherlands 91 I10
Macao China S.E. Asia 18 J7, 175 N14
Macao *Town* Macao China 175 N14
Macdonnell Ranges *Mountain range* Northern Territory, Australia 254 D10, 259 G7
Macedonia *Country* S.E. Europe 18 D5, 124 J8
Maceió *Town* Brazil 67 L6
Machala *Town* Ecuador 59 B6
Machu Picchu *Ancient site* Peru 59 E9
Mackenzie *River* Northwest Territories, Canada 11 S3, 21 H5, 27 D9
Mackenzie Mts. Northwest Territories, Canada 20 G5, 27 C9
Macon *Town* Georgia, USA 37 E10
Macquarie Island *Dependent territory* Pacific Ocean 265 D9
Madagascar *Country* Indian Ocean 10 F11, 18 F11, 203 D7, 205 K12
Madeira *Island* Atlantic Ocean 10 A6, 18 A6, 77 H5, 205 A2
Madgeburg *Town* Germany 95 I5
Madison *Town* Wisconsin, USA 37 C4
Madras *Town* India 167 F11
Madre de Dios *River* Bolivia/Peru 59 F8
Madrid *Town* Spain 100 F4
Madurai *Town* India 167 F12
Magellan, Strait of *Channel* Chile 41 G16, 71 H16
Maggiore, Lake Italy/Switzerland 103 C3, 106 D9
Mahajanga *Town* Madagascar 203 D7
Mahalapye *Town* Botswana 247 G8
Mahé *Island* Seychelles 203 E6, 205 L9
Mahilyow *Town* Belarus 111 K9
Maine *State* USA 37 K3
Mainz *Town* Germany 95 F8
Majorca *Island* Balearic Islands, Spain 100 L5
Makiyivka *Town* Ukraine 121 K7
Malabar Coast India 167 D11
Malabo *Town* Equatorial Guinea 232 C9
Malacca, Strait of S.E. Asia 203 I4
Málaga *Town* Spain 100 E8
Malang *Town* Java, Indonesia 196 H12
Malatya *Town* Turkey 145 H7
Malawi *Country* Africa 18 E10, 239 H13
Malaysia *Country* S.E. Asia 189 F15, 196 J6
Maldive Ridge Indian Ocean 203 G5
Maldives *Country* Indian Ocean 10 G8, 18 H9, 203 G4
Male *Town* Maldives 203 G5
Mali *Country* W. Africa 221 H6
Malmö *Town* Sweden 82 F11
Malta *Country* Europe 18 C6, 103 H15

Mammoth Caves Kentucky, USA 37 D7
Man, Isle of *Dependent territory* UK 87 H7
Manado *Town* Celebes, Indonesia 196 M8
Managua *Town* Nicaragua 44 E11
Manama *Town* Bahrain 153 F8
Manaus *Town* Brazil 67 E4
Manchester *Town* New Hampshire, USA 37 J4
Manchester *Town* UK 87 J9
Manchuria *Region* China 175 P5
Manchurian Plain *Region* China 10 K5, 133 L8
Mandalay *Town* Burma 189 C4
Manila *Town* Philippines 196 K3, 265 A5
Manisa *Town* Turkey 145 B7
Manitoba *Province* Canada 27 H11
Manizales *Town* Colombia 59 D3
Mannheim *Town* Germany 95 F9
Maputo *Town* Mozambique 247 I9
Mar del Plata *Town* Argentina 71 K9
Maracaibo *Town* Venezuela 59 E1
Maracaibo, Lake Venezuela 41 F3, 59 E1
Marañón *River* Peru 41 E6, 59 D6
Marathon *Ancient site* Greece 131 F7
Marbella *Town* Spain 100 E8
Mariana Trench Pacific Ocean 10 L8, 265 C4
Maribor *Town* Slovenia 109 G2
Marie Byrd Land *Region* Antarctica 269 D6
Maritsa *River* Bulgaria 127 I12
Mariupol' *Town* Ukraine 121 K8
Marka *Town* Somalia 215 I11
Marmara, Sea of Turkey 145 B5
Maroua *Town* Cameroon 232 F6
Marquesas Islands French Polynesia, Pacific Ocean 11 Q9, 255 R7, 265 H6
Marrakesh *Town* Morocco 208 G4
Marseille *Town* France 97 I9
Marshall Islands *Country* Micronesia, Pacific Ocean 11 N8, 19 N8, 255 J3, 265 D5
Martinique *Dependent territory* Caribbean Sea 45 V13
Maryland *State* USA 37 H7
Masai Steppe *Region* Tanzania 239 I7
Maseru *Town* Lesotho 247 H10
Mashhad *Town* Iran 153 J4
Massachusetts *State* USA 37 J5
Massif Central *Region* France 78 E11, 97 G7
Masterton *Town* New Zealand 262 F7
Matadi *Town* Zaire 232 E12
Matanzas *Town* Cuba 44 J5
Mato Grosso, Plateau of Brazil 11 W10, 41 H8, 67 F6
Maturín *Town* Venezuela 59 H1
Maui *Island* Hawaii, USA 33 G14
Mauritania *Country* W. Africa 18 B7, 220 D6
Mauritius *Country* Indian Ocean 18 F10, 203 E7, 205 L12
Mayagüez *Town* Puerto Rico 45 R10
Mayotte *Dependent territory* 18 E10, 203 D7, 205 J10
Mazar-e-Sharif *Town* Afghanistan 161 F8
Mazyr *Town* Belarus 111 J11
Mbabane *Town* Swaziland 247 I9
Mbandaka *Town* Zaire 232 G10
Mbeya *Town* Tanzania 239 H10
Mbuji-Mayi *Town* Zaire 232 I12
McKinley, Mt. *see* Denali
McMurdo *Research station* Antarctica 269 F8
Mead, Lake Arizona/Nevada, USA 33 J11
Mecca *Town* Saudi Arabia 153 B8
Medan *Town* Sumatra, Indonesia

196 B7
Medellín *Town* Colombia 59 D2
Medina *Town* Saudi Arabia 15 C7
Mediterranean Sea 10 C5, 77 J5, 78 G13, 103 F14, 131 H13
Meerut *Town* India 167 F4
Meknès *Town* Morocco 208 H3
Mekong *River* Asia 10 J7, 133 J12, 175 G11, I15, 189 E5, F6, H8
Melaka *Town* Malaysia 189 F16
Melanesia *Region* Pacific Ocean 255 I7, 265 D6
Melbourne *Town* Victoria, Australia 259 K12
Melilla *Spanish enclave* Morocco 209 I2
Melville Island Northwest Territories, Canada 11 TI, 21 J4, 27 F5, 267 D4
Memphis *Town* Tennessee, USA 37 C8
Mendoza *Town* Argentina 71 G7
Mérida *Town* Mexico 39 K7
Mérida *Town* Spain 100 D6
Mérida *Town* Venezuela 59 E2
Mersin *Town* Turkey 145 F8
Mesa *Town* Arizona, USA 33 K12
Meseta *Region* Spain 78 D12
Messina *Town* Italy 103 I12
Mestre *Town* Italy 103 F4
Meuse *River* W. Europe 78 E9, 91 H11, J8, 97 H2
Mexicali *Town* Mexico 39 A1
Mexico *Country* N. America 19 T7, 39 E5
Mexico City *Town* Mexico 39 G8
Mexico, Gulf of 11 U7, 21 L11, 39 I7
Miami *Town* Florida, USA 37 G13
Michigan *State* USA 37 E3
Michigan, Lake USA 21 L9, 37 D4
Micronesia, Federated States of *Country* Pacific Ocean 18 L8, 255 I5, 265 C5
Mid-Atlantic Ridge Atlantic Ocean 77 F5, F7, H10
Mid-Indian Ridge Atlantic Ocean 203 G8
Mid-Pacific Seamounts Pacific Ocean 265 D4
Middelburg *Town* Netherlands 91 F8
Midway Island *Dependent territory* Polynesia, Pacific Ocean 11 O6, 19 O6, 265 E4
Milan *Town* Italy 103 C3
Milford Sound *Town* New Zealand 255 I15, 262 B10
Milwaukee *Town* Wisconsin, USA 35 D4
Minbu *Town* Myanmar 189 B5
Mindanao *Island* Philippines 133 L14, 196 L5
Mindoro *Island* Philippines 196 K3
Minneapolis *Town* Minnesota, USA 35 J4
Minnesota *State* USA 35 J2
Minorca *Island* Balearic Islands, Spain 100 L5
Minsk *Town* Belarus 111 I9
Mississippi *River* USA 11 U6, 21 L9, 35 K4, K10, 37 B3, B9
Mississippi *State* USA 37 C10
Missouri *State* USA 35 K8
Missouri *River* USA 10 U5, 21 J8, 35 F2, I5, K7
Mitchell, Mt. Tennessee, USA 37 E8
Mitumba Mts. Zaire 232 J12
Mobile *Town* Alabama, USA 37 C11
Mogadishu *Town* Somalia 215 J11
Mojave Desert California, USA 33 H11
Moldova *Country* E. Europe 18 D5, 120 E7
Moluccas *Island group* Indonesia 10 K9, 197 N9
Mombasa *Town* Kenya 239 K7
Monaco *Country* Europe 97 J8
Mongolia *Country* E. Asia 18 I5, 175 I5

Monrovia *Town* Liberia 220 D12
Mons *Town* Belgium 91 G10
Mont Blanc *Mountain* France 78 E11, 97 J6
Montana *State* USA 35 D2
Monte Albán *Ancient site* Mexico 39 H9
Montenegro *Republic* Yugoslavia 124 H6
Montería *Town* Colombia 59 D1
Monterrey *Town* Mexico 39 G5
Montevideo *Town* Uruguay 71 K8
Montgomery *Town* Alabama, USA 37 D10
Montpelier *Town* Vermont, USA 37 J4
Montpellier *Town* France 97 H9
Montreal *Town* Québec, Canada 29 H7
Monywa *Town* Burma 189 C4
Morar, Loch *Reservoir* UK 87 H4
Moravia *Region* Czech Republic 115 F8
Morocco *Country* N.W. Africa 18 B6, 208 G3
Moroni *Town* Comoros 203 D6
Moscow *Town* Russian Federation 138 C5
Mosel (Moselle) *River* W. Europe 91 K13, 95 E8, 97 I3
Mosquito Coast Panama 41 D2
Mostar *Town* Bosnia and Herzegovina 124 G6
Mosul *Town* Iraq 153 E3
Moulmein *Town* Myanmar 189 D7
Mozambique *Country* Southern Africa 18 E10, 247 J6
Mozambique Channel Madagascar/ Mozambique 10 E10, 205 J12
Muang Phitsanulok *Town* Thailand 189 E7
Muchinga Mts. Zambia 239 F12
Mufulira *Town* Zambia 239 E12
Mulhacén *Mountain* Spain 100 F8
Multan *Town* Pakistan 167 D4
Munich *Town* Germany 95 I11
Münitz *Lake* Germany 95 J3
Münster *Town* Germany 95 E5
Murcia *Town* Spain 100 H7
Murmansk *Town* Russian Federation 138 F3
Murray *River* New South Wales/South Australia, Australia 10 L12, 254 F13, 259 I10
Mururoa Atoll *Island* French Polynesia, Pacific Ocean 255 R10, 265 G7
Musala *Mountain* Bulgaria 127 F12
Muscarene Islands Indian Ocean 10 F10, 203 F8
Muscat *Town* Oman 153 I9
Mwanza *Town* Tanzania 239 G6
Myanmar *Country* S.E. Asia 18 I7, 189 C5
Mycenae *Ancient site* Greece 131 E8
Mykolayiv *Town* Ukraine 120 G8
Mykonos *Island* Greece 131 H8
Mysore *Town* India 167 E11

N

N'djamena *Town* Chad 232 F6
Naberezhnyye Chelny *Town* Russian Federation 138 E7
Nacala *Town* Mozambique 247 L5
Naga *Town* Philippines 196 L3
Nagasaki *Town* Japan 185 B12
Nagorno Karabakh *Region* Azerbaijan 121 R14
Nagoya *Town* Japan 185 G9
Nagpur *Town* India 167 F7
Nairobi *Town* Kenya 239 I6
Nakhon Ratchasima *Town* Thailand 189 F8
Nakhon Sawan *Town* Thailand 189 E8

Nakhon Si Thammarat *Town* Thailand 189 E12
Nakuru *Town* Kenya 239 I5
Nam Dinh *Town* Vietnam 189 H5
Namib Desert *Namibia* 10 C10, 205 F12, 247 C7
Namibia *Country* Southern Africa 18 D11, 247 D7
Namp'o *Town* North Korea 175 P7
Nampula *Town* Mozambique 247 L5
Namur *Town* Belgium 91 H10
Nanchang *Town* China 175 N12
Nancy *Town* France 97 I3
Nanjing *Town* China 175 O10
Nanning *Town* China 175 L14
Nantes *Town* France 97 C5
Napier *Town* New Zealand 262 G5
Naples *Town* Italy 103 G9
Nashville *Town* Tennessee, USA 37 D8
Nasik *Town* India 167 D8
Nassau *Town* Bahamas 45 M4
Nasser, Lake Egypt 215 E4
Natal *Region* South Africa 247 I9
Natal *Town* Brazil 67 L5
Nauru *Country* Micronesia, Pacific Ocean 19 N9, 255 J6, 265 D6
Navoi *Town* Uzbekistan 161 F7
Naxos *Island* Greece 131 I9
Nazareth *Town* Israel 147 E7
Nazca *Ancient site* Peru 59 D9
Ndola *Town* Zambia 239 E12
Neagh, Lough *Lake* UK 87 G7
Nebraska *State* USA 35 H5
Negev Desert Israel 147 E10
Neiva *Town* Colombia 59 D4
Nelson *Town* New Zealand 262 E7
Nepal *Country* S. Asia 18 H6, 167 H5
Ness, Loch *Lake* UK 87 I4
Netherlands *Country* Europe 18 C4, 91 I7
Nevada *State* USA 33 I9
New Brunswick *Province* Canada 29 I6
New Caledonia *Dependent territory* Melanesia, Pacific Ocean 19 N11, 255 I9, 265 D7
New Delhi *Town* India 167 F4
New Guinea *Island* Indonesia/Papua New Guinea 10 L9, 133 N15, 254 E7, 265 B6
New Hampshire *State* USA 37 K4
New Jersey *State* USA 37 I6
New Mexico *State* USA 35 E9
New Orleans *Town* Louisiana, USA 35 L12
New Plymouth *Town* New Zealand 262 F5
New Siberian Islands Russian Federation 10 L1, 133 N2, 139 O3, 267 H3
New South Wales *State* Australia 259 K10
New York *State* USA 37 I4
New York *Town* New York, USA 37 I6
New Zealand *Country* Australasia 11 N12, 19 N12, 262 E8
Newark *Town* New Jersey, USA 37 I6
Newcastle *Town* New South Wales, Australia 259 L10
Newcastle upon Tyne *Town* UK 87 J7
Newfoundland *Island* Canada 10 X4, 21 P8, 29 K4
Newfoundland *Province* Canada 29 J3
Newfoundland Basin Atlantic Ocean 77 F5
Nha Trang *Town* Vietnam 189 J10
Niagara Falls *Waterfall* Canada/USA 21 M9, 29 G9, 37 G4
Niamey *Town* Niger 221 K8
Nicaragua *Country* Central America 19 U8, 44 F11

Nicaragua, Lake Nicaragua 41 D3, 44 E12
Nice *Town* France 97 J8
Nicobar Islands Indian Ocean 10 H8, 18 H8, 133 I13, 203 I4
Nicosia *Town* Cyprus 145 E9
Niger *Country* W. Africa 18 C7, 221 O7
Niger *River* W. Africa 10 B8, 205 C5, E6, 221 E9, G8, K9, MII
Niger Delta *River mouth* Nigeria 205 E7, 221 L13
Nigeria *Country* W. Africa 18 C8, 221 M10
Niihau *Island* Pacific Ocean 33 F14
Nijmegen *Town* Netherlands 91 J7
Nile *River* N.E. Africa 10 E7, 205 H3, I5, 215 E3, E5
Ninety East Ridge Indian Ocean 203 H7
Ningbo *Town* China 175 P11
Nis *Town* Serbia, Yugoslavia 124 K6
Niue *Dependent territory* Polynesia, Pacific Ocean 19 P10 265 F7
Nizhniy Novgorod *Town* Russian Federation 138 D6
Nkongsamba *Town* Cameroon 232 D8
Nome *Town* Alaska, USA 33 B2
Norfolk *Town* Virginia, USA 37 H8
Norfolk Island *Dependent territory* Pacific Ocean 19 N11, 255 J11, 265 D7
Normandy *Region* France 97 D3
North Albanian Alps *Mountain range* Albania/Yugoslavia 124 H7
North America *Continent* 11 T4, 20–21
North American Basin Atlantic Ocean 77 D5
North Cape Norway 78 H4, 82 J1
North Carolina *State* USA 37 G8
North Dakota *State* USA 35 G2
North European Plain Europe 78 G9
North Frisian Islands Denmark/ Germany 95 F1
North Island New Zealand 255 J13, 262 F5
North Korea *Country* E. Asia 18 K5, 175 P6
North Pole Arctic Ocean 267 F5
North Sea Atlantic Ocean 10 C4, 77 I3, 78 E8, 91 F7
North-Eastern Atlantic Basin Atlantic Ocean 77 H4
Northampton *Town* UK 87 K10
Northern Dvina *see* Dvina
Northern Ireland *Region* UK 87 G7
Northern Mariana Islands *Dependent territory* Micronesia, Pacific Ocean 10 L8, 18 L7, 254 F3, 265 C4
Northern Territory *Territory* Australia 259 G6
Northwest Territories *Province* Canada 27 F8
Norway *Country* Europe 18 C3, 82 G6
Norwegian Sea Atlantic Ocean 10 C3, 78 E5, 82 F5
Norwich *Town* UK 87 L10
Nottingham *Town* UK 87 J9
Nouakchott *Town* Mauritania 220 B6
Nova Scotia *Province* Canada 29 J6
Novaya Zemlya *Island group* Russian Federation 10 F2, 79 N2, 138 H3, 267 I7
Novgorod *Town* Russian Federation 138 C4
Novi Sad *Town* Serbia, Yugoslavia 124 I3
Novokuznetsk *Town* Russian Federation 139 J10
Novosibirsk *Town* Russian Federation 139 I9
Nubian Desert Sudan 205 I4, 215 E5

Nukus *Town* Uzbekistan 161 D6
Nullarbor Plain *Region* Western Australia, Australia 256 F10
Nuremberg *Town* Germany 95 H9
Nuuk *see* Godthåb
Nyasa, Lake Southern Africa 10 E10, 205 I10, 239 H11, 247 J4

O

Oahu *Island* Pacific Ocean 33 G14, 255 O2
Oakland *Town* California, USA 33 G10
Oaxaca *Town* Mexico 39 H9
Ob' *River* Russian Federation 10 G3, 132 F4, 133 G6, 138 H6, 139 I8
Oban *Town* UK 87 H5
Odense *Town* Denmark 82 E11
Oder *River* Germany 78 G9, 95 K4
Odessa *Town* Ukraine 120 G8
Odra *River* Central Europe 115 D4, F6
Ogbomosho *Town* Nigeria 221 L11
Ohio *River* USA 37 C7, F6
Ohio *State* USA 37 F6
Okavango *River* Southern Africa 205 H12, 247 D3
Okavango Delta Botswana 247 F6
Okayama *Town* Japan 185 E10
Okhotsk, Sea of Japan/Russian Federation 10 L4, 133 O6, 139 S7, 185 J1, 265 C2
Okinawa *Island* Japan 185 A16
Oklahoma *State* USA 35 I9
Oklahoma City *Town* Oklahoma, USA 35 I9
Öland *Island* Sweden 82 H11
Olduvai Gorge Tanzania 239 I7
Oloy Range *Mountain range* Russian Federation 133 Q4, 139 R4
Olympia *Ancient site* Greece 131 C8
Olympia *Town* Washington, USA 33 F5
Olympus, Mt. Greece 131 D4
Omaha *Town* Nebraska, USA 35 I6
Oman *Country* S.W. Asia 18 F7, 153 G11
Oman, Gulf of Arabia/Iran 10 G7, 132 E11, 203 F2
Omdurman *Town* Sudan 215 E7
Omsk *Town* Russian Federation 138 H9
Onega, Lake Russian Federation 10 E3, 78 K6, 138 E4
Onitsha *Town* Nigeria 221 M12
Ontario *Province* Canada 29 D6
Ontario, Lake Canada/USA 21 M9, 29 G8, 37 G4
Oodaaq Island Arctic Ocean 267 F7
Oradea *Town* Romania 127 E5
Oran *Town* Algeria 209 J2
Orange River Southern Africa 10 D11, 205 G13, 247 E10, G10
Ore Mountains Czech Republic/ Germany 95 I7, 115 C6
Örebro *Town* Sweden 82 G9
Oregon *State* USA 33 G6
Orenburg *Town* Russian Federation 138 E8
Orinoco *River* Venezuela 41 G4, 59 H2, F3, G3
Orizaba *see* Citlaltépetl
Orkneys *Island group* UK 78 D7, 87 J2
Orlando *Town* Florida, USA 37 F12
Orléans *Town* France 97 F4
Orsha *Town* Russian Federation 111 K8
Orumiyeh *Town* Iran 153 F3
Oruro *Town* Bolivia 59 F10
Osaka *Town* Japan 185 F10
Osh *Town* Kyrgyzstan 161 H7
Oshogbo *Town* Nigeria 221 L11
Osijek *Town* Croatia 109 K4

Oslo *Town* Norway 82 F8
Osmaniye *Town* Turkey 145 G8
Osorno *Town* Chile 71 F11
Ostend *Town* Belgium 91 E9
Ottawa *River* Ontario/Quebec, Canada 29 F7
Ottawa *Town* Ontario, Canada 29 G8
Ouagadougou *Town* Burkina 221 I9
Oued Chelif *River* Algeria 209 K2
Oujda *Town* Morocco 209 I3
Oulu *Town* Finland 82 J5
Outer Hebrides *Island group* UK 78 C7, 87 G3
Oviedo *Town* Spain 100 D1
Oxford *Town* UK 87 J10
Oxnard *Town* California, USA 33 H12

P

Pa-an *Town* Myanmar 189 D7
Pacific Ocean 11 Q7, 255 L3, 265 H4
Padang *Town* Sumatra, Indonesia 196 C9
Padua *Town* Italy 103 E4
Pagan *Ancient site* Myanmar 189 C5
Painted Desert Arizona, USA 33 K11
Pakambaru *Town* Sumatra, Indonesia 196 C9
Pakistan *Country* S. Asia 18 G6, 167 B4
Pakokku *Town* Myanmar 189 C5
Pakxé *Town* Laos 189 H9
Palau *Country* Micronesia, Pacific Ocean 18 L8, 254 D5, 265 B5
Palembang *Town* Sumatra, Indonesia 196 E10
Palenque *Ancient site* Mexico 39 J9
Palermo *Town* Italy 103 G12
Palmerston North *Town* New Zealand 262 F6
Palmyra Atoll *Dependent territory* Polynesia, Pacific Ocean 19 P8, 255 N5, 265 F5
Palu *Town* Celebes, Indonesia 196 K9
Pamir *River* Afghanistan/Tajikistan 161 H8
Pamirs *Mountain range* Tajikistan 133 G9, 161 H8
Pampas *Region* Argentina 11 W12, 41 G13, 71 H9
Pamplona *Town* Spain 100 H2
Panama *Country* Central America 19 V8, 44 G15
Panama Canal Panama 41 E3, 44 H15
Panama City *Town* Panama 44 I15, 77 C7, 265 L5
Panama, Isthmus of Panama 41 D4
Pancevo *Town* Serbia, Yugoslavia 124 J4
Pantelleria *Island* Italy 103 E14
Papua New Guinea *Country* Australasia 18 M9, 259 L2
Paraguay *Country* S. America 19 W11, 71 I3
Paraguay *River* S. America 41 H9, 71 J4
Paramaribo *Town* Suriname 59 K3
Paraná *River* Argentina/Paraguay/Brazil 11 W11, 41 H11, 67 G9, 71 J5, J7
Paranaiba *River* Brazil 41 I9
Paris *Town* France 97 F3
Parma *Town* Italy 103 D5
Parry Islands Northwest Territories, Canada 21 K3, 27 F4
Pasto *Town* Colombia 59 C4
Patagonia *Region* Argentina 11 V13, 41 F14, 71 H13
Patna *Town* India 167 H6
Patrai *Town* Greece 131 C7
Peary Land *Region* Greenland 21 R1, 267 E7

Pec *Town* Serbia, Yugoslavia 124 I7
Pegu *Town* Myanmar 189 C7
Peipus, Lake Estonia/Russian Federation 111 I4
Pelagie Islands Italy 103 F15
Pelée, Mt. *Volcano* Martinique 41 H2
Peloponnese *Island group* Greece 131 D8
Pematangsiantar *Town* Sumatra, Indonesia 196 B8
Pennines *Mountain range* UK 87 J7
Pennsylvania *State* USA 37 G5
Penza *Town* Russian Federation 138 C7
Penzance *Town* UK 87 G12
Peoria *Town* Illinois, USA 37 C6
Perm' *Town* Russian Federation 138 F7
Persian Gulf Saudi Arabia/Iran 132 D11, 153 F7, 203 E2
Perth *Town* UK 87 I5
Perth *Town* Western Australia, Australia 258 C10
Peru *Country* S. America 19 V10, 59 C6
Perugia *Town* Italy 103 F7
Peshawar *Town* Pakistan 167 D2
Petah-Tiqwa *Town* Israel 147 E7
Petra *Ancient site* Jordan 147 E10
Philadelphia *Town* Pennsylvania, USA 37 I6
Philippine Sea Philippines 10 K7, 196 L2, 254 C5, 265 B4
Philippines *Country* S.E. Asia 10 K8, 18 K8, 196 K5
Phnom Penh *Town* Cambodia 189 H11
Phoenix Islands Kiribati, Pacific Ocean 11 P9, 255 L6, 265 E6
Phoenix *Town* Arizona, USA 33 J12
Phuket *Town* Thailand 189 D12
Piatra-Neamt *Town* Romania 127 I5
Pico da Neblina *Mountain* Brazil 67 C3
Picton *Town* New Zealand 262 E7
Pierre *Town* South Dakota, USA 35 H4
Pietermaritzburg *Town* South Africa 247 H10
Pietersburg *Town* South Africa 247 H8
Pinar del Rio *Town* Cuba 44 H5
Pinatubo, Mt. *Volcano* Philippines 196 K2
Pindus Mountains Greece 131 C5
Pingxiang *Town* China 175 M12
Piraeus *Town* Greece 131 F8
Pisa *Town* Italy 103 D6
Pitcairn Islands *Dependent territory* Polynesia, Pacific Ocean 19 S11, 255 T11, 265 H7
Pitesti *Town* Romania 127 G8
Pittsburgh *Town* Pennsylvania, USA 37 G6
Piura *Town* Peru 59 B6
Plata, Rio de la *River* Argentina/Uruguay 41 H12, 71 J8
Pleven *Town* Bulgaria 127 G10
Ploiesti *Town* Romania 127 I8
Plovdiv *Town* Bulgaria 127 G11
Plymouth *Town* UK 87 H12
Po *River* Italy 78 F11, 103 B4, E4
Podgorica *Town* Montenegro, Yugoslavia 124 H7
Podlasie *Region* Poland 115 K4
Pointe-Noire *Town* Congo 232 E12
Poitiers *Town* France 97 E6
Poland *Country* Central Europe 18 D4, 115 H4
Poltava *Town* Ukraine 121 I6
Polynesia *Region* Pacific Ocean 255 N9, 265 F7
Pomerania *Region* Germany/Poland 115 E2
Ponce *Town* Puerto Rico 45 S10
Pontchartrain, Lake Louisiana, USA 35 L12

Pontianak *Town* Borneo, Indonesia 196 G9
Pontic Mountains Turkey 145 G5
Poopó, Lake Bolivia 41 G9, 59 F11
Popayán *Town* Colombia 59 C4
Popocatépetl *Volcano* Mexico 39 G8
Port Elizabeth *Town* South Africa 247 G11
Port Harcourt *Town* Nigeria 221 M13
Port Hedland *Town* Western Australia, Australia 258 C7
Port Louis *Town* Mauritius 203 E7
Port Moresby *Town* Papua New Guinea 259 K3
Port of Spain *Town* Trinidad & Tobago 45 U14
Port Said *Town* Egypt 203 C1, 215 E1
Port Sudan *Town* Sudan 215 F5
Port-au-Prince *Town* Haiti 45 O9
Port-Gentil *Town* Gabon 232 D10
Portland *Town* Oregon, USA 33 F5
Porto *Town* Portugal 100 B3
Pôrto Alegre *Town* Brazil 67 G12
Porto-Novo *Town* Benin 221 K12
Portoviejo *Town* Ecuador 59 B5
Portsmouth *Town* UK 87 J12
Portugal *Country* Europe 18 B5, 100 B6
Posadas *Town* Argentina 71 K5
Potosí *Town* Bolivia 59 G11
Potsdam *Town* Germany 95 J5
Poznán *Town* Poland 115 F4
Prague *Town* Czech Republic 113 D7
Praia *Town* Cape Verde 77 G6
Pravets *Town* Bulgaria 127 G11
Prespa, Lake Albania/Macedonia/Greece 124 J9, 131 B2
Preston *Town* UK 87 I8
Pretoria *Town* South Africa 247 H8
Prijedor *Town* Bosnia and Herzegovina 124 F3
Prince Edward Island *Province* Canada 29 J6
Prince Edward Islands Indian Ocean 10 E13, 18 E13, 203 E10
Pristina *Town* Serbia, Yugoslavia 124 J7
Prizren *Town* Serbia, Yugoslavia 124 J7
Prome *Town* Myanmar 189 C6
Provence *Region* France 97 I9
Providence *Town* Rhode Island, USA 37 J5
Pucallpa *Town* Peru 59 D7
Puebla *Town* Mexico 39 H8
Puerto Barrios *Town* Guatemala 44 D9
Puerto Montt *Town* Chile 71 F11
Puerto Natales *Town* Chile 71 G15
Puerto Rico *Dependent territory* Caribbean Sea 45 S10
Puerto Rico Trench Atlantic Ocean 77 D6
Puerto Santa Cruz *Town* Argentina 71 H14
Puncak Jaya *Mountain* Irian Jaya, Indonesia 197 R10
Pune *Town* India 167 D8
Punjab *Region* India 167 E3
Punta Arenas *Town* Chile 71 H15
Pusan *Town* South Korea 175 Q8
Putorana Mts. Russian Federation 139 L5
Pyinmana *Town* Myanmar 189 C6
Pyongyang *Town* North Korea 175 P7
Pyrenees *Mountain range* S.W. Europe 78 D11, 97 E10, 100 I2

Q

Qatar *Country* S.W. Asia 18 F7, 153 G8
Qazvin *Town* Iran 153 G4

Qena *Town* Egypt 215 E3
Qingdao *Town* China 175 O9
Qinghai Hu *Lake* China 175 H9
Qiqihar *Town* China 175 O4
Qolleh-ye-Damavand *Mountain* Iran 153 H4
Qom *Town* Iran 153 G4
Qornet es Saouda *Mountain* Lebanon 147 F5
Quang Ngai *Town* Vietnam 189 J8
Québec *Province* Canada 29 G6
Québec *Town* Québec, Canada 29 H7
Queen Charlotte Island British Columbia, Canada 20 G7, 27 A12
Queen Elizabeth Islands Northwest Territories, Canada 21 L2, 27 G4, 267 D5
Queen Maud Land *Region* Antarctica 269 F2
Queensland *State* Australia 259 J7
Queenstown *Town* New Zealand 262 B10
Querétaro *Town* Mexico 39 G7
Quezaltenango *Town* Guatemala 44 B9
Qui Nhon *Town* Vietnam 189 J9
Quito *Town* Ecuador 59 C5

R

Rabat *Town* Morocco 208 G3
Rach Gia *Town* Vietnam 189 H11
Rajkot *Town* India 167 C7
Rajshahi *Town* Bangladesh 167 J6
Raleigh *Town* North Carolina, USA 37 G8
Ramlat As Sab'Atayn *Desert region* Saudi Arabia/Yemen 153 D11
Râmnia Vâlcea *Town* Romania 127 G8
Rancagua *Town* Chile 71 F8
Ranchi *Town* India 167 I7
Rangoon *Town* Myanmar 189 C7
Rangpur *Town* Bangladesh 167 J6
Ras Dashen, Mt. Ethiopia 215 G7
Rasht *Town* Iran 153 G3
Rat Buri *Town* Thailand 189 E9
Ravenna *Town* Italy 103 F5
Rawalpindi *Town* Pakistan 167 D2
Razim *Lake* Romania 127 L8
Reading *Town* UK 87 J11
Recife *Town* Brazil 67 L5
Red River USA 21 K10, 35 H9
Red Sea 10 E7, 132 B11, 153 A7, 203 D2, 205 J4, 215 F3
Red Volta *River* W. Africa 221 I9
Regina *Town* Saskatchewan, Canada 27 G14
Reni *Town* Ukraine 120 E9
Rennes *Town* France 97 C4
Reno *Town* Nevada, USA 33 H9
Resistencia *Town* Argentina 71 J5
Resita *Town* Romania 127 D7
Resolute *Town* Northwest Territories, Canada 27 C5, 267 C5
Réunion *Dependent territory* Indian Ocean 18 F11, 203 E7, 205 L12
Revillagigedo Is. *Island group* Mexico 19 S7, 265 I4
Reykjavik *Town* Iceland 77 G3, 267 D10
Rheims *Town* France 97 G3
Rhine *River* W. Europe 10 C4, 78 E9, 91 J7, 95 D6, G10, 97 J3, 106 E7
Rhineland *Region* Germany 95 D8
Rhode Island *State* USA 37 J5
Rhodes *Island* Greece 131 L11
Rhodope Mts. Bulgaria/Greece 78 H11, 127 F12
Rhône *River* Switzerland/France 97 H8, 106 C9

Richmond *Town* Virginia, USA 37 H7
Riga *Town* Latvia 111 G6
Rijeka *Town* Croatia 109 E4
Rimini *Town* Italy 103 F5
Rio Cuarte *Town* Argentina 71 H7
Rio de Janeiro *Town* Brazil 67 I10
Rio Grande *River* Mexico/USA 11 T6, 21 J11, 35 F11, 39 G4
Rio Grande de Santiago *River* Mexico 39 E7
Riobamba *Town* Ecuador 59 C5
Rivadavia *Town* Argentina 41 G10, 71 H12
Rivne *Town* Ukraine 120 D4
Riyadh *Town* Saudi Arabia 153 E8
Rochester *Town* Minnesota, USA 35 K4
Rochester *Town* New York, USA 37 H4
Rockall *Island* UK, Atlantic Ocean 77 H3
Rockford *Town* Illinois, USA 37 C5
Rocky Mountains *N.* America 11 S4, 21 I7, 27 C11, 33 H5, 35 D6
Romania *Country* E. Europe 18 D5, 127 G6
Rome *Town* Italy 103, F8
Ronne Ice Shelf Antarctica 269 D4
Rosario *Town* Argentina 71 I7
Roseau *Town* Dominica 45 V13
Ross Ice Shelf Antarctica 269 E7
Ross Sea Antarctica 269 E8
Rostock *Town* Germany 95 I2
Rostov-na-Donu *Town* Russian Federation 138 B7
Rotorua *Town* New Zealand 255 K13, 262 G4
Rotterdam *Town* Netherlands 91 H7
Rouen *Town* France 97 E2
Rub 'al Khali (Empty Quarter) *Desert region* Saudi Arabia 10 F7, 132 C12, 153 E10
Rudolf, Lake *see* Turkana, Lake
Ruhr *River* Germany 95 F6
Ruse *Town* Bulgaria 127 I10
Russian Federation *Country* E. Europe/ N. Asia 18 D4, I3, 111 E8, 138–139
Ruwenzori Mts. Uganda/Zaire 205 H8, 239 E5
Rwanda *Country* Africa 18 D9, 239 F6
Ryazan *Town* Russian Federation 138 C6
Ryukyu Islands E. Asia 10 K7, 185 C15

S

Saarbrücken *Town* Germany 95 D9
Sabac *Town* Serbia Yugoslavia 124 I4
Sabah *Region* Borneo, Malaysia 196 J7
Sacramento *Town* California, USA 33 G9
Safi *Town* Morocco 208 F3
Sagaing *Town* Myanmar 189 C4
Sahara Desert *N.* Africa 10 C7, 205 D4, 209 M8, 221 H5
Sahel *Region* W. Africa 205 D6, 221 I7, 232 G5
Saimaa *Lake* Finland 10 D3, 78 I6, 82 K8
St. Étienne *Town* France 97 H7
St. George's *Town* Grenada 45 U15
St. George's Channel Ireland/UK 87 G10
St. Helena *Dependent territory* Atlantic Ocean 10 B10, 77 I9, 18 B10
St. John's *Town* Newfoundland, Canada 29 L4
St. Johns *Town* Antigua & Barbuda 45 V11
St. Kitts and Nevis *Country* West Indies 19 V7, 45 U11
St. Lawrence *River* Canada 21 N8, 29 H6

St. Lawrence Seaway *Canal* Ontario, Canada 29 G8
St. Lawrence, Gulf of Canada 21 O8, 29 I5
St. Louis *Town* Missouri, USA 35 L7
St. Lucia *Country* Caribbean Sea 19 W8, 45 V14
St. Malo *Town* France 97 C3
St. Paul *Island* Indian Ocean 18 H12, 203 G9
St. Paul *Town* Minnesota, USA 35 K4
St. Petersburg *Town* Florida, USA 37 F12
St. Petersburg *Town* Russian Federation 138 D4
St. Pierre and Miquelon *Dependent territory* 19 W5, 29 K5
St. Pierre *Town* St. Pierre and Miquelon 29 K5
St. Vincent and the Grenadines *Country* Caribbean Sea 18 V8, 45 V14
Sakhalin *Island* Russian Federation 133 N7, 139 S8
Salamanca *Town* Spain 100 D4
Salem *Town* Washington, USA 33 F6
Salisbury *Town* UK 87 J11
Salt Lake City *Town* Utah, USA 33 K8
Salta *Town* Argentina 71 G4
Salvador *Town* Brazil 67 K7
Salween *River* Burma/China 175 G11, H14, 189 D5
Salzburg *Town* Austria 106 H6
Samara *Town* Russian Federation 138 D7
Samarinda *Town* Borneo, Indonesia 196 J9
Samarkand *Town* Uzbekistan 161 F7
Samoa *Island* Pacific Ocean 255 M8
Samos *Island* Greece 131 J8
Samothraki *Island* Greece 131 I3
Samsun *Town* Turkey 145 G5
San Agustin *Ancient site* Colombia 59 C4
San Ambrosio Isla *Island* Chile 19 V11, 265 K7
San Antonio *Town* Texas, USA 35 I12
San Bernardino *Town* California, USA 33 H12
San Cristóbal *Town* Venezuela 59 E2
San Diego *Town* California, USA 33 H12
San Felix Isla *Island* Chile 19 V11, 265 K7
San Francisco *Town* California, USA 21 H10, 33 F10, 265 I3
San Jose *Town* California, USA 33 G10
San José *Town* Costa Rica 44 F13
San Juan *River* Utah, USA 33 K10
San Juan *Town* Argentina 71 G7
San Juan *Town* Peru 59 D10
San Juan *Town* Puerto Rico 45 S10
San Luis Potosí *Town* Mexico 39 F6
San Marino *Country* Europe 18 C5, 103 F6
San Miguel *Town* El Salvador 44 D10
San Miguel de Tucumán *Town* Argentina 71 H5
San Pedro Sula *Town* Honduras 44 D9
San Remo *Town* Italy 103 B6
San Salvador *Town* El Salvador 44 C10
San Salvador de Jujuy *Town* Argentina 71 G4
San Sebastián *Town* Spain 100 G1
San'a *Town* Yemen 153 C11
Sanandaj *Town* Iran 153 F4
Sandoway *Town* Myanmar 189 B6
Sankt Gallen *Town* Switzerland 106 D7
Sankt Pölten *Town* Austria 106 J5
Sanliurfa *Town* Turkey 145 I8
Santa Ana *Town* California, USA 33 H12
Santa Ana *Town* El Salvador 44 C10
Santa Clara *Town* Cuba 45 K6

Santa Cruz *Town* Bolivia 59 G10
Santa Fe *Town* Argentina 71 I7
Santa Fe *Town* New Mexico, USA 35 E9
Santa Marta *Town* Colombia 59 D1
Santander *Town* Spain 100 F1
Santiago *Town* Chile 71 F8, 265 L8
Santiago *Town* Dominican Republic 45 P9
Santiago *Town* Spain 100 B2
Santiago de Cuba *Town* Cuba 45 M8
Santiago del Estero *Town* Argentina 71 H5
Santo Domingo *Town* Dominican Republic 45 P10
São Luís *Town* Brazil 67 I4
São Paulo *Town* Brazil 67 I10
São Francisco *River* Brazil 11 X10, 41 K7, 67 I7
São Tomé *Town* São Tomé and Príncipe 232 C10
São Tomé and Príncipe *Country* Central Africa 18 C9, 232 C10
Sapporo *Town* Japan 185 H3
Sarajevo *Town* Bosnia and Herzegovina 124 G5
Saratov *Town* Russian Federation 138 C7
Sarawak *Region* Borneo, Malaysia 196 H8
Sarawak Chamber *Cave* Borneo, Indonesia 196 I7
Sardinia *Island* Italy 78 F12, 103 C10
Sargasso Sea Atlantic Ocean 77 E6
Sarh *Town* Chad 232 G7
Sari *Town* Iran 153 H4
Sarmiento *Town* Argentina 41 F14
Saskatchewan *Province* Canada 27 F12
Saskatoon *Town* Saskatchewan, Canada 27 F13
Satu Mare *Town* Romania 127 E4
Saudi Arabia *Country* S.W. Asia 18 E7, 153 D8
Sava *River* S.E. Europe 78 G11, 109 F3, I4, 124 G4
Savannah *Town* Georgia, USA 37 F10
Savannakhét *Town* Laos 189 H8
Scandinavia *Region* N. Europe 82
Schwerin *Town* Germany 95 H3
Scilly, Isles of UK 87 F12
Scotia Sea Atlantic Ocean 77 E12, 269 C2
Scotland *Region* UK 87 I5
Scott Base *Research station* Antarctica 269 F8
Scutari, Lake Yugoslavia/Albania 124 H7
Seattle *Town* Washington, USA 33 G4
Seikan Tunnel *Undersea rail tunnel* Japan 185 H4
Seine *River* France 78 D10, 97 F3, G3
Selvas *Region* Brazil 41 G7
Semarang *Town* Java, Indonesia 196 I52
Semnan *Town* Iran 153 H4
Sendai *Town* Japan 185 I7
Senegal *Country* W. Africa 18 A8, 220 C8
Seoul *Town* South Korea 175 Q8
Serbia *Republic* Yugoslavia 124 I5
Seremban *Town* Malaysia 189 F15
Serengeti Plain *Region* Tanzania 205 I9
Sétif *Town* Algeria 209 L2
Sevan *Lake* Armenia 121 Q14
Sevastopol' *Town* Ukraine 119 H10
Severn *River* UK 87 I10
Severnaya Zemlya *Island group* Russian Federation 10 I1, 139 L2, 267 H5
Seville *Town* Spain 78 C13, 100 D7
Seward Peninsula Alaska, USA 20 C5
Seychelles *Country* Indian Ocean 10 F9,

18 F9, 203 E6, 205 K9
Sfax *Town* Tunisia 209 N3
Shackleton Ice Shelf Antarctica 269 J6
Shamiyah Desert Syria 147 I5
Shandong Peninsula China 175 O8
Shanghai *Town* China 175 P10, 265 A3
Shannon *River* Ireland 87 F8
Shaoxing *Town* China 175 O11
Shaoyang *Town* China 175 M12
Sheffield *Town* UK 87 J9
Shenyang *Town* China 175 O6
's-Hertogenbosch *Town* Netherlands 91 I7
Shetlands *Island group* UK 78 D7, 87 K1
Shijiazhuang *Town* China 175 M8
Shikoku *Island* Japan 185 D11
Shinano *River* Japan 185 G8
Shiraz *Town* Iran 153 G6
Shkhara *Mountain* Georgia 121 O12
Sholapur *Town* India 167 E9
Shreveport *Town* Louisiana, USA 35 J10
Shumen *Town* Bulgaria 127 J10
Siauliai *Town* Lithuania 111 F7
Siberia *Region* Russian Federation 10 J3, 133 K5, 139 M7
Sibiu *Town* Romania 127 G7
Sicily *Island* Italy 78 G13, 103 G13
Sidi Bel Abbès *Town* Algeria 209 J2
Siena *Town* Italy 103 E6
Sierra Leone *Country* W. Africa 18 A8, 220 D10
Sierra Madre Del Sur *Mountain range* Mexico 39 G9
Sierra Madre Occidental *Mountain range* Mexico 21 J11, 39 D5
Sierra Madre Oriental *Mountain range* Mexico 11 T7, 21 J11, 39 F5
Sierra Nevada *Mountain range* California, USA 33 G9
Sierra Nevada *Mountain range* Spain 78 C12, 100 F8
Silesia *Region* Czech Republic/Poland 115 F6
Simferopol' *Town* Ukraine 121 I10
Simpson Desert Northern Territory/ South Australia, Australia 254 D11, 259 H8
Sinai Desert Egypt 147 C11, 215 E2
Sincelejo *Town* Colombia 59 D1
Sindh *Region* Pakistan 167 B5
Singapore *Country* S.E. Asia 18 J9, 189 G16
Sinuiju *Town* North Korea 175 P7
Sioux Falls *Town* South Dakota, USA 35 I4
Sistan, Lake Iran 153 J6
Sittwe *Town* Myanmar 189 A5
Sivas *Town* Turkey 145 G6
Skagerrak *Channel* Denmark/Norway 78 F7, 82 E10
Skiáthos *Island* Greece 131 F6
Skiros *Island* Greece 131 G6
Skopje *Town* Macedonia 124 J10
Skye *Island* UK 87 H4
Slavonski Brod *Town* Croatia 109 J5
Sliven *Town* Bulgaria 127 I11
Slovakia *Country* Central Europe 18 D4, 115 H9
Slovenia *Country* S.E. Europe 18 C5, 109 E3
Smederevo *Town* Serbia, Yugoslavia 124 J4
Smolensk *Town* Russian Federation 138 C5
Snake *River* Washington/Idaho, USA 21 I9, 33 H5
Society Islands French Polynesia, Pacific Ocean 11 P10, 255 P9, 265 G7
Socotra *Island* Yemen 133 E13, 203 E3
Sofia *Town* Bulgaria 127 F11

Sohâg *Town* Egypt 215 E3
Solomon Islands *Country* Pacific Ocean 10 M9, 19 N10, 255 J7, 265 D6
Solway Firth *Gulf* UK 87 I7
Somalia *Country* E. Africa 18 F8, 215 J10
Somme *River* France 97 F2
Songkhla *Town* Thailand 189 E13
Sonoran Desert Arizona, USA/Mexico 11 T6, 21 I10, 33 J12, 39 A1
Sosnowiec *Town* Poland 115 H7
South Africa *Country* Southern Africa 18 D11, 247 F9
South America *Continent* 11 W9, 41
South Australia *State* Australia 259 H9
South Bend *Town* Indiana, USA 37 D5
South Carolina *State* USA 37 F9
South China Sea 10 J7, 133 K13, 189 H12
South Dakota *State* USA 35 G4
South East Cape Tasmania 10 L13, 254 F15, 259 K13
South Georgia *Island group* Atlantic Ocean 77 G12
South Island New Zealand 255 J14, 262 B11
South Korea *Country* S.E. Asia 18 K6, 175 Q8
South Orkney Islands Pacific Ocean 77 F12, 269 B1
South Polar Plateau *Region* Antarctica 269 G5
South Pole Antarctica 269 F5
South Sandwich Islands *Dependent territory* Atlantic Ocean 77 G12
South Shetland Islands Atlantic Ocean 77 F12, 269 A1
Southampton *Town* UK 87 J11
Southeast Indian Ridge Indian Ocean 203 J10
Southend-on-Sea *Town* UK 87 K11
Southern Alps *Mountain range* New Zealand 255 J15, 262 C9
Southern Ocean 265 G10, 269 G1, F9
Southwest Indian Ridge Indian Ocean 203 E9
Soweto *Town* South Africa 247 H9
Spain *Country* Europe 18 B5, 100 E5
Spitsbergen *Island* Norway 267 G8
Split *Town* Croatia 109 H8
Spokane *Town* Washington, USA 33 H4
Sporades *Island group* Greece 131 F5
Springfield *Town* Illinois, USA 37 C6
Springfield *Town* Missouri, USA 35 K8
Srebrenica *Town* Bosnia and Herzegovina 124 H5
Sri Lanka *Country* S. Asia 10 H8, 18 H8, 133 G14, 167 F13
Srinagar *Town* India 167 E2
Stanley, Mt. Zaire 232 K11
Stanovoy Range *Mountain range* Russian Federation 133 K6, 139 N9
Stara Zagora *Town* Bulgaria 127 H12
Stavanger *Town* Norway 82 D9
Stewart Island *New Zealand* 255 J15, 262 B12
Stockholm *Town* Sweden 82 H9
Stockton *Town* California, USA 33 G10
Stoke-on-Trent *Town* UK 87 J9
Stonington Island Antarctica 269 B4
Strasbourg *Town* France 97 J3
Stratford-upon-Avon *Town* UK 87 J10
Stromboli *Volcano* Lipari Islands, Italy 103 H11
Stuttgart *Town* Germany 95 F10
Subotica *Town* Serbia, Yugoslavia 124 I2
Suceava *Town* Romania 127 I4
Sucre *Town* Bolivia 59 G11
Sudan *Country* N.E. Africa 18 D7, 215 D6
Sudd *Region* Sudan 215 D9

Sudeten Mountains Czech Republic/ Poland 115 F7
Suez *Town* Egypt 203 C1, 215 E1
Suez Canal Egypt 203 C1, 215 E1
Suez, Gulf of Egypt 147 C11, 215 E2
Sumatra *Island* Indonesia 10 I9, 133 J15, 196 C8
Sumbawa *Island* Indonesia 196 J12
Sumy *Town* Ukraine 121 I4
Sun City *Tourist resort* South Africa 247 G8
Superior, Lake Canada/USA 21 L8, 29 D8, 37 D2
Surabaya *Town* Java, Indonesia 196 H12
Surat *Town* India 167 D7
Suriname *Country* S. America 19 W8, 59 J3
Suzhou *Town* China 175 O11
Svalbard *Island group* Arctic Ocean 10 C1, 18 C1, 267 G7
Swabian Jura *Mountain range* Germany 95 F11
Swansea *Town* UK 87 H10
Swaziland *Country* Southern Africa 18 E11, 247 I9
Sweden *Country* Europe 18 C3, 82 G7
Switzerland *Country* Europe 18 C5, 106 D8
Sydney *Town* New South Wales, Australia 259 L10, 265 C8
Syracuse *Town* New York, USA 37 H4
Syria *Country* S.W. Asia 18 E6, 147 I4
Syrian Desert S.W. Asia 10 E6, 132 C10, 147 H6, 153 D5

T

Ta'if *Town* Saudi Arabia 153 B9
Ta'izz *Town* Yemen 153 C12
Table Mt. South Africa 247 E12
Tabora *Town* Tanzania 239 G8
Tabriz *Town* Iran 153 F3
Tacloban *Town* Philippines 196 L4
Tacna *Town* Peru 59 E10
Tacoma *Town* Washington, USA 33 F4
Taegu *Town* South Korea 175 Q8
Tagus *River* Spain/Portugal 78 C12, 100 C5, E5
Tahiti *Island* French Polynesia, Pacific Ocean 11 Q10, 255 P9, 265 G7
Tahoe, Lake California/Nevada, USA 33 G9
Tai'an *Town* China 175 N9
Taipei *Town* Taiwan 175 P13
Taiping *Town* Malaysia 189 E14
Taiwan *Country* E. Asia 18 K7, 133 L11, 175 P13, 265 A4
Taiyuan *Town* China 175 L8
Tajikistan *Country* Central Asia 18 GS, 161 G7
Tajumulco *Mountain* Guatemala 44 A8
Takla Makan *Desert* China 10 H5, 133 G9, 174 C8
Talca *Town* Chile 71 F9
Tallahassee *Town* Florida, USA 37 E11
Tallinn *Town* Estonia 111 H3
Tamale *Town* Ghana 221 I10
Tampa *Town* Florida, USA 37 F12
Tampere *Town* Finland 82 J8
Tana, Lake Ethiopia 215 G8
Tanami Desert Australia 254 D9
Tanga *Town* Tanzania 239 K8
Tanganyika, Lake Central Africa 10 E9, 205 I9, 232 K12, 239 F8
Tanggula Mts. China 175 F11
Tangier *Town* Morocco 208 H2
Tangshan *Town* China 175 N8
Tanjungkarang *Town* Sumatra,

Indonesia 196 E11
Tanta *Town* Egypt 215 D1
Tanzania *Country* Africa 18 E9, 239 H8
Taranto *Town* Italy 103 J9
Târgoviste *Town* Romania 127 H8
Târgu Mure *Town* Romania 127 G6
Tarragona *Town* Spain 100 J4
Tartu *Town* Estonia 111 I4
Tashkent *Town* Uzbekistan 161 G6
Tasman Sea Australia/New Zealand 10 M12, 255 I13, 262 D6, 265 D8
Tasmania *Island/State* Australia 254 F14, 259 K13
Tassili n'Ajjer *Mountain range* Algeria 205 E3, 209 M7
Tatar Strait Russian Federation 139 S9
Taunggyi *Town* Myanmar 189 D5
Taupo *Town* New Zealand 262 G5
Taupo, Lake New Zealand 262 G5
Tauranga *Town* New Zealand 262 G4
Taurus Mts. Turkey 10 E5, 145 E8
Tavoy *Town* Myanmar 189 D9
Taymyr Peninsula Russian Federation 133 I2, 139 K4, 267 I5
Tbilisi *Town* Georgia 121 P13
Te Anau, Lake New Zealand 262 B10
Tegucigalpa *Town* Honduras 44 D10
Tehran *Town* Iran 153 F4
Tel Aviv-Yafo *Town* Israel 147 E7
Tema *Town* Ghana 221 J12
Temuco *Town* Chile 71 F10
Tennessee *State* USA 37 D8
Tenochtitlán *see* Mexico City
Teotihuacán *Ancient site* Mexico 39 G8
Teresina *Town* Brazil 67 J4
Ternopil' *Town* Ukraine 120 C5
Tétovan *Town* Morocco 208 H2
Tetovo *Town* Macedonia 124 J8
Texas *State* USA 35 H11
Texcoco, Lake Mexico 39 G8
Thabana-Ntlenyana, Mt. Lesotho 247 H10
Thai Nguyen *Town* Vietnam 189 H5
Thailand *Country* S.E. Asia 18 I7, 189 F8
Thailand, Gulf of 10 I8, 189 E10
Thames *River* UK 78 D9, 87 J11
Thames *Town* New Zealand 262 G3
Thane *Town* India 167 D8
Thanh Hoa *Town* Vietnam 189 H6
Thar Desert India/Pakistan 10 G6, 133 G11, 167 C5
Tharthar, Lake Iraq 153 E4
Thasos *Island* Greece 131 G3
Thaton *Town* Burma 189 D7
The Hague *Town* Netherlands 91 G6
Thessaloniki *Town* Greece 131 E3
Thimphu *Town* Bhutan 167 J5
Thunder Bay *Town* Ontario, Canada 29 E7
Thuringian Forest *Region* Germany 95 H7
Tianjin *Town* China 175 N8
Tiber *River* Italy 103 F7
Tiberias, Lake Israel 149 E6
Tibesti *Mountain range* Chad/Libya 232 G3
Tibet, Plateau of Asia 10 H6, 133 H10
Tibetan Autonomous Region China 174 D10
Tien Shan *Mountain range* Kyrgyzstan/ China 10 H5, 133 H8, 161 I6, 174 C7
Tierra del Fuego *Island* Argentina/ Chile 41 F16, 71 H16
Tigris *River* S.W. Asia 132 C10, 145 I7, 153 E3
Tijuana *Town* Mexico 39 A1
Tikal *Ancient site* Guatemala 44 C7
Tilburg *Town* Netherlands 91 H8
Timaru *Town* New Zealand 262 D10
Timbuktu *Town* Mali 221 H7

Timisoara *Town* Romania 127 D7
Timor *Island* Indonesia 133 L16, 196 M12
Timor Sea Australia/Indonesia 10 K10, 197 N13, 254 C8
Tirana *Town* Albania 124 I9
Tisza *River* Hungary 78 H10
Titicaca, Lake Bolivia/Peru 11 W10, 41 F8, 59 F10
Toamasina *Town* Madagascar 203 E7
Toba *Volcanic Crater* Sumatra, Indonesia 196 B8
Togo *Country* W. Africa 18 C8, 221 J11
Tokelau *Dependent territory* Polynesia, Pacific Ocean 19 P9, 255 M7, 265 E6
Tokyo *Town* Japan 185 H9, 265 B3
Tol'yatti *Town* Russian Federation 138 D7
Toledo *Town* Ohio, USA 37 E5
Toledo *Town* Spain 100 F5
Tomsk *Town* Russian Federation 139 J9
Tonga *Country* Polynesia, Pacific Ocean 11 O10, 19 O10, 255 M9, 265 E7
Tongking, Gulf of China/Vietnam 175 L15
Tónlé Sap *Lake* Cambodia 189 G10
Topeka *Town* Kansas, USA 35 J7
Torkestan Mts. Afghanistan 161 F9
Toronto *Town* Ontario, Canada 29 F9
Torres Strait *Channel* Australia/Papua New Guinea 259 J3
Toulouse *Town* France 97 F9
Townsville *Town* Queensland, Australia 259 L6
Trabzon *Town* Turkey 145 I5
Transantarctic Mts. Antarctica 269 F6
Transvaal *Region* South Africa 247 H8
Transylvania *Region* Romania 127 F6
Trenton *Town* New Jersey, USA 37 I6
Trier *Town* Germany 95 D8
Trieste *Town* Italy 103 G3
Triglav *Mountain* Slovenia 109 D2
Trinidad and Tobago *Country* Caribbean Sea 19 W8, 45 U16
Trinidade *Island* Atlantic Ocean 19 Y10, 77 G9
Tripoli *Town* Lebanon 147 F4
Tripoli *Town* Libya 209 O4
Tristan Da Cunha *Dependent territory* Atlantic Ocean 10 A12, 18 B12, 77 H10
Trivandrum *Town* India 167 E12
Tromsø *Town* Norway 82 I2
Trondheim *Town* Norway 82 F6
Tropic of Cancer 11 Z7
Tropic of Capricorn 11 Y11
Troy *Ancient site* Turkey 145 A6
Trujillo *Town* Peru 59 C7
Tuamotu *Island group* French Polynesia, Pacific Ocean 11 Q10, 255 Q8
Tubuai Islands French Polynesia, Pacific Ocean 11 Q11, 255 P10
Tucson *Town* Arizona, USA 33 K13
Tula *Town* Russian Federation 138 C5
Tulsa *Town* Oklahoma, USA 35 I8
Tunis *Town* Tunisia 209 N2
Tunisia *Country* N. Africa 18 C6, 209 N3
Turin *Town* Italy 103 B4
Turkana, Lake Ethiopia/Kenya 205 J7, 215 F11, 239 I3
Turkey *Country* W. Asia 18 E5, 145 E6
Turkmenistan *Country* Central Asia 18 F5, 161 D7
Turks and Caicos Islands *Dependent territory* West Indies 45 P8
Turku *Town* Finland 82 I8
Tuscany *Region* Italy 103 D6
Tuvalu *Country* Pacific Ocean 11 N9, 19 O9, 255 L7, 265 E6
Tuzla *Town* Bosnia and Herzegovina

124 H4

Tyrrhenian Sea S. Europe 103 E9

U

Ubon Ratchathani *Town* Thailand 189 H8

Ucayali *River* Peru 59 D7

Udon Thani *Town* Thailand 189 G7

Ufa *Town* Russian Federation 138 E8

Uganda *Country* Africa 18 E9, 239 G4

Ujung Pandang *Town* Celebes, Indonesia 196 K11

Ukraine *Country* E. Europe 18 D4, 121 H6

Ul'yanovsk *Town* Russian Federation 138 D7

Ulan Bator *Town* Mongolia 175 J5

Uluru (formerly Ayers Rock) *Sacred site* Northern Territory, Australia 259 G8

Ungava Peninsula Québec, Canada 21 N6

United Arab Emirates *Country* S.W. Asia 18 F7, 153 G9

United Kingdom *Country* Europe 18 B4, 87 H7

United States of America *Country* N. America 19 T5, 33, 35, 37

Uppsala *Town* Sweden 82 H9

Ur *Ancient site* Iraq 153 E5

Ural *River* Kazakhstan 161 B3

Ural Mountains Russian Federation 10 F3, 79 N6, 132 E5, 138 F7

Uralsk *Town* Kazakhstan 161 C2

Urgench *Town* Uzbekistan 161 D6

Urmia, Lake Iran 153 F3

Urosevac *Town* Serbia, Yugoslavia 124 J7

Uruguay *Country* S. America 19 W11, 71 K7

Uruguay *River* S. America 41 H11, 71 J6

Ürümqi *Town* China 74 E6

Utah *State* USA 33 K9

Utrecht *Town* Netherlands 91 I6

Uxmal *Ancient site* Mexico 39 K7

Uzbekistan *Country* Central Asia 18 G5, 161 E6

V

Vadodara *Town* India 167 D7

Vaduz *Town* Liechtenstein 106 E7

Valdez *Town* Alaska, USA 33 D2

Valdéz Peninsula Argentina 41 G14, 71 I11

Valdivia *Town* Chile 71 F10

Valencia *Region* Spain 100 H5

Valencia *Town* Spain 100 I5

Valencia *Town* Venezuela 59 F1

Valladolid *Town* Spain E3

Valletta *Town* Malta 103 H15

Valparaíso *Town* Chile 71 F8

Van *Town* Turkey 145 K7

Van, Lake Turkey 145 K6

Vanadzor *Town* Armenia 121 P13

Vancouver *Town* British Columbia, Canada 27 C14, 265 H2

Vancouver Island British Columbia, Canada 21 H8, 27 B14

Vänern, Lake Sweden 78 G7, 82 G9

Vanuatu *Country* Melanesia, Pacific Ocean 11 N10, 19 N10, 255 I9, 265 D6

Varanasi *Town* India 167 H6

Varna *Town* Bulgaria 127 K10

Västerås *Town* Sweden 82 H9

Vatican City *Country* Rome, Italy 18 C5, 103 F8

Vatter, Lake Sweden 78 G7, 82 G10

Venezuela *Country* S. America 19 W8, 59 G2

Venice *Town* Italy 103 F4

Vereeniging *Town* South Africa 247 H9

Verkhoyansk Range *Mountain range* Russian Federation 133 M4, 139 O6

Verkhoyansk *Town* Russian Federation 133 M4, 139 P5

Vermont *State* USA 37 J4

Verona *Town* Italy 103 E4

Versailles *Town* France 97 F3

Vesterålen *Island group* Norway 78 G4, 82 H3

Viareggio *Town* Italy 103 D6

Victoria *River* Northern Territory, Australia 259 G5

Victoria *State* Australia 259 J11

Victoria *Town* Seychelles 203 E5

Victoria *Town* Vancouver Island, British Columbia, Canada 27 B14

Victoria Falls *Waterfall* Zambia/ Zimbabwe 205 H11, 239 C14, 247 G6

Victoria Island Northwest Territories, Canada 11 T2, 21 I4, 27 F6

Victoria Land *Region* Antarctica 269 G8

Columbia, Canada 27 C14

Victoria, Lake Tanzania/Uganda/Kenya 10 E9, 205 I8, 239 G5

Vienna *Town* Austria 106 K5

Vientiane *Town* Laos 189 G7

Viet Tri *Town* Vietnam 189 H5

Vietnam *Country* S.E. Asia 18 J8, 189 H7

Villavicencio *Town* Colombia 59 E3

Vilnius *Town* Lithuania 111 G8

Viña del Mar *Town* Chile 71 F8

Vinh *Town* Vietnam 189 H6

Vinnytsya *Town* Ukraine 120 E6

Vinson Massif *Mountain* Antarctica 269 D5

Virgin Islands *Dependent territory* Caribbean Sea 45 T10

Virginia *State* USA 37 H7

Visby *Town* Sweden 82 H10

Vishakhapatnam *Town* India 167 H9

Vistula *River* Poland 78 H9, 115 H2, J5, I7

Vitava, Lake Czech Republic 115 D8

Vitoria *Town* Spain 100 G2

Vitsyebsk *Town* Belarus 111 K8

Vladivostok *Town* Russian Federation 139 S11

Vojvodina *Province* Serbia, Yugoslavia 124 H3

Volga *River* Russian Federation 10 E3, 78 L8, L10

Volgograd *Town* Russian Federation 138 B7

Volta, Lake Ghana 205 D7, 221 I11

Voronezh *Town* Russian Federation 138 B6

Vosges *Mountain range* France 97 I4

Vostok *Research station* Antarctica 269 H8

Vukovar *Town* Croatia 109 K4

W

Waco *Town* Texas, USA 35 I11

Wad Medani *Town* Sudan 215 E7

Waddenzee *Sea* Netherlands 91 I4

Waikato *River* New Zealand 262 F4

Waipapakauri *Town* New Zealand 262 E2

Wairau *River* New Zealand 262 E7

Waitaki *River* New Zealand 262 C10

Waitangi *Town* New Zealand 262 F2

Wakatipu, Lake New Zealand 262 B10

Wake Island *Dependent territory* Micronesia, Pacific Ocean 19 N7, 255 J2, 265 D4

Wales *Region* UK 87 H10

Wallis and Futuna *Dependent territory* Polynesia, Pacific Ocean 19 O10, 265 E6

Walvis Bay Namibia 205 F10

Walvis Ridge Atlantic Ocean 77 I10

Wanganui *Town* New Zealand 262 F6

Warsaw *Town* Poland 115 I4

Wash, The *North Sea* UK 87 K9

Washington *State* USA 33 G4

Washington, D.C. *Town* USA 21 N10, 37 H6

Weddell Sea Antarctica 77 F13, 269 C3

Wellington *Town* New Zealand 262 F7, 265 E8

West Bank *Region* Near East 147 E7

West Frisian Islands Netherlands 91 I3

West Indies *Island group* Atlantic Ocean 41 G1, 77 C6

West Siberian Plain Russian Federation 132 E5, 138 H6

West Virginia *State* USA 37 F7

Western Australia *State* Australia 258 D8

Western Dvina *see* Dvina

Western Ghats *Mountain range* India 167 D10

Western Sahara *Disputed territory* N.W. Africa 18 A7, 208 C7, 220

Samoa *Country* Polynesia, Pacific Ocean 11 O10, 19 O10, 265 E6

Westport *Town* New Zealand 262 D7

Whangarei *Town* New Zealand 262 F2

White Nile *River* E. Africa 205 I6, 215 E7

White Sea Russian Federation 78 J5, 138 F4

White Volta *River* W. Africa 221 I10

Whitehorse *Town* Yukon Territory, Canada 27 B9

Wichita *Town* Kansas, USA 35 I8

Wicklow Mts. Ireland 87 G9

Wiesbaden *Town* Germany 95 F8

Wight, Isle of UK 87 J12

Wilhelm, Mt. Papua New Guinea 254 F7

Wilkes Land *Region* Antarctica 269 I8

Windhoek *Town* Namibia 247 D7

Windsor *Town* Ontario, Canada 29 F6

Windward Islands Caribbean Sea 45 U13

Winnipeg *Town* Manitoba, Canada 27 I14

Wisconsin *State* USA 37 C3

Wollongong *Town* New South Wales, Australia 259 L10

Wolverhampton *Town* UK 87 J10

Wrangel Island Russian Federation 133 S3, 139 Q1, 267 F2

Wroclaw *Town* Poland 115 F6

Wuhan *Town* China 175 M11

Wuppertal *Town* Germany 95 E6

Wuxi *Town* China 175 O10

Wyoming *State* USA 35 E5

Wyzyna Malopolska *Region* Poland 115 I7

X

Xi'an *Town* China 175 K10

Xiamen *Town* China 175 O13

Xiangfan *Town* China 175 L11

Xining *Town* China 175 I9

Xinjiang Uighur *Autonomous Region* China 174 D6

Xinyang *Town* China 175 M11

Y

Yalta *Town* Ukraine 121 I10

Yamoussoukro *Town* Ivory Coast 221 G12

Yangtze *River* China 10 J6, 133 K10, 175 L11, N11

Yaounde *Town* Cameroon 232 E9

Yarlung Zangbo *see* Brahmaputra

Yaroslavl' *Town* Russian Federation 138 D5

Yasuj *Town* Iran 153 G6

Yazd *Town* Iran 153 H6

Yekaterinburg *Town* Russian Federation 138 F7

Yellow River China 10 I5, 133 J9, 175 L8, M9

Yellow Sea China 10 K6, 133 L9, 175 O8

Yellowknife *Town* Northwest Territories, Canada 27 E9

Yellowstone *River* Montana/Wyoming, USA 21 J8, 35 F2

Yemen *Country* S.W. Asia 18 F7, 153 D11

Yenisey *River* Russian Federation 10 H2, 139 K8

Yerevan *Town* Armenia 121 P14

Yichang *Town* China 175 L11

Yinchuan *Town* China 175 J8

Yogyakarta *Town* Java, Indonesia 196 G12

Yokohama *Town* Japan 185 H9

York *Town* UK 87 J8

Yuan *River* China 175 L13

Yucatán Peninsula Mexico 39 K8, 41 C1

Yueyang *Town* China 175 M12

Yugoslavia *Country* S.E. Europe 18 D5, 124 I6

Yukon *River* Canada/USA 11 Q3, 20 E5, 27 A8, 33 D2

Yukon Territory *Province* Canada 27 B8

Z

Zadar *Town* Croatia 109 F6

Zagreb *Town* Croatia 109 G3

Zagros Mts. Iran 10 F6, 132 D10, 153 G6

Zahedan *Town* Iran 153 J7

Zaire *River see* Congo River

Zakynthos *Island* Greece 131 B8

Zambezi *River* Southern Africa 10 D10, 205 G11, I11, 239 B14, 247 H5, J5

Zambia *Country* Africa 18 D10, 239 D13

Zamboanga *Town* Philippines 196 L6

Zanzibar *Town* Zanzibar, Tanzania 239 K8

Zanzibar *Island* Tanzania 205 J9, 239 K8

Zaozhuang *Town* China 175 N9

Zaporizhzhya *Town* Ukraine 121 I7

Zaragoza *Town* Spain 100 H3

Zaria *Town* Nigeria 221 M10

Zenica *Town* Bosnia and Herzegovina 124 G5

Zhengzhou *Town* China 175 M10

Zhytomyr *Town* Ukraine 120 E5

Zibo *Town* China 175 N9

Zimbabwe *Country* Southern Africa 18 D10, 247 H6

Zonguldak *Town* Turkey 145 D5

Zrenjanin *Town* Serbia, Yugoslavia 124 I3

Zugspitze *Mountain* Germany 95 H12

Zurich *Town* Switzerland 106 D7

Zwolle *Town* Netherlands 91 J5

INDEX

Kremlin, Moscow, 138
krill, 269
Kuala Lumpur, Malaysia, 195
Kuba people, 237
Kurds, 144, 154
Kyrgyz people, 164

L

Lagos, Nigeria, 230
Lake Baikal, 143
Lake Chad, 235
Lake District, England, 79
Lake Kariba, 245
Lake Nasser, 214, 216
Lake Nicaragua, 49
Lake Nyasa, 244
Lake Titicaca, 40, **64**, 65
Lake Victoria, 204, 240
Lake Volta, 228
lakes
   Africa, 204, 239, 244
   Asia, 146, 160
   Europe, 86, 106, 126
   North America, 20
land reclamation, 91, **92**
land rights, Aboriginal, 260
land use, Panama, 51
Länder, 94, 270
landscape
   Africa, 246
   Australasia, 258
   Europe, 87, 97, 100, 103, 124
languages, 42
   in Africa, 235, 243
   in Asia, 160, 164, 196
   in Europe, 93, 101, 107
Lapland/Lapps 86
latitude, 14
Laurasia, 12
lead mining
   Africa, 245, 249
   Asia, 162, 191
   Europe, 120
   North America, 26
   South America, 65
leather goods, 68, 170
legends, Vietnamese, 189
Legoland, Denmark, 84
Leptis Magna, 213
Lhotsampa people, 173
Libreville, Gabon, 236
life expectancy, 81, 123, 186, 276
light engineering/industry
   Central America, 57
   Europe, 89, 105, 125
lignite, 96, 114
Lima, Peru, 64
limes, 56, 212; *see also* citrus fruit growing
linen, 110
linseed oil, 110
Lippizaner horses, 110
Lisbon, Portugal, 102
literacy, 75, 277
livestock, 116, 264
llamas, 58, 65, 73
logs/logging
   Asia, 143
   Europe, 86
   North America, 26, 32
   South America, 69
London, England, 88, 89
longitude, 14
lost worlds, South America, 59
Low Countries, 91
Luanda, Angola, 248
Luther, Martin, 96

M

Maçá Indians, 72
machinery manufacture
   Asia, 163, 180
   Europe, 89, 112, 116
   South America, 75
Machu Picchu, Peru, 64
mackerel, 64
Madagascar, 202
Madrid, Spain, 101
magnesium mining, 35
Magyars, 119
Malays, 194
Mali, 220, 225
Malinke people, 223, 225
Malvinas, Islas, 74
mambo, 52
Mandela, Nelson, 252
manganese mining, 69, 120, 236
mangoes, 56, 170
mangrove swamps, **63**
Manila, Philippines, 200
manufacturing industry, 90, 98, 104
Mao Zedong, 176
Maoris, 256, 257, 262, 263
maple syrup, 29
Mapuche Indians, 73
maquiladoras, 39
Marcos, Ferdinand, 201
market economy, 141
markets
   Africa, 228, 237
   Asia, 144, **148**
   Central America, **46**
   see also bazaars, *souks*
Maronites, 149
Marsh Arabs, **154**
marshland, Belarus, 112
Martinique, 45
Masai Mara, 238, 242
Masai people, 238
maté, 72
material, 253
Maya people/civilization, 23, 38, 43, 46, 47
meat industry
   Africa, 242
   Europe, 87, 92, 113, 117
   New Zealand, 262
   Uruguay, 72
   see also cattle ranching/rearing
Mecca, Saudi Arabia, 153, 156
media in Argentina, 74
medicine
   from rain forest plants, 69
   manufacture of, 54, 107
   preventive, 276
   traditional, 178, 234
   see also health care, immunization
Mediterranean climate, 15, 78, 79
Mekong Delta, 188
Melanesia, 254, 257, 264
Mende people, 226
Mennonites, 70
mercury, 164
Meseta, 100
Mesopotamia, 153
mestizos, 38, 48, 200
metals
   Asia, 142
   Europe, 116, 118, 119, 125
Metro in Moscow, 141
Meuse River, 91, 93
Mexico City, Mexico, 38
Micronesia, 254, 257, 264
Mid-Atlantic Ridge, 13, 76

Middle East, 137
midnight sun, 82
migrants
   to Australia, 257
   to Middle East, 157
   to South America, 66, 70
   see also, immigrants, settlers
migration
   in Central Asia, 162
   in North America, 31
   of humpback whales, 77
military government, 271
millet, 217, 221, 224, 231, **233**, 240
minarets, 148, 155
minefield in Cambodia, 193
minerals
   Africa, 222, 230, 253, 264
   Arctic Ocean, 266
   Asia, 140, 142, 162, 178, 193
   Australasia, 264
   Europe, 117, 132
   North America, 25
   South America, 61, 68, 69, 73
   see also under individual minerals
Minsk, Belarus, 112
Mississippi River, US, 21, 34
Mogadishu, Somalia, 219
mohair wool, 253
molasses, 52
Moluccas islands, 198
monarchy, 270, 271
Mongols, 141
monks, Buddhist, 190
monsoon, 166, 169, 188, 196, 202
Moreno Glacier, Argentina, 71
Mosel River, 91
mosques, 57, 146, 148, 155, 223
motorcycles, 110
mountain gorillas, 241
mountains, 13, 15
   Africa, 204
   Asia, 132
   Central and South America, 40
   Europe, 78, 100, 106, 123, 124
   North America, 20
   see also individual mountains and mountain ranges
MPLA (Angolan People's Liberation Movement), 248
Muhammad, 153, 156
mujahideen, 165
multicultural society, 88, 256, 257
multinational companies, 89, 280
multiparty democracy, 270
Museveni, Yoweri, 240
music
   Africa, 218, 224, 233, 236, 241, 251
   Central and South America, 52, 53, 57, 74
   Europe, 101, 114
   North America, 36
   see also opera
musical instruments
   Africa, 224, 233, 236, 248
   Asia, 181
   Europe, 101
   South America, 65
Muslims
   in Africa, 208, 213
   in Asia, 148, 167
   in Europe, 99, 123, 125
   see also Islam
Myanmar (Burma), 191

N

Nairobi, Kenya, 242
Namib Desert, 204, 249
Napa Valley, California, 32
national flower, Belize, 47
national identity, UK, 89
national parks
   Africa, 240, 241, 245
   Central America, 50
   Europe, 85, 115
   North America, 31, 34, 37
national symbol, Canada, 29
national wealth, 278
Native Americans, 23, 24, 26, 31
native Indians
   Central and South America, 42, 43, 66, 69, 70
   North America, 25
   see also Native Americans
native peoples, *see* peoples
natural gas, *see* gas
nature reserves
   Africa, 238
   Europe, 85
   see also game reserves, national parks
Ndebele, 252
Negroid people, 207
Nenets, 266
neon, 36
Netherlands Antilles, 45
neutral country, 107
New Australians, 261
New York, New York, 30, 36
Newars, 173
newspapers in Argentina, 74
Nguema, Macias, 234
Niagara Falls, 28
nickel, 25, 55, 62
Niger River, 205, 222, 223
Nile River, 204, **214–215**, 216
Nkrumah, Kwame, 228
nomads
   Arctic, 266
   Asia, 137, **160**, 164, 165, **181**
   Central Africa, 235, 238
   Middle East, 152, 156
   North Africa, 209, **217**, 219
   West Africa, 220, 222, 229
North European Plain, 78, 79
North Pole, 14, 15, 266
North/South divide, 280
Northern Ireland, 87, 89, 90
Nubans, 217
Nubian people, 217
nuclear
   accident, 122
   industry, 98, 112, 120, 129
   weapons testing, 256, 264
Nunavut, Canada, 25
nutmeg, 56, **57**, 198
nuts, 121, 163, 226

O

oasis, **213**
oats, 121, 122
ocean currents,
   see currents, ocean
Oceania, 254
Oceans
   Arctic, 266–267
   Atlantic, 76–77
   Indian, 202–203
   Pacific, 264–265
Oder River, 95
oil palm, 220, 230, 233
oil production/reserves/

refining
   Asia, 142, 160, 163, 164, 181
   Australasia, 259
   Central America, 53, 57
   Central Europe, 110, 120, 123, 125, 129
   Central, Southern and West Africa, 228, **230**, 233, 236, 237, 248
   Europe, **83**, 88, 112
   Middle East, **152**, 154, 155, 156, 157, 158, 159
   North Africa, 211, 212, 213, 216
   North America, 26, 34, 35, 39, 266
   South America, **60**, 62, 63, 75
   Southeast Asia, 191, 194, 195, **198**, 199
oil trade, 137, 281
Okavango Delta, 246
okra, 53, 56
Olduvai Gorge, Tanzania, 243
olive oil
   Greece, **130**
   Italy, 104
   Tunisia, 212
olives
   Africa, 208, 211, 212
   Europe, 101, 102, 119, 130
one-child policy, China, 177
one-party states, 270
OPEC (Organization of Petroleum Exporting Countries), 156, 273
opera, 104, 180
Operation Bootstrap, 54
opium poppies, 191, 193
oranges, 32, 66, 122; *see also* citrus fruit growing
Orthodox Churches, 130, 140, 274
Oslo, Norway, 83
Otavalo Indians, 63
Ottawa, Canada, 24
Ottoman Turks, 126, 208
outback, Australia, 254, 258
Ouverture, Toussaint, 55
Ovambo people, 249
overcrowding
   Cairo, Egypt, 216
   Central America, 48, 49
   Indian cities, 171
   Japan, 187
   Mexico City, 38
ozone layer, 73

P

Pacific Ocean, 264–265
Pacific peoples, 256, 264
Pacific Rim, 280
paddy fields, **176**, 188, 192, **197**;
   see also rice growing
Palestine, 146, 150
Palestine Liberation Organization (PLO), 146
Palestinian Arabs, 150, 151
palm
   kernels, 226
   oil, 194, 220, **230**
   see also coconuts, copra, dates
Palmyra, Syria, 148
Pamir Valley peoples, 163
pampas, Argentina, 15, 40, 70, 75
Pan-American Highway, 50, 70
Panama Canal, 41, **51**
Panama hat, 63

PICTURE SOURCES

The publisher would like to thank the following for their kind permission to reproduce the photographs.

t = top, b = bottom, c = centre, l = left, r= right,
a = above

Ace Photo Agency: Chris Middlebrook 89cl.

Allsport: Shaun Botterill 253tr, 257bc, Clive Brunskill 96tr, 242bc, Adrian Murrell 56tr, Pascal Rondeao 28tr.

Ancient Art & Architecture collection: 181tr.

Andes Press Agency: Carlos Reynes Manzo 66cr.

Art Directors: 71cl.

Asia Images: John Molloy 188tc.

Bridgeman Art Library: By courtesy of the board of trustees of the V&A 155br.

British Antarctic Survey: R. Mulvaney 268c.

Camera Press: 64br, 154cl, 146br, 168cr, Thierry Charlier 184c, J Allan Cash: 20bl, 75tr, 81tr, 96cla, 105br, 108clb, 108cr, 110tr, 110cr, 114ca, 144bl, 153br, 162bl, 195tl, 205clb, 219br, 220tc, 229bc, 230cr, 230br, 231c.David Rubinger 156tr.

Lester Cheeseman: 171bl, 172cl.

Cephas Picture Library: Mick Rock 119bc.

Churches Ministry Among the Jews: 150cb.

Stephanie Colasanti: 103br, 104cra.

Bruce Coleman: 53tr, 184cr, 239tl, 268br, Thomas Buchholz 81bc, 83clb, R. Campbell 206cl, Rob P. Carr 20bc, Brian J. Coates 197tl, 254cl, Alain Compost 133br, Raimund Cramm 21br, Gerald Cubitt 248cr, 250tr, Peter Davey 243tr, Keith Gunnor 63bl, Udo Hirsch 64cr, Harold Lange 24br, 94cr, Luiz Claudio Marigo 40bl, 69br, John Murray 204clb, Dr. Norman Myers 46bl, 228c, Carl Roessler 258bl, Jan Taylor 258cla.

Collections: Liba Taylor 88tr.

Colorific: Linda Bartlett 36cl, 124bl, M. Clark 90cr, Matrix /Robert Caputo 237cb /Sarah Leen 19tl, Claus Meyer 68clb, Kay Muldoon 219tr, Francois Perri 234cr, /Black Star: Peter Turnley 123cr, 123br.

Comstock: John Bulmer 61tr, Georg Gerster 2tl, 223tr.

Michael Copsey: 36tr, 37bc.

Corbis: 271cra; Tony Amuza 277cl; Adrian Arbib 281clb; Dave Bartruff 276tc; Yann Arthus-Bertrand 271tc, Bettmann / Reuter: 271tr, Jan Butchofsky-Houser 279bl; Ric Ergenbright 165crb; Macduff Everton 179cb; Franz-Marc Frei 54bc, Phillip Gould 277clb; Marc Granger 120br; Aaron Horowitz 273clb; Robbis Jack 74cr; Reed Kaestner 280clb; Stephanie Maze 279tl; Kelly-Mooney Photography 179tr; Carmen Redondo 118c; Vince Streano 277crb; Arthur Thevenart 279cra; David & Peter Tumley 276cl; David Turnley 121cra, 155cr, 277bc; Patrick Ward 271bl; Nik Wheeler 112crb; Janet Wishnesky 160tr; 272bl.

Corbis-Bettmann / Reuter: 271tr; /UPI: 228tr.

James Davis Travel Photography: 50tr, 57cr, 81tl, 100cb, 101tr, 101crb, 105tr, 110crb, 132cl, 132br, 140tr, 158bl, 260c, 262tr.

Ecoscene: Anthony Cooper 280br.

Empics: Stellan Danielsson 48br. 96tr; Tony Marshall 253tr.

Environmental Picture Library: Bob Edwards 141cla.

European Space Agency: 61bl.

Mary Evans Picture Library: 50cr, 65tr, 260 tr.

Eye Ubiquitous: David Cummings 101clb, 114cl, 138cb, 140br, Patrick Field 186cl, Steve Lindridge 91 bl, Steve Miller 70tr.

Ffotograff: Charles Aithie 152tr, Patricia Aithie 159tr.

Martyn Foote: 256tr, 258ca, 258c, 260cl.

Frederick Foster: 26cb.

Sir Norman Foster and Partners: Ian Lambot 179tr.

The Gambia Experience: 224bc.

Greenpeace: Green 256br, Morgan 264br.

Sonia Halliday Photography: T.C. Rising 134tr, 144tr.

Robert Harding Picture Library: 22tc, 23cla, 26cr, 28cr, 33cl, 42cb, 49bl, 57tl, 60cr, 60c, 74bl, 81crb, 85bl, 89cb, 92c, 98cl, 99cb, 102bl, 128tr, 129tr, 132cb, 142cr, 144cr, 147bc, 154tr, 155tl, 155bl, 163bl, 170tr, 172 cr, 179br, 183bc, 185bc, 190tr, 190c, 195cb, 198tr, 198cl, 198bl, 203bc, 207clb, 208ca, 209tr, 220bc, 222tr, 223cra, 225c, 230tr, 242tr, 245cr, 248bl, 249tr, 253bc, 267cb, 275bc, Felix. A, 219cra, J.R. Ashford 63tr, C. Bowman 73cl, Jeremy Bright 105ca, G. Corrigan 177br, Rob Cousins 23tc, Alain Evrard 191cb, 201cl, 201crb, Robert Francis 151clb, Odyssey, Chicago / Robert Frerck 23tr, Robert Frerck 38tr, K. Gillingham 51cl, Gavin Hellier 119cr, Wally Herbert 86tr, Paulo Koch 149bl, 176cr, David Lomax 22br, C. Martin 95br, Robert McLeod 194tr, H.P. Merten 95bl, Louise Murray 129crb, Gary Norman 61ca, Roy Rainford 93tr, Geoff Renner 204tr, 246cb, Christopher Rennie 141cr, Riffet 233cb, John G. Ross 70br, Sassoon 123ca, Michael Short 124tr, E. Simanor 148bl, James Strachan 47c, Luca Invernizzi Tettoni 189br, 190br, 198cr, Adam Woolfitt 31cb, 62br, 76bl, 79tr, 79 br, 127bl, 129cl, 216tr, Earl Young 47 cr.

Holt Studios International: 214tr, Mary Cherry 229cl, Inga Spence 32bc, 51br.

Jeremy Horner: 62cr, 62bl.

Hulton/Getty: /Reuter 252tr, 268bl.

Hutchison Library: 17br, 29cb, 52 cla, 58tl, 68bc, 157cr, 162cr, 164cl, 164bl, 172tr, 210 bl, 214cl, 214cr, 217ca, 217cl, 226crb, 226bl, 228clb, 234cla, 236cr, 247br, 249bl, Robert Aberman 144cl, Christina Dodwell 142tc, John G. Egan 81tr,138clb, Sarah Errington 17tl, 55tr, 235tr, 237bl, Andrew Evans 130bl, Robert Francis 73br, Norman Froggatt 115 bl, Réne-Nicolas Guidicelli 179ca, Maurice Harvey 227cr, 245cr, John Hatt 148tr, Jeremy Horner 62tl, Chris Johnson 229tr, R.Ian Lloyd 188bl, 191tr, M. Macintyre 201cr, Brian Moser 65br, 193bl, B. Régent 227tr, P.W.Rippon 155cl, Trevor Page 219cla, Christine Pemberton 178tl, Stephen Pern 43cr, 70bl, 156cl, 240tr, Bernard Régent 202bc, 236cla, Kerstin Rodgers 65bl, T. Souter 150br, Isabella Tree 259cr, Anna Tully 48tr, 230clb, Philip Wolmuth 54bl, 55bl.

ICCE: Robert Carlson 50bl, Glyn Davies 197tr

The Image Bank: 93br, 113tr, 180bl, 194bl, Luis Castenada 72bl, 274bl, Michael Coyne 259br, L.D. Gordon 39cb, Burton Mc Neely 32cr, Morrin E. Newman 36cr, Terje Rakke 83tr, J. Schmitt 38cr.

Images Colour Library: 98bl, 106bl /AGE Fotostock: 101cr, 108tr.

Impact: Christophe Bluntzer 164tr, Piers Cavendish 49cr, 76cr, 146bl /Clic Clap 45tc, 122cb, Sergio Doranles 39bl, Alain Evrard 136bl, Pilar Fernandez

37crb, Alain Le Garsmeur 49c, 49tr, 53cl, Robert Gibbs 42clb, Philip Gordon 182tr, Mark Henley Back cover cb, 2cb, 107br, 137cl, 192br, 195cl, Erol Houssein 126bl, Javed A. Jaffererji 136tr, Colin Jones 21bl, 51cb, 204cr, Alan Keohane 14bc, Geraint Lewis 114tr, M. Milivojevic 119cla, Vitaly Orlot 161br, Gary Parker 243bl, Caroline Penn 158tr, 213tr, 240cr, Christopher Pillitz 70cr, David Reed 225cr, 225tr, Ray Roberts 85tr, James Willis 157trb.

International Coffee Organisation: 66cb.

Japan Information and Cultural Centre: 184tr.

John R. Jones: 159cb, 188cra, 189tr, 192cl, 193tl, 193cr.

Katz: Rea Bellavia 180tr, Boisseaux-Chical 223bl, Bruno Hadjih 72cr, Randy G. Taylor 53br.

Kodia: I. Modic 109bl.

Link Picture Library: Orde Eliason 85bc

Roger Kohn: 75cra; **Korean Tourist Office:** 183bl.

Luxner News Inc: Larry Luxner 75cla.

Magnum Photos: Bruno Barbey 236tr, Steve McCurry 99cl.

National Cotton Council: 36crb.

Nature Photographers: Andrew Cleave 266cla.

Network: Homer Sykes 154c.

New Zealand Tourist Board: 263tl.

NHPA: Hellio and Van Ingen 132tc.

Novosti: 162tr, 162crb.

Christine Osborne Pictures: 148bc.

Oxford Scientific Films: Johnny Johnson 26crb.

Panos: M. Adler 235crb, 235bl, Trygve Bolstad 166bl, 251tr, Katri Burri 217tr, Neil Cooper 169cr, 169bl, 218tr, Jean-Léo Dugast 135clb,191cl, Mark Mc Evoy 149c, Alain le Garsmeur 137bl, 173bl, 178bl, Ron Giling 200cr, 200br, 222crb, Jeremy Hartley 115br, 207tr, 226tr, 224cr, Chris Johnson 251c, Rhodri Jones 121tc, Barbara Klass 169cr, N.Durrell McKenna 73bl, Micheal J O'Brien 122tr, Trevor Page 163cr, Bruce Paton 231bl, 246bl, 251bl, Betty Press 207cr, 241tr, 241c, Dominic Sansoni 202tr, Paul Smith 47tr, 251cr, Jon Spaull 136bc, Sean Sprague 48bl, 66tc, 128bl, 143cb, 218cr, 234bl, 241crb, Chris Stowers 144ca, 168bc, 170br, Penny Tweedie 208bl, 210bc, 244c, 244cr, 260cr, 68c.

Pearson Group: 74cl.

Performance Arts Library: Clive Barda 88cr.

Piaggio Veicoli Europei Spa: 104cr.

Pictor International Ltd: 23bl, 24tr, 25cb, 36bl, 41clb, 54c, 56cr, 56br, 59cr, 67bl, 68tr, 74br, 76br, 81c, 84tr, 93bc, 109tr, 116cb, 118br, 119cr, 129c, 130cr, 135br, 137tr, 186tr, 186bl, 190cb, 206br, 207tc, 209tl, 210tr, 212crb, 227br, 238bl, 243cl, 264bl, 268tr.

Pictures Colour Library: 25cb, 52tr, 52bl, 58br, 60tr, 168tr, 246cla.

Planet Earth Pictures: Andre Bartschi 43tl, Dave Lyons 78tc, Nigel Tucker 47br.

Popperfoto: 152cb/EPA, 48cb, Andrew Winning 273cla; Elio Ciol 275bl; Enny Nuraheni/Reuters 270cb; Kaz Nagasayu/Reuters 199bc; Muzammil/Reuters 281br; Patrick de Noirmont 137tc; Paul Cadenhead

ILLUSTRATORS

ACKNOWLEDGMENTS

Additional editorial assistance:
Bernadette Crowley, Christiane Gunzi, Terry Martin

Additional design assistance: Diane Clouting

Index and gazetteer: Lynn Bresler

Additional picture research: Giselle Harvey

DK Picture Researchers: Sarah Mills and Rose Horridge

Additional DTP assistance: Nicky Studdart

Film outputting: Brightside, London

**DK would like to thank the following people and organizations
for their help in the production of this book.**

Action Aid; The Algerian Embassy, London; The Arab British Center, London; The
Argentinian Embassy, London; The Australian High Commission, London; The Australian
Tourist Commission, London; BP Exploration, London; The Belguim Embassy, London;
The Brazilian Embassy, London; Bridgestone Corporation, Belgium; British Airways
Holidays, West Sussex; The British Consulate General, Rio De Janeiro; The British Embassy,
Argentina; The British Embassy, Philippines; The British Museum Education Service,
London; The Bulgarian Embassy, London; C. P. Rail System, Montreal, Canada; Chamber
of Mines of South Africa, Johannesburg, South Africa; China National Tourist
Administration, London; Coal World Magazine; The Coffee Museum, London; Cotton
Council International, London; The Council for the Advancement of Arab-British
Understanding, London; Cyprus Olive Products, Cyprus; The Cyprus Tourist Board,
London; The Danish Embassy, London; De Beers, London; The Embassy of Ecuador,
London; The Embassy of Jordan, London; The Embassy of Mexico, London; The Embassy
of the Republic of Estonia, London; The Embassy of the Republic of Yemen, London; The
Embassy of the Syrian Arab Republic, London; Farmers Weekly; The Financial Times,
London; The Finnish Embassy, London; The Football Association, London; Sir Norman
Foster and Partners, London; Fyffes Group Ireland Ltd.; Joss Graham; I. Hennig and Co.
Ltd., London; Hong Kong Government Office, London; The Indonesian Trade Center,
London; Institute of Civil Engineers, London; International Cocoa Organization, London;
International Coffee Organization, London; International Cotton Advisory Committee,
Washington, DC; Israeli Government Tourist Board, London; The Jordan Information
Bureau, London; Kew Gardens, London; Kibbutz Representatives, London; The Latvian
Embassy, London; The Lithuanian Embassy, London; The Luxembourg Embassy, London;
The Macao Tourist Information Bureau, London; The Malaysian Rubber Research and
Development Board; Menelik Restaurant, London; The Ministry of Agriculture, Grenada;
The Ministry of Tourism, Mexico; The Moroccan Embassy, London; Moss and Co., Timber
Importers, London; The Museum of Mankind, London; The National Cotton Council of
America, Memphis, Tennessee; Neal Street East, London; Northern Territory House,
London; The Royal Norwiegan Embassy, London; Oxfam, Oxford; Pilsner Urquell, Czech
Republic; Portuguese Trade and Tourism Office, London; The Queensland Tourist and
Travel Corporation, London; Railway Gazette International; The Romanian Embassy,
London; The School of African and Oriental Studies, University of London; Science
Museum Library, London; The Swedish Embassy, London; The Swiss Embassy, London;
The Taipei Representative's Office, London; The Trade Delegation of the Russian
Federation in the United Kingdom; The Tunisian Embassy, London; The Turkish
Information Office, London; Marion Turnock; Joan Twelves; UNICEF, Kampala; United
Nations High Commissioner for Refugees, London; Valley of the Kings Restaurant,
London; Wine and Spirit Education Trust, London.